Sustainable Finance

Series Editors

Karen Wendt, CEO. Eccos Impact GmbH, President of SwissFinTechLadies, President Sustainable-Finance, Cham, Switzerland

Margarethe Rammerstorfer, Professor for Energy Finance and Investments, Institute for Finance, Banking and Insurance WU Vienna, Vienna, Austria

Sustainable Finance is a concise and authoritative reference series linking research and practice. It provides reliable concepts and research findings in the ever growing field of sustainable investing and finance, SDG economics and Leadership with the declared commitment to present the theories, methods, tools and investment approaches that can fulfil the United Nations Sustainable Development Goals and the Paris Agreement COP 21/22 alongside with de-risking assets and creating triple purpose solutions that ensure the parity of profit, people and planet through choice architecture passion and performance. The series addresses market failure, systemic risk and reinvents portfolio theory, portfolio engineering as well as behavioural finance, financial mediation, product innovation, shared values, community building, business strategy and innovation, exponential tech and creation of social capital. Sustainable Finance and SDG Economics series helps to understand keynotes on international guidelines, guiding accounting and accountability principles, prototyping new developments in triple bottom line investing, cost benefit analysis, integrated financial first plus impact first concepts and impact measurement. Going beyond adjacent fields (like accounting, marketing, strategy, risk management) it integrates the concept of psychology, innovation, exponential tech, choice architecture, alternative economics, blue economy shared values, professions of the future, leadership, human and community development, team culture, impact, quantitative and qualitative measurement, Harvard Negotiation, mediation and complementary currency design using exponential tech and ledger technology. Books in the series contain latest findings from research, concepts for implementation, as well as best practices and case studies for the finance industry.

Sucharita Gopal · Josh Pitts

The FinTech Revolution

Bridging Geospatial Data Science, AI, and Sustainability

Springer

Sucharita Gopal
Boston University
Boston, MA, USA

Josh Pitts
Boston University
Boston, MA, USA

ISSN 2522-8285 ISSN 2522-8293 (electronic)
Sustainable Finance
ISBN 978-3-031-74417-4 ISBN 978-3-031-74418-1 (eBook)
https://doi.org/10.1007/978-3-031-74418-1

© The Editor(s) (if applicable) and The Author(s), under exclusive license to Springer Nature Switzerland AG 2024

This work is subject to copyright. All rights are solely and exclusively licensed by the Publisher, whether the whole or part of the material is concerned, specifically the rights of translation, reprinting, reuse of illustrations, recitation, broadcasting, reproduction on microfilms or in any other physical way, and transmission or information storage and retrieval, electronic adaptation, computer software, or by similar or dissimilar methodology now known or hereafter developed.
The use of general descriptive names, registered names, trademarks, service marks, etc. in this publication does not imply, even in the absence of a specific statement, that such names are exempt from the relevant protective laws and regulations and therefore free for general use.
The publisher, the authors and the editors are safe to assume that the advice and information in this book are believed to be true and accurate at the date of publication. Neither the publisher nor the authors or the editors give a warranty, expressed or implied, with respect to the material contained herein or for any errors or omissions that may have been made. The publisher remains neutral with regard to jurisdictional claims in published maps and institutional affiliations.

This Springer imprint is published by the registered company Springer Nature Switzerland AG
The registered company address is: Gewerbestrasse 11, 6330 Cham, Switzerland

If disposing of this product, please recycle the paper.

Preface

In a rapidly evolving global landscape marked by unprecedented challenges and opportunities, the role of FinTech has never been more crucial. At the nexus of technology, finance, and sustainability lies a path forward that can reconcile the often conflicting demands of economic growth and environmental stewardship. The title of our book "The FinTech Revolution—Bridging Geospatial Data Science, AI, and Sustainability" emphasizes the idea of moving beyond traditional barriers and forging new connections between these vital areas, all within the context of the sustainable FinTech industry.

This book embarks on a transformative journey designed for readers keen on understanding and navigating the intersection of sustainability, finance, and technology. The key objectives are:

- Significance of Sustainability and Resilience Strategy Data: Understand why sustainability and resilience have become critical components in today's financial landscape. Learn how these factors influence investment decisions and corporate strategies, making them indispensable for future-ready businesses.
- Introduction to Data Science, AI, and Analytics Tools: Dive into the world of data science and artificial intelligence (AI), where we explore the tools and techniques essential for accurate data collection, interpretation, and application in the financial sector. Discover how these technologies are reshaping the way we understand and act upon environmental, social, and governance (ESG) data.
- Exploration of the FinTech Landscape: Get a comprehensive overview of the current approaches within the FinTech space, particularly those that align with sustainability goals. This section offers insights into the evolving dynamics of financial technology and its role in promoting responsible business practices.
- Geospatial Technologies and Impact KPIs: Gain expertise in utilizing geospatial technologies and key performance indicators (KPIs) to assess impacts and risks. This guide will help professionals integrate these tools into their strategies for more informed decision-making.
- Risk Assessments and Regulatory Compliance: Understand the complexities surrounding risk assessments in the context of stringent global regulations. We

discuss frameworks such as the United Nations Sustainable Development Goals (UN SDGs), the U.S. Securities and Exchange Commission (SEC), and the European Union Sustainable Finance Disclosure Regulation (EU SFDR), offering guidance on navigating compliance challenges.
- Future of AI and Data Science in Finance: Explore the future of AI and data science in the realms of sustainability and finance. This discussion will equip readers with the knowledge to anticipate and adapt to emerging trends and technologies that will shape the industry.
- Real-World Case Studies: Engage with applied case studies that provide practical insights and actionable strategies. These examples offer a valuable reference for practitioners looking to implement sustainable practices in their organizations.

Organization of the Book

Our book provides a comprehensive exploration of how modern technologies are revolutionizing the financial sector's approach to sustainability. Each chapter builds on the previous one, creating a cohesive narrative that underscores the importance of integrating advanced technologies like AI, Big Data, blockchain, and geospatial data into sustainable finance practices. As the world continues to grapple with the challenges of climate change, this book offers valuable insights into the transformative potential of FinTech innovations in creating a more sustainable and resilient global financial system.

The first chapter sets the foundation for understanding the intricate strategies deployed to combat climate change, highlighting the critical role of global initiatives like the Principles for Responsible Investment (PRI) and the Sustainable Development Goals (SDGs). It explores how corporations are evolving their Environmental, Social, and Governance (ESG) practices to meet these global standards, driven by regulatory pressures, shareholder activism, and the ethical demands of younger generations. The chapter also examines the financial implications of materiality in the context of environmental risks, using the U.S. Inflation Reduction Act of 2023 as a case study to showcase the rise of eco-focused enterprises and technological innovation. Furthermore, it discusses the transformative impact of Artificial Intelligence (AI) and Big Data on ESG reporting, alongside how FinTech innovations like blockchain are enhancing transparency and accountability in financial services. Chapter 2 delves into the historical development of sustainable finance, identifying key stakeholders such as corporations, governments, NGOs, and financial institutions, and their roles in driving sustainability. It underscores the importance of ESG criteria in guiding the financial sector toward a sustainable future, highlighting both ethical and financial imperatives. The chapter further explores how advancements in digital measurement, reporting, and verification (MRV) are reshaping the financial landscape, offering new opportunities for alignment with global carbon reduction targets. It concludes with a look at significant innovations within Climate Tech and Ag Tech sectors that are driving the green transition.

Chapter 3 explores the Planetary Boundaries (PB) framework, a critical tool for understanding and maintaining Earth's system stability. It outlines the nine Earth system processes essential for ensuring a "safe operating space" for humanity and analyzes the severe consequences of transgressing these boundaries. The chapter provides a detailed examination of both successful and failed policies related to these boundaries and integrates these insights into the broader context of sustainable finance. The argument is made that adhering to the PB framework is not just an environmental concern but a fundamental economic imperative, aligning with regulatory frameworks and the objectives of the United Nations Sustainable Development Goals. Chapter 4 brings the conceptual foundations of the first three chapters into practical execution by entities such as companies, cities, and countries. This chapter focuses on the intersection of climate risks and business management, emphasizing the profound impact of changing environmental dynamics on organizations, industries, and economies. It explores how companies assess and mitigate climate-related threats, with a particular focus on the financial implications of extreme weather events and the role of the 2015 Paris Agreement in stabilizing global temperatures. The chapter also discusses the concept of "climate value at risk" (CVaR) and the growing recognition of climate risks by financial communities, which is driving changes in capital allocation and oversight practices.

Chapters 5 and 6 delve into geospatial technologies and data, the title of this book. How to incorporate such data into taking sustainable actions. Geospatial finance, a burgeoning field integrating spatial data and analysis into financial decision-making, is explored in the two chapters. These two chapters lay the foundations and methods relevant to geospatial finance. Chapter 5 highlights the importance of spatial context in financial assessments, particularly in identifying risks, optimizing locations, and making informed decisions. The chapter delves into the technical challenges of geospatial data interpretation and showcases the transformative potential of geospatial finance in aligning economic and environmental goals. Case studies, such as China's development finance, illustrate the practical applications and impact of geospatial finance. The chapter concludes by discussing the challenges of data quality and integration, underscoring the need for ongoing research and innovation. Chapter 7 examines geospatial finance through the lens of satellite imagery and geospatial data to provide detailed insights into the environmental impacts of investments, enabling informed and effective decision-making in sustainable finance. This approach facilitates the identification of risks and opportunities, while supporting the tracking of sustainable finance initiatives over time, thus promoting climate resilience. The chapter also uses case studies to illustrate the use of AI deep learning using satellite data for mangrove mapping.

Chapter 8 focuses on carbon. Carbon pricing is explored as a critical strategy to mitigate climate change by internalizing the costs associated with greenhouse gas (GHG) emissions. By implementing mechanisms like carbon taxes and cap-and-trade systems, carbon pricing incentivizes the reduction of emissions and fosters innovation in cleaner technologies. FinTech solutions enhance these efforts by utilizing geospatial data and blockchain technology to streamline carbon offset markets and improve data-driven carbon accounting, thereby accelerating the transition to a low-carbon economy.

Chapter 9 discusses the relevance of the newly emerging Generative AI (GenAI) as a powerful tool for navigating the complex landscape of sustainability data within FinTech. GenAI streamlines data reporting, ensures compliance with sustainability frameworks, and addresses challenges such as greenwashing. While GenAI offers significant advantages, the ethical implications and the need for human validation to mitigate biases are emphasized. The chapter also acknowledges the environmental impact of AI and suggests strategies for sustainable AI development. Together, these technologies are portrayed as essential tools driving transparency, sustainability, and innovation in the financial sector.

Expert Interviews

Each chapter is enriched by interviews with business leaders and scientific experts who bring valuable context and depth to the discussions, ensuring that readers not only grasp the issues but also appreciate the practical strategies being employed to overcome them. The book opens with a compelling call to action from Edward R. Saltzberg, Ph.D., co-founder and Executive Director of the Security and Sustainability Forum (SSF). Saltzberg underscores the critical importance of prioritizing sustainability as a cornerstone for humanity's long-term survival, setting the stage for a deep dive into sustainable practices that go beyond mere compliance and into transformative business strategies.

Mark Golovcsenko, a Principal in KPMG's US Strategy practice, brings a nuanced understanding of the regulatory landscapes across the US, Europe, Singapore, and other regions. He offers a detailed analysis of the opportunities created by the Inflation Reduction Act in the US, showing how these new regulations are reshaping business strategies and opening doors for companies willing to innovate.

In Chapter 2, Peter Fox-Penner, Ph.D., a distinguished Senior Fellow at Boston University's Institute for Global Sustainability (IGS) and Chief Impact Officer at Energy Impact Partners, shares his expertise on the burgeoning market for clean energy. His insights into investments in energy startups illustrate the accelerating demand for sustainable energy solutions, providing a roadmap for companies looking to enter this dynamic field. Mary Cerulli, founder of Climate Finance Action, adds depth to the discussion by sharing her expertise on sustainable finance, highlighting the critical role of education and advocacy in driving change.

Chapter 3 takes readers into the realm of planetary boundaries, where Severker Sorlin, one of the original authors of the planetary boundaries' framework, offers a cultural perspective on ecosystem services and their vital role in supporting local communities. Dr. Kevin P. Gallagher, Director of the Boston University Global Development Policy Center, complements this with a discussion on the challenges of achieving the UN's Sustainable Development Goals, providing a sobering yet hopeful view on the future of global development finance.

In Chapter 4, Dr. Madison Condon, a Professor at Boston University School of Law, delves into the significance of US SEC climate regulation rules and the critical need for integration across government sectors. She emphasizes the importance of decarbonization as part of fiduciary responsibility, while Graham Cook, an expert in catastrophic insurance modeling, explains the vital role of metrics and climate risk models in the development of solar and wind farm installations.

The narrative continues in Chapter 5 with insights from two industry veterans who explore the practice of sustainability in the hospitality and metal manufacturing sectors. P. Ashley Cimini Singh, President of GSM Metals Inc., provides a case study on responsible sourcing, illustrating how even small manufacturing businesses can lead in reducing greenhouse gas emissions. Peter Yesawich highlights the gap between consumer behavior and sustainability in the travel industry, noting that cost often outweighs environmental considerations in decision-making.

In Chapter 6, Manfred Fischer, Emeritus Professor of Economic Geography at Vienna University of Economics and Business, emphasizes the rising importance of geospatial data and its role in solving today's societal and environmental challenges. His discussion illuminates the transformative potential of geospatial sciences in creating more sustainable and resilient communities.

Chapter 7 brings back Mark Golovcsenko, who underscores the critical role of data and tools in effective reporting, setting the stage for the future of sustainability reporting.

Chapter 8 highlights the work of Nick Zwaneveld, CEO of Coorest, who introduces readers to the innovative world of NFTs and carbon tokens, explaining how these digital assets, powered by smart contracts and geospatial satellite data, are revolutionizing carbon pricing and sustainability efforts.

Finally, in Chapter 9, Per Edin, Board Committee Chair and AI Go-to-Market leader at KPMG in the US, shares insights on KPMG's GenAI initiatives. He discusses the opportunities and challenges of integrating GenAI across an organization, highlighting the importance of strategic adoption to maximize benefits and drive innovation.

Note the book is not just a collection of interviews; but rather, it is a comprehensive guide to understanding the future of sustainability in business, offering practical insights and case studies that can help organizations build resilience, improve returns, and gain a competitive edge in an increasingly sustainability-focused world.

Shaping the Future

This book encourages readers to be active participants in transforming the industry. By embracing a data-driven approach to resilience strategy, you can position your organization as a leader in innovation and responsible business practices, helping to shape a sustainable and prosperous future for the financial sector. This comprehensive approach aims to equip readers with the knowledge, tools, and inspiration to drive meaningful change in the FinTech industry, bridging the gaps between geospatial data science, AI, and sustainability.

You can stay ahead of global policy shifts with an in-depth analysis of the regulations affecting sustainable FinTech. You can learn how to navigate these regulations to ensure your organization not only compiles but thrives in a complex regulatory environment. Begin your journey today!

Boston, USA   Sucharita Gopal
                                                                                                                         Josh Pitts

Acknowledgments

In presenting this work, we take full responsibility for all the material contained herein. This book draws heavily from contributions across a wide range of fields, including finance, sustainable investment, spatial sciences, remote sensing, data science, and climate science, as well as policy reports. In our efforts to provide a comprehensive and inclusive perspective, we have made a concerted effort to incorporate literature and case studies from beyond the United States, recognizing that significant advancements in sustainability regulations and investments are occurring on a global scale.

We are deeply grateful to our colleagues from around the world, whose contributions have been instrumental in shaping the content and direction of this book. In particular, we would like to express our appreciation to Manfred Fischer for his critical review of the chapter on geospatial finance, which greatly benefited from our extensive discussions. We thank Edward Saltzberg for reviewing Chapter 1 and his early involvement in disseminating our research via the Security and Sustainability Forum webinars. We also extend our thanks to Magaly Koch for her rigorous critique of the chapter on remote sensing and to David Blitzer, the former chairman of S&P Dow Jones Indices, for his insightful contributions to Chapter 2 on ESG integration in sustainable finance. Chepuri Shri Krishna from Bangalore, India, provided invaluable insights on GenAI and agentic workflows. At the same time, Les Kaufman and Ethan Deyle, Boston University Marine Program, offered essential perspectives on planetary boundaries, which significantly informed Chapter 3. Their collective expertise allowed us to seamlessly integrate science, data analytics, and policy in this work.

Our early collaboration with Kevin Gallagher at the Global Development Policy Center at Boston University deepened our understanding of the environmental impacts of investments that underscored the relevance of the UN Sustainable Development Goals. Peter Fox-Penner provided significant feedback on the energy sector and the startup culture driving the transition from fossil fuels. Robert Kaufman was a consistently reliable sounding board for discussions related to economic models and energy. Petra Staufer-Steinnocher in Vienna offered valuable insights on global supply chains, and Gail Carpenter's discussions on the history and evolution of AI were particularly enlightening. We also wish to acknowledge Ron Nowak's editorial expertise, which significantly enhanced the quality of the manuscript.

We are incredibly grateful to our NSF-COPES associates, Les Kaufman, Ethan Deyle, and Roel Boumans, for their invaluable insights on marine and terrestrial ecosystems, ecosystem services, nature-based solutions, and systems modeling. Their critical input was crucial in shaping the discussions around these topics. We also extend our thanks to Nathan Phillips, whose expertise greatly influenced our thinking on the contexts of methane emissions. Additionally, we appreciate the support from Yaxiong Ma, a postdoctoral student, and Dhurv Toshniwal, a graduate researcher, for their research on deep learning using satellite data and GenAI, as well as from Mira Fair-Kelly, a graduate student, who supported our work on palm oil and mangroves. We also extend our gratitude to the Boston University Ignition Grant for providing funds to develop and design our data platform, the Pardee Center for the Study of the Longer-Range Future, and the Impact Measurement & Allocation Program at Boston University for supporting work related to ESG. We also thank the NSF COPES grant for funding our research on coastal communities, ecosystem services, and blue carbon.

The support of the Floodlight Inc. team—Nate Wyne, Matthew Fishman, and Chris Clancy—has been invaluable. Their insights into regulatory frameworks and investment strategies have offered practical, real-world applications of the methods discussed throughout this book, enhancing their relevance to current industry practices.

Gopal would like to express her gratitude to Devender, Vivek, Sreenivas, and her extended family for their unwavering support, love, and encouragement.

Pitts would like to thank Emily for her great care and love and the good friends and family surrounding us.

This book is the product of a collaborative effort shaped by diverse perspectives, and we hope it contributes meaningfully to the ongoing discourse on sustainability and responsible investment. Our goal is to remain optimistic and encourage businesses, banks, and nations to harness the data and insights emerging from geospatial technologies. We trust that this book will be both thought-provoking and informative, offering valuable insights at the intersection of FinTech and geospatial data, helping to drive positive change and innovation.

Contents

1 Background and Foundations: Sustainability, Fintech, Data Science, and AI 1
   1.1 Introduction 1
   1.2 Analyzing the Climate Crisis: Insights from Three Key Datasets 3
   1.3 Global Policy Approaches to Guide Collective Action 8
   1.4 From International SDGs to Corporate ESG Frameworks: Bridging Global Goals and Business Imperatives 10
      1.4.1 ESG Considerations 10
      1.4.2 Corporate Reporting and Trends 12
      1.4.3 ESG Reporting: Challenges and Standards 13
      1.4.4 Verification and Metrics in ESG Reporting 13
      1.4.5 Transitioning from ESG Frameworks to Financial Impact 14
   1.5 Shifting Realities for Business and Financial Institutions 15
      1.5.1 Compliance Regulations with Cross-Jurisdictional and Extraterritorial Implications 15
      1.5.2 ESG Litigation Around Greenwashing and Reporting 20
      1.5.3 Generational Differences in Investment Themes 21
      1.5.4 Materiality Really Matters—Financialization of ESG Risks 22
      1.5.5 Companies Sustainability Reports 25
   1.6 Federal Funds and Tax Incentives Usher the Climate Tech Revolution and Innovation 25
   1.7 Emerging Technologies and Emerging Economy 28
   1.8 Big Data and AI—New Frontiers 29
      1.8.1 Sources of Emerging ESG Data 29
      1.8.2 The Promise and Potential of AI 30
      1.8.3 Looking Forward: A Fintech Revolution 30

		1.8.4	Summary	31
	References			32
2	**ESG Integration: Unveiling Risk and Driving Innovation in Sustainable Finance**			35
	2.1	Introduction		35
	2.2	Sustainable Finance Timeline		40
	2.3	Various Stakeholders in Sustainable Finance Investment		42
		2.3.1	Consumers, Particularly Millennials and Younger Generations	43
		2.3.2	States, Cities, and Governments	43
		2.3.3	UN and Other International Organizations	44
		2.3.4	Corporates	44
		2.3.5	Pension Funds and Family Offices	45
		2.3.6	Regional, Global, Local Banks	48
		2.3.7	Private Investment Companies	49
		2.3.8	VC Firms and Philanthropists	49
	2.4	Implementing Sustainable Investment Strategies		50
		2.4.1	Sustainable Investment Strategies	50
		2.4.2	Fossil Fuel Divestment (FFC) as a Strategy	53
		2.4.3	Measurement and Benchmarking	54
		2.4.4	Example Funds	56
	2.5	Sustainable Investing as a Strategic Response to Demand and Increasing Awareness		57
		2.5.1	Physical Risks	57
		2.5.2	Comparative Generational Perspectives—Impact of Millennials	58
		2.5.3	Sustainable Reporting	59
	2.6	Regulations in Sustainable Finance		61
		2.6.1	EU's Regulation in Sustainable Finance	62
		2.6.2	The US Approach: Market-Driven Efforts and Regulatory Evolution	64
		2.6.3	Navigating the Regulatory Mosaic: Asia and Beyond	65
	2.7	Concluding Remarks—Is There a Brighter Future?		66
		2.7.1	Fintech Industry	66
		2.7.2	Innovations in Key Sectors Offering Hope for Our Survival	67
	References			73

3	**It's Changing: The Dynamics of the Modern World—Climate Change and Planetary Boundaries**	83
	3.1 Introduction—Planetary Boundaries	83
	3.2 Ecological Economics, Doughnut Economics, Piketty's Capital, and New Economics Inform on Planetary Boundaries	84
	3.3 The Evolution of the Planetary Boundaries Framework	88
	3.4 Planetary Boundaries Informs Policies and Frameworks Used by Countries, Financial Securities, and Companies	93
	3.5 Incorporating PB into Strategic Planning	95
	3.5.1 Climate Change	95
	3.5.2 Biosphere Integrity	98
	3.5.3 Land-System Change	100
	3.5.4 Freshwater Change	103
	3.5.5 Biogeochemical Flows	104
	3.5.6 Ocean Acidification	105
	3.5.7 Atmospheric Aerosol Loading	107
	3.5.8 Stratospheric Ozone Depletion	108
	3.5.9 Novel Entities	109
	3.6 Challenges and Solutions for Reporting on PB	110
	3.6.1 Addressing PB Problems Through Regulations and Guidelines	111
	3.6.2 Addressing PB Problems Through Nature-Based Solutions (NbS)	111
	3.6.3 Addressing PB Problems Through Finance	113
	3.7 Voluntary Carbon Markets	124
	3.8 The Emergence of Fintech and Climatetech	125
	3.8.1 Digital Payment Systems for Environmental Conservation	125
	3.8.2 Blockchain for Sustainable Supply Chains	126
	3.8.3 Crowdfunding for Environmental Projects	127
	3.8.4 Green Bonds and Sustainable Investments	127
	3.8.5 Carbon Trading	127
	3.8.6 InsurTech for Climate Resilience	129
	3.9 Summary and Conclusions	129
	References	130
4	**A Deep Dive into Climate Risks and Materiality**	135
	4.1 Introduction	135
	4.1.1 Value at Risk (VaR) and Climate Value at Risk (CVaR)	136
	4.1.2 Drivers and Strategies for Managing Climate Risks	141
	4.2 Physical and Transition Risks	143
	4.2.1 Chronic Physical Risks	145
	4.2.2 Acute Risks	146

		4.2.3	Economic Cost of Physical Risks	146
		4.2.4	Transition Risks	149
	4.3	Climate Scenario Models Assess Risk into the Future		150
		4.3.1	NGFS Scenarios	151
		4.3.2	Representative Concentration Pathways	151
		4.3.3	Shared Socioeconomic Pathways	153
		4.3.4	International Energy Agency (IEA) Scenarios	155
	4.4	Evaluating Physical Risk Hazard		158
		4.4.1	Proprietary Data Products Targeting Asset or Portfolio Climate Hazard Risks	159
		4.4.2	Climate Knowledge Data Portals	160
		4.4.3	Estimating Losses Due to Physical Risks	161
	4.5	Operationalizing Asset-Level Risk		162
		4.5.1	Asset-Related Customer Inputs	164
		4.5.2	Evaluate Climate Hazard	164
		4.5.3	Evaluate Exposure to Hazard	168
		4.5.4	Evaluate Vulnerability to Hazard	169
		4.5.5	Evaluate Direct Impacts in Absence of Adaptation	171
		4.5.6	Transition Risks via Scenario Modeling	172
	4.6	A Case Study Using Evaluation of Physical Risks at Asset Level		173
	4.7	Conclusions		179
	References			179
5	**Regulation and Frameworks: Current and Future Reporting Trends**			**183**
	5.1	Introduction		183
		5.1.1	Why Is Sustainability Reporting Good?	188
		5.1.2	Criticism of ESG Reporting	189
	5.2	Global Standard and Frameworks for Sustainability Reporting		191
		5.2.1	Sustainability Reporting	192
		5.2.2	Climate Disclosures	193
		5.2.3	ESG Frameworks	197
		5.2.4	ESG Rating Agencies	199
	5.3	Reporting Standards and Frameworks—The Case of the European Union		207
		5.3.1	ESRS and CSRD	208
		5.3.2	SFDR—Articles 6, 8, and 9	209
		5.3.3	SFDR Article 8 and 9 Funds	213
	5.4	Exploring the Evolution and Impact of ESG Disclosures in Corporate America		214
		5.4.1	To Be and Not to Be—New SEC Climate Regulations	215

		5.4.2 California's Climate Regulations	216
	5.5	Sustainability Reporting in Asia	217
	5.6	Summary	219
	References		221
6	**Geospatial Finance: Foundations and Applications**		**225**
	6.1	Introduction	225
		6.1.1 Financial Assessment Involves Spatial Context and Understanding	227
		6.1.2 What Is Geospatial Data?	228
	6.2	What's so Unique About Spatial Data?	230
		6.2.1 Types of Spatial Data and Geospatial Finance Applications	230
		6.2.2 Complex Geometries and Spatial Complexity	237
	6.3	The Vexing MAUP Problem in Spatial Data	239
	6.4	Spatially Explicit Models	242
		6.4.1 Spatial Neighborhood Representation	242
		6.4.2 Global and Local Spatial Autocorrelation Measures	243
		6.4.3 Applying Hot Spot Analysis in Finance	246
		6.4.4 Spatially Weighted Regression—Hedonic Models	247
		6.4.5 Geostatistics and Kriging Interpolation	249
		6.4.6 Spatial Econometrics	251
		6.4.7 Case Study: China's Development Finance Impacts	254
	6.5	Geospatial Finance Framework	256
		6.5.1 Unraveling the Property of Spatial Dependence in Spatial Finance	256
		6.5.2 A Spatial Hierarchical Framework for Geospatial Finance	258
		6.5.3 Geospatial Finance Use Cases	260
	6.6	Challenges and Limitations of Geospatial Data	265
	6.7	Summary	267
	References		268
7	**Satellite Remote Sensing: Pioneering Tools for Environmental Insight and Sustainable Investment**		**275**
	7.1	Introduction: Geospatial Finance and Satellite Remote Sensing	275
		7.1.1 Earth Observation and Remote Sensing—History and Evolution	277
		7.1.2 Commercial Satellites	278
	7.2	The Crucial Role of Geospatial Technologies in Addressing Climate Risks and Environmental Impacts	281
		7.2.1 Geospatial Finance: Navigating Climate Risks Across Asset Classes	282

		7.2.2	The Pivotal Role of Satellite Remote Sensing in Geospatial Finance	284
	7.3	Earth Observation via Remote Sensing		286
		7.3.1	Fundamentals of Remote Sensing	286
		7.3.2	Types of Remote Sensing Based on Satellite Characteristics	291
		7.3.3	Widely Used Satellites for Earth Observation (EO)—Landsat and Sentinel	296
		7.3.4	Satellites for Greenhouse Gas Emissions Accounting	297
	7.4	Satellite Data Access—Data Catalogs		300
		7.4.1	USGS EarthExplorer	301
		7.4.2	NASA LP DAAC Catalog	302
		7.4.3	EarthData Catalog	302
		7.4.4	NOAA Climate Data Online (CDO)	302
		7.4.5	EU Copernicus Access Portal	303
		7.4.6	Japan's Satellite Data Access	303
		7.4.7	India's Satellite Data Access	303
	7.5	Democratizing Global Access to Geospatial Data—Google Earth Engine Platform		303
	7.6	ML and Deep Learning in Remote Sensing		305
		7.6.1	Case Study: Enhanced Monitoring of Indonesian Mangrove Forests: Leveraging Deep Learning and Remote Sensing	306
		7.6.2	Significant Insights and Future Directions	309
	7.7	Advancements and Challenges in Remote Sensing		310
		7.7.1	Emerging ClimateTech Companies—With AI, This Sphere of Space Technologies Is Booming	310
		7.7.2	Sustainable Blue Bonds	311
		7.7.3	Financial Trading Platforms Use the Same Satellite Ground Stations	312
	7.8	Summary and Conclusions		312
	References			313
8	**The Intersection of Carbon Pricing, Fintech, and Blockchain Technology**			**317**
	8.1	Introduction—Addressing GHG Emissions by Carbon Pricing		317
	8.2	Climate Science and the Imperative for Carbon Pricing		319
		8.2.1	Current State of the Climate	320
		8.2.2	Future Projections of Emissions and Climate	322
	8.3	Economics of Carbon Pricing		324
		8.3.1	Economics of Carbon Pricing—Carbon Taxes and Cap-and-Trade Systems	324
		8.3.2	Rationale Behind Carbon Pricing	327

		8.3.3 Global Momentum and Challenges	329
		8.3.4 The Case of Canada	330
		8.3.5 The US, the EU, and Japan	332
	8.4	The Role of Fintech in Carbon Pricing—Blockchain and Digital MRV	333
	8.5	Case Study—Floodlight	338
	8.6	Conclusion	339
	References		340
9	**GenAI: Unlocking Sustainability Insights and Driving Change in Fintech**		**345**
	9.1	Introduction	345
		9.1.1 Alignment to Financial Stakeholder Interests	346
		9.1.2 Sustainability Reporting	349
		9.1.3 Issues in Automated Compliance Reporting	351
		9.1.4 Climate Risks and Environmental Impacts	354
		9.1.5 Validation and Increasing Compliance	354
	9.2	The GenAI Ecosystem and Its Transformative Impact	354
		9.2.1 GenAI Ecosystem	355
		9.2.2 Prompt Engineering: Unleashing GenAI's Potential	358
		9.2.3 Fundamentals of Fine-Tuning	359
		9.2.4 ABC's of Retrieval-Augmented Generation (RAG)	360
		9.2.5 The Emerging Agentic Workflow	363
	9.3	GenAI: A New Dawn for Sustainability Reporting	365
		9.3.1 Automating Routine Tasks	368
		9.3.2 Can GenAI Be Trained to Spot Greenwashing?	369
		9.3.3 GenAI for Complying to Different Standards and Frameworks	369
		9.3.4 Bridging Compliance and Reporting Gaps	370
		9.3.5 Competitive Intelligence	370
		9.3.6 Sovereign AI	370
	9.4	Overcoming Challenges with GenAI	371
		9.4.1 How Do Cognitive Biases and Fallacies in Human Decision-Making Impact GenAI Training?	372
		9.4.2 The Need for Human Validation	373
		9.4.3 Ethical Considerations and Bias	374
	9.5	Unlocking Potential: Prompt Engineering for Sustainable Fintech—Use Cases	375
		9.5.1 Mastering Effective Prompts: Extracting Insights from the Web with ChatGPT/Gemini	375
		9.5.2 What's in a Name? Few-Shot, Zero-Shot, and Multimodal Chain-Of-Thought Prompting	378

	9.5.3	Extracting Specific Information from US SEC 10-K Filings	384
9.6		The Elephant in the Room: Are GenAI and Other AI Models Increasing GHG Emissions?	386
9.7		Conclusion: Charting the Path Forward	389
References			390

10 Buds, Thorns, and Roses: Navigating the Landscape of Sustainable Finance and Climate Resilience ... 395

10.1	Introduction	395
10.2	Buds: Emerging Opportunities and Innovations	396
10.3	Thorns: The Challenges and Pitfalls	396
10.4	Roses: Success Stories and Positive Impacts	397
10.5	Conclusion: Navigating the Future of Sustainability	397

Acronyms

AI	Artificial Intelligence
AR6	IPCC's Working Group Sixth Assessment[1] Report (AR6)
AUM	Assets Under Management
CDP	Carbon Disclosure Project
CDSB	Climate Disclosure Standards Board
CMSA	Consolidated Metropolitan Statistical Area
CNN	Convolutional Neural Networks
CO_2	Carbon Dioxide
COP	Conference of the Parties
CSDDD	Corporate Sustainability Due Diligence Directive
CSR	Corporate Social Responsibility
CSRD	Corporate Sustainability Reporting Directive
CVaR	Climate Value at Risk
DEM	Digital Elevation Model
EMEA	Europe the Middle East and Africa
EMS	Electro Magnetic Spectrum
EPA	Environmental Protection Agency
ESA	European Space Agency
ESG	Environmental, Social, and Governance
ESRS	European Sustainability Reporting Standards
ETFs	Exchange Traded Funds
EU	European Union
EUAs	European Union Allowances
FEMA	Federal Emergency Management Agency
FFD	Fossil Fuel Divestment
FSB	Financial Stability Board
FTC	Federal Trade Commission
GDP	Gross Domestic Product
GEE	Google Earth Engine
GenAI	Generative Artificial Intelligence
GEO	Geostationary Orbit

GHG	Greenhouse Gas
GIS	Geographical Information System
GPT	Generative Pre-trained Transformer
GRI	Global Reporting Initiative
IAM	Integrated Assessment Model
IEA	International Energy Agency
IFRS	International Financial Reporting Standards
IIRC	International Integrated Reporting Council
IOSCO	International Organization of Securities Commissions
IPCC	Intergovernmental Panel on Climate Change
IR	Integrated Reporting
IRA	U.S. Inflation Reduction Act
ISSB	International Sustainability Standards Board
KPI	Key Performance Indicator
KPMG	Klynveld Peat Marwick Goerdeler
LEED	Leadership in Energy and Environmental Design
LiDAR	Light Detection and Ranging
LLaMA	Language Model Meta AI
LLMs	Large Language Models
M&A	Mergers & Acquisitions
MAUP	Modifiable Areal Unit Problem
N_2O	Nitrous Oxide
NASA	National Aeronautics and Space Administration
NFRD	Non-Financial Reporting Directive
NGA	National Greenhouse Accounting
NGFS	Network for Greening the Financial System
NGOs	Non-Government Organizations
NLP	Natural Language Processing
NOAA	National Oceanic and Atmospheric Administration
PAIs	Principal Adverse Impacts
PB	Planetary Boundaries
PCAF	Partnership for Carbon Accounting Financials
PM	Particulate Matter
PMSA	Primary Metropolitan Statistical Area
PRI	Principles for Responsible Investment
PwC	Price Waterhouse Coopers
R&D	Research and Development
RAG	Retrieval-Augmented Generation
SASB	Sustainability Accounting Standards Board
SBTi	Science-Based Targets initiative
SDGs	Sustainable Development Goals
SEC	Securities and. Exchange Commission
SFDR	Sustainable Finance Disclosure Regulation
SRI	Socially Responsible Investing
SSP	Shared Socioeconomic Pathway

TCFD	Task Force on Climate-related Financial Disclosures
TCs	Tropical cyclones
UK	United Kingdom
UN	United Nations
UNEP FI	UN Environment Programme Finance Initiative
UNEP	United Nations Environment Programme
UNFCCC	United Nations Framework Convention on Climate Change
US	United States
USGS	United States Geological Survey
VaR	Value at Risk
VC	Venture Capitalist
WBA	World Benchmarking Alliance

Chapter 1
Background and Foundations: Sustainability, Fintech, Data Science, and AI

> The future of life on earth depends on our ability to take action—David Attenborough

1.1 Introduction

In the current epoch, known as the Anthropocene[1] (the term used to describe the time during which humans have had substantial impact on the earth), human actions have caused dramatic changes to the Earth's natural processes, destabilizing the key elements—air, water, and natural resources—required for life to exist. This era is marked by a rapid increase in human population and the expansion of activities that disrupt the biosphere. These disturbances disrupt the natural balance and jeopardize the integrity of Earth's systems. According to the Intergovernmental Panel on Climate Change (IPCC, 2019), such anthropogenic impacts include, but are not limited to, industrialization, deforestation, and urban expansion.

Figure 1.1 depicts how human activities have exacerbated the greenhouse gas effect. This natural phenomenon, which is critical for keeping Earth's temperature within a range that supports life, has been aggravated by human activity, notably since the mid-twentieth century. The fundamental driver of this intensification is the use of fossil fuels (coal, oil, and natural gas) for energy and transportation, which dramatically increases atmospheric concentrations of carbon dioxide (CO_2), a potent greenhouse gas. Land use changes due to agriculture and urban development also contribute to the rise in greenhouse gases, albeit to a lesser extent. Figure 1.1 illustrates the connection between human activities (such as agriculture, transportation, heating, and industry) and greenhouse gas (GHG) emissions. Carbon dioxide (CO_2) is the most abundant GHG, accounting for well over 75% of GHG emissions, while

---

[1] The Anthropocene is a newly proposed geologic epoch, but current consensus is that the present era is the Holocene.

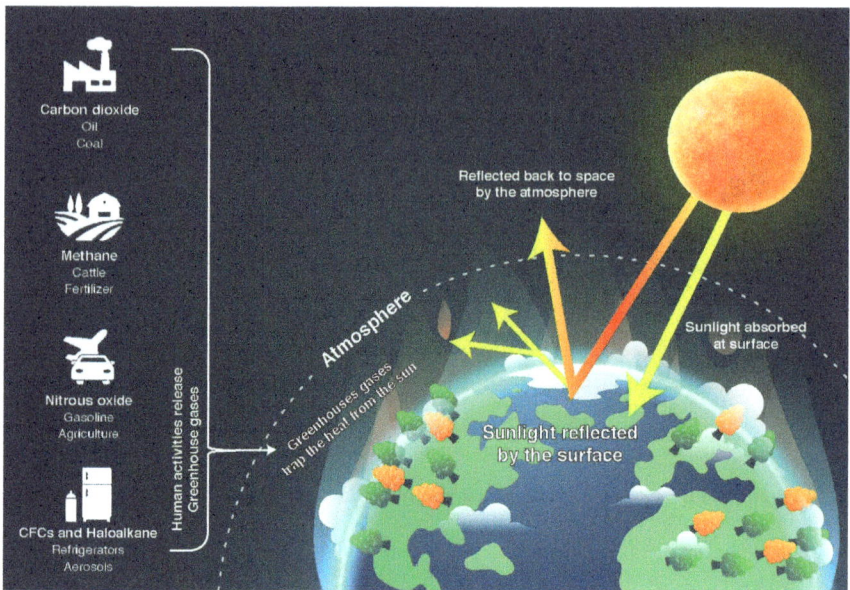

Fig. 1.1 The greenhouse effect resulting from the release of greenhouse gases, caused by human activities such as agriculture, transportation, heating, and manufacturing

methane is about 25 times more potent than CO2 over a 100-year period, and nitrous oxide (N20) is about 298 times that of CO2 over a 100-year period.

Greenhouse gases trap the sun's heat, preventing it from escaping into space, creating the greenhouse effect that keeps the Earth's temperature warmer than it would otherwise be. This alteration of the atmosphere's composition by GHG has led to several consequences. These include rising global average temperatures, increased frequency and intensity of extreme weather events, sea-level rise resulting from thermal expansion and glacier melt, oceanic circulation patterns and acidification changes, and heightened drought conditions.[2] These impacts are interconnected and can amplify each other, resulting in compound effects on the global climate system.

IPCC, in its Sixth Assessment Report (AR6) to policymakers, notes that "Human-induced climate change is already affecting many weather and climate extremes in every region across the globe. Evidence of observed changes in extremes such as heatwaves, heavy precipitation, droughts, and tropical cyclones, particularly their attribution to human influence, has strengthened since AR5" (IPCC, 2023).[3] Thus, the scientific consensus highlights a direct causal link between human activities and climate change, emphasizing the imperative for a detailed understanding of these relationships. To address this increase in global temperature, 196 countries signed

---

[2] For further details, see https://science.nasa.gov/climate-change/causes/.

[3] IPCC Sixth Assessment Report—Working Group I—The Physical Sciences Basis. Available online: https://www.ipcc.ch/report/ar6/wg1/downloads/report/IPCC_AR6_WGI_Headline_Statements.pdf accessed on May 19 2024).

the Paris Agreement (UNFCCC, 2015) to pursue efforts for "holding the increase in the global average temperature to well below 2 °C above pre-industrial levels and pursuing efforts to limit the temperature increase to 1.5 °C above pre-industrial levels."

A thorough understanding of these challenges is required for devising successful solutions to mitigate climate change and adapt to its inevitable consequences. The urgency of addressing these challenges highlights the need for a sustainable approach as defined by the UN World Commission on Environment and Development: "Sustainable development is a development that meets the needs of the present without compromising the ability of future generations to meet their own needs."[4] This definition, rooted in the principles of inter-generational equity and fairness, calls for a long-term perspective on the impacts of our environmental, social, and economic activities today. It acknowledges that the challenges we face, such as climate change driven by increased CO2 emissions, are not distant problems to be left for future leaders but immediate concerns that require concerted efforts across all sectors of society. The next section illustrates the rapid transformations occurring on earth, emphasizing the need for immediate action.

1.2 Analyzing the Climate Crisis: Insights from Three Key Datasets

This section uses three critical datasets to present a stark portrayal of the growing effects of climate change through rising global temperatures, escalating CO2 levels, and their immediate consequences on our environment and society. These datasets not only support the ongoing shifts in our planet's climate system but also highlight the immediate need for concerted global action. Figure 1.2, based on Berkeley Earth's analysis data, shows increasing global mean temperatures from 1850 to 2023.[5] There has been an increase in global temperatures of over 0.5 °C (compared with the reference period) from the 1980s onward. From 1990 to 2022, human-driven activities led to a roughly 47% surge in global annual CO2 emissions due to fossil fuels and land use changes, contributing significantly to climate change. The increase in greenhouse gases has led to a rise in the global average temperature by 0.86 °C (1.55°F) above the twentieth-century average, with 2022 having the sixth-highest temperature in the 1880–2022 record. However, 2023 is more significant as this was the first year that exceeded the key 1.5 °C (2.7°F) threshold. To be more precise, the global annual average for 2023 in this dataset was estimated as 1.54 ± 0.06 °C (2.77 ± 0.11°F) above the average estimated for the pre-industrial period, a significant global milestone.

---

[4] From UNESCO Glossary: https://whc.unesco.org/en/glossary/375.
[5] See Berkeley Earth for full data: https://berkeleyearth.org/global-temperature-report-for-2023/.

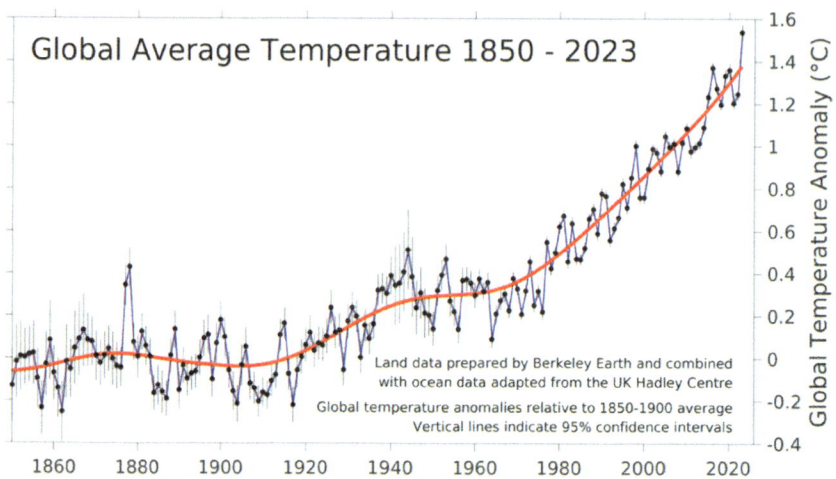

Fig. 1.2 Global anomalies in annual temperatures 1860–2023. The Y-axis represents the global temperature anomaly in degrees Celsius, running from −0.4 to 1.6. The X-axis shows years labeled from 1850 to past 2023. The reference period is the pre-industrial period, spanning 1850 to 1900. Anomalies are relative to the 1850–1900 average and show each year's relative change. Long-term trend shows an increase in anomaly value

Such changes highlight the urgency with which we must confront global warming, aiming to keep temperature increases far below 2 °C to ensure ecosystem resilience and vitality for future generations.

A second dataset reveals comparable anomalies over the summer months compared with historical averages based on NASA's surface temperature records.[6] Figure 1.3 displays the global temperature anomaly for the summer months (June, July, and August) from 1880 to 2023, compared to the 1951–1980 average. There is a clear upward trend in global temperature anomalies, particularly pronounced from the mid-twentieth century onward. Before the 1950s, most anomalies are negative, indicating cooler than average temperatures compared to the 1951–1980 baseline.[7]

---

[6] NASA assembles its temperature record, known as GISTEMP, from surface air temperature data acquired by tens of thousands of meteorological stations, as well as sea surface temperature data from ship- and buoy-based instruments. These raw data are analyzed using methods that account for the varied spacing of temperature stations around the globe and for urban heating effects that could skew the calculations. https://svs.gsfc.nasa.gov/cgi-bin/details.cgi?aid=14407&button=recent.

[7] The average is a statistic representing a dataset's central or typical value. There are different ways to measure the center: the mean, the arithmetic average (the sum of all values divided by the number of values), and the median (the middle value when all values are ordered). Usually, when "average" is used in the media, it refers to the mean. In the 2022 Global Temperature graph, the average is the sum of the global surface temperatures for 1951–1980 divided by 30. This average is the baseline represented by the horizontal line labeled 0 degree Celsius. The baseline is a reference point used for comparisons. An anomaly value is the difference between an individual value and the baseline. Go to the NASA climate website to learn more about how these averages are calculated.

1.2 Analyzing the Climate Crisis: Insights from Three Key Datasets

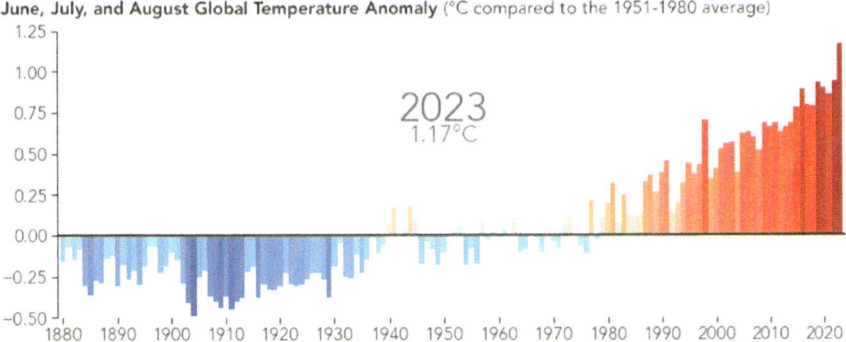

Fig. 1.3 Summer global temperature anomaly 1880–2023. The Y-axis is labeled temperature anomaly in degrees Celsius, running from −0.5 to 1.25. The X-axis spans from 1880 to 2023. *Source* NASA Earth Observatory image by Lauren Dauphin, based on data from NASA's Goddard Institute for Space Studies

There is a noticeable shift toward positive anomalies from the 1950s onward, indicating a trend toward warmer summers. The warming trend accelerates significantly, with the anomalies in the last few decades becoming increasingly positive. The highest anomaly of approximately 1.17 °C, indicating substantial warming recorded in 2023.

The summer of 2023 continued a long-term warming trend (from the 1980s), driven primarily by human-caused greenhouse gas emissions. The overall trend is rising temperatures compared with historical summertime temperatures, which, by 2023, were well above the 1-degree Celsius point.

The third dataset introduces the Keeling Curve from the Mauna Loa Observatory in Hawaii, which has been measuring and recording atmospheric CO_2 since the late 1950s. Named after Charles David Keeling, who initiated the monitoring, the Keeling curve shows a steady increase in CO_2 levels from year to year, and this increase is strongly correlated with global temperature increase. Figure 1.4 displays data from the Mauna Loa Observatory related to CO_2 levels. In addition to warming correlations, gas and pollutant emissions directly impact employee health and local environments. These, in turn, have reinforcing effects, often creating feedback loops that quickly worsen these problems. These impacts must be assessed to reduce emissions, monitored for temporal trends, and analyzed to find solutions. To summarize, the insights from these datasets show that the global community must take action.

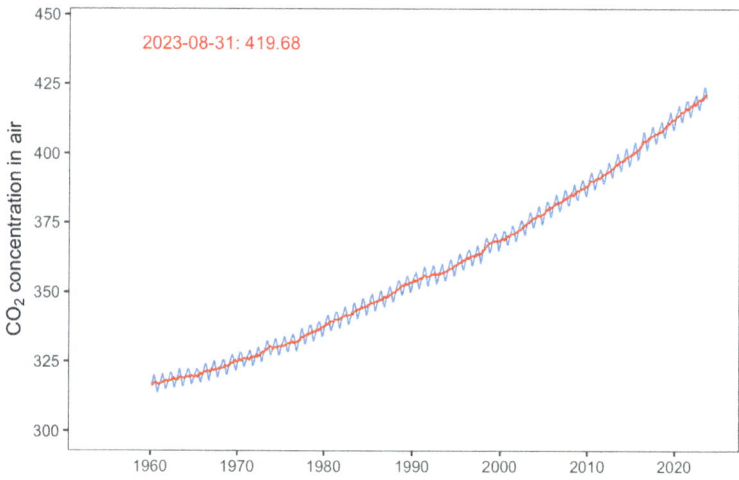

Fig. 1.4 Mauna Loa CO2 monthly mean concentration in air (parts per million) from 1960 to 2023. The line shows an upward trend of increasing CO2 concentrations *Source* NOAA/ESRL and Scripps Institution of Oceanography https://gml.noaa.gov/ccgg/trends/data.html

Expert in Focus: Edward Saltzberg

Edward R. Saltzberg, Ph.D., is a distinguished climate change leader and innovator who has held several impactful positions within the environmental and energy sectors. He is the executive director and a co-founder of The Security and Sustainability Forum (SSF). For 15 years, SSF has brought together global experts in online forums to address the threats to society from disruptions in natural and human systems, including climate change.

Dr. Saltzberg helps shape sustainability leaders as the director of Professional Education at George Washington University's Environmental and Energy Management Institute, where he manages non-degree courses on sustainability, energy, business, finance, risk management, policy, and governance. He is also a co-founder of Sovereign Resiliency Partners, where he leads sustainable economic development and energy resilience initiatives for Native American Tribes. Dr. Saltzberg holds a Ph.D. in Environmental Sciences from the University of Virginia, with a concentration in resource economics.

Humans have done a very poor job managing this side of our relationship with the Earth. We have overconsumed with little respect for the consequences. Our human nature, on the one hand, is very giving and loving, but on the other hand, it can be very selfish and take the earth's bounties for granted. Our nature has been to continue a behavior if the consequences don't affect us directly or immediately. This is the free rider problem, such as when the polluter is not held responsible, and pollution becomes a free input to production, and polluting makes money.

But we can't avoid a two-way street with the earth. The earth has a great regenerative capacity and can absorb man's impact, up to a point. As we have known for decades, continually taking the earth for granted gets to that point where something has to break, like the climate or healthy soils. So, maintaining a place for humans on the earth means caring about sustainability and biodiversity, and equitable allocation of resources, circularity in the economy, and reducing our negative footprint on the earth. The earth's going to survive over the millennium, but it may be a different biological mix. Humans could become just another failed biological experiment like the dinosaurs. This is something to think about. The dinosaurs, that failed experiment, lasted 140 million years. Humans have only been around for a few million years. The earth is going to continue unconcerned even if the current dominant species snuffs itself out. We don't want to be dinosaurs. What we do now will determine if humans are still walking the earth as long as they did.

The IPCC's Working Group Sixth Assessment[8] Report (AR6) made it clear: limiting global warming to 1.5 °C requires significant and immediate reductions in carbon dioxide (CO2) emissions along with other greenhouse gas emissions (IPCC, 2023). The AR6 lays out various outcomes depending on how effectively global societies mitigate emissions in the future. The report projects different warming possibilities based on various emission reduction methods.

According to the data used in the AR6, global temperatures have risen by approximately 1.1 °C above pre-industrial levels. There is an acknowledged possibility of temporarily reaching or surpassing 1.5 °C due to natural variability, in addition to human-induced warming; however, this differs from a continuous exceedance over

---

[8] https://www.ipcc.ch/report/sixth-assessment-report-cycle/.

time. The IPCC report outlines future scenarios in which temperatures might rise by roughly 3 °C by the end of the century if strong emissions-reduction measures are not implemented. These forecasts vary by scenario, indicating different levels of mitigation efforts. Such temperature changes have significant environmental impacts on agriculture, marine life, biodiversity, and vulnerable populations. In particular, island nations such as Mauritius and Fiji are experiencing increased beach erosion, land loss, and saltwater intrusion into freshwater systems. These issues threaten communities, crucial infrastructure, businesses, and tourism vital to island economies. Consequently, there is an urgent need for actions to reduce greenhouse gas emissions, mitigate and adapt to climate change, and integrate system-level transformations.

1.3 Global Policy Approaches to Guide Collective Action

The three climate datasets in the previous section provide factual evidence that supports the need for sustainable activities. In response to this critical need, global frameworks such as the United Nations Principles for Responsible Investment (PRI) and the Sustainable Development Goals (SDGs) have been formed to guide and accelerate global sustainability initiatives, as described next in this section. The PRI, introduced in 2006, represents a revolutionary strategy within the investment sector, calling for the incorporation of Environmental, Social, and Governance (ESG) issues into financial analysis and decision-making. The purpose was to get firms to focus on sustainability issues. This move fueled socially responsible investing (SRI) and green investments (a subset of SRI), which focus on companies dedicated to ecologically responsible business practices. Following the implementation of PRI, 63 investment firms with a combined USD 6.5 trillion in assets under management (AUM) agreed to incorporate ESG issues. With about 5500 signatories from over 100 countries and around USD 120 to USD 130 trillion in assets under management, the PRI members accounted for more than half of global institutional capital by the end of 2023.[9] Over the past 15 years, worldwide PRI AUM has increased by 1762%.

PRI has thus emerged as a pivotal framework within the global investment community, showing a paradigm shift toward responsible investment practices. This evolution can be attributed to a bottom-up response from the investment community, which has increasingly recognized the significance of incorporating ESG factors into risk assessment, value creation, and risk mitigation strategies. Traditional financial analysis often overlooks these factors, yet they hold substantial implications for long-term financial performance and risk management.

Simultaneously, the seventeen Sustainable Development Goals (SDGs) adopted in 2015 by all United Nations member states set forth a global agenda to address and mitigate the adverse effects of climate change among other pressing global challenges, by the year 2030. These goals serve as a blueprint for peace and prosperity,

---

[9] Further details and signatories can be seen here: https://www.unpri.org/download?ac=20150.

1.3 Global Policy Approaches to Guide Collective Action

Fig. 1.5 The United Nations Sustainable Development Goals (UN SDGs)[10] are a call to action encompassing 17 goals aimed at improving sustainability across various aspects of social, economic, and environmental development

targeting critical areas such as climate action, environmental sustainability, environmental degradation, and social equity, which are directly influenced by the trends depicted in the climate datasets. Figure 1.5 shows these goals.

The PRI recognizes the SDGs as a road map for achieving a sustainable future. The PRI framework encourages investors to align their practices with the goals outlined in the SDGs. The UN PRI and the SDGs are intrinsically linked as they prioritize a sustainable and equitable future. The PRI empowers investors to be active agents of change by providing the tools and resources to create positive impacts that align with the global goals set out in the SDGs. The principles of PRI have not only facilitated a more informed and holistic approach to investment but have also set a global standard for responsible investing, aligning financial objectives with broader societal and environmental goals.

Linking these global initiatives to the foundational climate data successfully demonstrates how empirical evidence of climate change has triggered a broad-based, international response. The increased connection between financial strategies and sustainability objectives, as evidenced by the increase in the PRI assets under management, demonstrates a greater understanding of the inherent link between environmental stewardship and economic success within the financial sector. This integrated approach not only highlights the direct impacts of climate change but also sets the stage for a discussion on how global financial and policy frameworks are adapting to these challenges, driving collective action crucial to sustainable development and mitigation of future risks. To summarize, SDGs outline the "what" of sustainable development or the universal goals we must achieve. ESG provides a critical method for the "how"—focusing on companies' actual practices and how those practices can work toward or against attaining the SDGs.

---

[10] UN SDGs: https://sdgs.un.org/goals

1.4 From International SDGs to Corporate ESG Frameworks: Bridging Global Goals and Business Imperatives

Understanding the different but complementary functions of the SDGs and ESG criteria is crucial for understanding how global sustainability goals are translated into corporate action. While the SDGs give a broad framework and specific targets for global sustainable development, ESG standards enable investors and other stakeholders to evaluate how well individual enterprises conform to these goals. This linkage motivates organizations to fully integrate sustainable practices into their operations, making ESG an important tool for translating the "what" of SDGs into the "how" of corporate sustainability.

1.4.1 ESG Considerations

Environmental (E) Considerations in ESG: Environmental metrics, which focus on aspects such as greenhouse gas (GHG) emissions, water usage and discharge, land impacts, and biodiversity impacts are integral for tracking corporate contributions to sustainability. These metrics are often quantifiable and provide a clear picture of a company's environmental footprint. For instance: Scope 1 and Scope 2 emissions: Scope 1 emissions are direct GHG emissions from operated assets by the company, such as fuel use, industrial processes, and machinery operation. Scope 2 emissions are indirect GHG emissions associated with emissions from the purchased electricity, steam, heat, or cooling. Fossil fuel companies will tend to have very high Scope 1 emissions. For example, Saudi Aramco (Oil & Gas) reported Scope 1 emissions of 55.7 MMtCO2e and Scope 2 emissions of 16.1 MMtCO2e.

On a broader scale, countries like China and the US contribute significantly to global GHG emissions, underscoring the need for targeted emission reduction strategies at both corporate and national levels. China accounted for 32.9% of CO2 emissions while the US accounted for 12.5% of total GHG emissions in 2021. Figure 1.6 illustrates the top ten countries by GHG emissions in 2021.[11]

Social (S) Considerations in ESG: The S in ESG focuses on a company's impact on its workforce and broader community. Although harder to quantify, these factors are used for assessing the broader societal impact of business operations. Often, regulations are contentious and are overthrown. For example, California's Women

---

[11] Source: IEA-EDGAR CO2. https://edgar.jrc.ec.europa.eu/report 2023, a component of the EDGAR (Emissions Database for Global Atmospheric Research) Community GHG database version 7.0 (2022) including or based on data from IEA (2021) Greenhouse Gas Emissions from Energy, www.iea.org/data-and-statistics, as modified by the Joint Research Centre, emphasizing the scale of emissions at a national level and underscoring the global nature of the challenge. Such data is essential for understanding the larger environmental impact and guiding targeted sustainability efforts in various regions or sectors of the economy.

1.4 From International SDGs to Corporate ESG Frameworks: Bridging ... 11

Fig. 1.6 Top ten countries in greenhouse gas (GHG) emissions in 2021. China and the United States are the two top countries. China is now emitting thrice the amount of GHG as the US

on Boards law (SB826) aimed to increase female representation (Greene et al. 2023) but was overturned in 2022 on constitutional grounds.[12] Despite being overturned, such regulations illustrate ongoing efforts and challenges to improving corporate social responsibility.

Governance (G) Considerations in ESG: The G in ESG focuses on a company's structures and processes that ensure responsible business management and alignment with stakeholders (suppliers, competitors, shareholders, and governments). These include employee health and safety measures, diversity of corporate board representation, and ethical business practices. ESG-driven action is exemplified by Engine No. 1, a hedge fund that campaigned to replace two Exxon Mobil Corp board members to force greater focus on climate change issues.[13]

1.4.2 Corporate Reporting and Trends

The rising trend in sustainability reporting, as evidenced by the increasing number of companies meeting ESG reporting standards, illustrates a growing corporate commitment to transparency.

The 2022 KPMG Survey of Sustainability Reporting (KPMG, 2022) analyzed the disclosure practices of the world's largest 250 companies by revenue (the G250) and a broader group of the top 100 businesses in each of 58 countries (the N100). It indicates that 78% of the G250 now use the GRI Standards for reporting, up from 73% in 2020. Among the 5800 N100 companies, 68% use GRI, an increase from 67% in 2020 when the N100 sample was smaller. About 96% of the G250 and 79% of the N100 report on sustainability or ESG issues, figures that have remained relatively stable since 2020. The KPMG report suggests that carbon reduction is widely reported, with 80% of the G250 and 71% of the N100 disclosing their efforts. However, less than half report on biodiversity, with 46% of the G250 and 40% of the N100 including this in their disclosures. Almost three-quarters of the surveyed companies (74% of the G250 and 71% of the N100) report on the Sustainable Development Goals (SDGs).

Corporate reporting aimed at addressing broader international goals, such as those set by frameworks like the SDGs, underscores the critical role businesses play in achieving global sustainability targets. By adhering to ESG standards, companies not only align with the environmental and social goals of the SDGs, emphasizes the vital role that businesses play in meeting global sustainability targets. Companies that adhere to ESG principles not only fit with the SDGs' environmental and social goals but also improve their long-term viability and market success in a fast-changing

---

[12] https://www.nytimes.com/2022/05/19/business/california-board-diversity-women.html.

[13] https://www.reuters.com/business/sustainable-business/shareholder-activism-reaches-milestone-exxon-board-vote-nears-end-2021-05-26/.

global economy. Despite these advancements, the KPMG survey also reveals significant room for improvement, particularly in integrating sustainability into leadership responsibilities and linking it to executive compensation, a practice currently adopted by 40% of the G250 companies.

1.4.3 ESG Reporting: Challenges and Standards

ESG reporting entails companies publicly sharing their environmental, social, and governance (ESG) impacts, often referred to as "sustainability reporting." Unlike financial reporting, which adheres to strict accounting standards and is obligatory for listed companies, ESG reporting is generally not as precisely regulated and is primarily optional. This variability in reporting standards among companies has sparked concerns regarding the consistency and reliability of the information shared, leading to varied application and interpretation of performance goals (Michelon et al., 2015; Morhardt, 2001; Sethi et al., 2017). Due to the need for comparable and trustworthy data, such discrepancies pose challenges for external stakeholders who aim to support companies excelling in sustainability.

1.4.4 Verification and Metrics in ESG Reporting

The ESG field distinguishes between process-focused verification and content-based indicators (Darnall et al., 2022). Process-focused verification determines whether a corporation follows reporting requirements and standards. Major guidelines including the Global Reporting Initiative (GRI), Sustainability Accounting Standards Board (SASB), Carbon Disclosure Project (CDP), International Integrated Reporting Council (IIRC), The World Benchmarking Alliance (WBA), and the Task Force on Climate-Related Financial Disclosures (TCFD) all endorse this approach to ensure that a company's reporting mechanisms are robust and reliable. The World Benchmarking Alliance (WBA), launched in 2018, provides a tool for measuring and comparing corporate performance relative to the UN SDGs. This initiative helps various stakeholders assess and influence corporate contributions toward these global goals. In a global context, companies, cities, and countries can record their emissions using estimation methods[14] (Akimoto et al., 2010), satellites (Crippa et al. 2021; Hakkarainen et al., 2016; Jacob et al., 2022), or a combination of the two (Gurney et al., 2020). This approach allows cities and countries to report and implement climate action goals.

Unlike process-focused verification, content-based measurements are critical for investors wishing to assess a company's unique ESG performance. These metrics

---

[14] https://ghgprotocol.org/sites/default/files/ghgp/Global-Warming-Potential-Values%20%28Feb; https://www.ipcc.ch/report/2006-ipcc-guidelines-for-national-greenhouse-gas-inventories/.

examine the correctness, dependability, and general quality of data supplied in ESG reports, evaluating the factual basis and precision of the disclosed information. One type of ESG data is global per capita emissions by sector, which are used to estimate total emissions for each industry. This necessitates a process-oriented method for estimating emissions per unit of production in each industry. These statistics are relevant for determining total GHG Scope 1 or Scope 2 emissions. MSCI, Refinitiv, S&P Global, Moody's Vigeo, RepRisk, and EcoVadis are some of the well-known ESG rating companies that prioritize content-based measures (further details on these ratings will be provided in subsequent chapters).

Despite the structure provided by these frameworks, the interpretation of ESG can vary, leading to diverse perspectives on what constitutes sustainable and ethical business practices. This disparity underscores the nuanced relationship between sustainability, ESG, and resilience, making ESG a term with multifaceted meanings that depend significantly on the observer's viewpoint. For example, while a business in the microprocessor industry may highlight its efforts to reduce water usage as a key sustainability initiative, a shareholder might focus on the company's ecological footprint related to the use of rare earth minerals (Berg et al., 2022; Christensen et al., 2022; Gibson Brandon et al., 2021). The perceived subjectivity surrounding ESG can sometimes lead to its dismissal as merely a moralistic judgment of a company's operations. However, the argument for the relevance of ESG extends beyond ethical considerations to include tangible impacts on long-term profitability and risk management. By employing precise data and metrics, businesses can better quantify the material risks associated with each ESG factor, thereby clarifying their significance for operations and investment decisions. This approach emphasizes the critical role of ESG considerations in determining the long-term viability and profitability of businesses, connecting closely with programs such as the UN's Principles for Responsible Investment (PRI).

1.4.5 Transitioning from ESG Frameworks to Financial Impact

The robust frameworks and verification processes discussed earlier not only enhance the credibility of ESG reporting but also significantly influence investment decisions. This connection is illustrated by recent data from Morningstar (2023), which underscore the increasing financial heft behind ESG principles in the asset management sector. As depicted in Fig. 1.7, BlackRock leads as the largest manager of sustainable investing funds, with a substantial USD 318 billion in ESG-focused open-ended assets and ETFs by the end of 2023.[15] Following closely are UBS (including Credit Suisse) and Amundi, highlighting a strong European presence in sustainable finance. These data not only reflect the scale of commitment among top asset managers to ESG

---

[15] https://assets.contentstack.io/v3/assets/blt4eb669caa7dc65b2/bltea603fae74386da2/65b7fb379 3cdf11bcb7cac4c/GlobalESGQ42023FlowReportfinalKG3.pdf.

principles but also demonstrate how these principles have been effectively translated into significant investment products.

Morningstar (2023) also highlights the diversity of ESG funds, saying that sustainable funds employ a variety of strategies based on their distinct ESG objectives. These tactics range from detecting material hazards and possibilities in sustainable investments to avoiding negative effect items. They also emphasize thematic sustainability investments, direct bonds intended for climate change mitigation or adaptation, and active participation through shareholder resolutions and proxy votes. This variety of techniques demonstrates the depth and breadth of ESG integration into financial strategies, providing investors with many options to contribute to societal and environmental changes.

These insights into the asset management landscape confirm that ESG metrics are not merely theoretical constructs but are critical tools for measuring and communicating sustainability efforts within the corporate world. They transition ESG from qualitative assessments to quantifiable, investment-worthy criteria, attracting substantial capital inflows into sustainable funds. This trend is crucial for companies seeking to align their operations with broader sustainability goals, thereby enhancing their long-term viability and appealing to a growing segment of socially conscious investors.

1.5 Shifting Realities for Business and Financial Institutions

The evolving landscape of climate change presents significant challenges and opportunities for business entities and financial institutions. These entities must adapt to new regulatory environments, shifting investment themes across generations, and the increasing importance of materiality in sustainability and climate change considerations. The following discussion aims to address these challenges.

1.5.1 Compliance Regulations with Cross-Jurisdictional and Extraterritorial Implications

In the changing landscape of global sustainability and climate accountability 2023 marked a significant milestone with the collaboration of five fundamental framework and standard-setting institutions: the Carbon Disclosure Project (CDP), the Climate Disclosure Standards Board (CDSB), the Global Reporting Initiative (GRI), the International Integrated Reporting Council (IIRC), and the Sustainability Accounting Standards Board (SASB). This coalition, in partnership with influential agencies such as the International Organization of Securities Commissions (IOSCO), the International Financial Reporting Standards (IFRS), the European Commission (EU), and

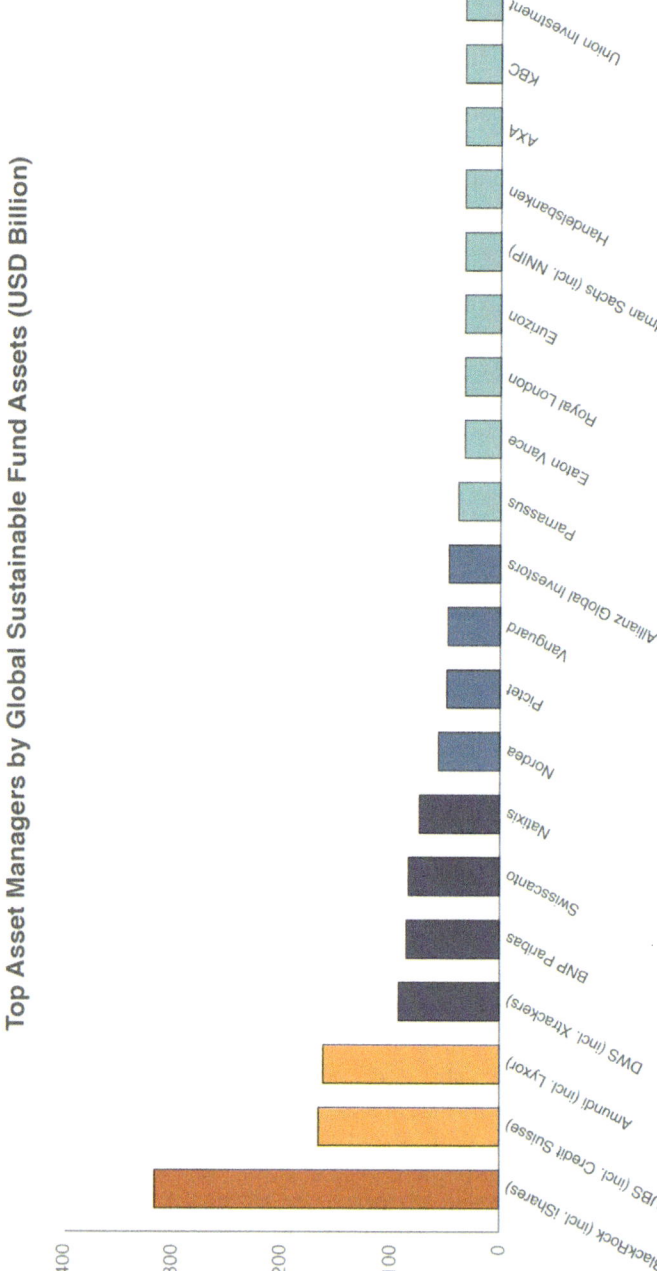

Fig. 1.7 Top asset managers by Global Sustainable Fund Assets (Morningstar, 2023)

1.5 Shifting Realities for Business and Financial Institutions

the World Economic Forum's International Business Council, aimed to consolidate and enhance integrated reporting standards.

This initiative mirrors a larger global trend of incorporating Environmental, Social, and Governance (ESG) factors into organizations' core operating and reporting frameworks. The goal is to move ESG from a largely voluntary or "soft law" framework to a more regulated or "hard law" approach, requiring compliance with increasingly complicated legal and financial disclosure requirements across various jurisdictions. This shift is particularly evident in the United States (US), the United Kingdom (UK), and the European Union (EU), where new and emerging ESG regulations underscore the transition.[16]

One of the notable challenges presented by these evolving regulations is their cross-jurisdictional and extraterritorial reach. For instance, the US companies or their subsidiaries might find themselves subject to the EU's Corporate Sustainability Reporting Directive (CSRD), which employs a double materiality standard, necessitating reporting not only on how sustainability issues affect the company (financial materiality) but also on the impact of the company's activities on society and the environment (environmental or impact materiality).

Moreover, the International Sustainability Standards Board's (ISSB) forthcoming standards, which are intended for adoption by various regions, further complicate the regulatory landscape. These standards aim to serve as the foundation for mandatory domestic ESG reporting requirements in multiple jurisdictions, thereby creating a layer of inter-jurisdictional regulatory implications.

The global push toward ESG accountability is not limited to Western countries; regions previously less focused on ESG, particularly in Asia, are introducing disclosure requirements for listed companies.[17] This expansion signifies a growing recognition of the importance of ESG considerations in corporate governance and reporting practices worldwide.[18] In Japan, the Tokyo Stock Exchange revised its Corporate Governance code to encourage ESG integration and improved climate risk reporting using the TCFD pillars. China introduced new guidelines for green bonds and the development of an ESG disclosure system for listed companies. Hong Kong made climate-related financial disclosures aligned with TCFD recommendations mandatory by 2025. Singapore is a leading sustainable finance hub in Southeast Asia with green finance initiatives and a road map for mandatory ESG reporting.

---

[16] Some regulations can have implications for companies in jurisdictions other than the jurisdiction in which the regulation was adopted. For example, the US Uyghur Forced Labor Prevention Act, the California Transparency in Supply Chains Act, and the New York proposed Fashion Sustainability and Social Accountability Act. In Europe, the UK Modern Slavery Act, the EU Corporate Sustainability Due Diligence Directive, the German Supply Chain Act.

[17] See for example https://www.adb.org/sites/default/files/institutional-document/823106/adbsr2021-part2-gri.pdf.

[18] The various laws, regulations, guidelines, and policy initiatives throughout Asia include corporate listing and reporting requirements including climate stress testing requirements in some sectors, green or sustainable taxonomies, fund-level disclosures, and an increased focus on ESG data providers.

Given the complex network of rules with potential gaps, overlaps, and conflicts, businesses are increasingly recommended to make an ESG regulatory mapping effort. This process entails examining how rules from many countries affect an organization's operations, such as emissions, water usage, social inclusion, value, and supplier chains. Such an approach is essential for navigating the complicated global ESG regulatory landscape, as it allows businesses to identify compliance duties, potential risks, and opportunities for alignment with global sustainability goals. This need for ESG regulatory mapping necessitates the collection of data, chief among them in the US is the methodology and framework of the Greenhouse Gas Reporting Program, which forms the basis of the US SEC's climate risk disclosure proposal and most existing corporate voluntary GHG emissions reporting.[19]

One of the experts interviewed for this chapter is **Mark Golovcsenko**, a Principal based in New York within KPMG's US Strategy practice. Golovcsenko offers perspectives on how businesses are dealing with regulations emerging around sustainability.

Expert in Focus: Mark Golovcsenko

Mark Golovcsenko is a Principal based in New York within KPMG's US Strategy practice. With over 15 years of experience in M&A-focused strategy consulting, Mark has successfully delivered growth strategies, M&A strategy development, commercial and operational due diligence, and post-close value creation for a diverse range of corporate and private equity clients.

His expertise spans B2B media, information businesses, and business service providers, where he supports clients in developing and executing value-creating M&A strategies, including due diligence, integration, and pricing.

---

[19] https://www.epa.gov/ghgreporting.

1.5 Shifting Realities for Business and Financial Institutions

Mark holds an MBA from Columbia Business School and a Bachelor of Science degree in Electrical Engineering from Marquette University.

Authors Question: The first thing that we wanted to ask is how do you envision the future of sustainability and resilience services evolving over the next few years, maybe five years, especially in light of this rapid technological advancement end and regulatory shifts that are taking place, especially coming from the US and Europe and Singapore and so on. How does KPMG stay ahead of the pack?

Sustainability is a broad concept. Personally, I focus primarily on the climate aspect of sustainability for various reasons. While I recognize that others in the sustainability field also consider non-climate-related impacts, I tend to concentrate on emissions and climate-related effects. My underlying assumption is that addressing climate issues will have positive ripple effects in other areas as well. We are somewhat supported in our sustainability efforts by several factors. For example, the recent European regulations, specifically the Corporate Sustainability Reporting Directive (CSRD), have a global impact. This directive affects many companies, including approximately 3,000 US companies.

Many of our clients subject to SEC regulations are also affected by the CSRD. Although we did not create this directive, it is one of the most comprehensive reporting standards, covering environmental, social, and governance (ESG) issues in great detail. Although we did not create this directive, it is one of the most comprehensive reporting standards, covering environmental, social, and governance (ESG) issues in great detail. We often tell our clients that if they comply with the CSRD, they will likely meet the SEC and California requirements as well. This effectively makes the CSRD a global standard, helping us achieve greater consistency in managing global clients.

However, there are significant differences in regulatory impacts. Some US companies are subject to the CSRD but not SEC or California regulations, and vice versa. This creates a complex regulatory landscape for companies to navigate. Despite this complexity, the need for regulatory triggers to enforce measurement across various sustainability topics is essential. Without these regulations, similar to how the SEC and accounting oversight boards were established following the Great Depression, we might lack the necessary data for investors to assess climate risk as a financial risk.

The SEC's climate rule, for instance, is a direct response to investor demands for data to evaluate the financial risks associated with climate change. Investors have clearly stated that climate risk is financial risk, and they need adequate data to make informed investment decisions.

1.5.2 ESG Litigation Around Greenwashing and Reporting

The integration of ESG considerations into corporate decision-making and investment practices has become a defining feature of contemporary business landscapes. This shift from peripheral concern to central strategic priority has given rise to a notable trend: the increase in ESG-related litigation within the context of M&A transactions. The rise of ESG considerations reflects a growing acknowledgment among businesses and investors of the pivotal role sustainability and responsible practices play in ensuring long-term success.

Recent research sheds light on a number of legal and regulatory challenges. Mispricing corporate climate risks has serious consequences for the environment and the global financial system (Condon, 2023). By failing to appropriately account for these risks, financial markets contribute to a cycle that prioritizes short-term gains over long-term sustainability, facilitating the detrimental effects of climate change. As businesses improve their reporting on Environmental, Social, and Governance (ESG) issues in response to market and shareholder demands, there has been a significant increase in successful legal actions challenging the veracity of corporate claims and disclosures regarding ESG achievements. Creative legal arguments are also being devised to target firms for alleged flaws in ESG operations and performance (Hackett et al., 2020). Furthermore, there is a growing tendency to hold firms accountable for their suppliers' conduct (Bueno & Bright, 2020). This spike in lawsuits over misrepresentations and performance concerns emphasizes the growing need for thorough management of ESG activities, outcomes, and communications (Pollman, 2022).

In Europe and beyond, regulatory bodies have intensified their focus on ESG, enacting more stringent regulations and guidelines. This evolving regulatory land scape heightens litigation risks, not only during but also after M&A transactions. The European Union's Corporate Sustainability Due Diligence Directive (CSDDD) exemplifies the expanding scope of transparency obligations, highlighting the importance of a proactive and comprehensive regulatory strategy in deal-making. A recent survey by the Berkeley Research Group (BRG) underscores the consensus on regulatory scrutiny of ESG metrics and commitments as a primary driver for ESG-related M&A litigation, with 64% of respondents echoing this sentiment.

ESG factors are increasingly influencing firm valuations, with a particular interest in transactions that provide exposure to ESG assets. A report by Price Waterhouse Coopers (PwC) indicates a growing emphasis on ESG activities[20] as drivers of value creation, necessitating appropriate assessment and disclosure of ESG elements during M&A discussions in order to minimize post-transaction disputes. Effective due diligence, which includes elements such as the CSDDD and EU Taxonomy, is critical for recognizing potential red flags and analyzing risks. KPMG's (2022) survey predicts an increase in due diligence efforts in the EMEA (Europe, the Middle East, and Africa) region, emphasizing the importance for thorough preparation to secure successful transaction outcomes.

---

[20] See https://www.pwc.com/gx/en/news-room/press-releases/2022/awm-revolution-2022-report.html.

1.5 Shifting Realities for Business and Financial Institutions

Shareholder activism (Boulton, 2023; Freund et al., 2023; Solana, 2020) represents another facet of the evolving ESG landscape, with institutional investors and shareholder groups increasingly demanding that M&A deals reflect broader ESG considerations. High-profile campaigns against companies such as Shell, BP, and Barclays illustrate the growing influence of environmental activism. The US remains the biggest market for activist investors, with 133 campaigns in 2023, compared with Europe at 69 and the Asia-Pacific region at 44.[21]

Thus, the emergence of ESG litigation within M&A transactions signifies a paradigm shift in how businesses approach sustainability and responsible governance. Navigating this complex landscape requires a multifaceted strategy encompassing regulatory compliance, meticulous due diligence, and engagement with shareholder activism. By prioritizing ESG considerations, companies and investors can mitigate litigation risks while fostering more resilient and sustainable business models for the future.

1.5.3 Generational Differences in Investment Themes

The investment landscape is increasingly influenced by generational shifts, particularly the values and priorities of Gen Z and Millennials. These younger generations exhibit a pronounced inclination toward sustainability and ethical considerations in their investment decisions. According to a Pew Research Center definition, Millennials are individuals born from 1981 to 1996, while Gen Z encompasses those born from 1995 to 2012.[22] A recent survey revealed that a significant portion of these generations prioritize sustainability, with about 46% of Gen Z and 55% of Millennials indicating its importance to their investment choices (SHRM survey 2022).[23] By 2025, Millennials are projected to constitute 75% of the global workforce, marking a shift in the demographic composition of investors and influencing investment themes. This generational transition underscores the need for businesses and financial institutions to align their strategies with the sustainability values of these influential cohorts, ensuring alignment with their ethical and environmental concerns.

---

[21] See https://www.reuters.com/business/finance/activist-investors-sights-set-corporate-europe-after-record-year-2024-01-08/.

[22] For the full report, see https://www.pewresearch.org/short-reads/2019/01/17/where-millennialsend-and-generation-z-begins/.

[23] See https://www.shrm.org/topics-tools/news/survey-esg-strategies-rank-high-gen-z-millennials.

1.5.4 Materiality Really Matters—Financialization of ESG Risks

The concept of materiality has gained prominence, highlighting the direct linkage between sustainability-related factors and financial risk. The mainstreaming of climate change concerns, societal sustainability values, and social considerations has enhanced the transparency and measurability of these connections. A KPMG survey of the global top 250 businesses by revenue indicates that 96% engage in some form of sustainability reporting, with 70% acknowledging direct financial benefits from their sustainability programs. This trend reflects a broader acknowledgment within the business community of the material impacts of sustainability initiatives on financial performance. As climate change realities become increasingly impossible to ignore, the ability to quantify and communicate the financial implications of sustainability-related factors is paramount. Businesses that effectively integrate these considerations into their reporting and operational strategies are better positioned to navigate the risks and opportunities presented by the evolving landscape of climate change and societal expectations.

A company's or entity's impact on the environment (e.g., GHG emissions, water depletion, deforestation) and its exposure to climate risks (e.g., heat waves, floods, droughts, earthquakes) are material to its operation. The Fukushima Daiichi accident in March 2011 shows both types of environmental impacts. Triggered by a magnitude 9 (on the Richter scale) earthquake and subsequent tsunami (15-m), the incident caused 2313 deaths and ongoing financial repercussions—the operator, Tokyo Electric Power Company (TEPCO), faces annual decommissioning costs of roughly USD 7.3 billion.

Research indicates that ESG characteristics are material to investments. Firms with strong ESG profiles tend to offer better risk-adjusted returns (Eccles et al., 2012), suggesting that ESG factors are significant in evaluating company performance and potential risks. This is further supported by studies showing that a robust commitment to ESG can lead to lower volatility in investment portfolios (Alareeni et al., 2020; Liang & Renneboog, 2017).

The financial sector's response to the material risks posed by ESG factors is significant, with major investment firms (Capital Group, Vanguard, Breckinridge Capital Advisors, and Pimco) incorporating ESG metrics into their overall risk assessment strategies. However, there are challenges and controversies, such as the shift in stance by BlackRock's CEO (2023) on the role of ESG, illustrating the complex and evolving nature of ESG integration in corporate governance and investment strategies.[24] Institutions like the World Bank have begun tying sustainability performance to their lending requirements, and there is increasing interest in green financing, reflecting a broader move toward integrating ESG factors into mainstream financial practices. Other investors and lenders are specifically interested in financing projects that are specifically "green financing" where the project itself has environmentally positive

---

[24] See https://www.reuters.com/business/environment/blackrocks-fink-says-hes-stopped-usingweaponised-term-esg-2023-06-26/.

outcomes, such as financing for wind energy projects. Though these issues are more intrinsically linked to sustainability, they are driven by unique investor perspectives and policy banking.

Specific metrics are emerging as a part of the mainstream investment process to better account for overall credit risk and ensure more stable (and sustainable) financial returns. According to projections by the World Economic Forum26, ESG assets will exceed USD 53 trillion globally by 2025, representing more than a third of the expected USD 141 trillion of global assets under management. PwC made similar projections. In 2023, some major meteorological, hydrological, climatological, and geophysical hazards caused losses of USD 250bn (Source: Munich Re, NatCatSERVICE 2023).

Table 1.1 itemizes natural hazard categories, costs, insured losses, overall losses, and fatalities. Meteorological events have the highest overall losses, with Typhoon Doksuri (Egay) causing damages of USD 25 billion. Geophysical Events follow closely, especially with the earthquake in Turkey and Syria, accounting for overall losses of USD 50 billion, the highest single event loss reported. The earthquake in Turkey and Syria on February 6 has the highest insured loss at USD 5.5 billion among all categories.

Table 1.1 Major natural disasters 2023 (caused overall losses of USD 250 bn worldwide)

Meteorological events	Hydrological events	Climatological events	Geophysical events
Severe storm		Lahaina Wildfire	Earthquake
1–4 Mar	Flash flood (Storm Daniel)	8–31 Aug	8 Sep
United States	4–12 Sep	United States	Morocco
Overall losses: USD 6bn	Libya, Bulgaria, Greece, Turkey	Overall losses: USD 5.5bn	Overall losses: USD 7bn
Insured losses: USD 4.2bn	Overall losses: USD 6.2bn	Insured losses: USD 3.5bn	Insured losses: USD 0.3bn
	Insured losses: USD 0.5bn	Fatalities: 100	Fatalities: 3,000
Tornado, winter storm	Fatalities: 4,300		
30 Mar–1 Apr			Earthquake
United States	Flood, severe storm		6 Feb
Overall losses: USD 5.5bn	12–23 May		Turkey, Syria
Insured losses: USD 4.3bn	Italy, Bosnia and Herzegovina, Croatia, Austria		Overall losses: USD 50bn
	Overall losses: USD 10bn		Insured losses: USD 5.5bn

(continued)

Table 1.1 (continued)

Meteorological events	Hydrological events	Climatological events	Geophysical events
Hurricane Otis	Insured losses: USD 1.1bn		Fatalities: 58,000
22–25 Oct			
Mexico			
Overall losses: USD 12bn			
Insured losses: USD 4bn			
Fatalities: 53			
Typhoon Doksuri (Egay)			
24 Jul-4 Aug			
China, Philippines, Taiwan, Vietnam			
Overall losses: USD 25bn			
Insured losses: USD 2bn			
Fatalities: 108			
Cyclone Gabrielle			
11–17 Feb			
New Zealand			
Overall losses: USD 2.8bn			
Insured losses: USD 1.9bn			

Source Munich Re, NatCatSERVICE 2023[25]

There's a significant gap between overall losses and insured losses across all events, indicating that many of the damages incurred from natural hazards remain uninsured. This discrepancy is especially pronounced in geophysical and hydrological events. For example, the Flash flood (Storm Daniel) had overall losses of USD 6.2 billion but insured losses of only USD 0.5 billion, showing a substantial gap between the economic impact of the event and the insured amount.

The growing trend of linking ESG performance to financial and project finance demonstrates that the financial sector recognizes the relevance of sustainability. The significant economic losses from natural disasters, as documented in the table from

---

[25] https://www.munichre.com/content/dam/munichre/mrwebsitespressreleases/MunichRe-Nat Cat-2023-world-map.pdf/_jcr_content/renditions/original./MunichRe-NatCat-2023-world-map.pdf

Munich Re, demonstrate the substantial financial implications of environmental and climate risks. The discrepancy between insured and overall losses, particularly in geophysical and hydrological events, underscores the challenges and financial risks that companies and insurers face, emphasizing the need for comprehensive risk management strategies that consider ESG factors.

1.5.5 Companies Sustainability Reports

Some companies consistently garner praise for their transparency, comprehensiveness, and stakeholder engagement in sustainability reporting. We list five illustrative examples in different industry sectors.

- Unilever, a consumer goods product company, publishes a detailed Integrated Annual Report that seamlessly blends financial and sustainability performance. They consistently achieve high rankings in sustainability indices and are lauded for their ambitious targets and clear action plans.
- Ørsted, the Danish renewable energy leader, has transitioned from a traditional fossil fuel company to a clean energy powerhouse. Their sustainability report is recognized for its transparency and data-driven approach, showcasing their significant contributions to decarbonization.
- Patagonia, the outdoor apparel company, champions environmental activism and transparency. Their annual "Footprint Report" goes beyond traditional metrics, delving into their environmental impact across their entire supply chain and advocating for systemic change.
- Tesla, the electric vehicle pioneer, focuses on sustainability by highlighting their impact on clean transportation and reducing greenhouse gas emissions. Tesla has adopted a data-driven approach and clear articulation of their long-term environmental goals.
- Trex, an outdoor decking and fencing company, promotes its sustainability commitment by reducing its environmental footprint and advancing waste recycling in its manufacturing.

1.6 Federal Funds and Tax Incentives Usher the Climate Tech Revolution and Innovation

The US Inflation Reduction Act (IRA), passed in 2022, represents an unprecedented advancement in the fight against climate change. The IRA aims to pivot American consumer and industrial behaviors away from fossil fuel dependency, introducing penalties for excessive methane emissions by fossil fuel enterprises and channeling funds into pollution mitigation.

Despite some provisions incentivizing oil leasing, the Act allocates USD 60 billion toward environmental justice and pollution reduction efforts, emphasizing support for low-income and disadvantaged communities. It also dedicates significant funding to domestic clean energy manufacturing, aiming to bolster US production of solar panels, wind turbines, and electric vehicles. It also promotes domestic manufacturing of these technologies while providing financial support for various climate priorities, including forest and coastal restoration and sustainable agriculture.

Figure 1.8 shows how the IRA introduces a comprehensive suite of tax incentives to reduce the prices of clean technologies such as solar, wind, and batteries, with the goal of accelerating renewable development in the most polluting sectors—transportation and electricity. Figure 1.8 shows two figure panels—A and B together illustrate how the Inflation Reduction Act seeks to tackle climate change by investing in clean energy technologies and lowering greenhouse gas emissions. The pie chart in Fig. 1.8 depicts a high-level overview of funding allocation across different program categories. The largest share of funding (42%) goes toward clean energy tax credits for individuals and businesses, which encourages investments in solar panels, electric vehicles, heat pumps, and other clean technologies. Clean energy generation and transmission receive 22% of the funding, with emphasis on grid modernization, renewable energy production, and clean energy demonstration projects. Energy efficiency receives 17% of the funding, with a focus on building efficiency upgrades, appliance rebates, and industrial decarbonization measures. Transportation electrification gets 13% of the funding, supporting electric vehicle charging infrastructure, zero-emission buses, and clean heavy-duty vehicles. Other categories, such as climate justice, methane emissions reduction, and forestry, receive less money. Panel B of Fig. 1.8 shows the available tax credits for clean energy investments. The value of the tax credits varies according to the technology and use case. Companies involved in solar, wind, and other renewable energy projects are beneficiaries.

Mark Golovcsenko, KPMG, introduced earlier in the chapter notes the following:

The Inflation Reduction Act (IRA) is a significant game changer. We've seen it influence businesses just as intended, altering the business case for many companies regarding investments in new technologies, building renewable power on-site, and other sustainability initiatives. This shift is evident in corporate boardrooms, with executives now asking how they can secure their share of the available funding.

The IRA has made investments that previously might not have been financially viable more attractive due to the various credits and incentives provided. This has revitalized corporate sustainability agendas, especially for forward-thinking companies that view sustainability as a core business strategy rather than an incremental change. These companies aren't just looking to cut costs with renewable power or find savings that reduce emissions; they're rethinking their entire business models. They're developing products that cater to consumer and business preferences for sustainability and finding new, innovative ways to operate.

We haven't yet discussed the carbon border adjustment mechanism in Europe, but it has the potential to shift competitive advantages significantly. It's more than just a tariff for exporting to Europe; it can make companies with less carbon-intensive value

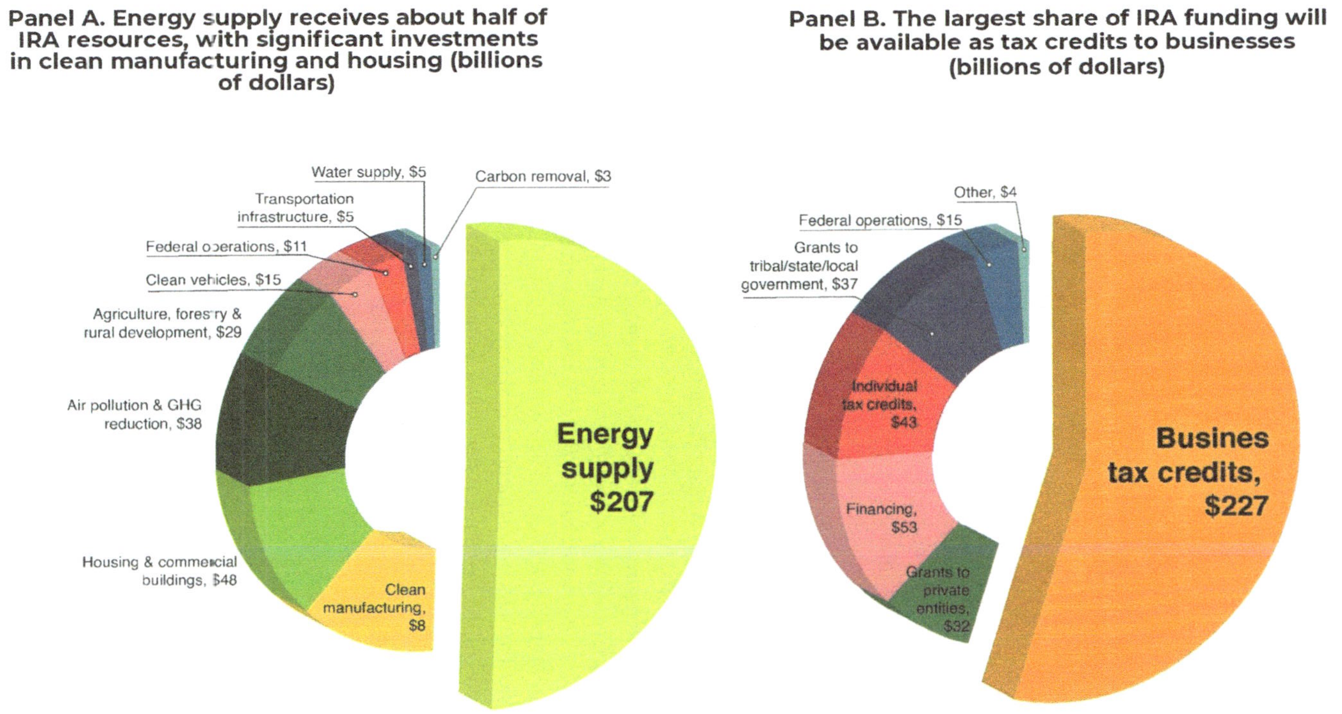

1.6 Federal Funds and Tax Incentives Usher the Climate Tech Revolution ... 27

Fig. 1.8 The Inflation Reduction Act (IRA) Investment in clean energy and climate change shows the US commitment to a new green economy with significant investments in clean manufacturing and housing. Panel A (left) shows sectors served by the IRA. Panel B (right) shows how these funds are being disbursed

chains more competitive. This mechanism might prompt companies to reconsider their sourcing choices to enhance their cost positioning for goods landed in Europe, relative to their competitors.

1.7 Emerging Technologies and Emerging Economy

This section discusses how sustainable finance might be used to drive needed reductions in greenhouse gas emissions, climate change mitigation and adaptation, and systemic transformation. Green technological breakthroughs frequently necessitate upfront capital. Sustainable finance is critical for funding energy research, creating carbon capture technologies and innovating more sustainable materials and production processes. Energy companies such as NextEra Energy Resources, First Solar, Fluence, Tesla (batteries for homes), electric vehicles from Rivian, Tesla, Ford, GM, and Lucid, and Charging infrastructure companies such as ChargePoint, and EVG are likely to gain and grow with both private and federal IRA funding. Beyond the specific examples above, countless other companies across the supply chain will benefit indirectly from the IRA's focus on clean energy and sustainability.

Energy Impact Partners is an investment company that targets investment into companies that have high chance of impact. Peter Fox-Penner, an energy expert and Chief Impact Officer of Energy Impact Partners, stated: *"The Inflation Reduction Act is gigantic. It is the most significant climate policy and investment package in the country's history. The figures we've looked at suggest that it will mobilize a trillion dollars' worth of private market investment capital. And that's essential. And it has a substantial effect on several areas. But it's not the only policy that we need. It's just the best and biggest package we've ever had."*

Energy Impact Partners' investments reveal major patterns in this emerging energy sector. At one end of the investment range is a company that utilizes artificial intelligence to solve an age-old problem: detecting and avoiding industrial accidents. Construction activities regularly result in the accidental rupture of subsurface gas pipes, which releases methane. Methane's powerful greenhouse effect (about 28 times greater than CO_2 over 100 years) exacerbates the climate change dilemma. Urbint offers smart incident prevention solutions. According to Peter Fox-Penner, Urbint uses artificial intelligence to examine utility applications linked to development projects near gas lines. The system's algorithms detect construction projects that pose a high risk of causing a gas line burst. This predictive risk assessment enables utility companies to prioritize these "high danger" projects, allowing them to commit more resources, issue improved warnings, and deploy more detailed maps. This tailored, AI-assisted method helps to reduce methane leak incidences. Several utility companies have used this software to proactively decrease damaging environmental leaks.

Another company in the Energy Impact Partners investment portfolio is Boston Metal, which has developed an innovative steelmaking process powered by clean electricity. Employing Molten Oxide Electrolysis (MOE) technology, this company offers a potential replacement for traditional blast furnaces, which rely heavily on coking coal, a significant source of emissions. When powered by clean energy sources (solar, wind, etc.), Boston Metal's process eliminates direct (Scope 1) and indirect (Scope 2) greenhouse gas emissions associated with electricity use. Compared to fossil-fuel-based steelmaking, this method achieves a 95% reduction in carbon dioxide emissions. The success of these transformational companies will shape the future of building, manufacturing, transportation, energy infrastructure, and other sectors, creating emerging business opportunities as societies seek a path to net zero and meet climate goals.

1.8 Big Data and AI—New Frontiers

ESG factors have become central considerations for investors, businesses, and policymakers. As the significance of sustainability issues within global economics increases, so too does the demand for high-quality data to monitor and track ESG performance. Traditional ESG assessments have often relied on self-reported metrics from companies, raising concerns about potential inconsistencies and subjectivity. The accurate assessment of ESG performance depends on access to reliable, comprehensive data. There are now diverse sources of ESG data, their integration through Big Data methodologies, and the types of analysis required to extract meaningful insights that inform decision-making and investment strategies.

Big Data approaches, encompassing the processing and analysis of large and diverse datasets, promise to transform this landscape. By gathering and combining data from various sources, Big Data provides the foundation for improved quality, robustness, and accuracy in ESG assessment. Advanced Big Data analytics offer immense potential to address this challenge, driving greater accuracy, transparency, and robustness in ESG accounting (explored in a subsequent chapter).

1.8.1 Sources of Emerging ESG Data

1. Satellite Imagery: Remote sensing satellites monitor Earth's surface and atmospheric conditions, yielding data on deforestation, land use changes, water quality, air pollution, and greenhouse gas emissions. Analysis of this imagery helps quantify environmental impacts associated with corporate operations.
2. Weather Stations and Ocean Buoys: This network of ground-based and oceanic sensors measures variables like temperature, precipitation, sea level, ocean currents, and salinity. Such data inform climate risk modeling and the ability of companies to predict disruptions to their supply chains and production facilities.
3. Social Surveys: Surveys and social sentiment analysis capture consumer and stakeholder perceptions on a range of ESG factors. These data are crucial for

companies to assess customer satisfaction, employee well-being, and broader community impacts.
4. Corporate Sustainability Reports and Filings: Businesses often disclose a significant amount of ESG data in their annual reports, sustainability statements, and mandatory filings (e.g., carbon emissions). Integration of such self-reported metrics with other data sources is critical for identifying discrepancies and potential greenwashing.
5. Social media data may provide employee sentiment, gender discrimination, product issues, or cyber threats instantaneously. Social media data can be subjective and reflect individual experiences, not always the complete picture. Context and nuance are important. Not all claims or accounts are authentic. Thorough verification and corroboration are essential.

1.8.2 The Promise and Potential of AI

The AI revolution, driven by advances in chip technology, data centers, Generative AI, and Large Language Models, is reshaping all facets of business operations, from sustainability and waste reduction to lifecycle management, supply chain optimization, and beyond. Over the past three decades, AI has been instrumental in advancing sustainability efforts, utilizing both conventional statistical models and innovative AI techniques. One of the author's (Gopal) earliest experiences with AI in the 1990s involved utilizing neural networks for various tasks including pattern recognition, unsupervised classification, predicting future trends, and anomaly detection in geospatial data.

The evolution of AI and deep learning has been a collaborative effort of academic research and commercial endeavors of leading companies, including Google, Microsoft, and Amazon. Commercial companies have played pivotal roles in propelling AI forward, offering resources, frameworks, and novel applications that have shaped the AI landscape.

The applications of AI and modern data science are far reaching across finance and sustainability. Novel approaches and new companies continue to emerge and innovate in this space, further compounding positive impacts and technologies. We will further discuss these topics and practical applications in later chapters.

1.8.3 Looking Forward: A Fintech Revolution

The Financial Stability Board (FSB) defines *Fintech* as "technologically enabled financial innovation that could result in new business models, applications, processes, or products with an associated material effect on financial markets and institutions, and the provision of financial services."[26] The Fintech revolution aims to improve and automate traditional forms of finance for businesses and consumers alike. Fintech refers to the use of software, mobile applications, and other technologies such as blockchain. With its data analytics, measurement metrics, and transparent accounting, Fintech is in a sweet spot to lead on financial and environmental sustainability. One of the emerging technological backbones of Fintech is Blockchain technology, which enables transparent and public reporting on critical issues that can be examined and audited globally. We will discuss the applications and ramifications of this technology in more detail in later chapters.

1.8.4 Summary

This chapter provides a comprehensive exploration of the multifaceted approach to addressing climate change, beginning with the presentation of three pivotal datasets that illuminate the accelerating warming of the Earth. It then transitions into a discussion of global initiatives, specifically highlighting the PRI and the SDGs, which mobilize global efforts toward sustainability. The chapter delves into how corporations are responding to these global calls to action through enhanced ESG reporting, aiming to significantly reduce their environmental footprints and bolster sustainability. This corporate shift is largely driven by a combination of regulatory compliance demands, increasing shareholder activism, and the evolving expectations of a younger demographic, particularly Millennials, who prioritize ethical and sustainable business practices.

Further, the chapter examines the concept of materiality in financial terms, underscoring how environmental risks are increasingly recognized as pivotal financial considerations. This segues into a discussion of the U.S. Inflation Reduction Act of 2023, illustrating its role in fostering a wave of new, environmentally focused businesses and technologies. Lastly, the chapter introduces the transformative potential of Artificial Intelligence (AI) and Big Data in refining sustainability and ESG reporting, coupled with an overview of how Fintech is revolutionizing financial services through innovations like blockchain to enhance transparency and accountability in environmental reporting. This integrated approach in this chapter underscores a dynamic shift in how businesses, governments, and individuals are converging to combat climate change and drive sustainability forward.

Further Readings: There are several authoritative and insightful books and reports for those readers seeking a deeper understanding of the complexities and nuances of climate change, its causes (IPCC, 2023; Masson-Delmotte et al., 2021), economics (Heal, 2016; Raworth, 2017; Stern, 2007; Tol, 2023), environmental history (Warde et al., 2018; Sörlin, 2022), and the political challenges in addressing

---

[26] https://www.fsb.org/work-of-the-fsb/financial-innovation-and-structural-change/fintech/.

it (Chomsky & Pollin, 2020; Giddens, 2009; Klein, 2015; Rosenbaum, 2016). AI books include Deep learning (Aggarwal, 2018; Domingos, 2015; Heaton, 2018).

References

Aggarwal, C. C. (2018). *Neural networks and deep learning*. Springer.
Akimoto, K., Sano, F., Homma, T., Oda, J., Nagashima, M., & Kii, M. (2010). Estimates of GHG emission reduction potential by country, sector, and cost. *Energy Policy, 38*(7), 3384–3393.
Alareeni, B. A., & Hamdan, A. (2020). ESG impact on performance of US S&P 500-listed firms. *Corporate Governance: The International Journal of Business in Society, 20*(7), 1409–1428.
Berg, F., Koelbel, J. F., & Rigobon, R. (2022). Aggregate confusion: The divergence of ESG ratings. *Review of Finance, 26*(6), 1315–1344.
Boulton, T. J. (2023, March 21). *Mandatory ESG disclosure, information asymmetry, and litigation risk: Evidence from initial public offerings*. Information Asymmetry, and Litigation Risk: Evidence from Initial Public Offerings.
Bueno, N., & Bright, C. (2020). Implementing human rights due diligence through corporate civil liability. *International & Comparative Law Quarterly, 69*(4), 789–818.
Chomsky, N., & Pollin, R. (2020). *Climate crisis and the global green new deal: The political economy of saving the planet*. Verso Books.
Christensen, D. M., Serafeim, G., & Sikochi, A. (2022). Why is corporate virtue in the eye of the beholder? The case of ESG ratings. *The Accounting Review, 97*(1), 147–175.
Condon, M. (2023). Climate services: The business of physical risk. *Arizona State Law Journal, 55*, 147.
Crippa, M., Solazzo, E., Guizzardi, D., Monforti-Ferrario, F., Tubiello, F. N., & Leip, A. J. N. F. (2021). Food systems are responsible for a third of global anthropogenic GHG emissions. *Nature Food, 2*(3), 198–209.
Cummins, T., Hamid, R., Reeves, E., Karalis, T., & Harnett, M. (2021). ESG litigation—How companies can get ready, respond and resolve claims. *Journal of Investment Compliance, 22*(5), 385–398.
Darnall, N., Ji, H., Iwata, K., & Arimura, T. H. (2022). Do ESG reporting guidelines and verifications enhance firms' information disclosure? *Corporate Social Responsibility and Environmental Management, 29*(5), 1214–1230.
Domingos, P. (2015). *The master algorithm: How the quest for the ultimate learning machine will remake our world*. Basic Books.
Eccles, R. G., Ioannou, I., & Serafeim, G. (2012). *The impact of a corporate culture of sustainability on corporate behavior and performance* (Vol. 17950, No. 1, pp. 2835–2857). National Bureau of Economic Research.
Freund, S., Nguyen, N. H., & Phan, H. V. (2023). Shareholder litigation and corporate social responsibility. *Journal of Financial and Quantitative Analysis, 58*(2), 512–542.
Gibson Brandon, R., Krueger, P., & Schmidt, P. S. (2021). ESG rating disagreement and stock returns. *Financial Analysts Journal, 77*(4), 104–127.
Giddens, A. (2009). *Politics of climate change*. Polity.
Greene, D., Intintoli, V., & Kahle, K. M. (2023, February 27). *How deep is the labor market for female directors? Evidence from mandated director appointments*. Evidence from Mandated Director Appointments.
Gurney, K. R., Liang, J., Patarasuk, R., Song, Y., Huang, J., & Roest, G. (2020). The Vulcan version 3.0 high-resolution fossil fuel CO_2 emissions for the United States. *Journal of Geophysical Research: Atmospheres, 125*(19), e2020JD032974.
Hackett, D., Demas, R., Sanders, D., Wicha, J., & Fowler, A. (2020). Growing ESG risks: The rise of litigation. *Environmental Law Reporter, 50*, 10849.

References

Hakkarainen, J., Ialongo, I., & Tamminen, J. (2016). Direct space-based observations of anthropogenic CO2 emission areas from OCO-2. *Geophysical Research Letters, 43*(21), 11–400.

Heal, G. (2016). *Endangered economies: How the neglect of nature threatens our prosperity.* Columbia University Press.

Heaton, J. (2018). Ian Goodfellow, Yoshua Bengio, and Aaron Courville: Deep learning: The MIT Press 2016, 800 pp, ISBN: 0262035618. *Genetic Programming and Evolvable Machines, 19*(1–2), 305–307.

IPCC. (2019). 2019 refinement to the 2006 IPCC guidelines for national greenhouse gas inventories. In E. Calvo Buendia, K. Tanabe, A. Kranjc, J. Baasansuren, M. Fukuda, S. Ngarize, A. Osako, Y. Pyrozhenko, P. Shermanau, & S. Federici (Eds.), Published: IPCC, Switzerland. Volume 5, Chapter 6. https://www.ipcc.ch/report/2019-refinement-to-the-2006-ipcc-guidelines-for-national-greenhouse-gas-inventories/

IPCC. (2023). https://www.ipcc.ch/report/sixth-assessment-report-cycle/

Jacob, D. J., Varon, D. J., Cusworth, D. H., Dennison, P. E., Frankenberg, C., Gautam, R., Guanter, L., Kelley, J., McKeever, J., Ott, L. E., Poulter, B., Qu, Z., Thorpe, A. K., Worden, J. R., & Duren, R. M. (2022). Quantifying methane emissions from the global scale down to point sources using satellite observations of atmospheric methane. *Atmospheric Chemistry and Physics, 22*(14), 9617–9646.

Klein, N. (2015). *This changes everything: Capitalism vs. the climate.* Simon & Schuster.

KPMG. (2022). *KPMG global survey sustainability reporting.* https://assets.kpmg.com/content/dam/kpmg/se/pdf/komm/2022/Global-Survey-of-Sustainability-Reporting-2022.pdf

Liang, H., & Renneboog, L. (2017). On the foundations of corporate social responsibility. *The Journal of Finance, 72*(2), 853–910.

Masson-Delmotte, V., Zhai, P., Pirani, A., Connors, S. L., Péan, C., Berger, S., Caud, N., C hen, Y., Goldfarb, L., Gomis, M. I., Huang, M., Leitzell, K., Lonnoy, E., Matthews, J. B. R., Maycock, T. K., Waterfield, T., Yelekci, O., Yu, R., & Zhou, B. (2021). Climate change 2021: the physical science basis. Contribution of working group I to the sixth assessment report of the intergovernmental panel on climate change, 2.

Michelon, G., Pilonato, S., & Ricceri, F. (2015). CSR reporting practices and the quality of disclosure: An empirical analysis. *Critical Perspectives on Accounting, 33*, 59–78.

Morhardt, J. E. (2001). Scoring corporate environmental reports for comprehensiveness: A comparison of three systems. *Environmental Management, 27*, 881–892.

Morningstar. (2023). *Global sustainable fund flows: Q4 2023 in review.* https://assets.contentstack.io/v3/assets/blt4eb669caa7dc65b2/bltea603fae74386da2/65b7fb3793cdf11bcb7cac4c/GlobalESGQ42023FlowReportfinalKG3.pdf

Pollman, E. (2022). *The making and meaning of ESG.* University of Pennsylvania, Institute for Law & Econ Research Paper (pp. 22–23).

Raworth, K. (2017). *Doughnut economics: Seven ways to think like a 21st-century economist.* Chelsea Green Publishing.

Rosenbaum, W. A. (2016). *Environmental politics and policy.* CQ Press.

Sethi, S. P., Martell, T. F., & Demir, M. (2017). Enhancing the role and effectiveness of corporate social responsibility (CSR) reports: The missing element of content verification and integrity assurance. *Journal of Business Ethics, 144*, 59–82.

Solana, J. (2020). Climate change litigation as financial risk. *Green Finance, 2*(4), 344–372.

Sörlin, S. (Ed.). (2022). *Resource extraction and arctic communities.* Cambridge University Press.

Stern, N. H. (2007). *The economics of climate change: The Stern review.* Cambridge University Press.

Tol, R. S. (2023). *Climate economics: Economic analysis of climate, climate change and climate policy.* Edward Elgar.

UNFCCC. (2015). UNFCCC/COP. *Paris Agreement*; UNFCCC. https://unfccc.int/process-and-meetings/the-paris-agreement

Warde, P., Robin, L., & Sörlin, S. (2018). *The environment: A history of the idea.* JHU Press.

Chapter 2
ESG Integration: Unveiling Risk and Driving Innovation in Sustainable Finance

Look deep into nature, and then you will understand everything better—Albert Einstein

2.1 Introduction

Building on the concepts introduced in Chapter 1, this section delves into the detailed mechanisms driving sustainable finance. It provides a clear definition of sustainable finance and outlines its evolving, holistic, and interdisciplinary nature. The chapter traces the historical evolution of sustainable finance, from its religious roots to a modern transformation that emphasizes achieving positive long-term social and environmental impacts. Sustainable finance is described as a dynamic concept that evolves through the incorporation of new practices and insights across different disciplines. The European Commission's definition of sustainable finance as a process integrating environmental, social, and governance (ESG) factors into financial and investment decisions is discussed, along with practical application of the process. The chapter also explores sustainable finance as an all-encompassing method of investing that champions environmental and social factors, including specialized segments such as environmental or green finance and socio-environmental finance. It emphasizes the importance of sustainability themes that transcend traditional environmental activism and have become firmly embedded in the financial and corporate sectors.

The concept of sustainable finance encompasses investing that prioritizes targeting one or more environmental challenges, social issues, climate, energy transition, and sustainable development. Sustainable finance includes environmental or green finance, which focuses on meeting environmental challenges such as reducing carbon footprints and preserving biodiversity. Another area of sustainable finance is socio-environmental finance, which avoids funding projects with adverse environmental effects and aims to achieve a balance between economic prosperity and environmental integrity.

Sustainable finance extends beyond financial metrics to include economic viability, environmental integrity, social responsibility, regulatory compliance, reputation management, and innovative advancement. Economic viability ensures that sustainability initiatives are financially sustainable and can generate long-term benefits without causing financial strain (Orieno et al., 2024). Environmental integrity focuses on conserving natural resources, minimizing pollution, and protecting biodiversity (Udeagha & Ngepah, 2023). Social responsibility encompasses the ethical treatment of employees, communities, and stakeholders (Masum et al., 2020). Regulatory compliance involves adhering to laws and regulations designed to promote sustainability (Condon, 2023a). Reputation management and innovative advancement are crucial for enhancing brand loyalty and driving progress through sustainable practices (Serafeim, 2020). Innovative advancement highlights the importance of developing new technologies and business models that support sustainable practices, driving progress and competitive advantage in a rapidly changing market (George et al., 2021).

These elements play a critical role in the decision-making processes of stakeholders involved in sustainability. Corporations prioritize economic viability and reputation management, while Non-Government Organizations (NGOs) focus on environmental integrity and social responsibility. Serafeim (2020) argues that businesses can achieve significant positive societal impact while also driving profitability and sustainable success. Moreover, companies integrating ESG considerations into their strategies tend to outperform their peers over the long term, emphasizing the importance of ESG integration for sustainable business success (Serafeim & Yoon, 2022a, 2022b). Governments emphasize regulatory compliance, and financial institutions balance economic viability with environmental and social criteria. Utilizing the IMF's Central Bank Legislation Database, a recent study (Dikau & Volz, 2021) examined 135 central banks. Only 12% of the central banks have explicit sustainability mandates, while 40% are required to support government policy priorities, which often include sustainability goals. The study concluded that it is essential for all central banks to integrate climate-related physical and transition risks into their policy frameworks to ensure macro-financial stability. Consumers, increasingly aware of sustainability issues, influence market trends by choosing products that align with their values.

Investor interest in sustainable finance is motivated by factors such as achieving positive environmental and social outcomes, aligning investments with personal values, and pursuing profitable opportunities. Several key motivations have kindled investor interest in sustainable finance, as illustrated in Fig. 2.1. Impact-driven investors focus on achieving positive ESG outcomes alongside financial returns. They integrate ESG criteria into their investment processes to generate measurable social or environmental impact. Adhering to principles of SRI, they emphasize long-term value creation and risk mitigation through ESG integration (Friede et al., 2015).

Sustainability-motivated investors derive personal satisfaction from aligning their investments with their values, particularly in terms of sustainability. They prefer "green" investments, which support environmentally sustainable practices, over "brown" investments associated with higher environmental risks. This behavior is

2.1 Introduction

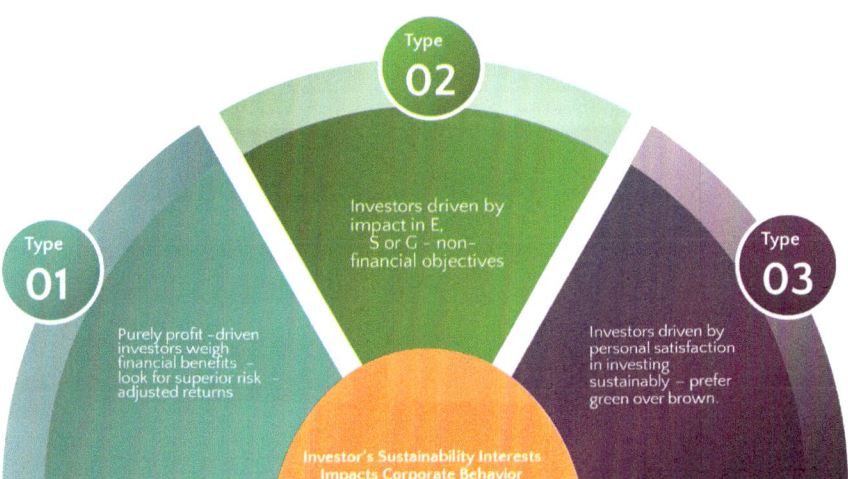

Fig. 2.1 Three groups of investors based on their motivations and investment criteria

often linked to ethical investing, in which personal values and sustainability considerations play a crucial role in investment decisions (Renneboog et al., 2008). These investors may select mutual funds or ETFs designed to include only companies meeting certain sustainability criteria. Thus, understanding these diverse aspects of sustainability is essential for developing strategies that meet the needs and expectations of all stakeholders involved.

Figure 2.2 illustrates the four types of strategies that profit-driven investors employ in sustainable investment. These investors aim to reduce risk exposure, increase profits from new opportunities, engage actively in corporate governance to effect changes, and undertake scenario analysis and stress testing to evaluate the impacts of climate change on their present and future portfolios.

Profit-driven investors, prioritize financial performance and aim to achieve superior risk-adjusted returns (as shown in Fig. 2.2). Their investment decisions are driven by the potential for financial gain, emphasizing metrics such as return on investment (ROI) and risk management. This group increasingly recognizes the importance of climate risks in their strategies due to potential impacts on financial performance and long-term value creation. They consider climate risks through various lenses and incorporate them into their investment theses in four ways, as discussed below and shown in Fig. 2.2.

Profit-driven investors assess the potential physical risks posed by climate change, such as extreme weather events, rising sea levels, and temperature changes. These risks can directly impact the operational efficiency, supply chains, and asset values of the companies they invest in. For example, properties in coastal areas might face increased flooding risks, leading to higher insurance costs and potential asset devaluation (IPCC, 2014). Additionally, these investors evaluate the risks associated with

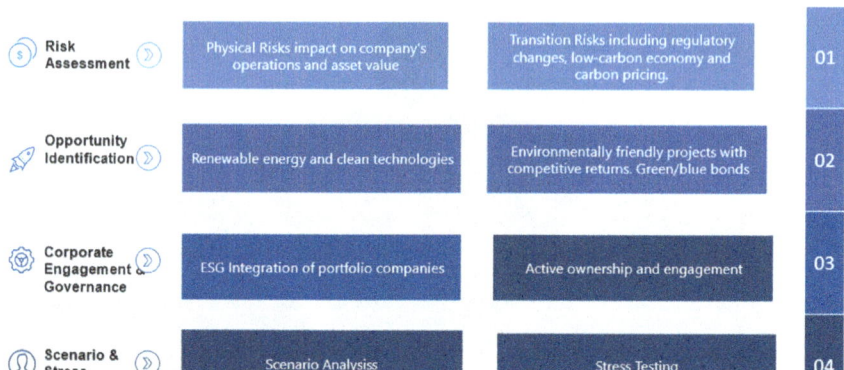

Fig. 2.2 Profit-driven investors have four types of strategies in sustainable investment

the transition to a low-carbon economy, including regulatory changes, technological advancements, and market shifts. Stricter environmental regulations, carbon pricing, and the phasing out of fossil fuels can affect the profitability of companies reliant on carbon-intensive processes (Board, 2017). For instance, the Amundi Just Transition for Climate Fund supports the transition to a low-carbon economy.

Profit-driven investors identify opportunities in sectors poised to benefit from the transition to a sustainable economy. Investments in renewable energy, energy efficiency technologies, and sustainable infrastructure projects are seen as avenues for growth and innovation, given the expected increased demand for cleaner energy sources (IEA, 2020). For example, the New Alternatives Fund (NALFX) invests in renewable energy, energy efficiency, and sustainable infrastructure projects. The growing market for green bonds and sustainable finance products presents opportunities for investors to support environmentally friendly projects while achieving competitive returns. Green bonds are debt instruments specifically earmarked for climate and environmental projects, offering both financial and environmental benefits (Harrison et al., 2022). An example is the iShares Global Green Bond ETF (BGRN), focusing on green bonds issued by corporations and governments.

The third strategy shown in Fig. 2.2 is corporate engagement and governance. ESG integration is a dominant theme here, as seen in the rising popularity of global sustainability funds. Profit-driven investors integrate ESG factors into their investment analysis and decision-making processes, both by purchasing individual equities or mutual funds. By assessing a company's ESG performance, investors identify potential climate-related risks and opportunities, ensuring that their portfolio companies are well-positioned to manage these challenges (Friede et al., 2015). Investors can purchase social impact funds such as the Calvert Impact Capital, focusing on community development and social enterprises, and the Nuveen ESG

2.1 Introduction

Large-Cap Growth ETF (NULG), investing in companies with strong social performance metrics. Investors also engage with companies to encourage the adoption of sustainable practices and improved climate risk disclosure. Through shareholder proposals, voting, and direct dialogue with management, investors can influence corporate behavior and promote greater transparency and accountability regarding climate risks (Dimson et al., 2015).

Profit-driven investors deploy scenario analysis to understand the potential impact of different climate change pathways on their investments. This involves modeling various climate scenarios, such as a 2 °C or 4 °C temperature rise, to assess how different outcomes could affect the financial performance of companies and sectors (TCFD, 2017). "Climate scenarios" encompass various forward-looking analyses exploring potential future climate conditions. Although climate scenario analysis is still emerging, regulators are beginning to mandate the reporting of certain climate scenario metrics. Financial institutions use these metrics for stress testing, risk management, and decision-making purposes. Climate scenarios aim to address two primary questions: what might happen to global warming due to specific actions, such as policy implementations or technological changes, and what measures are required to limit global temperature rise to a particular target. Investors use climate scenarios to evaluate the range of climate-related risks and opportunities and to measure and track their portfolios' alignment with specific temperature targets, such as limiting global warming to 1.5 °C above pre-industrial levels. Metrics like Climate Value at Risk (CVaR) and Implied Temperature Rise (ITR) are commonly used for stress testing or risk management and to assess proximity to these targets. Stress testing involves evaluating how extreme climate-related events could impact investment portfolios, helping investors identify vulnerabilities and develop strategies to mitigate potential losses (Bank of England, 2019).

Sustainable finance has now gone mainstream. According to Moody's Investors Service, despite a turbulent economic environment, sustainable bond issuance is projected to reach USD 950 billion in 2024, maintaining a similar level to the USD 946 billion issued in 2023. The agency anticipates that sustainable bonds will continue to represent about 14% of the global issuance market, consistent with their peak share in 2022 and 2023. Growing climate risks and the advancement of new technologies are driving the issuance of these bonds. The report also notes that rising investment in emerging green technologies and a stronger focus on transition finance are likely to boost green bond issuance, particularly in emerging markets. The Asia-Pacific region has seen significant growth in sustainable bond issuance, with volumes nearly tripling to USD 194 billion in 2021, and reaching record highs of USD 219 billion in 2022 and USD 234 billion in 2023. Moody expects this upward trend to continue, driven by increasing investments in green technologies and transition finance initiatives.

The following section examines the evolution of sustainable finance over the last 50 years, tracing development from its early ethical roots to the sophisticated, broad-spectrum sustainable finance approaches seen today. Initially driven by ethical considerations, sustainable finance has expanded to integrate environmental, social, and governance (ESG) factors into mainstream investment decisions. This evolution suggests that future innovations in renewable energy and sustainable AI may lead to even more transformative sustainable finance practices. As technologies advance and awareness of sustainability issues grows, we can expect new financial instruments and investment strategies that further align economic growth with environmental and social well-being, ultimately driving a more sustainable global economy.

2.2 Sustainable Finance Timeline

Historically, sustainable finance and investment (SFI) has evolved significantly. Before the 1970s, investments were driven primarily by religious groups that avoided "sin stocks" like alcohol, tobacco, and gambling due to ethical considerations (Schueth, 2003; Sparkes, 2001). Figure 2.3 shows the evolution of sustainable finance since before the 1970s to the present. The 1980s saw the rise of SRI, influenced by anti-war and anti-racism movements, focusing on corporate social responsibility (CSR) and divesting from companies associated with contentious issues like the Vietnam War or apartheid in South Africa (Moskowitz, 1972).

The 1980s introduced social investment, which expanded to broader societal concerns such as human rights and gender equality. Ethical investment also emerged, where corporations adopted negative screening based on moral values (Schwartz, 2003). The subsequent decade, the 1990s, witnessed the growth of green finance, emphasizing environmental impacts and promoting positive societal changes (Zhang et al., 2019).

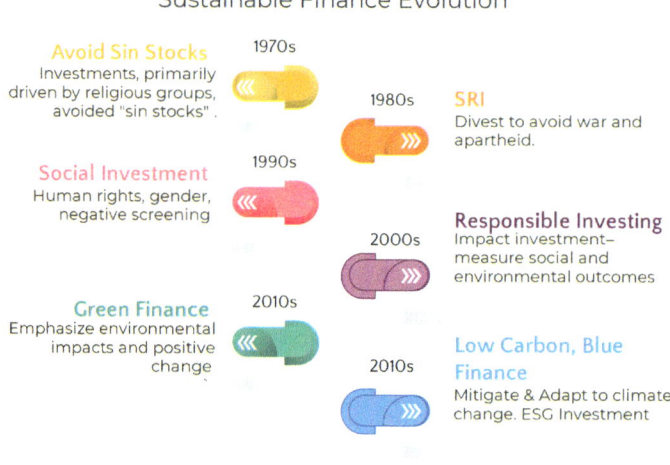

Fig. 2.3 Evolution of sustainable finance from the 1970s to the present time marked by negative and more recently, positive screening

The concept of ESG itself is not standardized and varies widely depending on the methodologies and metrics used by different data vendors (Eccles et al., 2020). The ESG vendors have developed their own systems to measure ESG performance, leading to divergent assessments of the same company. This diversity in ESG data interpretation and usage reflects the complex nature of the ESG data ecosystem (Kotsantonis & Serafeim, 2019). The variation is partly due to the different social origins of the data vendors, which influence how they construct and interpret ESG metrics (Eccles & Stroehle, 2018).

Two early innovators in this space were KLD Research & Analytics, Inc. (KLD) and Innovest Strategic Value Advisors, Inc. (Innovest). KLD, motivated by a commitment to sustainable development, focused on issues impacting external stakeholders and did not aggregate scores for companies, instead emphasizing a narrative-based approach (Chatterji et al., 2009; Eccles et al. 2020; Hatten et al. 2020; Kang, 2015). In contrast, Innovest prioritized financial materiality and used a quantitative methodology for its assessments, aiming to quantify the financial relevance of ESG factors. This difference highlights how the origins and motivations of ESG data providers shape the interpretation and application of ESG metrics.

In our view, the lack of a universal standard for ESG metrics poses both challenges and opportunities. On the one hand, the diversity of methodologies allows for a more comprehensive view of a company's performance, as different perspectives can highlight various aspects of ESG. On the other hand, the inconsistency and lack of comparability can be confusing for investors and may lead to misinterpretation of the data. Thus, while the rise in ESG interest is a positive development, there is a clear need for more standardized and transparent methodologies to ensure that ESG data is accurately and consistently interpreted across the industry.

Entering the 2000s, responsible investment gained traction, balancing social, environmental, and financial goals. This period also saw the introduction of impact investments, focused on achieving measurable social and environmental outcomes (Höchstädter & Scheck, 2015; Townsend, 2020). The concept of microfinance also emerged, providing financial services to underserved populations (Hudon & Sandberg, 2013).

The 2010s were defined by climate finance, which aimed at mitigating and adapting to climate change, and by the development of low-carbon and blue finance strategies, the latter focusing on ocean conservation (Diaz-Rainey et al., 2017; Wabnitz & Blasiak, 2019). ESG investment also became prominent, integrating environmental, social, and corporate governance factors into investment decisions (Busch et al., 2016).

Despite its evolution, sustainable finance remains a complex and multifaceted concept lacking a standardized definition, attributable to its holistic and interdisciplinary nature. This complexity has been reflected in the numerous terms used interchangeably in the literature to describe aspects of SFI, each emphasizing different facets of sustainability (Cunha et al., 2021). Sustainable finance research has predominantly employed qualitative methods due to the field's intricate nature (Kumar et al., 2022). Significant gaps remain in understanding the influence of formal and informal institutions on sustainable finance and how financial firms develop sustainable business models. Further research is needed to assess the effectiveness of these strategies and their long-term societal and environmental impacts. Evaluating these impacts is crucial to ensure that sustainable finance strategies promote economic growth and advance broader sustainability goals effectively.

2.3 Various Stakeholders in Sustainable Finance Investment

The development of SFI research needs to be more cohesive (Fabregat-Aibar et al., 2019), as the current fragmentation complicates the field's boundaries and distinguishes it from traditional finance and investment approaches. This fragmentation highlights the necessity for a more integrated approach to defining and understanding the unique aspects of sustainable finance and investment. This realization leads us to explore the unique "currency" of sustainability, a concept significantly relevant in finance and investment, impacting decision-making processes across economic spectra.

This section delineates how stakeholders, as shown in Fig. 2.4, including corporations, governments, NGOs, financial institutions, and consumers, contribute to and influence sustainability efforts. Corporations often drive sustainability through initiatives that improve energy efficiency, reduce waste, and promote sustainable supply chains. Governments set regulatory frameworks and policies that mandate or encourage sustainable practices, such as emission reduction targets and renewable energy incentives. NGOs advocate for environmental and social causes, often pressuring both corporations and governments to adopt more sustainable practices.

Financial institutions play a pivotal role by directing investments toward sustainable projects and incorporating environmental, social, and governance (ESG) criteria into their lending and investment decisions. Retail investors, who buy and sell securities for their personal accounts, exhibit varying preferences, with some favoring "green" over "brown" stocks (Ardia et al., 2023). This preference is distinct from non-financial objectives, as sustainable investors under this motive would avoid "brown" stocks, even if divestment did not directly impact the company's capital costs. This preference is rooted in the personal satisfaction derived from investing sustainably (Hafenstein & Bassen, 2016). On the other hand, institutional investors, such as banks, insurance companies, pension funds, hedge funds, mutual funds, and endowments, are increasingly integrating sustainability into their investment strategies due to growing awareness of ESG issues, regulatory pressures, and the potential for long-term financial performance.

2.3 Various Stakeholders in Sustainable Finance Investment

Fig. 2.4 Different stakeholders in sustainable finance with different perspectives

2.3.1 Consumers, Particularly Millennials and Younger Generations

Consumers, particularly Millennials and younger generations, are increasingly demanding sustainable practices. This shift in consumer preferences is mirrored in their demand for products and brands that commit to sustainable practices, reflecting their values toward preserving the planet for future generations (Curtis, 2019; Nielsen, 2018; Valente & Atkinson, 2019). This demographic shift significantly influences market trends and corporate behaviors. Surveys, such as one from Nielsen (2015), have shown that over 66% of consumers were willing to pay more for sustainable brands. About 72% of Generation Z (respondents under age 20) are willing to spend more on a product if it comes from a sustainable brand. Companies like Patagonia and Ben & Jerry's, which are committed to environmental responsibility, have notably strong followings among younger consumers.

2.3.2 States, Cities, and Governments

Governments at various levels play a crucial role in the adoption of sustainable finance policies. They do so to mitigate climate change impacts, improve quality of life, and ensure economic stability. The introduction of regulations and policies that incentivize or mandate sustainable practices reflect the degree of their commitment to sustainability. For example, the European Green Deal, an ambitious plan involving massive investment in environmental technologies, cleaner energy, and stricter emissions regulations, aims to make Europe climate-neutral by 2050. Cities like Copenhagen have ambitious goals to become carbon-neutral by 2025 through investments in renewable energy and green infrastructure (Damsø et al., 2017). The ambitious environmental policies of various governments set a precedent that international organizations are striving to uphold globally. These international efforts are crucial in supporting sustainable development, especially in developing countries, and help in financing climate resilience projects, as discussed next.

2.3.3 UN and Other International Organizations

International organizations such as the UN and World Bank are motivated by the need to support sustainable development globally, especially in developing countries. They focus on funding projects that promote environmental sustainability, reduce poverty, and build climate resilience. The Green Climate Fund, under the United Nations Framework Convention on Climate Change (UNFCCC), helps developing countries finance climate adaptation and mitigation practices (Bowman & Minas, 2019). The IMF and World Bank also integrate sustainability criteria into their lending and grants processes, emphasizing environmental impact and sustainable growth (Maldonado & Gallagher, 2022).

2.3.4 Corporates

Corporations are increasingly driven to adopt sustainable practices due to investor demand, recognition of climate-related financial risks, and regulatory requirements. These pressures influence business strategies and set market trends, creating both opportunities and challenges that require innovative approaches to address complex issues, often referred to as "wicked" or "super wicked" problems (Brønn & Brønn, 2018; De Salas et al., 2022; Kerekes, 2023; Klein, 2014; Lönngren & Van Poeck, 2021; Ostrom, 2009; Redgwell, 2012; Yearworth, 2016).

Companies should recognize that sustainability can drive business growth, innovation, and resilience. For example, Microsoft has committed to being carbon-negative by 2030, and Amazon has pledged to meet the Paris Agreement goals ten years early. These initiatives reflect compliance with regulatory standards and a strategic alignment of business models with sustainability to appeal to consumers and investors. The convergence of environmental changes, investor demands, and increasing regulation creates new opportunities and risks for businesses.

Many companies are setting targets across various sustainability factors, from climate risk mitigation to net-zero emissions (Fankhauser et al., 2022). These efforts require significant capital investment but can enhance long-term resilience. Businesses investing in sustainability are often rewarded through increased investor capital and market access due to regulatory compliance. New businesses are emerging to address these opportunities, bridging the gap between technology and expertise to meet these demands. Collectively, these actions across industries are starting to make a positive global impact. However, the question remains whether these initiatives are sufficient to combat the growing environmental crises. The pace of progress must accelerate to meet the urgent demands of climate change and sustainability. More ambitious goals, increased investments, and stronger regulatory frameworks are essential to ensure that the efforts made today will lead to a substantial and lasting reduction in the environmental crisis. Only through collective and intensified actions can we hope to achieve the necessary changes for a sustainable future.

Companies making a positive societal impact may benefit from better customer and employee attraction, access to business opportunities arising from societal shifts related to climate change, and financial inclusion. They also potentially avoid environmental penalties or regulatory crackdowns (Bodhanwala & Bodhanwala, 2019). If the benefits of these companies are undervalued, they can offer superior risk-adjusted returns, making them attractive to profit-driven investors (Aich et al., 2021). This alignment of business practices with sustainability is also evident in the banking sector, which faces similar regulatory pressures and market demands.

2.3.5 Pension Funds and Family Offices

Pension funds and family offices are pivotal in directing large pools of money toward sustainable investments (Hill, 2020; Townsend, 2020). Their motivations include responding to shareholder demands for ethical investments, complying with new regulatory frameworks, and recognizing that sustainable investments can offer competitive returns. Blackrock and its CEO, Lawrence Fink, have shifted their comments in the last few years in response to political pressures. The 2024 appointment of an oil executive to BlackRock's board has sparked a debate about the company's commitment to ESG principles.[1] BlackRock's declining support for environmental shareholder proposals, down from 28% in 2022 to 7% in 2023, reflects a broader trend among major asset managers like Vanguard, indicating a more cautious stance on aggressive ESG initiatives.[2]

In recent years, pension funds have increasingly incorporated climate risk assessments into their investment strategies. This shift is driven by the recognition that climate change poses systemic and material risks to the global economy and the financial stability of pension fund assets. Pension funds like CalPERS in the United States are factoring climate risk into their investment decisions (McDonnell, 2024; Muir, 2022). The New York City Employees' and Teachers' Retirement Systems have

---

[1] https://www.esgdive.com/news/blackrock-shareholders-appoint-aramco-ceo-nasser-board-larry-fink-climate-proposal/716358/.

[2] https://www.reuters.com/sustainability/climate-energy/blackrock-ceo-fink-woos-texas-after-esg-spat-2024-02-06/.

adopted comprehensive plans to achieve net-zero emissions across their investment portfolios by 2040. These plans include setting interim emissions reduction targets, engaging with portfolio companies and asset managers to align with net-zero goals, investing in climate solutions, and divesting from fossil fuel-related assets.[3]

States like Colorado, Illinois, Maine, and Maryland have enacted legislation encouraging the consideration of ESG factors in pension fund investment decisions. For example, Maryland's legislation mandates the assessment of climate-related risks and the inclusion of these considerations in investment strategies. This approach reflects a growing trend among states to incorporate ESG factors as a means of mitigating emerging financial risks.[4]

The expert in this context of pension funds is **Mary Cerulli,** founder of Climate Finance Action, whose interview excerpts are included in this section.

Pension funds represent beneficiaries concerned not only with retirement income but also with broader issues like environmental health and societal stability. These beneficiaries might endorse companies that enhance their social impact, even if it leads to a potential reduction in profits (Lewis et al., 2016). Senior citizens often express a strong desire to leave a better planet for their grandchildren. This sentiment stems from a deep sense of responsibility and care for future generations, motivating them to support environmental initiatives, choose green investments for their pension funds, and advocate for sustainable practices.

Expert in Focus: Mary Cerulli

Mary Cerulli is the founder of Climate Finance Action, established on May 6, 2020, following 18 months of dedicated climate finance work. Her efforts were in conjunction with an investor-led campaign initiated by former New York City Comptroller Scott Stringer, aimed at decarbonizing the 20 largest electric

---

[3] https://comptroller.nyc.gov/newsroom/new-york-city-pension-funds-adopt-implementation-plan-to-achieve-net-zero-investment-portfolio-by-2040/.

[4] https://www.pewtrusts.org/en/research-and-analysis/articles/2024/01/24/how-emerging-financial-risks-could-affect-public-pension-fund-assets.

generating utilities in North America. Mary holds an MBA from Boston University and a BA in Geology from Skidmore College. She completed the ESG: Navigating the Board's Role course at the University of California, Berkeley Law/Ceres.

Before transitioning to the nonprofit sector, Mary accumulated over twenty years of experience as an analyst and consultant in the financial services industry. She began her career at a subsidiary of New York Life, creating tax-advantaged packaged products in oil, gas, and real estate. Mary later co-founded Cerulli Associates, Inc., where she focused on retail distribution dynamics, packaged products, and retirement markets. She authored reports on the wealth management industry, high-net-worth market, and the annuity industry, and worked on client projects involving emerging manager expansion strategies and independent registered investment advisors (RIAs).

Mary now leverages her financial sector experience to research and decode financial information, empowering advocates to conduct effective campaigns that push the financial sector to address the climate crisis. She serves on the ESG Committee of the Massachusetts Pension Reserves Investment Management Board.

Expert Interview with Mary Cerulli

Can you elaborate on how incorporating climate change considerations into pension funds investments affects long-term retirement security for the beneficiaries? Are there any potential trade-offs or concerns that need to be addressed?

First, in terms of beneficiaries, the largest group typically comprises union workers, who are essential to our states and cities. These workers, who include members of the National Education Association, the American Federation of Teachers, the Service Employees International Union, and other federal unions, highly value a dignified retirement. Their retirement benefits are a critical component of their compensation for public service, and any threats to these benefits are a major concern, especially given the long history of attacks on public state pension plans.

While climate change might not be the top priority for these workers, its impact is becoming increasingly apparent due to the rise in physical disasters like wildfires, sea level rise, hurricanes, and storms. However, there is also significant resistance to integrating environmental and social risks into pension plans, especially from conservative states opposing what they perceive as "woke capitalism." This resistance has led to over 200 proposed legislative bills, which have constrained innovative approaches within pension plans in the U.S.

> *To address these challenges, we need to treat climate risk as part of the broader risk management framework of pension funds. This approach helps depoliticize the issue and focuses on the necessity of accounting for climate-related risks, which have become more volatile and unpredictable, much like the economic disruptions caused by events such as COVID-19. Climate risks are now a critical consideration for the stability and sustainability of our economy.*
>
> *Our strategy has been to integrate climate risk into the risk management processes of pension funds, presenting it as another essential factor to ensure the long-term security of retirement benefits. This approach has proven successful in several instances, despite the complex and constrained legislative environment. This is annoying because it highlights a disconnect that needs to be addressed. We need political will and public opinion to connect the dots between our bankruptcy system, ESG disclosure system, and corporate governance system, which currently operate in isolation. It will be interesting to see how the politics of bailing out these companies plays out when it happens, and hopefully, it will lead to significant reforms.*

2.3.6 Regional, Global, Local Banks

Banks are increasingly aware of the financial risks associated with climate change, including the potential for stranded assets in industries like fossil fuels. They are motivated to mitigate these risks by diversifying their portfolios toward more sustainable investments. Banks and financial institutions are facing growing regulatory pressures to incorporate sustainability into their practices (Monasterolo, 2020; Park & Kim, 2020). Global frameworks and national regulations encourage or mandate increased transparency on climate risks and opportunities. Both retail and institutional clients are demanding more green financial products, such as green bonds and sustainable asset funds, prompting banks to respond with appropriate offerings. Many major banks globally are part of initiatives like the Principles for Responsible Banking, which aligns banks' strategies with the UN Sustainable Development Goals (SDGs) and the Paris Agreement. For example, HSBC has pledged to achieve net-zero carbon emissions across all its operations and supply chains by 2030 and aims to support its clients in transitioning to net zero by 2050. To summarize, demonstrating leadership in sustainability can enhance a bank's reputation, attract customers, and improve relations with government regulators and the community.

2.3.7 Private Investment Companies

Like banks and other financial institutions, private investment companies are beginning to adapt to the changing landscape by embracing green financial products and sustainable asset funds. There is a growing recognition among private investment companies (e.g., Brookfield Asset Management) that sustainable investments can deliver competitive, if not superior, returns. Investment firms are motivated to capitalize on opportunities in renewable energy, resource-efficient technologies, and other sustainable industries. Institutional investors, including pension funds and endowments, are increasingly mandating that their capital be used in ways that align with environmental, social, and governance (ESG) criteria.

2.3.8 VC Firms and Philanthropists

The players in this space are venture capitalist (VC) firms such as Kleiner Perkins and Khosla Ventures and philanthropists including Michael Bloomberg, Bill Gates, and Jeff Bezos. These philanthropists recognize the interconnectedness of systemic global challenges and use their resources to catalyze significant changes. Their philanthropic strategies often involve funding high-risk, high-reward projects that might not attract traditional investments due to their nature, filling crucial gaps in the global response to climate change and sustainability challenges. Bloomberg is mainly focused on combating climate change and promoting energy efficiency. He advocates for sustainable cities through his work with C40 Cities, which connects cities worldwide to share strategies and implement solutions to climate challenges. Bloomberg champions financial transparency regarding climate risks and opportunities, facilitating better investment decisions. Bloomberg terminal now provides a wealth of ESG information.

VC firms are investing in the sustainability space. Kleiner Perkins has a long history of investing in innovative technology companies. In sustainability, it focuses on technologies that can scale effectively to address significant environmental challenges, such as renewable energy, green building technologies, and sustainable agriculture. Kleiner Perkins has made substantial investments in companies like Bloom Energy, which produces fuel cells for clean and reliable power, and Proterra, a manufacturer of electric buses. A second well-known venture company, Khosla Ventures, has invested in companies like LanzaTech, which converts carbon-rich waste and residues into valuable products, such as sustainable fuels.

The myriad activities of these stakeholders illustrate a dynamic network of forces promoting sustainability. To summarize, each stakeholder group, from consumers to philanthropists, plays a crucial role in steering the global economy toward sustainability, reinforcing the importance of integrated efforts across all sectors.

2.4 Implementing Sustainable Investment Strategies

Setting sustainable investment strategies is essential for aligning financial activities with environmental stewardship, social responsibility, and corporate governance. These strategies define the ambition behind investments, ranging from adhering to personal ethics and mitigating financial risks to addressing substantial ecological or social challenges. Classifying investment objectives is critical as it helps frame the screening methods used to achieve them, categorized into adherence to personal standards, risk mitigation, or direct engagement with real-world challenges.

According to a report by FTSE Russell (2023), after five years of consistent growth, there was a modest decrease (from 88% in 2022 to 80% in 2023) in the proportion of global asset owners actively implementing and evaluating sustainable investment strategies, attributed to significant macroeconomic challenges, such as heightened interest rates to curb inflation and geopolitical disruptions, particularly the conflict in Ukraine.[5] The report notes that global asset owners generally have a strong, long-term commitment to sustainable investments, reflecting the evolving maturity of this investment theme. This year's research underscores the maturation of sustainable investments, revealing that an equal proportion (73%) of asset owners employ passive and active strategies in sustainable investing. This balance illustrates how sustainable investment practices are increasingly becoming mainstream, aligning with the broader trend toward passive investment strategies. The report notes that data quality is a significant obstacle to sustainable investing, with 58% of respondents indicating that this issue needs to improve their ability to meet regulatory demands. Despite these hurdles, there is a clear pathway forward by strategically selecting high-quality data sources and effective data partners.

In summary, the asset owner community remains dedicated to advancing its sustainable investment strategies. This dedication persists despite the problematic macroeconomic and geopolitical climate impacting its short-term strategies and sentiments toward sustainable investing. The next section examines these strategies.

2.4.1 Sustainable Investment Strategies

Sustainable investment employs various screening strategies to achieve investment goals. Negative or exclusionary screening avoids sectors or companies based on unethical practices. In contrast, positive screening favors entities with superior ESG performance, potentially enhancing returns without compromising risk. Norms-based screening aligns investments with global standards like the United Nations Global Compact or the SDGs, ensuring compliance with international norms. ESG integrative screening thoroughly analyzes ESG risks and opportunities alongside

---

[5] https://www.lseg.com/en/ftse-russell/sustainable-investing-solutions/global-asset-owner-survey.

2.4 Implementing Sustainable Investment Strategies

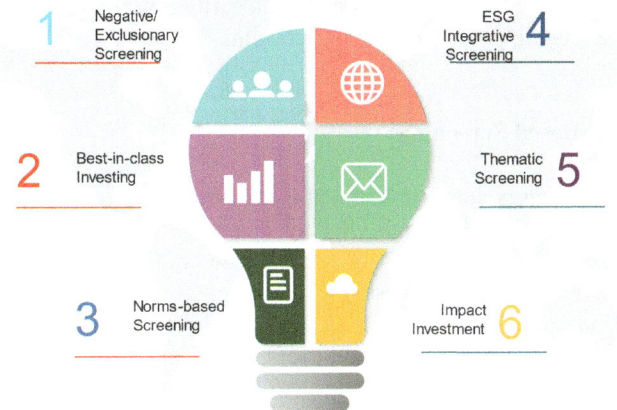

Fig. 2.5 International trends in sustainable investment showing interest around impact investment, ESG integrative screening, and negative screening

traditional financial assessments used by major financial institutions to enhance long-term value creation. Additionally, thematic screening focuses on specific sustainability themes, proving resilient during economic downturns and facilitating impact investments that generate measurable ESG outcomes. Figure 2.5 shows six main sustainable investment strategies, which are discussed below.

2.4.1.1 Negative/Exclusionary Screening

Negative screening in investing involves excluding sectors, companies, or practices from investment consideration based on selected criteria. In ESG investing, initially centered around "sin stocks," this strategy has evolved to avoid investments in entities engaged in activities considered unethical or detrimental to environmental and social values (Cai et al., 2021; Trinks & Scholtens, 2017). Despite potential impacts on financial performance, negative screening represents a step toward aligning investments with ethical and sustainability objectives. However, inconsistencies in ESG ratings pose challenges, underscoring the need for improved data and impact measures for effective screening (Liang & Renneboog, 2020).

2.4.1.2 Positive/Best-in-Class Screening

Positive or best-in-class screening demonstrates that selecting entities based on superior performance can enhance risk-adjusted returns. Focusing on entities with top ESG rankings, this strategy has yielded higher returns and lower risk without significantly compromising diversification (Verheyden et al., 2016). Machine learning and

AI advances are expected to refine this approach further by integrating qualitative data into ESG screening processes (De Franco et al., 2020).

2.4.1.3 Norms-Based Screening

Norms-based screening evaluates investments against specific international standards or norms, such as the United Nations Global Compact or the Sustainable Development Goals (SDGs). This approach aims to exclude entities violating established norms related to responsible business practices, including human rights, environmental protection, and anti-corruption (Polaschek, 2021). Norm-based screening aligns investment portfolios with ethical beliefs and international standards, potentially influencing investment decisions through legislation like the Uyghur Forced Labor Prevention Act.[6]

2.4.1.4 ESG Integrative Screening

This method systematically considers ESG risks and opportunities within investment decision-making processes. Entities like JP Morgan Chase exemplify this approach by incorporating ESG factors alongside traditional financial analysis to manage risk and enhance long-term returns. This methodology evaluates environmental, social, and governance aspects to inform investment choices (Larcker et al., 2022). Asset managers at firms like Vanguard, Fidelity, and BlackRock measure ESG metrics for managing fund portfolios using a variety of ESG data rating providers, including MSCI, Sustainalytics, and Refinitiv, and data providers such as Factset (business data and analytics).

2.4.1.5 Thematic Screening

Sustainability-themed investing focuses on themes and activities directly related to sustainability, often showing resilience during financial downturns (Ielasi & Rossolini, 2019). Impact investing aims to generate positive, measurable ESG outcomes, transitioning from philanthropy to investment strategies that yield above-market returns by integrating impact drivers (Lieberman, 2020).

2.4.1.6 Impact Investment

Impact investment is an investment strategy that aims to generate specific beneficial social or environmental effects and financial gains. Unlike traditional investment

---

[6] https://www.reuters.com/world/us-bars-imports-three-more-chinese-companies-over-uyghur-forced-labor-2023-12-08/.

approaches that focus primarily on financial returns, impact investments are made to achieve measurable positive impacts on society or the environment while also targeting a financial return. For example, the Government Pension Fund of Norway, one of the world's most significant sovereign wealth funds, is an excellent example of impact investing on a national scale. It is often called the "Oil Fund" and invests Norway's oil revenues to secure and grow financial assets for future generations (Gasparini, 2023). The fund is known for its strict investment criteria based on ethical guidelines, which include considerations related to human rights, corruption, severe environmental damage, coal, and other sustainability factors.

Collectively, these strategies foster a sustainable financial ecosystem and position investors to lead in the transition toward a greener and more equitable global economy. This approach to investment underscores a broader trend toward sustainability, influencing significant shifts in the financial landscape as more investors choose to divest from sectors like fossil fuels in favor of more sustainable alternatives. Whether exclusionary, norms-based, or integrative, investment screening strategies set the stage for targeted investment approaches such as FFC divestment. This strategy highlights how specific investment decisions, such as divesting from fossil fuels, can lead to significant shifts in the financial landscape and reflect broader market trends toward sustainability.

With a clear understanding of the various investment strategies and their objectives, the next logical step is to examine how they are measured and benchmarked. This step involves assessing the ESG or impact performance metrics crucial for categorizing investments and ensuring they meet their intended sustainability targets.

2.4.2 Fossil Fuel Divestment (FFC) as a Strategy

This topic of fossil fuel company divestment (FFC) merits its section, given its history and evolution and its financial impacts (Plantinga et al., 2021). In 2012, Bill McKibben proposed a radical concept to combat climate change: revoking the fossil fuel industry's social license by urging financial institutions and civil society to divest from fossil fuels collectively. This idea seemed particularly bold at the time, considering the dominance of companies like ExxonMobil in the global market, with most foundations and academic endowments heavily invested in the sector. Today, fossil fuel divestment has evolved from a marginal idea into a significant movement, where 1634 institutions are divesting assets worth approximately USD 40.76 trillion.[7] This shift has fundamentally altered the financial landscape, leading over a thousand significant investors, pension plans, and endowments to commit to environmentally sustainable funds. The divestment movement has questioned the long-term viability of fossil fuels, aiming to stigmatize the industry and diminish its financial attractiveness by increasing the capital costs for intensive activities like mining, exploration, and extraction. This financial recalibration is particularly evident

---

[7] https://divestmentdatabase.org/.

in the coal sector, which is recognized as highly polluting and inefficient, and is also gradually impacting oil and gas.

Scholars have explored various strategies by which investors influence FFCs. Activist investors have attempted to steer FFCs toward more sustainable practices (McDonnell et al., 2022), while high-profile divestment movements have sought to sway larger, less actively minded institutions (Ayling & Gunningham, 2017). Additionally, the potential for FFCs to leave unburnable fossil fuels in the ground presents complex challenges for institutional investors regarding stranded assets (Ansar et al., 2013). These concerns are echoed by financial leaders like Mark Carney, who underscore the importance of stable financial markets amid the climate crisis (Carney, 2015).

2.4.3 Measurement and Benchmarking

The next aspect of sustainable investing is measurement, which involves the various ESG or impact performance metrics required for categorizing an investment accordingly. Such metrics might include evaluating breaches of certain ethical standards or principles within business practices or through the products and services offered (e.g., the production of tobacco or alcohol, or human rights infringements).

A key aspect of measurement is being able to measure, which is frequently facilitated through public corporate disclosures and reports such as corporate sustainability reports. Reviewing and assessing these reports and disclosures can also be part of the investment or post-investment strategies. These reports involve active engagement with companies to promote better practices through dialogue, shareholder resolutions, and voting. Notable instances include shareholder activism at ExxonMobil, highlighting the importance of corporate engagement across environmental issues. However, legal challenges, such as ExxonMobil's lawsuit against activists, underscore the complexities in corporate engagement for outcomes (Tillotson et al., 2023).

When assessing materiality, performance metrics also encompass the assessment of ESG-related risks and prospects, commonly assessed through ESG ratings (considering financial or outside-in materiality). Several ESG rating companies, including MSCI, Bloomberg, Moody's, and MorningStar, provide ESG ratings for global companies. These agencies usually have proprietary methods that assess a company's practices to provide a score across various metrics.

Double materiality (Baumüller & Sopp, 2021) is gaining significant traction in sustainable finance, emphasizing the interconnectedness of financial and non-financial factors in corporate decision-making and reporting. Financial materiality, shown in Fig. 2.6, evaluates the impact of environmental, social, and governance (ESG) factors on a company's financial performance, such as costs associated with climate change regulations or reputational risks from poor labor practices. On the other hand, impact materiality assesses the broader impact a company's activities have on people and the planet, including greenhouse gas emissions, water usage, and

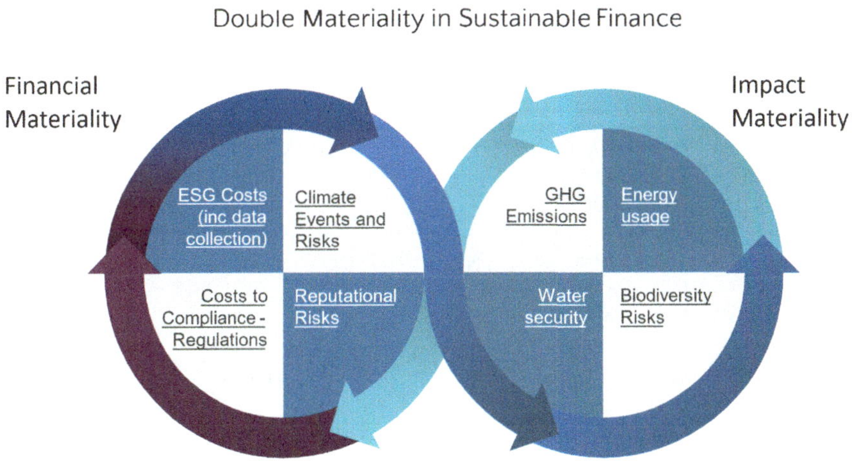

2.4 Implementing Sustainable Investment Strategies

Double Materiality in Sustainable Finance

Financial Materiality
- ESG Costs (inc data collection)
- Climate Events and Risks
- Costs to Compliance - Regulations
- Reputational Risks

Impact Materiality
- GHG Emissions
- Energy usage
- Water security
- Biodiversity Risks

Fig. 2.6 Double materiality refers to financial materiality that evaluates the impact of environmental, social, and governance (ESG) factors on a company's financial performance, while impact materiality assesses the broader impact of a company on people and planet

social justice issues. This can be thought of as impact *to the company* and impact *by the company*, respectively.

Double materiality requires companies to disclose financial and impact material information through sustainability reports, integrated reports, or other means of communication. Investors can make more informed decisions by considering companies' financial and impact performance. Double materiality aligns with the UN SDGs, promoting sustainable business practices and contributing to a more sustainable future. The European Union's (EU) Sustainable Finance Disclosure Regulation (SFDR) requires companies to disclose their sustainability risks and impacts, pushing double materiality further into the mainstream. As standards and frameworks evolve, double materiality is expected to become a key component of responsible investment and corporate reporting practices.

Various ESG research firms offer SDG assessments to quantify the beneficial and detrimental impacts of a company's services, products, and business modalities. There are challenges in reporting double materiality. Measuring and disclosing sustainability factors can be complex and resource-intensive, requiring companies to develop robust data collection and analysis systems. There is no single, universally accepted standard for double materiality reporting, which makes it challenging for companies to implement and for investors to compare different companies. Integrating double materiality into existing financial reporting frameworks requires careful consideration and adjustments to ensure seamless and transparent disclosures.

Table 2.1 Example ESG Funds, showing size in assets and fund return rate[8]

Fund (ticker)	Index	Expense ratio	Total assets	Fund three-year return as of December 31 2023
iShares ESG Aware MSCI USA ETF (ESGU)	MSCI USA Extended ESG Focus Index	0.15%	USD 13.3 billion	8.38%
iShares ESG Aware MSCI EAFE ETF (ESGD)	MSCI EAFE Extended ESG Focus Index	0.20%	USD 7.5 billion	4.00%
iShares ESG Aware MSCI EM ETF (ESGE)	MSCI Emerging Markets Extended ESG Focus Index	0.25%	USD 4.0 billion	−6.18%
Vanguard ESG US Stock ETF (ESGV)	FTSE US All Cap Choice Index	0.09%	USD 7.4 billion	7.94%
Vanguard ESG International Stock ETF (VSGX)	FTSE Global All Cap ex US Choice Index	0.12%	USD 3.5 billion	0.32%
iShares ESG Aware US Aggregate Bond ETF (EAGG)	Bloomberg Barclays MSCI US Aggregate ESG Focus Index	0.10%	USD 3.6 billion	−3.45%

2.4.4 Example Funds

Table 2.1 provides a detailed comparison of various ESG funds, highlighting their indices, expense ratios, total assets, and three-year returns as of December 31, 2023.

These ESG funds demonstrate varied performance and expense structures, offering investors different options based on their risk tolerance and investment goals. The iShares ESG Aware MSCI USA ETF (ESGU) and Vanguard ESG US Stock ETF (ESGV) showed the highest returns over the three-year period, with 8.38% and 7.94% respectively. The iShares ESG Aware MSCI EM ETF (ESGE) and iShares ESG Aware US Aggregate Bond ETF (EAGG) reported negative returns, with −6.18% and −3.45% respectively.

---

[8] https://www.usatoday.com/money/blueprint/investing/best-esg-funds/.

2.5 Sustainable Investing as a Strategic Response to Demand and Increasing Awareness

This section discusses current trends in sustainable investment and the rationale provided by experts for proactive financial strategies in the face of climate change. It emphasizes three topics that are accelerating interest in sustainable investment: the physical risks associated with climate change, changing investor perspectives, and regulatory environments. The regulatory environment plays a significant role in sustainable finance globally, with different approaches to climate disclosure regulations in the EU and the US reflecting the complex and evolving nature of ESG frameworks. On the demand side, consumers are also increasingly seeking sustainable products and practices and engaging with brands and companies with strong ESG credentials. These elements drive a marked increase in interest in various financial products such as bonds, equities, private investments, and sovereign debt.

2.5.1 Physical Risks

Financial commitments have been slow despite long-standing warnings from climate scientists about the physical risks of climate change. This sluggishness is now being countered by a growing awareness within the financial sector of the urgent need to adapt investment strategies to address these risks, underscored by the "Tragedy of the Horizon" (Carney, 2015). This concept extends the economic principle of the "tragedy of the commons" to climate issues, illustrating how the benefits of emission reductions accrue globally while the costs are borne individually, leading to underinvestment in mitigation measures. Recent developments, however, are beginning to shift the financial sector's approach as leaders recognize the pressing need to address climate-related risks.

The intersection of climate change and sustainable investment is rapidly evolving, driven by an increasing recognition of both the physical risks to assets and the strategic financial opportunities presented by a shift to a low-carbon economy. Traditionally, investors assumed a stable climate and predictable future; however, the increasing frequency of severe climate events disrupts this assumption. For example, the US faced significant climate disasters in 2021 alone, including wildfires, hurricanes, floods, and heatwaves, which underscored the direct threat to financial assets (Condon, 2023b). As climate change progresses, the relationship between asset values and environmental stability becomes increasingly nonlinear. Initially, asset values may appear stable, but they can plummet rapidly once certain environmental thresholds are crossed (Duqi, 2023; Thomas, 2023). Although the most severe physical impacts, such as rising sea levels and intense storms, may seem distant, they influence current asset valuations. Investments are valued based on projected cash flows discounted by a rate that reflects risk and uncertainty. As climate change introduces new variables affecting these projections, discount rates increase, signaling heightened risk and diminishing present asset values (Weitzman, 2013).

The establishment of the Task Force on Climate-related Financial Disclosures (TCFD), spearheaded by Michael Bloomberg, aims to standardize the assessment of climate risks across the financial sector (TCFD, 2017). The TCFD encourages companies to consider both the direct physical impacts of climate change and the risks associated with the transition to a low-carbon economy through scenario analysis, helping investors make more informed decisions (O'Dwyer & Unerman, 2020). Understanding the physical risks and the financial implications of climate events helps frame the urgency of integrating climate risks into financial planning.

The following section examines how generational shifts, particularly the influence of Millennials, are reshaping investment priorities toward sustainability. Chapter 4 discusses the risks associated with changing climate and material risks in various sectors of the economy.

2.5.2 Comparative Generational Perspectives—Impact of Millennials

An essential aspect of broad investment drivers is the pivotal role of generational wealth dynamics. As each generation moves into strong earning and investment years, it drives investment and consumption trends. Each generation has varying perspectives on investment strategy and future outlooks. Baby Boomers are individuals born from 1946 to 1964; members of Generation X were born from 1965 to 1980; Millennials were born from 1981 to 1996; and members of Generation Z were born from 1997 to 2012.

Millennials, constituting a significant portion of the current US population (24.2%), have an outsized interest in investment in ESG factors and are reshaping the investment landscape with a pronounced preference for sustainable and socially responsible-centric investment options (Bunting, 2021). Digital platforms serve as crucial mediums for their investment education and decision-making processes, marking a departure from traditional investment avenues. The "Robin Hood Effect," observed during the pandemic, exemplifies this shift, highlighting the role of financial technology in altering investment behaviors among younger investors (Welch, 2020). Despite access to ESG information, a gap persists between expressed sustainability interests and actual investment decisions, indicating a nuanced relationship between attitudes and behaviors (Moss et al., 2020; Uzsoki, 2020).

Contrasting with Millennials, Baby Boomers (21.8% of the total population) exhibit more conservative investment tendencies, prioritizing financial security over ESG factors, though they still express interest in sustainable investing. This divergence extends across global demographics, with variations in investment preferences observable between generational cohorts in different regions, including the EU and Japan. In emerging economies like India, Millennial engagement in the stock market influences broader investment patterns, suggesting a global trend toward sustainability in investment preferences across generations.

Figure 2.7 illustrates the population distribution by generation in various countries as of 2020. Millennials represent a substantial percentage of the population across all listed countries, particularly UK and Sweden, where they form the largest generational cohort. The relatively large size of the Millennial generation in most countries suggests that its preferences could influence the development of sustainable finance products and services as financial institutions seek to cater to this demographic's interests. Millennials across the world show striking patterns. In India, the investment environment, particularly in the stock market, has been influenced by the younger population, with Millennials becoming increasingly active. This change may indirectly affect the investment patterns of older generations, including Baby Boomers. In South Korea, there are intergenerational differences in perceptions of successful aging between Millennials and second-wave Baby Boomers, which may reflect differing attitudes toward investment and economic behaviors (Jing & Joo, 2021).

Generation Z (born 1997–2012) also constitutes a notable proportion of the population, especially in emerging economies like India and Indonesia. As this generation matures financially, its values and investment choices may further accelerate the focus on sustainable finance. These generational data support the idea that as these younger, more socially and environmentally conscious cohorts become the dominant force in the economy, their preferences could significantly shape the future direction of investment and corporate behavior, reinforcing the importance of sustainable finance in the global market.

The significant influence of Millennials on the investment landscape highlights broader demographic trends also reflected in evolving regulatory environments. These regulatory changes are crucial in shaping the frameworks that govern sustainable finance, mainly through initiatives like the EU's SFDR and the US's evolving regulatory approaches described in the next section.

2.5.3 Sustainable Reporting

Corporations are increasingly required to report on their sustainability practices, particularly their impacts related to GHG Scope 1, 2, and 3 emissions, to comply with growing regulation and scrutiny worldwide. They adhere to various standards such as the UN SDGs, GRI, and TCFD, among others, leading to an "alphabet soup" of standards and frameworks. International sustainability reporting involves companies disclosing ESG performance, often guided by frameworks like the Global Reporting Initiative (GRI) and Integrated Reporting (IR) frameworks, discussed in detail in Chapter 4. The effectiveness of these reporting practices has been debated among scholars and practitioners (Dey et al., 2024; Eccles & Krzus, 2010).

60 2 ESG Integration: Unveiling Risk and Driving Innovation in Sustainable Finance

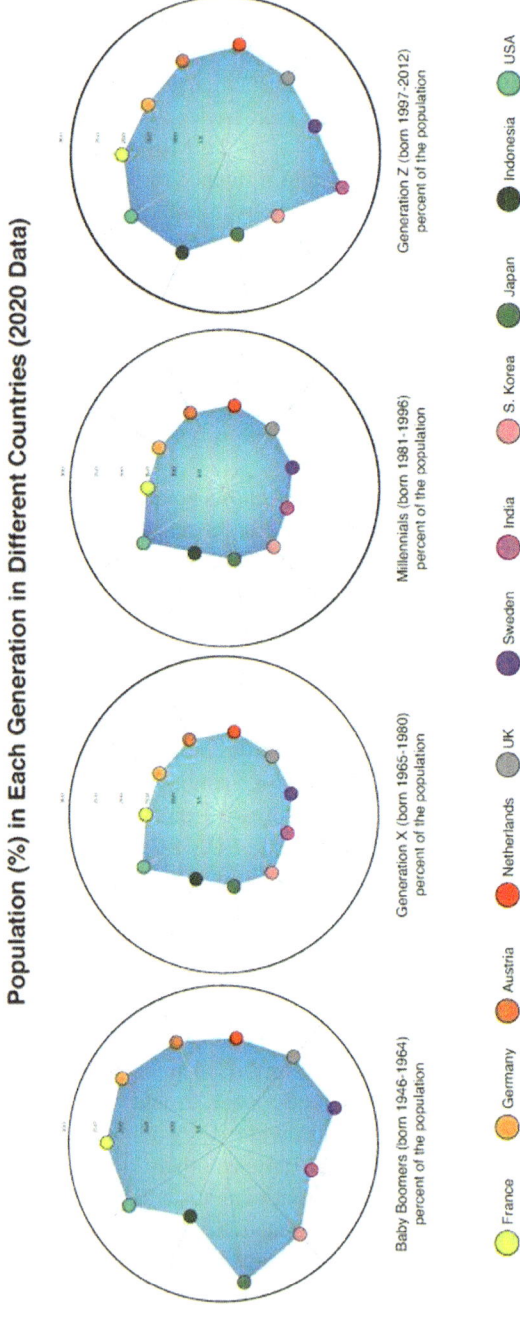

Fig. 2.7 Percentage of overall population by generational cohort. Colors show different countries presented for comparison

Sustainability reporting practices provide information on key performance indicators. The GRI has been successful in promoting the dissemination of sustainability reporting, especially among companies in Asia and South America. However, the content tends to be uniform across countries and sectors, not fully reflecting materiality considerations (Barkemeyer et al., 2015). Integrated reporting (IR) aims to provide a holistic view of sustainability management, but firms often offer biased IR disclosures, providing limited forward-looking and quantitative information and avoiding disclosure when social and environmental results are poor (Stacchezzini et al., 2016). While the adoption of GRI standards has influenced CSR management practices, it has also introduced unintended consequences, such as increased administrative burden and potential for superficial compliance (Vigneau et al., 2015). Existing sustainability indicator frameworks do not effectively address all aspects of sustainability, particularly in developing countries, where social criteria often receive less attention, limiting comprehensive assessments of sustainability performance (Labuschagne et al., 2005).

Effective reporting practices increase transparency and awareness. Sustainability reporting frameworks like GRI and IR have significantly enhanced corporate transparency and public awareness regarding ESG issues. These frameworks provide standardized guidelines that help compare the sustainability performance of different organizations globally. In regions like Europe and Japan, regulatory requirements have supported the persistent nature of sustainability reporting (Kolk, 2003).

However, the limitations of such reporting include superficial compliance, when companies sometimes engage in sustainability reporting as a form of impression management rather than a genuine commitment to sustainability, leading to biased and incomplete disclosures. Reports often fail to reflect material issues specific to different sectors and lack meaningful stakeholder engagement, limiting their effectiveness in driving actual sustainability improvements (Barkemeyer et al., 2015). Additionally, the separation of economic, environmental, and social dimensions in many reporting frameworks leads to compartmentalized assessments rather than a holistic view of sustainability (Lozano & Huisingh, 2011).

In summary, while international sustainability reporting has made strides in increasing transparency and standardization of ESG disclosures, issues like superficial compliance, lack of materiality, and insufficient stakeholder engagement limit its effectiveness. To truly drive corporate responsibility, these challenges need to be addressed through more rigorous standards and genuine integration of sustainability into corporate strategies. Chapter 4 presents new disclosure regulations from the EU and the context in the US.

2.6 Regulations in Sustainable Finance

In sustainable finance, regulatory frameworks are indispensable in sculpting the contours of ESG transparency. By establishing standardized accounting practices and imposing mandates for non-financial disclosures, such regulations facilitate informed decision-making among consumers and investors and propel companies toward adopting responsible practices conducive to long-term sustainability. The evolution of sustainability standards and frameworks over the past decades has led to various approaches—in some cases, incompatible. This has led to confusion for both consumers and sophisticated investors alike. Some of these nuances are discussed in later chapters, but this section explores the broad approaches primarily led by the EU and the US.

The regulatory landscape and thought leadership in sustainability are diverse, particularly in the US and EU. Each jurisdiction has taken a unique approach to climate disclosure standardization, transparency, and accountability. The EU, for instance, has adopted a comprehensive approach through initiatives like SFDR, setting a high bar for ESG transparency. In contrast, the US has initially relied on market-driven efforts, which are now being supplemented by more formal regulatory proposals, reflecting a global shift toward standardized climate disclosure regulations.

2.6.1 EU's Regulation in Sustainable Finance

The EU has been at the forefront of integrating sustainability into financial and corporate practices through comprehensive regulations. Two critical pieces of legislation, the Sustainable Finance Disclosure Regulation (SFDR) and the Corporate Sustainability Due Diligence Directive (CSDDD) show the EU's emphasis on promoting sustainable investments and corporate responsibility. The European Sustainability Reporting Standards (ESRS) are a set of standards being developed to enhance and standardize sustainability reporting across the European Union. These standards are part of the broader European Green Deal initiative and aim to support the Corporate Sustainability Reporting Directive (CSRD), which expands and strengthens the non-financial reporting requirements outlined in the Non-Financial Reporting Directive (NFRD).

The EU's stride toward ESG transparency is epitomized by the Sustainable Finance Disclosure Regulation (SFDR), a landmark regulation effective from March 10, 2021. Anchored within the European Commission's Sustainable Finance Action Plan, the SFDR mandates ESG disclosure obligations for asset managers and other financial market participants to foster transparency and promote environmental and social responsibility within the finance industry. This regulation, integral to the broader legislative package under the Commission's agenda, alongside the EU Taxonomy Regulation 2020/852 necessitates that financial entities such as banks, insurers, and investment firms report their sustainable investment practices in a standardized manner, thereby enabling informed investor decision-making (Gortsos, 2021; Malecki, 2021).

Non-compliance with the SFDR can have significant repercussions. It can lead to reputational damage, disciplinary action by local financial authorities, and a loss of trust among clients and investors. The regulation aims to level the playing field

2.6 Regulations in Sustainable Finance

for transparency in sustainability risks and impacts. It also includes guidelines on disclosure requirements and mandates that financial market participants and advisers disclose how they integrate ESG factors at both entity and product levels. These disclosures can be made through websites, prospectuses, or quarterly reports. The SFDR primarily applies to EU-based financial institutions but also indirectly affects non-EU firms through EU subsidiaries, services offered in the EU, and market pressures. Furthermore, investment managers or advisors outside the EU marketing their products to EU customers are required to comply with SFDR disclosures.

Principal Adverse Impacts (PAIs) on sustainability factors are a significant element of the EU's Sustainable Finance Disclosure Regulation (SFDR). The SFDR requires financial market participants and advisors to disclose how they consider the adverse impacts of investment decisions on sustainability factors. The SFDR aims to improve transparency, allowing investors to make more informed decisions based on non-financial considerations. Organizations with fewer than 500 employees can elect to comply with entity-level disclosure requirements regarding PAIs or provide an explanation for not considering the adverse effects of investment choices on sustainability factors (Pacces, 2021). Figure 2.8 shows some pros and cons of PAI reporting.

Proposed in February 2022, the Corporate Sustainability Due Diligence Directive (CSDDD) seeks to ensure that companies conduct due diligence regarding human rights and environmental impacts within their operations and value chains. This directive applies to large companies operating in the EU, including certain non-EU companies with substantial activity in the European market. The CSDDD is part of the European Green Deal and the European Commission's action plan on financing sustainable growth.

These new standards and frameworks, when combined, provide comprehensive guidance and enforcement for corporate reporting and investment criteria across much of Europe. Delving into the EU's robust approach to sustainability regulations through SFDR and other initiatives, it becomes evident that Europe is setting a

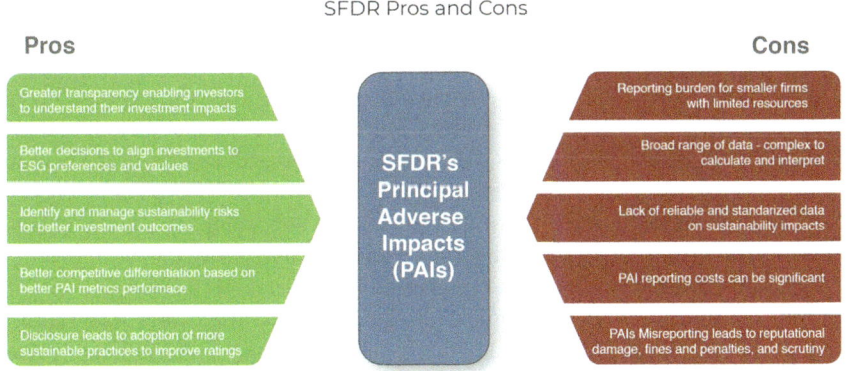

Fig. 2.8 Pros and Cons for entities electing to report Principal Adverse Indicators (PAIs)

stringent standard for ESG transparency. In stark contrast, the US has chosen a different route, marked by market-driven efforts that are now being bolstered by more formal regulatory proposals, signaling a global shift toward standardized climate disclosure regulations.

The pressing question remains, how can we leverage the vast amount of new regulation data to construct a new portfolio of ESG companies or funds? This is a significant challenge that must be met to create superior funds with SFDR compliance data. For instance, if a company has no PAIs on its operations, can we trust it enough to invest? This is the crucial connection that needs to be established between regulation and the sustainable finance practices of investors.

2.6.2 The US Approach: Market-Driven Efforts and Regulatory Evolution

Contrastingly, the US approach to similar matters has predominantly been characterized by voluntary, market-driven initiatives. However, a noticeable shift occurred throughout 2021 and 2022, with federal agencies, including the US Securities and Exchange Commission (SEC), the Federal Trade Commission (FTC), and the Treasury, alongside state-level regulations, embarking on new initiatives and proposals centered on environmental and social matters. In addition to these measures, President Biden issued an executive order in February 2021, accentuating the assessment, disclosure, and mitigation of climate pollution and related risks across the economy's sectors. The SEC's proposal for standardizing reporting frameworks for climate-related risks underscores an escalating regulatory focus on environmental considerations in public market investment decisions.

In May 2024, the SEC adopted a significant rule requiring public companies to disclose climate-related risks and their potential financial impacts. The final rule mandates that companies include information about material climate-related risks in their annual reports and registration statements, covering aspects like Scope 1 and Scope 2 GHG emissions, but notably excludes the more controversial Scope 3 emissions pertaining to supply chain impacts.

The SEC received over 24,000 comments during the rule's drafting process. Public comments reflect a wide range of opinions. Proponents of the rule, including many investors and environmental groups, argued that standardized climate disclosures are essential for assessing long-term risks and making informed investment decisions. They emphasized the importance of transparency in how companies are managing climate-related risks and transitioning to more sustainable practices.

On the other hand, some business representatives and trade groups voiced concerns about the feasibility and costs of implementing the required disclosures. They argued that the rule could lead to an overload of information that may not be uniformly relevant across all sectors, potentially resulting in "disclosure fatigue" among investors. Several companies and industry groups expressed strong opposition to the SEC's climate disclosure rule. Key concerns include the increased regulatory burden and potential legal liabilities arising from the new disclosure requirements. Opponents argue that the rule exceeds the SEC's statutory authority and could compel companies to disclose information that may not be directly material to their financial performance. Energy companies and business groups have been particularly vocal, citing the rule as an undue intrusion into their operations and warning about the high costs and complexities of compliance. Numerous legal challenges have been filed against the rule. A coalition of nine Republican-led states, along with several energy companies, have petitioned courts to block the rule, arguing that it is arbitrary and capricious and violates the Administrative Procedure Act. They also contend that the SEC lacks the authority to mandate such comprehensive climate disclosures, and that the rule imposes excessive burdens on businesses without clear statutory support.

Overall, while the SEC's rule is seen as a landmark step toward greater climate transparency, it faces significant opposition and legal hurdles that may shape its implementation and effectiveness in the coming years.

2.6.3 *Navigating the Regulatory Mosaic: Asia and Beyond*

The global narrative on ESG investing, while prominently featuring established economies, often overlooks the intricacies inherent within emerging markets (Singhania & Saini, 2022). This section delves into a comparative analysis of the ESG regulatory landscapes across five pivotal emerging markets: China, India, Brazil, Japan, and South Korea. Each jurisdiction exhibits unique regulatory approaches and challenges toward ESG reporting and disclosure, reflecting diverse maturity levels and focus within their respective frameworks.

From China's ambitious carbon neutrality goals and its struggle with transparency and international standards alignment, and India's evolving framework marked by the SEBI's (Securities and Exchange Board of India) Business Responsibility Reporting, to Japan's progressive stance on CSR and environmental regulations juxtaposed with financial integration challenges, South Korea's emphasis on transparency through mandatory disclosures, and Brazil's sector-specific focus amid growing investor and consumer pressure for responsible practices—these narratives underscore a dynamic and rapidly evolving ESG regulatory landscape across emerging markets.

To summarize, the transatlantic comparison of climate disclosure regulations between the EU and the US and the exploration of ESG regulatory frameworks in emerging markets highlights the diverse and evolving nature of global ESG regulatory landscapes. While challenges such as policy clarity, enforcement, and stakeholder engagement persist, the trajectory toward enhanced transparency, accountability, and sustainability in finance is evident. The dynamic interplay of regulations across jurisdictions underscores the significance of international collaboration and knowledge sharing in fostering robust and effective ESG frameworks, paving the path toward a more sustainable global financial ecosystem.

2.7 Concluding Remarks—Is There a Brighter Future?

The concluding section of this chapter offers glimmers of hope for humanity in facing the challenges of a catastrophic set of events and dire warnings of climate change. This section examines how technological advancements are transforming the financial services landscape, offering new avenues for sustainable growth and alignment with global carbon reduction targets. Significant developments within major Fintech companies, such as digital payment platforms offsetting carbon emissions and online lenders offering green loans, are highlighted. There follows a discussion of the technology transition happening in the US and elsewhere in the innovation and development of renewable energy, grid infrastructure, smart agriculture, green manufacturing, and green transport that will transform societies in the next decade.

2.7.1 Fintech Industry

The Fintech industry, known for its use of technology to enhance financial services, has become a crucial driver of sustainability (Antoncic, 2020; Macchiavello & Siri, 2022). Fintech companies are harnessing the power of Big Data and advanced analytics to analyze vast amounts of environmental, social, and governance (ESG) data. This enables them to assess sustainability risks and opportunities, develop sustainable investment strategies, and track the environmental impact of financial portfolios. For instance, advanced analytics help in evaluating ESG performance, identifying sustainable investment opportunities, and monitoring the ongoing impact of investments (Chueca Vergara & Ferruz Agudo, 2021; Puschmann et al., 2020). One of Fintech's key contributions to green finance is the development of sustainable investment platforms that enable investors to allocate capital toward environmentally friendly projects and companies. They utilize data analytics to screen investments based on ESG criteria, offering transparency into the environmental footprint of investments. This empowers investors to make sustainable choices that align with their values and preferences (Climate Bonds Initiative, 2021).[9]

Fintech innovations also facilitate the integration of green finance principles into traditional financial services such as banking, lending, and insurance. Blockchain technology, for example, enhances transparency, traceability, and efficiency in sustainable supply chains, carbon trading, and renewable energy financing. This technology ensures that transactions are secure and verifiable, fostering trust and accountability in sustainable practices.[10]

Despite these advancements, challenges remain in fully harnessing the potential of data-driven sustainability in Fintech. These include data privacy and security

---

[9] https://www.climatebonds.net/market/explaining-green-bonds.

[10] https://www.weforum.org/agenda/2021/06/blockchain-can-help-us-beat-climate-change-heres-how/.

2.7 Concluding Remarks—Is There a Brighter Future?

Fig. 2.9 Many sectors of the economy, including agriculture, transportation, construction, and energy, are being transformed due both to regulation and capital investment. The second expert interviewed for this chapter Peter Fox-Penner discusses private equity interest in clean technologies

concerns, regulatory uncertainties, and the need for greater collaboration and standardization among stakeholders. Addressing these challenges requires a concerted effort from regulators, industry players, and technology providers to create a supportive ecosystem for sustainable finance.

2.7.2 Innovations in Key Sectors Offering Hope for Our Survival

The transition to sustainable practices across various sectors is not only essential for environmental health but also creates new job opportunities and drives economic growth. Several key sectors are witnessing significant innovations that promise a greener future for humanity shown in Fig. 2.9.

2.7.2.1 Renewable Energy

NextEra Energy is a significant US player in the clean energy market, particularly in solar and wind energy. Ørsted, a leader in offshore wind energy from Denmark, continues to expand its global footprint with numerous projects in Europe, Asia, and North America. The company is set to achieve substantial growth, driven by a robust pipeline of offshore wind projects expected to come online by 2025. Plug Power, specializing in hydrogen fuel cells, has been making significant strides in the clean energy sector.

Newer and smaller nuclear companies include NuScale Power, developing small modular reactors (SMRs) to provide scalable and safer nuclear energy solutions, and TerraPower, focusing on advanced nuclear reactor designs including the traveling wave reactor and molten salt reactors.

2.7.2.2 Power Grids

Investments include enhancing grid infrastructure for better integration of renewable energy. US Companies such as Schneider Electric are providing digital grid solutions to optimize and automate utility grids, enhancing flexibility and resilience for integrating renewables. General Electric is developing technologies to modernize the grid, enabling the integration of renewable energy sources efficiently. Global Companies include Siemens (Germany), focusing on smart grid solutions that enhance efficiency and sustainability. An Israeli company, Brightmerge, develops software to automate and optimize the design and operation of microgrid systems, ensuring more sustainable decentralized energy production.

Expert in Focus: Peter Fox Penner

About Peter Fox-Penner: Peter Fox-Penner, Ph.D., is a distinguished Senior Fellow at the Boston University Institute for Global Sustainability (IGS) and holds the role of Principal at the Brattle Group and Chairman, and Chief Impact Officer at Energy Impact Partners, a leading clean energy private equity fund group. Additionally, he is an academic advisor to The Brattle Group and is actively involved with several organizations, including the global leadership council of the World Resources Institute, advisory boards of Mobility Impact Partners, and the National Regulatory Research Institute's Training Initiative. He is also affiliated with the Energy Futures Initiative. Earlier in his career,

2.7 Concluding Remarks—Is There a Brighter Future?

Fox-Penner held senior positions at the U.S. Department of Energy and the White House Office of Science and Technology Policy.

A renowned speaker on energy issues, Fox-Penner is the author of numerous articles and books. His notable works include "Smart Power: Climate Change, the Smart Grid, and the Future of Electric Utilities" (2010) and its sequel "Power After Carbon: Building a Clean, Resilient Grid" (2020), both receiving critical acclaim. His research, particularly in electric power strategy, regulation, governance, energy and climate policy, sustainable finance, and public-private economic dynamics, has been widely recognized and cited, including in a Supreme Court decision.

Interview with Peter Fox-Penner
With your extensive experience in energy consulting and as the Chief Impact Officer at Energy Impact Partners, how do you assess the potential of these new renewable energy technologies in terms of scalability and impact?

The process of evaluating the potential value of an investment based on its impact begins with selecting the appropriate metric. In social investing, numerous metrics are relevant, but at EIP Ventures, we prioritize carbon savings due to our mission at Energy Impact Partners to accelerate the clean energy transition. For this discussion, I will focus solely on carbon savings. To measure carbon savings, the first step is to establish a baseline scenario—what the world would look like without your investment. This involves considering additionality, or the degree of causality between your investment and changes in the energy system. You need to outline a baseline emissions trajectory and then model the same energy system incorporating your technology.

Building this model involves isolating the portion of the energy system impacted by your investment. It's crucial to establish a measurable chain of causality, as many investments may not have one. For foundational investments, we avoid quantifying carbon savings to prevent false precision, which we believe can border on greenwashing. However, for investments with a clear causality chain, we analyze which part of the energy system the technology will alter, the extent of the change, and the expected emissions without the investment. This requires a thorough examination from the investment to the company's business plan, realistic sales forecasts, competitive analysis, and alternative technology pathways. Modeling all these factors allows us to make credible calculations for investors to base their decisions on. At EIP, this framework is integral to our investment process. We primarily invest in startups, many of which lack such a framework. These companies, aligned with our mission, often welcome the framework, as it integrates them into our community and simplifies the learning process. We collaborate with them annually on these calculations, ensuring they grasp the framework. By the third or fourth year, they typically understand it well enough to continue independently post-exit.

Regarding investor interest in clean energy technologies, I believe there is significant attention across most verticals. However, energy efficiency has been chronically underfunded due to high transaction costs and institutional barriers. This broad area, spanning from heating electrification to simple solutions like attic insulation and smart energy-saving technologies, has substantial untapped potential.

AI is an invaluable tool for enhancing technology and processes. It accelerates the discovery of new battery compounds and rare earth metal substitutes, optimizes processes, and improves the efficiency and reliability of the power grid. AI's potential to drive process improvements is vast and already evident. For instance, Energy Impact Partners has invested in Urbint, a company leveraging AI in the clean energy sector. Urbint uses AI to tackle a significant issue: accidental ruptures of gas lines during construction, which release methane, a greenhouse gas 28 times more potent than CO_2. With thousands of construction projects near gas lines daily, Urbint's AI analyzes utility applications to predict and identify high-risk sites. This allows utilities to allocate resources more effectively, reducing leak rates and enhancing safety. This innovative use of AI has been validated over several years, showcasing AI's potential to solve complex challenges in the energy sector.

2.7.2.3 Energy Storage

Investments include technologies for storing energy, such as batteries. Two European companies Northvolt (Sweden) and Varta (Germany) play significant roles in the advancement of lithium-ion battery technology, each addressing different aspects of the market. Northvolt's efforts are vital for the scalability of renewable energy and the growth of the electric vehicle industry, while Varta's high-performance solutions support a wide range of applications that demand reliable and efficient battery technology.

2.7.2.4 CCS (Carbon Capture and Storage)

Investments are directed at technologies to capture and store carbon emissions. Climeworks (Switzerland) specializes in direct air capture (DAC) technology to remove CO_2 from the atmosphere, meaning that this approach is not limited to local emissions but targets global atmospheric CO_2 levels. On the other hand, a US company, Carbon Clean Solutions, provides modular carbon capture technology for industrial applications. This means the CO_2 is captured directly from the exhaust

2.7 Concluding Remarks—Is There a Brighter Future?

gases of factories, power plants, and other industrial sites. The goal here is to prevent the CO2 from entering the general atmosphere by capturing it at the point of emission. This approach is more localized, focusing on specific emission sources rather than the overall atmospheric CO2 levels.

2.7.2.5 Hydrogen

Hydrogen can be produced through various methods, primarily electrolysis (splitting water into hydrogen and oxygen using electricity) and natural gas reforming (mixing natural gas with steam). The former produces green hydrogen which has less emissions associated with it while the latter produces gray and blue hydrogen. Investments focus on hydrogen production and utilization technologies. Plug Power develops hydrogen fuel cell systems for various applications, including transportation and stationary power. Nel Hydrogen (Norway) provides solutions for the production, storage, and distribution of hydrogen from renewable energy sources. Both Plug Power and Nel Hydrogen produce green hydrogen.

2.7.2.6 Electrified Transport

Investments in electric vehicles (EV) and related infrastructure are well illustrated by Tesla, the leading manufacturer of electric vehicles and energy storage solutions in the US, and Nio (China) and BYD (China), which manufacture electric cars and trucks with advanced battery swapping technology. Another company in the US is Rivian. A Tesla Model 3 emits 110–150 g of CO2 per miles (Scope 2 emissions) compared with more than 350 g for gasoline cars.[11]

2.7.2.7 Electrified Heat

Investments in electric heating solutions are well represented by Dandelion Energy, providing geothermal heating and cooling solutions for residential homes, and BlocPower, retrofitting buildings with energy-efficient heating and cooling systems using heat pumps and other technologies. Geothermal systems such as Dandelion utilize table temperatures underground and offer a renewable and sustainable alternative to traditional HVAC systems. Thus, they have no on-site emissions and significantly reduce the carbon footprint of heating and cooling a home. BlocPower utilizes air source heat pumps to transfer heat between the inside of a building and the outside air. They can provide energy-efficient heating in the winter and cooling in the summer.

---

[11] https://climate.mit.edu/ask-mit/are-electric-vehicles-definitely-better-climate-gas-powered-cars; https://www.reuters.com/business/autos-transportation/when-do-electric-vehicles-become-cleaner-than-gasoline-cars-2021-06-29/.

2.7.2.8 Clean Industry

Innovative carbon reduction technologies are essential for transforming the industrial sector into a more sustainable and environmentally friendly industry. Investments are directed in making industrial processes cleaner. CarbonCure Technologies innovates in concrete production by injecting CO2 into the mix, which not only reduces CO2 emissions but also enhances the strength and durability of the concrete, making it a more sustainable building material. Boston Metal develops molten oxide electrolysis technology to produce steel without carbon emissions. H2 Green Steel (Sweden) focuses on producing steel without GHG emissions by using hydrogen instead of coal. Thus, industries developing and embracing these technologies are not only crucial for the environment but also for the long-term ty and competitiveness of industrial enterprises.

2.7.2.9 Clean Shipping

Reducing emissions from the shipping industry is crucial for combating climate change. A combination of cleaner fuels, innovative technologies, regulatory measures, and industry-wide commitment can significantly reduce the environmental impact of maritime transport. Investments are directed to reducing emissions from the shipping industry.[12] Crowley Maritime Corporation invests in LNG-powered ships and other low-emission maritime solutions. Maersk (Denmark) is committed to achieving carbon neutrality by 2050 with investments in alternative fuels and technologies. Swedish company Oceanbird aims to use large sails to harness wind power, potentially reducing CO2 emissions by up to 90% for certain routes.[13]

2.7.2.10 Smart Agriculture

Companies in this space use data and AI to provide smart climate, water, soil, and seed solutions to make agriculture more efficient and effective in dealing with drought and poor soils. This sector is sometimes referred to as Ag Tech. For example, Eat Neat Project (India) customizes aquaponics systems for urban environments, providing higher yields with significantly less water usage compared to traditional farming. Their systems help reduce the carbon footprint of urban agriculture. Refarmers (France) develop vertical aquaponic greenhouses, integrating automation and monitoring technologies to optimize indoor farming. Their solutions are tailored for urban environments and emphasize sustainability and waste-to-food recycling.

Prior research (Hayek et al., 2020; Ritchie, 2019; Sinke et al., 2023) indicates that plant-based meats may reduce land use by more than 60% as well as reducing more than 50% of air pollution. The two companies BeyondMeat, Planted Foods,

---

[12] https://terrapass.com/blog/5-ways-the-shipping-industry-can-reduce-its-carbon-emissions/.

[13] https://www.theoceanbird.com/the-oceanbird-concept/.

and Impossible Foods in the US developed whole cuts of plant-based meat, now sold in supermarkets and McDonalds. Switching to plant-based meats like those from Beyond Meat and Planted Foods can lead to reduction of annual emissions of greenhouse gas emissions, supporting broader efforts to mitigate climate change, improve air quality, and promote better health.[14]

The innovations in renewable energy, electrified transport, clean industry, and other sectors are encouraging trends that highlight the potential for a greener future. However, it is crucial to remain realistic about the challenges and the pace of change. Transforming our global systems to tackle climate change is a massive undertaking that requires coordinated efforts from governments, businesses, and individuals across the globe. Both international and national governments, agencies, corporates, and the public should continue to support and invest in these innovations, push for stronger policies and regulations, and foster global cooperation. As global temperatures are projected to rise over 1.5 °C in the next two decades, the advancements discussed in this chapter offer some hope for our survival and a more sustainable future.

While these efforts will not yield instant results, they are essential steps toward achieving a sustainable future. The journey is long, but the progress being made is a hopeful sign that humanity can rise to the challenge before it is too late.

Acknowledgements We would like to thank David Blitzer, Ph.D., for providing feedback on this chapter. Blitzer is a distinguished figure in the finance industry, renowned for his significant contributions to the S&P Dow Jones Indices. Blitzer led the index committee responsible for selecting stocks for major indices, including the S&P 500 Index and the Dow Jones Industrial Average. His role encompassed overseeing the selection process, conducting thorough index analysis, and managing the indices until his retirement in 2019.

References

Aich, S., Thakur, A., Nanda, D., Tripathy, S., & Kim, H. C. (2021). Factors affecting ESG towards impact on investment: A structural approach. *Sustainability, 13*(19), 10868.

Ansar, A., Caldecott, B., & Tilbury, J. (2013). *Stranded assets and the fossil fuel divestment campaign: What does divestment mean for the valuation of fossil fuel assets?* Smith School of Enterprise and the Environment, University of Oxford.

Antoncic, M. (2020). Uncovering hidden signals for sustainable investing using Big Data: Artificial intelligence, machine learning and natural language processing. *Journal of Risk Management in Financial Institutions, 13*(2), 106–113.

Ardia, D., Bluteau, K., Boudt, K., & Inghelbrecht, K. (2023). Climate change concerns and the performance of green vs. brown stocks. *Management Science, 69*(12), 7607–7632. https://doi.org/10.1287/mnsc.2022.4636

---

[14] https://www.un.org/en/actnow/food. The UN estimates that switching to a plant-based diet can reduce an individual's annual carbon footprint by up to 2.1 tons with a vegan diet or up to 1.5 tons for vegetarians. Using UN's estimates, by switching to a plant-based diet twice a week, an individual can save approximately 0.43 tons of CO2 emissions per year.

Ayling, J., & Gunningham, N. (2017). Non-state governance and climate policy: The fossil fuel divestment movement. *Climate Policy, 17*(2), 131–149. https://doi.org/10.1080/14693062.2015.1094729

Bank of England. (2019, April 17). *Open letter on climate-related financial risks*. https://www.bankofengland.co.uk/news/2019/april/open-letter-on-climate-related-financial-risks

Barkemeyer, R., Preuss, L., & Lee, L. (2015). On the effectiveness of private transnational governance regimes—Evaluating corporate sustainability reporting according to the Global Reporting Initiative. *Journal of World Business, 50*(2), 312–325. https://doi.org/10.1016/j.jwb.2014.10.008

Baumüller, J., & Sopp, K. (2021). Double materiality and the shift from non-financial to European sustainability reporting: Review, outlook and implications. *Journal of Applied Accounting Research, 23*(1), 8–28. https://doi.org/10.1108/JAAR-04-2021-0114

Board, F. S. (2017). *Recommendations of the task force on climate-related financial disclosures (TCFD)*. https://apo.org.au/node/97651

Bodhanwala, S., & Bodhanwala, R. (2019). Relationship between sustainable and responsible investing and returns: A global evidence. *Social Responsibility Journal, 16*(4), 579–594. https://doi.org/10.1108/SRJ-12-2018-0332

Bowman, M., & Minas, S. (2019). Resilience through interlinkage: The Green climate fund and climate finance governance. *Climate Policy, 19*(3), 342–353. https://doi.org/10.1080/14693062.2018.1513358

Brønn, C., & Brønn, P. S. (2018). Sustainability: A wicked problem needing new perspectives. In H. Borland, A. Lindgreen, F. Maon, V. Ambrosini, B. Palacios Florencio, & J. Vanhamme (Eds.), *Business strategies for sustainability*. Routledge.

Bunting, W. C. (2021). Against corporate activism: Examining the use of corporate speech to promote corporate social responsibility. *Oklahoma Law Review, 74*(3), 245.

Busch, T., Bauer, R., & Orlitzky, M. (2016). Sustainable development and financial markets: Old paths and new avenues. *Business & Society, 55*(3), 303–329. https://doi.org/10.1177/0007650315570701

Busch, T., van Hoorn, V., Stapelfeldt, M., & Pruessner, E. (2022). Classification scheme for sustainable investments. *EUROSIF White Paper, 163*, 1–30.

Cai, L., Cooper, R., & He, D. (2021). Socially responsible investing and factor investing, is there an opportunity cost? *The Journal of Portfolio Management, 48*(2), 181–197. https://doi.org/10.3905/jpm.2021.1.307

Carney, M. (2015). Breaking the tragedy of the horizon—Climate change and financial stability. *Speech given at Lloyd's of London, 29*, 220–230.

Chatterji, A. K., Levine, D. I., & Toffel, M. W. (2009). How well do social ratings actually measure corporate social responsibility? *Journal of Economics & Management Strategy, 18*(1), 125–169.

Christensen, D. M., Serafeim, G., & Sikochi, A. (2022). Why is corporate virtue in the eye of the beholder? The case of ESG ratings. *The Accounting Review, 97*(1), 147–175.

Chueca Vergara, C., & Ferruz Agudo, L. (2021). Fintech and sustainability: Do they affect each other? *Sustainability, 13*(13), 7012. https://doi.org/10.3390/su13137012

Cicchiello, A. F., Marrazza, F., & Perdichizzi, S. (2023). Non-financial disclosure regulation and environmental, social, and governance (ESG) performance: The case of EU and US firms. *Corporate Social Responsibility and Environmental Management, 30*(3), 1121–1128.

Climate Bonds Initiative. (2021). *Sustainable debt global state of the market 2021*. https://www.climatebonds.net/files/reports/cbi_global_sotm_2021_02h_0.pdf

Condon, M. (2023a, August 29). 'Green' Corporate Governance. In *Oxford handbook of corporate law and governance* (2nd ed.). Boston University School of Law Research Paper No. 4556184, Available at SSRN: https://ssrn.com/abstract=4556184

Condon, M. (2023b). Climate services: The business of physical risk. *Arizona State Law Journal, 147*. https://doi.org/10.2139/ssrn.4396826

Cunha, F. A. F. d. S., Meira, E., & Orsato, R. J. (2021). Sustainable finance and investment: Review and research agenda. *Business Strategy and the Environment, 30*(8), 3821–3838. https://doi.org/10.1002/bse.2842

References

Cunha, F. A. F. d. S., Oliveira, E. M., Orsato, R. J., Klotzle, M. C., Cyrino Oliveira, F. L., & Caiado, R. G. G. (2020). Can sustainable investments outperform traditional benchmarks? Evidence from global stock markets. *Business Strategy and the Environment, 29*(2), 682–697. https://doi.org/10.1002/bse.2397

Curtis, D. D. (2019). *Sustainability-related indices should be attuned to the cohort driving growth in sustainable investing—millennials* (Master's thesis, Harvard University).

Damsø, T., Kjær, T., & Christensen, T. B. (2017). Implementation of local climate action plans: Copenhagen—Towards a carbon-neutral capital. *Journal of Cleaner Production, 167*, 406–415. https://doi.org/10.1016/j.jclepro.2017.08.156

Daugaard, D. (2020). Emerging new themes in environmental, social and governance investing: A systematic literature review. *Accounting and Finance, 60*(2), 1501–1530. https://doi.org/10.1111/acfi.12479

De Franco, C., Geissler, C., Margot, V., & Monnier, B. (2020). *ESG investments: Filtering versus machine learning approaches.* arXiv preprint arXiv:2002.07477. https://doi.org/10.48550/arXiv.2002.07477

De Salas, K., Scott, J. L., Schüz, B., & Norris, K. (2022). The super wicked problem of ocean health: A socio-ecological and behavioural perspective. *Philosophical Transactions of the Royal Society B, 377*, 1854. https://doi.org/10.1098/rstb.2021.0271

Dey, D., Richards, L., Arora, M., Boyle, E., Bryson, R., Jackman, S., Patel, V., & Shirazi, C. (2024). Overview of climate disclosures. *British Actuarial Journal, 28*, e13.

Diaz-Rainey, I., Robertson, B., & Wilson, C. (2017). Stranded research? Leading finance journals are silent on climate change. *Climatic Change, 143*(1–2), 243–260. https://doi.org/10.1007/s10584-017-1985-1

Dikau, S., & Volz, U. (2021). Central bank mandates, sustainability objectives and the promotion of green finance. *Ecological Economics, 184*, 107022.

Dimson, E., Karakaş, O., & Li, X. (2015). Active ownership. *The Review of Financial Studies, 28*(12), 3225–3268. https://doi.org/10.1093/rfs/hhv044

DiPiazza Jr, S. A., & Eccles, R. G. (2002). *Building public trust: The future of corporate reporting.* Wiley.

Driessen, M. (2021). Sustainable finance: An overview of ESG in the financial markets. *Sustainable finance in Europe: Corporate governance, financial stability and financial markets* (pp. 329–350). Palgrave Macmillan.

Dumrose, M., Rink, S., & Eckert, J. (2022). Disaggregating confusion? The EU Taxonomy and its relation to ESG rating. *Finance Research Letters, 48*, 102928.

Duqi, A. (2023). *Banking institutions and natural disasters: Recovery, resilience and growth in the face of climate change.* Springer Nature.

Dye, J., McKinnon, M., & Van der Byl, C. (2021). Green gaps: Firm ESG disclosure and financial institutions' reporting Requirements. *Journal of Sustainability Research, 3*(1), e210006.

Eccles, R. G., Ioannou, I., & Serafeim, G. (2012). *The impact of a corporate culture of sustainability on corporate behavior and performance* (Vol. 17950, No. 1, pp. 2835–2857). National Bureau of Economic Research.

Eccles, R. G., & Krzus, M. P. (2010). *One report: Integrated reporting for a sustainable strategy.* Wiley.

Eccles, R. G., Lee, L. E., & Stroehle, J. C. (2020). The social origins of ESG: An analysis of Innovest and KLD. *Organization & Environment, 33*(4), 575–596.

Eccles, R. G., & Stroehle, J. C. (2018). *Exploring social origins in the construction of ESG measures.* Available at SSRN 3212685.

Edmans, A., & Kacperczyk, M. (2022). Sustainable finance. *Review of Finance, 26*(6), 1309–1313.

Fabregat-Aibar, L., Barberà-Mariné, M. G., Terceño, A., & Pié, L. (2019). A bibliometric and visualization analysis of socially responsible funds. *Sustainability, 11*(9), 2526. https://doi.org/10.3390/su11092526

Fang, M., Tan, K. S., & Wirjanto, T. S. (2019). Sustainable portfolio management under climate change. *Journal of Sustainable Finance & Investment, 9*(1), 45–67.

Fankhauser, S., Smith, S. M., Allen, M., Axelsson, K., Hale, T., Hepburn, C., Kendall, J. M., Khosla, R., Lezaun, J., Mitchell-Larson, E., Obersteiner, M., Rajamani, L., Rickaby, R., Seddon, N., & Wetzer, T. (2022). The meaning of net zero and how to get it right. *Nature Climate Change*, *12*(1), 15–21. https://doi.org/10.1038/s41558-021-01245-w

Ferrell, O. C., Thorne, D. M., & Ferrell, L. (2020). *Business & society: A strategic approach to social responsibility & Ethics*. Sage.

Fink, C. (2021). Why millennials gravitate to new brands in online investing. *Journal of Brand Strategy*, *9*(4), 401–407.

Freiberg, D., Rogers, J., & Serafeim, G. (2020). *How ESG issues become financially material to corporations and their investors* (Harvard Business School Accounting & Management Unit Working Paper [20–056]).

Friede, G., Busch, T., & Bassen, A. (2015). ESG and financial performance: Aggregated evidence from more than 2000 empirical studies. *Journal of Sustainable Finance & Investment*, *5*(4), 210–233. https://doi.org/10.1080/20430795.2015.1118917

FTSE Russell. (2023). *Asset owners commit to maturing sustainable investment strategies*. https://www.lseg.com/en/ftse-russell/sustainable-investing-solutions/global-asset-owner-survey

Gasparini, A. (2023). Norway's opportunities via the Sovereign wealth fund and the European green deal. *International Journal of Environmental Studies*, *80*(5), 1445–1455.

George, G., Merrill, R. K., & Schillebeeckx, S. J. (2021). Digital sustainability and entrepreneurship: How digital innovations are helping tackle climate change and sustainable development. *Entrepreneurship Theory and Practice*, *45*(5), 999–1027. https://doi.org/10.1177/1042258719899425

Global Sustainable Investment Alliance. (2019). *Global sustainable investment review 2018*. Retrieved from

Gortsos, C. V. (2021). The taxonomy regulation: More important than just as an element of the capital markets union. In D. Busch, G. Ferrarini, & S. Grünewald (Eds.), *Sustainable finance in Europe* (pp. 351–395). Palgrave Macmillan. https://doi.org/10.1007/978-3-030-71834-3_11

Goyal, P., Kumar, V., & Srivastava, R. (2021). A critical analysis of the SEBI's business responsibility reporting framework in India. *International Journal of Corporate Social Responsibility*, *5*(2), 38–52.

Guimaraes, T., & Leal, R. (2022). The rise of ESG investing in Brazil: Drivers, challenges, and opportunities. *Sustainability*, *14*(13), 8254.

Gupta, A., & Sharma, T. (2023). Environmental, social, and governance (ESG) integration in infrastructure financing: A case study of India. *Environmental Development*, *48*, 87–100.

Hafenstein, A., & Bassen, A. (2016). Influences for using sustainability information in the investment decision-making of non-professional investors. *Journal of Sustainable Finance & Investment*, *6*(3), 186–210. https://doi.org/10.1080/20430795.2016.1203598

Hale, J. (2021). Commentary: The DOL ESG rule: A chilling effect on ESG but a rollback is likely. *The Journal of Impact and ESG Investing*, *1*(3), 100–103.

Harrison, C., MacGeoch, M., & Michetti, C. (2022). *Sustainable Debt Global state of the market 2021*. Climate Bonds Initiative 2022.

Hatten, K. J., Keeler, J. P., James, W. L., & Kim, K. (2020). Reflecting on the methods used in KLD research. *The Journal of Business and Economic Studies*, *24*(1), 1–32.

Hayek, M. N., Harwatt, H., Ripple, W. J., & Mueller, N. D. (2021). The carbon opportunity cost of animal-sourced food production on land. *Nature Sustainability*, *4*(1), 21–24.

Hill, J. (2020). *Environmental, social, and governance (ESG) investing: A balanced analysis of the theory and practice of a sustainable portfolio*. Academic Press.

Höchstädter, A. K., & Scheck, B. (2015). What's in a name: An analysis of impact investing understandings by academics and practitioners. *Journal of Business Ethics*, *132*(2), 449–475. https://doi.org/10.1007/s10551-014-2327-0

Hockerts, K., Hehenberger, L., Schaltegger, S., & Farber, V. (2022). Defining and conceptualizing impact investing: Attractive nuisance or catalyst? *Journal of Business Ethics*, *179*(4), 937–950.

References

Hooghiemstra, S. N. (2020). *The ESG disclosure regulation–new duties for financial market participants & financial advisers.* SSRN 3558868.

Hsu, J., Liu, X., Shen, K., Viswanathan, V., & Zhao, Y. (2018). Outperformance through investing in ESG in Need. *The Journal of Index Investing, 9*, 18–26.

Huang, Y., Li, Y., & Zhou, L. (2020). Green finance in China: Policies, challenges, and prospects. *Sustainability, 12*(1), 359.

Hudon, M., & Sandberg, J. (2013). The ethical crisis in microfinance: Issues, findings, and implications. *Business Ethics Quarterly, 23*(4), 561–589. https://doi.org/10.5840/beq201323440

IEA. (2020). *World energy outlook 2020*, IEA, Paris. https://www.iea.org/reports/world-energy-outlook-2020, Licence: CC BY 4.0

Ielasi, F., & Rossolini, M. (2019). Responsible or thematic? The true nature of sustainability-themed mutual funds. *Sustainability, 11*(12), 3304. https://doi.org/10.3390/su11123304

Indahl, R., & Jacobsen, H. (2019). Private equity 4.0: Using ESG to create more value with less risk. mutual funds. *Journal of Corporate finance, 31*(2), 34–42.

Intergovernmental Panel on Climate Change (IPCC). (2014). *Fifth assessment report (AR5)*. Cambridge University Press. http://www.ipcc.ch/report/ar5/

Investors DiPiazza Jr, S. A., & Eccles, R. G. (2002). *Building public trust: The future of corporate reporting*. Wiley.

Jing, Z., & Joo, S.-H. (2021). Intergenerational comparison of successful aging perception, lifestyle and self-esteem. *Journal of Intergenerational Relationships, 19*(1), 92–108. https://doi.org/10.1080/15350770.2021.1868234

Kato, T., & Yoshino, N. (2020). *Corporate social responsibility in Japan: History, theory, and practice*. Springer.

Paraschi, E. (2022). Why ESG reporting is particularly important for the airlines during the Covid-19 pandemic. *Journal of Business and Management Studies, 4*(3), 63–67.

Kang, J. (2015). Effectiveness of the KLD social ratings as a measure of workforce diversity and corporate governance. *Business & Society, 54*(5), 599–631.

Kerekes, S. (2023). Chasing the impossible. Sustainable development is a wicked problem, but it can be and should be tamed! *World Futures, 79*(3), 394–405. https://doi.org/10.1080/02604027.2021.1974263

Klein, N. (2014). *This changes everything: Capitalism vs. the climate*. Simon & Schuster.

Kolk, A. (2003). Trends in sustainability reporting by the Fortune Global 250. *Business Strategy and the Environment, 12*(5), 279–291. https://doi.org/10.1002/bse.370

Koller, T., Nuttall, R., & Henisz, W. (2019, November 14). *Five ways that ESG creates value.* The McKinsey Quarterly.

Kotsantonis, S., & Serafeim, G. (2019). Four things no one will tell you about ESG data. *Journal of Applied Corporate Finance, 31*(2), 50–58.

Kramer, M. R., & Pfitzer, M. W. (2022). The essential link between ESG targets & financial performance. *Harvard Business Review, 100*(2), 128–137.

Kumar, S. (2022). A quest for sustainium (sustainability Premium): Review of sustainable bonds. *Academy of Accounting and Financial Studies Journal, 26*(2), 1–18.

Kumar, S., Sharma, D., Rao, S., Lim, W. M., & Mangla, S. K. (2022). Past, present, and future of sustainable finance: Insights from Big Data analytics through machine learning of scholarly research. *Annals of Operations Research*, 1–44. Advance online publication. https://doi.org/10.1007/s10479-021-04410-8

Labuschagne, C., Brent, A. C., & Claasen, S. J. (2005). Environmental and social impact considerations for sustainable project life cycle management in the process industry. *Corporate Social Responsibility and Environmental Management, 12*(1), 38–54. https://doi.org/10.1002/csr.76

Lambin, E. F., & Thorlakson, T. (2018). Sustainability standards: Interactions between private actors, civil society, and governments. *Annual Review of Environment and Resources, 43*, 369–393.

Larcker, D. F., Pomorski, L., Tayan, B., & Watts, E. M. (2022). *ESG ratings: A compass without direction* (Rock Center for Corporate Governance at Stanford University Working Paper Forthcoming).

Lewis, E., Pinchot, A., & Christianson, G. (2016). *Navigating the sustainable investment landscape*. World Resources Institute.

Liang, H., & Renneboog, L. (2020). *Corporate social responsibility and sustainable finance: A review of the literature* (European Corporate Governance Institute Finance Working Paper, no. 701).

Lieberman, D. (2020). Practical applications of impact investing 2.0—Not just for do-gooders anymore. *Practical Applications, 8*(2), 1–7. https://doi.org/10.3905/pa.8.2.398

Lin, L. (2022). Venture capital in the rise of sustainable investment. *European Business Organization Law Review, 23*(1), 187–216.

Lipton, A. M. (2020). Not everything is about investors: The case for mandatory stakeholder disclosure. *Yale Journal on Regulation, 37*, 499.

Lönngren, J., & van Poeck, K. (2021). Wicked problems: A mapping review of the literature. *International Journal of Sustainable Development & World Ecology, 28*(6), 481–502. https://doi.org/10.1080/13504509.2020.1859415

Lozano, R., & Huisingh, D. (2011). Inter-linking issues and dimensions in sustainability reporting. *Journal of Cleaner Production, 19*(2–3), 99–107. https://doi.org/10.1016/j.jclepro.2010.01.004

Luu, E., & Rubio, S. (2023). *Millennial managers*. Corporate Governance: An International Review.

Macchiavello, E., & Siri, M. (2022). Sustainable finance and fintech: Can technology contribute to achieving environmental goals? A preliminary assessment of 'green fintech' and 'sustainable digital finance.' *European Company and Financial Law Review, 19*(1), 128–174. https://doi.org/10.1515/ecfr-2022-0005

Maldonado, F., & Gallagher, K. P. (2022). *Climate change and IMF debt sustainability analysis*. The Task Force on Climate, Development and the IMF. https://www.bu.edu/gdp/2022/02/10/climatechange-and-imf-debt-sustainability-analysis

Malecki, C. (2021). The EU taxonomy regulation: Giving a good name to sustainable investment. *Environmental Liability, 26*(4), 149–156.

Masum, A., Hanan, H., Awang, H., Aziz, A., & Ahmad, M. H. (2020). Corporate social responsibility and its effect on community development: An overview. *Journal of Accounting Science, 22*, 35–40. https://doi.org/10.9790/487X-2201053540

McDonnell, C. (2024). Pension funds and fossil fuel phase-out: Historical developments and limitations of pension climate strategies. *International Environmental Agreements: Politics, Law and Economics, 24*(1), 169–191. https://doi.org/10.1007/s10784-024-09626-0

McDonnell, C., Rempel, A., & Gupta, J. (2022). Climate action or distraction? Exploring investor initiatives and implications for unextractable fossil fuels. *Energy Research & Social Science, 92*, 102769. https://doi.org/10.1016/j.erss.2022.102769

Meziani, A. S. (2020). It is still not easy being green for exchange-traded funds. *The Journal of Beta Investment Strategies, 10*(4), 6–23.

Miyahara, T., & Adelaja, A. (2020). Aging and economic growth in Japan: Differential effects of multiple generations. *Journal of Population Ageing, 15*, 239–258.

Monasterolo, I. (2020). Climate change and the financial system. *Annual Review of Resource Economics, 12*, 299–320. https://doi.org/10.1146/annurev-resource-110119-031134

Morningstar. (2024). *Global sustainable fund flows: Q1 2024 in review*. Flows improve in Europe but worsen in the United States. https://esgnews.com/wp-content/uploads/2024/04/Global_ESG_Q1_2024_Flows_Report.pdf

Moskowitz, M. (1972). Choosing socially responsible stocks. *Business and Society Review, 1*(1), 71–75.

Moss, A., Naughton, J. P., & Wang, C. (2020). *The irrelevance of ESG disclosure to retail investors: Evidence from Robinhood*. https://ssrn.com/abstract=3604847

Muir, D. M. (2022). Sustainable investing and fiduciary obligations in pension funds: The need for sustainable regulation. *American Business Law Journal, 59*(4), 621–677.

Nielsen. (2015, October). *The sustainability imperative*. New insights on consumer expectations. https://www.supplychain247.com/images/pdfs/nielsen_global-sustainability-report-oct-2015.pdf

Nielsen. (2018). https://nielseniq.com/global/en/insights/analysis/2018/was-2018-the-year-of-the-influential-sustainable-consumer/

O'Dwyer, B., & Unerman, J. (2020). Shifting the focus of sustainability accounting from impacts to risks and dependencies: Researching the transformative potential of TCFD reporting. *Accounting, Auditing & Accountability Journal, 33*(5), 1113–1141. https://doi.org/10.1108/AAAJ-02-2020-4445

Orieno, O. H., Ndubuisi, N. L., Eyo-Udo, N. L., Ilojianya, V. I., & Biu, P. W. (2024). Sustainability in project management: A comprehensive review. *World Journal of Advanced Research and Reviews, 21*(1), 656–677. https://doi.org/10.30574/wjarr.2024.21.1.0060

Ostrom, E. (2009). *A polycentric approach for coping with climate change*. Available at SSRN https://ssrn.com/abstract=1934353

Pacces, A. M. (2021). Will the EU taxonomy regulation foster sustainable corporate governance? *Sustainability, 13*(21), 12316. https://doi.org/10.3390/su132112316

Pachauri, R. K., Allen, M. R., Barros, V. R., Broome, J., Cramer, W., Christ, R., Church, J. A., Clarke, L., Dahe, Q., Dasgupta, P., Dubash, N. K., Edenhofer, O., Elgizouli, I., Field, C. B., Forster, P., Friedlingstein, P., Fuglestvedt, J., Gomez-Echeverri, L., Hallegatte, S., ... van Ypserle, J. P. (2014). *Climate change 2014: Synthesis report*. Contribution of Working Groups I, II and III to the fifth assessment report of the Intergovernmental Panel on Climate Change (IPCC) (p. 151).

Pallathadka, A., Sauer, J., Chang, H., & Grimm, N. B. (2022). Urban flood risk and green infrastructure: Who is exposed to risk and who benefits from investment? A case study of three US Cities. *Landscape and Urban Planning, 223*, 104417.

Park, H., & Kim, J. D. (2020). Transition towards green banking: Role of financial regulators and financial institutions. *Asian Journal of Sustainability and Social Responsibility, 5*(1), 1–25. https://doi.org/10.1186/s41180-020-00034-3

Pérez, L., Hunt, V., Samandari, H., Nuttall, R., & Biniek, K. (2022). *Does ESG really matter—and why*. McKinsey Quarterly.

Plantinga, A., & Scholtens, B. (2021). The financial impact of fossil fuel divestment. *Climate Policy, 21*(1), 107–119. https://doi.org/10.1080/14693062.2020.1806020

Polaschek, R. (2021). Responses to the Uyghur crisis and the implications for business and human rights legislation. *Business and Human Rights Journal, 6*(3), 567–575. https://doi.org/10.1017/bhj.2021.44

Purvis, B., Mao, Y., & Robinson, D. (2019). Three pillars of sustainability: In search of conceptual origins. *Sustainability Science, 14*, 681–695.

Puschmann, T., Hoffmann, C. H., & Khmarskyi, V. (2020). How green FinTech can alleviate the impact of climate change—The case of Switzerland. *Sustainability, 12*(24), 10691. https://doi.org/10.3390/su122410691

Raghutla, C., Shahbaz, M., Chittedi, K. R., & Jiao, Z. (2021). Financing clean energy projects: New empirical evidence from major investment countries. *Renewable Energy, 169*, 231–241.

Redgwell, C. (2012). UNCLOS and climate change. *Proceedings of the Annual Meeting (American Society of International Law), 106*, 406–409. https://doi.org/10.5305/procannmeetasil.106.0406

Renneboog, L., ter Horst, J., & Zhang, C. (2008). The price of ethics and stakeholder governance: The performance of socially responsible mutual funds. *Journal of Corporate Finance, 14*(3), 302–322. https://doi.org/10.2139/ssrn.1102706

Ritchie, H., & Roser, M. (2019). Land use. Our world in data. Our world in data.

Schoenmaker, D., & Schramade, W. (2023). Capital market adaptability, investor behaviour, and impact. In *Corporate finance for long-term value* (pp. 395–428). Springer International Publishing.

Schueth, S. (2003). Socially responsible investing in the United States. *Journal of Business Ethics, 43*(1), 189–194. https://doi.org/10.1023/A:1022981828869

Schwartz, M. S. (2003). The "ethics" of ethical investing. *Journal of Business Ethics, 43*(3), 195–213. https://doi.org/10.1023/A:102293391

Serafeim, G. (2020). Public sentiment and the price of corporate sustainability. *Financial Analysts Journal, 76*(2), 26–46. https://doi.org/10.2139/ssrn.3265502

Serafeim, G. (2022). *Purpose and profit: How business can lift up the world.* HarperCollins Leadership.

Serafeim, G., & Yoon, A. (2022a). Which corporate ESG news does the market react to? *Financial Analysts Journal, 78*(1), 59–78. https://doi.org/10.1080/0015198X.2021.1973879

Serafeim, G., & Yoon, A. S. (2022b). Understanding the business relevance of ESG issues. *Journal of Financial Reporting, 7*(2), 207–212. https://doi.org/10.2308/JFR-2022-010

Serafeim, G., & Yoon, A. (2023). Stock price reactions to ESG news: The role of ESG ratings and disagreement. *Review of Accounting Studies, 28*(3), 1500–1530.

Shan, C., & Tang, D. Y. (2023). The value of employee satisfaction in disastrous times: Evidence from COVID-19. *Review of Finance, 27*(3), 1027–1076.

Singhania, M., & Saini, N. (2022). Quantification of ESG regulations: A cross-country benchmarking analysis. *Vision, 26*(2), 163–171.

Sinke, P., Swartz, E., Sanctorum, H., van der Giesen, C., & Odegard, I. (2023). Ex-ante life cycle assessment of commercial-scale cultivated meat production in 2030. *The International Journal of Life Cycle Assessment, 28*(3), 234–254.

Soussane, J. A., Mansouri, D., Fakhouri, M. Y., & Mansouri, Z. (2023). Does climate change constitute a financial risk to foreign direct investment? An empirical analysis on 200 countries from 1970 to 2020. *Weather, Climate, and Society, 15*(1), 31–43.

Sparkes, R. (2001). Ethical investment: Whose ethics, which investment? *Business Ethics: A European Review, 10*(3), 194–205. https://doi.org/10.1111/1467-8608.00233

Stacchezzini, R., Melloni, G., & Lai, A. (2016). Sustainability management and reporting: The role of integrated reporting for communicating corporate sustainability management. *Journal of Cleaner Production, 136*, 102–110. https://doi.org/10.1016/j.jclepro2016.01.109

TCFD. (2017). TCFD. 2017. Final report—Recommendations of the task force on climate-related financial disclosures. https://assets.bbhub.io/company/sites/60/2020/10/FINAL-2017-TCFD-Report-11052018.pdf

Thomas, V. (2023). *Risk and resilience in the era of climate change.* Springer Nature.

Thompson, B. S. (2021). Corporate payments for ecosystem services in theory and practice: Links to economics, business, and sustainability. *Sustainability, 13*(15), 8307.

Tillotson, P., Slade, R. B., Staffell, I., & Halttunen, K. (2023). Deactivating climate activism? The seven strategies oil and gas majors use to counter rising shareholder action. *Energy Research & Social Science, 103*(1), 103190. https://doi.org/10.1016/j.erss.2023.103190

Townsend, B. (2020). From SRI to ESG: The origins of socially responsible and sustainable investing. *The Journal of Impact and ESG Investing, 1*(1), 10–25. https://doi.org/10.3905/jesg.2020.1.1.010

Trinks, P. J., & Scholtens, B. (2017). The opportunity cost of negative screening in socially responsible investing. *Journal of Business Ethics, 140*(2), 193–208. https://doi.org/10.1007/s10551-015-2684-3

Udeagha, M. C., & Ngepah, N. (2023). The drivers of environmental sustainability in BRICS economies: Do green finance and fintech matter? *World Development Sustainability, 3*, 100096. https://doi.org/10.1016/j.wds.2023.1000967

Uzsoki, D. (2020). *Sustainable investing. Shaping the future of finance.* International Institute for Sustainable Development.

Valente, A., & Atkinson, D. (2019). Sustainability in business: A millennials' perspective. *Journal of Modern Accounting and Auditing, 15*(6), 293–304. https://doi.org/10.17265/1548-6583/2019.06.002

Verheyden, T., Eccles, R. G., & Feiner, A. (2016). ESG for all? The impact of ESG screening on return, risk, and diversification. *Journal of Applied Corporate Finance, 28*(2), 47–55.

Vigneau, L., Humphreys, M., & Moon, J. (2015). How do firms comply with international sustainability standards? Processes and consequences of adopting the global reporting initiative. *Journal of Business Ethics, 131*(2), 469–486. https://doi.org/10.1007/s10551-014-2278-5

Wabnitz, C. C. C., & Blasiak, R. (2019). The rapidly changing world of ocean finance. *Marine Policy, 107*, 103526. https://doi.org/10.1016/j.marpol.2019.103526

References

Wang, S., Liao, Y. K., Wu, W. Y., & Le, K. B. H. (2021). The role of corporate social responsibility perceptions in brand equity, brand credibility, brand reputation, and purchase intentions. *Sustainability, 13*(21), 11975.

Weitzman, M. L. (2013). Tail-hedge discounting and the social cost of carbon. *Journal of Economic Literature, 51*(3), 873–882.

Welch, I. (2020). The wisdom of the Robinhood crowd. National Bureau of Economic Research. Working Paper 27866. https://doi.org/10.3386/w27866

Yearworth, M. (2016). Sustainability as a "super-wicked" problem; opportunities and limits for engineering methodology. *Intelligent Buildings International, 8*(1), 37–47. https://doi.org/10.1080/17508975.2015.1109789

Yoon, A. S., & Serafeim, G. (2022). Understanding the business relevance of ESG issues. *Journal of Financial Reporting, 7*(2), 207–212.

Yu, E. P. Y., Guo, C. Q., & Luu, B. V. (2018). Environmental, social and governance transparency and firm value. *Business Strategy and the Environment, 27*(7), 987–1004.

Zhang, D., Zhang, Z., & Managi, S. (2019). A bibliometric analysis on green finance: Current status, development, and future directions. *Finance Research Letters, 29*, 425–430. https://doi.org/10.1016/j.frl.2019.02.003

Chapter 3
It's Changing: The Dynamics of the Modern World—Climate Change and Planetary Boundaries

> The fact is that no species has ever had such wholesale control over everything on earth, living or dead, as we now have. That lays upon us, whether we like it or not, an awesome responsibility. In our hands now lies not only our own future, but that of all other living creatures with whom we share the earth—David Attenborough.

3.1 Introduction—Planetary Boundaries

Nature, in its entirety, consists of both living (biotic) and non-living (abiotic) components. This includes everything from significant oil reserves and mineral mines to varied ecosystems like tropical forests, savannas, grasslands, cities, and water bodies both fresh and saline. The complexity of nature is augmented by biodiversity, the diversity of lifeforms across these ecosystems, which is crucial for ecological balance and providing services vital for human survival and economic prosperity. The World Economic Forum notes that about half of the world's Gross Domestic Product or GDP (over USD 44 trillion) is significantly dependent on nature—a stark illustration of the deep economic ties to natural systems. This interdependence underscores the urgent need to understand and address the impact of human activities on our planet, for the sake of both environmental and economic sustainability. The central question is: *What parts of the planetary system are being most affected by human activities? What risks does this pose to companies, countries, and ultimately, the future of sustainable finance?*

This chapter delves into two key frameworks that guide our understanding of these risks and opportunities: the Planetary Boundaries (PB) and the UN Sustainable Development Goals (SDGs are presented in Chapter 1). Introduced in 2009 by the Stockholm Resilience Centre, the PB framework sets the environmental limits within which humanity can safely operate. It identifies nine key Earth system processes, such as climate stability and water cycle dynamics, and uses control and response variables to measure human impacts on the Earth system. Alarmingly, current assessments indicate that four of these nine boundaries have been crossed, signaling a shift toward the Anthropocene era, a period characterized by significant human influence on the planet, mentioned in Chapter 1 of this book.

The PB framework, in the spirit of the precautionary principle, aims to define a "safe operating space" within which humanity can operate without pushing the Earth system toward instability. For corporations, cities, states, and countries, understanding and integrating these boundaries into their strategic planning, reporting, and governance is crucial for achieving sustainable development. This proactive approach not only mitigates environmental risks but also aligns with emerging regulatory, financial, and societal expectations. The PB framework dovetails beautifully with the UN SDGs, highlighting the interconnectedness of environmental and social well-being. By incorporating nine dimensions that directly map onto the SDGs, the PB framework demonstrates how development can proceed without exceeding planetary boundaries. This integration underscores the essential link between achieving the SDGs and maintaining Earth system stability.

3.2 Ecological Economics, Doughnut Economics, Piketty's Capital, and New Economics Inform on Planetary Boundaries

Before delving into ecological economics or contemporary models of economic behavior, it is essential to understand how the frameworks differ from traditional economics. Classical economic theory, which forms the foundation of traditional economic thought, is built on three principal assumptions: (i) individuals act rationally, (ii) decisions are driven by self-interest, and (iii) individuals adjust their beliefs and perspectives based on new information.

Adam Smith, often heralded as the father of modern economics, introduced these foundational concepts in his seminal work, "An Inquiry into the Nature and Causes of the Wealth of Nations," published in 1776. Smith's contributions laid the groundwork for the classical economic paradigm, emphasizing the role of rational self-interest and the invisible hand in market dynamics (Hollander, 1973). However, the relevance of classical economic theory in addressing the complexities of today's socioeconomic and technological challenges is increasingly under scrutiny. The clear-cut and predictable nature of classical assumptions contrasts sharply with the intricate realities of human behavior and decision-making as we now understand them. This has led to the emergence of alternative economic models that embrace insights from psychology, acknowledging how cognitive biases, emotions, and social influences affect economic decisions. Pioneers like Kahneman and Tversky (1979) and Thaler (1980) have significantly contributed to these newer models, expanding our understanding of economic behavior beyond the classical constraints.

Ecological economics, relevant to this chapter, is a transdisciplinary field that combines ecological and economic principles to study the interactions between human economic activity and the natural world. An influential report, *The Limits to Growth* by the Club of Rome (Meadows et al., 1972), raised concerns about the environmental limits to economic growth and inspired calls for a more sustainable approach. The UN Stockholm Conference on the Human Environment (1972) brought together scientists and policymakers to discuss environmental challenges and emphasized the need for integrating environmental considerations into economic development (Costanza et al., 1997; Costanza et al., 2011; Daly, 2014).[1]

The term ecosystem services refer to the multitude of benefits ecosystems provide humanity, supporting our survival and quality of life. These services are often classified into four main categories: provisioning, regulating, cultural, and supporting services. Provisioning services are the products directly obtained from ecosystems, such as food, freshwater, timber, fiber, and genetic resources. Oceans, forests, and agricultural lands are vital for these services, providing the essential resources for human nutrition and economic activities (Daily, 1997).

Regulating services encompass the benefits derived from the moderation or control of ecosystem processes and environmental conditions through ecological functioning. These services include climate regulation, disease control, water purification, and pollination. For instance, wetlands are critical in purifying water by filtering pollutants. At the same time, bees and other pollinators are essential for the reproduction of many plants and crops, directly impacting food production (MEA, 2005). Cultural services encompass the non-material benefits people obtain from ecosystems through spiritual enrichment, cognitive development, recreation, and aesthetic experiences. These services highlight the cultural, spiritual, and recreational importance of natural landscapes and biodiversity (Costanza et al., 1997). Supporting services are necessary to produce all other ecosystem services, including soil formation, photosynthesis, nutrient cycling, and water cycling. These underpinning services maintain the conditions for life on Earth and are the basis upon which other services are built (De Groot et al., 2002).

The concept of ecosystem services has gained prominence as a framework for understanding and communicating the value of biodiversity and ecosystems to human well-being. By quantifying these services, researchers and policymakers aim to integrate natural capital into economic systems, highlighting the need for sustainable management of natural resources (Costanza et al., 1997; Daily, 1997; MEA, 2005). The Millennium Ecosystem Assessment (MEA, 2005) represents a significant effort to assess the consequences of ecosystem change for human well-being and to provide a scientific basis for action to conserve and sustainably use ecosystems and their services. In recent years, the ecosystem services concept has been instrumental in promoting a more holistic approach to environmental conservation, emphasizing the interconnectedness of human and ecological health. It advocates for strategies that protect biodiversity and enhance the benefits ecosystems provide to society (TEEB, 2010).

In this way, ecological economics offers a critical lens for understanding the connection between our economic activities and the planet's health. By recognizing

---

[1] https://www.un.org/en/conferences/environment/stockholm1972.

the essential role of ecosystem services and respecting planetary boundaries, we can build a more sustainable and resilient economy that benefits both people and nature in the long term. Unlike traditional economic models that often treat nature as an unlimited resource, ecological economics acknowledges the finite but essential contribution of nature's services to our economy. These services, like water purification, air filtration, and climate regulation, are crucial for maintaining a healthy planet and supporting economic activity.

More recently, Thomas Piketty's "Capital in the Twenty-First Century" (2014) offered valuable insights for discussing new economics considering planetary boundaries and wealth inequality. Piketty argues that wealth tends to concentrate over time due to the inherent rate of return on capital (r) exceeding the economic growth rate (g). This trend incentivizes further capital accumulation, potentially leading to increased resource extraction and environmental degradation. By highlighting this dynamic, Piketty encourages us to consider alternative economic models that decouple wealth accumulation from resource depletion and prioritize sustainability within planetary boundaries. Figure 3.1 shows the income inequality where the top 1% in Western Europe and the US own 22% and 37.5% of the share of total personal income in 2020 while in 1910, the top 1% in Western Europe and US owned 55% and 43% respectively. The data is based on World Inequality Report (Chancel et al., 2022).

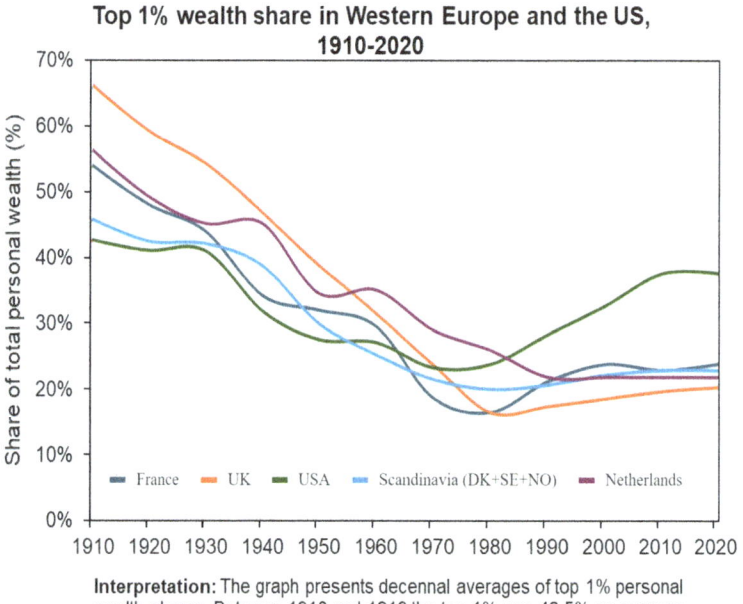

Fig. 3.1 This graph presents the decennial averages of top 1% share of total personal wealth shares in the US and Western European countries. *Source* Chancel et al. (2022) and World Inequality Report (2022)

3.2 Ecological Economics, Doughnut Economics, Piketty's Capital …

Figure 3.1 shows that in 1901, the top 1% in Europe owned 55% of the wealth while in the US, they owned 43% of the wealth. In 2020, wealth equality in the US has risen faster than in Western Europe. From 1901 to 2020, the bottom 50% of the population in terms of wealth shares in both US and Western Europe has been extremely low, less than 10%.

Kate Raworth's (2017) proposed doughnut economics, shown in Fig. 3.2, a visual model for sustainable development, resembling a doughnut or lifebuoy, that integrates planetary boundaries with social foundations for understanding the balance between ecological sustainability and social equity. The framework's name comes from its shape: a disc with a central hole. This hole represents the percentage of people lacking access to essential resources like health, food, water, education, and equity. The outer ring signifies the ecological limits crucial for maintaining life on Earth, which should not be exceeded (the focus of this chapter).

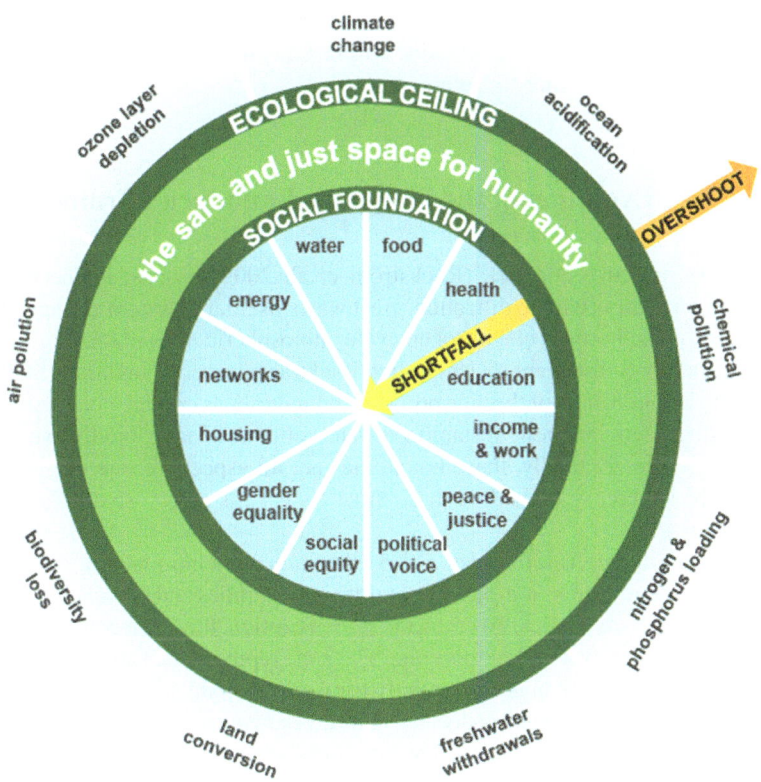

Fig. 3.2 Kate Raworth's Doughnut Economics is a visual model for sustainable development

If natural capital is underutilized (the center of the doughnut), then essential human needs aren't met; if natural capital is overutilized (outside the doughnut), then planetary boundaries have been crossed. The model advocates for a society where every individual has access to life's necessities, ensuring a dignified life without harming the planet's health. While traditionally associated with liberal viewpoints, often pejoratively termed as "Limousine liberals" engaging in "woke talk," the model's emphasis on universal access to planetary benefits extends beyond political labels, addressing a broader, inclusive approach to global sustainability.

These works by Piketty (2014) and Raworth (2017) define economic underpinnings of sustainable development. They highlight that current economic models are limited in their ability to address sustainable development effectively. This chapter focuses on understanding and applying these frameworks to move beyond simply mitigating environmental damage and toward a future where finance catalyzes a sustainable and equitable world. This journey requires a fundamental shift in perspective, acknowledging our deep connection to the natural world and embracing our responsibility to operate within its limits. As we navigate this path, the insights the PB framework and the SDGs provide will be crucial in guiding our investments and shaping a brighter future for future generations.

3.3 The Evolution of the Planetary Boundaries Framework

The 2009 initial framework (Rockström et al. 2009) proposed nine boundaries: climate change, ocean acidification, freshwater use, land-system change, biodiversity loss, phosphorus cycle, nitrogen cycle, atmospheric aerosol loading, and chemical pollution. Subsequent revisions identified transgressed boundaries. Steffen et al. (2015) identified three of the nine proposed boundaries as critical, potentially pushing the Earth system into new, destabilized states: climate change, biodiversity loss, and nitrogen cycle. Critically, these boundaries are all aspects of one single, interconnected biosphere, so exceeding these three also exerts a pervasive influence on the remaining ones.

In a 2015 update, (Steffen et al., 2015), the framework introduced a "zone of uncertainty" to acknowledge significant scientific uncertainties and the inherent variability of Earth system dynamics. To err on the side of caution, the framework positioned the boundary at the lower end of this zone. The zone represents an area of indeterminate risk, where crossing it could potentially trigger irreversible, abrupt changes to Earth system processes—a scenario deemed entering dangerous planetary territory. Hence, maintaining control variables within defined boundaries, away from the uncertainty zone, is crucial for staying within the Earth system's safe operating space. One of the authors of this paper **Sverker Sörlin's** interview for this book, is included in this chapter.

A case in point is the climate boundary, set at an atmospheric CO_2 concentration of 350 ppm to limit global temperature increases to below 1 °C, thereby ensuring system stability. The designated zone of uncertainty, 350–450 ppm CO_2, underscores the

3.3 The Evolution of the Planetary Boundaries Framework

escalating risk of adverse climate effects and the activation of Earth System tipping points as CO2 levels rise. With current CO2 concentrations surpassing 410 ppm, the Earth is witnessing an uptick in extreme weather events and the activation of tipping points that could push the Earth system toward a hotter state. Notably, while measures such as the ban on Chlorofluorocarbons (CFCs) have stabilized atmospheric ozone levels, indicating a potential recovery, most control variables for other boundaries are diverging from the safe operating space. Initially conceived as a framework to define safe operating space for humanity within environmental limits, the PB concept has proven influential in global sustainability policy.

The nine planetary boundaries model developed by the Stockholm Resilience Center and modified in subsequent versions is a framework designed to define the safe operating space for humanity with respect to the Earth system, shown in Fig. 3.3. Each boundary is associated with a critical threshold not to be crossed without risking severe environmental degradation. The model is typically represented with colors. Green indicates that the boundary has not been crossed and is within a safe operating space. Yellow represents a zone of uncertainty or increasing risk. Red signals that the boundary has been crossed.

The concept of planetary boundaries (PB) has evolved significantly since its initial introduction. Richardson et al. (2023) provide an updated and expanded analysis of the PB framework that quantifies all nine boundaries for the first time. Humanity has crossed six boundaries: climate change, biosphere integrity, land-system change, freshwater use, altered freshwater flows, and phosphorus cycle, further emphasizing the interconnectedness and cumulative pressures on the Earth system.

The boundaries presented in Richardson et al. (2023) are not identical to those in the original 2009 framework. The earlier framework included climate change, ocean acidification, freshwater use, land-system change, biodiversity loss, phosphorus cycle, nitrogen cycle, atmospheric aerosol loading, and chemical pollution. In the updated framework, only five boundaries remain the same: climate change, ocean acidification, freshwater use, land-system change, and atmospheric aerosol loading. Significant changes in the updated framework include:

- Biogeochemical Flows: The earlier boundaries of the phosphorus cycle and nitrogen cycle have been combined into a single category, biogeochemical flows.
- Novel Entities: Chemical pollution is no longer listed as a separate boundary but may have been replaced by the category of novel entities.
- Biosphere Integrity: The concept of biodiversity loss has been replaced or subsumed under biosphere integrity.
- Stratospheric Ozone Depletion: This has been added as a new boundary, recognizing its importance in Earth's system stability.
- Altered Freshwater Flows: Richardson et al. (2023) introduce "altered freshwater flows" in addition to "freshwater use," reflecting a more nuanced understanding of freshwater dynamics.
- Restoration of the Phosphorus Cycle: Despite its combination with the nitrogen cycle under biogeochemical flows, the phosphorus cycle is specifically highlighted again due to its critical role and current transgression.

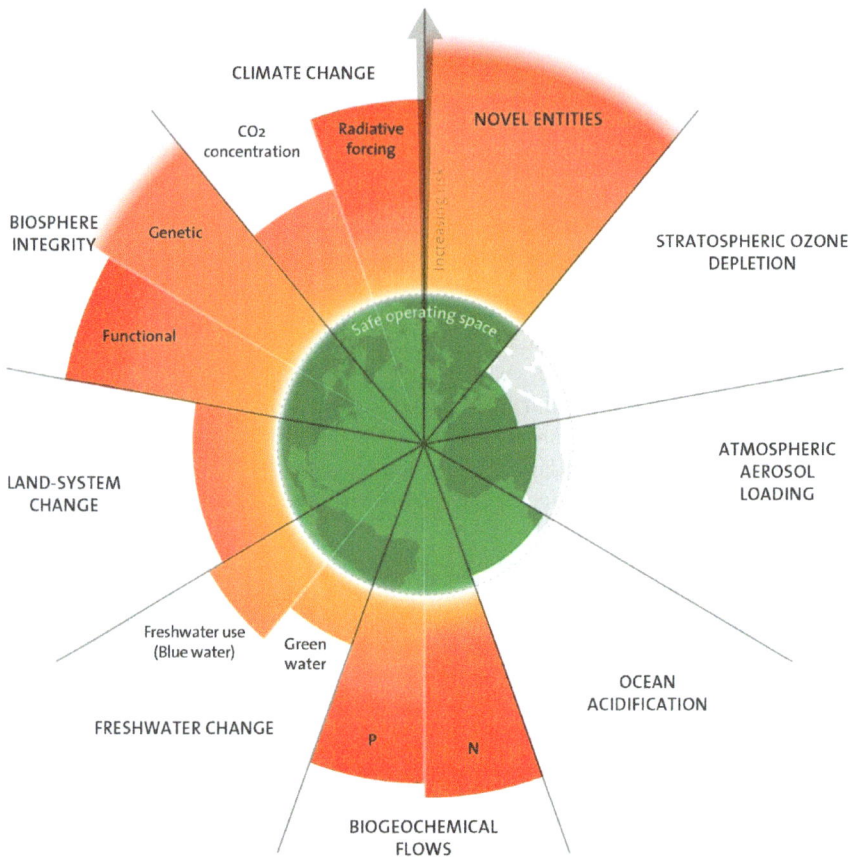

Fig. 3.3 The nine planetary boundaries model developed by the Stockholm Resilience Center. *Source* https://www.stockholmresilience.org/research/planetary-boundaries.html. Download the 2023 Planetary Boundaries illustration (Credit: Azote for Stockholm Resilience Centre, based on analysis in Richardson et al., 2023). Attribution: CC BY-NC-ND 3.0

These changes reflect an evolving understanding of Earth's system processes and the interconnected impacts of human activities. The updated framework aims to provide a more comprehensive and accurate assessment of planetary boundaries, highlighting areas where immediate action is required to prevent further degradation of the Earth system.

Figure 3.3 illustrates the state of planetary boundaries, a framework for assessing the Earth's limits to support human activity. This figure represents a dashboard for Earth's health, where exceeding boundaries poses risks that directly impact business and investments. The model is typically represented with colors to indicate the status of these boundaries. Green indicates that the boundary has not been crossed and is within a safe operating space. This suggests sustainable human activities that do not pose significant risk to the Earth's resilience. Yellow represents a zone of

3.3 The Evolution of the Planetary Boundaries Framework

uncertainty or increasing risk. It indicates that the boundary is being approached but not yet crossed. This zone suggests that caution is needed as the boundary is nearing the high-risk threshold. Red signals that the boundary has been crossed. This indicates a high risk of severe environmental change which could be irreversible and lead to undesirable states of the Earth system, affecting its capacity to support human life. Thus, each boundary's color status helps to quickly convey the urgency and magnitude of the planetary pressures in those areas, guiding policy and action toward sustainability.

Although originally articulated as such, these planetary boundaries are not just an environmental concern. They are crucial for investors to consider when assessing business sustainability, long-term risk exposure, and new market opportunities in transitioning to a truly sustainable economy. Three insights emerge out of this framework for informing business decisions.

- Systemic Risk: The global economy has exceeded safe limits in six critical areas including climate change, biodiversity loss, and pollution. This crossing signals significant instability for global markets and threatens supply chains, resource availability, and asset values.
- Increasing Uncertainty: Two factors, "novel entities" (new chemicals, pollutants) and loss of genetic diversity, (PB's biosphere integrity) have significant but poorly understood risks. Their impacts could be far-reaching and unpredictable, further increasing market uncertainty.
- Emerging Investment Focus: Investors increasingly seek companies that address planetary boundaries. This investor perspective involves shifting focus from just climate action to solutions for pollution, biodiversity conservation, renewable energy, and efficient resource management.

Expert in Focus: Sverker Sörlin

Since 2007, Sverker Sörlin, Ph.D., has been a distinguished professor of environmental history and environmental humanities at the Division of History of Science, Technology and Environment at the KTH Royal Institute of Technology in Stockholm." Sörlin served as an Associate Director for the Center for History of Science at the Royal Swedish Academy of Sciences from 1988 to 1990 and was the founding director of the Swedish Institute for Studies in Education and Research (SISTER) from 2000 to 2003. He chaired the Swedish committee for the International Polar Year from 2006 to 2009. Additionally, he was a member of the Swedish Government's Research Advisory Board during 1994–1998 and 2005–2009 and is currently part of the Government's Environmental Research Board.

Since January 1, 2018, Sörlin has been a member of the Climate Policy Council, an independent expert body. Sörlin's publications span across various fields, including the history of science, environmental history, forestry history, human ecology, environmental humanities, European history, research policy, innovation studies, and the history and politics of higher education. He is a frequent contributor to Swedish media and writes popular science and narrative non-fiction. His recent books include: Grounding Urban Natures: Histories and Futures of Urban Ecologies, with Henrik Ernstson (2019), Ice Humanities: Living, Working and Thinking in a Melting World, with Klaus Dodds (2022), Pathways: Exploring the Routes of a Movement Heritage, with Daniel Svensson and Katarina Saltzman (2022) Resource Extraction and Arctic Communities: The New Extractivist Paradigm (2023).

Expert Interview with Sverker Sörlin

What are the challenges in quantifying and monetizing ecosystem services? Your books cover numerous regions and a wide range of ecosystem services that benefit local indigenous communities. How do you address their needs in the context of monetizing nature's services?

Sörlin: I've been primarily interested in the development of ecosystem services as a concept because I think it's part of the, what I'm always interested in is the environmental history of different kinds, and this is part of the modern history of the environment, various methods to try and quantify it and monetize it. However, they should be separated, as the quantification has been going on for quite some time, to some extent, with ecosystem services identifying them. And, of course, you talk about spiritual, for example, and health-related services.

We can talk about ecosystem-related services. Once you start thinking about this, you come up with so many things that nature does without us asking anything. It just happens. And all these benefits are there. The big issue is

> *that quantifying is challenging but doable when it comes to monetization. It's usually about demand and supply to a very high degree in the market. But in some contexts, you don't have a market for a particular service. If you have a forest, a piece of land which is forested, and people go there to worship their various gods that there might be in the community, they, of course, think this is important when they say, yeah, now let's look at this as a service, instead of you just doing that. First, how do you quantify that value? And, how would you get a price for it? How would you monetize it? It isn't a scientific question that can get a straightforward scientific answer, at least not always.*
>
> *There was much ridicule thrown at an attempt by a group writing a paper in 1997 that became infamous, where the authors tried to calculate the entire benefit of the earth, the entire planet, and it turned out to be a very high number, but not higher than twice the size of the global GDP in 1997. And some thought, from the pure economic theory point of view, it was impossibly high because it couldn't be higher than twice the size of the global GDP in 1997. And some thought, from the pure economic theory point of view, it was impossibly high because it couldn't be higher than the worth of the entire planet. And it was twice. How about quantifying it, let alone monetizing it? But even small things are formidable to monetize.*

3.4 Planetary Boundaries Informs Policies and Frameworks Used by Countries, Financial Securities, and Companies

The concept of PB has proved influential in global sustainability policy development. While not the first attempt to define biophysical limits for human development, the PB framework stands out for its scientific rigor and widespread impact on policy discourse. The framework increasingly informs business practices and strategies, with companies integrating these principles to mitigate ecological risks and foster sustainable development. From shaping EU policies to redefining the fashion industry's approach to sustainability, the concept serves as a foundational framework for assessing and managing human impacts on the planet across various scales and sectors. The concept of planetary boundaries has been employed in various ways to define and navigate the safe operating space for humanity regarding Earth's life-supporting systems. Below is a synthesis of its utilization, particularly in sustainable business contexts:

EU Policy Development: The Stockholm Resilience Centre's technical report, in collaboration with the Stockholm Environment Institute and Netherlands Environmental Assessment Agency, marked an early attempt to translate the concept of planetary boundaries into operational guidelines at the EU level. This initiative aimed to integrate scientific understanding into policymaking, ensuring that European Union policies supported a sustainable balance within the Earth's biophysical limits. Increasingly, companies are asking for guidance on putting the planetary boundaries into business practice. Some recent studies highlight the use of planetary boundaries in assessments (Ryberg et al., 2020; Sala et al., 2020).

Circular Economy Integration: The Circularity Metric represents the share of secondary materials (those reintroduced into the economy after their initial use) in the total material input of an economy. This metric, expressed as a percentage, reflects the extent to which materials are cycled within the system rather than being extracted anew. As of 2023, the metric is around 7.2%, signifying a critical need for tackling declining circularity. Over 90% of materials are wasted, lost, or locked in long-term use (e.g., buildings, machinery), hindering resource efficiency. The global economy heavily relies on virgin material extraction, contributing to environmental degradation and resource depletion. The partnership between the Stockholm Resilience Centre, the Ellen MacArthur Foundation, and the H&M group, a global fashion and design company, is a notable business case illustrating the implementation of planetary boundaries in corporate strategy.[2] By integrating this framework with circular economy principles, H&M sought to redefine its business practices to minimize environmental impacts, focusing on sustainable material use and waste reduction represented in Fig. 3.4. According to its reporting, H&M's commitment to sustainability focuses on reducing environmental impact and promoting ethical practices throughout the lifecycle of its garments.

National and Regional Assessments: Reports to the Swedish Environmental Protection Agency and studies for the European Environment Agency have applied the planetary boundaries framework to evaluate national and regional contributions to global environmental limits. These assessments have helped to determine the environmental impact of activities within Europe and the consumption patterns of its citizens, informing policy and business strategies aimed at reducing ecological footprints.

Corporate Sustainability Strategies: The World Business Council on Sustainable Development, a forum for 200 companies, including some of the best-known brands worldwide, used the planetary boundaries framework to shape its Action 2020 strategy. This strategic plan highlights how multinational corporations can align their business operations with sustainability goals, influencing sectors like finance, food, textiles, building, technology, and household goods.

Sector-Specific Engagements: Companies across multiple sectors have sought guidance on incorporating planetary boundaries into their business practices. This engagement demonstrates a growing recognition within the corporate world of the need to operate within Earth's ecological limits. Companies are innovating in product design, supply chain management, and resource utilization to reduce their environmental impact and ensure long-term sustainability.

---

[2] https://hmgroup.com/sustainability/circularity-and-climate/circularity/.

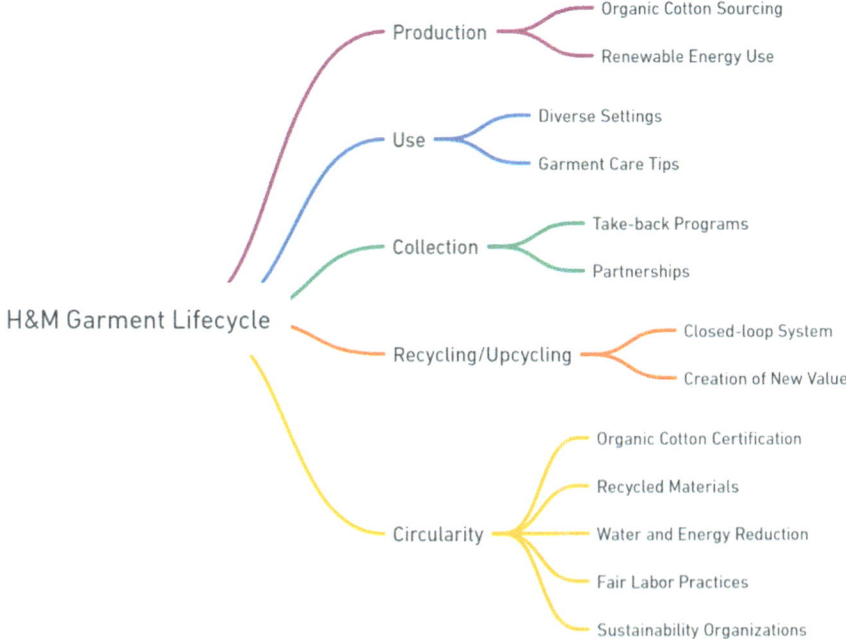

Fig. 3.4 An illustration of the lifecycle of H&M garments, focusing on various stages from production to circularity, within the context of sustainability

3.5 Incorporating PB into Strategic Planning

The concept of PB underscores the critical limits within which humanity must operate to preserve the Earth's ecological balance and stability. For corporations, cities, states, and countries, understanding and integrating PB into strategic planning, reporting, and governance is essential for sustainable development.

This approach mitigates environmental risks and aligns with emerging regulatory, financial, and societal expectations. This section describes each boundary, data variables relevant to measurement and analysis, successes and failures, policy, regulation, and a case study of an application of a sustainable finance instrument. Figure 3.5 shows the five elements of the template used to describe each PB to ensure consistency in explanation.

3.5.1 Climate Change

This boundary, shown in Fig. 3.3, focuses on the global mean rise in surface temperature. Crossing it could trigger abrupt and irreversible changes like ice sheet melt and ocean acidification.

Fig. 3.5 Five elements used to report on each PB including data variables and metrics for measuring success or failures.

Reporting Mechanisms: Corporations in the United States increasingly must disclose environmental risks and sustainability efforts, notably in their reporting to the Securities and Exchange Commission (SEC). The SEC mandates the disclosure of material risks, including those related to climate change, which could impact a company's financial performance. Corporations in the European Union have similar reporting following the new guidelines. This reporting is crucial for investors, regulators, and the public to evaluate a company's environmental impact, risk management strategies, and sustainability practices (Ameli et al., 2020; Carrington, 2020; IPCC, 2018, 2019; Lenton, 2019).

Data Variables: Data variables relevant to the climate change PB include greenhouse gas (GHG) emissions, energy consumption, carbon footprint, and exposure to climate-related risks such as supply chain disruptions or asset devaluation due to extreme weather events like sea-level rise. Companies report on these variables to assess and communicate their environmental impact and progress toward sustainability goals. Satellite observations can provide relevant data that can be processed to the level of an asset or site location.

Metrics: Successes and Failures: Success in managing the climate change boundary is measured by a company's ability to reduce GHG emissions, enhance energy efficiency, transition to renewable energy sources, and implement climate adaptation strategies. Conversely, failures are seen in increased emissions, lack of transparency in reporting, and inadequate risk management strategies that lead to environmental degradation and financial losses.

Policy, Regulation, and Sustainable Finance Instruments: Policies and regulations play a pivotal role in guiding corporate behavior toward sustainability. Examples include the Paris Agreement targets, the European Union's Green Deal,[3] and

---

[3] https://shorturl.at/korOV. "The European Green Deal is a package of policy initiatives, which aims to set the EU on the path to a green transition, with the ultimate goal of reaching climate neutrality by 2050. It supports the transformation of the EU into a fair and prosperous society with a modern and competitive economy."

3.5 Incorporating PB into Strategic Planning

carbon pricing mechanisms (e.g., carbon taxes and cap-and-trade systems). Sustainable finance instruments such as green bonds and sustainability-linked loans offer financial incentives for companies undertaking environmental projects.

- Significance of Reporting Climate Losses or Risks: Reporting climate losses or risks to the SEC or other bodies is crucial for several reasons.
- Transparency: It provides a clear picture of a company's exposure to climate-related risks, informing investors and stakeholders.
- Risk Management: Understanding these risks enables companies to develop more effective strategies for mitigation and adaptation.
- Compliance: It ensures compliance with evolving regulatory requirements, avoiding potential fines or sanctions.
- Investor Confidence: Transparent reporting attracts investors who are increasingly prioritizing sustainability in their investment decisions.
- Reputation: Companies that proactively address and report on climate risks are seen as leaders in sustainability, enhancing their brand value and customer loyalty.

Case Study: Climate change increases the frequency and intensity of extreme weather events. Island nations are particularly vulnerable to cyclones, storms, and heavy rainfall, which can cause extensive damage to infrastructure, homes, and livelihoods. Given the limited resources available for recovery and rebuilding, these events have significant economic and social impacts. The economies of the Maldives and Seychelles are heavily reliant on tourism and fisheries, sectors highly vulnerable to climate change impacts. Changes in sea temperature and acidity can affect fish stocks, while the loss of beaches and coral reefs can diminish the appeal of these destinations for tourists.

The Maldives and Seychelles are threatened by rising sea levels and consequent loss of land. The Maldives, for example, is the lowest-lying country in the world, with an average ground level of just 1.5 m above sea level. A study by the Intergovernmental Panel on Climate Change has projected significant sea-level rise over the twenty-first century, even if strong action is taken to curb emissions, which could submerge significant portions of these islands, leading to loss of habitat, infrastructure, and freshwater resources.[4] Simultaneously, these countries face climate threats to the coral reefs that surround them and are crucial for their protection, biodiversity, and tourism industries. Increased sea temperatures have led to widespread coral bleaching events. A notable instance was the global coral bleaching event from 2014 to 2017, which affected the Indian Ocean and severely impacted the coral reefs of the Maldives and Seychelles. Even when the living tissue of coral reefs recover, coral bleaching reduces the resilience of the reef ecosystem, affecting marine life and the livelihoods of communities dependent on them.

---

[4] https://www.ipcc.ch/report/ar6/wg2/chapter/chapter-15/.

3.5.2 Biosphere Integrity

The significance of the biodiversity integrity PB transcends ecological considerations, impacting economic, social, and governance aspects for corporations, cities, states, and countries. This boundary emphasizes the imperative to preserve biodiversity and ecosystem functions, as their degradation poses severe risks to food security, public health, and overall human well-being. Understanding and integrating biodiversity conservation into policy, regulation, and business operations becomes crucial.

Reporting Mechanisms: Globally, various reporting frameworks and guidelines have emerged to facilitate biodiversity-related disclosures by organizations. The Global Reporting Initiative[5] provides standards for sustainability reporting, including biodiversity impacts. The Task Force on Nature-related Financial Disclosures[6] (TNFD), modeled after the Task Force on Climate-related Financial Disclosures (TCFD), aims to provide a framework for organizations to report and act on evolving nature-related risks. CDP (formerly the Carbon Disclosure Project) offers a platform for companies and cities to disclose their environmental impact, including on biodiversity.[7] CDP scored over 21,000 companies on their environmental disclosures, with more than 400 companies earning an A for their leadership in environmental transparency and performance on climate change, deforestation, and water security. However, scoring varies across agencies and depends on the variables used for evaluation, making it challenging to gauge a company's score, especially given the lack of data on Scope 3 emissions. There is confusion about what to report for biodiversity and the availability of data at the asset level.

Data Variables: Key data variables for biodiversity reporting include species diversity indices, indicator species, habitat extent and condition, ecosystem services valuation, direct and indirect impacts on biodiversity, and conservation efforts. Companies also report on their dependency on biodiversity and the risks to their operations from biodiversity loss. There are not many asset-level data for this dimension but some recent work related to China's investments propose the methodology using geospatial datasets and analysis (Ma et al., 2023; Yang et al., 2021). The World Wildlife Foundation project provides some useful data on the Living Planet Index that needs to be processed for each study based on priorities.[8]

Metrics: Successes and Failures: Biodiversity varies from region to region, some of which is understood by broad principles (macroecology) but not always. It takes much work to choose what metrics to use (Jetz et al., 2019). For example, do invasive species "count"? (Simberloff, 2013). Successes in managing biodiversity integrity involve implementing and reporting on effective conservation strategies, restoration projects, sustainable supply chain practices, and achieving biodiversity-positive outcomes. Failures, conversely, are characterized by contributing to habitat destruction, species

---

[5] https://www.globalreporting.org/standards/.
[6] https://tnfd.global/.
[7] https://www.cdp.net/en.
[8] https://www.livingplanetindex.org/data_portal.

3.5 Incorporating PB into Strategic Planning

extinction, or food-web collapse and not engaging in or misreporting biodiversity conservation efforts.

Policy, Regulation, and Sustainable Finance Instruments: Many countries and regions have developed legal frameworks and policies to protect biodiversity. Examples include the EU's Biodiversity Strategy for 2030, the UK's Environment Bill, Brazil's Forest Code, Kenya's Wildlife Conservation and Management Act, and India's National Biodiversity Authority guidelines. Illegal wildlife crime is a global issue that is exacerbating the current biodiversity crisis proving that policy and regulation is ineffective in many countries. The World Economic Forum (2023) notes that more than 2000 animal and plant species are estimated to be threatened by the wildlife trade internationally.[9] This alarming statistic underscores the need for more robust and enforceable policies. The ineffectiveness of current regulations can lead to a lack of confidence among investors, as biodiversity loss represents a significant risk to long-term investment stability and returns. The persistence of illegal wildlife crime indicates gaps in governance and enforcement, which must deter investment in regions where natural resources are being unsustainably exploited.

Reporting on Biodiversity in Various Regions: In the EU, companies report under the Non-Financial Reporting Directive and will transition to the Corporate Sustainability Reporting Directive), which includes biodiversity considerations. While there is no federal mandate for biodiversity reporting, companies in the US voluntarily disclose through frameworks like the Global Reporting Initiative, the Task Force on Nature-related Financial Disclosures, and CDP. The Environment Bill in the UK includes provisions for biodiversity net gain, requiring developments to enhance biodiversity. In Australia, the Environment Protection and Biodiversity Conservation Act influences reporting for projects affecting biodiversity. The Brazilian Forest Code requires rural property owners to maintain or restore native vegetation, with reporting obligations. In Kenya, under the Wildlife Conservation and Management Act, activities impacting biodiversity require reporting and are regulated. In India, the Biological Diversity Act requires companies using biological resources to report and share benefits with local communities.

Case Study: The Amazon rainforest's biodiversity and the Coral Triangle's marine diversity[10] are unparalleled. The former houses approximately 10% of the world's known biodiversity. It is home to over 390 billion individual trees divided among 16,000 species, more than 2,500 species of fish, hundreds of reptile and mammal species, and tens of thousands of insect species (Ter Steege et al., 2013). The region is also incredibly rich in plant species, with estimates suggesting that one square kilometer may contain over 56,500 trees.[11]

At the same time, the Amazon is experiencing widespread deforestation and degradation, threatening its ability to function as a vital ecosystem and illustrating the

---

[9] https://www.weforum.org/stories/2023/02/biodiversity-nature-loss-cop15/

[10] https://oceanexplorer.noaa.gov/okeanos/explorations/10index/background/biodiversity/biodiversity.html.

[11] Steege et al. (2013) note an estimate of tree density yielded a total of 3.9×1011 individual trees or 56,500 trees.

potential consequences of transgressing the biosphere integrity boundary noted in several studies (Barlow et al., 2016; Da Silva et al., 2005; Food and Agriculture Organization of the United Nations The State of the World's Forests, 2022; Laurance et al., 2002). Three financial instruments for the Amazon are discussed below.

- Debt-for-Nature Swaps: The Tropical Forest Conservation Act in the United States has facilitated debt-for-nature swaps in several countries, including those within the Amazon basin. For instance, in 2010, the United States and Brazil agreed on a debt-for-nature swap that redirected USD 21 million of Brazil's debt payments to conservation efforts in the Amazon.
- Green Bonds: The Brazilian Development Bank issued its first green bond in 2017, raising USD 1 billion to finance sustainable projects, including those in the Amazon rainforest. These funds support initiatives such as sustainable agriculture, forest management, and renewable energy that contribute to the conservation of the Amazon.
- Payment for Ecosystem Services: The Bolsa Floresta Program in Brazil is one of the most extensive PES programs targeting the Amazon rainforest. It provides financial incentives to families living in state-designated conservation areas to support their involvement in forest conservation and sustainable development and improvement of their quality of life.

These examples illustrate the practical application of various financial instruments designed to mobilize resources for the conservation of the Amazon rainforest. Each initiative contributes to the broader goal of preserving the Amazon's unparalleled biodiversity and mitigating the effects of climate change.

3.5.3 Land-System Change

The PB related to land-system change is crucial for corporations, municipalities, regional governments, and nations. With the increasing availability of satellite data, it is now easier to examine and monitor land-system changes, resulting in a rich body of scientific literature in this area. This data underscores the necessity to judiciously plan and manage the transition of natural landscapes to areas dominated by agricultural, urban, and other human-centric activities. Such transitions carry the risk of undermining critical ecosystem services, including water regulation, soil fertility, and carbon sequestration, which are essential for environmental sustainability and human prosperity. Land-system changes can lead to habitat destruction, fragmentation, and a decline in biodiversity. For example, transforming forests into agricultural lands through slash-and-burn methods often lead to habitat destruction and a decline in biodiversity.

Reporting Mechanisms: Organizations globally employ several frameworks to disclose their impacts on land use and ecosystem services, enhancing transparency and accountability. Such disclosures enable companies to bolster their brand reputation, attract investment, and foster local partnerships. By openly sharing information

3.5 Incorporating PB into Strategic Planning

about their environmental impacts, organizations demonstrate their commitment to sustainability and responsible resource management, which can lead to increased trust and support from stakeholders. The Global Reporting Initiative provides sustainability reporting standards, including specific land use indicators as well as biodiversity indicators. CDP facilitates disclosure of environmental impacts, including deforestation and land use changes, helping companies manage environmental risks. The Sustainability Accounting Standards Board offers industry-specific sustainability accounting standards, including land use and biodiversity conservation metrics. European regulations and CSR frameworks emphasize the importance of biodiversity, prompting organizations to integrate biodiversity considerations into their sustainability practices. The European Union's Biodiversity Strategy and the Non-Financial Reporting Directive are examples of policies encouraging companies to disclose their impacts on biodiversity.[12] This heightened focus should guide businesses not only comply with regulations but also meet the growing expectations of stakeholders who prioritize environmental sustainability.

Data Variables: Essential data variables for reporting on land-system change encompass land conversion metrics (e.g., forest to agricultural land), land degradation rates, impacts on biodiversity, reforestation efforts, sustainable land management practices, and the carbon stock changes due to land use change. Satellite remote sensing provides spatial data for continuous monitoring of changes.

Metrics: Successes and Failure: Adopting sustainable land management and agricultural practices, initiating effective reforestation and afforestation, and maintaining or enhancing biodiversity and soil health demonstrate success in addressing the land-system change boundary. Failure is characterized by unchecked deforestation, habitat destruction, biodiversity loss, soil degradation, and no implementation of sustainable land use practices.

Policy, Regulation, and Sustainable Finance Instruments: There are numerous policies aimed at managing land use sustainably, such as the EU's Common Agricultural Policy (CAP), which includes measures for limiting for limiting soil erosion and enhancing biodiversity conservation; the United States Conservation Reserve Program (CRP); the UK's Agricultural Bill focusing on payments for public goods, including environmental benefits; and Brazil's Forest Code, requiring landholders to maintain a portion of their land as forest.

Green bonds, sustainability bonds, and environmental impact investments are financial mechanisms that support projects to mitigate land-system change and its impacts. These instruments fund sustainable agriculture, forest conservation, and land restoration projects. The World Bank issues green bonds that support projects promoting sustainable agriculture among smallholder farmers. These projects include improving water management, enhancing crop resilience to climate change, and reducing greenhouse gas emissions. The funds raised through these bonds directly support the transition to more sustainable agricultural practices. Increased agricultural productivity and reduced environmental footprint contribute to food security and climate change mitigation.

---

[12] https://environment.ec.europa.eu/strategy/biodiversity-strategy-2030_en.

In 2016, Starbucks issued a USD 500 million sustainability bond with proceeds aimed at enhancing the sustainability of its coffee supply chain by supporting coffee farmers in implementing sustainable agricultural practices, such as water and soil health conservation, and increasing their farms' resilience to climate change by leveraging technology and building social capital. The Althelia Climate Fund is an impact investment fund that finances projects to conserve tropical forests and restore degraded land.[13] One of its projects focuses on protecting and restoring the Peruvian Amazon through sustainable land use and agroforestry practices, combining conservation efforts with sustainable commodity production. Agroforestry refers to the land management system that integrates trees and shrubs into agricultural landscapes. This practice combines agricultural and forestry technologies to create more diverse, productive, sustainable, and resilient land use systems.

Reporting on Land-System Change in Various Regions: In the EU, the US, and many other countries, companies report on land-system change through national regulations and international frameworks that emphasize sustainability and environmental stewardship. The reasons for doing so are regulations, investor relations, corporate responsibility, and risk management. For example, investors are increasingly concerned with sustainability and environmental stewardship as part of their investment criteria. Reporting on land-system change demonstrates a company's commitment to sustainable practices, which can enhance its attractiveness to environmentally conscious investors and potentially improve access to capital.

Case Study: Expanding industrial agriculture and unsustainable land management practices contribute to soil erosion, desertification, and biodiversity loss, which are evident in regions like the Sahel in Africa, where land degradation threatens livelihoods and food security. The Sahel is characterized by variable climate, ranging from arid to semi-arid. It is home to millions of people who depend on subsistence agriculture and pastoralism for their livelihoods. However, the region has been facing increasing challenges due to changes in land use, exacerbated by the expansion of industrial agriculture and unsustainable land management practices such as deforestation, monocropping, and overgrazing (UNCCD Global Land Outlook 2020).[14] The Harita (Horn of Africa Risk Transfer for Adaptation) project in Ethiopia offers an innovative model providing microinsurance to farmers in exchange for their labor on public works projects that enhance water conservation and reduce erosion. This approach effectively links microinsurance with climate resilience activities, presenting a strategy that holds potential for replication in regions like the Sahel, where similar environmental challenges exist.

---

[13] https://www.eib.org/en/projects/all/20100720.

[14] https://www.unccd.int/resources/global-land-outlook/.

3.5.4 Freshwater Change

The PB related to freshwater use underscores the importance of managing freshwater resources sustainably to fulfill human requirements while preserving ecosystem integrity. This balance is crucial for corporations, cities, states, and countries to maintain water availability for agriculture, industry, and domestic use without compromising the health of aquatic ecosystems and the services they provide.

Reporting Mechanisms: Organizations report on freshwater use through various mechanisms. The Global Reporting Initiative (GRI) offers standards for sustainability reporting, including detailed indicators on water withdrawal, consumption, and discharge. CDP Water Security is a platform for companies to disclose water use, risks, and management strategies, emphasizing the importance of water stewardship. The EarthScan's Water Footprint Network provides tools and guidelines for assessing and reporting water footprints, helping organizations and individuals (in any country) understand their water use in the context of global water scarcity. For example, a female who is vegetarian, average and high meat eater in the US with gross yearly income of USD 30,000 (part of the family income consumed by the individual) will utilize 1581, 1994, and 2154 m^3 per year respectively.

Data Variables: Critical data variables for freshwater use reporting include total water withdrawal, water sources (surface water, groundwater, and rainwater), water consumption, recycling and reuse rates, and discharge quality. Companies also track water efficiency measures and the impact of their water use on local water resources.

Metrics: Successes and Failures: Reducing water withdrawal, increasing water use efficiency, enhancing water recycling and reuse, and improving wastewater treatment are successes in managing the freshwater use boundary. On the other hand, excessive water extraction, which contributes to local water scarcity, pollution of water bodies, and lack of investment in sustainable water management practices, is a failure.

Policy, Regulation, and Sustainable Finance Instruments: Many jurisdictions have implemented regulations promoting sustainable water use, such as the EU Water Framework Directive, which sets out a framework for water protection and management across Europe. The United States has the Clean Water Act and Safe Drinking Water Act, focusing on water quality and safety. Sustainable Finance Instruments, such as green bonds, and sustainability-linked loans can finance projects that aim to improve water efficiency, reduce pollution, and enhance water infrastructure. Public grants and subsidies are also available for water conservation projects.

Reporting on Stratospheric Ozone Depletion in Various Regions: In many countries, companies report on freshwater use through compliance with local environmental regulations and participation in global sustainability initiatives. Reasons for reporting include environmental stewardship, regulatory compliance, and risk management.

Case Study: Overexploitation of groundwater resources is critical in several regions, leading to falling water tables and land subsidence. The Aral Sea in Central

Asia has shrunk dramatically due to unsustainable water use for irrigation, environmental degradation (Loodin, 2020), and economic hardship, highlighting the potential consequences of exceeding the freshwater boundary. Some positive news is that Kazakhstan has taken significant steps toward restoring the northern part of the Aral Sea, known as the North Aral Sea. With support from the World Bank, Kazakhstan constructed the Kokaral Dam, which has been crucial in increasing water levels and reducing salinity in the North Aral Sea. This project, completed in 2005, has led to the revival of local fisheries and an increase in biodiversity.

3.5.5 Biogeochemical Flows

The PB, biogeochemical flows consist of nitrogen and phosphorus cycles, highlights the critical issue of human alterations to the natural balanced cycling and exchange of these essential nutrients. This relates to biogeochemical flows in Fig. 3.3. The excessive application of fertilizers in agriculture and also from the widespread cultivation of nitrogen fixing crops (soybeans, etc.) are primary dimensions of water pollution and the cause of aquatic ecosystem disturbances, leading to algal blooms and dead zones in aquatic environments. Excessive nitrogen is also associated with increased production of NO_x gases, which are potent greenhouse gases. Managing these boundaries is vital for corporations, cities, states, and countries aiming to sustain environmental health and agricultural productivity.

Reporting Mechanisms: Entities utilize various mechanisms to report their impact on nitrogen and phosphorus cycles. The Global Reporting Initiative provides reporting standards, including indicators for nutrient emissions and management practices. CDP Water Security offers a platform for companies to disclose water-related issues, including nutrient management and impacts on water quality. National environmental reporting systems in many countries require reporting on air and water emissions, including these nutrients.

Data Variables: Key data variables for reporting on these cycles include the amounts of nitrogen and phosphorus used in operations, the efficiency of nutrient use, runoff and leaching rates, and initiatives to reduce nutrient losses. Gathering accurate data on nutrient use and its impacts involves complex monitoring and measurement systems. Variability in farming practices and environmental conditions can make it challenging to obtain consistent data. Comprehensive data collection requires significant resources, both in terms of technology and manpower, which may not be feasible for all companies. Unilever, Nestle, Danone, and BASF have reported on their nutrient management.

Metrics: Successes and Failures: Implementing efficient fertilizer application techniques, adopting precision agriculture, improving wastewater treatment to remove nutrients, and restoring affected water bodies represent success. Conversely, failure is highlighted by continued nutrient runoff leading to eutrophication, not adopting best management practices, and a need for more innovation in nutrient recycling.

Policy, Regulation, and Sustainable Finance Instruments: Some jurisdictions and companies are implementing policies aimed at reducing nutrient pollution (Kanter, 2023). Once again, the reasons for doing so are regulations, investor relations, corporate responsibility, and risk management. But many companies do not provide these numbers.

Reporting on Nutrients in Various Regions: The EU's Nitrates Directive limits the amount of nitrogen applied to land in nitrate-vulnerable zones. The United States has the Clean Water Act, which includes provisions for managing nutrient pollution. Other countries have very few reporting regulations for managing nutrient pollution.

Case Study: Eutrophication of water bodies due to nutrient runoff from agricultural activities is a prevalent issue globally. The Gulf of Mexico is home to one of the world's largest "dead zones," an area of hypoxic waters with an oxygen concentration too low to support most marine life.[15] This dead zone is primarily the result of nutrient runoff from the Mississippi River Basin, which collects agricultural pollutants from across the central United States (Paudel & Crago, 2021). The nitrogen and phosphorus from fertilizers, combined with the River's discharge, feed the algal blooms in the Gulf that harm marine life and ecosystems (World Resources Institute, 2015). NOAA is collaborating with states to create advanced runoff risk forecasting tools. These tools assist farmers in deciding the optimal times to apply fertilizer by considering predicted rainfall amounts.

3.5.6 Ocean Acidification

Ocean acidification changes the chemical composition of seawater and disrupts the biogeochemical cycles of numerous elements and compounds (Doney, 2010). A notable consequence is the reduction in calcium carbonate saturation states, which adversely affects shell-forming marine organisms, including plankton, benthic mollusks, echinoderms, and corals. This change in the chemical composition of seawater poses significant risks to marine life, including coral reefs, shellfish, and the broader marine ecosystems, with cascading effects on fisheries, livelihoods, and global biodiversity. There have been three major global bleaching events to date that have impacted the Great Barrier Reef. The Reef is experiencing unprecedented coral bleaching and mortality due to rising ocean temperatures, illustrating the potential consequences of exceeding this boundary. Due to the dynamic and complex oceanography of coastal waters, hotspots of acidification are already beginning to approach ecologically significant thresholds (Jones et al., 2020). Addressing ocean acidification is imperative for corporations, cities, states, and countries committed to maintaining marine health and ensuring the sustainability of ocean-dependent economies.

Reporting Mechanisms: Entities worldwide utilize several frameworks and platforms to report their contributions to and actions against ocean acidification,

---

[15] https://oceantoday.noaa.gov/deadzonegulf/.

including GRI, which offers standards for environmental reporting and can include impacts related to carbon emissions and, indirectly, ocean acidification. TCFD encourages companies to disclose climate-related risks, including ocean acidification, due to its link with CO2 emissions. CDP provides a mechanism for disclosing environmental impacts, including those affecting oceans.

Data Variables: Ocean acidification is a complex process influenced by various factors, including local environmental conditions and global climate change. This complexity creates data gaps and uncertainties that make it difficult to draw definitive conclusions and develop effective mitigation strategies. Yet, systematic pH monitoring and reporting are not widespread, with exceptions like Norway's salmon farming industry, which has begun integrating environmental monitoring into their operations.

Metrics: Successes and Failures: Successes in addressing ocean acidification involve significant reductions in CO2 emissions, investment in carbon capture and storage technologies, and adopting sustainable marine practices. Continued high carbon emissions indicate failures, lack of actionable strategies for emission reduction, and insufficient investment in marine conservation efforts.

Policy, Regulation, and Sustainable Finance Instruments: International agreements such as the Paris Agreement aim to limit global warming and, by extension, reduce ocean acidification. National and local policies may also regulate emissions and promote marine conservation. Sustainable Finance Instruments include green bonds, blue bonds (aimed explicitly at financing marine and ocean-based projects), and environmental impact investing, which are mechanisms to fund initiatives that combat ocean acidification and its effects.

Reporting on Ocean Acidification in Various Regions: In the EU, US, UK, Australia, Brazil, Kenya, and India, companies report on their environmental impact, including ocean acidification, through a mix of regulatory compliance and voluntary sustainability initiatives. Reasons for reporting include environmental stewardship, regulatory compliance, and risk management.

Case Study: Coral reefs, vital marine ecosystems supporting biodiversity and livelihoods, are particularly vulnerable to ocean acidification. Indonesia is the center of the Coral Triangle, an area of unparalleled marine biodiversity including, and a product of, the coral reefs. Consequently, financial instruments like blue bonds could provide critical support for conservation efforts within the country and marine planning areas. This approach would help preserve biodiversity and support the livelihoods of millions of Indonesians who depend on healthy marine ecosystems for fishing, tourism, and coastal protection. The Coral Reef Rehabilitation and Management Program is funded by the World Bank and the Global Environment Facility; this project aims at coral reef conservation in Indonesia (IPCC, 2019).

3.5.7 Atmospheric Aerosol Loading

The PB of atmospheric aerosol loading concerns the concentration of fine particles in the atmosphere, and gaseous pollutants, which has significant implications for climate regulation, air quality, and public health. Managing aerosol emissions is crucial for corporations, cities, states, and countries to mitigate adverse environmental and human well-being effects, including exacerbating respiratory conditions and altering weather systems.

Reporting Mechanisms: The Global Reporting Initiative sets standards for sustainability reporting, with emissions-related indicators, including particulate matter (PM). The CDP offers a platform for corporations to disclose climate-related information, encompassing emissions that contribute to atmospheric aerosol loading. By means of National Emissions Inventories, countries often require reporting on air pollutants, including aerosols, through environmental protection agencies or equivalent bodies.

Data Variables: Key data variables for atmospheric aerosol loading include emissions of particulate matter, which are categorized by size (PM2.5 and PM10), sulfur dioxide (SO_2), nitrogen oxides (NO_x), and ammonia (NH_3), all of which can contribute to aerosol formation. The U.S. Environmental Protection Agency (EPA) has made significant strides in improving air quality since the Clean Air Act was enacted in 1970. The EPA monitors various pollutants, including PM2.5, PM10, SO_2, NO_x, and others, and has reported significant reductions in these emissions. Between 1970 and 2020, combined emissions of six common pollutants dropped by 78%, resulting in improved air quality and reduced health risks for Americans. The EPA uses a combination of regulatory and voluntary programs to achieve these results, continuously tracking and reporting on the progress. The Supreme Court in a 6-3 ruling overturned the Chevron doctrine, which had allowed courts to defer to federal agencies' interpretation of ambiguous statutes. This case, Loper Bright Enterprises v. Raimondo, is discussed in recent studies (Merrill, 2023; Beermann, 2024).

Metrics: Successes and Failures: Successes in managing atmospheric aerosol loading are marked by emissions reductions through the adoption of clean technologies, effective pollution control measures, and improvements in municipal or regional air quality. Failures manifest as increased emissions from industrial activities, transportation, and agriculture, leading to poor air quality and public health issues.

Policy, Regulation, and Sustainable Finance Instruments: Various regulations aim to reduce atmospheric aerosol loading, such as the Clean Air Act in the US, which sets standards for air quality and emissions. The EU's Air Quality Directive establishes air quality objectives for member states, including limits for aerosols. Sustainable Finance Instruments include green bonds and sustainability loans that can finance projects that reduce emissions contributing to atmospheric aerosol loading, such as renewable energy installations, energy efficiency improvements, and pollution control technologies.

Reporting on Stratospheric Ozone Depletion in Various Regions: In regions such as the EU, US, UK, Australia, Brazil, Kenya, and India, companies and governments report on emissions contributing to atmospheric aerosol loading to comply with local and international regulations. Reasons for reporting include regulatory compliance and risk management, public health, environmental protection, and corporate responsibility.

Case Study: Air pollution from fossil fuel combustion and industrial activities is a significant concern in many cities worldwide. Beijing, China, has notoriously high levels of air pollution caused by particulate matter, highlighting the potential consequences of exceeding the atmospheric aerosol loading boundary.[16] The Chinese government invested heavily in pollution control measures, including shutting down factories, reducing car usage, and implementing stricter emission standards. Significant funds were directed toward improving public transportation and increasing green spaces to reduce urban heat islands and pollution levels.

Many of the stringent pollution control measures were relaxed or removed after the Olympics, leading to a resurgence of pollution levels. The temporary nature of these measures indicates an unsustained financial commitment to long-term air quality improvement. While the financial instruments and policies deployed for the Beijing Olympics had a significant short-term impact on air quality, the lack of sustained efforts post-event led to a quick return to previous pollution levels. This underscores the importance of long-term commitments and continuous investments in sustainability to achieve lasting environmental improvements. The growing public awareness and demand for cleaner air led to increased pressure on the government to enforce stricter regulations. These regulations have included mandates to reduce coal usage and promote alternative energy sources, resulting in measurable improvements in air quality (Zheng et al., 2018).

3.5.8 *Stratospheric Ozone Depletion*

The PB of stratospheric ozone depletion emphasizes the critical role of the ozone layer in shielding the Earth from the Sun's harmful ultraviolet (UV) radiation. Its depletion poses severe risks, including heightened rates of skin cancer among humans and widespread ecological disturbances, thus requiring attention from corporations, cities, states, and countries worldwide.

Reporting Mechanisms: Organizations report on ozone depletion through various mechanisms, including the Global Reporting Initiative (GRI), which provides sustainability reporting standards that include indicators for emissions of ozone-depleting substances and particulate matter. The Montreal Protocol on Substances that Deplete the Ozone Layer requires countries to report their progress in phasing

---

[16] https://www.who.int/data/gho/data/themes/air-pollution/who-air-quality-database/2022.

out ozone-depleting substances. The CDP offers a platform for disclosing climate-related information, including emissions contributing to atmospheric aerosol loading and efforts to phase out ozone-depleting substances.

Data Variables: Stratospheric Ozone Depletion data variables include emissions of ozone-depleting substances (ODS), such as chlorofluorocarbons (CFCs), halons, and other related chemicals.

Metrics: Successes and Failures: Effective international agreements like the Montreal Protocol have significantly reduced the emissions of ODS, contributing to the gradual recovery of the ozone layer. In the context of atmospheric aerosol loading, advancements in emission-reduction technologies and stricter air quality regulations have helped decrease particulate emissions in many regions. Persistent use of ODS in some sectors and regions and inadequate enforcement of air quality regulations can lead to failures in mitigating ozone depletion and controlling aerosol emissions, respectively.

Policy, Regulation, and Sustainable Finance Instruments: The Montreal Protocol is a successful international treaty regulating ODS production and consumption. For atmospheric aerosol loading, national regulations like the Clean Air Act in the US set standards for air quality and limit emissions of harmful pollutants. Sustainable Finance Instruments can be effective in this context. Green bonds and sustainability-linked loans can finance projects to reduce emissions of ozone-depleting substances and particulate matter, such as transitioning to ozone-friendly technologies and implementing air quality improvement projects.

Reporting on Stratospheric Ozone Depletion in Various Regions: In regions such as the EU, US, UK, Australia, Brazil, Kenya, and India, companies and governments report on emissions contributing to stratospheric ozone depletion and atmospheric aerosol loading through national regulations and international agreements. Reasons for reporting include regulatory compliance, risk management, and environmental stewardship.

Case Study: The Montreal Protocol, an international treaty to phase out ozone-depleting substances, has been a success story (Gareau, 2010; Whitesides, 2020).

3.5.9 Novel Entities

The planetary boundary framework identifies novel entities as one of the critical boundaries that define the safe operating space for humanity. This boundary is concerned with the introduction and accumulation of substances that can cause irreversible harm to Earth's systems. Unlike other boundaries, novel entities do not have a clear quantitative threshold due to the vast diversity and complexity of these substances. However, their impact is significant, necessitating robust management and control measures (Persson et al., 2022; Steffen et al., 2015). Many novel entities, particularly persistent organic pollutants (POPs) and plastics, accumulate in the environment. These substances can persist for long periods, leading to bioaccumulation and biomagnification through the food chain, causing adverse effects on wildlife and ecosystems. Exposure to certain novel entities, such as endocrine-disrupting chemicals (EDCs) and heavy metals, can lead to severe health issues, including cancers, reproductive disorders, and neurological damage. Novel entities can disrupt ecosystem functions. For instance, plastic pollution affects marine life, while pesticides and herbicides can harm non-target species, leading to biodiversity loss.

Monitoring novel entities is challenging due to their diversity and the complex nature of their interactions with the environment. Effective measurement and monitoring require:

- Advanced Analytical Techniques: Technologies such as mass spectrometry and genomic analysis are crucial for detecting and quantifying novel entities.
- Standardized Reporting: Establishing consistent methods for reporting the presence and concentration of novel entities can help in tracking their distribution and impacts.
- International Collaboration: Global cooperation is essential for monitoring the transboundary movement of novel entities and sharing data and best practices (Clift et al., 2017).

3.6 Challenges and Solutions for Reporting on PB

Measuring, reporting, and taking action to prevent the crossing of planetary boundaries (PB) face significant challenges. Accurate data collection on environmental impacts, such as nutrient use, greenhouse gas emissions, and ocean acidification, requires complex monitoring and measurement systems. Variability in practices and environmental conditions can result in inconsistent and unreliable data. Comprehensive data collection demands significant resources, including advanced technology and manpower, which smaller companies often lack.

The absence of standardized methods for reporting environmental impacts leads to inconsistencies in data across different companies and regions. Furthermore, companies may define the scope of their reporting differently, complicating comparisons across firms or sectors.

Many sustainability initiatives depend on the adoption of new practices by farmers, companies, and other stakeholders. However, resistance to change, lack of awareness, and insufficient support can hinder effective implementation. Economic pressures often lead to prioritizing immediate gains over long-term environmental benefits, resulting in suboptimal management practices.

In some regions, weak or poorly enforced environmental regulations reduce the incentive for rigorous monitoring and reporting. Addressing these challenges requires coordinated efforts from companies, policymakers, farmers, and consumers. By investing in advanced monitoring technologies, developing international reporting standards, providing education and incentives for sustainable practices, and strengthening regulatory frameworks, we can move toward a more sustainable future that respects and preserves our planet's boundaries.

3.6 Challenges and Solutions for Reporting on PB   111

This chapter uses the planetary boundaries as a foundational framework to examine a vision in addressing issues that carry material risk. This section provides an overview of financial products that provide opportunities to address these risks.

3.6.1 Addressing PB Problems Through Regulations and Guidelines

The intersection of corporate responsibility, environmental sustainability, and regulatory compliance, such as those in the US and EU, presents a unique opportunity to bridge the gap between the ecological limits set by planetary boundaries and the socioeconomic considerations highlighted by critics. By embedding the concept of planetary boundaries within corporate sustainability strategies and regulatory frameworks, companies can move beyond the traditional focus on short-term financial returns to embrace a more sustainable and responsible business model. This action involves recognizing the finite nature of Earth's resources and the interconnectedness of environmental sustainability and socioeconomic well-being.

Regulations like the US Securities and Exchange Commission guidelines on environmental disclosures, the Sustainable Finance Disclosure Regulation in the European Union, and the European Sustainability Reporting Standards are pivotal in this context. They mandate transparency and accountability regarding environmental impacts and encourage companies to consider how their operations intersect with planetary boundaries. By aligning corporate strategies with these regulations, businesses can address both the scientific and social dimensions of sustainability, responding to the criticisms of the PB framework's initial formulation.

Incorporating planetary boundaries into corporate governance and reporting standards encourages a shift toward long-term environmental stewardship and socioeconomic resilience. It propels businesses to innovate in ways that reduce ecological footprints, enhance social equity, and ensure economic viability, thus fostering a more sustainable future. This approach exemplifies how the concept of planetary boundaries can be expanded to include broader socioeconomic factors and integrated into corporate and regulatory frameworks and consequently evolve from a purely ecological metric to a comprehensive guide for sustainable development across all sectors.

3.6.2 Addressing PB Problems Through Nature-Based Solutions (NbS)

While this is positive news, much remains to be done on the ground in terms of conserving nature. The road ahead is long and will require the participation of all citizens of this planet. The UNEP's annual "State of Finance for Nature" report

(UNEP, 2023), for the first time, quantifies the vast amounts of finance from both public and private sectors that negatively affect nature globally, revealing a staggering nearly USD 7 trillion annually, with a caution that this number might be on the conservative side since it only accounts for direct impacts.[17] The private sector's direct adverse financial impact on nature amounts to USD 5 trillion, dwarfing private investments in NbS by 140 times. This stark contrast highlights the urgent need for a global shift in financial priorities. To truly address the planet's environmental challenges, it is imperative that we reduce harmful investments and significantly increase funding toward sustainable practices and NbS. This endeavor will require coordinated action from governments, businesses, and individuals worldwide.

On the government front, subsidies harmful to the environment have surged by 55% to USD 1.7 trillion since the previous report in 2022, driven by increased support for fossil fuel usage, contrary to global commitments. This surge in nature-detrimental funding from both sectors poses a significant threat, negating potential gains in NbS financing. However, this discrepancy highlights a significant chance to redirect financial flows toward objectives set by the Rio Conventions. The Rio Conventions, established at the 1992 Earth Summit in Rio de Janeiro, are three international agreements that address key global environmental challenges. The Convention on Biological Diversity emphasizes the conservation of biological diversity, the sustainable use of its components, and the fair and equitable sharing of the benefits arising from the use of genetic resources. The United Nations Framework Convention on Climate Change aims to stabilize greenhouse gas concentrations in the atmosphere at a level that would prevent dangerous anthropogenic interference with the climate system. The third, United Nations Convention to Combat Desertification tackles desertification and mitigates the effects of drought through effective actions at all levels, supported by international cooperation and partnership arrangements. These conventions are intrinsically linked, operating within the same ecosystems and addressing interdependent issues such as climate change, biodiversity loss, and desertification. They emphasize sustainable development and have established mechanisms for collaboration and synergy to avoid duplication of efforts.

Despite the urgent need for enhanced funding, investments in NbS currently stand at USD 200 billion, merely a third of what is required to meet 2030 climate, biodiversity, and land restoration targets. Most NbS funding (82%) comes from governments. Although commitments such as zero deforestation in the agricultural sector are rising, funding for NbS has only seen an 11% increase since 2022.

NbS offers valuable investment avenues due to their multifaceted benefits, which increase their cost-effectiveness relative to purely engineered solutions so long as the co-benefits can be properly accounted. For instance, investments in sustainable land management could see a fourfold increase by 2050, reflecting the long-term profitability of sustainable agricultural and commodity production, which is crucial for attracting private capital. Moreover, conserving diverse ecosystems is an economical choice, accounting for 80% of the land area required for NbS while only needing

---

[17] https://www.unep.org/resources/state-finance-nature-2023.

20% of the projected NbS financing by 2030. Restoration efforts present significant opportunities to enhance ecosystem functionality and resilience, essential for maintaining the ecosystem services upon which humanity heavily depends. All of these efforts are enhanced from the financing side by frameworks like the planetary boundaries, which account for broadly distributed or multifaceted benefits.

However, the most effective measure to mitigate nature loss is adjusting the finance flowing toward activities that harm nature. Given their substantial volume, redirecting public and private funds away from such activities is paramount to prevent undermining NbS investments. While increasing public funding for NbS is vital, there is also a pressing need to reform detrimental subsidies. Concurrently, governments must implement regulations and incentives to steer private capital away from activities harmful to nature and toward NbS. The finance sector and businesses must immediately shift away from unsustainable practices, even without a fully supportive policy landscape. A significant shift in how nature is financed is imperative. "Greening finance" involves not only increasing financial support for environmentally beneficial activities but also reducing financial support for activities detrimental to nature. By reducing the financial backing for harmful activities and simultaneously boosting investments in NbS, efforts to address the challenges of climate change, biodiversity loss, and environmental degradation will remain robust.

3.6.3 Addressing PB Problems Through Finance

This section describes six financial instruments that assist in addressing PB issues.

3.6.3.1 Debt-for-Nature Swaps

Are innovative financial transactions in which a portion of a developing country's foreign debt is forgiven in exchange for commitments to environmental conservation measures. These swaps can be bilateral, involving two parties, or trilateral, involving the debtor country, a creditor country, and a third-party conservation organization. Historically, these financial mechanisms were primarily aimed at preserving tropical rainforests. However, such instruments also have been used to protect coral reefs and marine areas. Seychelles' Climate Adaptation and Impact Investment Debt Swap introduced several innovations (Esser et al., 2021; McFarland, 2021), marking it as the first of its kind in various aspects. It was the inaugural swap to support marine conservation financially, the first to leverage impact investment, the initial swap negotiated within the Paris Club, and the pioneering arrangement to embed policy commitments within its legal framework. The Paris Club is an informal assembly of creditor nations that work together to provide structured and sustainable solutions for countries struggling with debt repayment issues (Paris Club 2024).[18] The

---

[18] https://clubdeparis.org/en/.

Philippines, located within the biodiversity-rich Coral Triangle, benefited from debt-for-nature swaps facilitated by the World Wildlife Fund (WWF) in the late 1980s and early 1990s. These agreements mandated the Philippines to allocate funds toward conservation efforts, notably the management and preservation of the El Nido Marine Sanctuary and the Tubbataha Reef National Park.

Indonesia has been a notable participant in debt-for-development swaps, which can be considered a subset of or similar mechanism to debt-for-nature swaps. These swaps have been used as a government debt-relief policy and development finance strategy. Although the swaps have aimed to ease debt burdens and increase resources for sectoral purposes, including environmental conservation, their effectiveness has been mixed. A study by Cassimon et al. (2014) suggests that Indonesia could take a more proactive stance in negotiating the economic terms of its debt swaps, including nature conservation efforts. More recently, however, "debt-for-climate" swaps have been utilized whereby debtor countries are relieved from their contractual debt obligations in return for local climate-related spending commitments. Such instruments may help address debt and climate-related challenges (Essers et al., 2021).

The concept of pollution swapping, by which measures to reduce one pollutant inadvertently increase another, can offer insights into the complex trade-offs involved in environmental conservation efforts, including those funded by debt-for-nature swaps. Recognizing and addressing pollution swapping is crucial for the success of any environmental policy, including those financed through debt relief (Brennan et al., 2015; Stevens & Quinton, 2009).

Since 2008, the China Development Bank and the Export-Import Bank of China, China's international policy banks, have allocated USD 464 billion to governments globally, with merely USD 3 billion directed toward wealthier nations. Many nations that owe large debts to China are at a crossroads, facing the competing demands of economic revival, public health initiatives, and environmental sustainability (See Fig. 3.6). With prompt intervention to address this debt dilemma, these developing nations could avoid the prospect of allocating resources to external debt repayments over crucial needs such as combating the pandemic, safeguarding at-risk populations, and adhering to environmental sustainability pledges.

In determining the most suitable type of debt swaps for each country, it is essential to consider their specific threats. Countries including Angola, Cambodia, Laos, Myanmar, Uganda, and the Solomon Islands, shown in Fig. 3.6, can limit significant climate and biodiversity threats since their debt-for-nature and debt-for-climate swap potentials are the highest. Senegal, Sudan, and Zimbabwe might derive the most significant advantages from prioritizing debt-for-climate swaps. Given their heightened vulnerability to climate risks, this approach could mitigate their disproportionately high-carbon emissions and enhance investments in constructing climate-resilient communities.

The expert interviewed in this context is **Kevin Gallagher**, Boston University, Global Development Policy Center. His book (2016) on China's growing boom in Latin America traces the development finance in this region, and impacts, including deindustrialization and biodiversity. Gallagher discusses a wide range of topics in development finance and the debt crises.

3.6 Challenges and Solutions for Reporting on PB

Fig. 3.6 This map illustrates a global overview of the potential for debt swaps in countries with significant Chinese debt exposure. The interactive version of this map provides further insight into this analysis

3.6.3.2 Environmental Taxes and Charges

Environmental taxes and charges serve as pivotal instruments for steering economies toward sustainability, underpinning efforts in conservation, protection, and resilience against environmental challenges. By carefully designing these fiscal tools to reflect local conditions and mitigate potential negative impacts, governments can harness their revenue-generating capacity to fund critical environmental initiatives, thereby promoting a more sustainable and resilient future.

Environmental tax reform, which reallocates tax burdens toward environmental pollutants, has been studied for its potential to achieve a "double dividend"— enhancing environmental quality without compromising economic performance. Empirical evidence suggests that when revenues from environmental taxes are used to reduce labor taxes, and inflation is controlled, there can be a significant reduction in pollution, a modest increase in employment, and slight changes in production levels in the short to medium term. This finding indicates that environmental taxes can support conservation efforts while having a neutral or slightly positive effect on the economy (Bosquet, 2000). In Africa, green taxes hold the potential for promoting environmental sustainability and achieving Sustainable Development Goals (SDGs). These taxes face the challenge of balancing revenue mobilization for environmental protection with the risk of increasing inequality and energy poverty. The effectiveness of green taxes in Africa hinges on designing tax mechanisms that support green economic growth while minimizing adverse impacts on vulnerable populations (Mpofu, 2022).

Environmental tax reforms that focus on carbon and material productivity present an opportunity for substantial environmental benefits. For instance, a large-scale implementation of such taxes in the European Union, aimed at meeting emission reduction targets, resulted in improved carbon accounting and material productivity, suggesting a positive impact on environmental conservation and economic resilience. This approach demonstrates that environmental taxes can be cost-effective for reducing emissions and promoting sustainability (Wolde-Rufael, & Mulat-Weldemeskel, 2021). Payments for environmental services are a related financial mechanism that incentivizes the conservation of environmental services. PES schemes are voluntary, conditional agreements that compensate landowners for environmental services, translating environmental taxes and charges into direct conservation actions. These programs underscore the potential of financial incentives to foster environmental resilience by promoting sustainable land use practices (Reyes-Hernández 2023; Wunder, 2007; Wunder, 2008).

3.6.3.3 Green Bonds, Green Loans, Microcredits

These financial instruments are part of a broader strategy to integrate environmental considerations into financial decision-making. They provide critical funding for projects that might not be feasible through traditional financing methods, thus playing a vital role in the transition to a green economy. The growth of these instruments reflects a growing recognition of the importance of financial markets in addressing global environmental challenges and the need for innovative solutions to finance sustainable development projects effectively. Green bonds are debt securities issued to finance projects with positive environmental and climate benefits. The evolution of green bonds has made them a significant tool for sustainable finance, raising funds for environmentally friendly projects across various sectors such as renewable energy, sustainable agriculture, and water management. Green bonds have been highlighted as a potential support mechanism for post-pandemic recovery, emphasizing their role in sustainable development and environmental policy objectives (Malorgio et al., 2021).

Green loans have objectives similar to those of green bonds but are structured as loan agreements. They are designated for financing or refinancing projects with clear environmental benefits. While specific literature on green loans is less prevalent than on green bonds, their principle remains aligned with sustainable finance's goals. They support projects contributing to environmental sustainability, including energy efficiency improvements and sustainable resource use.

Expert in Focus: Kevin Gallagher

Dr. Kevin P. Gallagher is a Professor of Global Development Policy at the Frederick S. Pardee School of Global Studies at Boston University, where he also serves as the Director of the Boston University Global Development Policy Center (GDP Center). The GDP Center is dedicated to conducting policy-relevant research aimed at promoting financial stability, human well-being, and environmental sustainability worldwide. Professor Gallagher's expertise encompasses economic development, trade and investment policy, international environmental policy, and Latin American affairs.

3.6 Challenges and Solutions for Reporting on PB

Currently, Dr. Gallagher is the Lead Expert on Multilateral Development Bank Reform for the Brazilian Presidency of the G20. He is also a member of the Task Force on Climate, Development, and the International Monetary Fund, a group of experts focused on advancing development-centered climate policy at the IMF through rigorous empirical research. Additionally, he co-chairs the Debt Relief for a Green and Inclusive Recovery Project.

He participated in the US Department of State's Investment Subcommittee of the Advisory Committee on International Economic Policy and served on the National Advisory Council on trade policy at the US Environmental Protection Agency. His academic roles have included Visiting or Adjunct Professor position at the Paul Nitze School of Advanced International Studies at Johns Hopkins University, the Fletcher School of Law and Diplomacy at Tufts University, El Colegio de Mexico in Mexico, Tsinghua University in China, and the Center for State and Society in Argentina.

He is the author or co-author of seven books, his latest *The Case for New Bretton Woods* was co-authored with Richard Kozul-Wright. Other publications include *The China Triangle: Latin America's China Boom* and *the Fate of the Washington Consensus*. Previously, he served as co-chair for the T20 India Task Force on 'Refueling Growth: Clean Energy and Green Transition' under the Indian Presidency of the G20. Additionally, he was a member of the Chair's Council of the United States Export-Import Bank on China Competition and acted as the International Chair for the 'Greening the BRI Task Force' within the China Council for International Cooperation on Environment and Development (CCICED).

Expert Interview with Kevin Gallagher

What are some of the biggest challenges and opportunities that you see in achieving these sustainable development goals globally, particularly in light of the recent geopolitical and economic shifts that are happening in the world?

I believe that 2023 was a watershed year because, at the G20, the Indians introduced the International Experts Group on Development Finance (IEG), which produced a report called the Triple Agenda. This report was signed and approved by all G20 countries. The first significant outcome was the agreement on the scale of finance needed. According to the report, emerging market and developing countries (excluding China, which can manage on its own) need to mobilize $3 trillion annually to meet the SDGs and climate goals by 2030. Of this amount, $2 trillion should come from domestic sources, such as taxes and other internal revenues, while $1 trillion should come from international sources like JPMorgan and the World Bank.

This agreement has set the right scale and division of labor. Of the $1 trillion from international sources, $500 billion needs to come from public sources, including new capital for the World Bank and increased aid from organizations like USAID. There is a detailed agenda on how to achieve this $500 billion target, and a major discussion on this will take place at the next COP, which I believe is in Azerbaijan. Here, they will determine the new pledge amount from the UN, which will likely be between $100 billion and $500 billion. The remaining $500 billion is expected to come from the private sector, which is where your expertise is crucial.

To continue on an optimistic note, if we can secure $500 billion in public finance, it can play a significant role in de-risking and paving the way for international investment. This investment, which is typically risk-averse, could then be directed toward projects like building power plants in South Africa or Malawi, supported by guarantees from the World Bank and investments in technological logistics. Public finance could essentially create the pipeline for innovative green and SDG finance moving forward.

Looking ahead to 2024, I am even more hopeful because of Brazil's role. Brazil, as a democratic country committed to multilateralism, stands as a beacon of hope in an era where support for multilateralism is waning.

Climate Bonds Initiative (CBI) is an international non-profit organization that has significantly contributed to channeling capital toward climate solutions. It has helped establish clear standards, increase investor confidence, and fuel the enormous growth of the green bond market. The CBI's climate bond taxonomy provides guidance on climate-aligned assets and projects, aiding institutions and policymakers in identifying key investments essential for achieving a low-carbon economy. This taxonomy aims to support the development of a cohesive thematic bond market that promotes a low-carbon economy.

3.6 Challenges and Solutions for Reporting on PB

Table 3.1 identifies the elements of taxonomy that correspond to the PB framework. It identifies where there are available or pending certifications and areas where there are none in four categories, use of proceeds debt, assets, sustainability-linked debt, and entities. The categories that have full or partial certification and pending certification are left blank while gray cells show that no certifications are available as of now. For example, aviation (transport), bioenergy and nuclear (energy) have no bond initiatives as of 2024. Climate Bonds has played a significant role in the formulation of the EU Sustainable Finance Taxonomy. Financial instruments (bonds and loans) linked to these eligible assets, activities, and entities will be aligned with the Paris Agreement and the goal of keeping global temperature rises to no more than 1.5 °C above pre-industrial levels.

Climate Bonds recorded cumulative volume of USD 4.7 trillion in aligned green, social, sustainability, and sustainability-linked bonds, (collectively called Green, Social and Sustainability bonds) by March 31, 2024. The volume added just in Quarter 1 of 2024 was USD 272.7 billion, which was 15% more than in the same period in 2023. Since 2006, the percent in green, social, sustainability and sustainability-linked bonds is displayed in the Fig. 3.7. Green bonds continue to make the largest portion of the total aligned issuance, reaching 72% of the total, compared with 64% since 2006. Europe has the highest volume of these bonds, around 58% followed by Asia-Pacific (26%), and N. America (11%), shown in Fig. 3.8.

The CBI has been a significant force behind the rapid expansion of the green bond market. Since its founding, the market has grown from relative obscurity to a multi-trillion-dollar global asset class. The CBI has developed a detailed, science-based standard to determine which projects and assets qualify for green bond designation. This standard allows investors to identify investments that confidently genuinely address climate change. Its Climate Bonds Standard and certification process has increased transparency and trust in the market, attracting mainstream investors who want to support environmentally responsible projects. CBI-certified bonds help fund renewable energy, low-carbon transport, sustainable water management, and climate adaptation projects worldwide.

Muhammad Yunus (2007, 2010) is widely recognized as a pioneer in microfinance, specifically for introducing the concept of microcredit as a tool for poverty alleviation and economic empowerment, particularly among women in developing countries. Microcredits are small loans provided to individuals or groups in developing countries to empower them to generate sustainable income and engage in environmentally sustainable practices. Microcredits have been used to support small-scale environmental projects, such as organic farming and renewable energy installations, thereby contributing to poverty alleviation and sustainable development. However, the effectiveness of microcredit programs in achieving sustainable development can vary and may require careful design and implementation, focusing on environmentally sensitive business ventures (Desta, 2010).

Yunus's groundbreaking work began with the founding of the Grameen Bank in Bangladesh in 1983, which aimed to provide small loans to the rural poor without requiring collateral, thus enabling them to embark on small business ventures that

Table 3.1 CBI-certified climate bonds certification Source: Climate Bonds Initiative 3/2023[19]

Sector	Criteria Status	Use of Proceeds debt	Assets	Sustainability-linked debt	Entities
Energy	Solar				
	Wind				
	Geothermal			■	■
	Hydropower				
	Marine renewables				
	Electricity grids & storage				
	Mixed energy (utilities)				
	Bioenergy	■	■	■	■
	Nuclear	■	■	■	■
Transport	Public passenger transport				
	Private transport				
	Freight rail				
	Water-borne				
	Biofuels for transport			■	■
	Aviation	■	■	■	■
Water	Water monitoring			■	■
	Water storage			■	■
	Water treatment			■	■
	Water distribution			■	■
	Water desalination				
	Flood defence				
	Nature-based solutions				
Landuse and marine resources	Crop production				
	Livestock production				
	Commodity supply chains				
	Commercial forestry			■	■
	Ecosystem conservation & restoration			■	■

---

[19] https://www.climatebonds.net/files/reports/cbi_mr_q1_2024_01e_1.pdf.

3.6 Challenges and Solutions for Reporting on PB 121

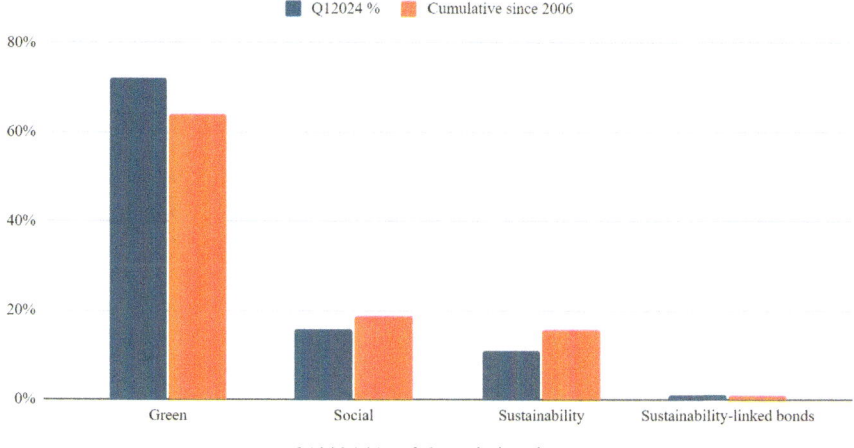

Fig. 3.7 Climate bonds by type in Q1 (2024) and cumulative since 2006 (Source: CBI)[20]

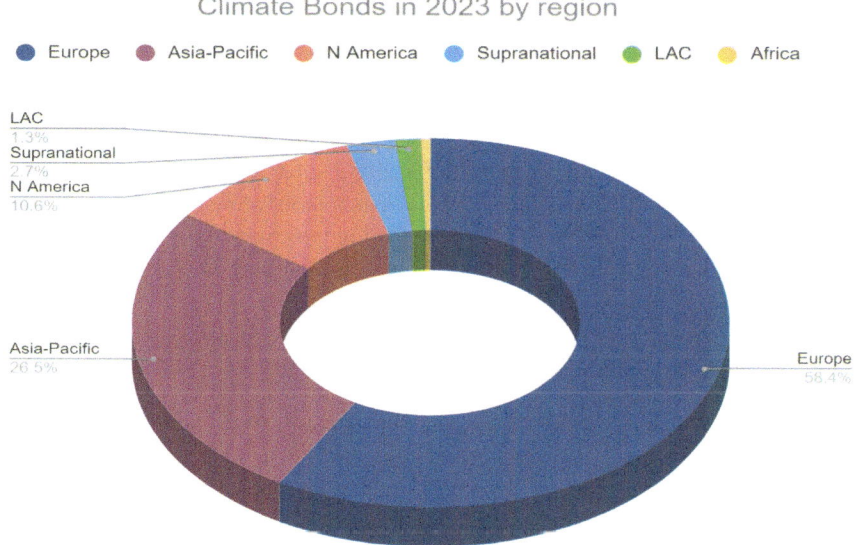

Fig. 3.8 Climate Bonds in different regions in 2023. LAC refers to Latin America and Caribbean, Supranational refers to UN and other international organizations (*Source* CBI)[21]

would have otherwise been inaccessible to them due to lack of traditional financial backing. The literature on microfinance often highlights its positive impacts,

---

[20] https://www.climatebonds.net/files/reports/cbi_mr_q1_2024_01e_1.pdf

[21] https://www.climatebonds.net/files/reports/cbi_mr_q1_2024_01e_1.pdf.

including increased income, enhanced self-esteem, and improved social standing for women. Yunus won the Nobel Peace Prize in 2006, which he received jointly with the Grameen Bank for their efforts to create economic and social development from below. Yunus's work underscores the potential of microfinance to address poverty by empowering individuals through access to financial services while highlighting the need for careful implementation and ongoing evaluation to ensure that microcredit achieves its intended outcomes. Ongoing Fintech applications in microfinance overcome some challenges in some countries (Leite et al., 2024).[22]

3.6.3.4 Payments for Ecosystem Services (PES)

Are a market-based approach to environmental conservation and sustainability designed to provide financial incentives to landowners or resource stewards for managing their land in ways that maintain or enhance ecosystem services. These ecosystem services include carbon sequestration, biodiversity conservation, water filtration, and erosion control, which are vital for the well-being of the environment and human society. The concept of PES is grounded in the principle that those who provide ecosystem services by conserving or restoring natural habitats should be compensated by those who benefit from these services.

Figure 3.9 shows the five comprehensive payments for ecosystems services (2008). This approach aims to create a financial value for the ecological goods and services that nature provides, which are often taken for granted (Jack et al., 2008; Suhardiman et al., 2013). PES schemes typically involve agreements by which the service providers are directly paid by service beneficiaries or by intermediaries such as governments, NGOs, or businesses interested in the conservation outcomes. For example, an income generated from carbon credits can help local stakeholders in Belize in maintaining resiliency of seagrass.

PES schemes have been implemented globally with varying degrees of success. In Latin America, for example, Costa Rica has pioneered using PES for forest conservation, funded through fuel tax revenues to compensate landowners for forest protection, reforestation, and sustainable management practices (Pagiola, 2008). In China, the Sloping Land Conversion Program pays farmers to plant trees on degraded lands to prevent erosion and improve water quality (Bennett, 2008). The effectiveness of PES in achieving conservation goals while supporting local economies highlights its potential as a flexible and integrative approach to managing ecosystem services. However, the design and implementation of PES schemes require careful consideration of ecological, socioeconomic, and institutional factors to ensure they are effective, equitable, and sustainable.

---

[22] https://knowledge.wharton.upenn.edu/article/how-is-fintech-transforming-microfinance/.

3.6 Challenges and Solutions for Reporting on PB

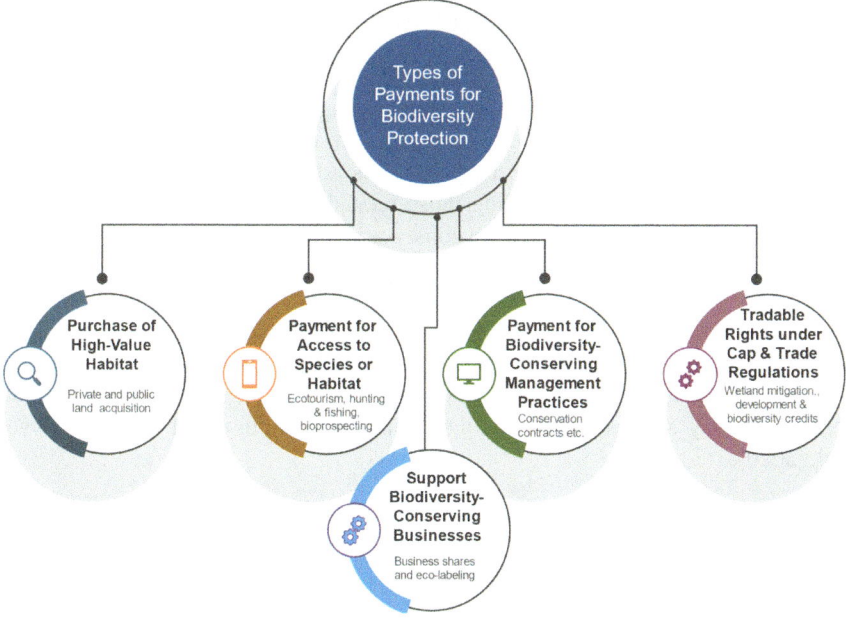

Fig. 3.9 UNEP describes the comprehensive payments for ecosystem services in five buckets, as shown above[23]

3.6.3.5 Biodiversity Offsets

Biodiversity offsets represent a promising but complex tool for achieving conservation objectives in the face of ongoing development. Their success depends on careful design, transparent and rigorous implementation, and ongoing monitoring and management to ensure they deliver genuine biodiversity benefits. Biodiversity offsets can be supported by various financial instruments, such as conservation banking in the United States (Gonçalves et al., 2015) or habitat banking in the European Union (Regnery et al., 2013). These mechanisms facilitate the trade of biodiversity credits, allowing developers to finance conservation activities that offset their impacts. Additionally, innovative financial mechanisms, including impact investments and blue carbon schemes, are being explored to enhance the financing of marine protected areas and other conservation initiatives.

Biodiversity offset policies are being advanced in various countries including the United States, Australia, Brazil, Colombia, and South Africa. These policies detail the conditions under which offsets are appropriate and how they should be implemented. However, the effectiveness of these policies in achieving conservation outcomes varies and is often subject to rigorous debate within the scientific community and among conservation practitioners.

---

[23] https://wedocs.unep.org/bitstream/handle/20.500.11822/9150/payment_ecosystem.pdf?sequence=1&isAllowed=y.

3.6.3.6 Public-Private Partnerships

Public-private partnerships (PPPs) are collaborative arrangements between governmental entities and private sector companies designed to finance, construct, and manage projects by combining the strengths of both sectors (Pinz et al., 2021). These partnerships leverage the private sector's efficiency, expertise, and capital to deliver public goods and services, including those related to environmental conservation and protection (Kim & Kwa, 2019). In conservation finance, PPPs involve initiatives that aim to preserve biodiversity, manage natural resources sustainably, and protect ecosystems, providing an innovative approach to addressing environmental challenges and offering economic opportunities. These PPPs can leverage private capital, allow for risk sharing, adopt innovative technologies for conservation, and contribute to achieving SDGs. Examples include protected area management (Lindsey et al., 2021; Thackway & Olsson, 1999) and sustainable agriculture and forestry (Dwyer et al., 2020).

3.7 Voluntary Carbon Markets

Voluntary carbon markets are financial instruments enabling entities to purchase carbon credits to offset their carbon emissions voluntarily. These markets differ significantly from cap-and-trade systems in their operational mechanisms, purpose, and regulatory frameworks. While both aim to reduce greenhouse gas (GHG) emissions, they operate under different principles, contributing uniquely to climate change mitigation efforts. Moreover, blockchain technology has emerged as a promising tool to enhance transparency, efficiency, and trust in voluntary carbon markets.

Regulatory Framework: Cap-and-trade systems are mandatory regulatory schemes that set a cap on the total level of GHG emissions and allow entities to trade emissions allowances within this cap. In contrast, voluntary carbon markets operate outside such regulatory mandates, allowing participants to buy carbon credits voluntarily to offset their emissions.

Purpose and Participants: Cap-and-trade systems target large emitters within regulated sectors, aiming to reduce emissions at the lowest possible cost. Voluntary carbon markets, however, cater to entities seeking to offset their emissions as part of corporate social responsibility initiatives beyond any legal requirement.

Flexibility and Scope: Voluntary carbon markets offer greater flexibility in projects that can generate carbon credits, including reforestation, renewable energy, and community-based projects, potentially across a broader geographical scope.

Evaluating the success of voluntary carbon markets versus cap-and-trade systems involves considering their respective goals and impacts. Cap-and-trade systems have been effective in particular jurisdictions at reducing emissions within the regulated sectors by setting a legal limit on emissions. Voluntary carbon markets, while not directly limiting emissions, play a crucial role in funding projects that might not otherwise receive support, contributing to GHG reductions and sustainable development goals.

Table 3.2 shows the carbon sequestration rate, which indicates how much carbon (in CO2 equivalent) each ecosystem could potentially remove from the atmosphere per hectare per year. Higher rates mean more potential for generating carbon credits. The "Carbon Credits Price" represents the current price per ton of CO2e on whichever carbon market (voluntary or compliant) the project operates within. This price is influenced by supply and demand. Income Potential calculates the potential revenue per hectare per year by multiplying the sequestration rate and carbon credit price. Table 3.2 shows that upper and lower ranges of carbon sequestration rates that depend on mangroves can sequester an estimated 1–4 tons of carbon per hectare per year, translating to approximately 3.67–14.68 tons of CO2 per hectare per year. Factors influencing sequestration rates depend on the species, age, health, and location. For example, some mangrove species are inherently faster growing or build denser biomass than others. Younger mangroves typically sequester carbon more rapidly, but mature forests store vast amounts in their soil. Degraded or stressed mangrove forests sequester little carbon. Geographic variability (climate, tidal flows, soil type) impacts sequestration potential. Mangroves are exceptional because most of their carbon storage is in their rich, waterlogged soil. At the same time, the immediate sequestration rate matters, and long-term protection of mangrove carbon stores is crucial.

3.8 The Emergence of Fintech and Climatetech

The research on Fintech solutions that preserve ecosystems' provisioning, regulating, cultural, and supporting services is still emerging, with few direct references to their impact on ecosystem services. However, Fintech's potential to support sustainable environmental outcomes, mainly through innovative financial products and services, is increasingly recognized. Here, we explore how Fintech solutions can contribute to preserving ecosystem services, drawing insights from broader Fintech literature and global examples.

3.8.1 Digital Payment Systems for Environmental Conservation

Fintech enables digital payment systems that support conservation efforts. For instance, platforms like Alipay's Ant Forest encourage users to adopt low-carbon activities by tracking their carbon savings, which are translated into virtual trees. Once a certain threshold is reached, real trees are planted in deforested areas,

Table 3.2 Carbon sequestration rate in each ecosystem per hectare per year, assuming that carbon credits price per ton of carbon is $20

Parameter	Carbon sequestration rate (average)- tons of carbon per hectare per year	CO2 conversion factor- tons of CO2e per hectare per year	Carbon sequestration in CO2e ton per hectare per year	Example project area- hectares	Estimated annual carbon sequestration- ton of CO2	Estimated annual income from carbon credits- Price in $ (using $20 pricing)
Peatlands	1	3.67	3.67	100	366.7	7334
Rainforests (upper)	40	3.67	146.68	100	14,668	293,360
Rainforests (lower)	4	3.67	14.67	100	1466.8	29,336
Coastal Marshes (upper)	20	3.67	73.34	100	7334	########
Coastal Marshes (lower)	5	3.67	18.34	100	1833.5	36,670
Seagrass	1.38	3.67	5.06	100	506.05	10,120.92
Mangroves (upper)	4	3.67	14.67	100	1466.8	29,336
Mangroves (lower)	1	3.67	3.67	100	366.7	7334

thus contributing to ecosystem provisioning and supporting ecosystem services by enhancing biodiversity and carbon sequestration (Bethlendi & Szőcs, 2022).

3.8.2 Blockchain for Sustainable Supply Chains

Blockchain technology, a key component of Fintech, enhances the transparency and traceability of sustainable supply chains. For example, platforms like IBM's Food Trust use blockchain to track the journey of food products from farm to table, ensuring they are sourced sustainably. This supports the regulation of ecosystem services by promoting sustainable agricultural practices and reducing environmental impact (Wójcik, 2020).

3.8.3 Crowdfunding for Environmental Projects

Fintech platforms such as Kickstarter and GoFundMe facilitate crowdfunding for environmental projects, enabling individuals and organizations to raise funds for conservation efforts, renewable energy projects, and sustainable development initiatives. This approach mobilizes resources to support ecosystem provisioning, regulating, and cultural services by funding projects that protect natural habitats, improve air and water quality, and promote environmental awareness (Sapian et al., 2021).

3.8.4 Green Bonds and Sustainable Investments

Fintech companies are increasingly facilitating investments in green bonds and other sustainable financial instruments. Platforms like Robinhood and Betterment allow individual investors to easily invest in portfolios that include green bonds, which fund projects with environmental benefits, including renewable energy, energy efficiency, and sustainable water management. Such investments support ecosystem services by channeling financial resources into projects with a positive environmental impact (Thompson, 2017).

3.8.5 Carbon Trading

As more jurisdictions globally implement CO_2 emissions trading schemes, carbon allowances have evolved into a liquid and fungible asset.[24] The European Union Emissions Trading Scheme (EU ETS) has been operational since 2005. Its trading unit, the European Union Allowance (EUA), is exchanged on the market among industrial polluters and represents the right to emit one ton of CO_2. A higher price of EUA indicates a greater cost for polluters per ton of CO_2 they release into the atmosphere.

Fintech companies such as Homaio[25] are viewing carbon allowances as financial instruments, examining their behavior in financial markets, comparing them to other assets, and exploring their appeal from a financial perspective. Homaio focused on EU Allowances (EUAs), which are permits that allow companies covered by the European Union Emissions Trading System (EU ETS) to emit a specified amount of carbon dioxide equivalent (CO2e). The fundamental purpose of EUAs is to provide a regulatory mechanism for controlling and reducing greenhouse gas emissions across Europe. However, their tradeable nature and fluctuating market price have attracted attention from financial market participants who see EUAs as a new class of asset. The variable market price of EUAs reflects the cost of reducing emissions. These

---

[24] https://medium.com/@valentin_98172/carbon-as-an-asset-class-9862e17b115c.

[25] https://www.homaio.com/.

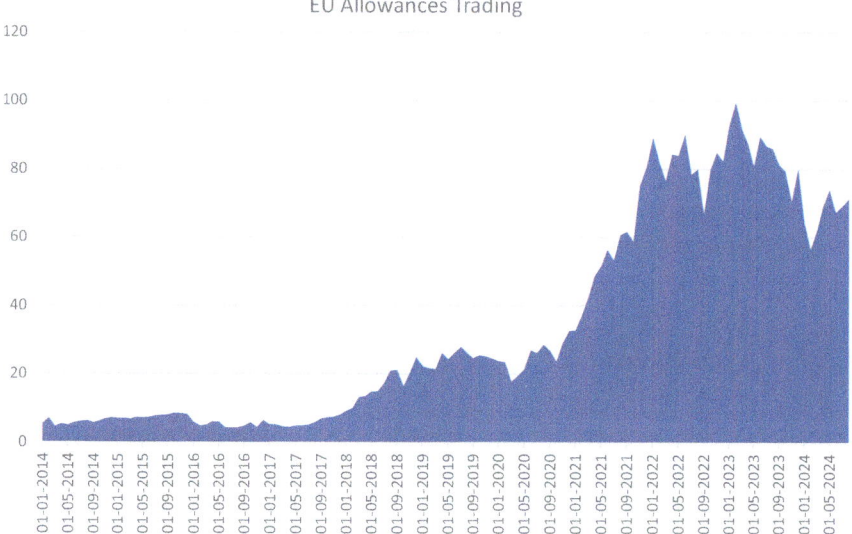

Fig. 3.10 European Union Allowances (EUAs) are exchanged on the market among industrial polluters. Y-axis shows the price in €[27]

companies are treating EUAs not just as compliance tools but as assets with distinct market behaviors, akin to commodities or other tradable financial instruments.

As shown in Fig. 3.10, currently, EUAs trade at approximately €72 per unit.[26] Over the past ten years, their price has surged significantly. In November 2017, they were valued around €8 per unit and traded as high as €99 at times in February 2023. The trend in Fig. 3.10 shows the increasing cost and value associated with carbon emissions rights in the EU market starting 2021.

The increasing focus on EUAs by Fintech companies like Homaio underscores the growing recognition of carbon allowances as a dynamic and potentially lucrative asset class within financial markets. As the EU continues to advance its climate goals and tighten emissions regulations, the role of EUAs in both environmental policy and financial strategy is likely to expand. This convergence of environmental and financial considerations makes EUAs a critical component of the EU's path to net-zero emissions, while also presenting new opportunities and challenges for investors and companies alike.

---

[26] https://www.investing.com/commodities/european-union-allowance-eua-year-futures-streaming-chart.

[27] https://www.investing.com/commodities/european-union-allowance-eua-year-futures-streaming-chart.

3.8.6 InsurTech for Climate Resilience

InsurTech, a subset of Fintech focusing on insurance, is leveraging technology to offer insurance products that improve climate resilience. Companies like Lemonade use AI and data analytics to offer insurance policies that incentivize sustainable behavior and cover climate-related risks, maintaining the regulating and supporting services of ecosystems by promoting risk reduction and adaptation to climate change (Abad-Segura et al., 2020).

In conclusion, while Fintech solutions are primarily associated with financial services innovation, their application extends to supporting ecosystem services through enhancing sustainability, transparency, and efficiency in environmental conservation efforts and sustainable development. Integrating Fintech into environmental initiatives represents a promising avenue for leveraging technology to preserve and enhance ecosystem services globally.

Blockchain technology offers several advantages that could enhance the functioning of voluntary carbon markets:

- Transparency and Trust: Blockchain's immutable ledger ensures that once a carbon credit is sold or retired, the transaction is recorded permanently, preventing double counting and enhancing market integrity.
- Efficiency and Lower Transaction Costs: Blockchain can lower transaction costs and make the market more accessible to a broader range of participants by automating transactions and reducing the need for intermediaries.
- Innovation in Carbon Trading: Blockchain enables the development of new platforms and applications that facilitate peer-to-peer trading of carbon credits, opening up new avenues for funding environmental projects.

Despite the potential benefits, integrating blockchain into voluntary carbon markets faces challenges, including technological complexity, regulatory uncertainty, and the need for widespread adoption among market participants. Addressing these challenges will be crucial for leveraging blockchain to its full potential in enhancing voluntary carbon markets' efficiency, transparency, and effectiveness.

3.9 Summary and Conclusions

The concept of planetary boundaries defines the safe operating space for humanity, beyond which irreversible damage can occur. This framework helps guide economic activities toward sustainability and resilience. Ecological economics critiques traditional models that prioritize endless growth and overlook the real costs of environmental degradation. In this chapter, each planetary boundary (PB) is detailed with examples, relevant data variables for measurement and analysis, successes and failures, policy implications, regulations, and a case study of a sustainable finance instrument application.

This chapter explains each PB in terms of reporting mechanisms, data variables, metrics, and sustainable finance instruments. The chapter takes an optimistic perspective by suggesting what is possible, with a warning: a lot of work needs to be done by individuals, financial institutions, national governments, and international organizations. Measuring, reporting, and taking action to prevent the crossing of planetary boundaries face significant challenges. Accurate data collection on environmental impacts, such as nutrient use, greenhouse gas emissions, and ocean acidification, requires complex monitoring and measurement systems. Variability in practices and environmental conditions can result in inconsistent and unreliable data. Comprehensive data collection demands significant resources, including advanced technology and manpower, which smaller companies often lack.

The absence of standardized methods for reporting environmental impacts leads to inconsistencies in data across different companies and regions. Furthermore, companies may define the scope of their reporting differently, complicating comparisons across firms or sectors. Many sustainability initiatives depend on the adoption of new practices by farmers, companies, and other stakeholders. However, resistance to change, lack of awareness, and insufficient support can hinder effective implementation. Economic pressures often lead to prioritizing immediate gains over long-term environmental benefits, resulting in suboptimal management practices. In some regions, weak or poorly enforced environmental regulations reduce the incentive for rigorous monitoring and reporting.

Addressing these challenges requires coordinated efforts from companies, policymakers, farmers, and consumers. By investing in advanced monitoring technologies, developing international reporting standards, providing education and incentives for sustainable practices, and strengthening regulatory frameworks, we can move toward a more sustainable future that respects and preserves our planet's boundaries.

The chapter then discusses research on Fintech solutions that preserve ecosystems' provisioning, regulating, cultural, and supporting services, noting that this field is still emerging with few direct references to its impact on ecosystem services. However, the potential of Fintech to support sustainable environmental outcomes through innovative financial products and services is increasingly recognized. The chapter explores how Fintech solutions can contribute to preserving ecosystem services, drawing insights from broader Fintech literature and global examples.

The goal is not to greenwash with great examples but to give the reader a sense of hope and new direction. It is essential to understand the risks if the PBs are crossed, while recognizing the potential for transformative change through coordinated efforts and innovative solutions.

References

Abad-Segura, E., Fuente, A. B. D. L., González-Zamar, M. D., & Belmonte-Ureña, L. J. (2020). Effects of circular economy policies on the environment and sustainable growth: Worldwide research. *Sustainability, 12*(14), 5792.

References

Ameli, N., Drummond, P., Bisaro, A., Grubb, M., & Chenet, H. (2020). Climate finance and disclosure for institutional investors: Why transparency is not enough. *Climatic Change, 160*, 565–589.

Barlow, J., Lennox, G. D., Ferreira, J., Berenguer, E., Lees, A. C., Nally, R. M., Thomson, J. R., Ferraz, S. F. B., Louzada, J., Oliveira, V. H. F., Parry, L., de Castro, R., Solar, R., Vieira, I. C. G., Aragão, L. E. O. C., Begotti, R. A., Braga, R. F., Cardoso, T. M., Jr., & R.C.O., Souza, C. M., Moura, N. G., ... Gardner, T. A. (2016). Anthropogenic disturbance in tropical forests can double biodiversity loss from deforestation. *Nature, 535*, 144–147.

Beermann, J. M. (2024). Loper bright and the future of Chevron deference. *William & Mary Law Review Online, 65*, 1.

Bennett, M. T. (2008). China's sloping land conversion program: Institutional innovation or business as usual? *Ecological economics, 65*(4), 699–711.

Bethlendi, A., & Szőcs, Á. (2022). Geographical and sectoral overview of the most valuable start-ups: What factors have increased the number of unicorns globally? *Információs Társadalom, 22*(4), 15.

Bosquet, B. (2000). Environmental tax reform: Does it work? A survey of the empirical evidence. *Ecological Economics, 34*(1), 19–32.

Brennan, R. B., Healy, M. G., Fenton, O., & Lanigan, G. J. (2015). The effect of chemical amendments used for phosphorus abatement on greenhouse gas and ammonia emissions from dairy cattle slurry: Synergies and pollution swapping. *PLoS ONE, 10*(6), e0111965.

Carrington, D. (2020). *Greenland ice sheet lost a record 1m tons of ice per minute in 2019.* https://www.theguardian.com/environment/2020/aug/20/greenland-ice-sheet-lost-a-record-1m-tons-of-ice-perminute-in-2019

Cassimon, D., Essers, D., & Fauzi, A. (2014). Indonesia's debt-for-development swaps: Past, present, and future. *Bulletin of Indonesian Economic Studies, 50*(1), 75–100.

Chancel, L., Piketty, T., Saez, E., & Zucman, G. (Eds.). (2022). *World inequality report 2022.* Harvard University Press.

Clift, R., Sim, S., King, H., Chenoweth, J. L., Christie, I., Clavreul, J., Mueller, C., Posthuma, L., Boulay, A.-M., Chaplin-Kramer, R., Chatterton, J., DeClerck, F., Druckman, A., France, C., Franco, A., Gerten, D., Goedkoop, M., Hauschild, M. Z., Huijbregts, M. A. J., & Murphy, R. (2017). The challenges of applying planetary boundaries as a basis for strategic decision-making in companies with global supply chains. *Sustainability, 9*(2), 279.

Costanza, R., d'Arge, R., de Groot, R., Farber, S., Grasso, M., Hannon, B., Limburg, K., Naeem, S., Oneill, R. V., Paruelo, J., Raskin, R. G., Sutton, P., & van den Belt, M. (1997). The value of the world's ecosystem services and natural capital. *Nature, 387*(6630), 253–260.

Costanza, R., Graumlich, L. J., & Steffen, W. (Eds.). (2011). *Sustainability or collapse? An integrated history and future of people on Earth.* MIT Press.

Da Silva, J. M. C., Rylands, A. B., & Da Fonseca, G. A. B. (2005). The fate of the amazonian areas of endemism. *Conservation Biology, 19*(3), 689–694.

Daily, G. C. (1997). Introduction: what are ecosystem services. *Nature's services: Societal dependence on natural ecosystems.* Island Press.

Daly, H. E. (2014). *Beyond growth: The economics of sustainable development.* Beacon Press.

De Groot, R. S., Wilson, M. A., & Boumans, R. M. (2002). A typology for the classification, description and valuation of ecosystem functions, goods and services. *Ecological Economics, 41*(3), 393–408.

Desta, A. (2010). Microcredit for poverty alleviation and fostering environmentally sustainable development: A review of African case studies. *International Journal of Business Research, 10*(2), 1–26.

Doney, S. C. (2010). The growing human footprint on coastal and open-ocean biogeochemistry. *Science, 328*(5985), 1512–1516.

Dwyer, J., Short, C., Berriet-Solliec, M., Déprés, C., Lataste, F. G., Hart, K., & Prazan, J. (2020). Fostering resilient agro-food futures through a social-ecological systems framework: Public–private partnerships for delivering ecosystem services in Europe. *Ecosystem Services, 45*, 101180.

Essers, D., Cassimon, D., & Prowse, M. (2021). Debt-for-climate swaps: Killing two birds with one stone? *Global Environmental Change, 71*, 102407.

Food and Agriculture Organization of the United Nations The State of the World's Forests 2022;

Gallagher, K. (2016). *The China triangle: Latin America's China boom and the fate of the Washington consensus*. Oxford University Press.

Gareau, B. J. (2010). A critical review of the successful CFC phase-out versus the delayed methyl bromide phase-out in the Montreal protocol. *International Environmental Agreements: Politics, Law and Economics, 10*, 209–231.

Gonçalves, B., Marques, A., Soares, A. M. V. D. M., & Pereira, H. M. (2015). Biodiversity offsets: From current challenges to harmonized metrics. *Current Opinion in Environmental Sustainability, 14*, 61–67.

Hollander, S. (1973). *The economics of Adam smith*. University of Toronto Press.

IPCC. (2018). *Global Warming of 1.5°C*. An IPCC Special Report on the impacts of global warming of 1.5°C above pre-industrial levels and related global greenhouse gas emission pathways, in the context of strengthening the global response to the threat of climate change, sustainable development, and efforts to eradicate poverty, A.1.1. https://www.ipcc.ch/sr15/chapter/spm/25.

IPCC. (2019). *Summary for policymakers*. In Climate Change and Land: an IPCC special report on climate change, desertification, land degradation, sustainable land management, food security, and greenhouse gas fluxes in terrestrial ecosystems, A.2.2. https://www.ipcc.ch/srccl/chapter/summary-for-policymakers/

Jack, B. K., Kousky, C., & Sims, K. R. (2008). Designing payments for ecosystem services: Lessons from previous experience with incentive-based mechanisms. *Proceedings of the national Academy of Sciences, 105*(28), 9465–9470.

Jetz, W., McGeoch, M. A., Guralnick, R., Ferrier, S., Beck, J., Costello, M. J., Fernandez, M., Geller, G. N., Keil, P., Merow, C., Meyer, C., Muller-Karger, F. E., Pereira, H. M., Regan, E. C., Schmeller, D. S., & Turak, E. (2019). Essential biodiversity variables for mapping and monitoring species populations. *Nature Ecology & Evolution, 3*(4), 539–551.

Jones, H. P., Nickel, B., Srebotnjak, T., Turner, W., Gonzalez-Roglich, M., Zavaleta, E., & Hole, D. G. (2020). Global hotspots for coastal ecosystem-based adaptation. *PLoS ONE, 15*(5), e0233005.

Kahneman, D., & Tversky, A. (1979). Prospect theory: An analysis of decision under risk. *Econometrica, 47*(2), 263–292.

Kanter, D. (2023). *A new approach to nutrient pollution governance in France and the EU*. LIEPP Policy Brief.

Kim, S., & Kwa, K. X. (2019). *Exploring public-private partnerships in Singapore: The success-failure continuum*. Routledge.

Laurance, W. F., Lovejoy, T. E., Vasconcelos, H. L., Bruna, E. M., Didham, R. K., Stouffer, P. C., Gascon, C., Bierregaard, R. O., Laurance, S. G., & Sampaio, E. (2002). Ecosystem decay of Amazonian forest fragments: A 22-year investigation. *Conservation Biology, 16*(3), 605–618.

Leite, Z. N., & Sá, E. S. (2024). Microfinance institutions managers' motivation towards environment protection through green microfinance: the case of the developing country of Cabo Verde. *International Journal of Bank Marketing, 42*(4), 725–744.

Lenton, T. et al. (2019). *Climate tipping points—Too risky to bet against*. https://www.nature.com/articles/d41586-019-03595-0

Lindsey, P., Baghai, M., Bigurube, G., Cunliffe, S., Dickman, A., Fitzgerald, K., Flyman, M., Gandiwa, P., Kumchedwa, B., Madope, A., Morjan, M., Parker, A., Steiner, K., Tumenta, P., Uiseb, K., & Robson, A. (2021). Attracting investment for Africa's protected areas by creating enabling environments for collaborative management partnerships. *Biological Conservation, 255*, 108979.

References

Loodin, N. (2020). Aral sea: An Environmental disaster in twentieth century in Central Asia. *Modeling Earth Systems and Environment, 6*(4), 2495–2503.

Ma, Y., Gopal, S., Ma, X., Gallagher, K., Koch, M., & Kaufman, L. (2023). The deforestation and biodiversity risks of power plant projects in Southeast Asia: A big data spatial analytical framework. *Sustainability, 15*(19), 14461.

Malorgio, A., Teti, E., & Dallocchio, M. (2021). Green bonds: The evolution of a sustainable financial instrument on the cutting edge. *International Review of Environmental and Resource Economics, 15*(1–2), 95–135.

McFarland, B. J., & McFarland, B. J. (2021). Debt conversions. *Conservation of tropical coral reefs: A review of financial and strategic solutions* (pp. 493–552).

Meadows, D.H., Meadows, D.L., Randers, J., & Behrens, W.W. (1972). *The limits to growth: A report for the Club of Rome's project on the predicament of mankind*. Universe Books.

Merrill, T. W. (2023). Response: Chevron's ghost rides again. *Boston University Law Review, 103*(1717).

Millennium Ecosystem Assessment (MEA). (2005). *Ecosystems and human well-being: Synthesis*. Island Press.

Mpofu, F. Y. (2022). Green Taxes in Africa: Opportunities and challenges for environmental protection, sustainability, and the attainment of sustainable development goals. *Sustainability, 14*(16), 10239.

Pagiola, S. (2008). Payments for environmental services in Costa Rica. *Ecological economics, 65*(4), 712–724.

Paudel, J., & Crago, C. L. (2021). Environmental externalities from agriculture: Evidence from water quality in the United States. *American Journal of Agricultural Economics, 103*(1), 185–210.

Persson, L., Carney Almroth, B. M., Collins, C. D., Cornell, S., De Wit, C. A., Diamond, M. L., Fantke, P., Hassellöv, M., MacLeod, M., Ryberg, M. W., Jørgensen, P. S., Villarrubia-Gómez, P., Wang, Z., & Hauschild, M. Z. (2022). Outside the safe operating space of the planetary boundary for novel entities. *Environmental Science & Technology, 56*(3), 1510–1521.

Piketty, T. (2014). *Capital in the 21st century* (Goldhammer, A., Trans.). Harvard University Press.

Pinz, A., Roudyani, N., & Thaler, J. (2021). Public-private partnerships as instruments to achieve sustainability-related objectives: The state of the art and a research agenda. *Sustainable Public Management*, 3–24.

Raworth, K. (2017). *Doughnut Economics: Seven ways to think like a 21st-century economist*. Chelsea Green Publishing.

Regnery, B., Couvet, D., & Kerbiriou, C. (2013). Offsets and conservation of the species of the EU habitats and birds directives. *Conservation Biology, 27*(6), 1335–1343.

Reyes-Hernández, H. (2023). Payment for environmental services: Forest conservation and poverty alleviation in a tropical region of Mexico. *Land Use Policy, 133*, 106847.

Richardson, K., Steffen, W., Lucht, W., Bendtsen, J., Cornell, S. E., Donges, J. F., Drüke, M., Fetzer, I., Bala, G., von Bloh, W., Feulner, G., Fiedler, S., Gerten, D., Gleeson, T., Hofmann, M., Huiskamp, W., Kummu, M., Mohan, C., Nogués-Bravo, D., … Rockström, J. (2023). Earth beyond six of nine planetary boundaries. *Science Advances, 9*(37), eadh2458.

Rockström, J., Steffen, W., Noone, K., Persson, Å., Chapin, F. S., III., Lambin, E., Lenton, T. M., Scheffer, M., Foley, J., & Schellnhuber, H. J. (2009). Planetary boundaries: Exploring the safe operating space for humanity. *Ecology and Society, 11*(2), 32.

Ryberg, M. W., Andersen, M. M., Owsianiak, M., & Hauschild, M. Z. (2020). Downscaling the planetary boundaries in absolute environmental sustainability assessments–A review. *Journal of Cleaner Production, 276*, 123287.

Sala, S., Crenna, E., Secchi, M., & Sanyé-Mengual, E. (2020). Environmental sustainability of European production and consumption assessed against planetary boundaries. *Journal of Environmental Management, 269*, 110686.

Sapian, S. M., Abdulkadir, N., & Ibrahim, N. (2021). Trade finance in digital era: Can FinTech harness the current risks and challenges? *The Journal of Muamalat and Islamic Finance Research, 18*(1), 78–89.

Simberloff, D. (2013). *Invasive species: What everyone needs to know*. Oxford University Press.

Steffen, W., Richardson, K., Rockström, J., Cornell, S. E., Fetzer, I., Bennett, E. M., Biggs, R., Carpenter, S. R., De Vries, W., De Wit, C. A., Folke, C., Gerten, D., Heinke, J., Mace, G. M., Persson, L. M., Ramanathan, V., Reyers, B., & Sörlin, S. (2015). Planetary boundaries: Guiding human development on a changing planet. *Science, 347*(6223), 1259855.

Stevens, C. J., & Quinton, J. N. (2009). Diffuse pollution swapping in arable agricultural systems. *Critical Reviews in Environmental Science and Technology, 39*(6), 478–520.

Suhardiman, D., Wichelns, D., Lestrelin, G., & Hoanh, C. T. (2013). Payments for ecosystem services in Vietnam: Market-based incentives or state control of resources? *Ecosystem Services, 5*, 94–101.

TEEB. (2010). *The economics of ecosystems and biodiversity: Ecological and economic foundations*. Earthscan.

Thompson, B. S. (2017). Can financial technology innovate benefit distribution in payments for ecosystem services and REDD+? *Ecological Economics, 139*, 150–157.

Ter Steege, H., Pitman, N. C., Sabatier, D., Baraloto, C., Salomão, R. P., Guevara, J. E., Phillips, O. L., Castilho, C. V., Magnusson, W. E., Molino, J. F., Monteagudo, A., Vargas, P. N., Montero, J. C., Feldpausch, T. R., Honorio Coronado, E. N., Killeen, T. J., Mostacedo, B., Vasquez, R., & Silman, M. R. (2013). Hyperdominance in the Amazonian tree flora. *Science, 342*(6156), 1243092.

Thackway, R., & Olsson, K. (1999). Public/private partnerships and protected areas: Selected Australian case studies. *Landscape and Urban Planning, 44*(2–3), 87–97.

Thaler, R. H. (1980). Toward a positive theory of consumer choice. *Journal of Economic Behavior & Organization, 1*(1), 39–60.

UNEP. (2023). *United Nations environment programme. State of finance for nature: the big nature turnaround—Repurposing $7 trillion to combat nature loss*. Summary for Decision-makers. Nairobi. https://doi.org/10.59117/20.500.11822/44278

Whitesides, G. (2020). Learning from success: Lessons in science and diplomacy from the Montreal protocol. *Science & Diplomacy, 9*(2), 1–13.

Wójcik, D. (2020). Financial and business services: A guide for the perplexed. In J. Knox-Hayes & D. Wójcik (Eds.), *The Routledge handbook of financial geography*. Routledge (forthcoming).

Wolde-Rufael, Y., & Mulat-Weldemeskel, E. (2021). Do environmental taxes and environmental stringency policies reduce CO2 emissions? Evidence from 7 emerging economies. *Environmental Science and Pollution Research, 28*(18), 22392–22408.

World Economic Forum. (2023). *50% of the global economy is under threat from biodiversity loss*. https://www.weforum.org/stories/2023/02/biodiversity-nature-loss-cop15/

WRI. (2015). *Eutrophication and hypoxia coastal areas*. WRI policy note.

Wunder, S. (2007). The efficiency of payments for environmental services in tropical conservation. *Conservation Biology, 21*(1), 48–58.

Wunder, S. (2008). Payments for environmental services and the poor: Concepts and preliminary evidence. *Environment and development economics, 13*(3), 279–297.

Yang, Q., Liu, G., Casazza, M., Gonella, F., & Yang, Z. (2021). Three dimensions of biodiversity: New perspectives and methods. *Ecological Indicators, 130*, 108099.

Yunus, M. (2007). *Banker to the poor: Micro-lending and the battle against world poverty*. PublicAffairs.

Yunus, M. (2010). *Building social business: The new kind of capitalism that serves humanity's most pressing needs*. Public Affairs. ISBN 978-1-58648-824-6.

Zheng, B., Tong, D., Li, M., Liu, F., Hong, C., Geng, G., Li, H., Li, X., Peng, L., Qi, J., & Yan, L. (2018). Trends in China's anthropogenic emissions since 2010 as the consequence of clean air actions. *Atmospheric Chemistry and Physics, 18*(19), 14095–14111.

Chapter 4
A Deep Dive into Climate Risks and Materiality

> If someone reports close to a 100% accuracy, they are either lying to you, made a mistake, forecasting the future with the future, predicting something with the same thing, or rigged the problem—Matthew Schneider

4.1 Introduction

This chapter bridges the concepts explored in prior chapters with practical considerations around how the changing environmental and planetary dynamics directly impact financial businesses and people. The chapter describes what climate risk is in the context of business management and how businesses approach risk assessment. In this context, it is useful to differentiate between two risks—*physical and transition risks*. Physical risks are associated with extreme weather events, natural disasters, and climate-related impacts that manifest as economic, operational, credit, and market risks. Transition risks are associated with the shift toward a lower-carbon economy, driven by policy changes, technological advancements, and evolving market conditions. These risks can lead to economic, geopolitical, market, and credit risks.

Scientific evidence indicates that extreme physical risk events, such as heatwaves, hurricanes, flooding, and droughts, are becoming more frequent and severe, significantly impacting organizations, industries, and economies. Many investors, banks, and financial regulators are increasingly aware of these climate risks and have pledged to support the UN Climate Change Conference (COP21) Paris Agreement (UNFCC, 2016). This agreement aims to mitigate these risks by stabilizing temperature increases well below 2 °C above pre-industrial levels, which is essential for keeping negative climate impacts manageable (Hoegh-Guldberg et al., 2018). Achieving these goals requires substantial structural changes across various sectors and actors (Lenton et al., 2022), which present transition risks. Some industries will need to rapidly expand, while others must transform their technological foundations or face contraction and potential obsolescence. Fossil fuel extraction and distribution sectors, along with industries reliant on fossil fuels for production, are particularly vulnerable. While some sectors, such as power production, have viable low-carbon alternatives, others, like steel and air travel, are in the early stages of developing sustainable solutions (IEA, 2019, 2023a).

Financial communities are increasingly recognizing the risks associated with both the physical effects of climate change and the regulatory actions required for transitioning to a net-zero economy. Physical risks are significant in agriculture, while transition risks are particularly significant for fossil energy companies, which are the main source of carbon emissions. Investor concerns about climate risks influence capital allocation and oversight practices, affecting companies in the energy sector. Different energy firms have responded to these climate-related pressures in various ways, reflecting the broader implications for financial markets and the energy industry (Fox-Penner, 2020; TCFD, 2021). As public opinion, governmental policies, business leadership, and institutional investment strategies align with the urgency of climate change mitigation, the transition from fossil fuels to renewable energy is accelerating. This transition, driven by commitments to carbon neutrality from over 100 countries, represents significant carbon-transition risks for companies dependent on fossil fuels. Transition risks encompass a range of shocks, including policy changes, reputational impacts, market shifts, and technological innovations, all of which contribute to the evolving landscape of climate risk management (UNEP, 2019).

4.1.1 Value at Risk (VaR) and Climate Value at Risk (CVaR)

From a financial perspective, it is equally critical to consider the direct impact of climate change on asset values. Prior analysis (Dietz et al., 2016) demonstrates how the expected "climate value at risk" (CVaR) for global financial assets changes across IPCC scenarios, with the best outcomes associated with mitigating emissions to limit global warming to no more than 2 °C. Similar findings are reported by another study (S&P Global, 2023). Companies currently exposed to extreme weather events and the physical impacts of climate change are projected to face increasingly significant financial costs in the coming decades. Without adaptation measures, these costs will annually average 3.3% of the value of real assets held by companies in the S&P Global 1200 by the 2050s, potentially rising to as much as 28% per annum.

It is useful to differentiate between VaR, a statistical measure used to assess the risk of loss for investments, and CVaR. The former estimates the maximum potential loss over a given time period within a certain confidence level. For example, a one-day VaR at the 95% confidence level indicates a 95% chance that the portfolio will not lose more than a specified amount in one day. In the insurance context, VaR is measured by the technical insurance premium, which captures the annual expected cost of climate-related damage relative to the replacement cost of dwellings. Therefore, VaR encompasses the costs associated with servicing housing, including

4.1 Introduction

insurance, repairs, replacement, and maintenance costs. It does not reflect a decline in the property's value itself. Since VaR = Annual Premium / Replacement cost, we can easily estimate replacement cost if the VaR of 0.5 percent equates to an annual premium of $3000 on a building. The replacement cost is equal to (3000/0.05)*100. The result is $600,000.

CVaR extends the concept of VaR by incorporating the financial impact of climate-related risks (MSCI, 2020). It not only considers potential financial losses due to extreme weather events (physical risks) but also includes losses related to the transition to a low-carbon economy (transition risks). CVaR provides a broader perspective on potential losses by including scenarios such as policy changes, market shifts, and technological advancements aimed at mitigating climate change (UNEP, 2019). There are multiple entities interested in Climate Value at Risk (CVaR) as shown in Fig. 4.1.

- Banks, asset managers, insurance companies, and other financial institutions are highly interested in climate-related and environmental risk management in the banking sector. These entities aim to assess and manage the financial risks associated with climate change in their investment portfolios and lending activities.
- Regulatory organizations like the European Central Bank (ECB, 2021), Financial Conduct Authority in the UK, Japan Financial Services Agency, and other national

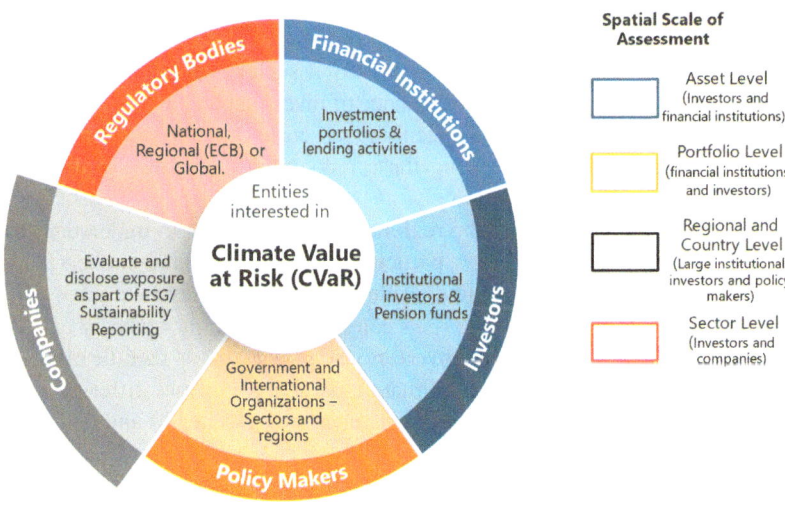

Fig. 4.1 Entities interested in Climate Value at Risk and their spatial scales of operation

regulatory bodies focus on Climate Value at Risk (CVaR) to ensure that financial institutions under their supervision are adequately managing climate-related risks. The Financial Stability Board (FSB, 2022) addresses global regulatory approaches to climate-related risks, including CVaR, to enhance the resilience of the financial system.

- Large corporations, particularly those in sectors highly exposed to climate risks (e.g., energy, agriculture, real estate), use CVaR to evaluate and disclose their exposure to climate risks as part of their environmental, social, and governance (ESG) reporting (ECB, 2022).
- Institutional investors and pension funds use CVaR to understand the potential impact of climate change on their long-term investments and to guide their engagement with portfolio companies on climate risk management. But there are some limitations in traditional economic and financial risk pricing models (Battiston et al., 2021; Monasterolo, 2020).
- Policymakers, including governments and international organizations, may use CVaR to inform climate policies and assess the economic impacts of climate change on various sectors and regions (Eckstein et al., 2021; Nordhaus, 2019).

Entities interested in CVaR typically assess climate risks at multiple spatial scales, including asset level, portfolio level, region, state, and country. Investors and financial institutions often analyze climate risks at the asset level to understand the specific vulnerabilities of individual properties or facilities. This granular analysis helps in identifying direct impacts of climate events such as flooding, extreme heat, and wildfires on specific assets.

Many financial institutions and investors aggregate asset-level risk scores to obtain portfolio-level risk scores, which aids in assessing the overall exposure of their investment portfolios to climate risks and in making informed decisions about asset allocation and risk management. At the portfolio or asset level, physical risks can significantly affect the valuation and performance of investments. For example, real estate portfolios in flood-prone areas or agricultural assets in drought-stricken regions may suffer substantial losses. Evaluating these risks allows investors to diversify and protect their investments appropriately.

Some assessments focus on the regional or country level to understand broader climatic trends and risks. This is particularly useful for policymakers and large institutional investors who need to consider how climate risks vary across different geographic regions and how these risks can impact economic stability and growth. On the other hand, companies and investors also look at sector-specific climate risks, which help in understanding how climate change may impact different industries differently. This sectoral analysis can guide investment strategies and risk mitigation efforts.

The impact of transition risks can vary widely between countries and regions based on their current reliance on fossil fuels and their regulatory environment. Countries heavily invested in fossil fuel industries may face significant economic disruptions as policies shift toward renewable energy. Understanding these regional differences is essential for policymakers to craft tailored transition strategies. For investors,

4.1 Introduction

transition risks can affect the financial performance of specific assets and portfolios. For example, investments in coal mining or oil extraction may face declining returns due to stricter environmental regulations and the adoption of cleaner technologies. Assessing these risks at the asset level enables investors to make informed decisions about divestment, reallocation, and engagement in sustainable investments.

Understanding both physical and transition risks from the perspectives of countries, regions, portfolios, and assets is necessary for several reasons. The entities and levels of assessment are shown in Fig. 4.1. Businesses and investors can implement targeted risk mitigation strategies such as diversifying investments, improving asset resilience, and engaging in climate adaptation measures. Staying informed about regional and national policies helps organizations ensure compliance with new regulations and avoid potential penalties. Accurate risk assessment supports long-term strategic planning, allowing businesses to anticipate market shifts and technological advancements. Investors can make more informed decisions by understanding how climate risks affect different sectors and regions, leading to better portfolio management and sustainable investment practices.

The first expert interviewed for this chapter **is Graham Cook**, a veteran of Catastrophic modeling for insurance. He discusses the major differences between this type of modeling and climate risk modeling. He also elaborated on estimating VaR and CvaR.

> **Expert in Focus: Graham Cook**
>
> Dr. Graham Cook, Principal, Insurance Consultant, who is on Floodlight's advisory team is the chief architect of the Floodlight CAT model. Dr. Cook is an industry veteran with over three decades of experience and practice in this field. He has published widely and has consulted to various re/insurance companies, various agencies, and startups on catastrophic risk in North America, Asia, and Europe. He has a PhD in Civil/Structural engineering from Johns Hopkins University. He is a member of the Engineers Australia, Working Group on Disaster Risk Reduction and Responses.
>
>

Graham is an experienced insurance and reinsurance professional. He is responsible for leading teams researching, developing and evaluating third party and in house catastrophe and financial models. He has lectured on catastrophe models and ESG for re/insurance companies in the US, Europe, Asia and Australia.

Graham works in the area of catastrophic (Cat) insurance models and climate risk models. Graham notes that CAT models utilize geospatial data and analysis in several key ways to assess and predict the potential impact of natural disasters on insured properties. Geospatial data collected from actual events is used to calibrate and validate CAT models, ensuring that the models accurately reflect real-world conditions and outcomes. Traditionally, CAT models are used to evaluate the financial impacts of natural disasters like hurricanes, earthquakes, and floods. They focus on the immediate risks posed by these events to insurance and reinsurance portfolios, estimating potential losses based on historical data and hazard analysis.

Expert Interview with Graham Cook

Can you elaborate on best practices in the context of CAT models?

To effectively manage catastrophic risks, it is essential to leverage the strengths of advanced insurance models. This begins with auditing and enhancing data quality, which ensures that the foundation of any model is accurate and reliable. Understanding the science behind these models, including the nuances of model changes, is crucial for interpreting results and making informed adjustments.

By comparing outputs from multiple models, we can identify inconsistencies and validate the reliability of predictions. Sensitivity analyses further refine these results, helping us understand how different variables impact outcomes. Blending these insights with expert judgments allows for a more comprehensive and nuanced approach to risk management. Adjusting models for non-modeled perils, such as unexpected or rare events, ensures that all potential risks are accounted for. Employing diverse metrics like Value at Risk (VaR) and Tail Value at Risk (TVaR) provides a robust framework for assessing these risks. These are relevant in climate risk models at the asset level. A commercial REIT or solar or wind farm's risk from multiple hazards can be estimated using similar procedure.

Simple deterministic methods offer additional insights, particularly in identifying exposure concentrations that could amplify losses. Finally, integrating underwriting and actuarial judgments into the process ensures that these models are not just theoretically sound but also practically applicable, making them powerful tools in the field of catastrophic insurance.

How do CAT models vary from climate models?

4.1 Introduction

> *Catastrophe models and climate models serve different purposes and have distinct limitations. Catastrophe models, while not designed as climate models, do implicitly account for moderate increases in losses attributed to climate change. However, they are focused on accurately modeling extreme weather events at a high spatial resolution (10 m to 10 km), making them more suitable for pricing risks in the insurance industry, which operates on an annual basis.*
>
> *In contrast, climate models, which divide the world into larger cells (ranging from a kilometer to hundreds of kilometers), struggle to accurately simulate the specifics of hurricanes—such as intensity, frequency, and landfall locations. Additionally, climate models are not practical for pricing risks due to their inability to precisely model extreme weather events and the high cost of running them over the necessary time and spatial dimensions. Moreover, since climate change occurs over extended periods, its impacts do not align directly with the annual pricing structure of insurance policies.*

4.1.2 Drivers and Strategies for Managing Climate Risks

Table 4.1 categorizes different entities such as investment banks, asset managers, and insurance companies, highlighting drivers that force these entities to take action, such as regulatory pressure, market demand, and risk exposure. For example, in row one of Table 4.1, increasing regulatory demands for the disclosure and management of climate risks are putting pressure on banks to integrate these considerations into their risk management processes. Maintaining a responsible investment image is crucial as stakeholders increasingly demand transparency and action on climate issues (UNEP, 2019). Thus, banks are developing and integrating climate risk assessment models into investment decisions to better understand and manage exposure (Nieto, 2019). Banks are also prioritizing green and sustainable investment opportunities to capitalize on the transition to a low-carbon economy (IFC, 2019). They are enhancing their climate risk disclosure in line with frameworks like TCFD (2021) to improve transparency and accountability.

Asset managers, row two in Table 4.1, have a fiduciary responsibility due to regulations in the EU or US, client demand, or market stability to undertake actions such as portfolio diversification, ESG integration, and active engagement with companies to address risks. They are using risk assessment models, green investments, and disclosure practices to address and communicate their actions. Another example is venture capital (VC) firms, row eight in Table 4.1, which aim to ensure the long-term stability and profitability of their investments, which can be threatened by climate-related physical and transition risks. VC firms comply with regulatory frameworks to access funding (e.g., U.S. Inflation Reduction Act) and avoid penalties. There is growing market demand for sustainable and green investments, driven by investor

Table 4.1 This table lists the drivers positioning various entities to manage climate and transition risks and the strategies or actions they adopt to address these drivers

Entities	Driver compelling entities to manage climate and transition risks				Strategies or actions taken to address the drivers (columns 2–4)			
Investment banks	Exposure to climate risk	Regulatory pressure	Reputation	Risk assessment models	Portfolio diversification	Green investments	Disclosure practices
Asset managers	Fiduciary Duty	Client demand	Market stability		Portfolio diversification	ESG integration	Engagement with companies
Insurance companies	Risk exposure	Premium adjustment	Long-term viability	Risk modeling	New products (parametric)		Reinsurance
Corporates	Operational impact	Transition costs	Reputation and compliance	Sustainability strategies	Resilient supply chains		Carbon reduction and offsets
Cities and states	Infrastructure vulnerability	Economic stability	Public safety	Urban planning	Policy frameworks		Public awareness
United Nations & international organizations	Global coordination	Policy development	Funding and support	Global agreements	Technical assistance		Monitoring and reporting
NGOs	Advocacy	Awareness and education	Grassroots mobilization	Campaigns and advocacy	Partnerships		Research and reporting
Venture capital firms	Investment stability	Regulatory compliance	Market demand	Due diligence	Diversification		Partnership
Central banks & financial regulators	Financial stability	Macroprudential policy:	Monetary policy	Stress testing	Green finance		Regulatory guidance

preference for environmentally responsible projects, including solar energy installation and production. VC firms must integrate climate risk assessment into the due diligence process to evaluate the exposure and resilience of potential investments. They can collaborate with experts in climate science, engineering, and sustainability to accurately assess and mitigate risks associated with investments. They can diversify the investment portfolio to include a mix of projects with varying levels of climate risk to balance potential returns and vulnerabilities.

In summary, physical and transition risks are crucial considerations for various entities due to their potential impact on financial stability, operational continuity, regulatory compliance, and reputational standing. Proactive risk management, informed by robust data and aligned with best practices, is essential to address these challenges effectively. Each entity—investment banks, asset managers, insurance companies, corporates, cities, and states—has unique motivations and strategies to manage climate risks, emphasizing the importance of tailored approaches and comprehensive planning.

In the following sections, physical and transition risk methodologies are discussed. Section 4.2 examines physical and transition risk classes along with sectors most vulnerable to these risks. Section 4.3 describes scenario models and time horizons (from present into the future, 2100). Section 4.4 outlines the evaluation of physical risk.

4.2 Physical and Transition Risks

Recognizing climate change as a financial risk is imperative for precise asset pricing. Physical climate risks involve the potential for asset damage and operational disruptions caused by weather events linked to climate change and variability. Investments must yield returns commensurate with the associated risks, necessitating higher risk premiums for greater risks. Without investor awareness or proper disclosure of climate-related risks, market prices cannot accurately reflect the risk-return trade-off (Table 4.2).

Accurate identification and assessment of these risks are essential for effective monitoring and management. Proper integration of these risks into financial markets facilitates efficient capital allocation and supports the transition to a low-carbon economy (Dietz et al., 2016).

Physical risks refer to adverse effects resulting from rising temperatures and an increasing frequency of extreme weather events, such as droughts, floods, and rising sea levels due to climate change. The Task Force on Climate-Related Financial Disclosures (TCFD, 2021) categorizes risks into chronic risks, which are associated with gradual changes such as rising sea levels and temperatures, and acute risks, which are tied to extreme weather events like floods and severe droughts. The frequency and intensity of these extreme events are expected to increase as climate change progresses. Chronic and acute risks are discussed in subsections 4.2.1 and 4.2.2. There is a significant risk of widespread mispricing in financial markets due

Table 4.2 The European Union Commission delegated regulation (EU) 2021/2139 classifies climate-related hazards into acute and chronic based on four categories

Classification of climate-related hazards

		Temperature related	Wind-related	Water-related	Solid mass-related
Chronic		Changing temperature (air, freshwater, marine water)	Changing wind patterns	Changing precipitation patterns and types (rain, hail, snow/ice)	Coastal erosion
		Heat stress		Precipitation or hydrological variability	Soil degradation
		Temperature variability		Ocean acidification	Soil erosion
		Permafrost thawing		Saline intrusion	Solifluction
				Sea level rise	
				Water stress	
Acute		Heat wave	Cyclones, hurricanes, typhoons	Drought	Avalanche
		Cold wave/frost	Storms (including blizzards, dust, and sandstorms)	Heavy precipitation (rain, hail, snow/ice)	Landslide
		Wildfire	Tornado	Flood (coastal, fluvial, pluvial, groundwater)	Subsidence
				Glacial lake outburst	

Source Commission delegated regulation (EU) 2021/2139

4.2 Physical and Transition Risks   145

to the inherent uncertainty of climate-related risks (Condon, 2022; FSB, 2020). This chapter features an interview with Condon related to climate risks. Subsection 4.2.3 examines the economic costs associated with physical risks. Transition risks, dealing with regulatory, policy, and other concerns, are examined in subsection 4.2.4.

4.2.1 Chronic Physical Risks

Chronic physical risks involve longer-term continuous shifts in climate patterns, including increasing temperatures, rising sea levels, and changes in precipitation. A recent study (Trancoso et al., 2024) analyzed wetter or drier future conditions with trends from 146 Global Climate Models simulated under two elevated greenhouse gas (GHG) emissions scenarios. The study findings highlighted future hotspots of increased aridity and excessive rainfall, particularly in regions already facing water scarcity or surplus. These projected changes are expected to affect a substantial portion of the global population, with an estimated three billion people (38% of the current global population) impacted under an *intermediate* emissions scenario, and five billion people (63% of the current global population) under a *high* emissions scenario by the end of the century. Other studies of climate scenario simulations had similar results.

Chronic risks, viewed in the socioeconomic context, show impacts in coastal zones vulnerable to hazards like sea-level rise and increasing populations. High urbanization and changing land use have resulted in significant risks. Neumann et al. (2021) examined how global and regional coastal populations may be impacted by 2030 to 2060, using baseline population data from 2000 and projecting changes based on different sea-level and socioeconomic scenarios. This analysis did not account for potential displacement of people from these areas but utilized current trends of urban growth to predict future demographic changes. The results indicate that Asia, particularly China, India, Bangladesh, Indonesia, and Vietnam, will continue to have the highest coastal population exposure to 100-year flood events. Meanwhile, Africa, especially Egypt and sub-Saharan nations, is expected to see the fastest coastal population growth and urbanization. This study (Neumann et al., 2021) underscored the urgent need for adaptive planning and policy interventions to mitigate the risks of coastal flooding. It highlighted areas requiring further research in scenario-based exposure assessments, as well as incorporating UN SDGs. Another chronic risk is the accelerating rate of ocean acidification, which is increasingly disrupting marine food webs and reducing coral cover (Doney et al., 2020). This was described in Chapter 3, Planetary Boundaries.

4.2.2 Acute Risks

Acute hazards are severe, short-term events with significant negative economic impacts, such as droughts, floods, heatwaves, hurricanes, tornadoes, and storms. For example, a flood may damage a business's data storage center (considered as a microeconomic transmission channel), leading to operational losses from system downtime or lost data. As acute hazards become more frequent due to climate change, their impacts may eventually resemble those of chronic hazards. For example, increased flooding of a river may render surrounding areas less habitable over time (TCFD 2017).

Tropical cyclones (TCs) are among the worst physical risks, and their frequency and severity are expected to rise due to climate change and socioeconomic development, despite substantial uncertainties. Since 1980, TCs have caused an average cost of $22.8 billion per event (CPI-adjusted) (NOAA, 2024). Future risks from TCs are modeled using scenario analysis, which considers significant interactions between climate change and socioeconomic development alongside various vulnerability functions (Meiler et al., 2023). These scenario analyses are crucial for effective mitigation and planning, enabling better preparedness and risk management strategies to address the anticipated increase in TC activity. Scenario analysis is described in Sect. 4.3.

Future TC impacts are projected to increase due to climate change and socioeconomic development. Climate change is expected to drive an increase in the most severe TCs, enhance precipitation rates, and amplify the destructive power of TC-induced flooding through rising sea levels. Concurrently, socioeconomic development will expand the population and assets exposed to TCs. Providing at-risk communities with transparent information about future TC risk changes is crucial for effective adaptation and mitigation strategies.

4.2.3 Economic Cost of Physical Risks

The economic cost of global natural disasters has been measured since 1980, indicating that the total economic cost of damages because of global natural disasters (measured in current US$) has increased from 1980 to 2000 and beyond (EM-DAT, 2024). The most expensive year was 2011 with a cost of $371.20 billion. Global disasters included drought, floods, extreme weather, extreme temperature, landslides, dry mass movements, and wildfires, as well as volcanic activity, and earthquakes. (Chapter 1 has a table xx of global disasters.)

Table 4.3 shows eight recent examples of physical risks faced by companies in terms of loss amounts and the years (information from various sources including Deloitte (2024), Zurich Insurance Group Annual Reports, and company financial reports). Figures 4.2 and 4.3 show the global damage costs from natural disasters.

4.2 Physical and Transition Risks

The worst year was 2011, when damages were caused by various events including earthquakes, which are not a climate risk.

According to the National Centers for Environmental Information, from 1980 to 2024 (NOAA, 2024), the US experienced 387 weather and climate disasters, each of which cost at least $1 billion and the total cost of which exceeded $2.740 trillion. Tropical cyclones inflicted the most damage, totaling $1,411.2 billion (adjusted for CPI), and had the highest average cost per event at $22.8 billion (CPI-adjusted) (NOAA, 2024). Other significant contributors to the overall damage include droughts

Table 4.3 Examples of companies directly impacted by physical risks

Company	Physical risk/ Hazard	Year	Loss amount
1. Archer Daniels Midland Company (ADM)	Severe droughts in the western United States	2021 2012	The droughts significantly impacted crop yields, leading to an estimated loss of hundreds of millions of dollars in agricultural supply and operational costs
2. Pacific Gas and Electric Company (PG&E)	Persistent drought conditions and heat waves in California increased the frequency and severity of wildfires	2018	The Camp Fire, the deadliest and most destructive wildfire in California's history, was caused by PG&E's electrical transmission lines. The fire resulted in extensive property damage and led to PG&E filing for bankruptcy in 2019 due to the liabilities
3. BP (British Petroleum)	Hurricane Ida disrupted offshore oil production in the Gulf of Mexico	2021	BP incurred estimated losses of around $1 billion due to production halts and infrastructure damage
4. Ford Motor Company	Flooding in key production areas in Southeast Asia	2022	The disruptions led to production delays and financial losses estimated at approximately $500 million
5. Turner Construction	Extreme weather events, including hurricanes and heavy rains	2021–2023	Project delays and increased costs resulted in estimated financial losses of over $200 million
6. CSX Corporation	Hurricane Ida and subsequent flooding	2021	The rail infrastructure damage led to operational disruptions and repair costs of approximately $300 million
7. Simon Property Group	Hurricanes and severe storms in the southeastern United States	2022	Property damage and temporary closures resulted in financial losses of around $100 million
8. Zurich Insurance Group	Increased frequency and severity of natural disasters	2021–2023	Higher insurance claims and payouts led to financial impacts of several billion dollars over these years

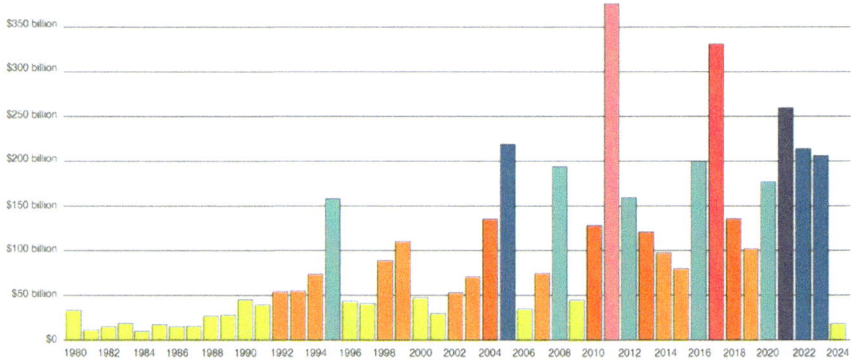

Fig. 4.2 Global disaster costs 1980–2024. *Source* EM-DAT, CRED/ UCLouvain (2024). *Note* Data includes recorded up to April 2024

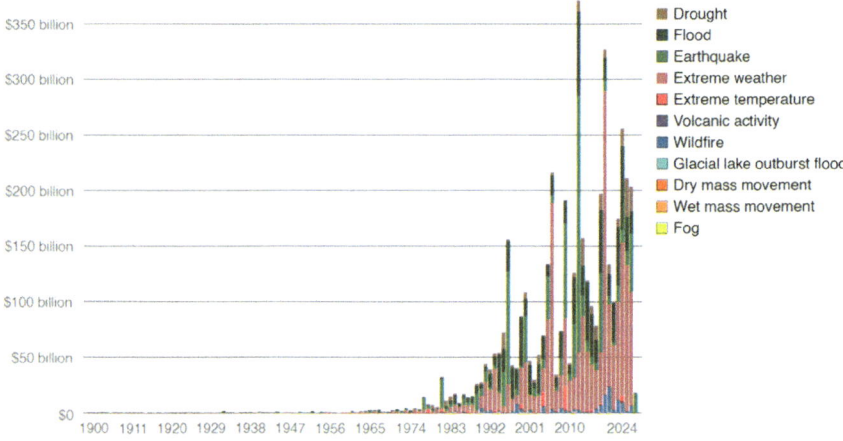

Fig. 4.3 Economic costs by disaster type 1900–2024 *Source* EM-DAT, CRED/ UCLouvain (2024). *Note* Data includes recorded up to April 2024

($360.2 billion, CPI-adjusted), severe storms ($485.2 billion, CPI-adjusted), and inland flooding ($200.2 billion, CPI-adjusted). Severe storms were the most frequent event type with 195 occurrences, followed by tropical cyclones with 62 occurrences and inland flooding with 44 occurrences. Tropical cyclones also caused the most fatalities, with 6,897 deaths, followed by drought/heatwave events with 4522 deaths and severe storms with 2,117 deaths.

4.2.4 Transition Risks

Transition risks related to climate change encompass policy and legal risks, technological risks, market risks, and reputational risks, all of which can significantly impact organizations depending on their ability to adapt and respond to evolving climate-related challenges. The following section examines each risk using examples.

4.2.4.1 Policy and Legal

Policy actions around climate change continue to evolve, generally falling into two categories: those that attempt to constrain activities contributing to climate change and those that promote adaptation to climate change. The risk and financial impact associated with policy changes depend on the nature and timing of these changes. As the value of loss and damage arising from climate change grows, litigation risk is likely to increase. This litigation may arise from organizations failing to mitigate climate impacts, failing to adapt to climate changes, or insufficiently disclosing material financial risks. Additionally, regulatory measures aimed at achieving climate targets, such as the goal of limiting global temperature rise to 2 °C above pre-industrial levels, set by the Paris Agreement to mitigate severe climate impacts, can increase credit costs due to their impact on the business models and performance of investees and borrowers. Changes in regulations in response to growing international concern regarding climate change also contribute to these risks (Bui & De Villiers, 2017). For example, the European Union's Green Deal aims to make Europe the first climate-neutral continent by 2050, significantly impacting industries reliant on fossil fuels. Compliance with these regulations can increase operational costs and require substantial investments in new technologies.

4.2.4.2 Technology

Technological improvements or innovations supporting the transition to a lower-carbon, energy-efficient economic system can significantly impact organizations. The displacement of old systems by new technologies can disrupt existing economic structures, resulting in "creative destruction" where winners and losers emerge. However, the timing of technology development and deployment is a key uncertainty in assessing technology risk (Lee & Geum, 2021; McHenry, 2013). For example, the development and adoption of electric vehicles (EVs) have disrupted the automotive industry, creating opportunities for companies specializing in EV technology while challenging traditional automakers to innovate or face decline.

4.2.4.3 Market

The effects of climate change on markets are varied and complex, with one major impact being shifts in supply and demand for certain commodities, products, and services as climate-related risks and opportunities are increasingly considered. Market risks are also influenced by changes in corporate performance and the supply-demand relationship for goods and services as markets become more decarbonized-oriented (Welton, 2018). The shift toward renewable energy sources like solar and wind has decreased demand for coal and oil, affecting the profitability and market value of companies in the fossil fuel sector while boosting the renewable energy market.

4.2.4.4 Reputation

Climate change is a potential source of reputational risk due to changing customer or community perceptions of an organization's contribution to or detraction from the transition to a lower-carbon economy (Agrawal & Cooper, 2015; Solana, 2020). For instance, if Amazon wants to appear green, it has to electrify its delivery trucks and use renewable energy in its data centers. Failing to implement these sustainable practices could result in consumer backlash, as well as competition from Walmart, which has local footprints in every major town in the US.

4.3 Climate Scenario Models Assess Risk into the Future

A requirement in the EU Sustainable Finance Disclosure Regulation (SFDR) mandates that climate risks be estimated in alignment with net-zero pathways. Scenario analysis is a useful tool used to evaluate the potential impacts of different future events and conditions on an organization, system, or environment. It involves creating various plausible scenarios, each representing different assumptions about key variables, to understand how these changes could affect outcomes. This method is often used in strategic planning, risk management, and policymaking to prepare for uncertainties and to develop robust strategies that can perform well under different future conditions.

Various climate stress tests conducted by central banks and scholars utilize scenario modeling (Cartellier, 2022). Climate stress testing has been developed to illuminate the financial system's exposure and vulnerability to climate-related risks. The ultimate goal is to evaluate the resilience of financial institutions to adverse climate-related scenarios and to support their role in financing the low-carbon transition.

Financial institutions consider the following time horizons in their future scenarios.

1. 1–5 years: Short-term analysis often focuses on immediate impacts and near-future changes, typically involving less uncertainty and more precise projections.
2. 5–10 years: Medium-term analysis covers a period when trends and patterns start to evolve and the impacts of ongoing changes become more visible.
3. 10–30 years: Long-term analysis spans a broader timeframe, capturing significant transformations and potential long-term effects of current actions.
4. 30 + years: Very long-term analysis considers distant future scenarios with high levels of uncertainty, which are often used for understanding the implications of large-scale trends and shifts.

The scenario models used the most in the banking and financial context are described below.

4.3.1 NGFS Scenarios

NGFS (Network for Greening the Financial System) is an international group of central banks and financial supervisors committed to promoting the integration of climate-related risks and opportunities into the financial system. The NGFS (2023) scenarios are designed to assess financial risks related to climate change. The NGFS key initiatives are developing climate-related stress tests for financial institutions to assess their resilience to climate risks **(See interview with expert Madison Condon)**, promoting the integration of climate-related factors into financial supervision practices, supporting the development of sustainable finance initiatives and products, and encouraging the disclosure of climate-related risks by financial institutions.

In Fig. 4.4, the two extreme scenarios are "Hot-House world," representing a future when no significant climate policies are implemented, leading to severe climate impacts, and "Disorderly Scenarios," describing futures when climate policies are implemented too late or inconsistently, causing economic and social disruptions. The scenario "Orderly" in the lower left quadrant assumes that climate policies are introduced early and both physical and transition risks are low. The upper right, "too little, too late" scenario, has the worst outcomes.

4.3.2 Representative Concentration Pathways

Representative Concentration Pathways (RCPs) are climate change scenarios developed to project future greenhouse gas concentrations. These pathways describe different potential climate futures based on varying levels of greenhouse gas emissions. The Intergovernmental Panel on Climate Change (IPCC) uses RCPs in its climate modeling and research (IPCC, 2023). Each RCP is labeled according to the

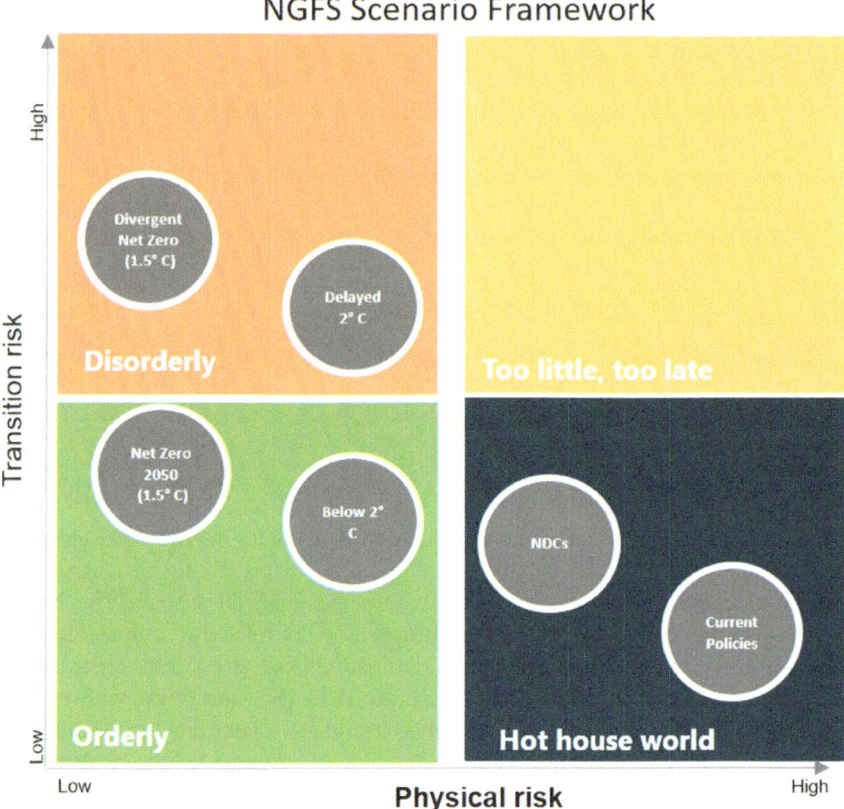

Fig. 4.4 The NGFS framework (2023) examines six scenarios defined by their levels of physical and transition risks. These risks are influenced by the degree of policy ambition, the timing and coordination of policies, and the implementation of technological measures

radiative forcing level (measured in watts per square meter) that it is expected to produce by the year 2100. The key RCP scenarios.

- RCP 1.9: This scenario aims to limit global warming to below 1.5 °C, aligning with the goals of the Paris Agreement. It requires significant reductions in greenhouse gas emissions and achieving negative emissions through carbon capture and sequestration technologies.
- RCP 2.6: Known as a very stringent pathway, this scenario requires CO_2 emissions to start declining by 2020 and achieve net zero by 2100. Methane emissions must be halved from 2020 levels, and sulfur dioxide emissions must be reduced to 10% of those from 1980 to 1990. This pathway is likely to keep global temperature rise below 2 °C by 2100.

- RCP 4.5: Another intermediate scenario, in which emissions peak around 2040 and then decline. It requires CO_2 emissions to start declining by approximately 2045 and methane emissions to stop increasing by 2050.
- RCP 8.5: Represents a high-emission scenario in which greenhouse gas emissions continue to rise throughout the twenty-first century. It is often used for worst-case scenario analysis and projects significant global warming by the end of the century.

In terms of physical and transitions risks, RCP scenarios can be applied to assess and manage risks. Higher RCP scenarios (such as RCP 8.5) predict severe climate impacts like increased frequency of extreme weather events, sea-level rise, and temperature increases. These physical risks can damage assets, disrupt supply chains, and impact economic activities. Banks and financial institutions need to assess and manage these risks to protect their investments and loan portfolios. Lower RCP scenarios (RCP 2.6 and RCP 1.9) require aggressive policy measures to reduce emissions, which can lead to significant economic shifts. Transition risks include policy changes, technological advancements, and market shifts toward low-carbon alternatives. Banks must anticipate these changes to manage their investment risks and opportunities.

4.3.3 Shared Socioeconomic Pathways

Shared Socioeconomic Pathways (SSPs) present IPCC models (Meinhausen et al., 2020) that describe different future societal developments, focusing on aspects such as economic growth, demographic changes, and technological advancement, shown in Fig. 4.5. Research using these models has proved useful in predicting well into the twenty-first century. The anticipated human-induced increase in atmospheric greenhouse gas levels throughout the twenty-first century far exceeds all observed variations from the past 2000 years (Meinhausen et al., 2020). The new SSP scenarios offer a wider range of future CO_2 concentrations, with the highest (SSP5-8.5) leading to greater concentrations than the previous RCP8.5 scenario, and the lowest (SSP1-1.9) projecting CO_2 (carbon dioxide) emissions dropping to 350 ppm (parts per million) by 2150.

Figure 4.5 shows the SSP models in terms of their adaptation and mitigation pathways. These pathways are used alongside RCPs to analyze how different socioeconomic conditions could impact climate change mitigation and adaptation efforts. SSPs in the financial and banking context, shown in Fig. 4.6, are described below.

- **Risk Management and Financial Planning**: Financial institutions use SSPs to assess both physical risks (e.g., impacts of climate change on infrastructure) and transition risks (e.g., policy shifts, technological changes) associated with different future scenarios. For instance, SSP1 (sustainability) assumes rapid technological development and strong global cooperation, leading to lower risks, while SSP3 (regional rivalry) foresees high conflict and low technological advancement, resulting in higher risks.

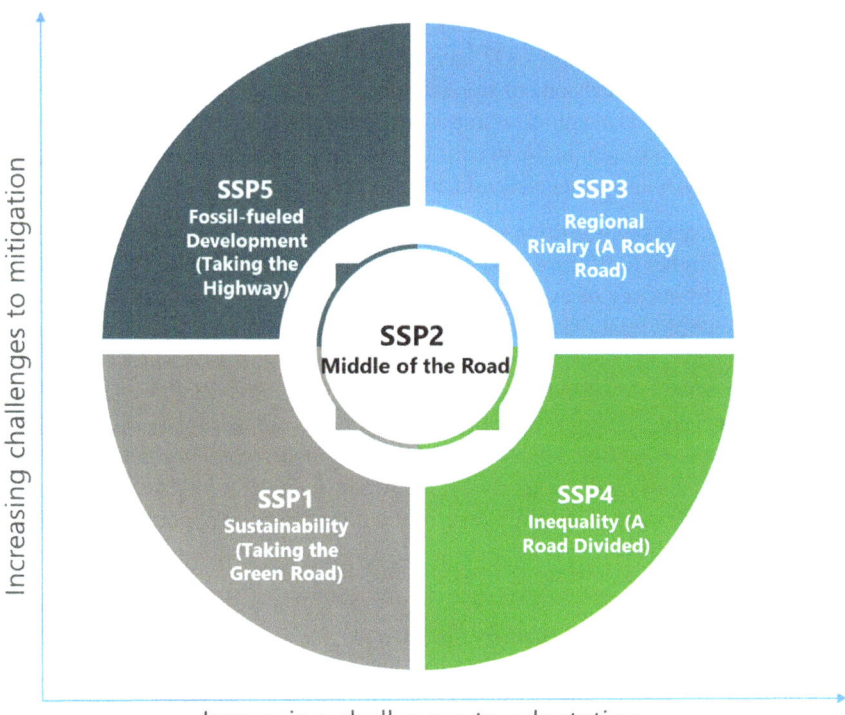

Fig. 4.5 Five different SSPs, each with a different focus marked in the figure. SSP2 shows the middle of the road pathways, continuing with current development patterns. (Figure adopted from https://climatedata.ca/resource)

- **Sustainable Investments**: SSPs help identify opportunities for sustainable investments, such as green and blue bonds and ESG investments. For example, under SSP1, there is a strong focus on green technologies and sustainability, encouraging investments in renewable energy and green bonds. Conversely, SSP3 may lead to higher investment risks in such sectors due to less global cooperation and slower technological progress.
- **Credit Risk and Lending in Different Sectors**: Different SSPs can impact various sectors differently in terms of credit risk and lending. Financial institutions analyze SSP scenarios to understand how sectors like agriculture, energy, and real estate might be affected by socioeconomic changes. This informs their lending practices and helps in managing credit risk in lending and loan portfolios.
- **Regulatory and Compliance**: Financial institutions must navigate changing regulatory landscapes influenced by SSPs. For instance, SSP1 aligns with strong climate policies and regulations, requiring banks to adapt their operations and reporting practices to comply with stricter environmental standards.
- **Scenario Analysis and Stress Testing**: Banks use SSPs for scenario analysis and stress testing to evaluate their resilience under different future conditions. This

4.3 Climate Scenario Models Assess Risk into the Future

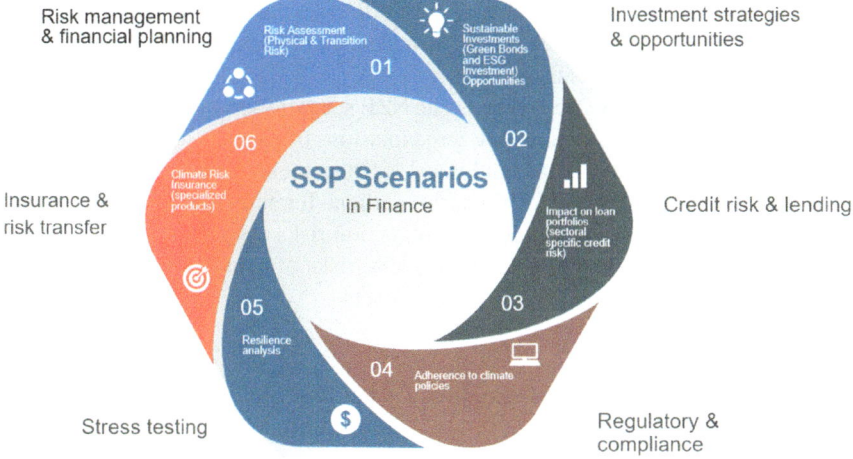

Fig. 4.6 SSP scenarios assist in a variety of ways including risk management and stress testing

helps in strategic planning and ensures that institutions are prepared for potential socioeconomic and environmental changes.

- **Insurance and Risk Transfer**: Insurance companies use SSPs to design insurance products that cater to varying levels of climate risk. For example, SSP5 (fossil-fueled development) might require more comprehensive coverage due to higher physical risks from climate impacts.

4.3.4 International Energy Agency (IEA) Scenarios

The International Energy Agency (IEA, 2023) develops various scenarios to model future energy markets, climate impacts, and policy outcomes. Some key IEA scenarios and their implications in the financial context are examined below.

- Stated Policies Scenario (STEPS): This scenario reflects current policy settings and measures announced by governments. It provides a baseline view of where the global energy system is heading under existing commitments. STEPS helps financial institutions understand the likely trajectory of energy markets and associated investment risks and opportunities. It highlights sectors that may face regulatory changes or shifts in consumer preferences.
- Sustainable Development Scenario (SDS): The SDS outlines a pathway to meet internationally agreed climate, air quality, and universal energy access goals. It aligns with the objectives of the Paris Agreement, aiming to keep global temperature rise well below 2 °C. This scenario underscores the need for significant

investments in renewable energy, energy efficiency, and low-carbon technologies. Banks and investors can use SDS to identify opportunities in green finance and sustainable investments.
- Net-Zero Emissions by 2050 (NZE): The NZE scenario sets out a roadmap for the global energy sector to achieve net-zero emissions by 2050. It includes a detailed analysis of the necessary technological advancements, policy measures, and investments required. The NZE scenario is crucial for assessing long-term investment strategies and understanding the transition risks associated with achieving net-zero emissions. It highlights the financial risks of continuing investments in fossil fuels and the potential for stranded assets.

Expert in Focus: Madison Condon
Madison Condon became an associate professor at Boston University School of Law in July 2020. She teaches courses in Environmental Law, Corporations, and a seminar on climate risk and financial institutions. Professor Condon is a recognized authority on climate change, financial risk, and regulation.

Her work has been featured in the top articles of the year across multiple fields, including environmental, corporate, and securities law. Her research has influenced rulemakings by the US Securities and Exchange Commission and the US Department of Labor. The President's Council of Advisors on Science and Technology has cited her critiques of financial models in their recommendations for managing extreme weather risk. In 2023, she joined the United Nations Principles of Responsible Investment Academic Network Advisory Committee.

Her scholarship is published in prestigious legal journals such as the UC Davis Law Review, Washington Law Review, and Utah Law Review. She also contributes to interdisciplinary publications like Finance & Society, NOMOS, Land Use Policy, and the Review of Environmental Economics and Policy. Her insights have been highlighted in media outlets including the New York Times, Bloomberg, NPR, Politico, The Atlantic, and The New Republic.

Expert Interview with Madison Condon

Right now, the way the SEC rules are structured is not very forward-looking when it comes to physical risks. Companies are mostly required to disclose substantial disaster-related impacts from the current year and the associated costs, without a requirement to project future risks. While I'm fortunate to be surrounded by people who think about these issues regularly, there's still no consensus on the best approach, and no one knows how companies should be handling this, either in the EU or the US.

In the EU, the disclosure regime is more prescriptive and forward-looking, but it seems overly broad. Companies are asked to assess and disclose every conceivable physical risk, such as soil fluctuations and glacier outbursts, without clear guidance on prioritization. This often leads to companies using extensive computing resources to analyze all their assets. The effectiveness of this approach remains to be seen, but as of now, it appears poorly designed.

A major issue is the lack of integration between different sectors of the government. For example, there should be more collaboration between economists in the US Treasury and climate impact scientists at NOAA. It was frustrating to see that the Federal Reserve's climate stress test did not include a single climate scientist, leading to basic errors like questioning the impact of hurricanes on New York under specific emission scenarios for 2050. I'm advocating for the US government to better incorporate scientific insights. While the EU does a somewhat better job integrating science, they too have not fully resolved the issue, and their risk scenarios are still incomplete.

European asset managers and institutional investors are more proactive about decarbonization, viewing it as part of their fiduciary duty. They understand the importance of internalizing externalities and acting as universal owners. In contrast, this mindset is less prevalent in the US, mainly seen in large public pension funds like CalPERS and the New York State Treasurer's fund. Interestingly, the leaders of CalPERS and CalSTRS are not necessarily driving the climate conversation but are reacting to pressure from the California legislature to divest from fossil fuels, which makes them more active on climate issues. This difference in attitude can be partly attributed to cultural factors, as Europeans have been more concerned about climate change for a longer time and are more willing to take action.

I believe Warren Buffett is not a positive influence on climate action. It was surprising to read his letter in the Financial Times, where he claimed that all utilities would eventually need government bailouts and ownership,

> *especially since just a year prior, he downplayed climate risks and criticized ESG reporting. This inconsistency is troubling because it highlights a broader disconnect that needs to be addressed. There needs to be political will and public opinion to bridge the gaps between our bankruptcy system, ESG disclosure system, and corporate governance system, which currently operate in isolation. It will be interesting to see how the politics of potential bailouts for these companies unfold and whether it will lead to meaningful reforms.*

Financial institutions use IEA scenarios to conduct climate risk assessments and stress tests, evaluating the resilience of their portfolios under different future energy and climate conditions. First, these scenarios guide investment strategies and decisions by highlighting sectors and technologies poised for growth or decline. For example, scenarios emphasizing renewable energy transitions can steer investments toward solar, wind, and battery storage technologies. Second, understanding IEA scenarios helps banks and financial institutions stay ahead of regulatory changes and align their operations with global climate goals. This is particularly relevant for compliance with frameworks like the Task Force on Climate-related Financial Disclosures (TCFD, 2021). Third, IEA scenarios identify emerging market opportunities in the energy transition, such as electric vehicles, hydrogen, and carbon capture and storage. Financial institutions can leverage these insights to develop new financial products and services that support sustainable development. Fourth, IEA scenarios help evaluate the potential effects of regulatory changes on industries and economic systems, emphasizing compliance and strategic adaptation.

To summarize, each model serves a unique purpose and is tailored to different aspects of scenario analysis, helping stakeholders understand and prepare for various future challenges and opportunities. The next section examines the models used in estimating economic impacts of risks that leverage the scenarios models.

4.4 Evaluating Physical Risk Hazard

Changes in climate change physical risks such as droughts, floods, and hurricanes are expected to vary widely across the globe, with existing hazards increasing in intensity in some regions and with other regions becoming subject to hazards not previously experienced. For example, scientific studies suggest that tropical cyclone rainfall rates and intensities are likely to increase due to climate change, and trends suggest that the locations at which cyclones reach maximum intensity are shifting poleward (Pointner & Ritzberger-Grünwald, 2019; Studholme et al., 2022). These changes, combined with the increasingly global nature of corporate operations and supply chains, may present significant variation in the intensity and range of physical risk exposures across capital markets in different regions.

4.4 Evaluating Physical Risk Hazard

Physical climate risk has become a major concern for governments, companies, and civil societies. There are both proprietary tools (e.g., Moody's ESG360, BlackRock Aladdin, Swiss Re CatNet, CLIMAFIN) and publicly available tools (e.g., the World Bank Climate Change Knowledge Portal, the World Resources Institute Aqueduct Water Risk Atlas) that aim to help their users understand and assess physical climate risks at a variety of spatial scales. Proprietary tools estimate risk at asset level and free tools at country or coarser spatial scale. Section 4.4.1 describes proprietary tools and 4.4.2 discusses some free tools. Section 4.4.3 operationalizes the hazard risk assessment model.

4.4.1 Proprietary Data Products Targeting Asset or Portfolio Climate Hazard Risks

MSCI's CVaR model helps investors understand the potential financial impacts of climate change on their portfolios.[1] The tool provides scenario analysis covering both physical risks (such as extreme weather events and long-term shifts in climate patterns) and transition risks (such as policy changes and technological advancements). MSCI's CVaR (MSCI, 2020) helps investors quantify the financial risks of climate change and integrate these considerations into their investment decision-making processes.

Moody's offers the ESG360 tool, which integrates environmental, social, and governance (ESG) factors into credit risk analysis.[2] This tool provides comprehensive data and analytics to assess the exposure of assets and portfolios to climate risks. Moody's climate risk products help financial institutions and investors evaluate how climate change might impact credit ratings and the overall risk profile of their investments.

Bloomberg's climate asset risk products provide detailed insights into the financial impacts of climate risks at the asset level.[3] Bloomberg's tools incorporate climate data into financial analysis and offer scenario analysis to project the potential impacts of various climate scenarios on investment portfolios. Bloomberg's solutions enable investors to assess and manage the risks associated with climate change and identify opportunities for sustainable investments.

CLIMAFIN helps institutional investors comply with climate-related reporting standards (TCFD, EU-NFRD, French Article 173) using evidence from leading scientific journals. The company team services include comprehensive climate risk

---

[1] https://www.msci.com/documents/1296102/16985724/MSCI-ClimateVaR-Introduction-Feb 2020.pdf.

[2] https://www.moodys.com/web/en/us/capabilities/climate-risk.html.

[3] https://www.bloomberg.com/professional/products/data/enterprise-catalog/esg/.

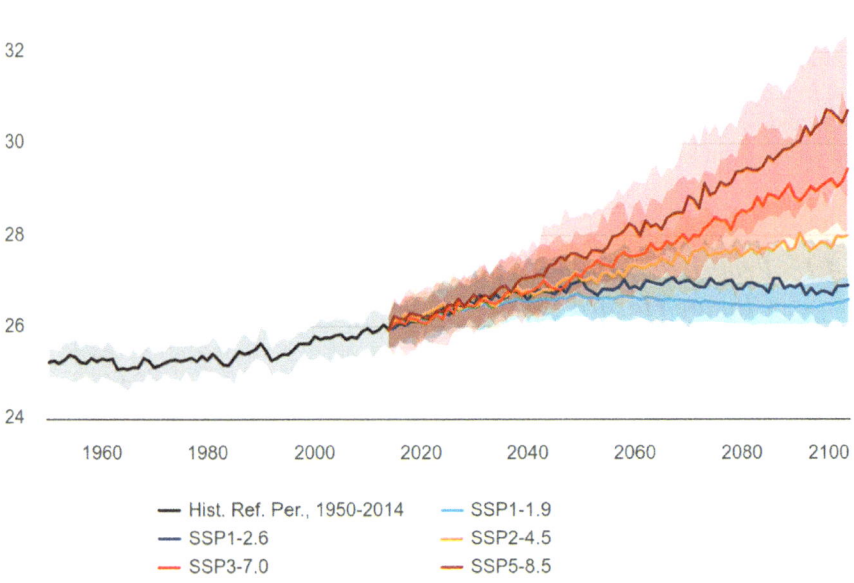

Fig. 4.7 Projected mean surface air temperature in Belize using multi-model ensemble predictions 1950–2100 (from World Bank Climate Portal)[5]

analytics and portfolio optimization across all asset classes and scenarios. Additionally, it assists financial institutions in incorporating climate risks into their internal models with tailored consulting and data access.[4]

4.4.2 Climate Knowledge Data Portals

World Bank's Climate Change Knowledge Portal (CCKP) provides global data on historical and future climate, vulnerabilities, and impacts at either country or watershed scale (World Bank, 2024). Figure 4.7 shows the projected average mean surface temperature for Belize, based on data of the reference period of 1995–2014. The multi-model ensemble pattern shows increases in Belize's temperature until the end of this century. The projected number of days with heat index above 41 °C also increases, resulting in economic and health impacts.

---

[4] https://climafin.com/#solution.
[5] https://climateknowledgeportal.worldbank.org/.

MIT's En-ROADS (Kapmeier et al., 2021; Rooney-Varga et al., 2020) provides a broad, interactive simulation of the global energy and climate system, highlighting the impact of different policies and interventions. The model includes interactions between resources, energy production, energy prices, the economy, and climate change. Operating at a global level, it makes broad assumptions about policy implementations and their impacts. For example, a scenario with moderate interventions assuming a diverse mix of energy sources, and a gradual increase in the use of renewables and new zero-carbon energy, predicts a temperature increase +2.6 °C (4.7°F) by 2100. In contrast, a scenario with a slower transition to renewable and zero-carbon energy, predicts a temperature increase +3.3 °C (6.0°F) by 2100. En-ROADS is designed for policymakers, educators, and stakeholders to explore the implications of various climate actions quickly and interactively. While En-ROADS offers useful interactive simulations of the global energy and climate system, it is not suitable for financial-focused metrics that can be applied to individual assets or portfolios, offering detailed insights into the financial impact of climate risks.[6]

4.4.3 Estimating Losses Due to Physical Risks

Quantifying physical climate risks is typically defined as a function of ***hazard, exposure, and vulnerability***, as shown in Fig. 4.8. The conceptual framework aims to explain the complex relationship between hazards, exposure, and vulnerability in specific geographic locations (Cutter, 2010, 2021). The framework emphasizes that the characteristics of a place significantly influence the community's risk to various hazards. The framework that was originally applied to analyze social exposure and vulnerability to risks can be applied to model risks to assets and financial portfolios.

For businesses, hazards may include natural disasters (e.g., floods, hurricanes, earthquakes), technological hazards (e.g., cyberattacks), and human-induced hazards (e.g., accidents, violence. Exposure, in a business context, refers to how much of a business's physical assets (e.g., buildings, equipment, inventory) and human resources (employees, customers) are at risk from identified hazards. For example, in agriculture or construction, the number of people exposed to a hazard (such as heat) is relevant variable. In contrast, for properties like hotels or other buildings along the coast, exposure to sea-level rise or hurricanes is a critical factor, along with the number of people at risk. Vulnerability pertains to the business's capacity to withstand, respond to, and recover from hazards. Factors influencing vulnerability can include the quality of the infrastructure (age and structure type), access to resources, staff training, and overall business continuity planning.

---

[6] https://en-roads.climateinteractive.org/scenario.html?v=24.7.0

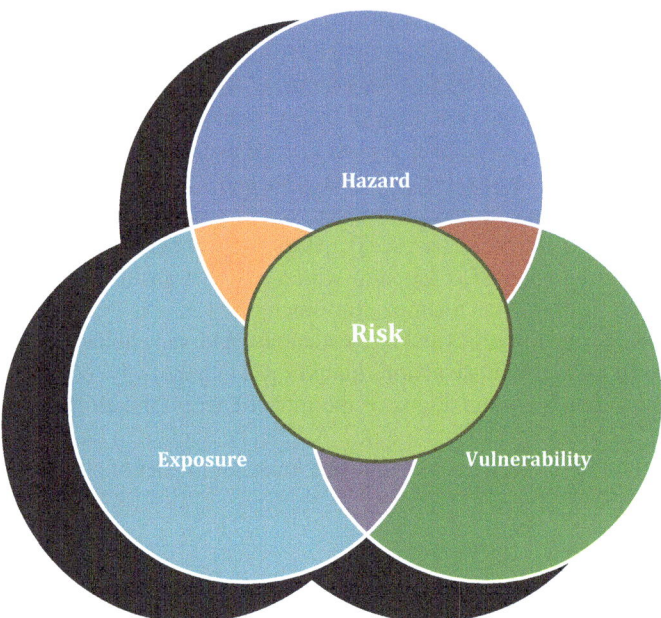

Fig. 4.8 Effective risk mitigation requires understanding and addressing all three components: reducing the hazard, minimizing exposure, and decreasing vulnerability

4.5 Operationalizing Asset-Level Risk

As discussed in Sect. 4.4, general climate risk assessment involves three key components: climate hazard, asset exposure, and asset vulnerability. The relationship between these three variables is nonlinear and neither additive nor multiplicative. Instead, it involves a complex interaction that is non-stationary and evolves over time. As sustainable Fintech strives to understand how assets will be impacted in a changing climate, risk modeling will become increasingly important both within and outside the industry. Therefore, it is crucial to communicate clearly and consistently about the approach to risk assessment, ensuring that the definition and understanding of risk are uniformly applied across the industry and beyond (Fig. 4.9).

Each of these components must be integrated, though the method of combining them can vary across data providers. A schematic framework of the methodology is shown in Fig. 4.8. Subsections 4.5.1 to 4.5.5 describe steps and rationale in the methodology while subsection 4.6 presents a case study with a dataset of actual assets.

4.5 Operationalizing Asset-Level Risk

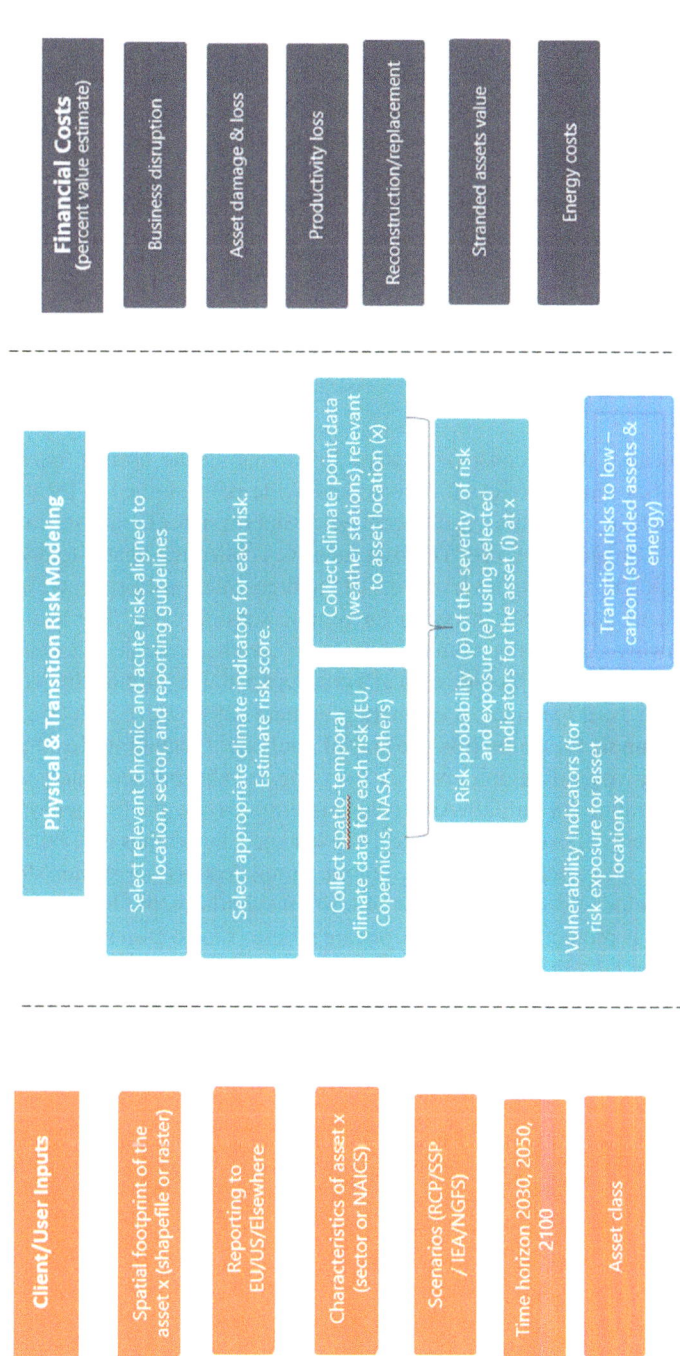

Fig. 4.9 The steps in operationalizing asset-level risk are shown in three panels. The panel on the left shows the client/user inputs into the process in terms of asset location and scenarios. The middle panel shows the physical and transition modeling and the left panel shows the financial costs in the calculation of overall risk to each asset

4.5.1 Asset-Related Customer Inputs

The first step in the process is for the client or user to input the spatial footprint of the asset (shapefile or raster) and the NAICS code or sector. A sector such as cement is different from the retail sector and so must be determined upfront. The address of the asset is then georeferenced to the map in the subsequent geospatial analysis. The client specifies the reporting requirements, such as EU's taxonomy, or climate scenarios. The time horizon for future scenarios 2030–2100 is also selected. The client can also specify further asset data on type and usage.

4.5.2 Evaluate Climate Hazard

In Fig. 4.8, the central panel consists of steps in evaluating the climate hazards impacting an asset or region. Relevant chronic and acute risks aligned to location, sector, and reporting guidelines are considered to select appropriate climate indicators for each risk and estimate risk score. This step involves collecting spatio-temporal climate data for each risk (using a variety of data sources such as European Space Agency's Copernicus and NASA missions for remote sensing data). The analysis can sometimes involve collecting climate data from weather stations relevant to asset location. Climate models provide data at a coarser spatial resolution that could be downscaled to an asset location for estimating climate risks.

What is the rationale for doing this geospatial analysis? Evaluating the climate hazards impacting an asset or region involves assessing each hazard separately such as changes in temperatures or rainfall. As global temperatures rise, the frequency and intensity of these events are subject to change. For instance, hurricanes may become more powerful due to warmer sea surface temperatures, leading to greater storm surges and higher wind speeds (Knutson et al., 2020). Similarly, the likelihood of extreme heat events is projected to increase, posing severe risks to human health and infrastructure (Masson-Delmotte et al., 2021). Thus, assessing the hazard involves understanding the changing patterns of these extreme events and their potential impact on specific geographical areas.

The calculation of hazard risks relies on climate data, primarily sourced from climate models. Climate datasets for the US are available at a county scale and station scale. For example, in the US, Federal Emergency Management Agency (FEMA) National Risk Index primarily focuses on immediate disaster response, preparedness, and recovery within the United States. The Risk Index utilizes available source data for natural hazard and community risk factors to define a baseline risk measurement for each county and census tract in the country.[7]

FEMA assesses risks to support emergency management and planning, often with a shorter-term perspective. Figure 4.10 has a map of US counties whose risks across sixteen hazards are aggregated using probability of the severity of the hazard

---

[7] https://hazards.fema.gov/nri/map.

using the FEMA guidelines. California, Florida, and Gulf coast counties are at a higher risk while those in the Dakotas, Maine, and Vermont have very low risk. Interested readers may learn more about FEMA's risk index methodology incorporating expected annual loss, social vulnerability, and community resilience. Expected Annual Loss measures the potential economic impact of natural hazards on a community's infrastructure, including buildings, agriculture, and population. It represents the average annual financial loss expected due to natural hazards. Social Vulnerability assesses the susceptibility of social groups within a community to harm from natural hazards. It takes into account the capacity of individuals and groups to prepare for, respond to, and recover from disasters.

Community Resilience measures the ability of a community to withstand and recover from natural hazards. It considers the strengths and resources available within the community to manage and mitigate risks in the US.

As discussed in Sect. 4.3, the European Union Commission Delegated Regulation (EU) 2021/2139, which is part of the Taxonomy Regulation, classifies climate-related hazards into acute and chronic categories to help identify and manage the four categories of climate risks associated with climate change (See Table 4.3). They are temperature, wind, water, and solid mass-related risks. It is therefore important to use this scale while reporting in EU.

Assessing risks at the asset level allows for a more detailed and accurate identification of vulnerabilities and potential financial impacts. This granular approach enables companies to implement targeted risk management strategies and adaptation measures, enhancing their resilience to climate change (Linnenluecke & Griffiths, 2012). Asset-level risk assessment provides investors with more precise information on the exposure of specific assets to physical and transitional risks. This information is essential for making informed investment decisions, aligning portfolios with sustainability goals, and mitigating potential financial losses (Caldecott et al., 2016). With increasing regulatory requirements on climate-related financial disclosures, asset-level assessments ensure compliance with frameworks such as the Task Force on Climate-related Financial Disclosures (TCFD).

Accurate risk assessments help companies meet these requirements and provide transparency to stakeholders (TCFD, 2021). Understanding the specific impacts of physical and transitional risks at the asset level allows companies to integrate climate risk into their corporate strategy. This proactive approach enhances long-term resilience and ensures sustainable growth (Weinhofer & Busch, 2013). Quantifying physical and transitional risks at the asset level provides a clearer picture of the potential economic and financial implications for companies, by identifying which assets are at risk for different hazards. This understanding is crucial for valuing assets accurately and for planning future capital expenditures and operational adjustments.

4.5.2.1 Evaluate Climate Hazard

The next step is calculating the risk probability based on severity of risk exposure for the asset using the selected climate indicators. Depending on the client's needs,

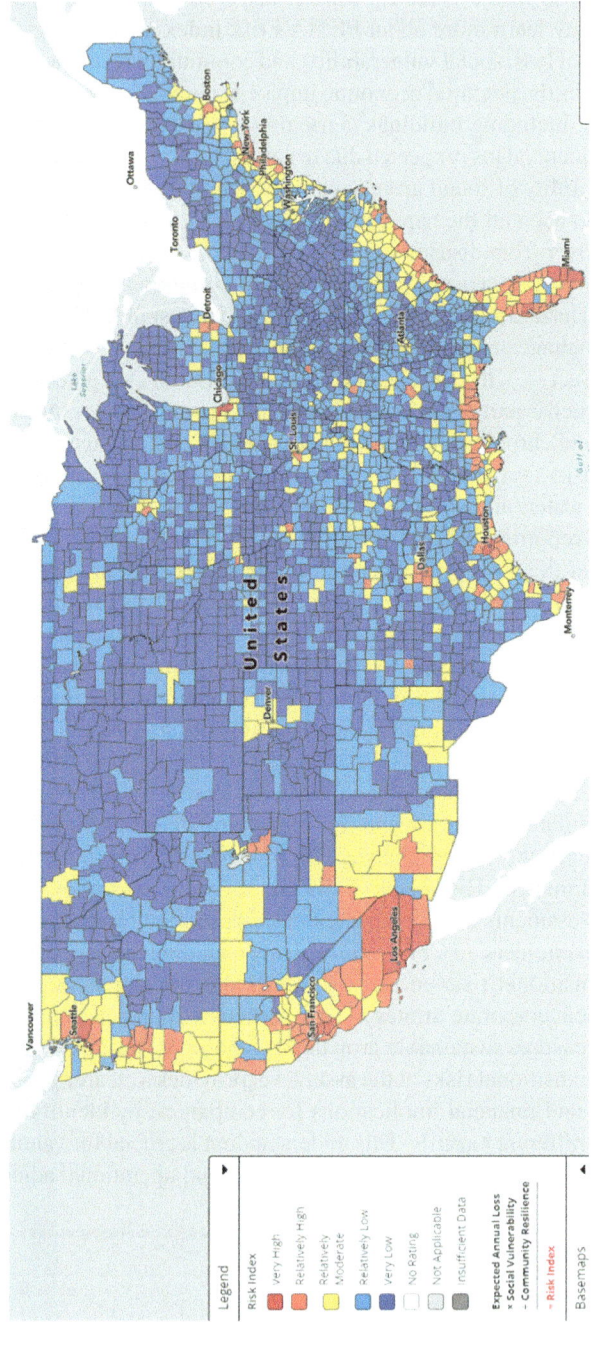

Fig. 4.10 Map of US counties showing risks across sixteen hazards using methodology described in the FEMA National Risk Index. Areas in red have very high risks

determining the vulnerability indicators that affect the asset's exposure to risk can be incorporated in the analysis.

Using climate data to determine climate hazards involves identifying the most relevant and priority climate hazards based on the asset's vulnerability. For instance, heatwaves would be very material for the construction sector but less so for non-material services. Natural hazard metrics are derived from raw climate data and are used to assess the frequency and intensity of climate hazards at the asset's location to determine the asset's exposure. For each hazard and sector, hazard metrics can be identified and, depending on data availability, can be specific to a sector/project or more generic. Examples of relevant sector-specific metrics have been compiled by projects like ClimINVEST (Gallo & Lepousez, 2020) and in prior scientific publications. Following is a partial list of such hazard metrics in agriculture, energy, and real estate.

1. Agriculture: Temperature extremes impact crops differently. The number of days with temperatures above 30 °C can impact crop yields and livestock health. The percent impact (loss of income) can be measured using the threshold temperature. Similarly, annual precipitation levels and seasonal variability are important in risk estimation. Changes in rainfall can impact water availability for irrigation and crop growth.
2. Energy: The number of cooling degree days above or below a standard temperature for the region indicates increased energy demand for air conditioning. Similarly, average annual wind speed is essential for the performance and planning of wind energy projects.
3. Real Estate: Flood Risk, which is measured using the metric flood return period (e.g., 1-in-100 year flood), is important for assessing the risk of property damage and insurance costs. Sea-level rise, which is measured by the metric projected increase in sea level by 2050 and 2100, is critical for coastal infrastructure and transportation networks.

4.5.2.2 Climate Indicators

The next step is to estimate risk exposure score based on the selection of appropriate climate indicators or metrics for each risk from the prior step. For example, increasing temperature can be measured as temperature variability, which refers to the fluctuations or changes in temperature over a specific time period in the location of the asset.

For locations outside the US and EU, climate indicators or metrics have been computed and are available on different data portals. Geospatial data from satellites like GOES (Geostationary Operational Environmental Satellites) or Copernicus are used to derive climate data. Such data may be at a coarse scale 0.25-degree resolution (~27.75 km), and can be downscaled to the asset location using nearby weather stations leveraging scientific knowledge.

Indicators can be asset/company-specific, sector-specific, or more generic. The more specific the indicators are, the more accurately they will describe the exposure of the asset. However, generic and sectoral indicators are usually more available on data portals, whereas asset-specific indicators might have to be defined through a co-construction process with sectoral experts or by downscaling using proximal weather station data. Weather stations (in any region) record data including daily maximum and minimum temperature, rainfall, wind, and relative humidity. Climate data can also be supplemented with local, contextual data (land use, specific aggravating factors) to capture climate-related hazards such as floods, landslides, coastal erosion, and biodiversity loss. The second step involving downscaling may often be beyond the scope of an investor's climate risk assessment.

There are well-established schemes for classifying each type of risk. For example, hurricane risks are measured using the Saffir-Simpson hurricane wind scale, drought risks using the Palmer drought severity index, and the standardized precipitation index. The fire weather index assesses fire danger based on weather conditions such as temperature, humidity, wind speed, and precipitation.

Climate indicators or metrics are provided and published online. Many indicators have been computed and are available on different data portals such as the Copernicus Climate Data Store. For example, temperature indicators include the following recorded at weather stations or estimated using scenarios.

- Maximum temperature: The highest temperature recorded during a specific period (e.g., daily, monthly, yearly).
- Minimum temperature: The lowest temperature recorded during a specific period.
- Average temperature: The mean temperature over a specified period.
- Number of heating degree days: Days when the temperature is below a certain threshold, indicating the need for heating.
- Number of cooling degree days: Days when the temperature is above a certain threshold, indicating the need for cooling.

4.5.3 Evaluate Exposure to Hazard

Evaluating exposure involves assessing the extent to which people, assets, or economic activities are exposed to identified climate hazards. This refers to the specific information about the asset including its location and financial value. It is essential to select proxies that accurately reflect the physical locations of the actual activities, particularly for companies. For example, in the pharmaceutical industry, the location of headquarters may not align with the locations of factories or markets where physical climate impacts are more likely to occur.

Exposure refers to the extent to which an asset is subject to a particular climate hazard. This is predominantly determined by the asset's geographical location. For example, coastal regions are more exposed to hurricanes and sea-level rise, while inland areas might face higher risks of heat waves or droughts (Oppenheimer et al., 2019). Accurate mapping of these hazards and identifying the specific locations of assets enable a detailed assessment of exposure. Tools such as Geographic Information Systems (GIS) and climate models are often employed to visualize and quantify exposure levels (Cutter, 2010).

For a business asset, exposure may be measured in terms of physical structures and infrastructure that may be impacted. Key aspects of this exposure involve various characteristics of the particular asset, which are essential to understand in order to accurately model the interactions between the hazard and vulnerability. Examples of these characteristics include method of construction, materials used, roof type and geometry, and deck construction and material. These building attributes are crucial components of exposure, providing a more comprehensive understanding of the risk, which allows for a more holistic and accurate risk modeling.

In case asset-level data are not available, sector or region wide estimates are often used. For example, for bond investments, economic activity impacts are measured by examining the businesses and economic operations affected by the hazard.

4.5.4 Evaluate Vulnerability to Hazard

Assessing vulnerability is often more complex since it is defined as the susceptibility or damageability of an asset to a given intensity of the hazard. Assessing this involves understanding how a climate event may impact an asset or system based on its specific characteristics, dependencies, and adaptive capacity. The vulnerability of an asset is influenced by various factors including its type, use, and physical properties. Buildings and infrastructure can vary widely in their susceptibility to damage from extreme weather events. For example, older buildings constructed with less resilient materials may be more vulnerable to damage from hurricanes compared to newer buildings designed to withstand high winds and flooding (Cutter, 2010). Additionally, the function of the asset—whether it is used for residential, commercial, or office purposes—also determines its vulnerability. Commercial buildings with critical operations might require more robust protection measures compared to residential buildings (Birkmann et al., 2013).

There is currently no established equation or catalog of impacts that can be used reliably across sectors to translate climate indicators into physical impact. Calculations, when they exist, are sector-specific; for example, the impacts of increasing temperature on crop yields have been calculated for some crops. These links between climate data and physical impacts are called impact functions or damage functions. The use of universal impact functions (e.g., a function linking temperature rise to the evolution of global GDP) is to be avoided. In theory, the physical impact of each climate hazard would be calculated for each asset. In practice, this quickly becomes too complex and unmanageable for investors at the portfolio level.

Vulnerability affects various parts of the value chain and financial aspects, such as capital and operational expenditures, and revenues. Specific thresholds, like temperature limits for winter tourism or maximum temperatures tolerated by systems, also play a role. For businesses, vulnerability depends on physical asset specifics (e.g., building materials, design), dependencies (e.g., water consumption), value chain links, and adaptive capacity. Comprehensive risk assessments must consider these factors to provide accurate evaluations. Large-scale analyses that ignore asset-level sensitivity or adaptive capacity may offer broad estimates but miss specific impacts. The detail and nature of a climate risk assessment can vary based on available information on impacts and vulnerabilities. There are different types of vulnerability:

- Physiological: Impact on human health and productivity, such as the percentage reduction in labor productivity at different temperatures relevant to coffee or palm oil cultivation. Studies have shown that labor productivity can decrease substantially as temperatures rise (Kenny et al., 2020). For example, at temperatures above 25–30 °C, labor productivity can decline due to increased fatigue and health risks. Turner Construction, like many other companies in temperature-sensitive industries, must pay close attention to the risks posed by rising temperatures. By understanding and mitigating the impacts of heat on labor productivity and worker health, Turner Construction[8] can ensure the safety of its workforce, maintain productivity, and manage operational costs effectively. This proactive approach is crucial for sustaining long-term success and resilience in the face of climate change.
- Ecological: Impact on ecosystems, such as the percentage reduction in crop yields at different temperatures. Research indicates climate change could impact the yields of maize (corn) and wheat by 2030 under a scenario of high greenhouse gas emissions. Projections indicate maize yields may decrease by 24%, while wheat yields might increase by approximately 17% (Jägermeyr et al. 2021), and reduction in agricultural total factor productivity based on modeled estimates particularly in Africa, Latin America, and the Caribbean (Ortiz-Bobea et al., 2021). As a leading global agribusiness, Archer Daniels Midland Company (ADM) must pay close attention to these facets of climate risk for several reasons including reduction in its supply, disruptions in the supply chain of grains, sourcing strategies and potential losses.
- Physical: Damage to infrastructure, such as the percentage of capital stock affected at specific flooding levels, is a critical factor in assessing exposure. Ford motor company has faced many flood-related damages and losses. In its TSFD disclosures (2023) report it notes that Winter Storm Uri in 2021 caused significant disruption to supplier facilities due to ice and subfreezing temperatures, leading to widespread power outages. Over 500 different parts and dozens of suppliers were affected, impacting most of Ford's North American assembly plants, including those in Kentucky, Michigan, Missouri, Canada, and Mexico. It notes

---

[8] https://www.turnerconstruction.com/insights/turner-studying-effects-of-rising-temperatures-on-construction-workers.

the following: Heavy precipitation (rain, hail, snow/ice); Risk Type: Acute Physical; Time Horizon: Short-term; Magnitude of Impact: Medium; Primary Potential Financial Impact: Decreased revenues due to reduced production capacity; Likelihood: About as likely as not.[9]

Ford motor company has this statement in a recent 10K filing December 31, 2023: "*Given the worldwide scope of our supply chain and operations, we and our suppliers face a risk of disruption or operating inefficiencies that may increase costs due to the adverse physical effects of climate change, which are predicted to increase the frequency and severity of weather and other natural events, e.g., wildfires, extended droughts, and extreme temperatures. In addition, in the event a weather-related event, strike, international conflict, or other occurrence limits the ability of freight carriers to deliver components and other materials from suppliers to us or logistics providers to transport our vehicles for an extended period of time, it may increase our costs and delay or otherwise impact both our production operations and customers' ability to receive our vehicles.*"[10] This suggests that Ford is acknowledging the role of climate risks in its operations, although no quantitative loss values are provided for such disruptions.

Quantitative risk assessment provides numerical results on expected physical and financial impacts. Qualitative approach utilizes rating or scale-based methods (e.g., high-medium–low) to understand asset vulnerability and estimate climate risk when detailed quantitative data are unavailable. Understanding vulnerability helps to quantify the extent of damage or impact that exposed entities might suffer due to climate hazards. For example, the decrease in worker productivity with increasing temperatures is an example of physiological vulnerability. This information is critical for developing effective mitigation and adaptation strategies.

To summarize, a comprehensive asset-level climate physical risk assessment necessitates a thorough understanding of hazard, exposure, and vulnerability. By integrating data on the changing nature of extreme weather events, the specific location of assets, and the unique characteristics of each asset, it is possible to develop effective strategies to mitigate risks and enhance resilience against climate change impacts, as examined in the next section.

4.5.5 *Evaluate Direct Impacts in Absence of Adaptation*

This step assesses the immediate impact of climate change on socioeconomic systems if no adaptation measures are taken. It assumes that exposure to hazards increases in line with historical trends and that vulnerability remains unchanged. The direct impacts are calculated as:

---

[9] https://corporate.ford.com/content/dam/corporate/us/en-us/documents/reports/2023-climate-change-report.pdf

[10] https://www.sec.gov/Archives/edgar/data/37996/000003799624000009/f-20231231.htm

$$\Sigma(p(s) \cdot E(s) \cdot V(s)) \tag{4.1}$$

where **p(s) is the probability of the hazard, E(s) is the exposure, and V(s) is the vulnerability**.

There are multiple perspectives on vulnerability. Fixing asset vulnerability is a critical component of climate adaptation, which involves making assets more resilient to the impacts of climate change. This process can include a range of strategies such as enhancing building designs, integrating sustainable technologies, and improving the overall robustness of infrastructure. The MIT-En-ROADS application demonstrates how various adaptation strategies in a country can reduce global emissions (see Sect. 4.4.2). The difference in outcomes before and after adaptation defines the transition risk and path to net zero for assets and companies.

Social vulnerability can be assessed using census data in the US, while asset or business vulnerability is measured differently. The Social Vulnerability Index (SVI) identifies census tracts or counties that are most socially vulnerable to disasters. The SVI uses US Census data to determine the social vulnerability of every county and tract, based on 15 social factors, including poverty, lack of vehicle access, and crowded housing (Flanagan et al., 2011). The SVI plays a crucial role in hazard risk modeling by providing a comprehensive understanding of how different aspects of society, measured by UN SDGS (Sustainable Development Goals), are affected by hazards (Depietri, 2020; Hagenlocher et al., 2018).

Broad social vulnerability is integral to hazard risk modeling as it provides insights into how different socioeconomic systems are affected by hazards. By considering factors such as livability, food systems, physical assets, infrastructure services, and natural capital, models can better predict impacts and guide effective mitigation and adaptation strategies for a county as a whole. This holistic approach ensures that risk assessments are comprehensive, inclusive, and capable of informing policies that protect both people and the environment. This broad perspective is also pertinent in assessing asset risks since the broader social milieu impacts the asset's vulnerability.

4.5.6 Transition Risks via Scenario Modeling

The next step is to assess transitional risks assessed using scenario models to estimate the potential financial impacts on assets, portfolios, and overall business operations. Regulators around the world are increasingly requiring financial institutions and companies to assess and disclose their exposure to climate risks, including transitional risks. Scenario analysis is a key tool in this process. These scenario models typically include climate scenarios exploring different pathways for global temperature increases, typically aligning with targets such as the Paris Agreement (e.g., 1.5 °C or 2 °C warming scenarios). The scenario models predict until 2100. Other types of scenarios, described below, are adopted if the company adopts a specific regulatory framework.

Policy scenarios help model the impact of various policy responses to climate change, such as the introduction of carbon taxes, subsidies for renewable energy, and other regulatory measures. Technology scenarios consider the impact of technological advancements and the adoption rates of low-carbon technologies. Economic scenarios assess the broader economic impacts of climate change and the transition to a low-carbon economy, including shifts in energy prices, changes in trade patterns, and impacts on different sectors.

The next step in the analysis involves comparing across scenarios described in Sect. 4.3. SSP or RCP scenarios are used for assets, while banks may prefer NGFS and energy companies may prefer IEA scenarios (O'Neill et al., 2017; Van Vuuren et al., 2011). By comparing these scenarios, it is possible to identify how different assumptions about future socioeconomic and environmental conditions can affect asset vulnerability and risk profiles (IEA 2020; NGFS 2020). For example, an asset might face higher risks under an RCP8.5 scenario due to increased frequency and severity of extreme weather events compared to an RCP2.6 scenario. Similarly, financial institutions can use NGFS scenarios to understand the potential impact of transition risks, such as policy changes and market shifts, toward a low-carbon economy.

Integrating the results from these scenario comparisons enables a more nuanced understanding of climate risks. This approach supports the development of targeted adaptation and mitigation strategies, ensuring that stakeholders across different sectors can make informed decisions to enhance resilience and sustainability. For instance, energy companies can align their strategic planning with IEA scenarios to optimize investments in renewable energy technologies, while banks can adjust their risk management frameworks based on NGFS scenario outcomes.

4.6 A Case Study Using Evaluation of Physical Risks at Asset Level

This case study illustrates the data and methodology for assessing the financial impact of physical climate risks at the asset level of companies. The objective is to highlight the data used for the analysis and the example outputs that are formulated through the work.

Based on the disaster risk described in Sect. 4.5, an asset's expected annual losses due to physical risks are estimated using hazard probability and magnitude in the region and asset exposure to a specific risk based on location and vulnerability (geography, asset building, use and structural components). Data and methodology include a mix of geospatial data including satellite data (Landsat, Sentinel, NOAA, Copernicus), publicly available databases (World Bank, UN, World Resource Institute), and machine learning (Random Forest and Support Vector Machine) and AI algorithms for the asset-loss-modeling.

Recording Asset Data in Geospatial Database: For a proper analysis of the many chronic and acute physical risks, a geospatial database or geodatabase needs to be designed, in which assets form individual records. Location-specific physical risks and vulnerabilities to these risks specific to the asset (based on North American Industry Classification System or NAICS code) are estimated or scored for each asset and recorded as columns in the geodatabase. Table 4.4 shows the assets that have addresses located as latitudes and longitudes; relevant NAICS codes are noted. The client may specify the regulatory framework and future climate scenarios, timelines, and net-zero goals for the transition phase.

Spatialization of the Asset. The first step in the process is the spatialization of the property boundaries of each asset either as a point (latitude, longitude, and elevation) or a polygon (vector data described in Chapter 5) on a map. Other attributes including distance or proximity to seacoast, rivers, roads, and forests and elevation, if deemed relevant, are derived from GIS operations and noted in the database. These may be relevant to the site or sector or NAICS risks.

Select Acute and Chronic Asset-Specific Risks. The second step is to select acute or chronic hazards at each asset location, relevant to the location or sector (NAICS code) or reporting framework. The choices of hazards relevant to the US, as listed by the Federal Emergency Management Agency (Zuzak et al., 2022), are utilized to estimate aggregate risks in 2023 for each asset location. Figure 4.11 shows the map of spatialized assets with NAICS codes and counties.

Impact Functions and Vulnerability

Published sector and regional values in the context of NAICS codes and regions in the US allow derivation of the following insights, the loss values of which then can be attributed to each asset. Annual losses in California for NAICS 488 (Support Activities for Transportation) and 481 (Air Transportation) are estimated as very high annual loss, the highest in the nation (in year 2023). Similarly, NAICS code 336,111 (Automobile Manufacturing) in Florida is very high. Any physical damage impacting building, agriculture, or other infrastructure in California, Florida, New York, and Massachusetts has associated costs that are high compared to those in some counties of Montana, Wyoming, and Northern Texas. NAICS 221,112 (Fossil Fuel Electric Power Generation) in Iowa and Indiana may have more property damage and disruption to business when impacted by physical risks. Overall losses are estimated at the sector and zip code level for the purpose of the case study.

In this case study, GenAI is utilized to derive insights on intensity in the NAICS sectors. It might be useful to derive similar AI-based insights based on training on major industry standards (for example, IEA Aviation, Carbon Disclosure Project), sustainability reports that mention intensities (Deutsche Telekom Annual Report), and leaders in a sector (such as Unilever in the food packaging or GM in the auto category).

4.6 A Case Study Using Evaluation of Physical Risks at Asset Level

Table 4.4 List of NAICS codes and relative risks for regions marked

NAICS_Code	Description	State	County	Final_Risk_Rating
481	Air Transportation headquarters	Georgia	Fulton	Relatively Moderate
488	Support Activities for Transportation	Georgia	Clayton	Relatively Moderate
481	Air Transportation	Minnesota	Hennepin	Relatively High
492,110	Couriers and Express Delivery Services	Tennessee	Shelby	Relatively High
492,110	Couriers and Express Delivery Services	Indiana	Marion	Relatively Moderate
492,110	Couriers and Express Delivery Services	Texas	Dallas	Relatively High
336,212	Truck Trailer Manufacturing	Kentucky	Jefferson	Relatively High
336,111	Automobile Manufacturing	Missouri	Clay	Relatively Moderate
336,111	Automobile Manufacturing	Kentucky	Scott	Relatively Low
811,121	Automotive Body, Paint, and Interior Repair and Maintenance	California	Los Angeles	Very High
221,112	Fossil Fuel Electric Power Generation	North Carolina	Person	Very Low
221,112	Fossil Fuel Electric Power Generation	Indiana	Gibson	Relatively Low
221,112	Fossil Fuel Electric Power Generation	North Carolina	Gaston	Relatively Low
221,112	Fossil Fuel Electric Power Generation	California	San Bernardino	Very High
221,122	Electric Power Distribution	California	San Bernardino	Very High
221	Utilities	California	Los Angeles	Very High
221,112	Fossil Fuel Electric Power Generation	California	Contra Costa	Very High
333,415	Air-Conditioning and Warm Air Heating Equipment	Indiana	Marion	Relatively Moderate
333,415	Air-Conditioning and Warm Air Heating Equipment	Tennessee	Shelby	Relatively High
333,999	All Other Miscellaneous General Purpose Machinery	Ohio	Cuyahoga	Relatively Moderate

(continued)

Table 4.4 (continued)

NAICS_Code	Description	State	County	Final_Risk_Rating
518,210	Data Processing, Hosting, and Related Services	Kentucky	Jefferson	Relatively High
333,618	Other Engine Equipment Manufacturing	North Carolina	Durham	Relatively Moderate
334,510	Electromedical and Electrotherapeutic Apparatus Manufacturing	Wisconsin	Milwaukee	Relatively Moderate
423,830	Industrial Machinery and Equipment Merchant Wholesalers	Florida	Polk	Relatively High
493,110	General Warehousing and Storage	Virginia	Warren	Very Low
311	Food Manufacturing	Texas	McLennan	Relatively Moderate
326,122	Plastics Pipe and Pipe Fitting Manufacturing	Texas	Harris	Very High
31–33	Manufacturing	Minnesota	Mower	Relatively Low
311,920	Coffee and Tea Manufacturing	Iowa	Marion	Very Low
311,821	Cookie and Cracker Manufacturing	Colorado	Boulder	Relatively Moderate
311,821	Cookie and Cracker Manufacturing	Louisiana	Orleans	Relatively High

4.6 A Case Study Using Evaluation of Physical Risks at Asset Level 177

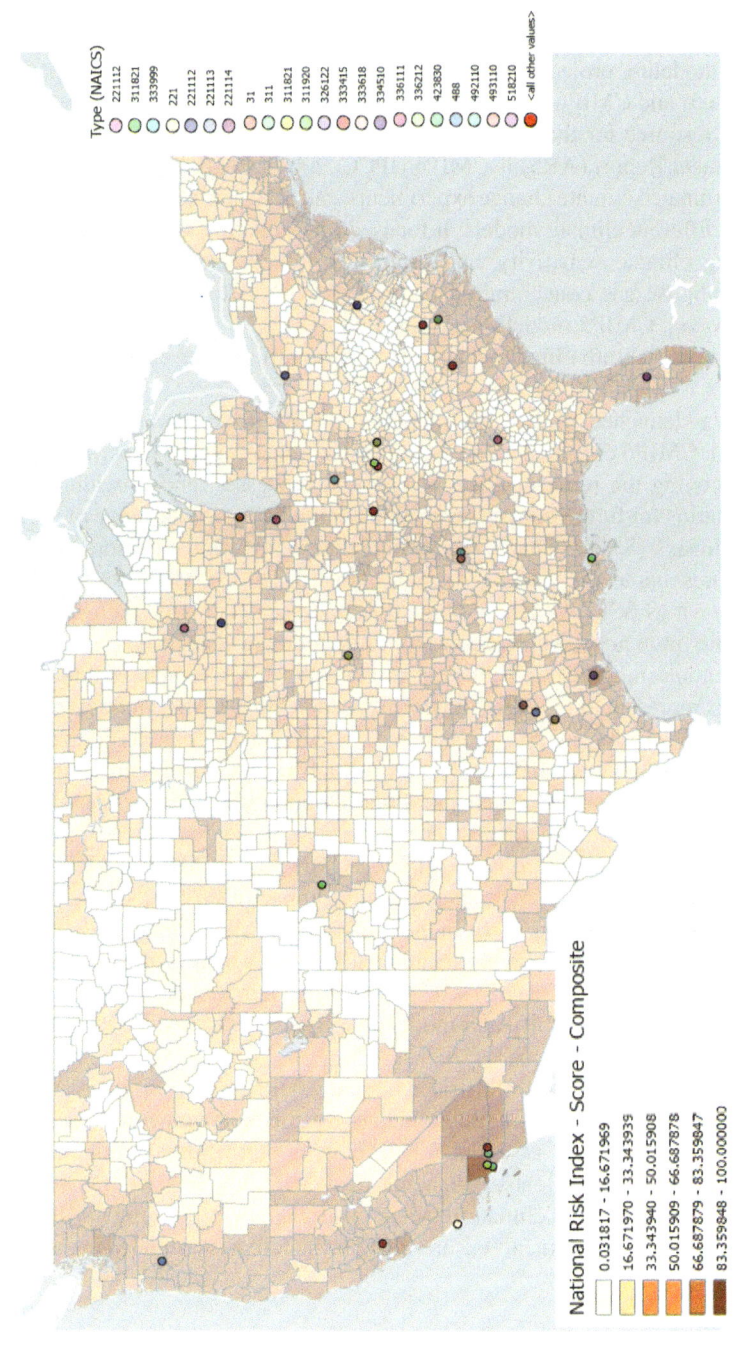

Fig. 4.11 Asset locations with NAICS codes on a map of National Risk Index (2023)

Transition Risks via Scenario Modeling

Certain future-looking variables can be selected using models that have been previously run. The World Climate Research Programme (WCRP) coordinated extensive climate modeling projects known as CMIP5 (Coupled Model Intercomparison Project Phase 5) and CMIP6 (Coupled Model Intercomparison Project Phase 6).[11]

A critical resource for the Intergovernmental Panel on Climate Change (IPCC) Fifth Assessment Report (AR5) is CMIP5 (IPCC, 2007). CMIP5 provided a framework for coordinated climate change experiments, called scenarios, enabling comparisons across different climate models. It focused on evaluating model performance, understanding climate sensitivity, and projecting future climate scenarios under various greenhouse gas concentration pathways (RCPs—Representative Concentration Pathways). CMIP5 models used four RCPs (RCP2.6, RCP4.5, RCP6.0, and RCP8.5) to project future climate changes based on different levels of greenhouse gas emissions.

CMIP6 was launched in 2013 to support the IPCC Sixth Assessment Report (IPCC, 2021). CMIP6 expands upon CMIP5 by incorporating new experiments and models, improving the representation of physical processes, and providing more detailed scenarios for future climate projections. It includes a wider range of socioeconomic pathways (SSPs—Shared Socioeconomic Pathways) to explore different possible futures based on varying societal choices. Thus, CMIP6 uses updated scenarios known as SSPs, which combine different socioeconomic pathways with RCPs to create more nuanced projections of future climate change.

To differentiate the two, CMIP6 models generally have higher resolution and more complex representations of Earth system processes than CMIP5 models. CMIP6 introduces SSPs, which provide more detailed socioeconomic contexts compared to the RCPs used in CMIP5. CMIP6 models include advancements in representing key processes like aerosols, land use changes, and carbon cycle feedback, leading to potentially more accurate climate projections.

This step of assessing future risks utilizing CMIP5 and CMIP6 models yields valuable insights into how climate change could impact each asset in the future. By integrating climate projections from these models, we can estimate the potential exposure of assets to various climate-related risks, such as increased frequency and intensity of extreme weather events, sea-level rise, and temperature changes. These projections enable us to quantify and model the physical risks that assets may face under different climate scenarios.

While this specific step is not illustrated here, it would provide critical results for transition modeling by helping identify which assets are most vulnerable to climate change. This information is essential for developing strategies to mitigate risks, such as diversifying investments, enhancing resilience measures, or transitioning toward more sustainable and climate-resilient portfolios. Incorporating CMIP5 and CMIP6 data into these assessments ensures that the modeling is grounded in the latest

---

[11] https://wcrp-cmip.org/cmip-overview/#:~:text=What%20is%20CMIP%3F,a%20digital%20analogue%20to%20Earth.

4.7 Conclusions

This chapter provides a comprehensive exploration of the multifaceted risks posed by climate change to businesses, financial institutions, and economies. It highlights the increasing frequency and severity of extreme weather events and the profound financial implications for organizations. The chapter delineates between physical risks—such as those from hurricanes, floods, and heatwaves—and transition risks linked to the shift toward a low-carbon economy driven by policy changes, technological advancements, and market conditions.

The discussion underscores the importance of the 2015 Paris Agreement in stabilizing global temperatures and outlines the extensive structural changes needed across various sectors to achieve rapid decarbonization. It also addresses the concept of "Climate Value at Risk" (CVaR), emphasizing the need for financial communities to recognize and manage climate-related risks, which include both physical impacts and transition challenges.

Furthermore, the chapter explains the methodologies for evaluating these risks, including the use of scenario models and the assessment of physical and transition risks at asset levels. It emphasizes the necessity for tailored risk management strategies and comprehensive planning to enhance resilience against climate change impacts. The integration of climate risk considerations into financial decision-making processes is presented as essential for long-term financial stability and sustainable growth.

Overall, this chapter serves as a crucial guide for understanding and mitigating the complex risks associated with climate change, advocating for proactive and informed approaches to climate risk management.

References

Agrawal, A., & Cooper, T. (2015). Insider trading before accounting scandals. *Journal of Corporate Finance, 34*, 169–190.
Battıston, S., Dafermos, Y., & Monasterolo, I. (2021). Climate risks and financial stability. *Journal of Financial Stability, 54*, 100867.
Birkmann, J., Cardona, O. D., Carreño, M. L., Barbat, A. H., Pelling, M., Schneiderbauer, S., Kienberger, S., Keiler, M., Alexander, D., & Welle, T. (2013). Framing vulnerability, risk and societal responses: The MOVE framework. *Natural Hazards, 67*, 193–211.
Bui, B., & De Villiers, C. (2017). Business strategies and management accounting in response to climate change risk exposure and regulatory uncertainty. *The British Accounting Review, 49*(1), 4–24.
Caldecott, B., Harnett, E., Cojoianu, T., Kok, I., & Pfeiffer, A. (2016). *Stranded assets: A climate risk challenge*.

Cartellier, F. (2022). *Climate stress testing, an answer to the challenge of assessing climate-related risks to the financial system?*. Available at SSRN 4179311.
Condon, M. (2022). Market myopia's climate bubble. *Utah Law Review, 63*.
Cutter, S. L. (2010). *Social science perspectives on hazards and vulnerability science* (pp. 17–30). Springer.
Cutter, S. L. (2021). The changing nature of hazard and disaster risk in the anthropocene. *Annals of the American Association of Geographers, 111*(3), 819–827.
Depietri, Y. (2020). The social–ecological dimension of vulnerability and risk to natural hazards. *Sustainability Science, 15*(2), 587–604.
Dietz, S., Bowen, A., Dixon, C., & Gradwell, P. (2016). 'Climate value at risk' of global financial assets. *Nature Climate Change, 6*(7), 676–679.
Doney, S. C., Busch, D. S., Cooley, S. R., & Kroeker, K. J. (2020). The impacts of ocean acidification on marine ecosystems and reliant human communities. *Annual Review of Environment and Resources, 45*(1), 83–112.
ECB. (2021). *The state of climate and environmental risk management in the banking sector*. ISBN 978-92-899-4882-1. https://doi.org/10.2866/917135
ECB. (2022). *Good practices for climate related and environmental risk management Observations from the 2022 thematic review*. ISBN 978-92-899-5407-5, https://doi.org/10.2866/417808
Eckstein, D., Künzel, V., & Schäfer, L. (2021). *The global climate risk index 2021*. Germanwatch.
EN-DAT. (2024). *EM-DAT, CRED / UCLouvain*, Brussels, Belgium – www.emdat.be
Flanagan, B. E., Gregory, E. W., Hallisey, E. J., Heitgerd, J. L., & Lewis, B. (2011). A social vulnerability index for disaster management. *Journal of Homeland Security and Emergency Management, 8*(1), 0000102202154773551792.
Fox-Penner, P. (2020). *Power after carbon: Building a clean, resilient grid*. Harvard University Press.
FSB. (2020). *The implications of climate change for financial stability*. https://www.fsb.org/uploads/P231120.pdf
FSB. (2022). *Supervisory and regulatory approaches to climate-related risks* (Final report). https://www.fsb.org/wp-content/uploads/P131022-1.pdf
Gallo, F., Lepousez, V., Dejonckheere, S., Sillmann, J., Clapp, C., Stackpole Dahl, M., Marginean, L., Budding, M., Hubert, R., & Cardona, M. (2020). *Assessing climate physical risks for financial decision makers. Common methodologies, challenges and case studies*. Clim INVEST-Tailored climate risk information for financial decision makers.
Hagenlocher, M., Renaud, F. G., Haas, S., & Sebesvari, Z. (2018). Vulnerability and risk of deltaic social-ecological systems exposed to multiple hazards. *Science of the Total Environment, 631*, 71–80.
Hoegh Guldberg, O., Jacob, D., Taylor, M., Bindi, M., Brown, S., Camilloni, I., Diedhiou, A., Djalante, R., Ebi, K. L., Engelbrecht, F., Guiot, J., Hijioka, Y., Mehrotra, S., Payne, A., Seneviratne, S. I., Thomas, A., Warren, R., Zhou, G. (2018). *Impacts of 1.5 C global warming on natural and human systems*.
IEA. (2019). *World energy outlook 2019*. IEA. https://www.iea.org/reports/world-energy-outlook-2019, Licence: CC BY 4.0
IEA. (2023a). *World energy outlook 2023*. IEA. https://www.iea.org/reports/world-energy-outlook-2023, Licence: CC BY 4.0 (report); CC BY NC SA 4.0 (Annex A)
IEA. (2023b). *Global energy and climate model documentation—2023*. International Energy Agency. https://iea.blob.core.windows.net/assets/ff3a195d-762d-4284-8bb5-bd062d260cc5/GlobalEnergyandClimateModelDocumentation2023.pdf
IFC—International Finance Corp. (2019). *Investing for impact* (Annual report 2019). https://www.ifc.org/en/insights-reports/2010/ifc-ar-2019
IPCC. (2007). *The physical science basis: Contribution of Working Group I to the fourth assessment report of the Intergovernmental Panel on Climate Change*. Intergovernmental Panel on Climate Change (IPCC), Climate change 2007, 996.

References

IPCC. (2023). *Summary for policymakers*. In: Climate Change 2023: Synthesis Report. Contribution of Working Groups I, II and III to the Sixth Assessment Report of the Intergovernmental Panel on Climate Change [Core Writing Team, H. Lee and J. Romero (eds.)]. IPCC, Geneva, Switzerland, pp. 1–34, https://doi.org/10.59327/IPCC/AR6-9789291691647.001

Jägermeyr, J., Müller, C., Ruane, A. C., Elliott, J., Balkovic, J., Castillo, O., ... & Rosenzweig, C. (2021). Climate impacts on global agriculture emerge earlier in new generation of climate and crop models. *Nature Food, 2*(11), 873–885.

Kapmeier, F., Greenspan, A., Jones, A., & Sterman, J. (2021). Science-based analysis for climate action: How HSBC Bank uses the En-ROADS climate policy simulation. *System Dynamics Review: THe Journal of the System Dynamics Society, 37*(4), 333–352.

Kenny, G. P., Notley, S. R., Flouris, A. D., & Grundstein, A. (2020). Climate change and heat exposure: impact on health in occupational and general populations. *Exertional Heat Illness: A Clinical and Evidence-Based Guide*, 225–261.

Knutson, T., Camargo, S. J., Chan, J. C., Emanuel, K., Ho, C. H., Kossin, J., Mohapatra, M., Satoh, M., Sugi, M., Walsh, K., & Wu, L. (2020). Tropical cyclones and climate change assessment: Part II: Projected response to anthropogenic warming. *Bulletin of the American Meteorological Society, 101*(3), E303–E322.

Lee, S., & Geum, Y. (2021). How to determine a minimum viable product in app-based lean start-ups: Kano-based approach. *Total Quality Management & Business Excellence, 32*(15–16), 1751–1767.

Lenton, T. M., Benson, S., Smith, T., Ewer, T., Lanel, V., Petykowski, E., Powell, T., Abrams, J., Blomsma, F., & Sharpe, S. (2022). Operationalising positive tipping points towards global sustainability. *Global Sustainability, 5*, e1.

Linnenluecke, M. K., & Griffiths, A. (2012). Assessing organizational resilience to climate and weather extremes: Complexities and methodological pathways. *Climatic Change, 113*, 933–947.

Masson-Delmotte, V., Zhai, P., Pirani, A., Connors, S. L., Péan, C., Berger, S., ... & Zhou, B. (2021). Climate change 2021: The physical science basis. *Contribution of Working Group I to the Sixth Assessment Report of the Intergovernmental Panel on Climate Change, 2*(1), 2391.

McHenry, M. P. (2013). Technical and governance considerations for advanced metering infrastructure/smart meters: Technology, security, uncertainty, costs, benefits, and risks. *Energy Policy, 59*, 834–842.

Meiler, S., Ciullo, A., Kropf, C. M., Emanuel, K., & Bresch, D. N. (2023). Uncertainties and sensitivities in the quantification of future tropical cyclone risk. *Communications Earth & Environment, 4*(1), 371.

Meinshausen, M., Nicholls, Z. R. J., Lewis, J., Gidden, M. J., Vogel, E., Freund, M., Beyerle, U., Gessner, C., Nauels, A., Bauer, N., Canadell, J. G., Daniel, J. S., John, A., Krummel, P. B., Luderer, G., Meinshausen, N., Montzka, S. A., Rayner, P. J., Reimann, S., & Wang, R. H. J. (2020). The shared socioeconomic pathway (SSP) greenhouse gas concentrations and their extensions to 2500. *Geoscience Model Development, 13*, 3571–3605. https://doi.org/10.5194/gmd-13-3571-2020

Monasterolo, I. (2020). Climate change and the financial system. *Annual Review of Resource Economics, 12*(1), 299–320.

MSCI. (2020). *Climate value-at-risk*. https://www.msci.com/documents/1296102/16985724/MSCI-ClimateVaR-Introduction-Feb2020.pdf

Neumann, J. E., Chinowsky, P., Helman, J., Black, M., Fant, C., Strzepek, K., & Martinich, J. (2021). Climate effects on US infrastructure: The economics of adaptation for rail, roads, and coastal development. *Climatic Change, 167*(3), 44.

NGFS. (2023). *NGFS climate scenarios for central banks and supervisors—Phase IV*. https://www.ngfs.net/en/ngfs-climate-scenarios-phase-iv-november-2023

Nieto, M. J. (2019). Banks, climate risk and financial stability. *Journal of Financial Regulation and Compliance, 27*(2), 243–262.

NOAA National Centers for Environmental Information (NCEI) U.S. Billion-Dollar Weather and Climate Disasters. (2024). https://www.ncei.noaa.gov/access/billions/, https://doi.org/10.25921/stkw-7w73

Nordhaus, W. (2019). Climate change: The ultimate challenge for economics. *American Economic Review, 109*(6), 1991–2014.

O'Neill, B. C., Kriegler, E., Ebi, K. L., Kemp-Benedict, E., Riahi, K., Rothman, D. S., van Ruijven, B. J., van Vuuren, D. P., Birkmann, J., Kok, K., Levy, M., & Solecki, W. (2017). The roads ahead: Narratives for shared socioeconomic pathways describing world futures in the 21st century. *Global Environmental Change, 42*, 169–180.

Oppenheimer, M., et al. (2019). Sea level rise and implications for low-lying islands, coasts and communities. In *IPCC Special Report on the Ocean and Cryosphere in a Changing Climate*.

Ortiz-Bobea, A., Ault, T. R., Carrillo, C. M., Chambers, R. G., & Lobell, D. B. (2021). Anthropogenic climate change has slowed global agricultural productivity growth. *Nature Climate Change, 11*(4), 306–312.

Pointner, W., & Ritzberger-Grünwald, D. (2019). Climate change as a risk to financial stability. *Financial Stability Report, 38*, 30–45.

Rooney-Varga, J. N., Kapmeier, F., Sterman, J. D., Jones, A. P., Putko, M., & Rath, K. (2020). The climate action simulation. *Simulation & Gaming, 51*(2), 114–140.

S&P Global. (2023). https://www.spglobal.com/en/research-insights/market-insights/sustainability/climate-risk-resilience

Solana, J. (2020). Climate change litigation as financial risk. *Green Finance, 2*(4), 344–372.

Studholme, J., Fedorov, A. V., Gulev, S. K., Emanuel, K., & Hodges, K. (2022). Poleward expansion of tropical cyclone latitudes in warming climates. *Nature Geoscience, 15*(1), 14–28.

TCFD. (2017). *Recommendations of the task force on climate-related financial disclosures*. https://assets.bbhub.io/company/sites/60/2021/10/FINAL-2017-TCFD-Report.pdf

TCFD. (2021). *Task force on climate related financial disclosures status. Guidance on metrics, targets and transition plans*. Basel Switzerland. https://assets.bbhub.io/company/sites/60/2021/07/2021-Metrics_Targets_Guidance-1.pdf

Trancoso, R., Syktus, J., Allan, R. P., Croke, J., Hoegh-Guldberg, O., & Chadwick, R. (2024). Significantly wetter or drier future conditions for one to two thirds of the world's population. *Nature Communications, 15*(1), 483.

UNEP. (2019). *The climate risk landscape: Mapping climate-related financial risk assessment methodologies*. https://www.unepfi.org/themes/climate-change/the-climate-risk-landscape/

UNFCC. (2016). *Report of the Conference of the Parties on its twenty-first session, held in Paris from 30 November to 13 December 2015*. Addendum. Part two: Action taken by the Conference of the Parties at its twenty-first session. COP 21, https://unfccc.int/documents/9097

Van Vuuren, D. P., Edmonds, J., Kainuma, M., Riahi, K., Thomson, A., Hibbard, K., Hurtt, G. C., Kram, T., Krey, V., Lamarque, J.-F., Masui, T., Meinshausen, M., Nakicenovic, N., Smith, S. J., & Rose, S. K. (2011). The representative concentration pathways: An overview. *Climatic Change, 109*, 5–31.

Weinhofer, G., & Busch, T. (2013). Corporate strategies for managing climate risks. *Business Strategy and the Environment, 22*(2), 121–144.

Welton, S. (2018). Electricity markets and the social project of decarbonization. *Columbia Law Review, 118*(4), 1067–1138.

World Bank. (2024). *User manual Climate Change Knowledge Portal (CCKP)*.

Zuzak, C., Mowrer, M., Goodenough, E., Burns, J., Ranalli, N., & Rozelle, J. (2022). The national risk index: Establishing a nationwide baseline for natural hazard risk in the US. *Nat Hazards, 114*, 2331–2355. https://doi.org/10.1007/s11069-022-05474-w

Chapter 5
Regulation and Frameworks: Current and Future Reporting Trends

You can't manage what you can't measure—Peter Drucker

5.1 Introduction

There is a clear distinction between planetary and corporate sustainability. Planetary sustainability refers to the broader goal of preserving the Earth's ecological balance, which includes mitigating climate change, protecting biodiversity, and ensuring long-term environmental health. Chapter 3 discusses the topic of planetary sustainability in the context of planetary boundaries. In contrast, corporate sustainability focuses on how businesses operate in ways that consider their impact on the environment, society, and governance (ESG) while still pursuing profitability. The difference is crucial: planetary sustainability is a global imperative seeking to avert catastrophic environmental outcomes, while corporate sustainability is a subset reflecting how businesses contribute to or mitigate these global issues.

Climate change, driven largely by human activities, has led to dangerous global warming, manifesting in extreme weather events, rising sea levels, and disruptions to critical infrastructure. The Paris Agreement, a landmark in international climate negotiations held during COP21 in 2015, set a long-term goal to limit global warming to well below 2 °C above pre-industrial levels, with efforts to limit the temperature increase to 1.5 °C (UNFCC, 2016). The 1.5 °C target emerged as a critical threshold beyond which the impacts of climate change would become significantly more severe, leading to irreversible changes to ecosystems and more frequent extreme weather events. Countries committed to submitting nationally determined contributions, which are climate action plans outlining efforts to reduce greenhouse gas emissions and adapt to climate change. These contributions are to be updated every five years, with the expectation that countries will increase their ambition over time. Thus, reducing corporate carbon footprints is essential for meeting the Paris Agreement targets. Carney introduces the concept of the "tragedy of the horizon," highlighting the mismatch between the short-term focus of financial markets and policymakers and the long-term implications of climate change. He argues that while climate risks are clear and escalating, the financial system does not yet account adequately for these risks due to their long-term nature (Carney, 2015).

The Greenhouse Gas (GHG) Protocol (Wbcsd WRI, 2004) is a corporate accounting and reporting standard, which categorizes emissions into three "scopes" for organizational reporting:

- Scope 1 includes direct GHG emissions that occur from sources that are owned or controlled by the organization. This includes CO_2 emissions from on-site fuel combustion (e.g., natural gas heating, company-owned vehicles) and other GHG emissions (e.g., methane from landfills or refrigerants).
- Scope 2 consists of indirect GHG emissions from the generation of purchased electricity, steam, heating, and cooling consumed by the organization.
- Scope 3 consists of all other indirect emissions that occur in the value chain of the reporting company, including both upstream and downstream emissions.

In many countries, corporations are significant sources of GHG Scope 1 emissions, particularly in the industry, electricity and heat production, and agriculture and forestry as shown in Fig. 5.1. The industrial sector is the largest contributor to global GHG emissions, accounting for 24% of the total. This includes emissions from manufacturing, construction, and various industrial processes. Efforts to green this sector involve adopting cleaner technologies, improving energy efficiency, and transitioning to low-carbon processes. Innovations such as carbon capture and storage and the use of alternative materials are crucial in reducing the carbon footprint of industries. Electricity and heat production is the second-largest emitter, responsible for 23% of GHG emissions. This sector's emissions primarily come from the burning of fossil fuels like coal, oil, and natural gas. The transition to renewable energy sources, such as wind, solar, and hydroelectric power, is central to greening this sector. Additionally, improving grid efficiency and expanding energy storage solutions are critical steps in reducing emissions from electricity and heat production.

The third largest sector in global GHG is agriculture, forestry, and other land use contribute 22% of global GHG emissions. This sector includes emissions from livestock, deforestation, and land use changes. Greening this sector involves promoting sustainable agricultural practices, reducing deforestation, and enhancing carbon sequestration through reforestation and soil management. Innovations in precision agriculture and the development of alternative proteins are also contributing to emissions reductions in this sector. The next sector, transportation, accounts for 15% of global GHG emissions, driven by the use of fossil fuels in cars, trucks, ships, and airplanes. Efforts to reduce emissions in this sector focus on electrification, the development of more efficient vehicles, and the use of alternative fuels such as hydrogen and biofuels. Additionally, investments in public transportation and urban planning are crucial to reducing reliance on high-emission vehicles. Other Energy (10%) category includes emissions from energy sources that do not fall into the above sectors, such as the production and refining of fuels. Greening this sector involves improving

5.1 Introduction

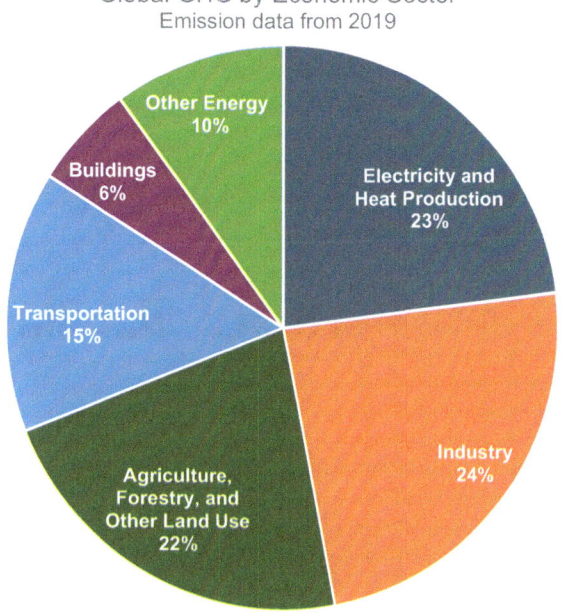

Fig. 5.1 Source of global GHG by economic sector, caused by human activities including industry, electricity and heat production, and agriculture and forestry constitute 69% of total emissions transition to a net-zero economy

the efficiency of energy extraction, refining processes, and reducing methane emissions from oil and gas production. The shift toward renewable energy and the phasing out of coal plants are key strategies in reducing emissions from this sector.

The buildings sector, contributing 6% of global GHG emissions, includes emissions from the energy used in residential and commercial buildings for heating, cooling, lighting, and appliances. Efforts to green this sector include improving energy efficiency through better insulation, adopting energy-efficient appliances, and incorporating renewable energy sources like solar panels into building designs. The move toward net-zero energy buildings and the use of sustainable construction materials are also significant trends.

While each sector is making strides toward reducing its carbon footprint, the pace and scale of these efforts vary. The transition to a low-carbon economy is complex and requires coordinated action across all sectors. Challenges such as the high cost of new technologies, regulatory barriers, and the need for substantial investments in infrastructure continue to hinder progress. However, the ongoing innovation in clean energy, sustainable practices, and carbon capture technologies offers hope for significant reductions in global GHG emissions in the coming years.

Achieving global climate targets will depend on the continued commitment of these sectors to adopt greener practices and technologies. The integration of sustainability into business models, driven by regulatory frameworks and consumer demand, will be crucial in accelerating this transition.

In Fig. 5.2, the annual fossil fuel CO_2 emissions (Friedlingstein, 2022) resulting from the burning of fossil fuels (such as coal, oil, and natural gas) and the production

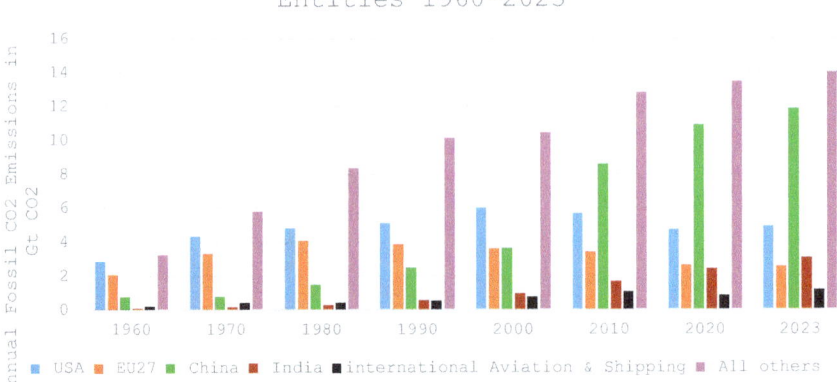

Fig. 5.2 Trends in annual fossil CO2 emissions in Gt CO2 selected countries and entities. *Source* Global Carbon project

of cement are plotted for period 1960 to 2023. In terms of annual fossil CO2 emissions, the rapid rise of China after 2000 and India starting in 2010 contrasts with the low to moderate decreases in the US and EU. The category of all other countries is increasing from 1960. The Global Carbon Project tracks and reports these emissions annually as part of their efforts to monitor global carbon levels and trends.

Corporations are identified as "principal agents" of GHG emissions, with a small number of companies contributing disproportionately to annual CO2 emission levels. Consequently, corporations are indispensable in achieving the goals of the Paris Agreement (IPCC, 2022). By reducing emissions, adopting renewable energy, managing sustainable supply chains, engaging in transparent reporting, and investing in green finance, corporations can significantly contribute to global efforts to combat climate change. Increasingly, companies are adopting Science-Based Targets that align their emission reduction pathways with the Paris Agreement goals (SBTI, 2024). By setting targets consistent with what climate science deems necessary to limit warming to 1.5 °C or 2 °C, companies contribute directly to global efforts. Their role extends beyond merely reducing their own carbon footprint; it also involves leading systemic changes across economies and societies that align with the Paris objectives. However, this responsibility requires corporations to act with urgency and ambition, ensuring that their commitments result in real, measurable progress toward global climate goals.

The triple bottom line—people, planet, profit—is a framework that encourages businesses to measure their success not just in financial terms but also in social and environmental outcomes. However, this approach has led to a complex landscape of sustainability reporting, where companies are expected to account for their impacts across these three dimensions. While various reporting frameworks and standards may have different focal points, they share a common goal of enhancing transparency

5.1 Introduction

and accountability regarding an organization's environmental and social impacts. These frameworks are essential for investors, regulators, and other stakeholders to assess a corporation's performance and sustainability practices.

From a corporate perspective, integrating sustainability metrics and reporting is becoming increasingly vital as the investment community seeks to assess risks, opportunities, and the broader impact of their decisions on society and the environment. Initially, interest in non-financial information was minimal, but since the 1970s, there has been a significant increase in demand for such disclosures, driven by the growth of sustainable and responsible investing (GSIA, 2022). Carney introduces the concept of the "tragedy of the horizon," highlighting the mismatch between the short-term focus of financial markets and policymakers and the long-term implications of climate change. He argues that while climate risks are clear and escalating, the financial system does not yet account adequately for these risks due to their long-term nature. A study by State Street Global Advisors (2019) indicated that 46% of institutions viewed ESG as a fiduciary duty, while 46% wanted to get ahead of regulation, and 44% used it to mitigate ESG risks. The choice of a reporting framework often depends on the corporation's goals, the stakeholders they need to communicate with, and the specific regulatory environment they operate in. Navigating the diverse landscape of sustainability reporting regulations is challenging for companies, a complexity exacerbated by the various perspectives on corporate sustainability, each with its own requirements and expectations.

Sustainability reporting frameworks vary, offering different focuses and methodologies. For example, the Global Reporting Initiative (GRI) Standards provide comprehensive disclosure guidelines, while others, like the GHG Protocol, focus on specific issues such as emissions. This diversity in reporting standards poses challenges for companies, regulators, and stakeholders, leading to inconsistencies and confusion in reporting practices (Berg et al., 2022; Christensen et al., 2022). It also complicates efforts to achieve transparency and trust among investors and stakeholders.

The regulatory landscape for sustainability reporting includes both voluntary and mandatory disclosures. Some regulations, like modern slavery legislation, require disclosure without enforcing compliance measures, while others, such as those concerning conflict materials, mandate due diligence and remediation actions (Darendeli et al., 2022). The push for standardized, mandatory disclosures has grown, particularly in the European Union and the United States. The EU's Corporate Sustainability Reporting Directive and the US Securities and Exchange Commission (SEC) climate-related disclosure rules are examples of efforts to harmonize reporting standards (Fiechter et al., 2022). However, as of 2024, political sentiments in the US have stalled the SEC's climate disclosure regulations.

In summary, while sustainability reporting is crucial for addressing global environmental challenges, its current form is often inadequate. A streamlined, more standardized approach is essential to ensure that corporate actions align with the broader goals of planetary sustainability. Subsections 5.1.1 and 5.1.2 discuss the pros and cons of sustainability reporting.

5.1.1 Why Is Sustainability Reporting Good?

Sustainability reporting offers corporations several benefits that are increasingly being recognized through recent research. These benefits begin with the role of transparency. Reporting compels companies to disclose their environmental and social impacts, thereby increasing transparency for stakeholders, which fosters trust and accountability, as businesses are held responsible for their actions and decisions (Ioannou & Serafeim, 2017; Serafeim, 2013). For example, a greater focus on sustainability reporting has led to more transparency regarding the long-term economic situation and non-financial information in some European banks (Buallay, 2019). However, there are ongoing concerns about the quality of such disclosures (Boiral et al., 2019). Experienced reporters tend to provide a significant volume of disclosure, and their quality of risk disclosure is positively influenced by their international presence and reporting experience (Truant et al., 2017).

By identifying and reporting on ESG risks, companies can better anticipate and mitigate potential negative impacts. This proactive approach to risk management helps protect companies from future liabilities, regulatory fines, and reputational damage. For instance, understanding a corporation's GHG emissions is crucial for investors assessing the opportunities, challenges, and risks associated with climate change, both historically and in the future. The disclosure of non-accounting information gives investors an indicator of how well a firm controls business risks, with higher ESG scores often correlating with lower business risks (Sharfman & Fernando, 2008). Companies with high sustainability scores tend to demonstrate superior operational performance and face lower risks (Clark et al., 2015).

Furthermore, companies engaged in sustainability reporting often outperform their peers financially. Sustainability-conscious businesses are more likely to attract ethical investors and consumers and talented employees. Additionally, these companies are often better prepared for future regulations and shifts in market demand (Atz et al., 2023; Eccles & Serafeim, 2013).

Sustainability reporting also enables companies to engage with a broader range of stakeholders, including investors, employees, customers, and local communities. This engagement can lead to valuable insights, helping businesses improve their sustainability practices and strengthen relationships with key stakeholders. Engaging with stakeholders can further improve the quality of sustainability reports (Stocker et al., 2020). Recent studies show that Millennials and other investor groups increasingly consider ESG factors when making investment decisions (Ricci & Sautter, 2021). As more investors across generations follow this example, ESG-focused voting is expected to gain momentum, encouraging citizens to invest directly in corporate stock to gain voting power.

There is growing evidence that prospective investors prefer companies that include sustainability reports, reflecting a shift toward rational investment behaviors based on ESG considerations (Garel & Petit-Romec, 2021). The association between sustainability scores and mutual fund performance reveals that funds investing in companies with higher ESG scores experience better risk-adjusted performance, underscoring the positive impact of sustainable investing on financial returns (Durán-Santomil et al., 2019). On an individual decision-making level, the willingness to pay for sustainable investments may be driven primarily by an emotional, rather than a purely calculative, valuation of impact (Heeb et al., 2023).

Companies that prioritize sustainability are better positioned for long-term success. Sustainability reporting enhances the value relevance of financial statements, which show that companies recognized for their sustainability reporting have a stronger association between earnings per share and stock price returns compared to those that do not emphasize sustainability reporting (Eccles & Serafeim, 2013; Eccles et al., 2012; Sutopo et al., 2018). Incorporating ESG indicators into financial reporting can transform sustainability into tangible value for all stakeholders, further underscoring the financial significance of non-financial reporting practices (Oncioiu et al., 2020).

Corporate reputation is a valuable intangible asset, and negative ESG disclosures through media channels have been shown to significantly lower firm valuation. Recent findings highlight that smaller, less liquid firms, especially those not included in the S&P 500, are particularly vulnerable to stock price declines following adverse media coverage. Companies in industries like candy & soda, steelworks, banking, and insurance are more likely to experience substantial negative reactions from investors. These results suggest that the impact of negative ESG coverage on stock performance varies depending on firm size, liquidity, reputation, and industry, offering new insights into how different factors influence investor responses to adverse media reports (Wong & Zhang, 2022).

5.1.2 Criticism of ESG Reporting

Despite the positive aspects of sustainability reporting, ESG reporting has faced criticism on several fronts: A primary criticism of ESG reporting is the lack of standardized metrics and frameworks. Different companies use various methodologies to measure and report their ESG performance, making it difficult for stakeholders to compare data across companies and industries. This inconsistency can undermine the credibility of ESG reports. The variability and inconsistency in how companies report ESG data, particularly employee health and safety, lead to significantly different outcomes when analyzing the same set of companies. This inconsistency stems from the diverse methods companies use to report such data, resulting in over 20 different reporting approaches. Additionally, the way data providers define and benchmark peer groups can heavily influence a company's performance ranking, yet the lack of transparency in these practices creates inconsistencies across the market (Billio et al., 2021; Cort & Esty, 2020).

Measuring social and environmental impact poses challenges, even for companies within the same industry. Local conditions can significantly influence both the intended and actual impacts achieved (Gary, 2019). The European Non-Financial Reporting Directive (NFRD, 2021) mandates that large companies disclose certain non-financial information, yet the implementation of such directives often varies, leading to inconsistencies in how sustainability is reported and understood.

While sustainability reporting is intended to promote transparency and accountability, some companies may use ESG reporting as a tool for "greenwashing," by which they exaggerate or misrepresent their sustainability efforts to appear more environmentally friendly or socially responsible than they actually are. Recent investigation into the determinants of selective disclosure highlights that this practice is more prevalent in specific areas, notably labor rights/supply chain and human rights/community (Roszkowska-Menkes et al., 2024). These are crucial aspects of sustainability, and the tendency to selectively disclose information in these areas raises concerns about the authenticity and completeness of sustainability reports. This deceptive practice can mislead investors and consumers and diminish the overall trust in ESG reporting (Yu et al., 2020). The quality and reliability of ESG data are often questioned. Since many of the data are self-reported by companies, there are concerns about accuracy and potential biases. Independent verification and auditing of ESG data are not always conducted, leading to skepticism about the validity of the reported information (Del Giudice & Rigamonti, 2020).

Critics argue that ESG reporting can sometimes prioritize short-term gains over long-term sustainability. Companies might focus on quick wins or easily achievable goals to boost their ESG ratings, rather than making substantial, long-term commitments to sustainability (Kotsantonis et al., 2016).

In the US, many conservatives view ESG reporting as part of a broader political agenda that promotes progressive values.[1] They argue that ESG focuses on social issues, such as diversity and climate change, which they believe should not be the primary concern of businesses. This perception leads to resistance against what they see as the politicization of corporate governance (Painter, 2024). Some conservatives believe that ESG reporting imposes additional costs and regulatory burdens on businesses, potentially hindering economic growth and innovation.[2] They argue that companies should focus on maximizing shareholder value rather than diverting resources to ESG initiatives that may not yield immediate financial returns.

Conservatives often champion free market principles, by which businesses operate with minimal government intervention. ESG reporting, especially when mandated or encouraged by government policies, is seen as a form of interference that disrupts the natural functioning of the market. Certain conservatives remain skeptical about the severity of climate change and the importance of social justice issues. As a result, they may view ESG reporting, which often emphasizes these areas, as unnecessary or even harmful. ESG reporting can negatively impact traditional industries, such as fossil fuels, by highlighting their environmental and social risks. Conservatives who support these industries may oppose ESG reporting as they see it as a threat to jobs and economic stability.

---

[1] https://news.law.fordham.edu/jcfl/2023/02/24/a-critical-look-at-the-politicization-of-esg/.

[2] https://www.forbes.com/sites/jamesbroughel/2023/03/09/republicans-are-making-A-mistake-by-waging-war-on-esg-investing/.

5.2 Global Standard and Frameworks for Sustainability Reporting

In summary, while sustainability reporting offers numerous benefits, it is not without its challenges and criticisms. The opposition to ESG reporting, particularly from conservatives, stems from concerns about politicization, economic impact, and free market principles. As the debate around ESG continues, it is essential to strike a balance between promoting sustainability and addressing these valid concerns. As sustainability reporting grows in importance, it becomes a critical factor for organizations aiming to align their strategies and operations with sustainable practices. Thus, despite challenges related to standardization and transparency, evidence suggests that sustainability reporting can significantly enhance financial performance and investment decisions. This underscores the importance of adopting robust ESG practices and reporting frameworks to support sustainable development goals and.

5.2 Global Standard and Frameworks for Sustainability Reporting

Sustainability reporting has evolved as a critical practice for companies to communicate their economic, environmental, and social performance to stakeholders. This process includes disclosing non-financial information such as climate change impact, water management, ethical practices, and supply chain management. This practice supports global initiatives such as the United Nations Sustainable Development Goals and the transition to a net-zero economy. The scheme for standards and frameworks is shown in Fig. 5.3 and is briefly discussed below.

Fig. 5.3 The scheme for standards and frameworks for sustainability reporting

5.2.1 Sustainability Reporting

Sustainability reporting is the practice of disclosing an organization's economic, environmental, and social impacts. The GRI is an independent international body that facilitates uniform reporting, helping organizations meet stakeholder demands for comparable data. GRI is one of the most widely used frameworks for sustainability reporting, designed to empower organizations to produce comprehensive reports on their influence on sustainable development. GRI provides guidelines for reporting on a wide range of sustainability topics, including energy use, emissions, labor practices, and community impact, with an emphasis on transparency and accountability to stakeholders such as investors, customers, employees, and the community. It offers standardized metrics and indicators for consistent reporting and comparison across organizations. About 78% of the world's largest 250 companies by revenue have adopted GRI for sustainability reporting, and GRI standards are referenced in over 289 policies from 102 countries.

GRI has set standards for 40 sectors, grouped into four priority categories. For example, Group 2, Industrial, includes sectors such as construction materials, aerospace and defense, automotive, construction, chemicals, machinery and equipment, pharmaceuticals, and electronics. Some examples of companies reporting within these priority groups are:

- Basic Materials: Companies like BP, ExxonMobil, and Shell in the oil and gas sector, or BHP and Rio Tinto in mining, have historically reported using GRI standards.
- Industrial: Companies such as BASF in chemicals, Boeing in aerospace, and General Motors in automotive are known to report under GRI.
- Transport and Infrastructure: Airlines like Delta and transportation companies like DHL often use GRI for their sustainability reports.
- Other Services and Light Manufacturing: Retail giants like Walmart and service providers like Johnson & Johnson in medical equipment might use GRI standards for reporting.

UNGC: The second organization, shown in Fig. 5.3, is the United Nations Global Compact (UNGC), a voluntary initiative based on CEO commitments to implement universal sustainability principles and undertake partnerships in support of UN goals. Launched in 2000, the UNGC is the world's largest corporate sustainability initiative, with thousands of corporate participants and other stakeholders from over 160 countries.

The UNGC's ten principles, derived from broader UN declarations and conventions, are grouped into four categories:

1. Encourages businesses to uphold human rights within their sphere of influence and avoid involvement in human rights violations.
2. Focuses on fair treatment of workers, protecting their rights, and promoting a safe, inclusive, and equitable working environment.

3. Advocates for environmental stewardship, urging companies to minimize their environmental impact and invest in sustainable practices and technologies.
4. States that businesses should work against corruption in all its forms, including extortion and bribery, emphasizing transparency, integrity, and accountability.

Participation in the UNGC is voluntary, with companies joining through a commitment made by their CEOs or other top executives. This commitment involves integrating the principles into business strategies, policies, and practices, and embedding them into the company culture while addressing sustainable development goals.

For example, Tiffany & Co., a luxury jeweler, has made ambitious sustainability commitments focused on traceability, responsible material sourcing, craftsmanship, and innovation, with specific targets set for 2021 through 2025. By 2025, Tiffany aims to achieve 100% traceability of individually registered diamonds to their mine of origin or an approved supplier. By 2021, Tiffany had already achieved 100% traceability of all gold, silver, and platinum used in their jewelry to either the mine or the recycler. In this chapter, an expert interview with **Ashley Cimini Singh,** a supplier to Tiffany, discusses the company's commitment to responsible sourcing. This interview demonstrates that some small businesses in manufacturing, which are significant GHG emitters, are utilizing standards and frameworks to reduce their emissions.

ISO Standards: The third reporting organization discussed is ISO, specifically ISO 14001, 14,064, and 26,000. ISO 14001 is an internationally recognized standard for Environmental Management Systems. It provides a framework that organizations can follow to effectively manage their environmental responsibilities and minimize their environmental impact. ISO 14064 is a set of standards for quantifying and reporting GHG emissions. ISO 26000 offers guidance on how businesses and organizations can operate in a socially responsible way, acting ethically and transparently. Many entities now comply with these third-party verification standards in their reporting.

5.2.2 *Climate Disclosures*

Carbon Disclosure Project (CDP): The Carbon Disclosure Project (CDP), now simply known as CDP, is a not-for-profit charity that runs a global disclosure system for investors, companies, cities, states, and regions to manage their environmental impacts. Founded in 2000, CDP has become a pivotal platform for disclosing environmental information, especially concerning climate change, water security, and deforestation. It focuses on climate change, water security, and deforestation, with the goal of promoting environmental risk management and reporting within the business community. Its strategy is to help investors avoid holdings with risks related to climate change.

By participating in CDP, organizations commit to disclosing their GHG emission levels, setting reduction targets, implementing initiatives to achieve these targets, and assessing the associated risks and opportunities from global warming. CDP has over 700 capital market signatories representing more than USD 142 trillion in assets; the latter consisting of banks and investment firms, request companies to disclose information on climate change, forests, and water security through CDP. Additionally, over 330 major buyers, with a combined purchasing power of USD 6.4 trillion, have asked their suppliers to disclose environmental information through CDP.

Expert in Focus: Ashley Cimini Singh

Ashley Cimini Singh is President of GSM Metals Inc., located in Cranston, Rhode Island, a family-owned and operated business. Ashley is a graduate of Yale University and was elected President of the Boston Jewelers Club in 2022.

GSM was acquired in 2002 with the initial vision of providing a stable, high-quality supply of precious metal raw materials to its sister company, Cimini and Associates, Inc. (C&A), founded in 1992. In 2008, GSM relocated to a state-of-the-art, 76,000 square foot manufacturing facility in Cranston. This move included the acquisition of advanced equipment, significantly enhancing capabilities from melting to final fabrication. From 2009 to 2011, GSM integrated jewelry fabrication and finishing into its operations, greatly improving efficiencies in quality, delivery, and cost. Today, GSM has approximately 100 non-union employees. GSM manufactures a wide range of mill products and precision-engineered precious metal jewelry, specializing in raw materials and components that require precise tolerances and are challenging to produce. Its premier client base includes leaders in the jewelry, aerospace, electronics, automotive, and musical arts industries. One of its key strengths is that all products, across these diverse sectors, are manufactured on the same equipment, providing business stability and reducing susceptibility to economic fluctuations.

Beyond its technical and engineering expertise, GSM has a competitive edge in its ability to design and manufacture products from start to finish, maintaining strict lot integrity and traceability back to the mine. It produces raw materials and can machine components, extrude, draw, solder, laser engrave, polish, inspect, and ship to the industry's highest quality standards. Additionally, GSM recycles its own scrap into new melts for the next batch of products, avoiding costly refining and processing expenses. These savings are directly reflected in prices, benefiting customers.

Expert Interview with Ashley Cimini Singh

The question we wanted to ask you is aligned with your work with Tiffany and several other companies, including those in the aerospace industry. Do these companies typically require your company to comply with sustainability guidelines? What kinds of standards related to emissions are they using?

That's a great question. In my industry, most of the emphasis on sustainability has traditionally focused on the sourcing of raw materials. We deal with silver, gold, and platinum alloys in various forms for different industries. Since these materials are extracted from the Earth, there is significant concern about the methods used for extraction. This has become increasingly important over the years, especially for major clients like Tiffany & Co.

Tiffany has been proactive in understanding the origins of the metals and stones used in their products for about 20 years now, emphasizing sustainability in their sourcing. Recently, however, our customer base has been looking deeper into our practices. They are interested not only in where our raw materials come from but also in how we handle them, what is created inside our plant, and what emissions we release.

Over the past few years, there has been a growing emphasis on setting sustainability goals related to emissions and hazardous waste generation. Although we haven't yet adopted a specific standard for emissions, we are collaborating with our clients to develop these goals. The reason they are asking us to do this is that we are a critical link in their supply chain. They are responsible for reporting sustainability compliance, and they need us to align with their goals to ensure they meet their overall sustainability commitments. By helping us come on board, they ultimately help themselves achieve their sustainability targets.

In my industry, there are two forms of recycling, one of which is less harmful than the other. The first method is called refining, which is somewhat analogous to oil refining. In refining, an alloy or a mixture of metals, which includes not just pure gold, silver, or platinum but also other elements like copper, germanium, and zinc, is processed to strip it back to its pure form. This is the process used in "cash for gold" programs where old jewelry is refined to extract pure gold, silver, or platinum. The refining process can be dirty, involving the use of

> *chemicals like cyanide and impacting the environment, but there are cleaner ways to do it. The second method is called the clean scrap process. This involves taking back scrap material from our customers' processing, melting it, and reusing it without any chemical stripping. This method is much cleaner as it simply involves melting and reforming the metal. About three years ago, I implemented this process with Tiffany & Co., and it has been hugely successful for them.*
>
> *Approximately a year and a half ago, Tiffany initiated a groundbreaking mandate that all materials used must be 100% recycled, prohibiting the use of metals directly extracted from the Earth. This was a significant shift in our industry, which many found challenging because not all manufacturing facilities are equipped to handle such requirements. As Tiffany's largest supplier, we had to lead the way and persuade the rest of the industry to adopt this approach.*
>
> *This initiative has started to influence others in the industry. Clients from various sectors, including the arts, are now beginning to request 100% recycled materials. While there are additional costs associated with this process, which can be prohibitive for some customers, the trend is growing. We are seeing an increasing number of clients who are willing and able to manage these costs to align with more sustainable practices.*

The CDP aims to foster investor engagement with companies on environmental issues and leverage the published data to identify opportunities and mitigate risks. CDP's collaboration with pension funds and banks (CDP, 2024) demonstrates how it helps financial organizations use data to achieve low-carbon goals. CDP is now aligned with International Financial Reporting Standards (IFRS) S2 Climate-related Disclosures and the European Sustainability Reporting Standards (ESRS). It is also partially aligned with the Task Force on Nature-Related Financial Disclosures recommendations and the US Securities and Exchange Commission (SEC) climate disclosure rule. Additionally, it aligns with the TCFD recommendations.

The CDP scoring system offers a comprehensive evaluation of a company's environmental transparency and performance. It emphasizes the importance of starting with a clear and open assessment of a company's environmental impact, paving the way for significant environmental initiatives. CDP scores provide organizations and their stakeholders with a clear indication of their progress toward achieving goals such as limiting global warming to 1.5 °C, zero deforestation, and water security. By consistently disclosing their environmental data over time, companies can more accurately track their progress and understand their environmental impact trajectory.

CDP employs a scoring methodology that encourages companies to quantify and manage their environmental impacts by responding to specific questionnaires on climate change, forests, and water security. This disclosure process motivates companies to take meaningful action. The scoring system categorizes companies from D- to A, guiding them through the stages of disclosure, awareness, management, and, ultimately, leadership in environmental stewardship. It is crucial to recognize that achieving an A score does not signify the culmination of a company's environmental efforts but rather highlights their high level of transparency and performance concerning climate change, deforestation, and water security. Aligned with TCFD and major environmental standards, CDP's scoring methodology offers a dataset that facilitates market-wide comparison.

In March 2024, CDP noted that 101 companies made it to its 2023 Water Security A list and 353 companies made it to its Climate Change A list. Table 5.1 shows the different global companies that received an A grade for climate, forest, and water metrics using CDP indicators. Notable A-listers in all three categories include Danone (Europe), Klabin S/A (South America), Philip Morris International (USA), and Sekisui House Ltd (Asia). The inclusion of Philip Morris International is controversial, given that it continues to sell tobacco products, which contribute to addiction and public health issues worldwide. Table 5.1 also some B and C grades. These scores provide transparency and action toward sustainability by measuring and analyzing environmental letter scores.

5.2.3 ESG Frameworks

Global Real Estate Industry Benchmark (GRESB): The GRESB is an investor-driven organization that assesses ESG performance of real assets globally, including real estate portfolios and infrastructure assets. Established in 2009, GRESB is an independent organization providing validated ESG performance data and peer benchmarks for investors and managers to enhance business intelligence, industry engagement, and decision-making. Its primary aim is to assess the ESG performance of real assets, offering standardized and validated data to investors, asset managers, and other stakeholders interested in the sustainability performance of their investments.

Through its rigorous assessment process, GRESB provides a comprehensive view of the sustainability performance of real estate portfolios, encouraging transparency and driving improvements in ESG practices within the global real estate sector. It evaluates ESG performance across a broad range of indicators, including energy consumption, carbon emissions, resource management, and adherence to social and governance best practices. GRESB also offers comparative performance analysis, allowing participants to benchmark their ESG performance against peers, which is instrumental in identifying strengths and opportunities for improvement. This framework supports the growing demand from investors for sustainable and responsible investment opportunities, contributing to the broader goal of promoting sustainable development in the real estate industry.

A prime example of a company excelling in the GRESB is GLP, which showed significant improvement in its 2021 GRESB assessment, achieving more than a 13% increase in its performance compared to 2020. All of GLP's fund submissions received Green Stars, surpassing the average peer score. Notably, GLP J-REIT and

Table 5.1 CDP scores of major brands in climate, forests and water impacts

Company	Climate	Forests	Water
Beiersdorf AG	A	A	A
Danone	A	A	A
KAO Corporation	A	A	A
Kering	A	A	A
Klabin S/A	A	A	A
Lenzing AG	A	A	A
L'Oréal	A	A	A
Mayr-Melnhof Karton Aktiengesellschaft	A	A	A
Philip Morris International	A	A	A
Sekisui House, Ltd.	A	A	A
GE Aerospace	C		F
Toyota Motor Corp.	A-		B
Nestle	A-	B	B
Proctor & Gamble	A	A-	B
Coca-Cola	A-	B-B-	A-
PepsiCo	A-	BB	A
Blackberry	B-		

5.2 Global Standard and Frameworks for Sustainability Reporting

GLP Japan Income Partners I received the highest five-star rating, underscoring GLP's commitment to ESG excellence within real estate.

Comprehensive investment in sustainability, as measured by the GRESB rating, benefits Real Estate Investment Trusts by improving operational performance and reducing risk exposure and volatility (Fuerst, 2015; Keeris & Langbroek, 2019). In contrast, more traditional approaches to property development and management tend to yield less favorable outcomes. Prologis, a real estate investment trust, participates in GRESB assessments to benchmark its ESG performance against industry standards.

International Financial Reporting Standards (IFRS): In 2024, a significant consolidation occurred in sustainability reporting due to the merger of the Task Force on Climate-related TCFD and the IFRS into the International Sustainability Standards Board (ISSB). This merger represents a major step forward in the global sustainability reporting landscape. The Climate Disclosure Standards Board (is also now part of IFRS, contributing to the effort to simplify and standardize the reporting of sustainability-related financial information (IFRS, 2024).

The ISSB, established by the IFRS Foundation in November 2021, aims to develop a comprehensive global baseline of sustainability-related disclosure standards, integrating existing frameworks and standards, including those from TCFD and the Value Reporting Foundation (VRF), which resulted from the merger of the Sustainability Accounting Standards Board (SASB) and the International Integrated Reporting Council (IIRC). The ISSB's standards, namely IFRS S1 and IFRS S2, align closely with TCFD recommendations, ensuring continuity and coherence in climate-related financial disclosures. This integration addresses the "alphabet soup" of ESG initiatives, providing clarity for companies and investors. The ISSB's establishment marks a milestone in creating a unified global approach to sustainability reporting, offering a comprehensive framework for companies to disclose sustainability-related financial information.

The ISSB's global sustainability disclosure framework benefits from SASB's established expertise and relevance to financial reporting. Table 5.2 shows the relevant SASB metrics for Danone and Nestlé in terms of their GHG emissions and water withdrawal. The intensity of per € 1b revenue enables comparison of the two companies. It is evident that Nestlé has higher intensities of these metrics. This effort illustrates their commitment to transparency and sustainability in their operations, providing stakeholders with detailed insights into their ESG performance.

5.2.4 ESG Rating Agencies

The rise of ESG rating agencies has become crucial in assessing and quantifying a company's adherence to ESG principles. These agencies serve as third-party intermediaries, providing transparent, quantitative evaluations of a company's ESG performance. This information is invaluable for stakeholders who rely on clear data to make

Table 5.2 Comparison of Danone and Nestle based on 2021 SASB Key Metrics

	Danone		Nestlé	
Revenue (2022)	€ 27.7 bn		CHF 94.4 bn (~ €94.4 bn)	
	total	per € 1b revenue	Total	per € 1b revenue
GHG Emissions	24.7 MtCO2eq	0.89 MtCO2eq	118.68 MtCO2eq	1.22 MtCO2eq
Scope 1	0.68 MtCO2eq	0.02 MtCO2eq	3.37 MtCO2eq	0.03 MtCO2eq
Scope 2	0.3 MtCO2eq	0.01 MtCO2eq	1.61 MtCO2eq	0.02 MtCO2eq
Scope 3	23.7 MtCO2eq	0.86 MtCO2eq	113.70 MtCO2eq	1.17 MtCO2eq
Water Withdrawal	67.8 Mio m^3	2.45 Mio m3 (equal to 980 Olympic pools)	98 Mio m^3	1.01 Mio m3 (equal to 980 Olympic pools)
Packaging Waste	115,000 t	4,152 t	3.8 Mio t	40,000 t

informed financial and investment decisions. The growing influence of ESG rating agencies reflects the increasing demand for accountability and sustainable practices in the corporate sector. However, the field of ESG ratings faces challenges, particularly the substantial disagreements that often arise among different rating agencies regarding a company's ESG performance (Dimson et al., 2020). This discord can create confusion and uncertainty among investors and stakeholders, potentially undermining the utility of ESG ratings.

To address these challenges, many US companies have begun voluntarily issuing ESG reports. These reports aim to provide greater transparency and detail about their ESG practices and performance, potentially bridging the gap between different rating agencies. Similar to the way voluntary disclosures, such as management forecasts and conference calls, have reduced discrepancies among capital market intermediaries, ESG reports could help achieve a consensus among ESG raters.

Research suggests that companies that proactively disclose ESG reports experience less disagreement among ESG rating agencies (Kimbrough et al., 2024). The study reveals a negative association between the issuance of ESG reports and rater disagreement, indicating that these reports can fulfill the information needs of stakeholders monitoring a firm's ESG performance. Raters disagree more about ESG outcome metrics than input metrics or policies (Christensen et al., 2022). The effectiveness of ESG reports in reducing rater disagreement depends on the quality and credibility of the information provided (Conway, 2019). High-quality ESG reports, particularly those verified by third-party attestations, are more likely to be associated with reduced disagreement among ESG raters. The linguistic attributes of these reports—such as length, tone, and consistency—also play a significant role (Caglio et al., 2020). Reports that are longer, less positive, and consistent in tone tend to foster greater consensus among raters (Melloni et al., 2017).

The voluntary issuance of ESG reports emerges as a promising strategy for companies aiming to reduce disagreements among ESG rating agencies. By providing detailed and credible information about their ESG practices and performance, companies not only enhance transparency but also contribute to the development of a more coherent and reliable ESG rating ecosystem. This, in turn, supports more informed decision-making by investors and stakeholders, fostering a culture of accountability and sustainability in the corporate world.

Key ESG rating agencies include MSCI ESG Ratings, S&P Global (formerly RobecoSAM), Sustainalytics (a Morningstar company), Vigeo Eiris (part of Moody's ESG Solutions), Refinitiv (formerly Thomson Reuters), and ISS ESG (Institutional Shareholder Services).

Hotels and tourist destinations submit their own ESG scores, and both Marriott and Hilton have received a "B" rating for their CDP climate and water security scores. These corporations also prepare their own sustainability reports. The second expert interviewed for this chapter, Dr. **Peter Yesawich**, a hospitality industry veteran, provided insights based on a global survey of hotels. His findings indicate that sustainability is not a primary factor in consumer decision-making when choosing travel options. As a result, the responsibility for sustainability is often not prioritized in travel and hospitality sectors, potentially leading to increased Scope 3 emissions from vacation-related activities. Consumers choose the cheapest flight and not the flight with the least carbon footprint, even if the information is provided to the consumer.

Expert in Focus Peter Yesawich

Peter C. Yesawich is Chairman of Yesawich Holding, LLC, and Co-founder and former Vice Chairman of MMGY Global, the world's largest integrated marketing communications company, serving clients in the travel, leisure, and entertainment industries from 13 offices across the Americas, Europe, and the Middle East.

Yesawich holds three degrees from Cornell University, including a doctorate in psychology, and completed post-graduate studies at both Yale and Stanford.

A leading authority on the evolving habits, preferences, and intentions of travelers, Yesawich frequently comments on travel trends in both domestic and international media. His resume includes the development of marketing programs for many of the industry's most prominent destinations and admired brands including the Bahamas, Bermuda, Costa Rica, Dominican Republic, Mexico, Fairmont Hotels & Resorts, Hilton International, Leading Hotels of the World, Outrigger Resorts & Hotels, Ritz-Carlton Hotel Company, Sandals Resorts, Trump Hotel Collection, Atlantis Paradise Island, Baha Mar, The Breakers, The Broadmoor, Gaylord Hotels, New York Palace, Wynn Las Vegas, Universal Orlando Resort, Walt Disney Parks & Resorts, and the US Olympic Committee.

The recipient of numerous industry awards, Yesawich served on the national board of directors of the Travel Industry Association of America and as a Visiting Associate Professor of Marketing at Cornell University. He has authored numerous articles in both trade and professional journals, and is a co-author of "*Marketing Leadership In Hospitality*" published by Prentice-Hall and "*Hospitable Healthcare: Just What the Patient Ordered!*" published by Indigo River Press.

From 2010 to 2020, Yesawich served as Chief Growth Officer (CGO) of Cancer Treatment Centers of America® (CTCA), a national network of specialty hospitals and outpatient clinics treating adults with complex or advanced-stage cancer. CTCA became the most widely recognized national cancer treatment provider in the US and third most positively perceived hospital system in the country under his tenure as CGO.

We thought it was wonderful to talk to you about tourism industry and how it's balancing the need for economic growth in a changing world, as well as the imperative in reducing their environmental footprint and making a difference in acting as the stewards for the next generation? We wanted to see your reaction and wanted to get your insights on those.

I still conduct a national survey called the Portrait of American Travelers, which I believe is the longest continuous examination of lifestyle and travel preferences in America. This survey provides a comprehensive database on various subjects, including sustainability.

We included questions on sustainability because many clients were curious about the importance of being LEED certified when building a new hotel, or having policies that promote sustainability for ecotourism destinations. We started tracking awareness and motivations related to these issues.

What we discovered, and what continues to be disappointing for many, is that although the stated importance of environmental issues among travelers has increased over the past 10 to 12 years, this awareness has not translated

> *into behavior. Travelers acknowledge the importance of things like LEED certification and environmental sensitivity, but when asked if they are willing to pay a premium for suppliers who demonstrate these qualities, the numbers drop significantly.*
>
> *Only about one-third of respondents admit they are prepared to pay a premium, and even then, they are generally willing to pay a very modest premium—less than 10%. So, despite increased sensitivity to environmental issues, it hasn't become a standard consideration in travel decisions. For instance, when booking flights, most travelers still opt for the cheaper option over one that offers carbon offsets.*
>
> *The conclusion we've drawn is that while it's essential for destinations to acknowledge and address environmental issues to remain competitive, they shouldn't expect to charge a premium for these efforts because the market is not yet willing to pay for them.*
>
> *For example, if you're booking a flight from Boston to Cancun and you see American Airlines offering a deal while Copa Airlines offers carbon offsets, most people will choose the cheaper option, even if they care about sustainability. This shows that the concern for environmental issues often doesn't translate into financial behavior.*

This shift highlights the challenge for the hospitality industry: without strong consumer demand for sustainable options, hotels may lack incentives to go beyond basic sustainability measures. Consequently, it underscores the importance of raising awareness and creating incentives that encourage both businesses and consumers to prioritize sustainability in their travel choices.

ESG scores are designed to evaluate the impact of a company's activities on the environment, society, and its governance structure. These scores have become a significant focus in the financial industry as non-financial metrics are increasingly seen as crucial for assessing the long-term viability and ethical grounding of businesses. ESG investing encompasses various approaches, often referred to as sustainable investing, responsible investing, or impact investing. Some of these themes were examine in Chapter 2 of this book. However, the precise classification of ESG factors from a financial standpoint remains challenging, reflecting broader uncertainties around the legal definition of sustainability.

Among the numerous ESG data providers, four major companies dominate the market: MSCI, Sustainalytics, Refinitiv, and RobecoSAM. MSCI, a spin-off of Morgan Stanley, is a leading player, leveraging its established position in the indexing business to offer ESG indices such as MSCI World ESG Leaders and MSCI ACWI ESG Leaders, launched in 2007 and 2013, respectively.[3] Sustainalytics, founded in 1992, is a European-based research and rating firm that focuses exclusively on sustainability ratings. In 2016, Morningstar acquired a 40% stake in Sustainalytics, further enhancing its market presence. Refinitiv, a London-based company, emerged

---

[3] https://www.msci.com/sustainable-investing/esg-ratings.

from a spin-off of Reuters' financial and risk business.[4] It is now controlled by Blackstone and Thomson Reuters and has recently been acquired by the London Stock Exchange Group (LSEG) in a USD 27 billion all-shares transaction aimed at creating a leading market infrastructure provider. RobecoSAM, a Swiss asset management firm founded in 1995, is dedicated solely to sustainable investments, with S&P Global recently acquiring its ESG rating business.[5]

Each of these companies employs distinct methodologies for calculating ESG scores. MSCI, for example, combines a quantitative model based on 35 ESG key issues with qualitative assessments from analysts, resulting in a rating scale that ranges from CCC to AAA. MSCI provides updated details on several frameworks and standards using its vast database of company sustainability reports. For example, it shows the following aggregate sector figure of companies that have a dependency to report on biodiversity loss.[6] The highest is reported from agriculture, fishery and aquaculture, food, forestry, and construction while banking and digital communications show no impact.

Refinitiv's ESG ratings are based on a database of over 630 ESG metrics, although only 186 are used in calculating the scores, which range from D- to A+. Refinitiv emphasizes transparency in its methodology, though the complexity and volume of data make replication challenging. RobecoSAM's approach involves a proprietary questionnaire covering economic, environmental, and social dimensions, complemented by a media stakeholder analysis. Sustainalytics, on the other hand, provides an absolute assessment of ESG risks, allowing comparisons across different sectors. Their methodology involves a top-down assessment of sub-industries to identify material ESG issues, followed by a company-specific analysis and a continuous review of media reports.

The divergence in ESG ratings across providers is notable, with significant variations observed in how companies are evaluated. Unlike credit ratings, which show a high correlation of 99% between agencies like Moody's and S&P, ESG ratings exhibit an average correlation of only 71% (Berg et al., 2022; Gibson Brandon et al., 2021). This variation can be attributed to differences in methodologies, criteria, and the weight given to various ESG factors. As a result, a company involved in controversial activities such as tobacco or alcohol production might receive a high ESG rating if it performs well relative to its industry peers. This lack of standardization in ESG ratings presents challenges for investors seeking to make informed decisions based on these scores (Dell'Erba & Doronzo, 2023).

As the demand for ESG ratings and data products continues to evolve, so does the landscape of ESG rating providers. New topics of interest, such as green initiatives, contributions to the UN Sustainable Development Goals, and broader areas like environmental changes, diversity, inclusion, and biodiversity, are shaping the development of ESG ratings. The ongoing evolution of ESG metrics and the increasing focus

---

[4] https://www.sustainalytics.com/about-us.

[5] https://www.robeco.com/en-us/.

[6] https://www.msci.com/documents/1296102/23003857/MSCI+Response+to+EC+Draft+Delegated+Act+on+the+ESRS.pdf.

5.2 Global Standard and Frameworks for Sustainability Reporting

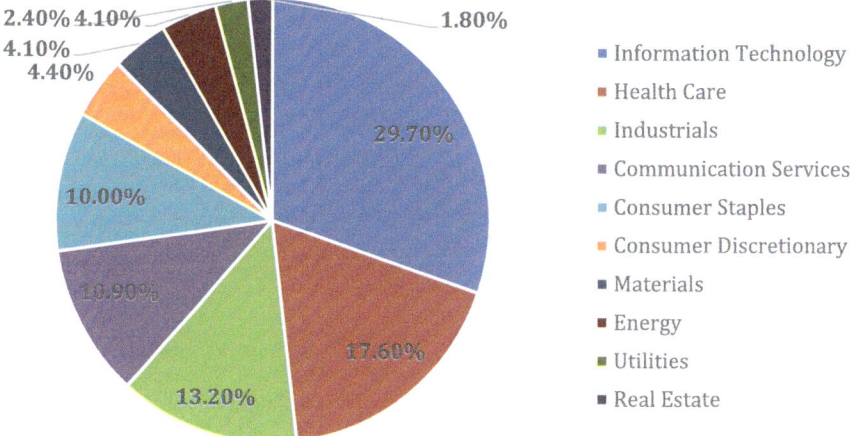

Fig. 5.4 Dow Jones Sustainability World Index (DJSWI) Sectors in 2023 (in percent)

on financial materiality highlight the dynamic nature of this field, which remains critical for investors and companies alike.

A quick analysis of the S&P Global Dow Jones Index provides some insights.

S&P Global Dow Jones Index: Leaders identified by S&P Global through its corporate sustainability assessment. These companies are the top 10% of the 2500 companies in the S&P Global BMI (Broad Market Index) based on long-term ESG criteria. Details are described in the factsheet of the website.[7] This index weighting by sector is shown in Fig. 5.4. Information technology, health care, and industrials make up more than 50% of the global index. The top 10 companies are Microsoft, Alphabet A, Taiwan Semiconductor, UnitedHealth Group, ASML Hlding, Abbvie, Salesforce, Adobe, Tencent Holdings, and Linde. Most companies are information technology, healthcare, or communication services. Only Linde is in the materials sector. This suggests that information technology companies have a smaller GHG Scope 1 footprint and may have a larger Scope 3 footprint that is not included in the calculations.

As part of its commitment to supporting ESG transparency, S&P Dow Jones Indices (different from Global BMI mentioned in the last paragraph) provides four carbon exposure metrics for its global indices to help market participants understand, measure, and manage carbon risk.

- The first measure is carbon footprint, carbon to value invested, which adjusts the index's total GHG for the amount of money invested in it, offering a measure of carbon accountability. Specifically, it quantifies the GHG emissions linked to every USD 1 million invested in the index. This allows for equitable comparisons regardless of the investment's scale or duration or the specific index in question. The calculation involves dividing the total GHG emissions of all the assets

---

[7] https://www.spglobal.com/spdji/en/indices/esg/dow-jones-sustainability-world-index/#data.

Table 5.3 Dow Jones Sustainability World Index Characteristics

Dow Jones Sustainability World Index	
Number of Constituents	322
Constituent Total Market Cap	
Largest Market Cap	3,074,280.85
Smallest Market Cap	95.61
Mean Market Cap	49,702.64
Median Market Cap	14,746.05
ESG Characteristics	
Carbon to Value Invested (metric tons CO2e/$1 M invested)*	55.19
Carbon to Revenue (metric tons CO2e/$1 M revenues)*	136.37
Weighted Average Carbon Intensity (metric tons CO2e/$1 M revenues)*	131.35
Fossil Fuel Reserve Emissions (metric tons CO2/$1 M invested)	1,003.52

within the index by the index's total investment value, expressed in millions of US dollars. This value in Table 5.3 shows the Dow Jones sustainability world index characteristics value invested (metric tons CO2e/$1 M invested), which is 55.19.

- The second measure is Carbon to Revenue (expressed in metric tons CO2e/$1 M revenues) metric that adjusts the total GHG emissions owned by the index to the revenue generated by its constituents, expressed in millions of US dollars associated with an investment in the index. This method reveals the carbon risk level of an index by measuring the correlation between the revenue of its constituents and their emissions. The calculation is done by dividing the total GHG emissions owned by the constituents by their total allocated revenues, both measured in millions of US dollars.

Dow Jones Sustainability World Index[8]: This index consists of global sustainability companies.

- The third measure is Weighted Average Carbon Intensity, which gauges the index's exposure to companies with high carbon emissions. This metric is calculated by determining the carbon intensity (measured in tCO2e per USD 1 million) of each index constituent and then multiplying it by the constituent's respective weight within the index. The overall carbon intensity of the index is then derived by summing up these individual contributions. This metric differs from the previously mentioned ones as it allocates GHG emission intensities based on the proportional representation of each constituent within the index, rather than attributing them based on ownership or responsibility.
- The fourth measure is Fossil Fuel Reserve Emissions. This metric quantifies the potential GHG emissions stemming from the combustion of proven (1P) and probable (2P) fossil fuel reserves held by the constituents of an index. It serves as an

---

[8] https://www.spglobal.com/spdji/en/documents/additional-material/spdji-esg-carbon-metrics.pdf.

indicator of the relative risk of stranded assets across various indices. Expressed in terms of emissions per USD 1 million invested in the index, it facilitates comparisons across investments of varying magnitudes, durations, or different indices. The calculation is performed by dividing the total emissions embedded in the owned fossil fuel reserves of the index constituents by the index's total investment value, measured in millions of US dollars. In Table 5.3, global fossil fuel reserve emissions (metric tons CO2/$1 M invested) is 1,003.52.

To summarize, Companies utilize services from Bloomberg Terminal ESG Analysis, Institutional Shareholder Services (ISS) E&S Quality Score, MSCI, and Sustainalytics to analyze and benchmark their ESG performance. These platforms aggregate data from public disclosures, providing insights and ratings that help investors make informed decisions.

5.3 Reporting Standards and Frameworks—The Case of the European Union

The regulations in the EU are introduced in Chapter 2 of this book. Section 2.6 examines regulation in the EU, US, and Asia. In this section, the SFDR is elaborated further.

Central to the EU reporting system is the EU Taxonomy, which provides a clear classification of what constitutes environmentally sustainable activities. It sets environmental goals and criteria for sustainable economic activities. It aligns financial and non-financial reporting with sustainability objectives. This is linked to the European Sustainability Reporting Standards (ESRS), a set of standards developed to guide companies in reporting their sustainability performance. The ESRS incorporates requirements that ensure companies disclose information about how their activities align with the EU Taxonomy, as shown in Fig. 5.5.

Figure 5.5 includes details on the extent to which their operations and investments meet the Taxonomy's criteria for being environmentally sustainable. They aim to ensure transparency, standardize reporting, and support stakeholders. The EU Taxonomy offers a standardized definition of economic activities that are considered environmentally sustainable. It sets criteria for what can be labeled as green or sustainable, guiding companies and investors in identifying truly sustainable investments and operations. The ESRS provides standardized and detailed information on companies' sustainability practices and impacts. These data are crucial for financial market participants to fulfill their SFDR obligations, particularly in assessing and disclosing the sustainability risks and impacts of their investments.

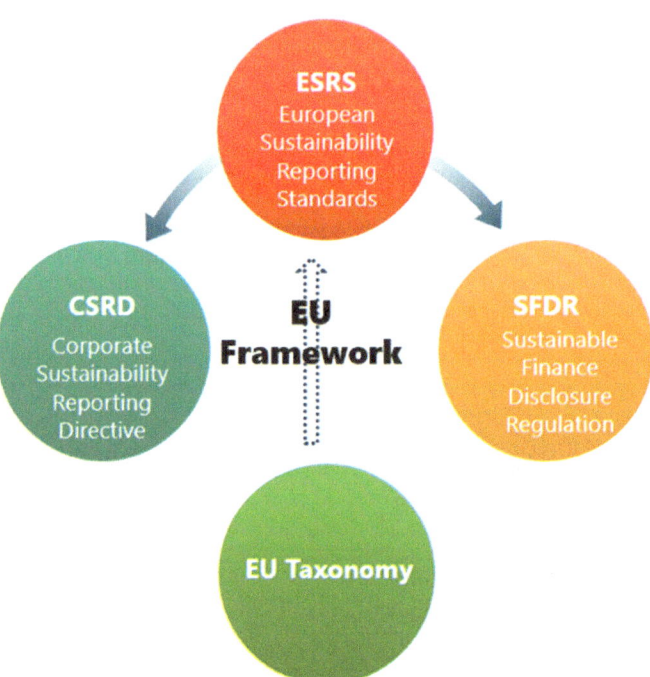

Fig. 5.5 The EU framework includes the EU taxonomy informing the ESRS which in turn guides CSRD aimed at corporations and SFDR aimed at financial disclosure regulations

5.3.1 ESRS and CSRD

The relationship between all elements of the EU sustainability framework is displayed in Fig. 5.6. ESRS and the taxonomy support both the Corporate Sustainability Reporting Directive (CSRD) and the Sustainable Finance Disclosure Regulation (SFDR) by providing aligned metrics for their reporting and disclosure requirements. The CSRD mandates that companies disclose their sustainability performance in detail, specifically in line with the EU Taxonomy. It requires comprehensive reporting on how their activities impact the environment and society, ensuring that their sustainability claims are verifiable and consistent with the EU's sustainability goals. The SFDR focuses on transparency within the financial markets. It compels financial market participants to disclose how their products align with the EU Taxonomy. This regulation aims to increase the transparency of sustainable investment products, making it easier for investors to understand and trust the sustainability claims made by financial institutions.

Companies must report how their economic activities contribute to the six environmental objectives of the EU Taxonomy: climate change mitigation, climate change

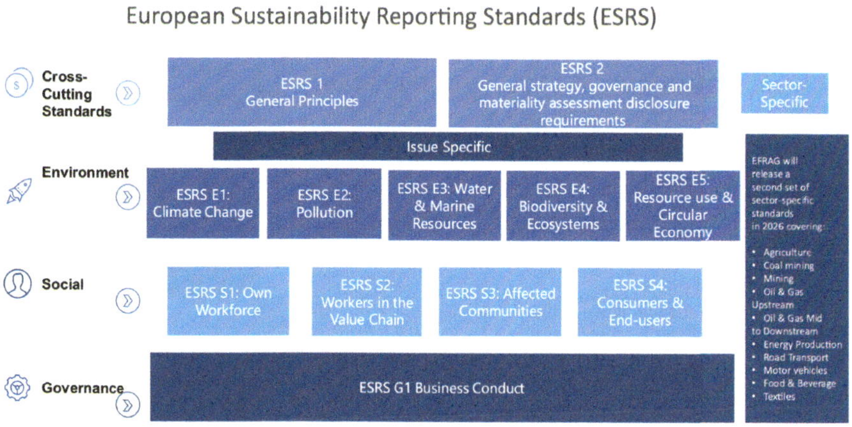

European Sustainability Reporting Standards (ESRS)

Fig. 5.6 Shows ESRS general principles and specifics of disclosure requirements. The cross cutting standards consist of ESG standards. The future sector specific standards are expected to come to practice in 2026

adaptation, pollution, sustainable use and protection of water and marine resources, biodiversity and ecosystems, and transition to a circular economy. The ESRS provides standardized and detailed information on companies' sustainability practices and impacts, which are displayed in Fig. 5.6. These data are crucial for financial market participants to fulfill their SFDR obligations, particularly in assessing and disclosing the sustainability risks and impacts of their investments. By integrating these regulations, the EU creates a streamlined approach to compliance and promotes sustainable investment. Companies benefit from a clear set of guidelines for reporting, while investors gain a reliable framework to evaluate the sustainability of their investments. This holistic strategy not only simplifies regulatory adherence but also enhances the attractiveness of sustainable investments for companies and investors alike.

5.3.2 SFDR—Articles 6, 8, and 9

The Sustainable Finance Disclosure Regulation (SFDR) is a pivotal piece of legislation introduced by the European Commission as part of its Action Plan on Sustainable Finance. Aiming to promote transparency and combat greenwashing, the SFDR requires financial market participants (FMPs) and financial advisors (FAs) to make disclosures about sustainability in their processes and products, focusing on a defined set of Principle Adverse Impact (PAI) indicators. Table 5.4 shows the SFDR disclosure template.

If an agricultural company such Dannon Adopted in response to the growing demand for sustainable investment products, the SFDR, alongside the Taxonomy Regulation, seeks to enhance transparency within the EU financial sector regarding

Table 5.4 The Majority of the PAI Indicators will be reported subject to materiality (green)

PAI Indicators	Mandatory Reporting Regardless of Materiality	Reporting Required only Subject to Materiality
1. GHG Emissions		✓
2. Carbon footprint		✓
3. GHG intensity of investee companies		✓
4. Exposure to companies active in the fossil fuel sector	✓	
5. Share of non-renewable energy consumption and production		✓
6. Energy consumption intensity per high impact climate sector		✓
7. Activities negatively affecting biodiversity-sensitive areas		✓
8. Emissions to water		✓
9. Hazardous waste and radioactive waste ratio		✓
10. Violations of UN Global Compact principles and Organisation for Economic Cooperation and Development (OECD) Guidelines for Multinational Enterprises		✓
11. Lack of processes and compliance mechanisms to monitor compliance with UN Global Compact principles and OECD Guidelines for Multinational Enterprises		✓
12. Unadjusted gender pay gap		✓
13. Board gender diversity	✓	
14. Exposure to controversial weapons	✓	

the sustainability of investment products. From 10 March 2021, entities are required to disclose the ESG characteristics of their funds, classifying them into one of three categories: Article 6, 8, or 9, based on their sustainability objectives and impacts.

5.3.2.1 Classification and Obligations

Article 6: The Baseline, whose scope includes all managed products, regardless of ESG focus. Disclosure requirements call for basic information on sustainability and climate risks.

Article 8: Light Green Classification, whose products that promote environmental or social characteristics, with investments not undermining these characteristics. The disclosure requirements call for enhanced disclosure on how ESG factors are integrated and do not significantly harm the sustainability objectives.

Article 9: Dark Green Classification, whose scope includes products targeting sustainable investment as their primary objective. The disclosure requirements must demonstrate active contribution to the EU Taxonomy objectives and report comprehensively on sustainability impacts.

Table 5.4 shows the majority of PAI indicators that will be reported by companies. It shows some PAI indicators are mandatory while on a majority (shown in green) reporting is required subject to materiality. For example, technology companies are not going to have biodiversity impacts while their energy consumption might be high.

Articles 8 and 9 of the SFDR outline specific requirements for different financial products: Article 8 products refer to financial products that promote, among other characteristics, environmental or social characteristics, or a combination of those characteristics, and where companies follow good governance practices. However, achieving a sustainable investment objective is not the main purpose for these products. Article 9 products, on the other hand, have sustainable investment as their objective. A sustainable investment refers to an investment in an economic activity that contributes to an environmental objective, or an investment that contributes to a social objective (for example, tackling inequality or fostering social cohesion, social integration and labor relations), and where, in both cases, the investment does not significantly harm any of those objectives and the investee companies follow good governance practices. In terms of disclosures, both Articles 8 and 9 products require firms to disclose information about how sustainability risks are integrated into their investment decisions and the potential impacts of sustainability risks on the returns of the financial products. Companies are required to disclose:

In terms of disclosures, both Articles 8 and 9 products require firms to disclose information about how sustainability risks are integrated into their investment decisions and the potential impacts of sustainability risks on the returns of the financial products. Companies are required to disclose:

- A description of the environmental or social characteristics or the sustainable investment objective. (See table below).
- The methodologies used to assess, measure, and monitor the environmental or social characteristics or the impact of the sustainable investments selected for the financial product.
- The data sources and processing actions.
- The limitations to the methodologies and data.

- The due diligence and actions taken for monitoring the ongoing impact of the investments.
- In terms of obtaining data, companies may need to rely on both internal resources and external providers to gather all the required information, which might include ESG ratings, climate data, social impact measurements, etc.

The implementation of these new regulations is a two-stage process. The first stage (level 1) started in March 2021. The second stage (level 2) started in January 2023.

SFDR is closely linked with the EU Taxonomy and the Task Force on Climate-related Financial Disclosures (TCFD), requiring periodic reporting against the EU taxonomy. Despite criticism regarding the dilution of criteria within the EU Taxonomy, SFDR and TCFD together represent a comprehensive approach to ESG disclosure, covering a broader spectrum of risks than TCFD's focus solely on climate change (Alessi et al., 2022; De Oliveira, 2022).

A recent Morningstar report, SFDR Article 8 and Article 9 Funds: Q4 2023 in Review, provides an in-depth analysis of the development and status of Article 8 and Article 9 funds as of December 2023, focusing on fund flows, assets, new launches, reclassifications, and their sustainability disclosures and impacts.[9] In the final quarter of 2023, the asset management landscape experienced significant shifts, particularly within the domains of Article 8 and Article 9 funds. This period marked the largest quarterly outflows ever for Article 8 funds and the inaugural quarterly outflows for Article 9 funds. The findings in the Morningstar report imply a complex and dynamic environment for Articles 8 and 9 funds. The volatility in fund flows could be attributed to a mix of factors, including changing investor preferences, market uncertainty, and geopolitical risks. However, the continued growth in assets and market share points to a sustained interest in sustainable investments, even as the market undergoes significant adjustments. Investors and fund managers will need to navigate these challenges carefully, balancing the demand for sustainability with the need to manage risk and maintain investor confidence.

While the SFDR marks a critical step toward embedding sustainability in the financial sector, its implementation poses considerable challenges. First, greenwashing, the practice of overstating an investment product's environmental or sustainable characteristics, stands at the forefront of SFDR's challenges (Yu et al., 2020. The regulation introduces a classification system for financial products (Article 8 and 9 funds) aimed at distinguishing genuine sustainable investments from others. However, the broad criteria for these classifications have inadvertently allowed some entities to market their products as "sustainable" without substantial evidence of their sustainability impact. This ambiguity undermines investor confidence and dilutes the effectiveness of the regulation in promoting genuine sustainable finance initiatives.

Second, a pivotal aspect of SFDR is its requirement for detailed ESG disclosures, intending to provide investors with clear insights into the sustainability risks and impacts of their investments (Alessi et al., 2022; De Oliveira, 2022). This

---

[9] https://www.morningstar.com/en-uk/lp/sfdr-article8-article9.

requirement, however, collides with the current ESG data landscape, characterized by fragmentation, varying reporting standards, and the occasional absence of relevant data. The inconsistency in ESG metrics across companies and industries complicates the compliance process, making it challenging for financial entities to aggregate and report the required information accurately. This situation places a considerable burden on financial market participants, particularly smaller firms with limited resources, potentially stifling their ability to compete in an increasingly sustainability-focused market.

Third, the implementation of SFDR necessitates significant adjustments in internal systems, processes, and documentation for financial institutions. The regulation demands an unprecedented level of detail in sustainability-related disclosures, requiring entities to enhance their data collection, analysis, and reporting capabilities (Pinson, 2023). This transformation is resource-intensive, posing a particular challenge for smaller market participants and possibly leading to market consolidation. Moreover, the evolving nature of SFDR—with updates and clarifications still being issued—adds to the regulatory uncertainty, complicating compliance efforts. Thus, addressing issues of greenwashing, data standardization, and the regulatory burden on market participants is essential for realizing the regulation's full potential. Future amendments and guidance should aim to refine classification criteria, promote data consistency, and support market participants through the transition. Ultimately, the success of SFDR hinges on a collaborative effort among regulators, financial institutions, and investors to foster a transparent, sustainable financial ecosystem.

5.3.3 SFDR Article 8 and 9 Funds

MSCI offers a range of ESG and sustainability-focused funds that are classified under SFDR Articles 8 and 9. These funds are designed to meet various ESG criteria, where Article 8 funds promote environmental or social characteristics, and Article 9 funds have sustainable investment as their objective. For example, Calvert Sustainable climate aligned fund invests in information technology, financial, health care and industrial. About 70% of funds are related to US companies while Japan, France and Switzerland contribute much less. Goldman Sachs has also been involved in SFDR Article 8 and 9 classifications.[10] They have research reports and funds that align with these articles, providing investors with opportunities to invest in companies that meet certain ESG standards. They note that the shift of capital into SFDR ESG funds is significantly influencing capital flows. Goldman focuses on the most commonly held and overweight stocks in Articles 8 and 9 funds, which continue to show a strong preference for thematically aligned companies. Since Articles 8 and 9 funds must report their alignment with the EU Taxonomy, Goldman expects taxonomy adoption

---

[10] https://www.goldmansachs.com/pdfs/insights/pages/gs-research/sfdr-two-years-on-trends-and-anatomy-of-article-8-and-9-funds-in-2023/report.pdf.

to become a key driver for investing in these companies and sectors, channeling essential capital toward enhancing sustainable outcomes.

AllianceBernstein has analyzed what to look for in Articles 8 and 9 portfolios, highlighting how investors and companies are responding to ESG issues.[11] They emphasize the importance of shareholder support for environmental initiatives within these funds. Additionally, they point out that, given the ambiguity of regulatory guidelines, asset managers must establish a transparent framework to demonstrate how their products align with sustainable investing classifications.

As asset managers improve their ability to interpret data in alignment with Articles 8 and 9, some uncertainty is likely to persist until more accurate classifications for sustainable investing are established.

5.4 Exploring the Evolution and Impact of ESG Disclosures in Corporate America

The landscape of corporate responsibility and transparency has undergone a remarkable transformation with the rise of ESG disclosures. Once a peripheral aspect of corporate reporting, ESG reports have burgeoned into a near-ubiquitous phenomenon among large US firms, marking a significant shift in business practices. This surge in ESG reporting, (Christensen et al., 2022; Serafeim & Yoon, 2023), reflects a growing demand from a broad spectrum of stakeholders for a deeper understanding of corporate activities beyond traditional financial metrics. Companies now invest substantial resources in crafting these reports, employing expert consultants, and allocating considerable funds to ensure their reports' accuracy, relevance, and presentation. This trend underscores a pivotal evolution in the informational ecosystem surrounding corporate entities, spotlighting the increasing importance of sustainability and ethical governance in the modern business ethos.

Despite the widespread adoption of ESG disclosures, much question remains regarding their true utility to investors, regulators, and society at large. The voluntary nature of these reports, coupled with a lack of auditing standards and uniformity, introduces variability in disclosure quality and depth. This scenario breeds skepticism regarding the actual content of ESG reports and their comparative relevance and reliability. As these reports become more prevalent, the imperative to scrutinize their financial materiality through empirical research grows, potentially guiding future regulatory frameworks and enhancing the overall utility of ESG disclosures.

A recent study (Kimbrough et al., 2024) used machine learning techniques to dissect the content of these disclosures at a granular level. A detailed examination of the amassed dataset revealed a noteworthy trend: on average, firms disclosed significantly more material than immaterial information in their ESG reports, with both the

---

[11] https://www.alliancebernstein.com/corporate/en/insights/investment-insights/sfdr-unpacked-what-to-look-for-in-article-8-and-9-portfolios.html.

quantity and relative amount of material information showing a recent uptake. Additionally, the study observed a convergence in the language used within ESG reports across industries, indicating a move toward standardization in how firms communicate their sustainability and governance efforts. This finding not only highlights the increasing emphasis on material ESG disclosures but also suggests a gradual harmonization of reporting practices within sectors. Companies engaged in following standard-setting process (Rouen et al., 2023) demonstrated high levels of significant disclosures before those standards were made public. Conversely, companies that did not participate in the standard-setting disclosures enhanced their significant disclosures after these standards were introduced.

5.4.1 To Be and Not to Be—New SEC Climate Regulations

On March 6, 2024, the US Securities and Exchange Commission (SEC) introduced climate risk disclosure rules, marking a significant development in the integration of climate risk analysis within the business and climate sectors. This move was pivotal as it enabled companies, nonprofits, and agencies that provide climate risk data to evaluate environmental issues affecting financial outcomes. The SEC's guidelines focus on the direct carbon emissions of companies (GHG Scope 1 and 2) and their vulnerability to extreme weather and climate events, thus urging corporations to consider the impact of climate change on their operations and to account for their emissions. This regulatory push is expected to enhance corporate engagement with a growing network of specialized entities that offer insights into climate risk, aiding businesses in quantifying the effects of climate change on their operations.

The SEC climate risk disclosure rules give investors and the public a much closer look at companies' contributions to, and impact on, climate change.[12] It works by requiring so-called large accelerated filers and "accelerated filers" to file securities disclosures of emissions from their direct operations (Scope 1), and the energy that powers them (Scope 2). They must also offer analysis of physical risks to their business from climate change, like extreme weather, and "transition risks" like climate policies and changing consumer preferences.[13] However, the SEC's decision to potentially exclude Scope 3 emissions (indirect emissions) from the disclosure requirements indicates a cautious approach amid political and legal challenges. This development occurs as various US states actively debate the role of ESG criteria in investment decisions, with some proposing legislation against ESG considerations. "Scope 3" emissions are often the largest category of emissions for many consumer facing companies. The adoption of this rule is seen as a response to the increasing

---

[12] https://www.sec.gov/newsroom/speeches-statements/gensler-statement-mandatory-climate-risk-disclosures-030624.

[13] https://www.sec.gov/newsroom/speeches-statements/cresnshaw-statement-mandatory-climate-risk-disclosures-030624.

frequency and severity of extreme weather events and reflects a broader trend toward more rigorous climate disclosure requirements globally.

The SEC rules represent a significant step toward greater transparency and accountability in corporate climate reporting. By mandating the disclosure of emissions and climate-related risks, the SEC aims to provide investors with crucial information on the environmental impact of companies. Larger public companies will be forced to disclose certain emissions and climate-related risks to their business, which will provide a much closer look at their impact on climate change. This regulatory move has thus been highly contested and heavily lobbied and has prompted litigation from groups across the political spectrum, underscoring the contentious nature of climate-related disclosures.

On March 14, 2024, the US Chamber of Commerce filed a lawsuit against the SEC over its new disclosure rules.[14] The nation's largest business lobby group thus joined several others, from the left and the right, in filing litigation against the measure, including the Sierra Club and Republican attorneys general from 10 states. The outcome of these legal challenges and the final form of the SEC rules will be pivotal in shaping the future of corporate climate accountability and the role of climate risk analysis in business strategy and investment decision-making.

In its reporting of March 12, 2024, CNBC interviewed Citadel founder Ken Griffin, who discussed "unintended consequences" of this rule.[15] Griffen believes that fewer companies would go public with this ruling, public companies would be paying more taxes, and it would stifle Research & Development activity as Venture Capitalists are not likely to invest in this landscape. He also said the public would pay for it. As companies prepare, they may need to consider the global regulatory environment, as the SEC rule is one of many that could apply to US companies.

5.4.2 California's Climate Regulations

On October 7, 2023, California Governor Gavin Newsom signed two groundbreaking climate disclosure bills that are set to transform climate reporting practices in the United States. These new regulations will impact over 10,000 US companies, including both public and private entities, as well as subsidiaries of international companies operating within California. The two climate laws are SB 261, known as the *Climate-Related Financial Risk Act*, and SB 253, the *Climate Corporate Data Accountability Act*. These laws require public and private companies doing business in California to disclose their greenhouse gas emissions and assess climate-related

---

[14] https://www.uschamber.com/cases/capital-markets-and-corporate-law/sec-climate-disclosure-rule.

[15] https://www.cnbc.com/2024/03/12/watch-citadels-ken-griffin-talk-about-the-markets-economy-and-the-feds-rate-cutting-path.html.

financial risks. SB 253 specifically mandates that all US-based companies generating revenues over $1 billion report their greenhouse gas emissions, promoting transparency and accountability in climate impacts.

- Carbon Offsets and Emissions Claims: Companies are required to disclose information about specific emissions claims and the sale and use of carbon offsets.

These requirements are in line with the standards set by the SEC climate disclosure proposal, the European Sustainability Reporting Standards, and the IFRS Sustainability Disclosure Standards. However, the scope of these California bills extends beyond the SEC proposal, covering both public and private companies engaged in business activities in the state. It would be a major step forward for climate disclosure (Gerrard & Orts, 2023). Environmental justice became integrated into the state's climate action efforts and may show the rest of the country how to proceed on this front (Pastor et al., 2024).

The bills are relatively concise but leave some questions unanswered regarding the specifics of implementation and timing. The California Air Resources Board is expected to issue more comprehensive regulations for SB 253 and SB 261 before January 1, 2025.[16] California Assembly Bill No. 1305 aims to ensure the authenticity and effectiveness of voluntary carbon offsets (VCOs) used by businesses to compensate for their emissions. The bill is designed to confirm that these offsets represent genuine emission reductions and removals, promoting high-quality offsets in the market. The legal mandate became effective as of January 1, 2024, under California law.[17] Non-compliance with AB 1305 includes potential civil penalties of up to $2,500 per day with a maximum penalty of $500,000. Companies are advised to review the applicability and requirements of these bills based on the available information and prepare for their mandatory climate-related disclosures.

5.5 Sustainability Reporting in Asia

Although many Asian economies currently lack a comprehensive climate taxonomy, the adoption of such frameworks is becoming more widespread. According to a recent survey, seven out of twelve countries reported not having a climate taxonomy that defines sustainable economic activities and financial instruments. The People's Bank of China introduced the region's first climate taxonomy in 2015, which has since been supplemented with additional guidelines (Zhang, 2020). Transitioning to net zero: Full potential of sustainable finance taxonomies not yet exhausted (Marchewitz et al., 2024). DIW Weekly Report, 14(28), 189–197.). Other countries, including Korea, Indonesia, Malaysia, and Mongolia, have finalized their taxonomies, while several others are in the process of developing theirs (IMF, 2023). In Japan, the government

---

[16] https://leginfo.legislature.ca.gov/faces/billNavClient.xhtml?bill_id=202320240SB253.

[17] https://www.persefoni.com/blog/ab-1305.

provides high-level guidance on climate finance, with the development of a taxonomy under consideration (IMF, 2024).

Governments are encouraged to establish robust climate information architectures, which include three key components: climate finance taxonomies, climate disclosure standards, and climate-related statistics. This architecture is essential for accurate market pricing of risks, informed investment decisions, and the growth of climate finance (Prasad et al., 2022). According to the International Monetary Fund (IMF, 2023), these components facilitate the development of a strong climate finance sector, particularly in emerging markets.

Climate Finance Taxonomies: Climate finance taxonomies are frameworks designed to align investments with globally agreed climate goals. Adhering to such principles can attract cross-border climate finance and leverage regional economies of scale, even as the stages of economic development vary significantly across countries (IMF, 2023). For example, transition taxonomies can help identify activities that reduce greenhouse gas (GHG) emissions over time, providing a pathway for industries to move toward sustainability (IMF, 2024). Cross-border climate finance, typically transferred from developed to refer to the financial flows that are transferred from one country to another to support climate change mitigation and adaptation efforts. Typically, these funds are transferred from developed countries to developing countries, which are often more vulnerable to the impacts of climate change and may lack the financial resources necessary to address these challenges. These include funds provided by governments through bilateral agreements, multilateral development banks (e.g., World Bank, Asian Development Bank), and international climate funds (e.g., Green Climate Fund, Global Environment Facility).

Climate-Related Data: High-quality, timely, reliable, and comparable data are crucial for making informed climate-related investment and finance decisions. Governments must invest in their statistical agencies to collect these data and develop macro-critical aggregates. These agencies play a key role in aligning taxonomies at the business level with international statistical classifications and standards.

Strengthening the capacity to conduct climate risk analyses is crucial for properly assessing the physical and transition risks associated with climate change. Ongoing efforts by the ASEAN Capital Markets Forum to assess the feasibility of adopting ISSB standards based on their jurisdictions' legal and regulatory frameworks are a positive step forward. Notwithstanding such efforts to improve the quality and reliability of data for climate stress tests in the region, financial regulators should continue to expedite their work in examining the potential impacts of these risks using available data, scenarios, and risk analyses. In the meantime, financial regulators could develop a range of in-house models at macroeconomic, microeconomic, and sectoral levels to evaluate the systemic impact (IMF, 2022).

Based on a survey by the Network for Greening the Financial System (NGFS, 2022) and the Financial Stability Board (FSB, 2022), several financial regulators in the Asia-Pacific region have already conducted scenario and risk analysis exercises to raise awareness. These could serve as best practices for other jurisdictions in the region.

Public investment management reforms are crucial for directing investment toward climate mitigation and adaptation goals. Inefficiencies in public investment processes can result in about 30 percent lower potential gains from such investments (IMF, 2015). Strengthening public investment management involves conducting public investment management assessment (PIMA), a framework that evaluates the planning, resource allocation, and implementation stages of the public investment cycle. PIMA also assesses the legal and regulatory frameworks, staff capacity, and information technology systems involved.

Public financial management reforms can assist governments in identifying viable projects aligned with national climate strategies, setting numerical targets for green technologies, and estimating the financing needs for these projects. Additionally, improving the capacity to assess climate-related debt costs and risks, as well as evaluating infrastructure resilience, can help address adaptation gaps. These reforms are essential for enhancing institutional capacity to manage public investment processes effectively, generating economic returns, and attracting private capital for financing (Aligishiev et al. 2022).

5.6 Summary

This chapter covered the evolving landscape of sustainability reporting, encompassing global standards, frameworks, and regulatory requirements, reflects a growing recognition of the importance of integrating ESG Sustainability reporting offers numerous benefits, including enhanced transparency, improved risk management, and the ability to attract long-term investors. By disclosing sustainability-related information, companies can demonstrate their commitment to ethical practices and environmental stewardship, which, in turn, strengthens their reputation and competitiveness in the market. Moreover, sustainability reporting provides a framework for companies to assess and communicate their progress toward achieving sustainability goals, fostering a culture of continuous improvement, considerations into corporate strategy and reporting. The increasing focus on sustainability reporting is driven by the need for greater transparency, accountability, and the alignment of business practices with global sustainability goals.

Despite its advantages, ESG reporting has faced criticism for its lack of standardization, the potential for greenwashing, and the variability in the quality and comparability of reported data. Critics argue that the proliferation of different ESG frameworks and the lack of a universally accepted standard can lead to inconsistencies and confusion among stakeholders. Additionally, concerns have been raised about the reliability of ESG ratings, which often vary significantly between rating agencies due to differing methodologies and criteria.

Global standards and frameworks for sustainability reporting, such as the Global Reporting Initiative (GRI) and the International Sustainability Standards Board (ISSB), have been developed to provide guidance on how companies should disclose sustainability-related information. These frameworks aim to harmonize reporting practices across industries and regions, enabling stakeholders to make informed decisions based on consistent and comparable data. However, the effectiveness of these standards largely depends on their adoption and implementation by companies worldwide.

Despite its advantages, ESG reporting has faced criticism for its lack of standardization, the potential for greenwashing, and the variability in the quality and comparability of reported data. Critics argue that the proliferation of different ESG frameworks and the lack of a universally accepted standard can lead to inconsistencies and confusion among stakeholders. Additionally, concerns have been raised about the reliability of ESG ratings, which often vary significantly between rating agencies due to differing methodologies and criteria.

The European Union has taken a proactive approach to sustainability reporting through initiatives such as the ESRS and CSRD. These regulations aim to enhance the quality and consistency of sustainability disclosures across the EU, mandating that companies report on a wide range of ESG factors. By setting a high bar for transparency and accountability, the EU is positioning itself as a leader in the global push for sustainable business practices. The Sustainable Finance Disclosure Regulation (SFDR) further strengthens the EU's regulatory framework for sustainability reporting. By classifying financial products based on their sustainability characteristics (under Articles 6, 8, and 9), the SFDR aims to combat greenwashing and ensure that investors have access to reliable information about the sustainability impact of their investments. This regulatory approach not only promotes transparency but also encourages the financial sector to align with the EU's broader sustainability goals. As companies start to report in the coming years, it would be useful to study their reporting to gain insights as the EU's investments and trade change.

In the United States, ESG disclosures have gained momentum, driven by both regulatory pressures and growing investor demand for transparency. Corporate America is increasingly recognizing the importance of ESG factors in building resilient, sustainable businesses. However, the evolution of ESG disclosures in the US is marked by ongoing debates about the role of regulation versus voluntary disclosure, as well as the challenges of creating a unified reporting framework in a diverse and dynamic market. California has emerged as a pioneer in climate regulation within the US, setting ambitious targets for reducing greenhouse gas emissions and promoting sustainable practices. The state's climate regulations, which often exceed federal standards, serve as a model for other jurisdictions and underscore the role of state-level action in driving national progress on climate issues. California's approach highlights the importance of strong regulatory frameworks in achieving meaningful environmental outcomes and demonstrates the potential for subnational leadership in the fight against climate change.

References

Alessi, L., Alemanni, B., & Frati, G. (2022). Financial regulation for sustainable finance in the European landscape. In N. Linciano, P. Soccorso, & C. Guagliano (Eds.), *Information as a driver of sustainable finance*. Palgrave Studies in Impact Finance. Palgrave Macmillan. https://doi.org/10.1007/978-3-030-93768-3_8.

Aligishiev, Z., Bellon, M., & Massetti, E. (2022). *Climate change and long-term growth: scenarios for the European Union*. International Monetary Fund.

Atz, U., Van Holt, T., Liu, Z. Z., & Bruno, C. C. (2023). Does sustainability generate better financial performance? Review, meta-analysis, and propositions. *Journal of Sustainable Finance & Investment, 13*(1), 802–825.

Berg, F., Koelbel, J. F., & Rigobon, R. (2022). Aggregate confusion: The divergence of ESG ratings. *Review of Finance, 26*(6), 1315–1344.

Billio, M., Costola, M., Hristova, I., Latino, C., & Pelizzon, L. (2021). Inside the ESG ratings:(Dis)agreement and performance. *Corporate Social Responsibility and Environmental Management, 28*(5), 1426–1445.

Boiral, O., Heras-Saizarbitoria, I., & Brotherton, M. C. (2019). Assessing and improving the quality of sustainability reports: The auditors' perspective. *Journal of Business Ethics, 155*, 703–721.

Buallay, A. (2019). Is sustainability reporting (ESG) associated with performance? Evidence from the European banking sector. *Management of Environmental Quality: An International Journal, 30*(1), 98–115.

Caglio, A., Melloni, G., & Perego, P. (2020). Informational content and assurance of textual disclosures: Evidence on integrated reporting. *European Accounting Review, 29*(1), 55–83.

Carney, M. (2015). *Breaking the tragedy of the horizon—Climate change and financial stability*. Speech given by Mark Carney, Governor of the Bank of England, at Lloyd's of London.

CDP. (2024). *CDP full corporate scoring introduction 2024—Version control*. https://cdn.cdp.net/cdpproduction/comfy/cms/files/files/000/009/176/original/CDP_Full_Corporate_Scoring_Introduction_2024.pdf

Christensen, D. M., Serafeim, G., & Sikochi, A. (2022). Why is corporate virtue in the eye of the beholder? The case of ESG ratings. *The Accounting Review, 97*(1), 147–175.

Clark, G. L., Feiner, A., & Viehs, M. (2015). *From the stockholder to the stakeholder: How sustainability can drive financial outperformance*. Available at SSRN 2508281.

Conway, E. (2019). To agree or disagree? An analysis of CSR ratings firms. *Social and Environmental Accountability Journal, 39*(3), 152–177.

Cort, T., & Esty, D. (2020). ESG standards: Looming challenges and pathways forward. *Organization & Environment, 33*(4), 491–510.

Darendeli, A., Fiechter, P., Hitz, J. M., & Lehmann, N. (2022). The role of corporate social responsibility (CSR) information in supply-chain contracting: Evidence from the expansion of CSR rating coverage. *Journal of Accounting and Economics, 74*(2–3), 101525.

de Oliveira Neves, R. (2022). The EU taxonomy regulation and its implications for companies. In P. Câmara & F. Morais (Eds.), *The Palgrave handbook of ESG and corporate governance*. Palgrave Macmillan. https://doi.org/10.1007/978-3-030-99468-6_13

Del Giudice, A., & Rigamonti, S. (2020). Does audit improve the quality of ESG scores? Evidence from corporate misconduct. *Sustainability, 12*(14), 5670.

Dell'Erba, M., & Doronzo, M. (2023). Sustainability gatekeepers: ESG ratings and data providers. *University of Pennsylvania Journal of Business Law, 25*, 355.

Dimson, E., Marsh, P., & Staunton, M. (2020). *Divergent ESG ratings*. https://api.repository.cam.ac.uk/server/api/core/bitstreams/c498bbb7-9f03-4c52-b86a-1f4229dc60ed/content

Durán-Santomil, P., Otero-González, L., Correia-Domingues, R. H., & Reboredo, J. C. (2019). Does sustainability score impact mutual fund performance? *Sustainability, 11*(10), 2972.

Eccles, R. G., Ioannou, I., & Serafeim, G. (2012). *The impact of a corporate culture of sustainability on corporate behavior and performance* (Vol. 17950, pp. 2835–2857). National Bureau of Economic Research.

Eccles, R. G., & Serafeim, G. (2013). The performance frontier. *Harvard Business Review, 91*(5), 50–60.

Fiechter, P., Hitz, J. M., & Lehmann, N. (2022). Real effects of a widespread CSR reporting mandate: Evidence from the European Union's CSR Directive. *Journal of Accounting Research, 60*(4), 1499–1549.

A Critical Look at the Politicization of ESG. https://news.law.fordham.edu/jcfl/2023/02/24/a-critical-look-at-the-politicization-of-esg/

Friedlingstein, P. (2022). Global carbon budget 2022. *Earth System Science Data, 14*, 4811–4900. https://doi.org/10.5194/essd-14-4811-2022

FSB. (2022). *Financial stability implications of climate change: An overview*. Financial Stability Board.

Fuerst, F. (2015). *The financial rewards of sustainability: A global performance study of real estate investment trusts*. Available at SSRN 2619434.

Garel, A., & Petit-Romec, A. (2021). Investor rewards to environmental responsibility: Evidence from the COVID-19 crisis. *Journal of Corporate Finance, 68*, 101948.

Gary, S. N. (2019). Best interests in the long term: Fiduciary duties and ESG integration. *Univeristy of Colorado Law Review, 90*, 731.

Gerrard, M., & Orts, E. W. (2023). *New California legislation would be a major step forward for climate disclosure*. Columbia Law School Sabin Center for Climate Change Law.

Gibson Brandon, R., Krueger, P., & Schmidt, P. S. (2021). ESG rating disagreement and stock returns. *Financial Analysts Journal, 77*(4), 104–127.

GSIA. (2022). *Global sustainable investment alliance (GSIA) review*. https://www.gsi-alliance.org/wp-content/uploads/2023/12/GSIA-Report-2022.pdf

Heeb, F., Kölbel, J. F., Paetzold, F., & Zeisberger, S. (2023). Do investors care about impact? *The Review of Financial Studies, 36*(5), 1737–1787.

IFRS. (2024). *IFRS taxonomy illustrated*. https://www.ifrs.org/issued-standards/ifrs-taxonomy/ifrs-taxonomy-illustrated/

IMF. (2015). *Making public investment more efficient*. International Monetary Fund.

IMF. (2022). *Climate-related financial disclosures and the role of financial supervisors in promoting transparency*. International Monetary Fund.

IMF. (2023). *Global financial stability report: Financial stability implications of climate change*. International Monetary Fund.

IMF. (2024). *Unlocking climate finance in Asia-Pacific: Transitioning to a Sustainable Future*. https://www.imf.org/en/Publications/Departmental-Papers-Policy-Papers/Issues/2024/01/29/Unlocking-Climate-Finance-in-Asia-Pacific-Transitioning-to-a-Sustainable-Future-541458

Ioannou, I., & Serafeim, G. (2017). *The consequences of mandatory corporate sustainability reporting*. Harvard Business School Research Working Paper (11–100).

IPCC. (2022). Summary for policymakers. In H.-O. Pörtner, D. C. Roberts, E. S. Poloczanska, K. Mintenbeck, M. Tignor, A. Alegría, M. Craig, S. Langsdorf, S. Löschke, V. Möller, A. Okem, H.-O. Pörtner, D. C. Roberts, M. Tignor, E. S. Poloczanska, K. Mintenbeck, A. Alegría, M. Craig, S. Langsdorf, S. Löschke, V. Möller, A. Okem, & B. Rama (Eds.), *Climate change 2022: Impacts, adaptation, and vulnerability. Contribution of working group II to the sixth assessment report of the intergovernmental panel on climate change* (pp. 3–33). Cambridge University Press. https://doi.org/10.1017/9781009325844.001

Keeris, W. G., & Langbroek, R. A. (2019). Global real estate sustainability benchmarking: An essential tool for real estate management. *Sustainable real estate: Multidisciplinary approaches to an evolving system* (pp. 165–196). Palgrave Macmillan.

Kimbrough, M. D., Wang, X., Wei, S., & Zhang, J. (2024). Does voluntary ESG reporting resolve disagreement among ESG rating agencies? *European Accounting Review, 33*(1), 15–47.

Kotsantonis, S., Pinney, C., & Serafeim, G. (2016). ESG integration in investment management: Myths and realities. *Journal of Applied Corporate Finance, 28*(2), 10–16.

Marchewitz, C., Schütze, F., & Ballesteros, F. (2024). Transitioning to net zero: Full potential of sustainable finance taxonomies not yet exhausted. *DIW Weekly Report, 14*(28), 189–197.

Melloni, G., Caglio, A., & Perego, P. (2017). Saying more with less? Disclosure conciseness, completeness and balance in integrated reports. *Journal of Accounting and Public Policy, 36*(3), 220–238.

NFRD. (2021). European Commission. *Proposal for a Directive of the European Parliament and of the Council amending Directive 2013/34/EU, Directive 2004/109/EC, Directive 2006/43/EC and Regulation (EU) No 537/2014, as regards corporate sustainability reporting.* Available at https://eur-lex.europa.eu/legal-content/EN/TXT/?uri=CELEX:52021PC0189. Accessed 28th May 2022.

NGFS. (2022). *NGFS scenarios for climate risk assessment: Global data and methodological challenges.* Network for Greening the Financial System.

Oncioiu, I., Petrescu, A. G., Bîlcan, F. R., Petrescu, M., Popescu, D. M., & Anghel, E. (2020). Corporate sustainability reporting and financial performance. *Sustainability, 12*(10), 4297.

Painter, R. W. (2024). The conservative case for ESG. *University of Pennsylvania Journal of Law and Public Affairs, 9*, 151.

Pastor, M., Cha, J. M., Méndez, M., & Morello-Frosch, R. (2024). California dreaming: Why environmental justice is integral to the success of climate change policy. *Proceedings of the National Academy of Sciences, 121*(32), e2310073121.

Pinson, S. (2023). Revamping green securitization frameworks in the EU. *University of Miami International and Comparative Law Review, 31*, 201.

Prasad, A., Aligishiev, Z., & Massetti, E. (2022). *Climate finance: Mobilizing private investment to support green growth.* International Monetary Fund.

Ricci, S. A., & Sautter, C. M. (2021). Corporate governance gaming: The collective power of retail investors. *Nevada Law Journal, 22*, 51.

Roszkowska-Menkes, M., Aluchna, M., & Kamiński, B. (2024). True transparency or mere decoupling? The study of selective disclosure in sustainability reporting. *Critical Perspectives on Accounting, 98*, 102700.

Rouen, E., Sachdeva, K., & Yoon, A. (2023). *The evolution of ESG reports and the role of voluntary standards.* Available at SSRN 4227934.

Science Based Targets Initiative. (2024, March). *Getting started guide for science based target setting.*

Serafeim, G. (2013). *The role of the corporation in society: An alternative view and opportunities for future research.* Available at SSRN 2270579.

Serafeim, G., & Yoon, A. (2023). Stock price reactions to ESG news: The role of ESG ratings and disagreement. *Review of Accounting Studies, 28*(3), 1500–1530.

Sharfman, M. P., & Fernando, C. S. (2008). Environmental risk management and the cost of capital. *Strategic Management Journal, 29*(6), 569–592.

State Street Global Advisors. (2019). *Into the mainstream ESG at the tipping point.* https://www.ssga.com/library-content/pdfs/insights/into-the-mainstream.pdf

Stocker, F., de Arruda, M. P., de Mascena, K. M., & Boaventura, J. M. (2020). Stakeholder engagement in sustainability reporting: A classification model. *Corporate Social Responsibility and Environmental Management, 27*(5), 2071–2080.

Sutopo, B., Kot, S., Adiati, A. K., & Ardila, L. N. (2018). Sustainability reporting and value relevance of financial statements. *Sustainability, 10*(3), 678.

Truant, E., Corazza, L., & Scagnelli, S. D. (2017). Sustainability and risk disclosure: An exploratory study on sustainability reports. *Sustainability, 9*(4), 636.

UNFCC. (2016). *Report of the Conference of the Parties on its twenty-first session, held in Paris from 30 November to 13 December 2015.* Addendum. Part two: Action taken by the Conference of the Parties at its twenty-first session. COP 21. https://unfccc.int/documents/9097

Wbcsd, W. R. I. (2004). *The greenhouse gas protocol. A corporate accounting and reporting standard* (Rev. ed.). Washington, DC.

Wong, J. B., & Zhang, Q. (2022). Stock market reactions to adverse ESG disclosure via media channels. *The British Accounting Review, 54*(1), 101045.

Yu, E. P. Y., Van Luu, B., & Chen, C. H. (2020). Greenwashing in environmental, social and governance disclosures. *Research in International Business and Finance, 52*, 101192.

Zhang, H. (2020). Regulating green bond in China: Definition divergence and implications for policy making. *Journal of Sustainable Finance & Investment, 10*(2), 141–156.

Chapter 6
Geospatial Finance: Foundations and Applications

> A map says to you. Read me carefully, follow me closely, doubt me not …… I am the earth in the palm of your hands—Beryl Markham

6.1 Introduction

The advent of geospatial finance marks a significant evolution in financial analysis, integrating geospatial data to augment traditional economic theories and practices. This advancement builds upon the concept of spatial finance, first introduced by the Sustainable Finance Group at Oxford University in 2019 (Caldecott, 2019). Spatial finance explicitly acknowledges the interplay between economic outcomes, the natural environment, and geographical information.

In this text, we adopt the term "geospatial finance," focusing on a data-centric approach encompassing data from a diverse geospatial technology, including satellites, LiDAR, sensors, and other sources which combine sensor readings with spatial locations. These new datasets range from ocean-based buoy data to social media inputs such as Yelp reviews tagged with spatial information like zip codes. This novel amalgamation is propelled by significant strides in Earth observation technologies, remote sensing, social media analytics, and machine learning. These technologies allow financial analysts to process large and complex datasets more accurately and quickly, improving their decision-making ability and providing new insights into business processes. Such advancements enable these entities to refine risk assessments, identify investment opportunities, and evaluate impacts with heightened accuracy. By providing insights into the spatial dynamics of various markets and assets, geospatial data is poised to revolutionize investment decision-making.

Moreover, geospatial data offers details on the physical locations and characteristics of assets (such as buildings or vehicles), infrastructure, and resources on the Earth's surface, thus augmenting investment capabilities and providing market insights based on environmental metrics. Advanced spatial data analysis techniques, such as change detection, hotspot identification, segmentation or classification, and spatial regression, give investors deeper insights into our changing planet's spatial dynamics.

At the core of geospatial finance's appeal is its potential to address reputational and regulatory risks, especially those associated with environmental, social, and governance (ESG) criteria. Employing Geographic Information System (GIS) and location intelligence allows financial institutions to meticulously assess their investments' environmental impacts. Increasing use of satellite imagery from the US, European Union, China, Japan, and other countries is resulting in increasing use of deforestation, biodiversity risk, land cover, and climate risk mapping to determine the financial impacts of risks and vulnerabilities. Moreover, advances in spatial analysis, data visualization, spatial econometrics, and environmental and climate sciences make it possible to develop and design relevant metrics to describe risk and impacts stemming from investment from stakeholders of finance. Some typical questions in geospatial finance are:

- What is the spatial pattern of risky coastal assets in Florida? How many face the highest insurance risk claims now and over the next five years?
- Where are the optimal areas for carbon sequestration initiatives in the Amazon?
- Can hotspots of elevated urban heat island effects be identified in Austrian cities?
- Which areas in Indonesia are experiencing the most severe biodiversity loss due to timber harvesting? Which species are most at risk?
- What is the spatial impact of GHG emissions from fossil fuel in Guyana? How do these emissions affect ecosystem services such as fisheries and mangroves?

Geospatial finance plays a crucial role within credit analysis, insurance, and risk assessment, and impact analysis. S&P is one of three big US credit-rating companies. It utilizes environmental information processed from NASA satellite data to examine debt metrics related to water utilities. A simple analysis of the location of water utilities on a land cover map revealed that evergreen forests were associated with better debt metrics.[1] S&P Global noted, "Within the context of credit, we typically consider geography in terms of whether a credit is geographically diversified or concentrated. Our rating criteria across all practices—governments, insurance, corporates, structured finance, and financial institutions—mention geography. Our credit analysis may examine the locations of assets, risk exposures, revenues, earnings, suppliers, and underlying assets in assessing a structured finance transaction, potential insurance claims, and so on."[2] This statement underscores the significance of geographic diversification in mitigating location-based risks, such as local economic trends or

---

[1] https://www.seattletimes.com/business/satellites-are-helping-the-municipal-bond-market-assess-climate-risk/.

[2] https://www.spglobal.com/ratings/en/research/articles/200122-space-the-next-frontier-spatial-finance-and-environmental-sustainability-11317146.

6.1.1 Financial Assessment Involves Spatial Context and Understanding

The increasing prevalence of climate change disruptions and the pressing need for a green economy are steering financial decision-makers toward new methodologies for evaluating investments and partnerships. Quantifying and analyzing the interplay between business and the natural environment has become a crucial competitive edge for global economic leaders. A financial assessment incorporating spatial context and understanding involves analyzing financial data with a focus on specific geographic areas. This approach is valuable for detecting trends, patterns, and disparities in economic activities, investment opportunities, market growth, and consumer behavior across different regions. For instance, Geographic Information System (GIS) technology can be employed to visualize financial data, such as income levels, property values, and business locations. This visualization helps businesses, investors, policymakers, and researchers gain insights into the financial health of specific areas, enabling them to make informed decisions based on spatial data.

Emerging geospatial finance employs advanced technologies such as GIS, remote sensing, and AI, the focus of this book. These tools facilitate the collection and analysis of real-time data from satellites, drones, and IoT sensors. This integration allows for the rapid processing of environmental data to detect patterns and anomalies on a global to local scale (Nowak et al., 2020; Pei et al., 2021; Sippel et al., 2020). Financial institutions increasingly use geospatial finance to anticipate climate risks before they manifest. For example, the use of satellite imagery combined with climate data helped assess wildfire risks in Australia, highlighting the potential of spatial finance tools to predict and mitigate natural disaster impacts (Gibson et al., 2020; Sulova & Jokar Arsanjani, 2020). Spatial finance also plays a role in monitoring regulatory compliance and reputational risks. Financial contracts often include ESG guidelines, and GIS-powered dashboards enable banks and investors to monitor environmental impacts across their portfolios, ensuring adherence to these standards (Posth et al., 2024; Zhang et al., 2024). Geospatial technologies enable financial analysts to map, model, and analyze data related to business infrastructure, supply chains, and insurance policies, providing a comprehensive view of the operational environment. This geographic approach supports the identification of areas where business and sustainability priorities intersect or diverge, aiding in strategy development. Environmental Systems Research Institute (ESRI), the leading geospatial company provides many examples of such applications on its website.[3]

---

[3] https://www.esri.com/about/newsroom/publications/wherenext/spatial-finance/.

6.1.2 What Is Geospatial Data?

Geospatial data or geographic information embodies any data that directly or indirectly references a specific geographical area (such as a city or county) or location (address of a store or office building). It represents physical objects within a geographic coordinate system, providing essential information about the location of features and boundaries on Earth. Historically, the cartographic tradition laid the groundwork for the utilization of spatial data, with ancient civilizations employing rudimentary forms of spatial analysis for navigation and the exploration of unknown territories. The Age of Discovery, characterized by extensive voyages and exploration, further cemented the importance of cartography and spatial data in navigation and territorial mapping. Similarly, spatial data's strategic significance was recognized in military planning and warfare during the Second World War, when it was instrumental in strategizing and executing military operations. More recent conflicts, particularly in Ukraine, have showcased a significant advancement in military technology with the employment of drones. These systems are notable for their spatial precision and accuracy, crucial factors that have reshaped battlefield tactics and strategic planning.

The term "spatial accuracy" refers to the closeness of a measurement to the true value of the location of the spatial asset being mapped. It is affected by systematic errors and indicates the veracity of the measurement relative to a standard or known value asset based on geographical coordinates. Spatial precision relates to the reproducibility of measurements. It describes the variability in measurements when repeated under unchanged conditions, indicating the consistency or repeatability of the measurements. This term does not necessarily imply that measurements are accurate. The integration of advanced geospatial technologies, such as precise sensors or drones, allows them to perform with a high degree of both attributes. Figure 6.1 shows the concepts of accuracy and precision. Being both accurate and precise is preferred in many financial applications while accuracy may be the requirement in some applications. Regulations generally dictate the nature of accurate data.

The application spectrum of spatial data significantly broadened with technological advancements, extending beyond tactical and navigational uses to encompass environmental monitoring and management. Global climate models, for instance, rely heavily on spatial data to simulate and predict climate dynamics across different geographical regions. This transition marks a pivotal shift toward leveraging spatial data for global sustainability and spatializing environmental risk, vulnerability, and resilience. Financial institutions are increasingly using precise spatial data to assess and manage risks related to climate change. This includes analyzing flood risks, wildfire hazards, and other climate-related vulnerabilities that could impact the financial stability of investments. For example, using high-resolution imaging and data analysis, banks can identify properties at risk of flooding and adjust mortgage and insurance products accordingly.

The contemporary relevance of spatial data is profoundly underscored by the ongoing climate crisis and the pressing need for sustainable development. The

6.1 Introduction

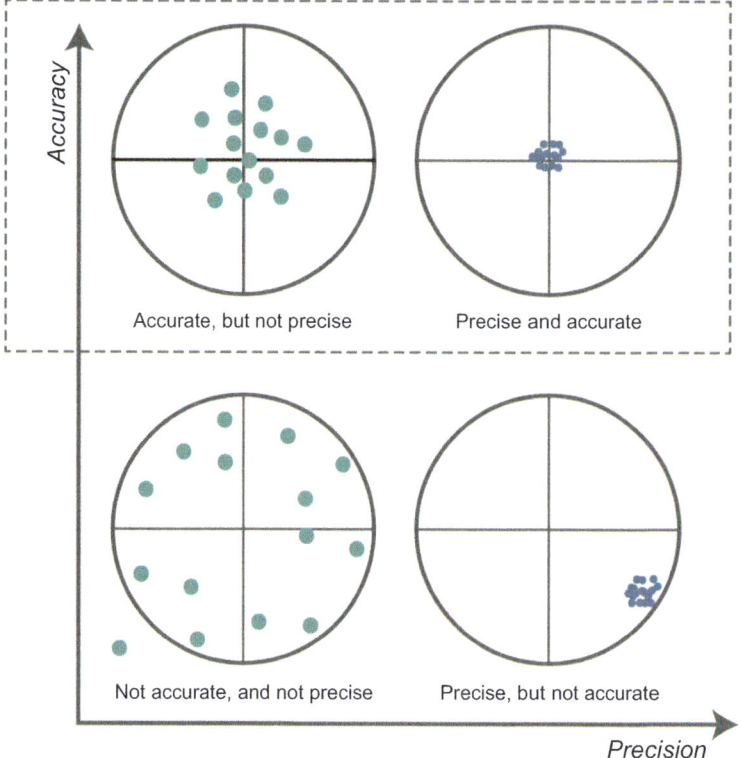

Fig. 6.1 Accuracy measures how close a value is to the true value while precision measures how close values are to each other

adverse effects of climate change, including rising sea levels, extreme weather events, and biodiversity loss, pose significant risks to island nations and marginalized communities worldwide. In this context, spatial data analysis emerges as a crucial tool for assessing environmental changes, assessing vulnerabilities, and informing policy and action toward mitigating climate impacts. This type of data is crucial for sustainable finance and climate risk analysis, as it enables the processing and analysis of geographical and environmental information. Moreover, spatial data plays an instrumental role in guiding sustainable finance initiatives. By providing insights into environmental risks, resource distribution, and conservation opportunities, spatial analysis supports the allocation of financial resources toward projects and investments that promote environmental sustainability and resilience against climate change.

Governments and agencies across many countries are already providing or developing a wide range of climate and environmental data services useful in monitoring forest, agriculture, and other ecosystems, water (both inland and oceanic), public health, disasters, energy sourcing, transportation and infrastructure, and urban issues.

For example, GEO Forest Carbon Tracking and Global Forest Observation Initiative (GFOI) integrates in-situ observations with advanced remote sensing data to estimate global forest cover and carbon content. This initiative plays a crucial role in providing tools for monitoring, reporting, and verification to support global climate mitigation policies. These efforts are essential for tracking and managing forest carbon stocks, thereby aiding countries in meeting their emissions-reduction targets as outlined in international agreements like the Paris Accord. Such work demonstrates the utility of spatial data in addressing environmental and climate-related challenges. Caldecott et al. (2022) noted that spatial finance applications so far include commodities trading, insurance assessments, and economic data analyses. They emphasized that spatial finance data is often lacking to run country or sector level analysis.

The above examples illustrate the indispensable role of spatial data in enriching our understanding and management of climate risks and sustainable finance. By harnessing spatial data, researchers and practitioners can develop more effective strategies for climate change mitigation and adaptation, contributing to the overarching goals of sustainable development.

6.2 What's so Unique About Spatial Data?

Spatial data is special and unlike traditional economic data. Spatial data, which comes in multiple forms as point, line, polygon, and raster data, is examined in Sect. 6.2.1. Spatial data is often correlated. Such is based on the principle that locations near each other are more likely to exhibit more similar attributes or behaviors than those farther apart, a phenomenon often summarized by the phrase "everything is related to everything else, but near things are more related than distant things," attributed to Waldo Tobler as the "First Law of Geography." In the 1990s, scholars debated the uniqueness of spatial data and its challenges (DeSmith et al., 2024; Fischer & Getis, 2013). The realization that spatial dependency significantly influences the accuracy and relevance of models has led to a concerted effort to develop spatially explicit models that account for the geographic context of data (Anselin, 2022). Today, the focus has shifted toward leveraging its unique properties to address complex problems, from sustainable finance to climate change impacts.

6.2.1 Types of Spatial Data and Geospatial Finance Applications

Spatial data, pivotal to a myriad of applications ranging from navigation to climate analysis and conservation, is organized into two primary categories: vector and raster data models. These models facilitate the representation, analysis, and processing of spatial entities across various spatial scales and contexts.

6.2.1.1 Vector Data Model (Feature Data)

Vector data, or feature data, encapsulates the geometric representation of specific real-world entities as points, lines, or polygons, each with distinct attributes detailing their characteristics. This model is adept at depicting discrete objects with precise boundaries and locations.

Point Data: Points represent specific locations defined by coordinates (x, y, and possibly z) without occupying an area. Examples include the locations of companies or emission facilities, which can be "spatialized" or mapped to estimate greenhouse gas emissions, as illustrated in Fig. 6.2a by Environmental Protection Agency (EPA) disclosures for all facilities in 2023.

These point data provide a quick visualization of density as well as quantity of emissions using different dot sizes as shown in Fig. 6.2b.

The association of these geometric representations with attribute tables enables a detailed and structured analysis of spatial features, linking geometric forms to their descriptive data. For multipart features, multiple geometries can be amalgamated to represent a single entity in the attribute table, facilitating complex spatial analyses. Table 6.1 shows the corresponding emission facility data.

Line Data: Lines connect sequences of points to outline linear features like rivers, roads, supply chains, and boundaries, capturing routes with defined directions and lengths but without thickness. Centrality, degree, betweenness, and other network metrics have been well studied (Andris & O'Sullivan, 2021). Network optimization is a focus in network analysis and operations research. The vulnerability of supply chains, highlighted by recent incidents such as the bridge collapse at the Port of Baltimore in March 2024[4] and the ongoing geopolitical tensions affecting Taiwan's semiconductor industry (Gopal et al., 2022), illustrates how both accidents and political instability can lead to significant uncertainties. The map in Fig. 6.3 shows the global network of shipping lanes. Oil, sourced in large part from North America, Russia, and the Middle East, travels along these marine paths to reach energy-consuming nations in Europe, Asia, and beyond. The dense web of lines crossing the Arabian Sea and Indian Ocean and going through the Strait of Malacca emphasizes the critical chokepoints and preferred maritime routes for oil transport. Many of the semiconductors manufactured in Taiwan also are supplied to the US and Europe via the maritime routes shown in Fig. 6.3.

Polygon Data: Polygons are closed loops of lines enclosing an area, used to represent zones like zip codes or parks. This model enables detailed spatial analysis and mapping, as demonstrated by emission maps delineating emissions per county using CDC (Center for Disease Control) data and reports.[5] Figure 6.4 shows a bivariate map of two indicators—low income and particulate matter (PM) 2.5. Some examples of counties with high income and low PM 2.5 (2020 US County Census) include Piscataquis (Maine), Broward (Florida), Humboldt (Nevada), Val Verde (Texas), and Vermilion (Louisiana). Some counties that have high unemployment and high PM 2.5

---

[4] https://www.nytimes.com/2024/03/26/us/key-bridge-collapse-baltimore-what-to-know.html.

[5] https://www.atsdr.cdc.gov/placeandhealth/eji/indicators.html.

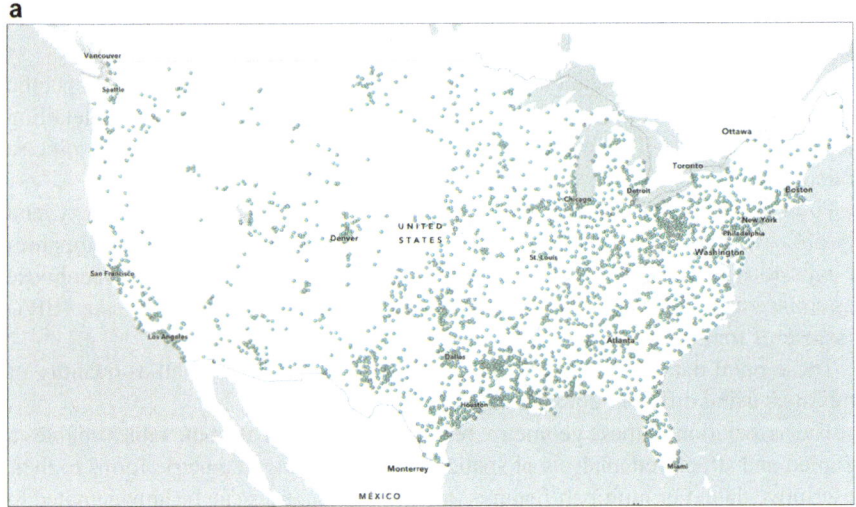

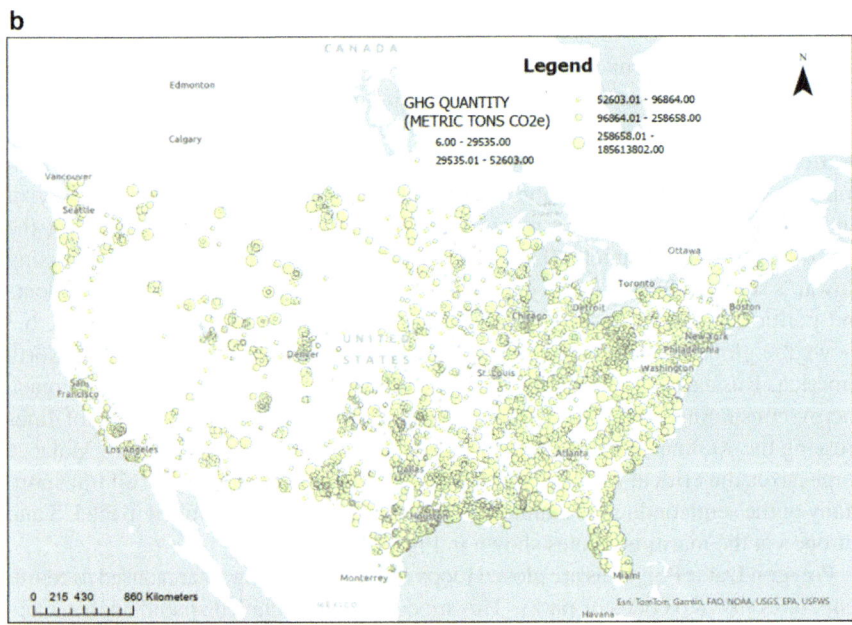

Fig. 6.2 a Greenhouse Gas (GHG) Emissions reported to the EPA in 2023, as shown by points of equal size. **b** GHG Emissions reported to the EPA in 2023. This visualization represents GHG emissions as circles of varying sizes, corresponding to the amount of emissions. The smallest circles indicate emissions less than 29,535 metric tons of CO2e, while the largest circles denote emissions exceeding 258,658 metric tons of CO2e (Carbon Dioxide equivalent)

Table 6.1 Table accompanying the GHG emission map (Figs. 1a and 1b) showing all details including names of the parent companies (column 3), state (column1), zip code (column 2), coordinates, (columns 4 and 5), identification (column 6), GHG quantity in metrics tons (column 7), and sector and subsector details (last two columns) associated with each point location

STATE	ZIP CODE	PARENT COMPANIES		DisplayX	DisplayY	GHGRP ID	GHG QUANTITY (METRIC TONS CO2e)	SUBPARTS	SECTOR-SUBSECTOR
LA	70805	EXXON MOBIL CORP (1...	::	−91.169693	30.486161	1007643	185613802	C,MM,X,Y	Chemicals-Petrochemi...
TX	77520	EXXON MOBIL CORP (1...	::	−95.022739	29.734969	1007542	183532155	C,MM,X,Y	Chemicals-Petrochemi...
IN	46394	BP AMERICA INC (100%)	::	−87.483197	41.662088	1007339	134491151	C,D,DD,MM,P,Y	Chemicals-Hydrogen P...
TX	77701	EXXON MOBIL CORP (1...	::	−94.074667	30.059751	1007959	121951161	C,D,MM,X,Y	Chemicals-Petrochemi...
TX	77520	TARGA RESOURCES C...	::	−94.89538	29.843039	1004614	120903054	C,NN,W	Natural Gas and Natur...
IL	62084	PHILLIPS 66 (100%)	::	−90.074743	38.83719	1007518	91734057	C,MM,P,PP,T,Y	Chemicals-Hydrogen P...
CA	90013	SEMPRA ENERGY (100...	::	−118.253197	34.050094	1005209	85473805	NN,W	Natural Gas and Natur...
CA	94105	PG&E CORP (100%)	::	−122.396033	37.791831	1005256	82386631	NN,W	Natural Gas and Natur...
TX	79720	DELEK US HOLDINGS I...	::	−101.421122	32.267181	1006961	78592047	C,MM,T,Y	Petroleum Product Su...
NJ	7036	PHILLIPS 66 (100%)	::	−74.219906	40.641122	1004305	74960181	C,MM,P,Y	Chemicals-Hydrogen P...
LA	70079	SHELL PETROLEUM IN...	::	−90.407168	29.994366	1005911	73653819	C,MM,X,Y	Chemicals-Petrochemi...
WA	98230	BP PRODUCTS NORTH...	::	−122.734978	48.888819	1006468	72512777	C,MM,P,PP,Y	Chemicals-Hydrogen P...
OK	74601	PHILLIPS 66 (100%)	::	−97.089795	36.691572	1001920	66033734	C,MM,P,Y	Chemicals-Hydrogen P...
TX	77547	TARGA RESOURCES C...	::	−95.196591	29.744802	1004454	58323300	C,MM	Petroleum and Natural...
NC	28210	DUKE ENERGY CORP (1...	::	−80.840207	35.151777	1001583	56361412	NN,W	Natural Gas and Natur...
IL	60563	THE SOUTHERN CO (1...	::	−88.195506	41.806357	1004163	54485243	NN,W	Natural Gas and Natur...
TX	77580	ENERGY TRANSFER LP (...	::	−94.89191	29.85032	1011018	52460352	C,NN,W	Natural Gas and Natur...
TX	78407	VALERO ENERGY CORP...	::	−97.444464	27.813375	1006959	48253837	C,MM,P,Y	Chemicals-Hydrogen P...
TN	38109	VALERO ENERGY CORP...	::	−90.079555	35.086557	1008271	47333931	C,MM,P,Y	Chemicals-Hydrogen P...
TX	79086	VALERO ENERGY CORP...	::	−101.877692	35.95861	1007936	47248533	C,MM,P,Y	Chemicals-Hydrogen P...
KS	67042	HF SINCLAIR CORP (10...	::	−96.867245	37.800232	1004291	46631656	C,MM,P,Y	Chemicals-Hydrogen P...
IL	60439	PDV AMERICA INC (100...	::	−88.04865	41.64098	1000343	44995670	C,MM,P,Y	Chemicals-Hydrogen P...
OH	43986	MPLX LP (100%)	::	−80.936963	40.33231	1010771	44327661	C,NN,W	Natural Gas and Natur...

Fig. 6.3 The map depicts global shipping routes with lines of varying widths, where each width corresponds to the volume of trade along each route. *Source* Arcgis.com[6]

are Zapata (Texas), Eddy (New Mexico), and Lincoln (Montana). These are counties with low incomes facing high PM 2.5 exposure.

6.2.1.2 Raster Data—Satellites

In contrast, the raster model approximates geographical areas through a grid of square pixels, each pixel holding a value that denotes a specific attribute, such as elevation, temperature, or land use, based on classification processes. This model is particularly suited for representing continuous data, including environmental and climate variables, and supports the layering of multiple raster datasets to create composite images or analyses. Examples include aerial photographs, digital elevation models (DEMs), and thematic maps showcasing land cover classifications.

Each pixel in a raster dataset can hold a value representing a particular attribute of the object within that pixel's area. These values might be numerical, such as integers or floating-point numbers, to denote various characteristics like elevation, temperature, or luminosity, or they could signify land use categories determined by classification processes. Figure 6.5 shows the land cover classes in a hypothetical

---

[6] https://www.arcgis.com/apps/mapviewer/index.html?layers=12c0789207e64714b9545ad30fca1633.

6.2 What's so Unique About Spatial Data?

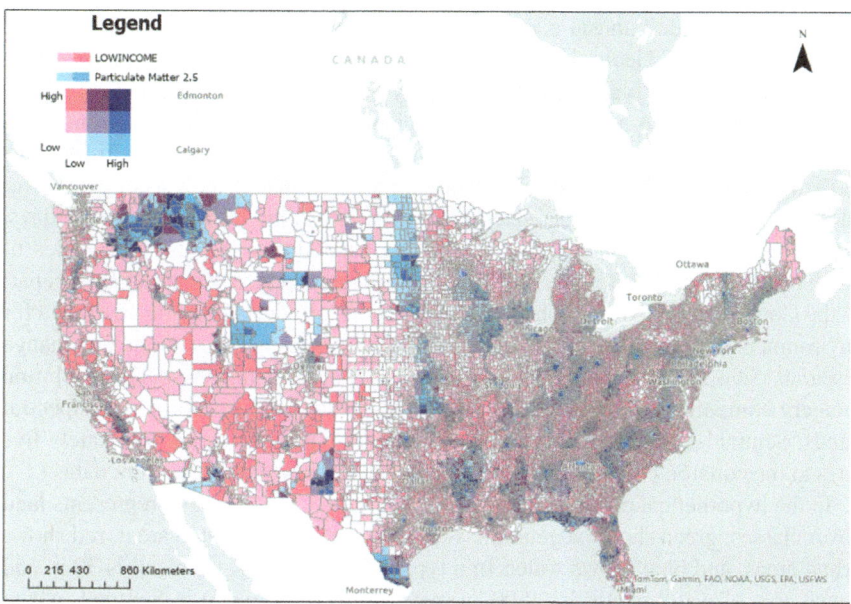

Fig. 6.4 This map visualizes the intersection of low income and exposure to particulate matter across US counties. Darker pink hues indicate areas predominantly characterized by low income. In contrast, darker blues highlight regions where both low income and high levels of Particulate Matter 2.5 coexist

image and a Sentinel land cover map centered on Riedenburg, Austria, where green shows vegetation, yellow shows non-vegetated areas, and blue shows water.

Satellites provide the geospatial data at a variety of spatial and temporal scales. Satellites are the only viable option for monitoring changes happening on the overall

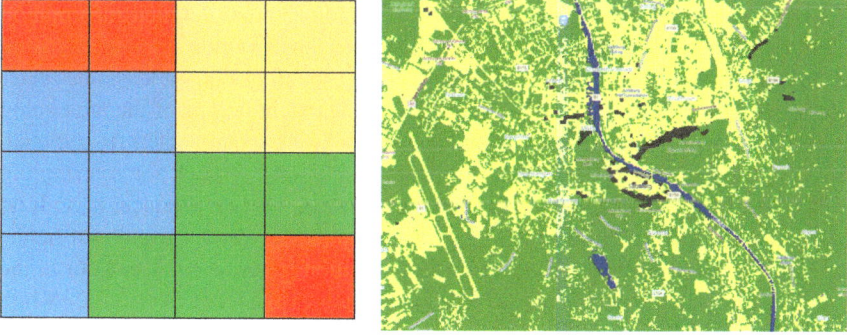

Fig. 6.5 Left panel: Displays cells as depicted in a typical remote sensing imagery. Right panel: Features a raster image (Sentinel Map dated 2024–04-27) focused on Riedenburg, Austria. In both images, green indicates vegetation, yellow represents non-vegetated areas, red highlights urban development, and blue denotes water bodies

surface of the Earth. Landsat is a series of Earth-observing satellite missions jointly managed by the US Geological Survey (USGS) and NASA. Landsat satellites have provided continuous, high-resolution imagery of the Earth's surface, making significant contributions to agriculture, forestry, land use planning, and environmental monitoring. Landsat satellites typically offer a spatial resolution of 30 m for most of their spectral bands, allowing for detailed observation and analysis of land cover and land use changes. Landsat satellites[7] revisit the same location every 16 days, providing consistent and periodic monitoring capabilities. Sentinel is a series of Earth observation satellites developed by the European Space Agency (ESA) as part of the Copernicus Program.[8] The Sentinel missions provide a wide range of data for environmental monitoring and management, disaster response, and climate change research. Sentinel satellites, particularly Sentinel-2, offer higher spatial resolution imagery compared to Landsat, with resolutions as fine as 10 m for several spectral bands. Sentinel-2 satellites have a more frequent revisit time of approximately five days at the equator, enhancing monitoring capabilities with more current data.

In the hypothetical raster representation of Fig. 6.5, the left panel represents land cover classes: green shows vegetation, yellow shows non-vegetated areas, red shows urban areas, and blue shows water. In a typical Landsat map, each cell is 30 m and hence area of water would be 4500 sq meters (30*30*5) while in Sentinel, where the cell size is 10 m, the same area of water would be 500 sq meters (10*10*5). This comparison highlights the importance of spatial resolution in remote sensing analysis. Higher resolution imagery, like that provided by Sentinel-2, allows for more detailed and precise observations of smaller features on the Earth's surface. This is displayed in Fig. 6.5 along with a typical raster representing land cover, where green indicates vegetation and yellow shows non-vegetated areas while blue shows water.

In remote sensing, the concepts of spatial scale and resolution of a satellite sensor are closely interrelated and are key to understanding how well we can detect, identify, and analyze features on the Earth's surface. Spatial resolution refers to the smallest object that can be resolved by a sensor. It is essentially the pixel size of an image, representing the area on the ground that each pixel covers. A sensor with a high spatial resolution has small pixel sizes, allowing it to capture more detailed information about the surface features. For example, a satellite sensor with a one-meter spatial resolution can distinguish between objects on the ground that are at least one meter apart. Spatial scale, on the other hand, refers to the extent or size of the area being observed or analyzed. It can range from local scales (a few square meters) to regional, national, or even global scales. The scale of observation is crucial for determining what kind of phenomena can be studied and understood. For instance, a study at a local scale might focus on monitoring individual buildings or agricultural fields; this would involve a sensor with one-meter resolution (relevant for Tier Four in the World Bank classification of Spatial Finance products explained in Sect. 6.5.2), while a study at a larger scale, MODIS sensor at 500-m resolution, might look at urban expansion or deforestation across an entire region.

---

[7] https://landsat.gsfc.nasa.gov/.

[8] https://www.esa.int/Applications/Observing_the_Earth/Copernicus/Sentinel-2.

6.2 What's so Unique About Spatial Data?

The integration of vector and raster data models enhances spatial analysis capabilities, enabling comprehensive environmental assessments, urban planning, and climate change studies. For instance, combining detailed vector-based outlines of land use with raster-based climate data allows for nuanced analyses of climate impacts on urban and natural environments. This integrative approach addresses the complexities of spatial phenomena, offering versatile tools for representing and analyzing the diverse aspects of geographical spaces.

Prior research on spatial data models elucidates the inherent strengths and applications of vector and raster data in capturing the complexities of the physical world, underscoring their indispensable role in environmental analysis, conservation efforts, and climate change mitigation. Recent advancements in spatial data analysis, (Bivand, 2022; De Smith, 2021; De Smith et al., 2024); underscore the critical role of choosing appropriate data models and the potential of integrating vector and raster data for enhanced spatial analysis. The exploration of new data models and operations (Singla et al., 2021) further illustrates the evolving landscape of spatial data processing, paving the way for innovative applications in environmental science, urban planning, and beyond. The intersection of spatial data science with responsible AI highlights the importance of integrating ethical principles into spatial computing to mitigate potential negative effects on society (Gupta & Shekhar, 2023). Recent trends in spatial computing, including the use of drones and driverless cars (Shekhar & Vold, 2020), drone and sensors (Penglase et al., 2023), high performance computing (Tang & Wang, 2020), virtual reality of urban landscapes (Ma et al., 2020), are covered.

To summarize, spatial objects and representation directly affect how data are stored and used to analyze the complex relationships between different financial entities and their geographical context. The detail of spatial data varies across the globe, resulting in issues in merging for financial applications. Basic GIS texts cover spatial analysis in detail (De Smith et al., 2024[9]; Fischer & Getis, 2010; Grekousis, 2020).

6.2.2 Complex Geometries and Spatial Complexity

The nature of spatial data is also characterized by its complex geometries (such as line strings and polygons) and inherent spatial relationships (like proximity and adjacency), which complicate analysis. A primary challenge is mapping and simulating data for complex spatial fields using conventional GIS data structures. The difficulty in scientifically representing and understanding multi-scale spatial fields that fluctuate rapidly, suggests the need for multi-scale techniques to capture spatial complexity (Jochem et al., 2021; Bian, 2023). The challenges posed by geospatial Big Data encompass spatial datasets beyond the capacity of current computing systems (Cao et al., 2024; Li, 2020). They underscored the importance of analytics

---

[9] Free text online. https://www.spatialanalysisonline.com/.

in leveraging the benefits of geospatial Big Data for applications like urban planning and healthcare, emphasizing the need for new platforms for sharing and analyzing the data (Gopal & Fischer, 2023; Mete, 2023).

How does this impact finance? The complexity of spatial data impacted by the challenges of dealing with complex geometries and spatial relationships inherent in spatial data is indeed a significant factor that influences spatial finance, particularly in areas like real estate market analysis, urban planning, and environmental risk assessment, which often rely on geographic information systems (GIS) for decision-making. The following challenges are worth mentioning.

Multi-Scale Representation: Financial analysis that relies on spatial data requires accurate representation across different scales. For example, real estate valuation in a specific portfolio may depend on data ranging from the drone and individual property level to broader market trends across a region. The difficulty in representing multi-scale spatial fields can lead to misinterpretation of market dynamics if not addressed properly (Kortas et al., 2022; Chi et al., 2021).

Computing Capacity: The complexity and size of geospatial Big Data exceed the capacity of current computing systems (Jiang & Shekhar, 2017; Shekhar & Vold, 2020). Interpreting this wealth of information is vital for gaining insights into Earth's complexities. The evolution of the geospatial industry hinges on the adoption of cloud-native data standards and formats. Institutions such as NASA are already moving toward cloud-native solutions, reflecting a wider shift in the scientific community's approach to managing substantial geospatial datasets. Upcoming satellite projects like NISAR and SWOT are projected to generate approximately 85 terabytes of data each day.[10] To adequately address pressing issues related to climate change and conservation, there is an urgent need to develop more advanced tools with greater efficiency and speed. This presents a challenge for financial institutions that must process large datasets for risk assessment, portfolio management, and investment strategy development.

Geospatial Dynamics: Advanced analytics are needed to extract meaningful insights from spatial data for applications like investment targeting and risk management. However, the complex nature of spatial relationships can hinder the application of conventional data mining techniques, requiring specialized approaches tailored for spatial analysis. GenAI (Generative AI) models are built incorporating these types of information to address this need.

Geometric and Topological Complexity: Spatial finance must account for the geometric and topological characteristics of space, as these can influence economic activity and financial transactions. This includes considerations of proximity, adjacency, and connectivity, which can affect asset valuation and investment decisions.

Dynamic Topological Structures: Prior research (Albert & Barabási, 2002; Bardoscia et al., 2021) investigated the representation of uncertain and dynamic topological structures, which are key in spatial finance for capturing the evolving

---

[10] https://developmentseed.org/blog/2024-03-19-combining-cloud-gpu-native.

nature of financial markets, investment networks, and economic activities that have a spatial component. These methodologies that jointly capture geometry and dynamics are crucial in developing tools for spatial data fusion and mining, which can enhance the predictive power and analytical capabilities of spatial finance models tackling spillover effects (Chen et al., 2022; Wang et al., 2021).

Financial entities often need to collaborate and share spatial data. The need for new platforms for sharing and analyzing geospatial Big Data suggests that current systems may not be adequate for the interoperability and security requirements of financial data.

Spatial Ontology: Spatial ontology concerns the precise definition and categorization of geographic terms and features, which is critical for effective data analysis and application in various fields, including finance (Bateman, 2010; Frank, 1997; Goodchild, 2010). Consider these questions: How do we categorically define a service area of a bank? What specific criteria differentiate a city from suburb? For investors, understanding the true extent of Boston's geographical boundaries is essential to accurately evaluate the area's financial or innovation (research and development) potential.

In the context of the United States Census, terminologies like Primary Metropolitan Statistical Area (PMSA), Consolidated Metropolitan Statistical Area (CMSA), and "city" are not just labels but are essential in classifying and interpreting data.[11] A PMSA signifies a highly populated core area with significant economic ties to adjacent areas. When several PMSAs combine, they form a CMSA, representing a larger interconnected region. A "city," as recognized by the census, is an established jurisdiction with government authority. In finance, the clarity provided by spatial ontology is indispensable. It aids in the integration of diverse datasets, enables sophisticated spatial reasoning, and enhances the deployment of financial insights, particularly for challenges entangled with geographic and environmental factors. Defining these terms is not merely an academic exercise; it is a practical necessity for efficient data mining and analysis, which in turn informs investment decisions and financial strategies. Thus, by leveraging spatial ontology, financial institutions and investors can gain deeper insights into geographic factors affecting their operations and investments, leading to more strategic and informed decisions.

6.3 The Vexing MAUP Problem in Spatial Data

Traditional data science and AI methodologies, including machine learning, often face challenges when applied to spatial datasets (Shekhar, 2021). Spatial data exist within a continuous domain, making classical statistical measures like correlation susceptible to issues such as the modifiable areal unit problem. The Modifiable

---

[11] https://www2.census.gov/geo/pdfs/reference/GARM/Ch13GARM.pdf.

Areal Unit Problem (MAUP)[12] presents a significant challenge in spatial data analysis, manifesting when varying results emerge from the same dataset under different aggregation strategies. MAUP splits into two distinct phenomena: the scale effect and the zone effect (Manley, 2021). The scale effect arises when analytical outcomes differ upon altering the aggregation units' scale without changing the underlying data. For instance, data aggregated at a county level may yield different insights compared to data aggregated by census tract. This variation often reflects legitimate differences in analytical perspectives attributed to the scale of analysis. On the other hand, the zone effect occurs when the analysis's scale remains constant but the shapes of the aggregation units vary. An example of this would be the disparity in results between using square grid cells and hexagonal cells for data aggregation. The challenge with the zone effect lies in its potential to reflect the characteristics of the chosen aggregation scheme rather than the actual data, complicating the interpretation of the analysis.

Figure 6.6 shows the impact of MAUP as a source of statistical bias composed of two related effects:

- Scale Effect: The variation in results that occurs when the same analysis is applied to the same underlying data aggregated at different scales. Figure 6.6a, b, c (top panel) demonstrate the scale effect by showing how different groupings of the same data can lead to different variances (δ^2) while maintaining the same mean ($\bar{x}$). Each panel shows data aggregated into fewer groups (from left to right). Hence as the aggregation becomes coarser (less detailed), the variance decreases.
- Zoning Effect: The variation in results that arises when the same total area is divided into a different number of zones or different configurations of zones. The lower panel of Fig. 6.6 demonstrates the zoning effect by showing how different configurations of zones (Figs. 6.6d, e, f) within the same scale can also result in different variances, affecting the mean in some cases.

To use an example from finance, consider a scenario in which a bank wants to analyze the average credit score by geographical area to analyze mortgage-backed securities. Using GIS, we can aggregate the credit score data at different levels, such as by neighborhood (microscale), city (mesoscale), or region (macroscale). At a neighborhood level, there can be significant variability in credit scores (high variance), suggesting that some neighborhoods are much riskier than others. At a city level, this variability might lessen because the differences are smoothed out when averaged over a larger area (lower variance). At a regional level, the variability might disappear altogether, suggesting uniform creditworthiness across the region (very low or zero variance). MAUP shows that the scale and zoning of data can lead to misleading conclusions about the area's creditworthiness. A bank may decide not to serve what appears to be a risky neighborhood, not realizing that within that neighborhood are pockets of high creditworthiness that are simply overshadowed by the broader data aggregation.

---

[12] https://support.esri.com/en-us/gis-dictionary/maup.

6.3 The Vexing MAUP Problem in Spatial Data

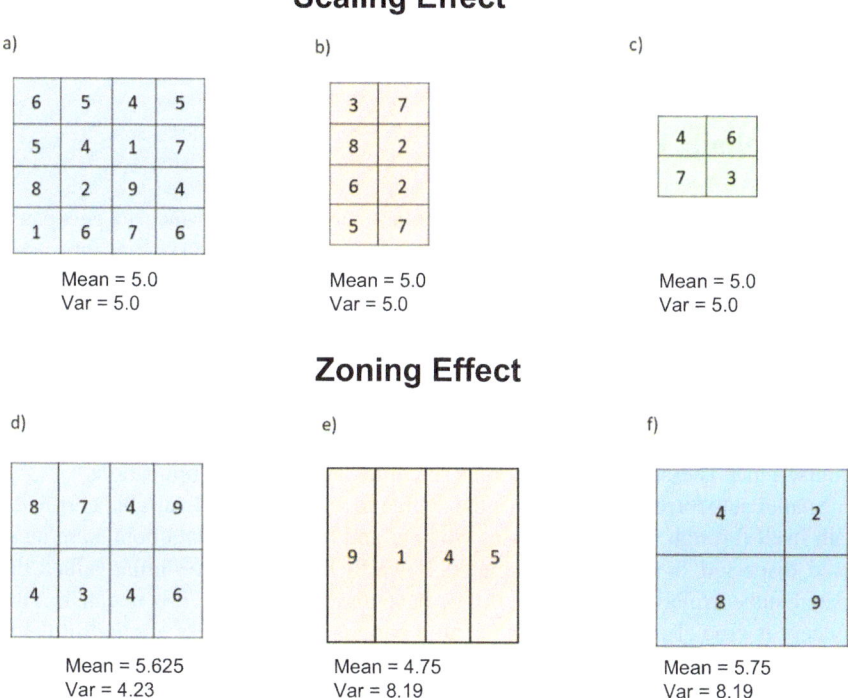

Fig. 6.6 Modifiable Areal Unit Problem: Scaling and Zoning Effects. The upper panels (a to c) demonstrate the scaling effect through varying levels of data aggregation. Despite different aggregations, the arithmetic mean remains consistent at 5 in each panel, though the variance differs across panels from a to c. The lower panels (d to f) illustrate the zoning effects with varying arithmetic means and variances. Note that the total area remains the same across each of the lower panels

To mitigate the effects of MAUP, one must carefully consider the scale and zoning used in spatial analyses and recognize that different configurations can reveal or obscure trends in the data. In other words, MAUP can lead to a different sort of greenwashing when an area's credit worthiness is being estimated for investment. Thus, the analyst needs to critically assess the spatial units chosen for the study to ensure that the results are indeed reflective of the real-world phenomena being studied, rather than artifacts of the arbitrary division of space into units. MAUP leads to similar misinterpreting using aggregated financial data. During the banking crisis of 2008, banks and financial institutions packaged individual subprime mortgages into mortgage-backed securities (MBS) and collateralized debt obligations (CDOs), which were then given high credit ratings and sold to investors (Markham, 2013; Pezzuto, 2012). This process was akin to the aggregation of data in MAUP, by which individual details can become obscured when data is combined into larger units. Similar to how MAUP can lead to misleading conclusions about spatial phenomena due to the scale and zoning of data, the financial instruments created from subprime mortgages masked the true risk of the individual loans they contained, leading investors and regulators to underestimate the risk involved.

6.4 Spatially Explicit Models

This section describes some spatially explicit models of relevance to geospatial finance. First, the section examines spatial neighborhood effect and spatial autocorrelation. The former refers to the influence that a geographic area's characteristics have on the properties of nearby locations discussed in the introduction to the "First Law of Geography" (Sect. 6.2). The spatial neighborhood effect acknowledges spatial dependence. Spatial autocorrelation is a key concept in spatial analysis, offering a framework to understand how georeferenced data points are related in space. This concept helps researchers analyze the spatial arrangement and relationships of data points, which is essential for numerous scientific and practical applications.

Spatial autocorrelation measures the degree to which a spatial variable correlates with itself through space. It assesses whether and how spatial data points are clustered, dispersed, or randomly distributed. If nearby locations have similar values, the spatial autocorrelation is positive; if they have dissimilar values, it is negative. This concept is crucial in understanding spatial patterns and is widely applied in fields such as geography, ecology, and urban planning. This section explores how spatial autocorrelation is assessed using various statistical measures and methods, such as Moran's I, the Getis-Ord G statistic, and the semivariogram. Each measure has its unique formulation and application, helping to identify and quantify spatial patterns at different scales.

6.4.1 Spatial Neighborhood Representation

The spatial neighborhood effect acknowledges that spatial dependencies exist; values at any given location can be influenced by values at surrounding locations, leading to patterns of spatial autocorrelation where similar (or dissimilar) values cluster together in space. The spatial autocorrelation of n georeferenced observations is described using a cross-product matrix composed of $\mathbf{W}$, shown in Eq. 6.1, a matrix of values that represent spatial relationships of a variable $\mathbf{Y}$ at location i with all other realizations at all other sites j. Defining the spatial neighborhood (sites j) is a crucial step in measuring neighborhood effects. Getis (2009) discussed the various schemes used to capture the spatial relationships captured in the $\mathbf{W}$ matrix.

$$\Gamma_{ij} = \sum_{i=1}^{n} \sum_{j=1}^{n} W_{ij} Y_{ij} \qquad (6.1)$$

In many applications, spatially contiguous neighbors are used to describe spatial relationships. Other schemes include inverse distance raised to some power (distance decline function), n nearest neighbors, bandwidth distance decay (required for geographically weighted regression), and lengths of share borders divided by perimeter. In raster analysis, contiguous neighbors in cardinal or all directions are used. In geospatial finance, the nature of the variables being studied for spatial effects will be key to the selection of the appropriate **W**. Schemas such as inverse weighted distance or bandwidth distance decay are pertinent while considering assets in a vector map while contiguous neighbors are suitable for climate risk or biodiversity loss assessments using raster data.

6.4.2 *Global and Local Spatial Autocorrelation Measures*

Spatial autocorrelation measures and tests serve distinct purposes, but both evaluate spatial effects in georeferenced data analyses. Moran's I is the foremost method and test for spatial autocorrelation (Getis, 2009). This statistic is designed similarly to the Pearson product-moment correlation coefficient, but with a significant modification: it incorporates spatial context through a spatial weight's matrix, **W**. Instead of analyzing the correlation between two different variables, it evaluates the correlation of a single variable with itself, considering the spatial relationships defined by the W matrix. In this setup, Y represents the covariance matrix, where Moran's I statistic measures each observation's deviation from the overall mean of all observations. To compute Moran's I, assign W as the chosen spatial weights matrix and set Y to the auto-covariance $(y_i - \bar{y})(y_j - \bar{y})$, where y_i and y_j are observations and $\bar{y}$ is the mean of all observations. The statistic is then scaled, using a Pearson correlation structure, by multiplying through appropriate normalization.

Spatial autocorrelation techniques are classified into "global" and "local" categories based on their analytical scope. Global measures involve the entire set of spatial units within the W (spatial weights) and Y (variable of interest) matrices, producing a single spatial autocorrelation value for the entire dataset. This global approach accounts for all spatial unit interactions. In contrast, local measures focus on individual spatial units, often assessing spatial autocorrelation specific to one unit by considering just one row of the W matrix and the corresponding row of the Y matrix, though they may also consider interactions between other elements as a broader context. Lenders use spatial autocorrelation to assess property values (Deppner & Cajias, 2024). If property values in a neighborhood are highly correlated, the valuation of a new property can be estimated more accurately based on nearby properties. Spatial autocorrelation helps in identifying areas with high default rates (Lee & Sohn, 2021). If defaults are clustered spatially, lenders might adjust their lending criteria or interest rates for those areas.

Ripley's K function in GIS is a measure of spatial point pattern analysis that assesses the clustering or dispersion of events at various scales (Bailey & Gatrell, 1995). It helps to determine whether points (such as trees in a forest, buildings in a city, or disease cases in a region) are randomly distributed, clustered, or regularly spaced at different scales. Ripley's K function is used to assess the spatial pattern of points by analyzing how point densities change with distance. It provides insight into the spatial arrangement and interaction of points over varying scales, identifying if points are more clustered or dispersed than expected under complete spatial randomness (CSR). In spatial finance, understanding the clustering of economic activities, such as the concentration of high-tech firms in a tech hub, is vital for deciding where to invest. This approach can guide investors to identify potential "hot spots" that might yield higher returns due to the benefits of agglomeration economies. Ripley's K nearest neighbors' analysis can also help identify the optimal location for a new store or service based on the proximity to customers or complementary businesses.

Local measures in spatial autocorrelation focus on the specific characteristics and interactions of individual sites or areas. Unlike global measures, which summarize spatial patterns across an entire study region, local measures provide detailed insights into spatial relationships at specific locations. The first measure proposed by Anselin (1995) is Local Indicators of Spatial Autocorrelation (LISA) that decomposes global measures like Moran's I and Geary's C into their local components, helping to identify influential observations and local outliers.

The second set of local statistics, G and G* statistics, developed by Getis and Ord (1992), measure local spatial association by focusing on the sum of values in the vicinity of a specific location. The Getis-Ord G and G* statistics are local measures of spatial autocorrelation used to identify clusters of high or low values within a spatial dataset. Both statistics assess the spatial concentration of similar values around a specific location, but they differ in how they incorporate the focal point (the location being analyzed) into the calculation. G focuses on the sum of values within a defined distance from a location i, excluding i's own value. G* includes the value at i itself, making it suitable for studying clusters where the focal point is part of the cluster.

The Getis-Ord G* statistic, or simply G*, assesses the spatial clustering of high or low values. (Getis & Ord, 1992, 2010). Unlike Moran's I, which considers spatial autocorrelation broadly, the Getis-Ord G* focuses on identifying "hot spots" and "cold spots" of significantly high or low values. It highlights areas where high values cluster together (hot spots) and where low values cluster together (cold spots), providing a more nuanced understanding of spatial patterns (Fig. 6.7).

Hotspot and coldspot analysis involves identifying geographic areas where observed phenomena (e.g., crime rates, disease incidence) are significantly higher or lower than average, respectively. Hotspots are areas with a high concentration of high values, indicating an aggregation of similar high-intensity events. Conversely, coldspots are areas where low values cluster. These analyses are instrumental in various fields, including public health, crime analysis, and environmental science, allowing researchers and policymakers to target interventions and resources effectively.

While both Moran's I and the Getis-Ord G assess spatial autocorrelation, their main difference lies in their focus and output. Moran's I measures overall spatial autocorrelation, providing a global view or localized patterns of similarity without distinguishing between high or low value clustering. Getis-Ord G, on the other

6.4 Spatially Explicit Models

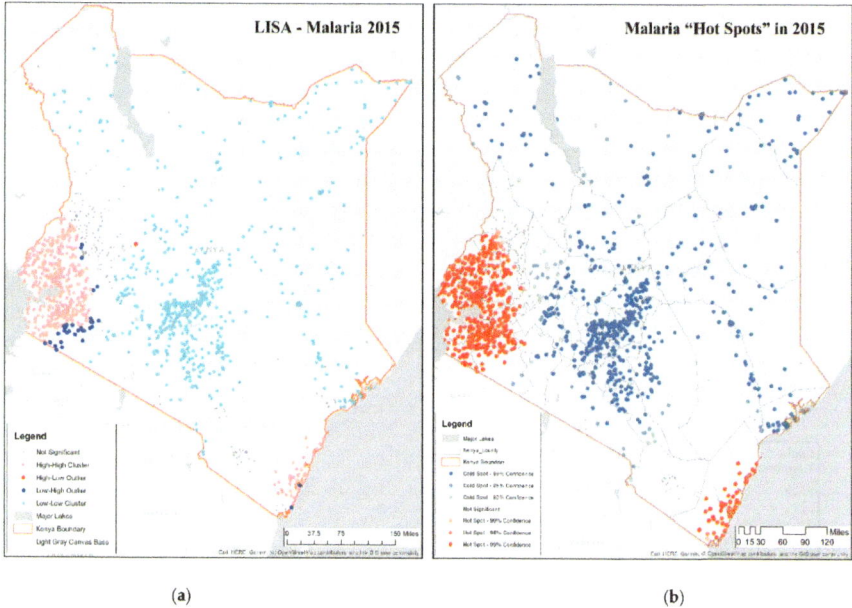

Fig. 6.7 Analysis of Local Spatial Autocorrelation in 2015 Malaria Incidence Rates in Kenya. The map in Panel a (LISA hotspots) identifies high-high clusters indicating significantly elevated malaria incidence near Lake Victoria in the west and on the eastern coast. The map in Panel b (Getis-Ord G) displays hot- and coldspots at three levels of statistical significance, visualizing areas with notably high and low malaria incidence rates

hand, specifically identifies regions of significant high value (hotspots) or low value (coldspots) clustering, offering a clearer direction for targeted analysis or intervention. In summary, spatial autocorrelation measures like Global and Local Moran's I and Getis-Ord G are pivotal in uncovering and understanding the spatial patterns inherent in geographical data. The choice between these measures and the specific parameters used, such as distance and neighborhood definitions, should be guided by the research question and the nature of the spatial data at hand. Figure 6.8 shows a case study of spatial autocorrelation of malaria in Kenya in 2015. The map in the left panel of Fig. 6.8 identifies high-high clusters indicating significantly elevated malaria incidence near Lake Victoria in the west and on the eastern coast. The map in the right panel shows Getis-Ord G, displaying hot- and coldspots at three levels of statistical significance and visualizing areas with notably high and low malaria incidence rates.

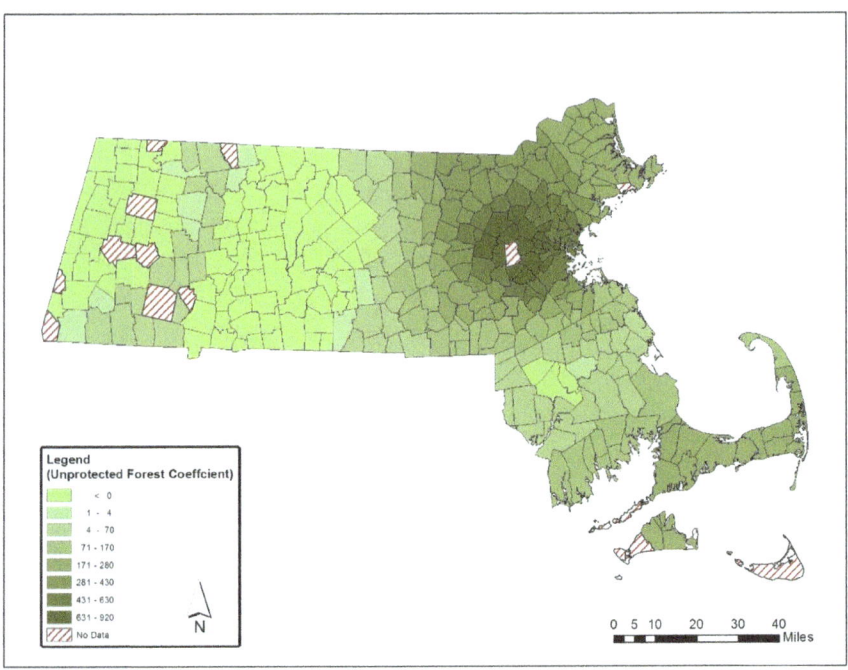

Fig. 6.8 Unprotected forest in this GWR model (2013 data) is a significant non-stationary variable, with higher coefficients (in darker green) centered around Boston in the east

6.4.3 Applying Hot Spot Analysis in Finance

Hotspot analysis has intriguing application beyond traditional fields like criminology and public health into the realm of finance and investment strategy. The transformation of Eastern Europe from a coldspot during the 1980s to a more favorable investment destination post-communism exemplifies how political and economic transitions can alter the investment landscape. Similarly, China's Belt and Road Initiative (BRI) represents a contemporary example of strategic investment in resource-rich regions, turning them into hotspots for infrastructure and resource extraction investments. Hotspot analysis has applications in the following facets in geospatial finance.

Strategic Investment and Geopolitical Influence: China's BRI serves dual purposes—securing China's access to crucial natural resources and expanding its geopolitical influence (Gopal et al., 2018). By investing in hydroelectric projects, mines, and other infrastructure in Southeast Asia and Africa, China not only ensures a steady supply of resources like coal, hydro, and minerals but also positions itself as a key economic partner in these regions. This strategic investment approach can be analyzed through hotspot analysis by mapping the concentration of Chinese investments globally and correlating these with regions rich in natural resources (Shi et al., 2023; Yang et al., 2021).

Shifts in Global Investment Patterns: The transition of Eastern Europe from an investment coldspot to a hotspot with the fall of communism underscores the impact of political changes on investment flows. A similar analysis can be applied to understand how global events, such as trade agreements, sanctions, and political alliances, influence investment patterns. Hotspot and coldspot analysis could reveal emerging investment frontiers and declining markets, offering insights into the dynamic nature of global finance.

Sustainable Development and Investment Hotspots: As global attention shifts toward sustainable development, regions with potential for renewable energy projects (such as solar and wind power) might emerge as new investment hotspots. An extension of the hypothesis could involve analyzing investment flows into green energy projects and identifying regions that are becoming hotspots for sustainable development investments. This would include not only hydroelectric power, as seen in China's investments, but also other forms of renewable energy.

Technology and Infrastructure Development as Hotspots: Beyond natural resources, the development of technology and infrastructure also attracts significant investments. Regions showing rapid growth in technological innovation or infrastructure development (e.g., 5G networks, smart cities) could be analyzed as hotspots. This extension of the hypothesis would explore how investments in technology and infrastructure fuel economic growth and transform investment landscapes.

Risk Analysis and Investment Strategy: Hotspot and coldspot analysis can also inform risk assessment and investment strategy. By identifying regions with high concentrations of investments (hotspots) and areas neglected by investors (coldspots), financial analysts can assess geopolitical risks, market saturation, and untapped opportunities. This nuanced understanding of global investment patterns can guide strategic investment decisions, diversification strategies, and risk management.

In conclusion, extending the hotspot hypothesis to include these dimensions illustrates the versatility of hotspot and coldspot analysis in finance. By applying these concepts to analyze investment patterns, geopolitical strategies, and emerging markets, investors and policymakers can gain valuable insights into the complex dynamics of global finance.

6.4.4 Spatially Weighted Regression—Hedonic Models

Spatial hedonic models and Geographically Weighted Regression (GWR) are two advanced econometric techniques used to analyze spatial data, particularly in the context of real estate and environmental economics. Both methods are designed to address the complexities that arise from the spatial dimension inherent in such data.

Spatial hedonic models are econometric tools used to estimate the value of a good or service by examining its attributes and the spatial (geographical) context in which it exists. These models are particularly useful in real estate and urban economics to analyze how various factors affect property prices while accounting for spatial dependencies. Hedonic pricing models break down the price of a good or service into the value of its constituent attributes. For example, in real estate, the price of a property can be considered as a function of characteristics like size, number of rooms, age, and location. These models help in understanding how each attribute contributes to the overall price, which is particularly useful for policy analysis and market assessments. Spatial dependence refers to the concept that observations close to each other in space are likely to be more similar than those farther apart. This is due to shared environmental or socioeconomic factors. It includes spatial autocorrelation (i.e., where the value of a variable at one location depends on values at nearby locations) and spatial heterogeneity, which is the variation in relationships over space (Lesage & Pace, 2009).

Geographically Weighted Regression is a spatial analysis technique that allows local rather than global parameters to be estimated (Comber et al., 2024; Fischer & Getis, 2010; Wheeler, 2021). Unlike traditional regression models that generate a single equation to describe the relationship between variables across all observations, GWR generates parameters that vary across the study area. This approach is particularly useful for data with non-stationarity, in which the relationships between variables vary across space. GWR addresses spatial heterogeneity by fitting a separate regression equation for every location in the data, using a subset of nearby data points weighted according to their proximity to the location in question. The result is a local model that can adapt to local idiosyncrasies in the data, providing a more nuanced understanding of spatial relationships. This is particularly important in urban economic studies in which factors influencing property values can vary significantly even over short distances.

$$y_i = \beta_{i0} + \sum_{k=1}^{p-1} \beta_{ik} x_{ik} + \varepsilon_i \qquad (6.2)$$

In Eq. 6.2, from Wheeler and Páez (2010), y is the dependent variable value at location i, x_{ik} is the value of the kth covariate at location i, β_{i0} is the intercept, β_{ik} is the regression coefficient for the kth covariate, p is the number of regression terms, and i ε is the random error at location i. In GWR, regression coefficients are estimated at each data location, while in the standard regression, the coefficient is global (one value).

Housing serves as a critical component of urban sustainability, with significant implications for regional economic stability and investment potential. From a financial investment and risk management perspective, GWR and the more general spatial econometric models (for a review and discussion, see Fischer & Nijkamp, 2021, pp. 2053–2282) capture spatial dependencies, which is crucial for investors and policymakers aiming to capitalize on real estate investments while mitigating economic risks associated with urban development. The correlation between home values and various determinants is shown by an assessment of the influence of spatial determinants on median home prices in Massachusetts towns (Ma & Gopal, 2018). Factors including the extent of unprotected forest land, educational attainment, vehicle ownership, school district performance, and demographic elements like the senior population, show different spatial effects across the region. Figure 6.8 shows that unprotected forest in this GWR model (2013 data) is a significant non-stationary variable, meaning that its spatial effect is strong. The coefficients vary across the region with higher coefficients (in darker green) centered around Boston in the east. This means that higher unprotected forest values are associated with higher housing values in that Boston metro area, while lower coefficients in the western part of the state suggest the opposite. Thus, unprotected forest regions in the Boston metro area add to the total house value.

6.4.5 Geostatistics and Kriging Interpolation

Geostatistics is a branch of statistics focusing on analyzing and predicting spatially distributed environmental and social data (Oliver, 2009). The semivariogram is a foundational tool in geostatistics for analyzing spatial autocorrelation and provides insights into how spatially associated units vary with distance (Getis, 2009). This concept plays a crucial role in understanding spatial patterns and dependencies within georeferenced data (Cressie, 2015).

The semivariogram function describes the degree of spatial dependence between observations as a function of distance. Specifically, it measures how the similarity between values decreases as the distance between them increases. The semivariogram has three main components: sill, range, and nugget. The variogram typically starts low at short distances (indicating strong similarity) and increases with distance until it stabilizes (indicating that points are less related as they get further apart). Figure 6.9 shows the semivariogram plot. Nugget represents measurement error or micro-scale variation at very small distances. Sill is the point where the variogram levels off, indicating the limit of spatial correlation. Range is the distance over which spatial correlation is significant; beyond this range, the spatial correlation is negligible. The variogram helps in understanding and quantifying spatial variability, which is crucial for effective kriging. It informs how weights should be assigned to data points based on their spatial relationship (Oliver & Webster, 2014).

In spatial finance, the semivariogram can be used in estimating carbon sequestration in soils (Alaboz & Dengiz, 2024) or studying pollution dispersion (Ballabio et al., 2021). These types of applications help in the analysis of the environmental impacts of a bank's investments or a company's operations in meeting regulations or reporting.

The mathematical form of the semivariogram, $\gamma(h)$, where h is the lag distance between pairs of observations, can be expressed as:

Fig. 6.9 The semivariogram plot with range, sill, and nugget on a plot where distance is marked on the X-axis and semivariance is plotted on the Y-axis

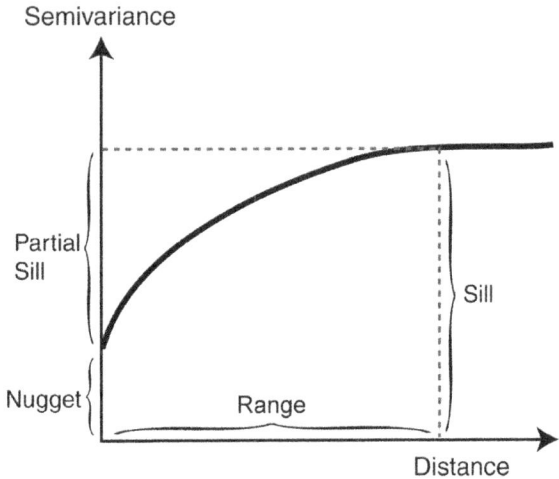

$$\gamma(h) = \frac{1}{2N(h)} \sum_{i=1}^{N(h)} [Z(x_i) - Z(x_i + h)]^2 \qquad (6.3)$$

In Eq. 6.3, $Z(x_i)$ is the value of the variable at location x_i, and $N(h)$ is the number of pairs of observations separated by distance h.

Kriging is a geostatistical interpolation technique that uses the semivariogram to make predictions about unknown values at unsampled locations. It is an advanced method that provides not only the predicted values but also the estimation of their uncertainty. The kriging estimator can be expressed as:

$$\hat{Z}(x_0) = \sum_{i=1}^{N} \lambda_i Z(x_i) \qquad (6.4)$$

where $\hat{Z}(x_0)$ is the predicted value at location x_0, $Z(x_i)$ are known values at sampled locations, and λ_i are the weights, shown in Eq. 6.4.

There are several types of kriging. Simple kriging assumes a known constant mean throughout the area. Ordinary kriging assumes an unknown but constant mean within the local neighborhood of each estimated point. Universal Kriging incorporates a deterministic trend along with the spatial correlation. Kriging is widely used in fields such as environmental science for pollution mapping, mining for estimating ore grades, and agriculture for soil property mapping.

Getis (2009) described the utility of the semivariogram, a foundational tool in geostatistics, for analyzing spatial autocorrelation and providing insights into how spatially associated units vary with distance. This concept was thoroughly discussed by Cressie (2015), and it plays a crucial role in understanding spatial patterns and dependencies within georeferenced data. The semivariogram assumes that the differences between spatially associated units decrease with increasing proximity. This means that points close to each other are more similar (exhibit smaller differences) than points farther apart. This concept is graphically represented by the shape of the semivariogram, typically resembling a positive exponential distribution.

Kriging is a fundamental geostatistical method widely utilized in the oil industry to predict the spatial distribution of oil reserves. This technique interpolates data from various sampling locations, incorporating both the distance and variation between known data points to forecast values at uncharted locations, thereby effectively modeling spatial phenomena such as oil reservoirs (Atkinson & Lloyd, 2021). Additionally, variogram analysis is employed to measure the spatial dependence within a dataset, allowing geostatisticians to construct more accurate subsurface models crucial for effective drilling operations (Isaaks & Srivastava, 1989). The inclusion of spatial dependence in models for oil exploration significantly refines reserve estimates, a critical component in the financial decision-making process within the oil industry. Advanced spatial modeling techniques not only mitigate the financial risks associated with drilling but also enhance operational efficiency by optimizing drill site locations to maximize success probabilities (Oliver & Webster, 2014).

Kriging allows developers to accurately predict the locations of geothermal reservoirs by analyzing the spatial distribution of subsurface temperatures and geological features (Stutz et al., 2015). This method helps in pinpointing areas with high geothermal potential, which are crucial for the efficient extraction of geothermal energy. By interpolating sparse data points, kriging provides a continuous surface estimation of geothermal resources. This continuous model aids in the assessment of the energy potential and sustainability of geothermal reservoirs, ensuring that the locations chosen for development have sufficient energy reserves to justify the investment. The use of kriging in geothermal exploration reduces the risk associated with drilling. By offering a detailed predictive model of subsurface conditions, kriging minimizes the uncertainty in drilling decisions, leading to better outcomes and reduced costs associated with unsuccessful drills. Accurate geospatial analysis through kriging also supports the optimal design and placement of infrastructure.

6.4.6 Spatial Econometrics

Spatial econometrics is a subfield of econometrics that deals with spatial interdependence and spatial heterogeneity in data (LeSage & Pace, 2009). Spatial heterogeneity refers to the variation in relationships or processes over space, which means the effect of an independent variable on the dependent variable may differ across locations. Spatial Lag Model (SLM) incorporates spatial dependence in the dependent variable. Spatial Error Model (SEM incorporates spatial dependence in the error terms. Spatial econometrics can be particularly useful in finance for analyzing data that exhibits spatial dependence and heterogeneity. Books by Elhorst (2014), LeSage and Pace (2009), and Rey and Anselin (2014) provide complete coverage of spatial econometric modeling.

Spatial econometric models can improve the accuracy of real estate price predictions by accounting for spatial dependencies among property values. Investors can use spatial econometrics to identify regions with uncorrelated economic activities, aiding in diversification strategies. Financial institutions can use spatial econometrics to model the clustering of loan defaults, improving the assessment of credit risk. Incorporating spatial dependence in loan performance can lead to more accurate pricing of loans and better risk management. Spatial econometric models can analyze how stock prices in one region affect those in another, considering regional economic and trade linkages. Understanding spatial patterns in stock returns can provide insights into regional economic dynamics and investment opportunities.

The interview with Dr. Manfred M. Fischer Emeritus Professor of Economic Geography at Vienna University of Economics and Business highlights the advances in spatial econometrics that can further inform geospatial finance.

Expert in Focus: Manfred Fischer

Dr. Manfred M. Fischer is Emeritus Professor of Economic Geography at Vienna University of Economics and Business, and Adjunct Professor at the Institute for Geographical Sciences and Natural Resources Research, Chinese Academy of Sciences in Beijing.

Dr. Fischer has been a pioneering figure in the field of Regional Science, contributing significantly as a researcher, educator, and editor.

Throughout his career, Dr. Fischer has published over 400 works, including journal articles, books, and encyclopedia entries. He has been instrumental in developing and leading academic programs such as the Supply Chain Management Master Program and the Innovation Economics Vienna Program. His research has spanned a wide range of topics, including regional and urban economics, spatial behavior, transportation systems, and Geographic Information Systems (GIS), earning him recognition as one of the most cited scholars in his field.

Dr. Fischer has served on numerous international committees and editorial boards, including as co-founder and editor-in-chief of the Journal of Geographical Systems. He has also been deeply involved in organizing international conferences and fostering research collaborations across the globe.

His work has been widely recognized with numerous honors and awards, including the RSAI Fellows Award, the European Prize in Regional Science, the Jean-Paelinck Award, and the RSAI Founder's Medal, among others. Dr. Fischer has also been elected as a Foreign Member of the Royal Netherlands Academy of Arts and Sciences, a Corresponding Member of the Austrian Academy of Sciences, and an Academician of the International Academy of Sciences for Europe and Asia.

Expert Interview with Manfred Fischer

What is the role of geospatial sciences in solving societal and environmental challenges today?

The role of geospatial sciences has undergone a profound transformation, driven by the increasing availability of data, advancements in computing power, and innovations in spatial econometric modeling, artificial intelligence, and cross-disciplinary collaborations. Today, geospatial analysis is more integral than ever, highlighting the critical importance of spatial relationships in a wide range of fields, including human interactions, international trade, geopolitics, and sustainable finance.

The recognition of spatial neighborhood effects and spatial autocorrelation has become essential in understanding complex processes, such as the environmental impacts of human activities and the assessment of climate risk on the ground. These spatial dynamics offer invaluable insights into how location and proximity influence outcomes, shaping our ability to develop more effective strategies for addressing global challenges.

In my recent work with colleagues, I have explored these themes in depth, focusing on how advanced geospatial methods can be applied to analyze and address pressing issues in environmental sustainability, economic development, and social equity. Our research underscores the growing importance of geospatial sciences in crafting solutions that are both spatially aware and sensitive to the intricate interconnections that define our world today.

My recent papers on government bond yields contribute significantly to the expanding body of knowledge on how advanced econometric models, when integrated with geospatial analysis, can enhance financial practices. By incorporating spatial dynamics, regional heterogeneity, and the intricate interplay between financial variables and local conditions, these studies emphasize the critical role of spatial relationships in shaping economic outcomes. The

> *insights gained from this research underscore the value of considering regional differences and spatial interactions in financial modeling. These approaches are particularly relevant to the emerging field of geospatial finance, where they can be applied to develop more robust predictive models, ultimately leading to more informed and resilient financial strategies.*

6.4.7 Case Study: China's Development Finance Impacts

China has emerged as a major player in overseas development finance, becoming one of the world's leading lenders in this field. Its financed projects—including roads, railways, and power plants—are critical for development but pose significant risks to biodiversity and Indigenous lands (Simmons et al., 2022). Further analysis reveals that 63% of projects financed by China are situated within or adjacent to areas crucial for biodiversity or Indigenous communities, potentially impacting up to 24% of the world's threatened birds, mammals, reptiles, and amphibians (Yang et al., 2021). The main risk hotspots are located in northern sub-Saharan Africa, Southeast Asia, and parts of South America. The environmental risks from China's projects, especially within the energy sector, are found to be higher than those associated with World Bank projects. This study provides a global view of the socio-ecological risks, offering vital insights to enhance the sustainability of China's international development finance.

Furthermore, geospatial data analysis, based on change detection of satellite images, indicates the deforestation and biodiversity impacts of energy investments in Southeast Asia from 2000 to 2018 (Ma et al., 2023). This study examined different types of power plants and their financing sources, identifying critical buffer zones and forest structures impacted by these investments, in line with International Union for Conservation of Nature (IUCN) criteria and spatial ecology principles. Categorizing forests more accurately—distinguishing core areas, edges, islands, and bridges—enables a better understanding of deforestation (Ma et al., 2023). Figure 6.10 shows the deforestation in SE Asia. This research offers important insights into the trade-offs between financed energy development and biodiversity conservation, providing actionable recommendations for policymakers, conservationists, and development banks to prioritize forest and habitat preservation in Southeast Asia and beyond.

Both domestic and foreign multinationals play a role in the cultivation and production of palm oil (Gopal et al., 2023).[13] These companies are responsible for reporting and helping to address the crisis of GHG and biodiversity loss stemming from deforestation in and around plantations. Figure 6.9 shows the location of palm oil refineries. This change detection study identifies the biodiversity and forest loss due to commercial palm oil cultivation in Southeast Asia. Many multinational companies are signatories of Roundtable on Sustainable Palm Oil (RSPO) and align to better business

---

[13] https://www.bu.edu/imap/research/projects/.

6.4 Spatially Explicit Models

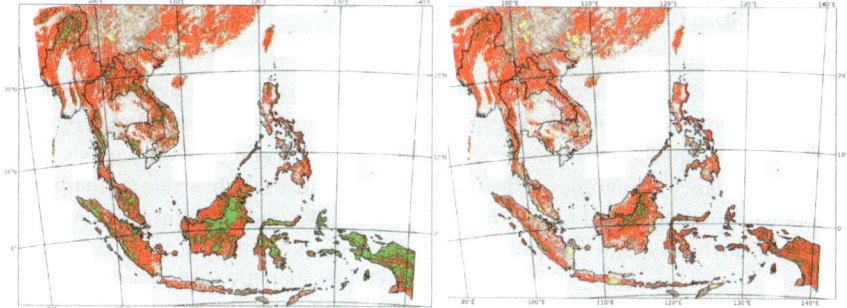

Fig. 6.10 Deforestation trends in Southeast Asia. The map on the left shows forested areas in green in 2006 while the map on the right shows forested areas in 2018. Deforestation impacting core forests and corridors in the forests is linked to mining and commercial agriculture (palm oil)

practices including sustainability in palm oil cultivation, addressing environmental concerns, and ensuring responsible business practices within the palm oil industry. Further study incorporating differentiation of RSPO and non-RSPO refineries can lead to targeted decisions and policies to guide sustainability in this sector (Fig. 6.11).

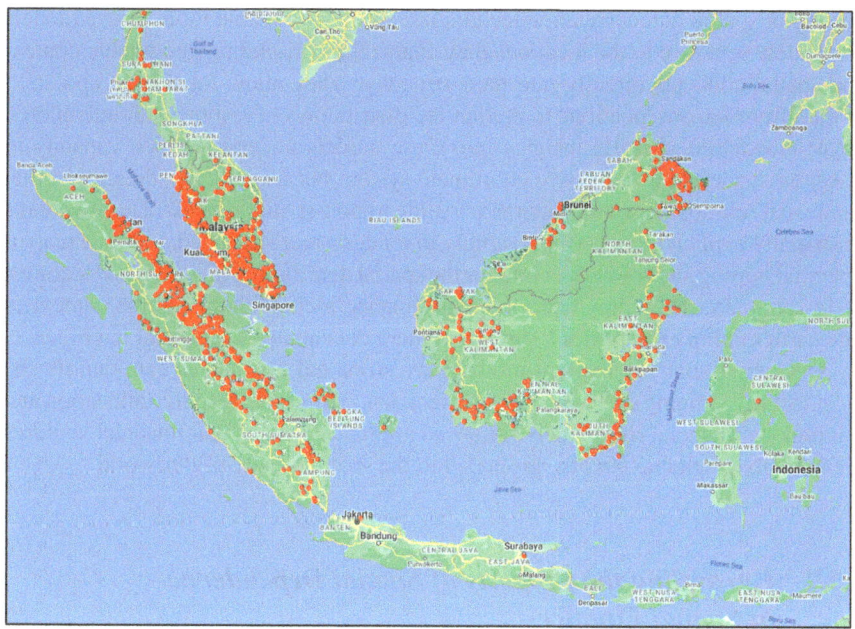

Fig. 6.11 Mapped locations of 1,400 palm oil plantations and refineries in Malaysia and Indonesia. Palm oil plantations have led to deforestation and forest degradation and biodiversity loss

6.5 Geospatial Finance Framework

The previous sections provide some insight into how the emerging field of geospatial finance can address the complex interplay between financial activities and geographical location, emphasizing that space is not a mere backdrop but an active agent influencing financial outcomes. When applied to industries such as rare earth mining, the sophistication of spatial finance becomes especially evident. Mining investments cannot rely on the evaluation of isolated sites due to the possibility of spurious patterns that may mislead investors. Spatial data often exhibits such deceptive patterns, which could be mistakenly interpreted as indicative of valuable resources. To circumvent these misleading cues, rigorous statistical significance testing is employed, filtering out false discoveries and focusing on genuinely promising locations. The inherent nature of spatial data, characterized by spatial autocorrelation and heterogeneity, defies traditional statistical models that assume data points to be independent and identically distributed (i.i.d.). This violation of i.i.d. assumptions in spatial datasets can lead to skewed analytical outcomes, rendering conventional models unreliable. For example, the presence of a valuable mineral deposit in one location does not guarantee similar findings in a nearby area due to the complex geological processes that distribute minerals unevenly across the landscape.

To address these challenges, spatially explicit models, such as those utilizing kriging or spatial autocorrelation techniques, are indispensable tools. These models are acutely sensitive to the locations they analyze, incorporating geographic context and spatial concepts directly into their structure. They allow for the extrapolation of data from known locations to predict the distribution of resources in unexplored areas. Goodchild's (2001) insights into these models underscore their capacity to integrate space not as a passive coordinate system but as an active dimension that can reveal relationships and patterns invisible to non-spatial models. The advantage of spatially explicit models is their ability to render a more nuanced, accurate map of potential mining sites by accounting for the spatial distribution of geological features.

In summary, the deployment of spatial finance methodologies in the context of rare earth mining exemplifies a shift from mere data analysis to spatial intelligence. By leveraging spatially explicit models, investors and companies can identify the most lucrative mining sites with greater precision, optimizing resource allocation and minimizing financial risks. Such a nuanced approach ensures that financial ventures are not only profitable but also grounded in the spatial reality of our world.

6.5.1 Unraveling the Property of Spatial Dependence in Spatial Finance

Spatial dependence, a core concept in spatial finance, poses a considerable challenge to traditional data science frameworks that typically presume observational independence. This principle stipulates that the value of a variable at a specific geographic point is not isolated but is influenced by values at adjacent locations (Anselin, 2003; Getis, 2009). The failure to integrate spatial dependence into financial models can significantly impair both the predictive accuracy and the interpretative power of these models, particularly when analyzing geographically defined phenomena.

As discussed in Sect. 6.4, in the realm of mining activities or oil drilling, spatial dependence is a crucial consideration. The distribution of mineral resources is not random but is influenced by geological processes that induce spatial autocorrelation of resource quantities (Griffith & Paelinck, 2011). Models that do not account for this correlation, such as those predicting the profitability of mining investments, risk overlooking the nuanced geological patterns that characterize resource deposits. In the context of Real Estate Investment Trusts (REITs), spatial dependence implies that events affecting one property can have repercussions on the valuation and risk profile of nearby properties. For instance, a burglary or water damage in one building could potentially alter the perceived safety or desirability of the surrounding area, thus influencing the market value of neighboring real estate (Basu & Thibodeau, 1998). Companies such as Zillow harness spatial finance principles by employing spatial econometric models to estimate home values. These models take into account not just the characteristics of individual homes but also the prices of nearby properties, acknowledging the principle of spatial autocorrelation where the value of a property is related to the value of its neighbors (Fischer et al., 2021). This spatial interdependence is particularly salient in REIT portfolios, where the aggregated performance can be affected by spatially clustered events. By incorporating spatial data into financial analyses, REIT investors and managers can better predict risks and returns, accounting for the non-random distribution of real estate values influenced by regional factors such as economic conditions, demographic shifts, and local environmental events (Pace et al., 1998).

Investing in areas with notable agglomeration effects has become a common strategy to mitigate risks and capitalize on the potential for economic growth. Agglomeration economies refer to the benefits firms accrue by being in proximity to each other, often leading to clusters, particularly in high-tech sectors (Porter, 1998). The locational choices of firms are frequently determined by the characteristics of surrounding regions, including the presence of similar firms, infrastructure, and labor markets (Krugman, 1991). Spatial econometric models that incorporate these factors are better suited to capturing the reality of such spatial interactions (Fischer & Nijkamp, 2021).[14] Furthermore, the spatial dynamics of firm location highlight the essential role of accessibility. Accessibility to transportation networks, consumer markets, and knowledge centers is a significant factor influencing the distribution of firms, particularly high-tech firms that rely heavily on innovation and skilled labor (Audretsch & Feldman, 2004). Prior empirical studies have frequently used proximity to central business districts, highways, and universities as indicators of accessibility, substantiating its significance in firm location decisions (Marshall, 1920; Ricardo, 1817).

---

[14] For a summary of spatial econometric models, see Fischer and Nijkamp (2021) Section IX.

Regions striving to attract high-tech industries result in a heterogeneous landscape of these firms across territories. This non-uniform distribution underscores the importance of embracing spatial context in examining high-tech firms' locational preferences, which are often guided by the cumulative and localized economic benefits (Scott & Storper, 2003). The emergence of data centers in 2023–2024 underscores the importance of cross-site externalities in determining firms' locational choices, suggesting these factors are more critical than the analysis of broader regions or states as homogeneous units might indicate. Firm location data, being georeferenced, implies that the locations are tied to spatial characteristics likely influenced by nearby sites' attributes. Consequently, analytical frameworks that overlook spatial variables are unable to detect the presence of spatial spillovers (LeSage & Fischer, 2012). Agglomeration economies, as the probably most cited locational determinant, describe the benefits firms gain by locating near one another. These economies are categorized into localization economies, arising from the proximity of firms within the same industry, and urbanization economies, stemming from inter-industry knowledge spillovers.

In conclusion, the acknowledgment of spatial effects is not merely an academic adjustment but a practical necessity that aligns with the principles of new economic geography. It emphasizes that the localized and cumulative advantages of agglomeration economies are most pronounced at the local level and can significantly shape economic landscapes (Rosenthal & Strange, 2020). Neglecting spatial factors in financial analysis and modeling risks a profound misunderstanding of the economic phenomena and potentially leads to suboptimal investment decisions.

6.5.2 A Spatial Hierarchical Framework for Geospatial Finance

A World Bank report (2022) highlighted three primary obstacles to the broader application of geospatial finance: a lack of reliable asset-level data with the necessary detail and frequency, a deficiency in granular supply chain information, and inadequate integration of observational climate and environmental data into financial models. To address these challenges, the World Bank proposed a hierarchical tier system to systematically categorize data according to detail and application specificity within spatial finance (see Fig. 6.12).

The hierarchy delineates distinct tiers of data analysis, commencing with Tier Four, which consists of sub-asset-level data that is possible to collect now with IoT sensors and smart meters. This granularity enables companies to prepare detailed ESG reports, providing asset managers and other stakeholders with project-specific financial insights. However, generating Tier four metrics is resource-intensive, requiring significant data processing capabilities.

Tier three is the asset-level information where one can spatialize the asset and assess GHG emissions using satellite remote sensing at multiple spatial scales.

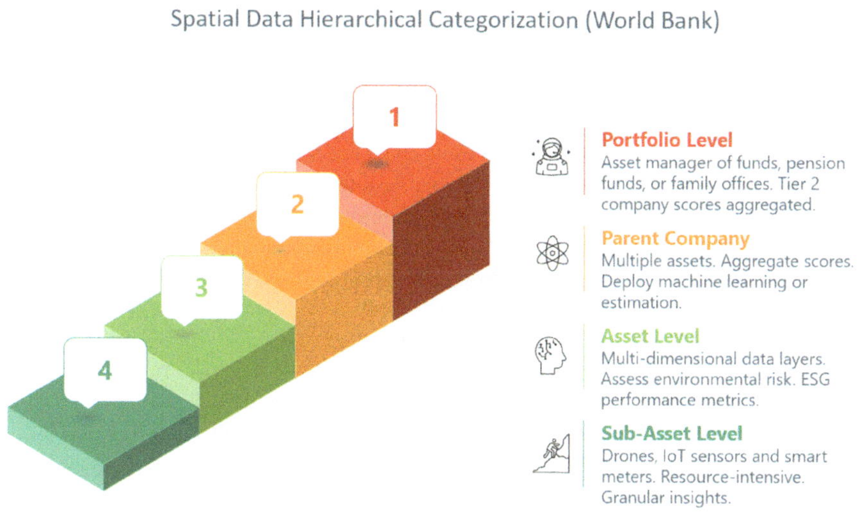

6.5 Geospatial Finance Framework

Spatial Data Hierarchical Categorization (World Bank)

1 Portfolio Level
Asset manager of funds, pension funds, or family offices. Tier 2 company scores aggregated.

2 Parent Company
Multiple assets. Aggregate scores. Deploy machine learning or estimation.

3 Asset Level
Multi-dimensional data layers. Assess environmental risk. ESG performance metrics.

4 Sub-Asset Level
Drones, IoT sensors and smart meters. Resource-intensive. Granular insights.

Fig. 6.12 The World Bank's Hierarchical Tier System to categorize data according to spatial scale (detail) within spatial finance

This tier enables the synthesis of multi-dimensional data layers, including remote sensing outputs, to evaluate environmental risk factors associated with a commercial asset, such as water scarcity, deforestation risk, carbon and methane emission levels, and production and trade dynamics implications. Tier three represents a maturing domain within spatial finance, with several commercial entities offering specialized observational data services that provide sector-wide, Tier three-level insights to clientele. This tier's development signifies spatial finance methodologies' increasing sophistication and applicability in delivering actionable ESG performance metrics.

The assets must be spatialized to utilize remote sensing sensors. Specifically, Tier three analyses facilitate the assessment of an asset's proximity to critical environmental landmarks, such as World Heritage Sites, Protected Areas, and ecologically sensitive zones, through Geographic Information System (GIS) technologies. The two authors of this book have first-hand experience and expertise, having worked on various research projects, assessing impact of hydroelectric dams in Cambodia (Pitts et al., 2020), urban expansion in Indonesia, (Kelly-Fair et al., 2022) environmental and social governance in Belize (Gopal et al., 2015), ESG US (Gopal et al., 2021), EU, and other contexts, relying on geospatial data, AI, and other analyses.

Tier two is the parent company with multiple assets' summed or aggregate scores. For instance, large companies like Walmart and Starbucks, with extensive global operations, face complexities in accounting for emissions across their numerous locations.

Tier one is the portfolio level required by an asset manager of funds, pension funds, or family offices. This portfolio data is aggregated using Tier 2 company scores, encompassing broad, macro-scale analyses conducive to deriving national-level insights for applications such as sovereign debt assessment. The tiered analytical model within geospatial finance underscores the critical role of observational data in the comprehensive evaluation of ESG performance metrics. The model facilitates a structured approach to navigating the extensive and heterogeneous data landscape by categorizing data according to specificity and application. The tier system enhances the precision of asset-level ESG assessments and broadens the scope of spatial finance applications, from national macro-scale evaluations to micro-scale, project-specific analyses. The ongoing development and refinement of this tiered framework can augment spatial finance's accuracy, relevance, and applicability in the pursuit of sustainable and responsible asset management practices.

6.5.3 Geospatial Finance Use Cases

Geospatial technologies and data play a pivotal role in sustainable finance by enhancing environmental risk assessment, resource allocation, and supply chain optimization. These applications offer detailed insights that are crucial for informed decision-making in sustainable finance projects that require a nuanced understanding of environmental and logistical factors.

6.5.3.1 Location Siting and Optimization

Spatial data can be crucial for identifying optimal locations for renewable energy projects, such as solar farms or wind turbines (Farr et al., 2021; Shao et al., 2020). By analyzing solar irradiance, wind patterns, land use, proximity to transmission lines, and environmental impact, investors can assess the viability and potential return on investment for projects in various locations. This analysis is called Location Siting. For instance, a solar energy company might use satellite imagery and climate data to pinpoint areas with the highest year-round solar irradiance for their installations, thereby maximizing energy production and investment returns (Mokarram et al., 2020; Saraswat et al., 2021). Similarly, Müller et al. (2023) demonstrated how geospatial cost modeling optimizes locations for green hydrogen production in Kenya, utilizing PV potential data to site renewable facilities effectively. Increasingly, trade-offs between renewable energy and biodiversity and forest loss are estimated (Cohen et al., 2021; Marin et al., 2022; Popescu et al., 2020). These considerations of environmental trade-offs are particularly relevant under frameworks like the EU's Principal Adverse Impacts (PAI) reporting, which mandates transparency in environmental impact assessments. Similarly, geospatial data has played a role in broader geopolitical projects, such as influencing decisions in China's Belt and Road initiative to halt coal mining projects due to identified environmental risks.[15] It should be emphasized that there are challenges related to spatial accuracy, data access, and

---

[15] https://www.bu.edu/gdp/2023/09/18/how-innovative-financing-mechanisms-can-green-the-belt-and-road-initiative/.

interpretation. More accurate data is more expensive and large companies such as Bloomberg, Refinitiv, Factset, and S&P 500 provide geospatial data at great costs. Affordability of such data is a limitation in driving sustainable finance solutions in developing countries.

6.5.3.2 Climate Risk Assessment

Financial institutions are increasingly using precise spatial data to assess and manage risks related to climate change. This includes analyzing flood risks, wildfire hazards, and other climate-related vulnerabilities that could impact the financial stability of investments. For example, using high-resolution imaging and data analysis, banks can identify properties at risk of flooding and adjust mortgage and insurance products accordingly. A recent study illustrated how geospatial analysis could predict the increasing risks to wine cultivation in California due to heightened wildfire threats, aiding in preemptive risk management (Gopal et al., 2021).

These risk assessments also present business opportunities. For example, by analyzing areas with increased UV exposure, companies can strategically establish dermatology clinics in locations with higher risks of non-melanoma skin cancer, targeting potential patient populations effectively. Leveraging GIS and remote sensing data, Gopal and Pitts (2022–2023) identified zip codes with a potential patient population of older white adults (above 70) frequently exposed to UV rays from the sun for a healthcare business specializing in non-melanoma skin cancer. Increasingly, climate change and evolving migration patterns create new opportunities for services in new locations.

6.5.3.3 Buying Carbon Credits on the Blockchain

Geospatial data and analysis can help financial institutions and investors identify areas where investment in agriculture or forest conservation could yield carbon credits. Investors can estimate the carbon offset value of growing fruit trees in Africa or Latin America, conserving certain forest areas by analyzing deforestation rates, biomass, and carbon storage data. A case in point is the use of remote sensing data to monitor the Amazon rainforest's health, guiding investments in conservation projects that generate carbon credits and contribute to biodiversity preservation.

Figure 6.13 shows the above and below-ground carbon sequestration, estimated using allometric equation specified by US Department of Agriculture.[16] An allometric equation for estimating the carbon sequestration of olive trees, considering both above- and below-ground biomass, would typically involve measuring specific physical parameters like the diameter at breast height (DBH), tree height, and possibly root spread or volume for below-ground calculations. The general form of such an equation might be:

---

[16] https://www.fs.usda.gov/nrs/pubs/gtr/gtr_nrs200-2021.pdf.

$$Cabon\,Sequestration = a \times (DBH)^b + c \times (Root\,Parameter)^d \quad (6.5)$$

where: a, b, c, and, d are coefficients derived from empirical data specific to olive trees, DBH is the diameter at breast height. Root Parameter could be root volume or spread, depending on available data.

Equation 6.5 requires calibration with local data to accurately predict carbon storage in both the biomass above ground and the root systems below ground.

Sofo et al. (2005) estimated that mature olive groves stored an average of 9.54 metric tons of CO2 per hectare per year, while younger groves stored less, at 2.74 metric tons per hectare per year. This indicates that older, denser groves are more effective at capturing CO2 from the atmosphere. For precise application, it is important to refer to specific studies that provide the coefficients based on measurements from olive trees grown in conditions similar to those of interest.

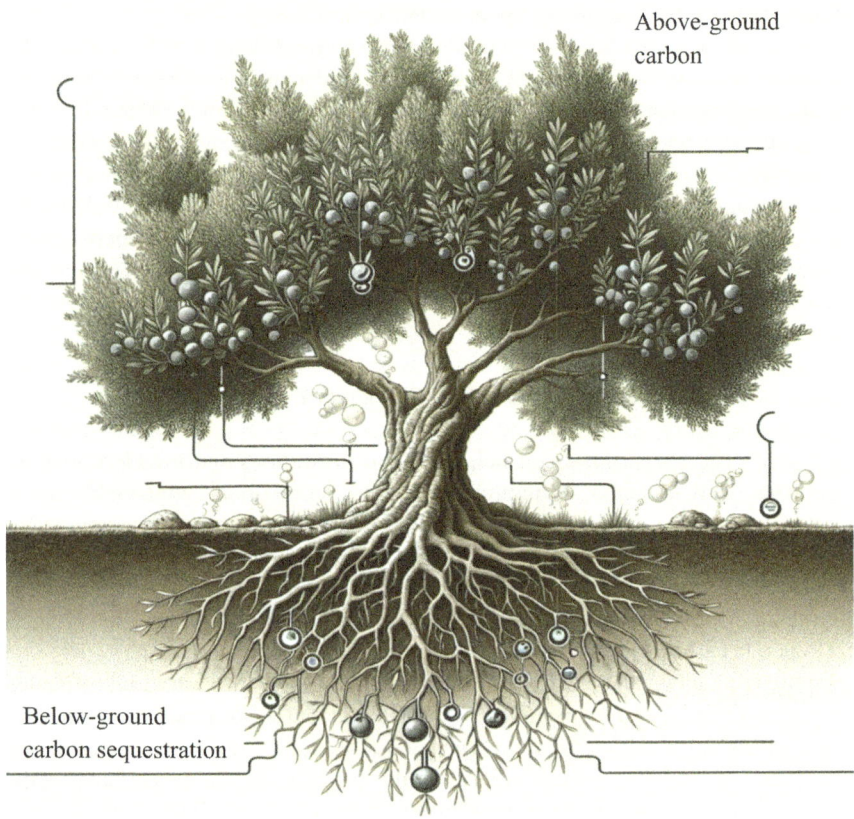

Fig. 6.13 Estimating the carbon sequestration of olive trees, considering both above- and below-ground biomass

Often it may be impossible to measure individual trees. Now analysts use unmanned aerial vehicles (UAVs) or drones equipped with RGB cameras to extract tree canopy structure at Level 4 resolution or remote sensing satellites at Level 3 resolution. Several carbon financing mechanisms traded on blockchain are actually trading carbon credits from fruit trees to mangroves. Blockchain is detailed in Chapter 8 of this book.

Coorest, a Dutch enterprise, introduced NFTrees—a carbon traded fund that streamlines the traditionally opaque and complex voluntary carbon market (VCM). This market has been challenging to navigate for both individuals and businesses due to its lack of transparency, traceability, and prevalence of low-quality carbon offset projects. With Coorest, carbon compensation becomes straightforward, swift, and transparent. By leveraging blockchain technology, Coorest enables anyone to offset their CO_2 emissions instantaneously from any location globally. This approach ensures each compensation is recorded in an immutable and traceable manner, enhancing reliability and accountability.

6.5.3.4 Precision Agriculture

Geospatial finance in agriculture benefits farmers by enabling risk assessment, resource management optimization, access to financial resources, and precision farming techniques. In the same vein, it provides insights for investors, lenders, and policymakers to assess and manage risks associated with agricultural properties. Emerging AgTech or Agritech or Farmtech companies (e.g., Pasture.io; EarthDaily; woolly.io) utilize satellite sensors to leverage the carbon cycle, extract carbon from the atmosphere, and store it in the soil. This new kind of farming uses technologies like satellite imaging, remote sensing, and AI procedures to analyze soil carbon stocks efficiently. It benefits farmers by increasing yields, improving soil health, and earning revenue through carbon markets. This transformation is called carbon farming, which builds climate resiliency in the long run. The biggest challenge is the need for a global framework for accurately measuring soil carbon stocks Climate Adapt EU is promoting precision agriculture as part of its green deal.

6.5.3.5 Insurance and Reinsurance

Companies use geospatial data to assess the flood risk of individual properties more accurately (e.g., Insurity, Ventivtech, Iceeye, Floodmapp). By analyzing topographical data, historical flood records, and climate models, insurance companies can adjust premiums based on the specific risk level of each property. For example, a property insurance company might use detailed floodplain mapping and rainfall data to identify properties at high risk of flooding, adjusting their insurance premiums and coverage terms accordingly. Geospatial data can help insurers assess and mitigate risks associated with climate change on agricultural productivity. By using satellite imagery to monitor crop health, precipitation data to predict drought likelihood, and temperature data to anticipate heatwaves, insurers can tailor insurance products to the specific needs of farmers. A notable application is the use of satellite data to implement index-based insurance for farmers in drought-prone regions, where payouts are triggered by specific, verifiable changes in climate conditions rather than traditional loss assessment methods.

6.5.3.6 Supply Chain Optimization

Geospatial data is a critical tool for companies seeking to enhance the efficiency and sustainability of their supply chains (Gopal et al., 2021; Murray, 2021). By leveraging this data, companies can optimize transportation routes and methods, leading to significant cost reductions and a decreased environmental footprint. Furthermore, precise tracking ensures that materials are sustainably sourced, preventing the supply chain from unintentionally contributing to environmental harm. In industries like semiconductor manufacturing,[17] which is classified under North American Industry Classification System (NAICS) code 33,441, the complexity of supply chains is notably high. This sector includes companies that produce a range of electronic components, such as capacitors, resistors, microprocessors, both bare and loaded printed circuit boards, electron tubes, electronic connectors, and computer modems. The production of a single DRAM chip, for example, involves over 1000 steps and crosses international borders multiple times, potentially passing through more than 70 countries before reaching the final consumer. The AI revolution has brought this into greater focus as Nvidia's latest AI servers require more than 35,000 parts from countries all over the world, including Taiwan (Chen & Leong, 2022). This intricate process complicates tasks such as risk assessment and logistics planning, making them challenging to execute effectively (Ezel, 2021; Gopal et al., 2022).

6.5.3.7 Nature-Based Solutions

Nature-based solutions like mangrove restoration are gaining recognition for their effectiveness in enhancing coastal resilience in countries like Belize, Indonesia, and Bangladesh. These projects are supported by a range of stakeholders including international organizations like the World Bank and UNEP, NGOs such as the Global Mangrove Alliance[18] and the IUCN,[19] and various governmental and private sector partners. The World Bank, for instance, has incorporated mangrove restoration in its

---

[17] https://www.csis.org/analysis/mapping-semiconductor-supply-chain-critical-role-indo-pacific-region.

[18] https://www.mangrovealliance.org/wp-content/uploads/2023/12/GMA-Policy-Brief_V6.pdf#:~:text=URL%3A%20.

[19] https://www.iucn.org/story/202211/mangrove-breakthrough-call-action-critical-ecosystem.

6.6 Challenges and Limitations of Geospatial Data

broader climate resilience strategies, acknowledging their role in protecting coastlines and supporting local economies (World Bank[20]) (UNEP—UN Environment Programme).

The economic valuation of ecosystem services provided by mangroves, like coastal protection, carbon sequestration, and support for fisheries and tourism, is complex. The authors are part of a larger group of scientists funded on a National Science Foundation grant called Strong Coasts.[21] The team is examining pricing of such services including direct market pricing, cost-saving, replacement costs, and benefit transfer among others. Investments in mangrove restoration are seen as cost-effective strategies for climate change adaptation and mitigation. The Belize Blue Carbon project (Morrissette et al., 2023) estimated that the mangrove systems in Belize stored 25.7 Tg of carbon, based on the first national mangrove carbon stock assessment for Belize.[22] Financial mechanisms being explored include carbon credits, blue bonds, and various forms of blended finance that combine private and public funding. These efforts aim to de-risk investments and provide a sustainable financial model for long-term ecosystem management (Climate Champions[23]) (UNFCCC[24]). Such strategic investment not only supports environmental goals but also boosts local economies through job creation and enhanced fisheries and tourism.

To summarize, the relevance of geospatial data extends significantly into the realms of sustainable finance and climate change. Spatially explicit models enable the identification of vulnerable regions, the assessment of environmental risks, and the optimization of resource allocation for sustainable development projects. In climate change research, these models are indispensable for predicting climate impacts, modeling disaster scenarios, and planning mitigation and adaptation strategies. The integration of spatial data into these fields enhances the precision and effectiveness of interventions aimed at achieving sustainability goals.

6.6 Challenges and Limitations of Geospatial Data

Despite the advancements in spatial data science, several challenges remain. While geospatial technologies offer transformative potential for sustainable finance and environmental management, several challenges must be acknowledged to appreciate the full scope of their application. The complexity of spatial dependence requires sophisticated space-time models that can accurately capture the spatial dynamics of phenomena. Additionally, the integration of vast amounts of spatial data from various sources necessitates robust data management and processing capabilities especially in

---

[20] https://www.worldbank.org/en/news/feature/2021/07/26/mangrove-conservation-and-restoration-protecting-indonesia-climate-guardians.

[21] http://people.bu.edu/suchi/.

[22] https://www.si.edu/newsdesk/releases/getting-root-blue-carbon-storage-belizes-mangroves.

[23] https://climatechampions.unfccc.int/system/mangroves/.

[24] https://unfccc.int/news/finance-for-nature-based-solutions-must-triple-by-2030.

financial models dealing with environmental risk and opportunity. Looking forward, the development of more intuitive spatially explicit models, along with improved methodologies for integrating domain knowledge, will be crucial in harnessing the full potential of spatial data.

The precision of geospatial data is crucial for effective decision-making. However, high-resolution spatial data often comes at a significant cost, which can limit the accessibility for smaller projects or organizations (Goodchild & Janelle, 2010; Guptill & Morrison, 2013). Errors in data, such as outdated information or incorrect measurements, can lead to poor decision-making, potentially jeopardizing project outcomes (Goodchild & Gopal, 1989; Shi, 2002). High-quality geospatial data is often expensive and controlled by large corporations like Bloomberg, Refinitiv, Factset, and S&P Global. The high cost of data can be a significant barrier, especially for stakeholders in developing countries where financial resources are more constrained. This creates a disparity in the ability to leverage advanced geospatial technologies between developed and developing regions. The affordability of geospatial data is a critical limitation that can hinder the adoption of sustainable finance solutions in developing countries. Without equitable access to this data, there is a risk of widening the gap between countries that can afford to invest in such technologies and those that cannot. This disparity could potentially delay global efforts toward sustainability.

Even with access to accurate data, the ability to interpret and utilize this information effectively poses another challenge. This requires specialized skills and knowledge, which may not be readily available in all organizations, particularly those in regions without robust educational infrastructure supporting geospatial sciences. Recently, the utility of spatial knowledge graphs in facilitating data analysis and improved data structure management and retrieval was investigated (Del Mondo et al., 2021; Mai et al., 2022).

Addressing these challenges is essential for maximizing the effectiveness of geospatial technologies in sustainable finance. Initiatives to improve the affordability, accessibility, and accuracy of geospatial data will be key in enabling broader adoption and ensuring that these technologies contribute positively to global sustainability goals. Geospatial data's "where," "what," "why," and "how" questions can be answered in the context of sustainable finance and risk insurance. By leveraging geospatial analysis's rich insights, financial institutions, investors, and insurers can make more informed decisions that account for the complex interplay between geographical factors and financial outcomes. Financial data providers such as Factset, Refinitv, S&P 500, and Bloomberg provide geospatial data for their corporate clients. And the EU regulations have driven the arrival of new startups to provide climate risk, emissions, and impact data.

6.7 Summary

This chapter provides background on geospatial data and geospatial analysis. This data represents physical objects within a geographic coordinate system, providing essential information about the location of features and boundaries on Earth. Spatial data's precision and accuracy are critical in various applications. Spatial accuracy refers to how close a measurement is to the true value, influenced by systematic errors. Spatial precision, on the other hand, describes the reproducibility of measurements under unchanged conditions. Both attributes are crucial for advanced geospatial technologies like sensors and drones. Technological advancements have broadened spatial data's application spectrum, extending its use to environmental monitoring and management. For instance, global climate models rely heavily on spatial data to simulate and predict climate dynamics. Financial institutions use precise spatial data to manage risks related to climate change, such as analyzing flood risks and wildfire hazards. High-resolution imaging and data analysis allow banks to identify properties at risk and adjust financial products accordingly.

Spatial data is also pivotal in sustainable finance, guiding investments in projects that promote environmental sustainability and resilience against climate change. Governments and agencies provide climate and environmental data services for monitoring various ecosystems and urban issues. For example, the Global Forest Observation Initiative (GFOI) integrates in-situ observations with remote sensing data to estimate global forest cover and carbon content, supporting global climate mitigation policies. Overall, spatial data is indispensable for understanding and managing climate risks, sustainable finance, and the allocation of resources toward environmentally sustainable projects. It enables researchers and practitioners to develop more effective strategies for climate change mitigation and adaptation, contributing significantly to sustainable development goals.

Spatial data science has evolved from theoretical debates to practical applications that address some of the most pressing challenges of our time. The development of spatially explicit models represents a utilitarian approach to leveraging the unique characteristics of spatial data. By incorporating spatial dependence and domain knowledge into these models, spatial data science can continue to support meaningful decision-making processes in sustainable finance, climate change, and beyond. The journey of geospatial data science, heavily incorporating satellite data, is far from complete, but its trajectory points toward an increasingly impactful role in shaping a sustainable and informed future.

References

Alaboz, P., & Dengiz, O. (2024). Evaluation of the soil carbon sequestration potential and toward digital soil mapping under semi-arid Mediterranean ecological condition. Euro-*Mediterranean Journal for Environmental Integration*, 997–1007. https://doi.org/10.1007/s41207-024-00512-4

Albert, R., & Barabási, A. L. (2002). Statistical mechanics of complex networks. *Reviews of Modern Physics, 74*(1), 47.

Andris, C., & O'Sullivan, D. (2021). Spatial network analysis. In *Handbook of regional science* (pp. 1727–1750). Springer Berlin Heidelberg.

Anselin, L. (1995). Local indicators of spatial association—LISA. *Geographical Analysis, 27*(2), 93–115.

Anselin, L. (2003). Spatial externalities, spatial multipliers, and spatial econometrics. *International Regional Science Review, 26*(2), 153–166.

Anselin, L. (2022). Spatial econometrics. *Handbook of spatial analysis in the social sciences* (pp. 101–122). Edward Elgar.

Atkinson, P. M., & Lloyd, C. D. (2021). Geostatistical models and spatial interpolation. In M. M. Fischer & P. Nijkamp (Eds.), *Handbook of regional science* (Vol. 3, pp. 1813–1827). Springer.

Audretsch, D. B., & Feldman, M. P. (2004). Knowledge spillovers and the geography of innovation. In *Handbook of regional and urban economics* (Vol. 4, pp. 2713–2739). Elsevier.

Bailey, T. C., & Gatrell, A. C. (1995). *Interactive spatial data analysis* (Vol. 413, No. 8). Longman Scientific & Technical.

Ballabio, C., Jiskra, M., Osterwalder, S., Borrelli, P., Montanarella, L., & Panagos, P. (2021). A spatial assessment of mercury content in the European Union topsoil. *Science of the Total Environment, 769*, 144755.

Bardoscia, M., Barucca, P., Battiston, S., Caccioli, F., Cimini, G., Garlaschelli, D., Saracco, F., Squartini, T., & T. & Caldarelli, G. (2021). The physics of financial networks. *Nature Reviews Physics, 3*(7), 490–507.

Basu, S., & Thibodeau, T. G. (1998). Analysis of spatial autocorrelation in house prices. *The Journal of Real Estate Finance and Economics, 17*, 61–85.

Bateman, J. (2010). Situating spatial language and the role of ontology: Issues and outlook. *Language and Linguistics Compass, 4*(8), 639–664.

Bian, L. (2023). Multiscale nature of spatial data in scaling up environmental models. In *Scale in remote sensing and GIS* (pp. 13–26). Routledge.

Bivand, R. (2022). R packages for analyzing spatial data: A comparative case study with areal data. *Geographical Analysis, 54*(3), 488–518.

Cao, K., Zhou, C., Church, R., Li, X., & Li, W. (2024). Revisiting spatial optimization in the era of geospatial big data and GeoAI. *International Journal of Applied Earth Observation and Geoinformation, 129*, 103832.

Caldecott, B. (2019). *Viewpoint: Spatial finance has a key role*. Investment and Pensions Europe.

Caldecott, B., McCarten, M., Christiaen, C., & Hickey, C. (2022). Spatial finance: Practical and theoretical contributions to financial analysis. *Journal of Sustainable Finance & Investment, 1–17*,. https://doi.org/10.1080/20430795.2022.2153007

Chen, M.-J., & Leong, J. (2022). *Nvidia and the Great East–West semiconductor game* (Darden Case No. UVA-S-0374). Available at SSRN: https://ssrn.com/abstract=4085010 or https://doi.org/10.2139/ssrn.4085010

Chen, S., Guo, L., & Qiang, Q. (2022). Spatial spillovers of financial risk and their dynamic evolution: Evidence from listed financial institutions in China. *Entropy, 24*(11), 1549.

Chi, B., Dennett, A., Oléron-Evans, T., & Morphet, R. (2021). Shedding new light on residential property price variation in England: A multi-scale exploration. *Environment and Planning B: Urban Analytics and City Science, 48*(7), 1895–1911.

Cohen, B., Cowie, A., Babiker, M., Leip, A., & Smith, P. (2021). Co-benefits and trade-offs of climate change mitigation actions and the sustainable development goals. *Sustainable Production and Consumption, 26*, 805–813.

References

Comber, A., Harris, P., & Brunsdon, C. (2024). Multiscale spatially varying coefficient modeling using a geographical gaussian process GAM. *International Journal of Geographical Information Science, 38*(1), 27–47.

Cressie, N. (2015). *Statistics for spatial data.* Wiley.

Del Mondo, G., Peng, P., Gensel, J., Claramunt, C., & Lu, F. (2021). Leveraging spatio-temporal graphs and knowledge graphs: Perspectives in the field of maritime transportation. *ISPRS International Journal of Geo-Information, 10*(8), 541.

De Smith, M. (2021). Geospatial analysis and geocomputation: Concepts and modeling tools. In *Handbook of regional science* (pp. 1615–1627). Springer.

De Smith, M. J., Goodchild, M. F., & Longley, P. A. (2024). *Geospatial analysis: A comprehensive guide to principles, techniques and software tools* (7th ed., pp. 1535–1538). Troubador Publishing. https://www.spatialanalysisonline.com/

Deppner, J., & Cajias, M. (2024). Accounting for spatial autocorrelation in algorithm-driven hedonic models: A spatial cross-validation approach. *The Journal of Real Estate Finance and Economics, 68*(2), 235–273.

Elhorst, J. P. (2014). *Spatial econometrics: From cross-sectional data to spatial panels* (Vol. 479, p. 480). Springer.

Ezel, S. (2021). *Moore's Law under attack: The impact of China's policies on global semiconductor innovation.* ITIF Information Technology & Innovation Foundation. Retrieved May 29, 2021, from https://itif.org/publications/2021/02/18/moores-law-under-attack-impact-chinas-policies-global-semiconductor

Farr, H., Ruttenberg, B., Walter, R. K., Wang, Y. H., & White, C. (2021). Potential environmental effects of deepwater floating offshore wind energy facilities. *Ocean & Coastal Management, 207*, 105611.

Fischer, M. M., & Getis, A. (Eds.). (2010). *Handbook of applied spatial analysis: Software tools, methods and applications.* Springer.

Fischer, M. M., & Getis, A. (Eds.). (2013). *Recent developments in spatial analysis: Spatial statistics, behavioural modelling, and computational intelligence.* Springer.

Fischer, M. M., Huber, F., Pfarrhofer, M., & Staufer-Steinnocher, P. (2021). The dynamic impact of monetary policy on regional housing prices in the United States. *Real Estate Economics, 49*(4), 1039–1068.

Fischer, M. M., & Nijkamp, P. (Eds.). (2021). *Handbook of regional science.* Springer. https://doi.org/10.1007/978-3-662-60723-7_133

Frank, A. U. (1997). *Spatial ontology: A geographical information point of view.* Springer. https://doi.org/10.1007/978-0-585-28322-7_5

Getis, A. (2009). Spatial autocorrelation. In *Handbook of applied spatial analysis: Software tools, methods and applications* (pp. 255–278). Springer Berlin Heidelberg.

Getis, A., & Ord, J. K. (1992). The analysis of spatial association by use of distance statistics. *Geographical Analysis, 24*(3), 189–206.

Getis, A., & Ord, J. K. (2010). The analysis of spatial Association by use of distance Statistics. In *Perspectives on spatial data analysis* (pp. 127–145). Springer.

Gibson, R., Danaher, T., Hehir, W., & Collins, L. (2020). A remote sensing approach to mapping fire severity in south-eastern Australia using sentinel 2 and random forest. *Remote Sensing of Environment, 240*, 111702.

Goodchild, M. F. (2001). Models of scale and scales of modelling. In N. J. Tate & P. M. Atkinson (Eds.), *Modelling scale in geographical information science* (pp. 3–10). Wiley.

Goodchild, M. F. (2010). Formalizing place in geographic information systems. In *Communities, neighborhoods, and health: Expanding the boundaries of place* (pp. 21–33). Springer New York.

Goodchild, M. F., & Gopal, S. (Eds.). (1989). *The accuracy of spatial databases.* Taylor & Francis.

Goodchild, M. F., & Janelle, D. G. (2010). Toward critical spatial thinking in the social sciences and humanities. *GeoJournal, 75*(1), 3–13.

Gopal, S., & Fischer, M. M. (2023). Opioid mortality in the US: Quantifying the direct and indirect impact of sociodemographic and socioeconomic factors. *Letters in Spatial and Resource Sciences, 16*(1), 29.

Gopal, S., Kaufman, L., Pasquarella, V., Ribera, M., Holden, C., Shank, B., & Joshua, P. (2015). Modeling coastal and marine environmental risks in Belize: The marine integrated decision analysis system (MIDAS). *Coastal Management, 43*(3), 217–237.

Gopal, S., Kelly-Fair, M., & Ma, Y. (2023). Palm oil–the increasing materiality of deforestation and biodiversity risks in Indonesia and Malaysia. In *IGARSS 2023–2023 IEEE International Geoscience and Remote Sensing Symposium* (pp. 2374–2377). IEEE.

Gopal, S., Pitts, J., Inampudi, K., Xu, Y., & Cook, G. (2021). The evolving landscape of big data analytics and ESG materiality mapping. *The Journal of Impact and ESG Investing, 2*(2), 77–100.

Gopal, S., Pitts, J., Li, Z., Gallagher, K. P., Baldwin, J. G., & Kring, W. N. (2018). Fueling global energy finance: The emergence of China in global energy investment. *Energies, 11*(10), 2804.

Gopal, S., Staufer-Steinnocher, P., Xu, Y., & Pitts, J. (2022). Semiconductor supply chain: A 360-degree view of supply chain risk and network resilience based on GIS and AI. In *Supply chain resilience: Insights from theory and practice* (pp. 303–313). Springer International Publishing.

Grekousis, G. (2020). *Spatial analysis methods and practice: Describe–explore–explain through GIS*. Cambridge University Press.

Griffith, D., & Paelinck, J. (2011). *Non-standard spatial statistics and spatial econometrics*. Springer-Verlag.

Gupta, J., An, S., & Shekhar, S. (2023). Towards responsible spatial data science and Geo-AI. In *Proceedings of the 2023 Fifteenth International Conference on Contemporary Computing* (pp. 545–551).

Guptill, S. C., & Morrison, J. L. (Eds.). (2013). *Elements of spatial data quality*. Elsevier.

Isaaks, E. H., & Srivastava, R. M. (1989). *An introduction to applied geostatistics*. Oxford University Press.

Jiang, Z., & Shekhar, S. (2017). *Spatial big data science*. Springer International Publishing AG.

Jochem, W. C., Leasure, D. R., Pannell, O., Chamberlain, H. R., Jones, P., & Tatem, A. J. (2021). Classifying settlement types from multi-scale spatial patterns of building footprints. *Environment and Planning b: Urban Analytics and City Science, 48*(5), 1161–1179.

Kelly-Fair, M., Gopal, S., Koch, M., Pancasakti Kusumaningrum, H., Helmi, M., Khairunnisa, D., & Kaufman, L. (2022). Analysis of land use and land cover changes through the lens of SDGs in Semarang, Indonesia. *Sustainability, 14*(13), 7592.

Kortas, F., Grigoriev, A., & Piccillo, G. (2022). Exploring multi-scale variability in hotspot mapping: A case study on housing prices and crime occurrences in Heerlen. *Cities, 128*, 103814.

Krugman, P. (1991). Increasing returns and economic geography. *Journal of Political Economy, 99*(3), 483–499.

Lee, J. W., & Sohn, S. Y. (2021). Evaluating borrowers' default risk with a spatial probit model reflecting the distance in their relational network. *PLoS ONE, 16*(12), e0261737.

LeSage, J., & Pace, R. K. (2009). *Introduction to spatial econometrics*. Chapman & Hall.

LeSage, J. P., & Fischer, M. M. (2012). Estimates of the impact of static and dynamic knowledge spillovers on regional factor productivity. *International Regional Science Review, 35*(1), 103–127.

Li, Z. (2020). Geospatial big data handling with high performance computing: Current approaches and future directions. In *High performance computing for geospatial applications* (pp. 53–76). Springer.

Ma, Y., & Gopal, S. (2018). Geographically weighted regression models in estimating median home prices in towns of Massachusetts based on an urban sustainability framework. *Sustainability, 10*(4), 1026.

Ma, Y., Gopal, S., Ma, X., Gallagher, K., Koch, M., & Kaufman, L. (2023). The deforestation and biodiversity risks of power plant projects in Southeast Asia: A big data spatial analytical framework. *Sustainability, 15*(19), 14461.

Ma, Y., Wright, J., Gopal, S., & Phillips, N. (2020). Seeing the invisible: From imagined to virtual urban landscapes. *Cities, 98*, 102559.

Mai, G., Huang, W., Cai, L., Zhu, R., & Lao, N. (2022). Narrative cartography with knowledge graphs. *Journal of Geovisualization and Spatial Analysis, 6*(1), 4.

Manley, D. (2021). Scale, aggregation, and the modifiable areal unit problem. In *Handbook of regional science* (pp. 1711–1725). Springer Berlin Heidelberg.

Marin, F. R., Zanon, A. J., Monzon, J. P., Andrade, J. F., Silva, E. H. F. M., Richter, G. L., Antolin, L. A. S., Ribeiro, B. S. M. R., Ribas, G. G., Battisti, R., Heinemann, A. B., & Grassini, P. (2022). Protecting the Amazon forest and reducing global warming via agricultural intensification. *Nature Sustainability, 5*(12), 1018–1026.

Markham, J. W. (2013). Chapter 11: Regulating credit default swaps in the wake of the subprime crisis. In Current developments in monetary and financial law, Volume 6. Restoring Financial Stability--The Legal Response. International Monetary Fund. Legal Dept. ISBN: 9781616350819. Publication Date: 08 Feb 2013 Publisher: International Monetary Fund. https://www.elibrary.imf.org/display/book/9781616350819/ch011.xml

Marshall, A. (1920). Industrial organization, continued. The concentration of specialized industries in particular localities. In *Principles of economics* (pp. 222–231). Palgrave Macmillan UK.

Mete, M. O. (2023). Geospatial big data analytics for sustainable smart cities. *The International Archives of the Photogrammetry, Remote Sensing and Spatial Information Sciences, 48*, 141–146.

Mokarram, M., Mokarram, M. J., Khosravi, M. R., Saber, A., & Rahideh, A. (2020). Determination of the optimal location for constructing solar photovoltaic farms based on a multi-criteria decision system and Dempster-Shafer theory. *Scientific Reports, 10*(1), 8200.

Morrissette, H. K., Baez, S. K., Beers, L., Bood, N., Martinez, N. D., Novelo, K., Andrews, G., Balan, L., Scott Beers, C., Betancourti, S. A., Blanco, R., Bowden, E., Burns-Perez, V., Carcamo, M., Chevez, L., Crooks, S., Feller, I. C., Galvez, G., Garbutt, K., & Canty, S. W. (2023). Belize Blue Carbon: Establishing a national carbon stock estimate for mangrove ecosystems. *Science of the Total Environment, 870*, 161829.

Müller, L. A., Leonard, A., Trotter, P. A., & Hirmer, S. (2023). Green hydrogen production and use in low-and middle-income countries: A least-cost geospatial modeling approach applied to Kenya. *Applied Energy, 343*, 121219.

Murray, A. T. (2021). Contemporary optimization application through geographic information systems. *Omega, 99*, 102176.

Nowak, M. M., Dziob, K., Ludwisiak, Ł., & Chmiel, J. (2020). Mobile GIS applications for environmental field surveys: A state of the art. *Global Ecology and Conservation, 23*, e01089.

Oliver, M. A. (2009). The variogram and kriging. In *Handbook of applied spatial analysis: software tools, methods and applications* (pp. 319–352). Springer Berlin Heidelberg.

Oliver, M. A., & Webster, R. (2014). A tutorial guide to geostatistics: Computing and modeling variograms and kriging. *CATENA, 113*, 56–69.

Pace, R. K., Barry, R., & Sirmans, C. F. (1998). Spatial statistics and real estate. *The Journal of Real Estate Finance and Economics, 17*, 5–13.

Pei, T., Xu, J., Liu, Y., Huang, X., Zhang, L., Dong, W., Qin, C., Song, C., Gong, J., & Zhou, C. (2021). GIScience and remote sensing in natural resource and environmental research: Status quo and future perspectives. *Geography and Sustainability, 2*(3), 207–215.

Penglase, K., Lewis, T., & Srivastava, S. K. (2023). A new approach to estimate fuel budget and wildfire hazard assessment in commercial plantations using drone-based photogrammetry and image analysis. *Remote Sensing, 15*(10), 2621.

Pezzuto, I. (2012). Miraculous financial engineering or toxic finance? The genesis of the US subprime mortgage loans crisis and its consequences on the global financial markets and real economy. *Journal of Governance and Regulation, 1*(3), 114–125.

Pitts, J., Gopal, S., Ma, Y., Koch, M., Boumans, R. M., & Kaufman, L. (2020). Leveraging big data and analytics to improve food, energy, and water system sustainability. *Frontiers in Big Data, 3*, 13.

Popescu, V. D., Munshaw, R. G., Shackelford, N., Montesino Pouzols, F., Dubman, E., Gibeau, P., Horne, M., Moilanen, A., & Palen, W. J. (2020). Quantifying biodiversity trade-offs in the face of widespread renewable and unconventional energy development. *Scientific Reports, 10*(1), 7603.

Porter, M. E. (1998). Clusters and competition. *On Competition, 7*, 91. https://citeseerx.ist.psu.edu/document?repid=rep1&type=pdf&doi=2cbe5b01c61edee8dc7cd97fdeb8b7bf9ed3a117

Posth, J. A., Schwendner, P., Laube, P., & Orpiszewski, T. (2024). *Bio-value-at-risk: A Concept to assessing the implications of biodiversity risks on portfolio management using geospatial analysis.* Available at SSRN.

Rey, S. J., & Anselin, L. (2014). *Modern spatial econometrics in practice: A guide to GeoDa.* Geoda Press LLC.

Ricardo, D. (1817). *On the principles of political economy and taxation.* Available online at the Library of Economics and Liberty: www.econlib.org/library/Ricardo/ricP.html

Rosenthal, S. S., & Strange, W. C. (2020). How close is close? The spatial reach of agglomeration economies. *Journal of Economic Perspectives, 34*(3), 27–49.

Saraswat, S. K., Digalwar, A. K., Yadav, S. S., & Kumar, G. (2021). MCDM and GIS based modeling technique for assessment of solar and wind farm locations in India. *Renewable Energy, 169*, 865–884.

Scott, A., & Storper, M. (2003). Regions, globalization, development. *Regional Studies, 37*(6–7), 579–593.

Shao, M., Han, Z., Sun, J., Xiao, C., Zhang, S., & Zhao, Y. (2020). A review of multi-criteria decision making applications for renewable energy site selection. *Renewable Energy, 157*, 377–403.

Shekhar, S. (2021, July). What is special about spatial data science and GeoAI? *Proceedings of the 33rd International Conference on Scientific and Statistical Database Management.* https://doi.org/10.1145/3468791.3472263

Shekhar, S., & Vold, P. (2020). *Spatial computing.* MIT Press.

Shi, K., Yang, L., Zhang, L., Chapman, C., & Fan, P. (2023). Transboundary conservation hotspots in China and potential impacts of the belt and road initiative. *Diversity and Distributions, 29*(3), 338–348.

Shi, W. (2002). *Spatial data quality.* CRC Press.

Simmons, B. A., Butt, N., O'Hara, C. C., Ray, R., Ma, Y., & Gallagher, K. P. (2022). China's global development finance poses heterogeneous risks to coastal and marine socio-ecological systems. *One Earth, 5*(12), 1377–1393.

Singla, S., Eldawy, A., Diao, T., Mukhopadhyay, A., & Scudiero, E. (2021, April). Experimental study of big raster and vector database systems. In *2021 IEEE 37th International Conference on Data Engineering (ICDE)* (pp. 2243–2248). IEEE.

Sippel, S., Meinshausen, N., Fischer, E. M., Székely, E., & Knutti, R. (2020). Climate change now detectable from any single day of weather at global scale. *Nature Climate Change, 10*(1), 35–41.

Sofo, A., Nuzzo, V., Palese, A. M., Xiloyannis, C., Celano, G., Zukowskyj, P., & Dichio, B. (2005). Net CO2 storage in Mediterranean olive and peach orchards. *Scientia Horticulturae, 107*(1), 17–24.

Sulova, A., & Jokar Arsanjani, J. (2020). Exploratory analysis of driving force of wildfires in Australia: An application of machine learning within Google Earth engine. *Remote Sensing, 13*(1), 10.

Stutz, G. R., Shope, E., Aguirre, G. A., Batir, J., Frone, Z., Williams, M., Reber, T. J., Whealton, C. A., Smith, D. J., Richards, M. C., Blackwell, D. D., Tester, J. W., Stedinger, J. R., & Jordan, T. E. (2015). Geothermal energy characterization in the Appalachian Basin of New York and Pennsylvania. *Geosphere, 11*(5), 1291–1304.

Tang, W., & Wang, S. (Eds.). (2020). *High performance computing for geospatial applications* (pp. 53–76). Springer International Publishing.

Wang, G. J., Yi, S., Xie, C., & Stanley, H. E. (2021). Multilayer information spillover networks: Measuring interconnectedness of financial institutions. *Quantitative Finance, 21*(7), 1163–1185.

Wheeler, D. C. (2021). Geographically weighted regression. In M. M. Fischer, & P. Nijkamp (Eds.), *Handbook of regional science* (Vol. 3). (pp. 1435–1461). Springer.

Wheeler, D. C., & Páez, A. (2010). Geographically weighted regression. In M. Fischer & A. Getis (Eds.), *Handbook of applied spatial analysis*. Springer. https://doi.org/10.1007/978-3-642-03647-7_22.

World Bank. (2022). *Spatial finance: Challenges and opportunities in a changing world (English). Equitable Growth, Finance and Institutions Insight*. World Bank Group. http://documents.worldbank.org/curated/en/850821606884753194/Spatial-Finance-Challenges-and-Opportunities-in-a-Changing-World

Yang, H., Simmons, B. A., Ray, R., Nolte, C., Gopal, S., Ma, Y., Ma, X., & Gallagher, K. P. (2021). Risks to global biodiversity and indigenous lands from China's overseas development finance. *Nature Ecology & Evolution, 5*(11), 1520–1529.

Zhang, W., Liu, X., Zhao, S., & Tang, T. (2024). Does green finance agglomeration improve carbon emission performance in China? A perspective of spatial spillover. *Applied Energy, 358*, 122561.

Chapter 7
Satellite Remote Sensing: Pioneering Tools for Environmental Insight and Sustainable Investment

The stories that you can tell around the [Landsat] images, along with the images, make something very, very powerful. And you need both to make the kind of impact that we need to make today to help people understand the devastation we've caused. But [also] to give them hope that we can turn things around. And that's what these satellite images show so clearly—Jane Goodall.[1]

7.1 Introduction: Geospatial Finance and Satellite Remote Sensing

In the realm of sustainable finance, satellite technology has evolved from a mere tool to a necessity. Satellite data play a crucial role in sustainable finance by providing critical insights into the environmental impact of investment activities. Satellite data help investors identify potential risks and opportunities while also monitoring the effectiveness of sustainable finance initiatives over time. The integration of Earth observation data into financial decision-making allows for a more accurate and timely assessment of various environmental factors such as deforestation, water pollution, and greenhouse gas emissions.

Traditionally, the financial sector has relied on self-reported data from companies, often inconsistent and susceptible to greenwashing. By incorporating satellite data, financial institutions can independently verify these reports and hold companies accountable for their environmental impacts. This approach reduces the reliance on potentially biased self-reporting and provides a more objective basis for sustainability assessments.

Satellite data aid in evaluating climate and environmental risks, ensuring compliance, facilitating reporting, and providing real-time intelligence. Most importantly, these data contribute to the development of climate resilience. As entities strive

---

[1] https://landsat.gsfc.nasa.gov/news/quotes-to-note/ September 13, 2023.

toward a net-zero future, satellite technology has a significant role, providing crucial data and insights that can guide us toward a more sustainable world. This rationale advocates for leveraging satellite data in environmental reporting, highlighting the potential to enrich sustainability investment decisions and influence ongoing discussions around standardization and transparency in climate change disclosures.

Geospatial finance plays a critical role in guiding asset management strategies across various asset classes, including equities, bonds, real estate, and commodities. This guidance is geared toward fostering sustainable investment practices. By blending insights from satellite imagery with financial analytics, geospatial finance opens new avenues for asset managers and investors to pursue alignment with environmental, social, and governance (ESG) objectives. This alignment is increasingly sought after by asset managers, banks, and investors who are keen on understanding the ESG attributes of their assets, exploring responsible investment options, and navigating the evolving landscape of investment that prioritizes sustainability.

For proper sustainability accounting in financial decisions, identifying and utilizing the right datasets is essential. The use of satellite imagery, which provides high- (less than 1–10 m) resolution, offers a significant advantage over traditional, often outdated, and less precise data sources. These real-time data enable a better understanding of the actual impact of investment activities on the environment. However, satellite data should be seen as one tool among many in the broader toolkit needed to achieve sustainable finance goals. While enhancing the overall process, it must be complemented with other tools and methods (such as AI) to form a comprehensive approach.

Overall, satellite data enhance the precision and timeliness of environmental impact assessments in sustainable finance, providing a powerful tool for driving environmentally sound investment decisions across government, investor, and industry levels. Despite the challenges associated with technology and regulation, continuous progress and collaborative endeavors are key to expanding the adoption of geospatial finance in environmental sustainability efforts. This chapter traces the history of Earth observation and satellite remote sensing. It provides a brief introduction to the fundamentals of remote sensing, widely used satellites, and data catalogs for remote sensing data. Since remote sensing is a mature science, interested readers are encouraged to seek basic texts and websites for more information on this growing field. Section 7.6 of the chapter also highlights the significant role of Artificial Intelligence (AI) and machine learning, including deep learning, in analyzing multispectral satellite data (as shown in a case study on mangrove mapping). These technologies are crucial for identifying and classifying such data, ultimately enhancing climate resilience through applications like carbon sequestration.

7.1.1 Earth Observation and Remote Sensing—History and Evolution

Global satellite use has become ubiquitous, fundamentally transforming how societies operate, from Global Positioning System navigation and satellite television to various information and communication technology applications. The journey toward advanced satellite monitoring began during World War I with the deployment of aircraft-mounted cameras, which laid the groundwork for aerial observation. This trajectory of technological evolution reached a pivotal milestone with the launch of Sputnik 1 by the Soviet Union in October 1957. This event marked the advent of the space age and intensified the space race between the superpowers during the Cold War, signaling a significant shift in global technological capabilities (Anderson, 2023). The Sputnik launch also led directly to the National Aeronautics and Space Administration (NASA) creation in 1958. The subsequent launch of the first US remote sensing satellite in 1960, aimed at observing weather patterns over North America, marked the beginning of using satellites for environmental monitoring. Today, satellites fulfill an extensive range of functions, from astronomical observations to environmental monitoring and military and civilian surveillance, showcasing the advanced capabilities developed over decades.

The field of satellite remote sensing (Jensen, 2015; Lillesand et al., 2015; Mather & Koch, 2022) emerges as a cornerstone in our capability to observe and analyze the Earth's surface from afar, negating the need for direct contact. This scientific domain encompasses the methodologies for identifying, measuring, and assessing characteristics of objects by detecting the energy they emit or reflect. Through earth observation (EO), remote sensing technologies allow for comprehensive monitoring of vast land, sea, and atmospheric systems. Satellite imagery is indispensable for myriad scientific, governmental, and commercial purposes, with over seven thousand satellites currently in orbit (Anderson, 2023). These devices are integral to communication and data gathering on a global scale, with the declining costs of satellite launches propelling a surge in commercial missions that began to outnumber government launches in 2017.

Satellite technology's advancements have also paved the way for significant applications in assessing climate and environmental risks, compliance and reporting, and providing real-time intelligence, notably in site and commodity monitoring (McKenna et al., 2020; Werner et al., 2020), supply chain tracking (Heldt & Beske-Janssen, 2023; Whitcraft et al., 2015), and energy intelligence (Ma et al., 2023), providing hedge funds, fund managers, and others with crucial information for strategic investment decisions. For instance, the Japanese Greenhouse Gases Observing Satellite "IBUKI" (GOSAT),[2] launched in 2009, was the earliest to measure concentrations of carbon dioxide (CO_2) and methane (CH_4) (Imasu et al., 2023). The European Space Agency (ESA) and the European Union's (EU) Copernicus program aim to monitor human-made greenhouse gas sources, with launches

---

[2] https://global.jaxa.jp/projects/sat/gosat/topics.html.

planned by 2026. Moreover, satellites like ESA's METOP-A series, equipped with the TROPOMI[3] instrument, are pivotal in measuring atmospheric composition, including carbon monoxide, thus contributing to our understanding of air quality and climate dynamics (Geddes et al., 2021). The launch of the Chinese TECIS 1 satellite[4] in 2022, designed to assess forest vegetation biomass, aerosol distribution, and solar-induced chlorophyll fluorescence, alongside NASA's OCO-2 satellite,[5] which provides open-access, high-resolution daily observations, underscores the expanding capabilities of satellite technology in environmental monitoring.

Landsat satellites play a crucial role in Earth observation by providing consistent, high-quality imagery of the Earth's surface over an extended period. The Landsat program, a joint initiative of NASA and the US Geological Survey (USGS), has been operating since 1972, making it one of the longest-running satellite programs dedicated to Earth observation. Figure 7.1 shows the Landsat-9 image of flooding in southeastern South Dakota and northwestern Iowa on June 24, 2024. Water had overtopped the banks of the Big Sioux River, inundating adjacent farmland. The images are false-color to emphasize the presence of water, which appears dark blue. Landsat provides critical data for assessing the impact of natural disasters such as floods, wildfires, hurricanes, and earthquakes. It aids in disaster response and recovery efforts.

This evolution in satellite technology and its integration with advanced AI and machine learning techniques, such as those applied in mangrove mapping for climate resilience, discussed in this chapter, represent a quantum leap in our ability to detect, track, and evaluate activities, shifts, and patterns from space. These technological advancements are invaluable for various applications, from agriculture and climate change monitoring to financial services, including insurance and real estate. For example, high-resolution satellite imagery is increasingly utilized to observe activities and stockpiles at ports, which is crucial for understanding market trends in supply and demand (Bauman, 2020). As space technology advances and space access costs decrease, the launch of numerous Earth observation satellites is becoming more feasible, making satellite imagery increasingly integral to the financial sector.

7.1.2 Commercial Satellites

Recent published literature (Anderson, 2023; Jacobson, 2020) discusses the growing commercial potential of space for businesses and investors. The shift from government-dominated space activities to a future driven by private innovation in various space industries, including satellite technologies, has opened up the potential for detailed Earth observation, resource extraction, space tourism, and more. For example, in 2014, Planet became the first private Earth observation satellite company

---

[3] https://www.esa.int/Applications/Observing_the_Earth/Copernicus/Sentinel-5P/Tropomi.

[4] https://www.space.com/china-launches-carbon-ecosystem-satellite-tecis-1.

[5] https://ocov2.jpl.nasa.gov/.

7.1 Introduction: Geospatial Finance and Satellite Remote Sensing

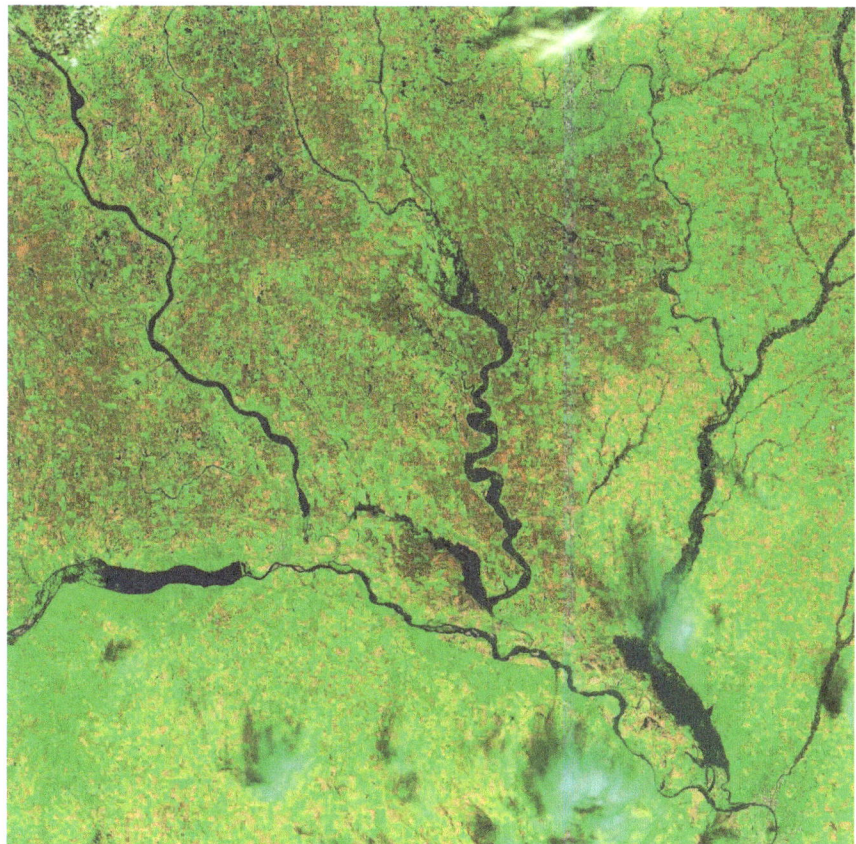

Fig. 7.1 Iowa flooding that began June 20–21 2024. Metadata Sensor(s):Landsat 9—OLI-2. Landsat 8—OLI. Visualization Date: June 25, 2024

to successfully deploy earth-sensing satellites (CubeSats or Doves). Planet now has the largest commercial Earth observation satellite constellation, with over 180 satellites in space. Its website notes: "... *Planet.org*[6]— *a non-profit affiliated with Planet Labs, designed to use space, earth imagery, and technology to better understand our dynamic planet; advance humanitarian causes; and ensure the sustainability and welfare of life on Earth.*" Another company, SkiFi,[7] offers diverse satellites and sensors on one easy-to-use platform with a simple interface. This company offers near real-time imagery with multiple resolutions and sensors, applicable in agriculture, construction, and carbon emission reduction.

---

[6] https://www.planet.com/pulse/loveearth/#more-1760.

[7] https://www.skyfi.com/blog/applications-of-satellite-imagery offers high resolution optical, multispectral, synthetic aperture radar, as well as night imaging.

Fig. 7.2 Commercial satellites selling geospatial data at finer spatial resolutions. This market is worth over USD 6.8 billion (2024)[12]

The Starling[8] satellite initiative (developed by Airbus and The Forest Trust) helps companies verify "No Deforestation" commitments. It leverages high-resolution imagery and radar sensing for all-weather monitoring. A recent startup, Planet-Watchers,[9] employs satellite data and machine learning for agricultural monitoring, providing insurers with up-to-date crop data. Global coral reef health is now monitored via satellite systems, aiding in the identification of resilient coral varieties for restoration efforts.[10]

The Global Footprint Network's report[11] on humanity exploiting natural resources faster than the Earth's ecosystems can rejuvenate highlights the urgent need for sustainable resource management. Satellite imagery is revolutionizing how businesses, especially global manufacturing giants in sectors like palm oil and paper products, monitor and protect natural resources. This technology enables corporations to oversee their supply chains with unprecedented clarity, facilitating responsible sourcing practices that align with global sustainability goals. Through the strategic use of satellite data, companies are not only enhancing their environmental stewardship but are contributing to a more sustainable future, underscoring the indispensable role of satellite technology in global conservation efforts. These private companies represent the tremendous opportunities in space technology for Earth observation. Some of the other commercial satellites are shown in Fig. 7.2.

---

[8] https://intelligence.airbus.com/industries/forest-and-environment/starling/.

[9] https://www.planetwatchers.com/.

[10] https://allencoralatlas.org/.

[11] https://www.footprintnetwork.org/.

[12] https://www.factmr.com/report/4632/earth-observation-market.

This chapter presents the crucial role of satellite data for investors, asset managers, and funds in their exposure to climate risks and their path to net zero, and a description of applications in sustainable finance. There follows a brief primer on remote sensing fundamentals and a case study demonstrating AI's application in satellite image processing.

7.2 The Crucial Role of Geospatial Technologies in Addressing Climate Risks and Environmental Impacts

The imperative for individual investors, asset managers, pension and sovereign funds, and other stakeholders to engage with geospatial technologies emerges from their unparalleled capacity to provide accurate and timely data on environmental risks, including greenhouse gas (GHG) emissions and climate change impacts. Traditional methods of environmental risk accounting are predominantly retrospective, offering a lagged view of impacts. In contrast, satellite technology facilitates digital measurement reporting and verification, ensuring real-time insights into environmental parameters.

Corporations and asset managers are increasingly pressured to demonstrate their commitment to sustainability through detailed reports to attract investor and shareholder interest. However, these reports often rely on disparate frameworks and standards, leading to inconsistencies and, at times, accusations of greenwashing. Geospatial finance, through satellite data, provides a solution to this challenge. It enables the direct observation of environmental impacts and human activities, including illicit practices such as slavery and child labor. These data are crucial for creating transparent, verifiable sustainability reports that genuinely reflect an entity's environmental and social impact.

Moreover, satellite technology offers data at various spatial resolutions, now enhanced by private satellite missions that extend coverage to even the most remote locations. This capability is vital for monitoring specific environmental issues, such as the effects of deforestation on biodiversity in regions like the jungles of Borneo or the replacement of peat bogs with palm oil plantations. The granularity of these data allows for precise, localized environmental assessments, providing stakeholders with the detailed information necessary for informed decision-making. The availability of satellite data on a global scale also supports standardized comparisons of environmental impacts across different regions and industries. This "apples to apples" comparison is facilitated by the uniformity of digital data, enabling stakeholders to objectively assess and compare environmental risks and practices worldwide.

Remote sensing technology relies on the acquisition and analysis of the radiation reflected or emitted by various terrestrial objects (Mather & Koch, 2022). The interaction between solar radiation and surface features of these objects varies according to their material composition, physical and chemical states (e.g., moisture content), surface roughness, and the geometric conditions of radiation incidence (e.g., the angle of solar radiation). The science of remote sensing, which underpins geospatial finance, is well-established and traditionally dominated by governmental space agencies. However, the recent influx of private venture capital into satellite technology indicates a shift toward a more diversified and innovative approach to environmental monitoring. This evolution reflects the growing recognition of the importance of accurate, timely data for managing climate risks.

Climate risk poses a significant threat to the financial bottom line of corporations and asset managers, necessitating strategies for resilience and optimization. Satellite data are instrumental in this context, offering insights that support the development of robust risk management and optimization strategies. By leveraging the capabilities of geospatial finance, stakeholders can not only mitigate environmental risks but also align their investment strategies with broader sustainability goals, ultimately contributing to a more sustainable and resilient global economy.

7.2.1 Geospatial Finance: Navigating Climate Risks Across Asset Classes

The advent of geospatial finance heralds a new era in asset management, offering invaluable insights into the multifaceted impacts of climate change across various asset classes. Leveraging satellite data, stakeholders can now navigate the complexities of environmental risks with unprecedented precision, enabling informed decision-making and strategic investment realignment toward sustainability and resilience.

Fixed Interest (Corporate or Government Bonds): The creditworthiness of bond issuers is increasingly under the microscope as climate change poses direct and indirect threats to their financial stability. Entities operating in industries or regions particularly vulnerable to climate change may face higher credit spreads. Moreover, evolving regulatory landscapes, including efforts by the US SEC (halted at the time of this writing), the EU's SFDR, and other frameworks, are poised to escalate operational costs, potentially hampering issuers' debt servicing capabilities. The cumulative effect of these dynamics is a gradual yet discernible shift in investor portfolios, moving away from assets heavily exposed to climate risks (Dafermos et al., 2021).

Equities: The valuation of equities is not immune to the repercussions of climate change. Growth-oriented assets, such as stocks, are projected to diminish in value under adverse climate scenarios, with the impact exhibiting significant variance across countries and sectors. Industries directly confronted by climate change, like agriculture and insurance, stand at a higher risk threshold. A strategic portfolio adjustment, favoring assets and regions with better risk-adjusted returns, especially in specific emerging markets, becomes imperative for resilience (Tokat-Acikel et al., 2021).

Real Estate: In the realm of real estate, particularly US real estate investment trusts, climate change introduces heightened volatility in returns. The sector's susceptibility to temperature anomalies underscores the critical role of technological innovation in mitigating these challenges (Salisu et al., 2024). It emphasizes the dual threat and opportunity climate change presents to the real estate business, pointing to technological advancements as a linchpin for adaptation and mitigation efforts. Asset managers, recognizing the immediacy of these risks, are diligently working to comprehend and adjust their portfolios accordingly.

Commodities: The commodities market experiences a complex interplay of climate change effects, impacting supply and demand dynamics. Agricultural productivity alterations and shifting weather patterns herald increased volatility in commodity prices. Some commodities may witness price surges due to scarcity, whereas others, associated with high carbon emissions, could see a decline in value. The recent global shortfalls of maple syrup and cocoa (Bergin & Peng, 2024) in Spring 2024 exemplify the tangible impacts of climate change on commodity availability and pricing.[13]

Alternative Investments: The inherent flexibility of alternative investments, such as private equities and hedge funds, positions them advantageously in the face of climate change. These investment vehicles enable selective backing of companies and projects dedicated to climate change mitigation or adaptation, potentially yielding superior returns as the global economy pivots toward lower carbon dependency.

Cryptocurrency: The relationship between cryptocurrency and climate change predominantly revolves around the environmental footprint of mining activities (Siddique et al., 2023). Cryptocurrency mining is the process of verifying and adding transactions to a blockchain (the digital ledger that records all transactions). Bitcoin and several other cryptocurrencies use a consensus mechanism requiring substantial computational power, which involves using specialized hardware or powerful graphics processing units.[14] With growing awareness and concern over climate change, cryptocurrencies face increasing pressure to adopt energy-efficient consensus mechanisms or to implement measures offsetting their carbon output. These pressures could significantly influence the market value and regulatory landscape for cryptocurrencies. With the growing use of ChatGPT AI, the same is now happening with data centers and their demand for energy (Chien, 2023).

Thus, the intersection of geospatial finance and climate change underscores the critical need for asset managers, investors, and stakeholders to harness satellite data. These data provide a robust foundation for assessing and managing environmental risks across different asset classes, facilitating a strategic pivot toward more sustainable and resilient investment portfolios.

---

[13] https://www.farmcrediteast.com/en/resources/todays-harvest-Blog/240305MapleOutlook2024.

[14] https://www.investopedia.com/tech/how-does-bitcoin-mining-work/.

7.2.2 The Pivotal Role of Satellite Remote Sensing in Geospatial Finance

With thousands of satellites currently orbiting the Earth, we now have access to a continuous stream of data that can significantly enhance the accuracy and timeliness of environmental reporting. These satellite-derived data provide a reliable basis for climate change disclosures, offering insights into direct emissions from corporate facilities, energy providers, and extensive supply chains. In the era of digital transformation and environmental accountability, the pivot toward geospatial finance signifies a notable shift in the landscape of environmental, social, and governance (ESG) reporting. This transition is not merely a change of guard but a fundamental evolution toward embracing digital methodologies and frequently updating crucial environmental data.

The Corporate Sustainability Reporting law of the EU mandates that all large companies, as well as all listed companies (excluding listed micro-enterprises), must disclose information regarding the risks and opportunities they identify from social and environmental issues, along with the impact their activities have on people and the environment. The following text highlights the numerous benefits of incorporating satellite remote sensing into geospatial finance, emphasizing how this technology can improve the quality, accuracy, and reliability of environmental impact assessments, and evaluate the effects of physical risks on assets and regions.

Traditional methods of environmental reporting, often characterized by retrospective analysis and reliance on self-disclosures, have faced significant challenges in accurately quantifying environmental impacts. This inadequacy is particularly pronounced within the environmental dimension of ESG reporting, where quantifying impacts necessitates precise and real-time data. For example, carbon reporting traditionally relies on estimations and self-reported data from companies regarding their greenhouse gas emissions. This approach can lead to significant inaccuracies due to underreporting or misreporting. By integrating satellite remote sensing, companies can obtain precise and real-time data on carbon emissions. Satellites equipped with sensors can measure the concentration of carbon dioxide and other greenhouse gases in the atmosphere, providing an accurate picture of a company's emissions over time.

Additionally, remote sensing can monitor deforestation, land degradation, and changes in land use, which are critical factors in carbon accounting. For instance, a company involved in large-scale agriculture can use satellite data to track the extent of deforestation resulting from its activities. These data can then be used to quantify the carbon emissions associated with land use changes, providing a more comprehensive and accurate assessment of the company's environmental impact. Therefore, the potential of satellite data to combat greenwashing and enable targeted investor and shareholder actions toward genuine environmental sustainability is profound.

Transforming raw satellite pixel data into actionable insights is a critical process that involves sophisticated analysis and interpretation. Commercial entities specializing in satellite data play a vital role in this transformation, offering detailed data

7.2 The Crucial Role of Geospatial Technologies in Addressing Climate ...

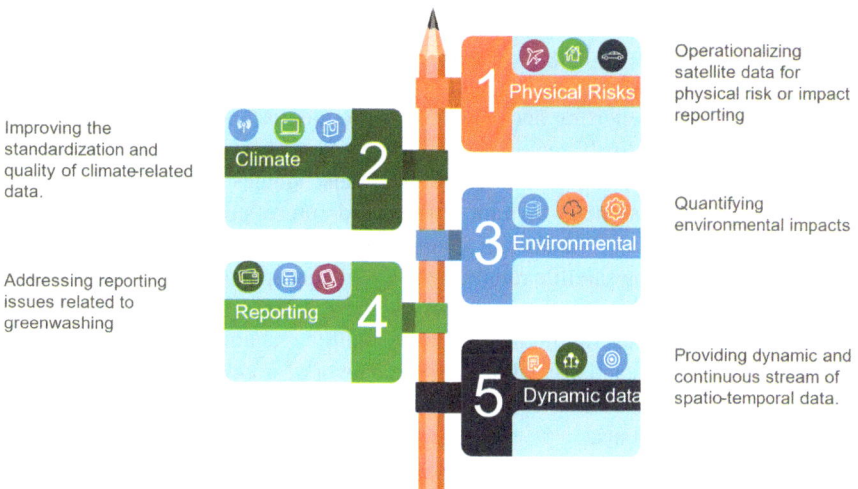

Fig. 7.3 Remote sensing data and analysis are critical in five ways in geospatial finance

reports and ongoing provision services for specific geographic areas. This process not only enables the integration of current satellite imagery with historical data but also facilitates the combination of imagery at different scales with additional data sources, enhancing the comprehensiveness and utility of the information provided.

Moreover, satellite data can enhance the assessment of physical risks on assets and regions. For example, a company with infrastructure in coastal areas can use remote sensing to monitor sea-level rise, coastal erosion, and the frequency of extreme weather events. This information is vital for evaluating the vulnerability of assets to climate-related risks and implementing measures to mitigate these risks as shown in Fig. 7.3.

Satellite remote sensing presents a promising avenue for improving the standardization and quality of climate-related data. By offering a viable, real-time, and universally accessible data source, satellites can serve as a benchmark for climate change reporting. This capability is critical for investors concerned about climate change, as it provides them with accurate, comparable information on greenhouse gas emissions, essential for informed decision-making. The existing US SEC 10-K filings often provide qualitative descriptions of physical risks. Investors have no clear way of assessing these statements. By incorporating geospatial data and AI technology, companies can better quantify and articulate these risks, leading to more precise and actionable disclosures. This enhancement not only aids in compliance with regulatory requirements but also strengthens investor confidence by providing a clearer understanding of the potential impacts of climate change on business operations and assets.

A significant hurdle in contemporary business practices is the authentication of ESG efforts, particularly in the environmental sphere. The reliance on diverse frameworks and standards for sustainability reporting has led to inconsistencies and a growing risk of greenwashing. The use of satellite data, which can provide real-time and accurate environmental metrics, emerges as a critical tool in standardizing environmental reporting and verifying corporate disclosures. However, leveraging these data effectively requires training and educating financial professionals on their use and interpretation. This requirement also suggests that universities and educational institutions need to train current and future students in satellite and geospatial technologies to deal with greenwashing and the sustainability marketplace. Thus, integrating satellite remote sensing into geospatial finance and environmental reporting heralds a new era of transparency, accuracy, and accountability in ESG disclosures. By leveraging the power of satellite technology, stakeholders can move toward a more standardized, reliable framework for environmental reporting, effectively addressing the challenges of greenwashing and enhancing the efficacy of sustainability investments.

7.3 Earth Observation via Remote Sensing

Most Earth observation data come from spaceborne platforms with remote sensing tools. Earth observation through satellites relies on their mounted payloads, which collect and transmit images or other data showing the Earth's characteristics. Earth observation satellites are typically launched to relatively low altitude orbits, about 600–800 km from the surface of the Earth. The interaction of solar energy with materials on Earth is complex, involving processes such as transmission, absorption, reflection, scattering, and emission, each affecting the energy in distinct ways. Furthermore, radiance and reflectance are integral to remote sensing, providing brightness and the ratio of reflected to total energy, respectively. The spectral signature of materials, defined as reflectance across different wavelengths, from short ultraviolet rays to long radio waves, enables the classification of materials based on their unique signatures. Several texts provide excellent explanations of the science of remote sensing, including Richards and Richards (2022), Jensen (2015), Lillesand et al. (2015), and Mather and Koch (2022). Much of the material in this section draws from these introductory remote sensing texts.

7.3.1 Fundamentals of Remote Sensing

The remote sensing imaging system encompasses multiple stages, beginning with the emission or scattering of energy by the surface of an object (Fig. 7.4). This energy travels through the atmospheric layer to the sensors on a remote sensing platform. After capture, the data are transmitted back to ground stations and processed into

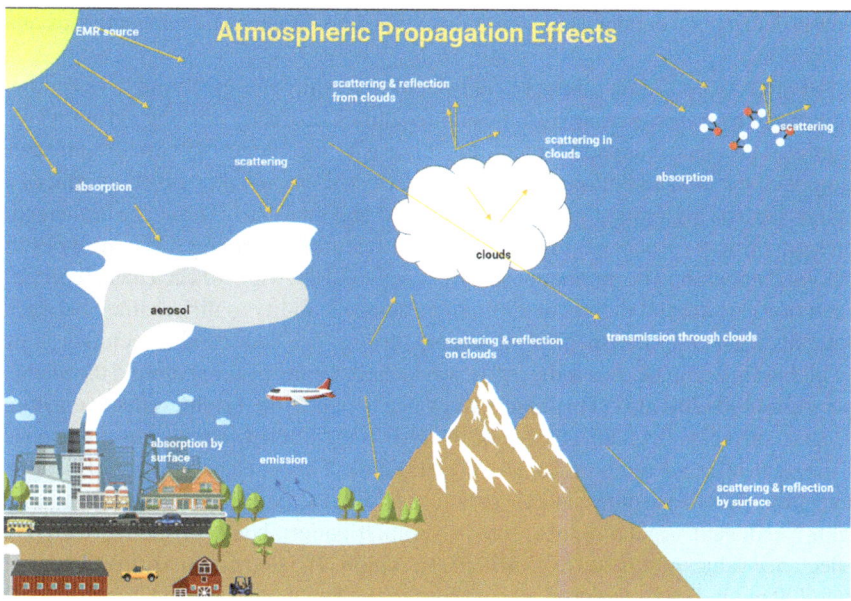

Fig. 7.4 Illustration of the various pathways and interactions of electromagnetic radiation (EMR) as it travels from its source to a sensor. Key processes include absorption, scattering, transmission and emission

usable image formats for end-users to analyze (Jensen, 2015). A crucial element of the data collected by a remote sensing system is the range of wavelengths used during image acquisition. The choice of wavelengths critically affects the type and quality of data collected, as different wavelengths interact variably with materials and conditions on Earth, being absorbed, transmitted, or reflected to varying degrees (Lillesand et al., 2015).

7.3.1.1 Interaction of Electromagnetic Energy with Matter

Electromagnetic energy that interacts with matter is known as incident radiation. This interaction may alter the radiation's intensity, direction, wavelength, polarization, and phase. Campbell and Wynne (2011, p. 4) define remote sensing as "the practice of deriving information about the Earth's land and water surfaces using images acquired from an overhead perspective, using electromagnetic radiation in one or more regions of the electromagnetic spectrum, reflected or emitted from the Earth's surface." The data and images thus obtained are analyzed to deduce the properties of the matter that interacted with the incident electromagnetic energy. Surface phenomena such as emission, scattering, and reflection are influenced predominantly by the surface characteristics of the matter, such as color and texture. In contrast, internal properties such as density and conductivity determine volume phenomena like transmission and absorption.

All objects on Earth interact with electromagnetic energy through reflection, absorption, or transmission, with these interactions distinctly varying across wavelengths. The electromagnetic spectrum represents the range of wave frequencies comprised by solar radiation. Each kind of terrestrial material or object produces a unique spectral signature that can be quantified and analyzed. These spectral signatures are critical for identifying various Earth features, including different types of rocks and minerals. The number of spectral bands and the width of each band (spectral resolution) are crucial factors determining a sensor's ability to differentiate between materials based on their spectral signatures. In Fig. 7.5, snow and ice, clouds show the highest reflectance across the entire wavelength range, peaking around the visible spectrum (400–700 nm). This high reflectance is due to the bright, reflective nature of these surfaces. Broadleaf vegetation shows a significant increase in reflectance in the near-infrared region (around 700–800 nm). This is characteristic of healthy vegetation due to the internal cell structure of leaves, which reflects near-infrared light. Needleleaf vegetation also shows a similar pattern but with slightly different reflectance values compared to broadleaf vegetation. The sharp increase in reflectance after 700 nm indicates the presence of chlorophyll and is a good indicator of vegetation health. Clear water shows low reflectance throughout the spectrum, especially in the near-infrared region where water strongly absorbs light, resulting in almost negligible reflectance.

The concept of albedo, a measure of the reflectivity of a surface, is directly related to the relationship between the percent reflectance and the reflective wavelengths of different components of the Earth's surface (Fig. 7.5). It is the ratio of the amount of electromagnetic radiation (usually solar radiation) reflected by a surface to the amount of radiation incident upon it. Thus, albedo is the percentage of the incoming solar radiation that is reflected back into the atmosphere. The albedo of different components of the Earth's surface, such as land, water, and vegetation, varies significantly based on the reflective wavelengths of those components. Figure 7.5 shows that snow and ice have very high albedo values, while clear water has low reflectance. Vegetation exhibits distinct absorption due to chlorophyll, as seen in both the broadleaf and needleleaf vegetation curves in Fig. 7.5.

These spectral signatures serve as a basis for remote sensing applications in environmental monitoring, agriculture, and hydrology, allowing for the detailed characterization and tracking of terrestrial and aquatic environments. The precision with which these features can be identified and monitored hinges on the spectral resolution of the remote sensing instruments employed, underscoring the crucial role of advanced imaging technologies in environmental sciences.

7.3.1.2 Path Length and Atmospheric Impact

Electromagnetic radiation emitted from energy sources passes through a portion of Earth's atmosphere before being detected by remote sensing instruments. This

7.3 Earth Observation via Remote Sensing

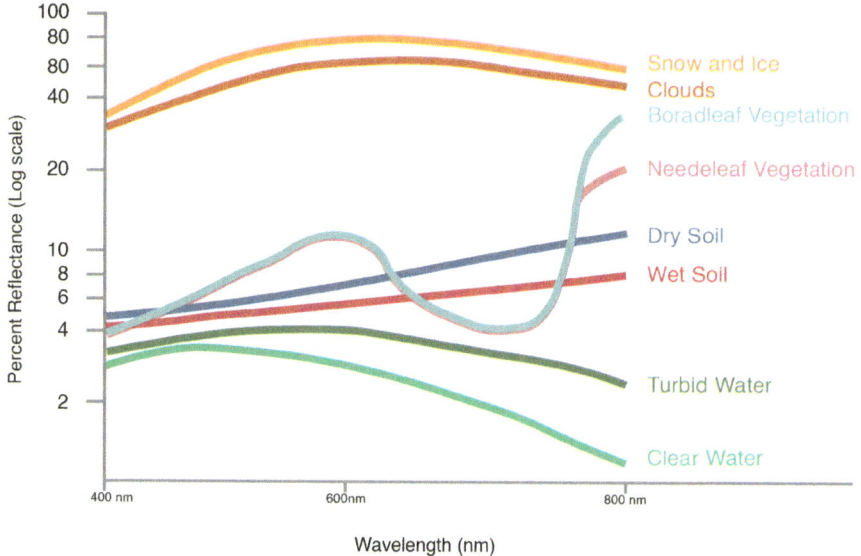

Fig. 7.5 Spectral signatures of different components of the Earth's surface. The wavelength is shown in nanometers (nm). The graph shows the percentage reflectance (on a logarithmic scale) against wavelength (in nanometers) for various components like snow and ice, clouds, different types of vegetation, soils, and water

distance, known as the path length, varies depending on the specific remote sensing technique and the energy source. For example, in space photography utilizing sunlight, the path length is equivalent to twice the thickness of Earth's atmosphere. In contrast, for airborne thermal sensors detecting energy emitted from terrestrial objects, the path length is the distance from the Earth's surface to the sensor, which is considerably shorter (Lillesand et al., 2015).

The impact of the atmosphere on radiation involves alterations to its intensity and spectral composition due to interactions such as scattering or absorption by atmospheric particles. Scattering processes, which do not alter the energy but change its spatial distribution, are classified into three types (Aggarwal, 2004; Mather & Koch, 2022). Rayleigh scattering is predominantly caused by atmospheric molecules and tiny particles smaller than one-tenth the wavelength of the interacting radiation. This scattering disproportionately affects shorter wavelengths, explaining why the sky appears blue during the day and takes on reddish hues at sunrise and sunset. Mie scattering occurs when the particle sizes are about the same as the wavelength of the radiation. Unlike Rayleigh scattering, Mie scattering can also affect longer wavelengths. Non-selective scattering occurs when particles are significantly larger than the wavelength, such as in the case of water droplets, leading to scattering that is relatively independent of wavelength, contributing to the white appearance of clouds.

Absorption involves retaining radiation from atmospheric particles, resulting in net radiative energy loss. This process is primarily facilitated by water vapor, carbon dioxide, and ozone, selective absorbers of specific wavelengths. The arrangement of molecular energy levels dictates the specific wavelengths these gases absorb (Mather & Koch, 2022).

7.3.1.3 Electromagnetic Spectrum

The electromagnetic spectrum (EMS) encompasses a comprehensive array of electromagnetic radiation, from the extremely short wavelengths of gamma rays to the much longer wavelengths of radio waves. This spectrum includes the familiar visible light, constituting only a minuscule portion of the range. The EMS is characterized by a correlation between wavelength and energy: shorter wavelengths, such as gamma rays and X-rays, possess higher energy, whereas longer wavelengths, like microwaves and radio waves, exhibit lower energy as shown in Fig. 7.6.

Remote sensing involves acquiring information about objects or areas from a distance, typically via satellites or aircraft, without physically contacting the subjects of interest. This technology leverages the EMS by utilizing the unique ways different surfaces on Earth reflect and absorb various wavelengths. By analyzing the spectral signatures produced by the energy reflected back or emitted to the sensors, we can derive information crucial for multiple applications. Visible light sensors function within the spectral range analogous to the human eye's perception, capturing imagery

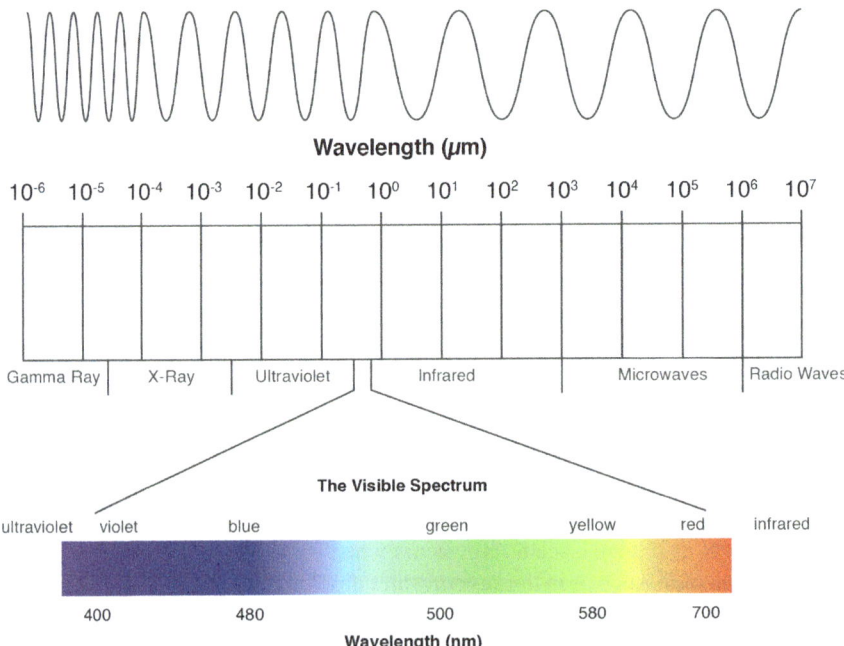

Fig. 7.6 The electromagnetic spectrum (EMS)

miming visual human observation. Visible light is characterized as electromagnetic radiation with wavelengths approximately from 0.4 to 0.7 μm (Mather & Koch, 2022). The spectrum's shorter wavelength end (0.4 μm) represents the "blue" portion, while the longer wavelength end (0.7 μm) corresponds to the "red" portion of the visible spectrum.

Electromagnetic radiation (EMR) has three distinct spectral regions with wavelengths shorter than visible light (less than 0.4 μm): gamma rays, X-rays, and ultraviolet radiation. Due to atmospheric scattering and absorption, these wavebands are not utilized in satellite remote sensing. Wavelengths longer than the visible spectrum's red end are divided into infrared (IR), microwave, and radio frequency bands.

Infrared (IR) sensors are subdivided into near-infrared, mid-infrared, and thermal infrared bands. IR sensors are particularly valuable for assessing vegetation health and detecting thermal variances, which are useful in applications such as wildfire management.

Unlike passive sensors, active microwave sensors (e.g., radar systems) emit signals and measure the reflection of surfaces. This technology is adept at assessing soil moisture levels and surface roughness, and it can perform effectively regardless of weather conditions.

Remote sensing significantly extends our perceptual capabilities beyond the visible spectrum. Each segment of the EMS provides unique insights critical for understanding various natural and human-made phenomena. The selection of the appropriate sensor type is driven by the specific requirements of the study, such as using infrared for vegetation analysis or radar for oceanographic measurements. This multifaceted approach enables a deeper understanding of the Earth's surface and atmosphere, contributing substantially to environmental monitoring and management.

7.3.2 Types of Remote Sensing Based on Satellite Characteristics

Remote sensing involves collecting and analyzing radiation reflected or emitted by Earth's surfaces. How solar radiation interacts with these surfaces depends on their material, state (like moisture content), and surface roughness, and the angle at which the radiation hits. Factors such as the objects' color, structure, and texture play crucial roles. Understanding these spectral reflectance properties is essential for accurately identifying and analyzing Earth's materials and features, a topic well-covered in several remote sensing texts (Lillesand et al., 2015; Richards & Richards, 2022; Sabins & Ellis, 2020).

The role of sensors, whether mounted on aircraft or satellites, is pivotal in remote sensing. These sensors are designed to measure electromagnetic radiation at specific wavelengths, or bands, and then convert these measurements into digital images. Each pixel in these images represents a digital number which is a measure of the intensity of detected radiation. The quality of these digital images is determined by various types of resolution: spatial, spectral, radiometric, and temporal. These resolutions influence the sensor's ability to differentiate features, capture spectral variety, assess brightness levels, and track changes over time. By analyzing spectral signatures across various wavelengths, remote sensing supports a wide range of applications such as environmental monitoring, agricultural assessment, and water quality evaluation. Next, relevant terms are defined including orbits, active and passive remote sensing, and resolution.

7.3.2.1 Satellite Orbits

Geostationary Orbit (GEO) satellites are critical to global communications and meteorological observations. They are positioned approximately 36,000 km above the Earth's equator and maintain an orbital period that matches the Earth's rotation period of roughly 24 h. This unique positioning allows these satellites to remain fixed over a specific point on the Earth's surface, providing consistent and continuous coverage of the same geographical area.

Satellites that instead traverse the Earth in polar or nonpolar orbits unleash a world of possibilities and serve a myriad of scientific and practical applications. One of the most intriguing aspects of satellites in such orbits is their ability to achieve global or near-global coverage. As the Earth gracefully rotates, different parts of the planet come into view of the satellite's sensors, enabling comprehensive mapping and monitoring.

Polar Orbit satellites, a cornerstone of environmental monitoring, travel at a relatively low altitude, crossing over both poles on each revolution around the Earth. Their unique orbit allows them to sweep across the entire Earth's surface over a sequence of passes, as the planet rotates beneath it. Widely acclaimed polar orbiting satellites include the Landsat series and Terra. The Landsat series of Earth observation satellites are designed to gather data in multiple spectral bands for global environmental monitoring, with a keen focus on changes in Earth's surface and atmosphere. Terra, a part of NASA's Earth Observing System (EOS), provides crucial data for research about the atmosphere, land, and oceans, underscoring the vital role of polar orbiting satellites in our understanding of the planet.

On the other hand, nonpolar orbits do not pass over the poles but can have various inclinations depending on their specific mission needs. For example, the International Space Station follows a nonpolar orbit. Another example is the Global Precipitation Measurement mission, a network of satellites that provides near-global precipitation measurements crucial for weather forecasting, studies of climate patterns, and precipitation tracking.

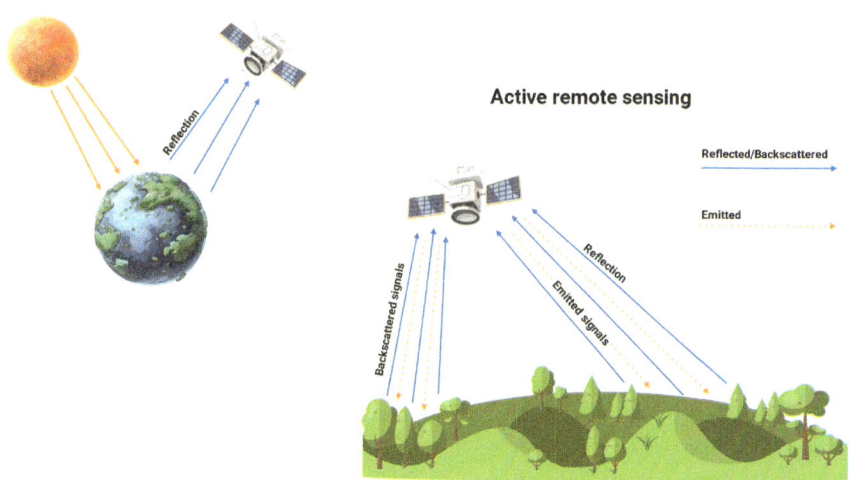

Fig. 7.7 Active and passive remote sensing

7.3.2.2 Energy Source—Passive vs. Active

Remote sensing technology fundamentally measures energy emitted from Earth and is divided into two main types: passive and active remote sensing, shown in Fig. 7.7. Passive remote sensing detects solar energy reflected off the Earth's surface, often captured as digital images (Richards, 2022). This method uses optical and thermal sensors, primarily focusing on visible light, near-infrared, short-wave infrared, and thermal infrared parts of the electromagnetic spectrum. Notable examples of passive sensors are the Landsat satellites launched by NASA in the early 1970s and the Sentinel-2 satellites developed by the ESA for environmental monitoring.

Active remote sensing does not rely on the sun but instead uses energy sources within the satellite, like radar sensors in the microwave range (Richards, 2022). Systems such as Synthetic Aperture Radar (SAR) are vital for this type. They can penetrate clouds to collect data, making them essential for surveying regions frequently obscured by clouds, like the Amazon rainforest. Understanding this distinction between passive and active remote sensing is critical to appreciating their various applications and capabilities.

7.3.2.3 What Is Spatial Resolution?

The clarity and detail in satellite imagery, termed resolution, are influenced by the configuration of the satellite's orbit and the design of its onboard sensors. Several factors, including the number and specificity of a sensor's spectral band signals, characterize resolution. Spatial and spectral resolutions are described next.

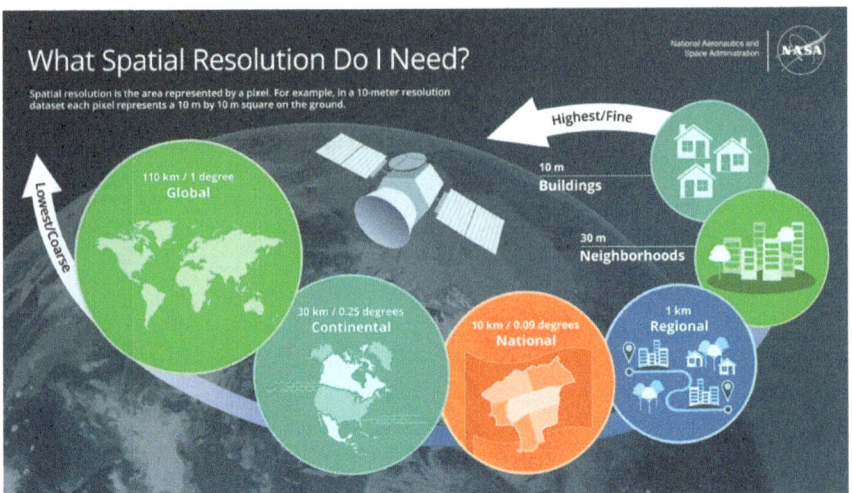

Fig. 7.8 Different spatial resolutions can be used for specific observational or research needs. This image shows spatial resolution examples for common NASA sensor products and a research scale for which they are suited (regional, national, continental, etc.). Credit: NASA Earthdata[15]

Remote sensing tools are indispensable for observing changes on the Earth's surface and managing agricultural developments, enabling informed decisions regarding crop management. Satellite sensors are capable of capturing Earth surface images at different spatiotemporal resolutions, ranging from low to high (see Fig. 7.8). Images with high spatial resolution cover smaller areas and provide less frequent updates, while those with high temporal resolution cover larger areas but offer reduced spatial detail. Striking a balance between spatial and temporal resolutions poses a technical challenge due to the interplay between scanning swath and pixel size. Currently, no single satellite constellation provides free access to images with both high temporal and high spatial resolution.

Spatial Resolution measures the smallest discernible detail in an image. It is typically quantified as the length of one side of a square pixel. For instance, the Landsat 8 satellite provides a spatial resolution of 30 m, which implies that each pixel in an image from Landsat 8 covers a ground area 30 m across. Each Landsat pixel has an area of 30 m X 30 m or 900 m^2. Moderate Resolution Imaging Spectroradiometer (MODIS) has a spatial resolution of 250–1000 m, while Sentinel-2 has a resolution of 10–60 m. ASTER has a resolution of 15 m.

Spectral Resolution describes the number of spectral bands an instrument captures and the bandwidth of each, defined by the range of wavelengths a single band encompasses. For example, black and white photographs utilize a single band covering all visible wavelengths, whereas color images use three bands. Landsat 8 features 11 bands, each with a broader range of wavelengths. In contrast, the MODIS achieves

---

[15] https://www.earthdata.nasa.gov/learn/backgrounders/remote-sensing#spectral-resolution.

7.3 Earth Observation via Remote Sensing

higher spectral resolution with 36 narrower bands that span from 0.4 to 14 μm, thus providing more detailed spectral information than Landsat 8. A higher spectral resolution means each band can capture a narrower range of wavelengths, allowing for more detailed observation and discrimination of different materials or conditions on the Earth's surface. The following sensors can be differentiated:

- Multispectral sensors typically have from 3 to 10 bands, which means they can capture images across a few broad wavelength ranges. This capability is sufficient for general classification tasks and basic remote sensing applications.
- Hyperspectral sensors, on the other hand, consist of hundreds to thousands of much narrower bands. This high spectral resolution enables detailed detection and identification of various surface materials and phenomena, making it ideal for advanced scientific research and applications.
- Panchromatic sensors use a single broad band encompassing a wide range of wavelengths, which is effective for capturing high-resolution grayscale images.

These differences in sensor design are crucial for tailoring satellite data to specific observational needs, from broad-scope surveillance and monitoring to detailed environmental and geological studies.

Radiometric Resolution refers to the granularity with which a satellite or sensor measures the radiation intensity in each spectral band. Higher radiometric resolution enables the sensor to differentiate and capture a broader range of radiation intensities. It is typically quantified in terms of bits per band. While 8-bit data were once standard in remote sensing, newer sensors, such as those used in Landsat 8, now employ 16-bit data, allowing for more detailed and accurate measurements.

Temporal Resolution refers to the interval between consecutive data collection sessions over the same area, often termed "return time" or "revisit time." The platform largely determines this resolution; for instance, satellites typically have fixed return times based on their orbital characteristics, including altitude (low versus high orbit), swath width, and sensor pointing capabilities. In contrast, sensors on aircraft or unmanned aircraft systems (UAS) usually offer more flexible return times. For example, the Landsat satellites revisit an area every 16 days, whereas the MODIS sensor can collect near-daily data.

7.3.2.4 The Instantaneous Field of View and Field of View

Image attributes like pixel size and frame size depend on the sensor's technical specifications. The Instantaneous Field of View indicates the sensor's highest angular resolution, determining the smallest ground area it can distinctly capture from a specific altitude. Conversely, the Field of View is the total angular range a sensor can observe, which translates to the swath width on the ground (Richards & Richards, 2022).

As remote sensing platforms move, they typically capture imagery continuously along their path. This imagery is divided into segments equal to the swath width for spacecraft to create square frames. In contrast, aerial systems on aircraft often keep the imagery in strip format for the entire flight (Campbell & Wynne, 2011).

7.3.3 Widely Used Satellites for Earth Observation (EO)—Landsat and Sentinel

Landsat and Sentinel-2 exemplify the application in sustainable finance and environmental research. These platforms offer multispectral imaging capabilities across various spectral bands and resolutions, providing invaluable data for a myriad of Earth observation applications (ESA 2015). The open data policies of NASA/USGS's Landsat and ESA's Sentinel missions provide significant opportunity for extensive crop monitoring. With their 10–30 m spatial resolution, weekly to biweekly data availability, and spectrum coverage, Landsat 8, Landsat 7, Sentinel-2, and Sentinel-1 form the best available moderate-resolution satellite dataset globally. Particularly, optical data from Landsat 8 OLI (The Operational Land Imager) and Sentinel-2 MSI (Multispectral Instrument) could create a "virtual constellation" with a 3–5 day revisit frequency, although sensor differences, satellite platforms, processing algorithms, and misalignments pose compatibility challenges. Ongoing research aims to produce a Harmonized Landsat Sentinel-2 (HLS) dataset—a consistent record of surface reflectance from both satellite sources, integrated through a unified workflow.

Example Using Landsat: The full archive of Landsat includes data from 1972 to present day, with data from 1982 onward at 30 m resolution (Landsat 4–9). Spectral signatures are depicted through spectral reflectance curves, which represent reflectance as a function of wavelength. Figure 7.9 shows green vegetation, dry bare soil, and clear water, highlighting their distinctive spectral behaviors. Green vegetation is characterized by its strong absorption of red wavelengths and high reflectance in the near-infrared (NIR) spectrum, a feature that characterizes the vibrancy and health of foliage. In contrast, water absorbs most of the incoming light, especially in the infrared and red wavelengths, making it appear dark in those spectral bands. Dry bare soil, meanwhile, exhibits moderate reflectance across a broad range of wavelengths, but with distinct peaks and troughs that vary depending on its composition and moisture content, distinguishing it from the other classes through its spectral behavior.

Other commonly used sensors are Sentinel-2 with 10–20 m spatial resolution and a 5-day revisit with much less temporal coverage. Sentinel-2 land applications are very similar to those of Landsat. Remote sensing technology has advanced to allow comprehensive monitoring and analysis of the Earth's surface. Sentinel-2's 10 m resolution composite stands out by providing high-quality, multispectral data, crucial for various environmental and urban planning studies. The Sentinel-2 image composite consists of a pixel-based global scale raster grid incorporating four spectral bands: Blue (B2), Green (B3), Red (B4), and Near Infrared (B8). Each band contributes to the composite's utility in deriving indices such as the normalized vegetation index

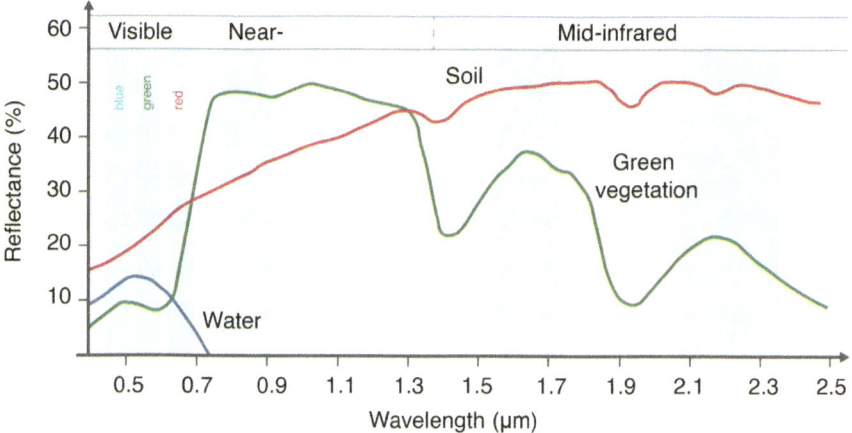

Fig. 7.9 Spectral signatures of soil, vegetation, and clear water as a function of wavelengths from visible to mid-infrared. Numbers 1–7 indicate visible, NIR, and MIR wavelength ranges, respectively

and supports automated land cover classification. Figure 7.10a shows an image of an area in Chennai, India. The composite in Fig. 7.10b shows the same area at a finer scale, which was generated using only four of Sentinel-2's thirteen bands, selected for their effectiveness in representing spatial features at 10 m resolution.

Sentinel imagery stored on the Joint Research Centre Big Data and processed on Google Earth Engine offers an efficient solution for handling extensive image classification and analysis tasks related to environmental monitoring and urban development projects.

7.3.4 Satellites for Greenhouse Gas Emissions Accounting

Greenhouse gas (GHG) monitoring from space has become an indispensable tool in understanding and addressing global climate change. Several satellite missions have been pivotal in GHG monitoring. The Greenhouse Gases Observing Satellite (GOSAT)[16] series, developed by the Japan Aerospace Exploration Agency (JAXA), and the Orbiting Carbon Observatory (OCO) series from NASA, are notable examples. These satellites use high-resolution spectrometers capable of detecting CO_2 and CH_4 concentrations by measuring the absorption of sunlight reflected off Earth's surface.

Satellites like the ESA's Sentinel-5 Precursor, with the TROPOspheric Monitoring Instrument (TROPOMI), have extended capabilities for monitoring air quality and GHG in high resolution. These missions provide data critical for tracking emissions

---

[16] https://www.gosat.nies.go.jp/en/.

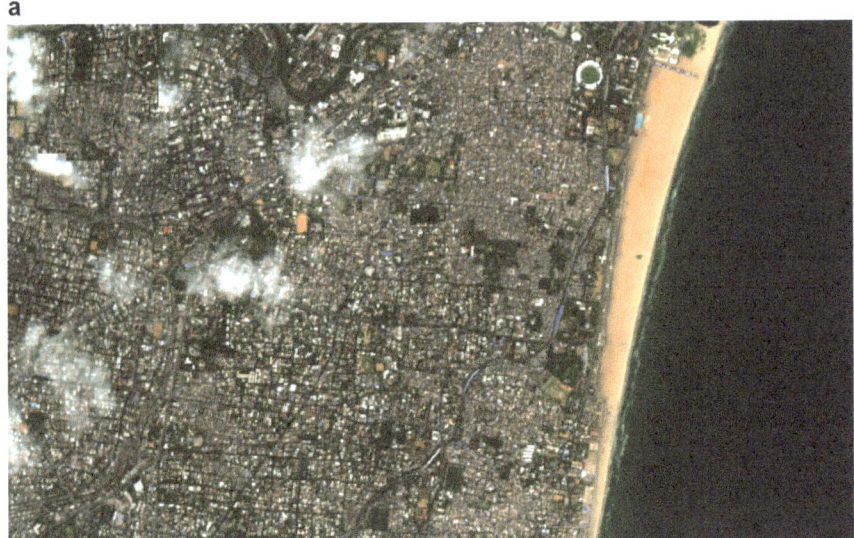

Fig. 7.10 a A Sentinel image over the region. (after user signs in) **b** An image of Chennai, India showing dense urban agglomeration with the waters of the Bay of Bengal in the extreme right *Source* https://developers.google.com/earthengine/datasets/catalog/COPERNICUS_S2_SR_HARMONIZED

from point sources over large geographic scales, offering insights into regional and global carbon cycles.

Over the next five years, the future of sustainability and resilience services will be shaped by rapid technological advancements and increasingly stringent regulatory frameworks, particularly in the US, Europe, and Singapore. The expert interviewed for this chapter is Mark Golovcsenko, a Principal based in New York within KPMG's US Strategy practice. Golovcsenko interview on sustainability is found in Chapter 1. This part of the interview talks about advances in technology that are helping companies report on emissions.

> **Expert in Focus: Mark Golovcsenko**
>
> *When thinking about the context of climate, whether it involves adapting or mitigating emissions-related issues, it's essential to consider the evolution of sustainability services. Historically, these services have been driven by regulations, first in Europe and more recently in the US, with a primary focus on measuring emissions and climate risk. Despite significant progress, comprehensive emission measurement, particularly Scope 3 emissions, remains challenging and incomplete.*
>
> *Advancements in technology have helped companies move beyond spreadsheets to more sophisticated tools for measuring emissions. However, the future focus should be on the actual impact—reducing emissions and adapting to climate change. Service providers that excel in this area will prioritize impact over mere compliance with measurement requirements.*
>
> *There is a growing need for tangible impact rather than just measurement. Making a real impact is undoubtedly more challenging than measurement, especially as we move towards a more non-voluntary reporting regime. Some executives have expressed concerns about the complexity and burden of European-inspired regulations like the CSRD. One executive pointed out that every dollar spent on measurement is a dollar less available for reducing emissions, emphasizing that the ultimate goal is to effect change, not just to measure it.*

Use Case: Advancing Climate Accountability: The Crucial Role of Satellites in GHG (Greenhouse Gas) Emissions Monitoring—Floodlight Perspective (Fig. 7.11).

Floodlight, inc. is a startup that has solved assessing asset-level greenhouse gas emissions using remote sensing data. Floodlight uses satellites and AI to remotely measure asset-level greenhouse gas emissions at highly precise resolutions, accounting for meteorological factors like wind and outside emissions sources. They offer full global, high-resolution coverage, including historical data and the ability to breakdown greenhouse gases into sub-gases, such as methane. Figure 7.11 showcases output of the analysis for an example company.

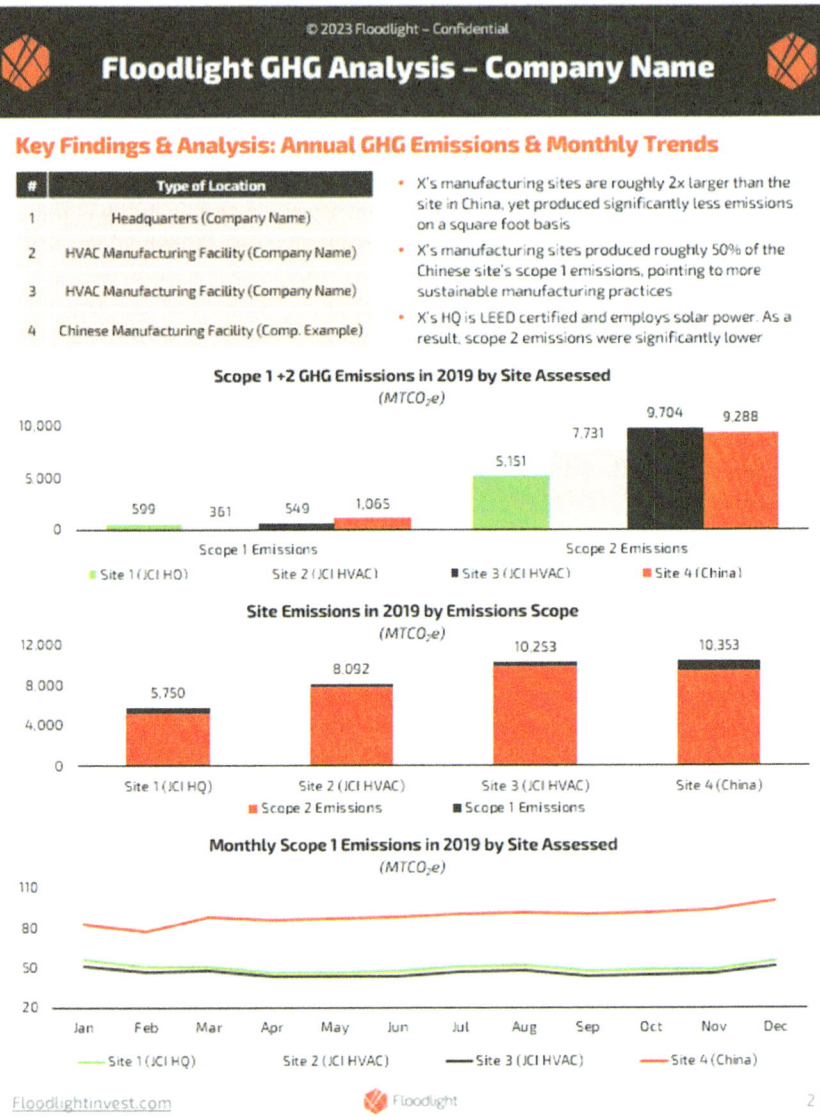

Fig. 7.11 Floodlight data product of GHG Scope 1 and Scope 2 emissions across sites. Scope 1 and 2 are explained in Chapter 1

7.4 Satellite Data Access—Data Catalogs

Remote sensing platforms such as the USGS EarthExplorer, NASA's LP DAAC Catalog, EarthData Catalog, NOAA Climate Data Online (CDO), the EU Copernicus Access Portal, and data access services provided by JAXA and the Indian Space

7.4 Satellite Data Access—Data Catalogs

Fig. 7.12 Shows the EOS Interface with menu-driven options for users to download relevant satellite data. *Source* https://earthexplorer.usgs.gov/

Research Organisation play a pivotal role in monitoring and understanding various environmental phenomena. These platforms or portals are integral for tracking global warming indicators such as greenhouse gas emissions, land cover changes, sea-level rise, forest fires, ice melt, and floods, as well as aiding in urban green planning and smart agriculture. These portals are not just gateways to satellite data, but user-centric platforms designed to cater to a wide range of applications. From academic research to practical implementations in environmental and resource management, each platform is tailored to the specific missions of its satellites and the data needs of its users. They are equipped with tools and resources to maximize the utility of the information provided, making them accessible and beneficial to all.

Earth Observation System (EOS) Level 1 and 2 data products, with the highest spatial and temporal resolution, are the most detailed and accurate. Level 3 and 4 products, while derived and therefore not as precise, still offer valuable insights with equal or lower spatial and temporal resolution than Level 2 products. They are also easier to use. EOS data access is provided by a number of searchable data repositories (EOS data gateways) such as the EarthExplorer (Fig. 7.12). They usually include: (1) an integrated search interface; (2) provision for searching by dataset, sensor, data type, location, and date; (3) a download option; and (4) an online manual and tutorial.

7.4.1 USGS EarthExplorer

The USGS EarthExplorer is a comprehensive online search, discovery, and ordering tool for various types of remote sensing data. It provides access to an extensive archive of satellite and aerial imagery. The EarthExplorer user interface allows for the selection of specific datasets through criteria such as data type, location, and date. Users can search for data from a range of sensors and satellites, including Landsat and MODIS, and historical aerial photos. The portal is known for its detailed search capabilities that cater to environmental research, planning, and management needs.

7.4.2 NASA LP DAAC Catalog

The NASA Land Processes Distributed Active Archive Center (LP DAAC) operates within the Earth Observing System Data and Information System (EOSDIS). This portal provides data and services related to land-based satellite imagery and remote sensing data, which are crucial for studying Earth's terrestrial surfaces. Tools like NASA's AppEEARS offer users the ability to explore and download a tailored selection of geospatial data from multiple satellite and environmental datasets. It is particularly useful for academic and scientific research that involves land dynamics influenced by natural and human-induced processes. Each of these portals is equipped with user guides and tutorials to assist new users in navigating and utilizing the available data effectively, making them invaluable resources for anyone involved in the study of Earth's systems.

7.4.3 EarthData Catalog

NASA's EarthData Catalog is part of the EOSDIS and offers access to a wealth of information on Earth's atmosphere, oceans, land, and more. This portal serves as a gateway to a suite of NASA Earth science data, information, and services. Users can search, discover, visualize, refine, and access NASA Earth Observation data through sophisticated search tools and Application Programming Interface (API). It also integrates with other NASA data tools and applications, providing a comprehensive resource for educators, scientists, and policymakers engaged in climate and Earth system research.

7.4.4 NOAA Climate Data Online (CDO)

The NOAA Climate Data Online portal is designed to provide public access to one of the most comprehensive datasets covering the Earth's climate. The data available include temperature, wind, atmospheric pressure, precipitation, and other climatic elements collected from ground-based observing systems and satellites. Users can request data through an easy-to-use interface, capable of filtering by various factors such as geographic region and time period. CDO is extensively used for climate research and helps in understanding long-term climate changes and patterns.

7.4.5 EU Copernicus Access Portal

The Copernicus Open Access Hub provides comprehensive access to Earth observation data from the Copernicus program, which is the EU's Earth observation and monitoring program. This portal offers data from the Sentinel series of satellites, which include capabilities for land, ocean, and atmospheric monitoring. Users can search, view, and download a wide range of data products that are crucial for environmental monitoring, natural disaster response, and climate studies. The portal is designed to cater to a diverse user base including scientists, policymakers, and educators, offering both real-time and historical data.

7.4.6 Japan's Satellite Data Access

The JAXA provides access to its satellite data through several portals, depending on the type of data and mission, for example, the Global Change Observation Mission for environmental monitoring data, and the Advanced Land Observing Satellite series for land monitoring. JAXA's data portals typically provide tools for searching, processing, and downloading satellite imagery and other data products, supporting both scientific research and practical applications in areas like disaster management and urban planning.

7.4.7 India's Satellite Data Access

The Indian Space Research Organisation provides satellite data through the Bhuvan portal, among others. Bhuvan is a platform offering multiple layers of Indian remote sensing satellite data for various applications. These applications range from thematic services to disaster services, and from ocean services to base map services. Users can access detailed satellite images of the Indian subcontinent, which help in numerous applications such as urban planning, agriculture, water resources, and environmental management. Bhuvan's user-friendly interface allows for extensive data exploration and supports both academic and development-oriented projects.

7.5 Democratizing Global Access to Geospatial Data—Google Earth Engine Platform

The Google Earth Engine (GEE) platform epitomizes the democratization of global access to geospatial data, harnessing the power of cloud computing to offer an unparalleled repository of satellite imagery and analytical tools (Tamiminia et al., 2020).

This platform consolidates a vast array of satellite data, enabling users to employ remote sensing techniques and visualize analysis outcomes all in one integrated environment. The foundation of GEE's user accessibility lies in its sophisticated API technology, which simplifies the execution of complex land cover monitoring algorithms and classifications through straightforward coded commands.

At the core of GEE's functionality is the Earth Engine JavaScript API, which stands as the predominant tool for engaging with the platform's capabilities. This API facilitates a user-friendly environment for conducting satellite imagery analysis, appealing to a broad spectrum of users with varying levels of expertise in remote sensing. Additionally, GEE offers a Python API accessible through Google Colaboratory for those who prefer or require Python for their analytical tasks. While the Python API introduces a layer of complexity compared to the direct interactions possible within the GEE code editor using JavaScript, it significantly expands the platform's versatility and application.

GEE includes satellite imagery from Landsat, Sentinel, MODIS, and many others, and climate and weather data such as precipitation, temperature, and humidity. Geophysical data include elevation and land cover, among others. Hence, GEE's operational capabilities extend to a wide range of applications, fundamentally changing the landscape of satellite imagery analysis. These include the automation of data processing and display, enabling users to streamline their workflows and achieve efficient analysis outputs. The platform supports near real-time monitoring, contingent on the data availability within its extensive catalog, offering timely insights into environmental changes and phenomena. Moreover, GEE facilitates the application of machine learning algorithms, empowering users to conduct sophisticated analyses that can uncover patterns and trends not immediately visible. The integration of a graphical user interface enhances the platform's usability, making advanced remote sensing methodologies accessible to a broader audience.

GEE excels in land applications, providing critical tools for the long-term monitoring of landscape changes and land cover types. Users can compute various normalized difference indices relevant to land management, including those for vegetation, water, snow, soil, and urban areas (Mutanga & Kumar, 2019). This capability is pivotal for environmental conservation, urban planning, and agricultural management. The platform also supports landscape time series analysis and change detection, enabling the identification of environmental trends over time. Summary statistics and validation and accuracy assessment methods further bolster the reliability and applicability of GEE's data outputs, ensuring that users can confidently utilize the information for research, policymaking, and operational decision-making.

In essence, Google Earth Engine[17] stands as a transformative platform in the field of geospatial science, offering an accessible, powerful, and versatile toolset for global users. By democratizing access to satellite data and advanced analysis tools, GEE empowers a diverse range of stakeholders to harness the potential of remote sensing for environmental monitoring, land management, and beyond. The earth engine catalog is ever increasing and includes a variety of standard Earth science

---

[17] https://developers.google.com/earth-engine/datasets/catalog.

raster datasets. The datasets can easily be imported into the user's script environment for a variety of applications.

7.6 ML and Deep Learning in Remote Sensing

The integration of machine learning (ML) and artificial intelligence (AI) into satellite remote sensing marks a pivotal shift toward the digital era, significantly enhancing the ability to process, analyze, and generate actionable insights from satellite imagery (Cheng et al., 2020; Maxwell et al., 2018). These advanced technologies are revolutionizing the field by improving the accuracy, efficiency, and applicability of satellite data across various sectors.

Machine Learning techniques are crucial in refining the analysis of satellite imagery. By modeling and extracting valuable information from vast datasets, ML algorithms facilitate the identification of specific features, track changes over time, and forecast future scenarios with the support of AI. This capability not only streamlines the complex processes involved in data verification and interpretation but also enables the development of models that can effectively parse through satellite images to deliver more relevant insights.

Artificial intelligence, particularly through its dependency on extensive datasets for training, has been fundamental in advancing satellite remote sensing. However, the challenge of sourcing, verifying, and processing data for machine learning is significant, often leading to inaccuracies due to data bias. Despite these hurdles, the evolution of synthetic data offers promising solutions, allowing data scientists to access large-scale, high-quality training datasets. This advancement is set to redefine AI's role in driving the future of remote sensing, as synthetic data moves from being a supplementary source to a primary driver of AI innovations.

Image classification within satellite remote sensing has benefitted greatly from the application of AI and ML techniques. Two primary methods, supervised and unsupervised classification, utilize algorithms to categorize satellite imagery into distinct land cover classes. Supervised ARTMAP, a network architecture designed for pattern recognition tasks, developed in the nineties, found significant application in remote sensing, enabling efficient learning and classification. This technology is instrumental in land cover and use classification, change detection, crop monitoring, and various environmental monitoring tasks, providing detailed analysis and insights for informed decision-making.

The realm of remote sensing has been transformed by the advent of AI, with over a hundred research papers highlighting AI's contributions across machine learning, data mining, and more. The development of deep learning architectures, especially convolutional neural networks (CNNs), has revolutionized image classification, detection, and prediction tasks, offering more profound insights than previously possible. Before the widespread adoption of deep learning, traditional machine learning algorithms like support vector machines and Random Forests laid the groundwork for AI in remote sensing, each contributing unique strengths to the field.

In summary, the role of machine learning and artificial intelligence in satellite remote sensing is undeniably transformative, offering unparalleled capabilities for analyzing and interpreting satellite data. By leveraging these advanced technologies, stakeholders in various sectors can derive accurate, timely, and actionable insights from satellite imagery, significantly improving decision-making processes and outcomes in environmental monitoring, agriculture, urban planning, and beyond. The future of remote sensing is bright, with AI and ML at the forefront of this digital and analytical revolution.

7.6.1 Case Study: Enhanced Monitoring of Indonesian Mangrove Forests: Leveraging Deep Learning and Remote Sensing

Despite occupying less than 0.1% of the Earth's terrestrial surface, mangrove forests are indispensable to the ecological and economic health of coastal communities across more than 110 nations. As detailed by Bunting et al. (2022), significant shifts in mangrove distribution from 1990 to 2020 in the top 20 countries with the largest areas of mangrove underscore the pressing need for effective conservation strategies. These ecosystems, characterized by their dense and complex nature, play a pivotal role in carbon sequestration, climate stabilization, and protecting coastal areas against environmental hazards. However, the relentless march of deforestation, driven by unsustainable agricultural, aquacultural, and urban development practices, coupled with the exacerbating effects of climate change, has put these vital habitats in jeopardy, with a 20% reduction observed from 1980 to 2005.

The unique challenges posed by mangrove ecosystems, especially in Indonesia, demand the adoption of more sophisticated observation and analysis methods. This necessity has catalyzed the exploration of remote sensing and machine learning technologies, with a particular emphasis on deep learning (DL) to navigate these complexities. This case study harnessed multispectral and multi-temporal satellite data from Sentinel-2, spanning from 2016 to 2023, to map and analyze the dynamics within Indonesian mangrove forests. The high spatial resolution and rich spectral data of Sentinel-2 were instrumental in this endeavor, enabling a nuanced understanding of mangrove transformations.

Data & Methodology: Our research (Gopal et al. 2023) compiled a comprehensive dataset to include optical bands, spectral indices, terrain, and proximity data. This dataset served as the foundation for applying convolutional network training, which relied on expert-selected labeled data to achieve high accuracy in delineating mangrove structure and types. The attributes and indices used in the analysis encompass:

7.6 ML and Deep Learning in Remote Sensing

- Cloud-free composite,
- Normalized vegetation index (NDVI),
- Normalized difference water indices,
- Automated water extraction index,
- Proximity to coastline, and
- Various terrain variables.

Each pixel/cell contained 17 attributes relevant to the study, facilitating detailed analysis. This approach ensured a nuanced understanding of the mangrove ecosystem's condition and changes over time. An expert field-validated shapefile map of mangrove distribution was utilized to create training data.

Methodology: Fig. 7.13 illustrates a workflow diagram for processing Sentinel-2 satellite images using various image processing, data preparation, and machine learning techniques to achieve cloud-free composite images and perform coastal area analysis. Here's a detailed description of each step in the workflow:

Satellite Imagery Acquisition: The process began with the collection of Sentinel-2 satellite images. Image processing included checking for cloud probability, based on an algorithm assesses the probability of cloud presence in the images. The images were then passed through a filter to reduce noise or unwanted data. Relevant spectral indices were computed from the filtered images. A composite of the images free from cloud cover was created, specifically for 1,227 tiles labeled as "fishnet."

Geographic Information System (GIS) processing was used to overlay country boundaries and specifically select coastal regions for further analysis. Digital Elevation Models (DEM) from Aster were used for terrain analysis. Training data includes mangrove areas identified in field surveys in 2019, which are represented as polygons in the spatial data along with two other classes, water, other land cover categories (including urban and forest).

AI deep learning used, as input, the processed data from the previous steps and mangrove labels as training labels. Two instances of a PyTorch-based convolutional neural network (CNN) with a 64×64 pixel filter were used to process the input data, potentially for feature extraction or classification tasks. The resulting accuracy estimates were examined and if the accuracy was satisfactory, the process moved to validation, else it might have cycled back to an earlier step for adjustments. The final validated results displayed the accuracy of the classifications or analyses performed by the model. This workflow is indicative of a systematic approach combining remote sensing, GIS, and AI to enhance the accuracy and utility of environmental data analysis, particularly in mapping and monitoring coastal ecosystems like mangroves. CNNs were particularly effective due to their ability to handle multi-dimensional data and detect complex patterns, shapes, and textures. The CNN training used expert-selected labeled data, ensuring high accuracy in characterizing mangrove structure and type (Fig. 7.13). The study also included traditional learning models for comparison and benchmarking, providing a comprehensive analysis of the effectiveness of various methodologies.

In Convolutional Neural Networks (CNNs), ReLU (Rectified Linear Unit) and Softmax are two types of activation functions that serve different purposes in the

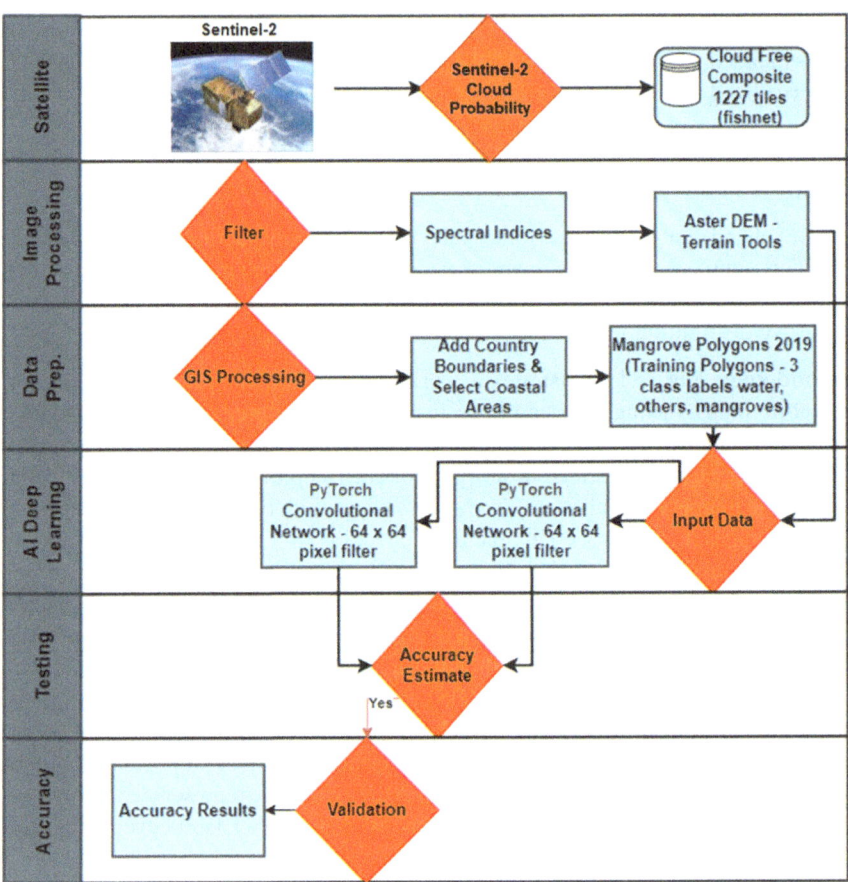

Fig. 7.13 Deep learning architectures and methodologies

network shown in Fig. 7.14. In brief, ReLU is used in hidden layers to introduce nonlinearity and help the model learn complex patterns, while also addressing issues like the vanishing gradient. Softmax is used in the output layer for multi-class classification tasks, converting the network's output into a probability distribution over the possible classes. Interested readers can check out a vast literature including Bengio et al., 2017; Aggarwal, 2018; Sejnowski, 2018; Heaton et al., 2017; Huang et al., 2020.

The results clearly demonstrate that CNNs are valuable tools for mangrove mapping across Indonesia. This exercise facilitated studying dynamic changes in mangrove cover using available field surveys from 2019 in order to train the algorithm for mapping mangroves in 2023. The next phase of our research will focus on evaluating the generalization capabilities of the CNN model to identify and monitor mangroves globally, which is crucial for estimating blue carbon. Given the significant threat to mangroves—often due to urban expansion or fish farming

7.6 ML and Deep Learning in Remote Sensing

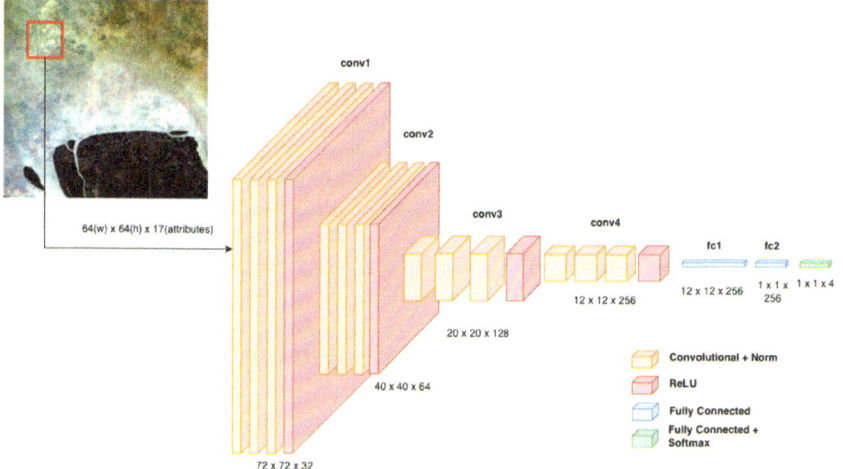

Fig. 7.14 Convolutional neural network architecture

Table 7.1 Preliminary results of CNN architecture in identifying mangroves

Approach	Model	Accuracy	Considerations
Node-based Regression	Random Forest	99.99%	Overfitting and inability to scale to many scenes and regions
Hyperplane Classification	Support Vector Machine	99.39%	Classes must be highly distinct, likely to fail on species specific scaling
Pixel-wise Deep Artificial Network	Feed Forward Neural Network (Tensorflow)	41.44%	Sensitive to Training Data and Architecture/Hyperparameter choice
Computer Vision Classification	CNN (PyTorch)	99.89%	Input Image Training size reduces Information Capture and Resolution

in some countries—this research ultimately aims to automate the identification of mangrove structure and species for more efficient mapping and monitoring worldwide (Table 7.1).

7.6.2 Significant Insights and Future Directions

This case study demonstrates the efficacy of integrating deep learning with remote sensing for environmental monitoring, particularly in the context of mangrove conservation in Indonesia. Looking forward, the study advocates for the integration of these technological methodologies with physical field surveys to refine training datasets further and enhance model accuracy. Such collaborative efforts promise to yield deeper insights and foster more effective conservation strategies.

Advancements in AI and remote sensing are proving instrumental in supporting the valuation and impact assessment of blue bonds. Specifically, the use case presented in this section is deep learning (AI) algorithms for mangrove mapping. The integration of multisensor data significantly refined the estimates of mangrove ecosystem values and their carbon sequestration capacities, critical for blue carbon accounting.

7.7 Advancements and Challenges in Remote Sensing

The following subsection discusses the emerging technologies related to the field of satellite remote sensing.

7.7.1 Emerging ClimateTech Companies—With AI, This Sphere of Space Technologies Is Booming

Several leading satellite companies have ventured into creating their own marketplaces, such as Airbus with its UP42 and OneAtlas platforms, and Maxar with its GBDX Notebooks initiative. These platforms were designed to enable developers and data scientists to access satellite imagery and utilize machine learning tools. Nonetheless, these marketplaces have struggled to achieve widespread acceptance. A key reason for this is their failure to compile data from various providers, as competitors were reluctant to share their data. Google, on the other hand, maintains an extensive catalog of satellite imagery and geospatial data, capable of planetary-scale analysis, and has used this advantage to enhance its in-house tools and strengthen its developer relationships.

The intricate nature of geospatial data becomes apparent through the involved multiple stages of transformation, processing, and customization. The integration of cloud technologies, edge computing, and AI/ML innovations, and the development of more robust geospatial APIs are making these data more approachable. Developers are now equipped to create specialized applications for unique customer needs without the necessity of mastering image capture, data processing, or object recognition. This shift mirrors the widespread accessibility of GPS technology following the introduction of Apple's App Store. We are witnessing the emergence of a new era when the demand for geospatial data not only becomes more measurable but also influences the development of new sensors and platforms.

7.7.2 Sustainable Blue Bonds

Sustainable bonds, as distinct financial instruments, are gaining traction among investors due to their targeted contributions to environmental and social initiatives. The sustainable bond market, especially within government securities, has seen robust growth due to escalating demand and supply, with issuances peaking at US$129 billion in 2021. Investment funds like the Norwegian Global Fund and Denmark's ATP Pension Fund have significantly incorporated sustainable securities into their portfolios. There are three common types of sustainable bonds:

1. Thematic Bonds: These include green, social, sustainability, SDG, and transition bonds. They are structured to finance projects that directly impact environmental or social goals with proceeds specifically allocated to such projects. Noteworthy, thematic investments are predicted to rise, driven by sustainability goals and potential returns, with significant expansion observed in the government securities sector. According to the 2023 BNP Paribas Thematics Barometer, 70% of thematic investors plan to increase their investments in thematic funds within three years, driven by the dual objectives of promoting sustainability and enhancing returns.
2. Sustainability-Linked Bonds: These bonds create a financial incentive structure by linking returns to the achievement of predefined sustainability targets.
3. ESG-Compliant Bonds: Typically lacking specific labels, these bonds meet general criteria for environmental, social, and governance factors and are often validated through second-party opinions.

In recent years, British International Investment has issued Blue bonds related to mangrove restoration. They partnered with Zephyr Power, a renewable energy business, to implement a mangrove restoration project at a wind power plant in Pakistan. This project is projected to bring significant economic benefits. The initiative could save up to $7 million in maintenance costs over 25 years, while also doubling the income of local communities. Additionally, a report by Earth Security proposes a business case for investing in mangrove restoration. It suggests that such investments, if done at scale, could return $11.8 billion by 2040. The creation of a Municipal Mangrove Bond Fund is also proposed as a new mechanism for cities to access adaptation finance.

Scottish Widows, a pension fund, has also recognized the potential of similar investments. It reports the role pension funds can play in driving responsible investment into nature-positive assets, which include projects like mangrove restoration. The report emphasizes that pension funds, controlling nearly $60 trillion globally, can significantly contribute to natural regeneration efforts and guide capital flows into projects that restore nature while providing financial returns.

These cases illustrate a growing trend of funds recognizing the importance and potential profitability of investing in nature-based solutions like mangrove restoration.

7.7.3 Financial Trading Platforms Use the Same Satellite Ground Stations

Ground station networks[18] include KSAT and SSC, which are prominent providers of ground station networks facilitating communications for satellites in various orbits, including radio and cell phone communication. These networks enable a range of services beyond traditional satellite communication, including Earth observation, environmental monitoring, and data relay for various applications. Competition and innovation in ground station services are rapidly evolving.[19] The same satellite ground stations are increasingly being used in financial trading platforms to gain competitive advantages, primarily through reduced latency in high-frequency trading. Financial trading platforms utilize satellite communications to transmit data across long distances faster than traditional fiber-optic cables. The speed at which trading orders are executed can significantly impact the profitability of trades, especially in markets where prices fluctuate rapidly.

High-frequency trading firms utilize satellite networks to establish direct and quicker paths between trading hubs, such as those between New York and London. By minimizing the delay caused by longer terrestrial routes, these firms can execute trades in a small fraction of the time taken by competitors relying on conventional internet connections. This ability to act quicker on market data can translate into substantial financial gains. The technology underlying this usage includes both geostationary (GEO) and low-earth orbit (LEO) satellites. LEO satellites, in particular, offer lower latency because they orbit closer to the Earth, reducing the time it takes for data to travel back and forth. Additionally, the advancement in satellite ground station technology, such as the development of electronically steered antennas and improvements in satellite-to-ground optical communications, has made satellite communications more reliable and quicker, further benefiting the financial trading sectors.[20]

7.8 Summary and Conclusions

This chapter has explored the intersection of geospatial finance, satellite remote sensing, and advanced technologies such as machine learning and deep learning, highlighting their pivotal roles in addressing climate risks and environmental impacts. We began by tracing the history and evolution of Earth observation and remote sensing, emphasizing the increasing importance of commercial satellites in this

---

[18] https://www.nasa.gov/smallsat-institute/sst-soa/ground-data-systems-and-mission-operations/.

[19] spacenews.com/smallsat-ground-station-operators-expect-consolidation-eye-new-antennas-optical-links/.

[20] https://www.gminsights.com/industry-analysis/satellite-ground-station-sgs-market; https://interactive.satellitetoday.com/via/august-2021/uber-ization-of-ground-stations-the-small-satellite-markets-enabling-aggregator-wave/.

domain. The discussion then shifted to the crucial role of geospatial technologies in navigating climate risks across various asset classes, where satellite remote sensing emerged as a key enabler in geospatial finance.

Delving deeper into the fundamentals of remote sensing, we examined the interaction of electromagnetic energy with matter, the impact of atmospheric conditions, and the characteristics of different remote sensing satellites. This section also reviewed widely used satellites like Landsat and Sentinel, along with those specifically designed for greenhouse gas emissions accounting.

The chapter further highlighted the accessibility of satellite data through various data catalogs and platforms, such as the USGS EarthExplorer, NASA's LP DAAC, and the EU Copernicus Access Portal. The democratization of geospatial data, particularly through platforms like Google Earth Engine, was also discussed as a significant advancement in making these powerful tools available to a global audience.

A case study on the enhanced monitoring of Indonesian mangrove forests demonstrated the practical application of deep learning and remote sensing for mapping and monitoring, offering significant insights into how these technologies can be leveraged for environmental monitoring. The discussion on the emerging ClimateTech companies and the growth of sustainable blue bonds showcased the ongoing advancements and challenges in the field.

In conclusion, the integration of geospatial technologies, satellite remote sensing, and advanced computational methods is driving transformative changes in how we understand and manage climate risks and environmental impacts. As these technologies continue to evolve, they will play an increasingly vital role in supporting sustainable finance and fostering a more resilient global environment. This evolution not only offers a solution to the long-standing challenges of quantifying environmental impacts but also paves the way for more credible, consistent, and actionable climate-related financial disclosures, marking a significant step forward in the journey toward sustainable investment and corporate responsibility. In conclusion, the transition to geospatial finance, underscored by the utilization of satellite remote sensing, represents a pivotal development in environmental reporting.

References

Aggarwal, C. C. (2018). *Neural networks and deep learning* (Vol. 10, p. 3). Springer.
Aggarwal, S. (2004). Principles of remote sensing. *Satellite Remote Sensing and GIS Applications in Agricultural Meteorology, 23*(2), 23–28.
Anderson, C. (2023). *The space economy: A guide for investors, entrepreneurs, and aspiring professionals*. Wiley. ISBN-10:1119903726
Bauman, J (2020). *High-fidelity insight from medium-resolution imagery* (pp. 20–21). ArcUser.
Bengio, Y., Goodfellow, I., & Courville, A. (2017). *Deep learning* (Vol. 1). MIT Press.
Bergin, C., & Peng, I. (2024, May 13). *Cocoa plunges 19% as rain forecasts stoke market volatility*. Bloomberg. https://www.bloomberg.com/news/articles/2024-05-13/cocoa-sli des-with-forecast-of-rains-in-key-growing-nations?embedded-checkout=true

Bunting, P., Rosenqvist, A., Hilarides, L., Lucas, R. M., Thomas, N., Tadono, T., Worthington, T. A., Spalding, M., Murray, N., & Rebelo, L. M. (2022). Global Mangrove Extent Change 1996–2020: Global mangrove watch version 3.0. *Remote Sens, 14*, 3657.

Campbell, J. B., & Wynne, R. H. (2011). *Introduction to remote sensing*. Guilford Press.

Cheng, G., Xie, X., Han, J., Guo, L., & Xia, G. S. (2020). Remote sensing image scene classification meets deep learning: Challenges, methods, benchmarks, and opportunities. *IEEE Journal of Selected Topics in Applied Earth Observations and Remote Sensing, 13*, 3735–3756.

Chien, A. A. (2023, August). GenAI: Giga$$$, TeraWatt-Hours, and GigaTons of CO2. *Communications of the ACM, 66*(8), 5.

Dafermos, Y., Gabor, D., Nikolaidi, M., Pawloff, A., & van Lerven, F. (2021). *Greening the Eurosystem collateral framework*. New Economics Foundation.

Geddes, J. A., Wang, B., & Li, D. (2021). Ozone and nitrogen dioxide pollution in a coastal urban environment: The role of sea breezes, and implications of their representation for remote sensing of local air quality. *Journal of Geophysical Research: Atmospheres, 126*(18), e2021JD035314.

Gopal, S. (2023, December). *Deep learning architectures for characterization of mangrove forests in the tropics using sentinel-2 and landsat 8 imagery (invited)*. American Geophysical Union.

Heaton, J. B., Polson, N. G., & Witte, J. H. (2017). Deep learning for finance: Deep Portfolios. *Applied Stochastic Models in Business and Industry, 33*(1), 3–12.

Heldt, L., & Beske-Janssen, P. (2023). Solutions from space? A dynamic capabilities perspective on the growing use of satellite technology for managing sustainability in multi-tier supply chains. *International Journal of Production Economics, 260*, 108864.

Huang, J., Chai, J., & Cho, S. (2020). Deep learning in finance and banking: A literature review and classification. *Frontiers of Business Research in China, 14*(1), 13.

Imasu, R., Matsunaga, T., Nakajima, M., Yoshida, Y., Shiomi, K., Morino, I., Saitoh, N., Niwa, Y., Someya, Y., Oishi, Y., Hashimoto, M., Noda, H., Hikosaka, K., Uchino, O., Maksyutov, S., Takagi, H., Ishida, H., Nakajima, T. Y., Nakajima, T., & Shi, C. (2023). Greenhouse gases Observing SATellite 2 (GOSAT-2): Mission overview. *Progress in Earth and Planetary Science, 10*(1), 33.

Jacobson, R. C. (2020). *Space is open for business*. ISBN: 978–1734205107

Jensen, J. (2015). *Introductory digital image processing: A remote sensing perspective* (Pearson Series in Geographic Information Science, 4th ed.). ISBN: 978–0–13–405816.

Lillesand, T., Kiefer, R. W., & Chipman, J. (2015). *Remote sensing and image interpretation* (7th ed.). Wiley.

Ma, Y., Gopal, S., Ma, X., Gallagher, K., Koch, M., & Kaufman, L. (2023). The deforestation and biodiversity risks of power plant projects in Southeast Asia: A big data spatial analytical framework. *Sustainability, 15*(19), 14461.

Mather, P. M., & Koch, M. (2022). Computer Processing of Remotely-Sensed Images, 5th Edition. Wiley-Blackwell. ISBN: 978-1-119-50282-1.

Maxwell, A. E., Warner, T. A., & Fang, F. (2018). Implementation of machine-learning classification in remote sensing: An applied review. *International Journal of Remote Sensing, 39*(9), 2784–2817.

McKenna, P. B., Lechner, A. M., Phinn, S., & Erskine, P. D. (2020). Remote sensing of mine site rehabilitation for ecological outcomes: A global systematic review. *Remote Sensing, 12*(21), 3535.

Mutanga, O., & Kumar, L. (2019). Google earth engine applications. *Remote Sensing, 11*(5), 591.

Richards, J. A., & Richards, J. A. (2022). *Remote sensing digital image analysis* (Vol. 5, pp. 256–258). Springer.

Sabins, F. F., Jr., & Ellis, J. M. (2020). *Remote sensing: Principles, interpretation, and applications*. Waveland Press.

Salisu, A. A., Ogbonna, A. E., & Vo, X. V. (2024). Climate risks and the REITs market. *International Journal of Finance & Economics*. https://doi.org/10.1002/ijfe.2983

Sejnowski, T. J. (2018). *The deep learning revolution*. MIT Press.

References

Siddique, I., Smith, E., & Siddique, A. (2023). Assessing the sustainability of bitcoin mining: Comparative review of renewable energy sources. *Journal of Alternative and Renewable Energy Sources, 10*(1), 1–12.

Tamiminia, H., Salehi, B., Mahdianpari, M., Quackenbush, L., Adeli, S., & Brisco, B. (2020). Google Earth Engine for geo-big data applications: A meta-analysis and systematic review. *ISPRS Journal of Photogrammetry and Remote Sensing, 164*, 152–170.

Tokat-Acikel, Y., Aiolfi, M., Johnson, L. D., Hall, J., & Jin, Y. (2021). *Top-down portfolio implications of climate change.* Available at SSRN 3816939.

Werner, T. T., Mudd, G. M., Schipper, A. M., Huijbregts, M. A., Taneja, L., & Northey, S. A. (2020). Global-scale remote sensing of mine areas and analysis of factors explaining their extent. *Global Environmental Change, 60*, 102007.

Whitcraft, A. K., Becker-Reshef, I., & Justice, C. O. (2015). A framework for defining spatially explicit earth observation requirements for a global agricultural monitoring initiative (GEOGLAM). *Remote Sensing, 7*(2), 1461–1481.

Chapter 8
The Intersection of Carbon Pricing, Fintech, and Blockchain Technology

> Some solutions are relatively simple and would provide economic benefits: implementing measures to conserve energy, putting a price on carbon through taxes and cap-and-trade and shifting from fossil fuels to clean and renewable energy sources—David Suzuki

8.1 Introduction—Addressing GHG Emissions by Carbon Pricing

Climate change is one of the most critical challenges facing humanity today. A series of reports by the UN's Intergovernmental Panel on Climate Change (IPCC) has documented a worrying trend of rising global temperatures driven by human activity. Since the IPCC was created in 1988, there have been six Synthesis Reports, the latest published in 2023. These reports, based on vast amounts of data, paint a clear picture: the ever-increasing concentration of carbon emissions in the atmosphere traps heat, causing a cascade of effects like melting glaciers, rising sea levels, and more extreme weather events (Boyce, 2019; Stern, 2007). The 2023 report highlighted the significant role human activities play in driving climate change by increasing the concentration of greenhouse gases (GHGs) in the atmosphere, primarily due to the burning of fossil fuels, deforestation, and industrial processes (IPCC, 2023).

Carbon pricing is a pivotal strategy in the fight against climate change. It involves assigning a cost to carbon emissions, thereby incentivizing polluters to reduce their carbon footprint. This can be achieved through two primary mechanisms: carbon taxes and cap-and-trade systems. A carbon tax directly sets a price on carbon by defining a tax rate on GHG emissions or the carbon content of fossil fuels. This straightforward approach provides a clear economic signal to emitters to reduce their emissions or face higher costs. On the other hand, cap-and-trade systems establish a market for emission permits. Governments set a cap on the total level of GHG emissions and allocate or auction off permits to emitters. Companies that can reduce their emissions at lower costs can sell their excess permits to those facing higher reduction costs, creating a market-driven approach to achieving emission reductions. By making carbon emissions a cost, carbon pricing creates a powerful market force that drives innovation toward cleaner technologies and reduced emissions. The financial implications of carbon pricing incentivize companies to invest in energy efficiency, renewable energy, and other low-carbon technologies. As a result, carbon pricing not only helps in reducing emissions but also promotes development of a sustainable, low-carbon economy.

To effectively address this monumental challenge and move companies and the public on a path of carbon emission-reduction roadmap, there is an urgent need to move beyond outdated information and outdated strategies. This new era demands advanced climate infrastructure, powerful new tools, and innovative approaches for carbon pricing and financial technology (Fintech) solutions, the central goal of this chapter.

There are data gaps. In spite of significant advancements in climate science, policy decisions and mitigation strategies have often relied on historical data and broad-scale observations. While these methods have been invaluable, they fall short of providing the granularity and real-time insights necessary to fully comprehend and address the complexities of our rapidly changing climate. Hence, using relevant data and transparency in estimation are critical in this context.

Fintech plays a crucial role in mobilizing capital and accelerating the transition to a low-carbon economy. Climate Fintech companies are at the forefront of developing solutions for data-driven carbon accounting, facilitating investments in renewable energy projects, and streamlining carbon offset markets. These solutions are essential for unlocking new sources of funding, connecting investors with sustainable projects, and ultimately accelerating the pace of decarbonization. One of the key contributions of Fintech to climate action is in the realm of carbon accounting. Accurate measurement, reporting, and verification (MRV) of carbon emissions are essential for the integrity of carbon markets and the effectiveness of carbon pricing mechanisms. Fintech solutions leverage advanced data analytics, artificial intelligence, and blockchain technology to enhance MRV processes, ensuring that emissions data are accurate, transparent, and tamper-proof.

In spite of the potential of carbon pricing and Fintech solutions, existing carbon markets face several challenges. One critical issue is ensuring the integrity and effectiveness of carbon offsets. Carbon offsets are tradable units representing a reduction in carbon emissions, and their credibility is crucial for the success of carbon markets. Ensuring that carbon offsets are genuine and represent real, additional, and verifiable emission reductions is essential for maintaining trust in the market. Blockchain technology can address these challenges by providing a transparent and tamper-proof record of carbon offset transactions. Blockchain technology, in particular, holds significant promise for enhancing the integrity of carbon markets (Al Sadawi et al., 2021; Howson, 2019; Kim & Huh, 2020). Blockchain's decentralized and immutable ledger can provide a transparent and reliable record of carbon transactions, reducing the risk of fraud and ensuring that carbon offsets represent genuine emission reductions. This technology can also streamline the trading of carbon credits, making it easier for companies to participate in carbon markets and for regulators to oversee these transactions (Chen, 2018a; Chen et al., 2019). Integrating blockchain with MRV processes enhances the credibility of carbon offsets and ensures the delivery of real environmental benefits (Chen, 2018b; Woo et al., 2021). This integration can also reduce transaction costs, increase market efficiency, and encourage greater participation in carbon markets.

By combining advanced climate infrastructure, innovative financial technologies, and robust carbon pricing mechanisms, we can create a sustainable path forward in the fight against climate change. The integration of these approaches will be essential for achieving the emission reductions needed to safeguard our planet for future generations.

The chapter is organized as follows: Sect. 8.2 presents IPCC findings on the current state of the climate and recent reports and key projections. Section 8.3 discusses the rationale behind carbon pricing, including internalizing the external costs of emissions and economic theories supporting carbon pricing mechanisms. It highlights the two key mechanisms: carbon taxes and cap-and-trade systems and the advantages and limitations of each approach. Section 8.4 focuses on the role of Fintech in carbon pricing and describes the use of blockchain technology in carbon pricing. Section 8.5 details the implementation of blockchain in a case study.

8.2 Climate Science and the Imperative for Carbon Pricing

Climate change science examines the factors contributing to climate alterations, focusing on anthropogenic greenhouse gas (GHG) emissions, their impacts, and mitigation strategies. Human activities, particularly the burning of fossil fuels, deforestation, and industrial processes, have significantly increased GHGs like CO_2, methane, and nitrous oxide in the atmosphere (IPCC, 2023). These gases trap heat, leading to global warming and altering weather patterns, sea levels, and ecosystems. Chapters 1–3 discuss the science as well as the impact of climate change.

The Intergovernmental Panel on Climate Change (IPCC) reports emphasize the severity of current climate trends. These assessments, including the Sixth Assessment Report (AR6), highlight the unprecedented levels of atmospheric GHGs and the resultant temperature rise (IPCC, 2023). The reports project significant future warming and associated impacts such as more frequent and severe weather events, loss of biodiversity, and risks to human health and food security. The scientific community overwhelmingly agrees on the urgency of immediate, large-scale actions to reduce GHG emissions and limit global warming to 1.5 °C above pre-industrial levels (IPCC, 2018). This consensus underscores the critical need for comprehensive policies and international cooperation to mitigate climate change and adapt to its inevitable impacts.

8.2.1 Current State of the Climate

Using the data from the Emissions Database for Global Atmospheric Research (Edgar), global CO2 emissions by sector over time are plotted to analyze trends (Crippa et al., 2023). Figure 8.1 displays the world CO2 emissions by sector over time, from around 1970 to approximately 2022. The left axis measures CO2 emissions in gigatons per year. There are several sectoral trends over time. Overall, there has been a general increase in CO2 emissions over the years across all sectors. The power industry sector appears to have grown the most in terms of emissions, expanding significantly and contributing the largest portion by 2022. Industrial combustion and waste have also experienced moderate increases. The agriculture sector, while increasing slightly, has remained relatively consistent compared to the other sectors, suggesting that its emissions have not grown as dramatically as those of other industries.

In addition, the right axis of Fig. 8.1 measures tons of CO2 per capita GDP per year, with the red dashed line indicating per capita emissions over the period. This line shows fluctuations with a general upward trend starting from around 2005. This suggests that while emissions have grown in absolute terms, the efficiency of emissions relative to economic output (GDP) has improved, meaning that for each unit of economic output, fewer emissions are being produced over time. This

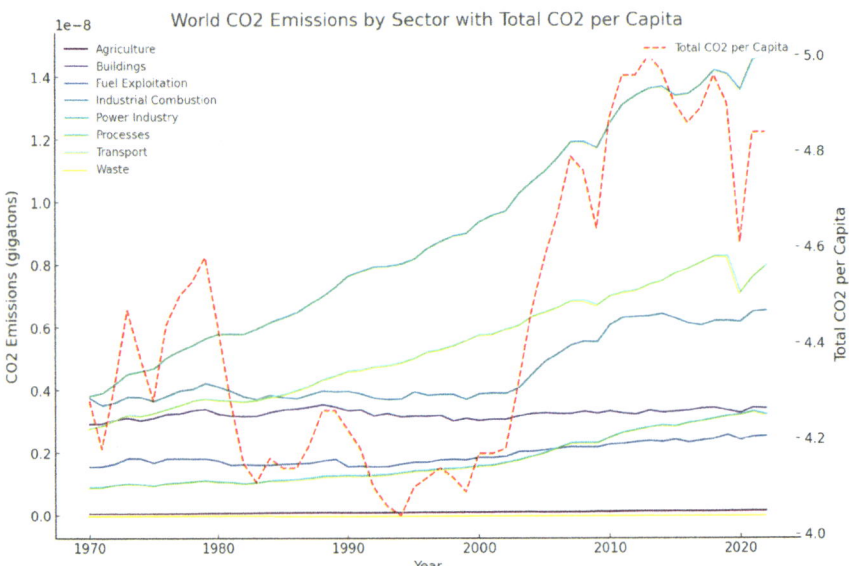

Fig. 8.1 This graph shows the CO2 emissions by various sectors in gigatons on the primary Y-axis (left); Agriculture, Buildings, Fuel Exploitation, Industrial Combustion, Power Industry, Processes, Transport, and Waste. The secondary Y-axis (right) displays the total CO2 emissions per capita. Data from https://edgar.jrc.ec.europa.eu/climate_change. EDGAR products are licensed under a Creative Commons Attribution (CC BY 4.0) license

8.2 Climate Science and the Imperative for Carbon Pricing

may reflect a decoupling of emissions from economic growth, potentially due to advancements in technology, energy efficiency improvements, or a shift toward less carbon-intensive industries (Hubacek et al., 2021; Schandl et al., 2016). It's also possible that there have been changes in the calculation or reporting of these values that contribute to this trend.

Figure 8.2a and 8.2b shows the top emitting countries in 1991 and 2020, respectively. This figure can be compared to infer the state of the world in terms of CO_2 emissions. The most important trend is the rise of China and India, the world's most populous countries. In 1991, China was the second-highest emitter, with emissions just over half that of the United States. By 2020, China's emissions had increased significantly, surpassing the United States to become the highest emitter by a considerable margin. India, which had emissions comparable to Ukraine and Canada in 1991, saw a significant increase by 2020, becoming the third-highest emitter. This reflects India's rapid industrialization and economic growth over these three decades.

Although the United States has been overtaken by China, it remains a major emitter. Both Russia and Japan have seen decreases in their emissions. Russia, in particular, has gone from being a close third to the United States and China in 1991, to a distant fourth in 2020, likely due to the post-Soviet economic contraction and subsequent changes in industrial activities. Germany's emissions have decreased, reflecting the country's efforts toward sustainability and renewable energy. Ukraine shows a dramatic decrease, which can be associated with the decline in heavy industry following the dissolution of the Soviet Union.

The lower panel of Fig. 8.2 shows that the 2020 emissions are more concentrated among the top two emitters (China and the United States) compared to 1991 (top panel of Fig. 8.2), when the emissions were more evenly distributed among several top-emitting countries. The trends shown are indicative of broad economic and political changes, including the rapid development of emerging economies, the deindustrialization of some developed nations, and international efforts to combat climate change through more efficient technologies and renewable energy sources.

To summarize, there is a clear upward trend in global emissions, with developing countries increasing their share of emissions as they grow economically. Advanced economies have either plateaued or slightly decreased in emissions, potentially due to efficiency gains, economic shifts, or deindustrialization. The global challenge is to balance economic growth, particularly in developing countries, with the need to reduce emissions to mitigate climate change. The challenges in tackling emission reduction include managing growth with sustainability; developing countries need to grow economically but must do so in a sustainable way. Energy transition must take place; there is a need for a massive shift from fossil fuels to renewable energy sources to reduce emissions from the power and transport sectors. Technological innovations in energy, agriculture, and manufacturing are required, alongside investments in sustainable infrastructure. Climate change is a global issue requiring coordinated international efforts and policies.

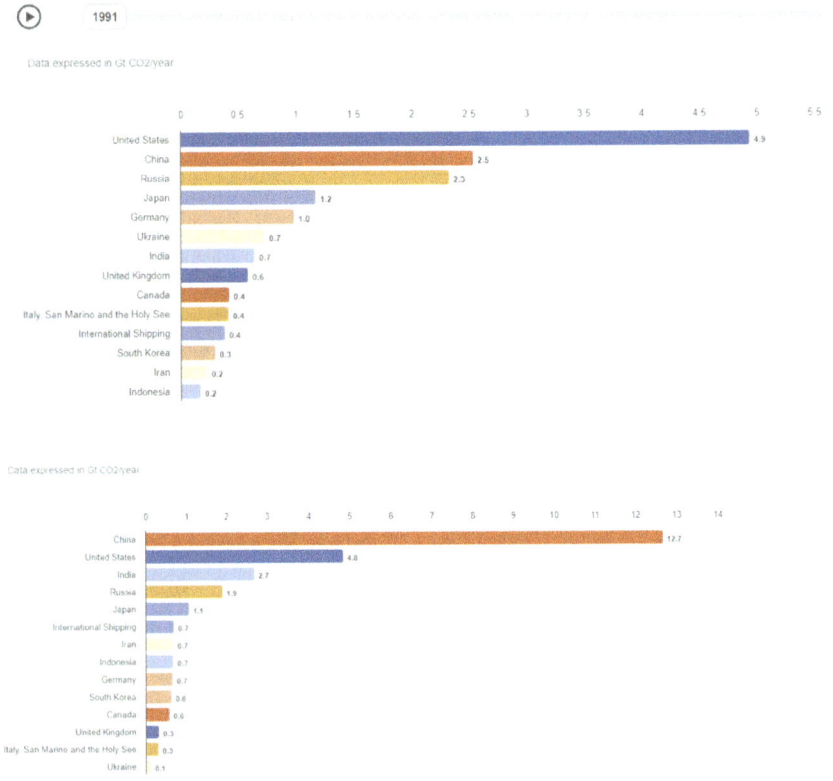

Fig. 8.2 Top CO2 emitting countries and international shipping in the years 1991 (top panel) and 2020 (lower panel) Data from Edgar. https://edgar.jrc.ec.europa.eu/country_profile. EDGAR products are licensed under a Creative Commons Attribution (CC BY 4.0) license

8.2.2 Future Projections of Emissions and Climate

The International Energy Agency (IEA) published the report *World Energy Outlook 2023*. The IEA (2023) proposed the integrated framework of the Global Energy and Climate Model (GEC Model), which is used to explore various future scenarios, each of which is built on a different set of underlying assumptions about how the energy system might evolve over time. It should be noted that these scenarios are not predictions and do not contain a single view about what the long-term future might hold. The following are the models:

- Net-Zero Emissions (NZE) by 2050 Scenario outlines a pathway for the global energy sector to achieve net-zero CO2 emissions by 2050 without relying on emissions reductions outside the energy sector. It aims for universal access to electricity and clean cooking by 2030 and was fully updated in 2023.

8.2 Climate Science and the Imperative for Carbon Pricing

- Announced Pledges Scenario (APS) assumes that all climate commitments made by governments and industries worldwide by the end of August 2023, including Nationally Determined Contributions (NDCs) and long-term net-zero targets, as well as targets for electricity access and clean cooking, will be fully met on time.
- Stated Policies Scenario (SPS) reflects current policy settings based on a detailed sector-by-sector and country-by-country assessment of energy-related policies in place as of the end of August 2023, along with those under development. It also considers currently planned manufacturing capacities for clean energy technologies.

The overall trend shown in Fig. 8.3 (left panel) is that CO_2 emissions in IEA scenarios vs. IPCC 1.5 °C scenarios start decreasing significantly after 2025 in both highlighted scenarios, with the green line (Net-Zero Emissions by 2050 Scenario) reaching net zero around 2050 and going slightly negative afterward, indicating net-negative emissions. The yellow line (Announced Pledges Scenario) shows a more gradual decrease, not reaching net zero by 2050. The right panel shows CO_2 emissions in IEA scenarios vs. IPCC 2.0 °C scenarios. While overall trend is similar, the decrease in CO_2 emissions is slower compared to the 1.5 °C scenario, but both highlighted scenarios still show a downward trend. The green line approaches net zero by 2050 but does not go negative, while the yellow line again shows a slower decrease and does not reach net zero by 2050. These data plots compare the downward trend of global emissions if certain emissions reductions are made under NZE, APS, and SPS scenarios. This leads into the next section where the rationale for carbon pricing is discussed.

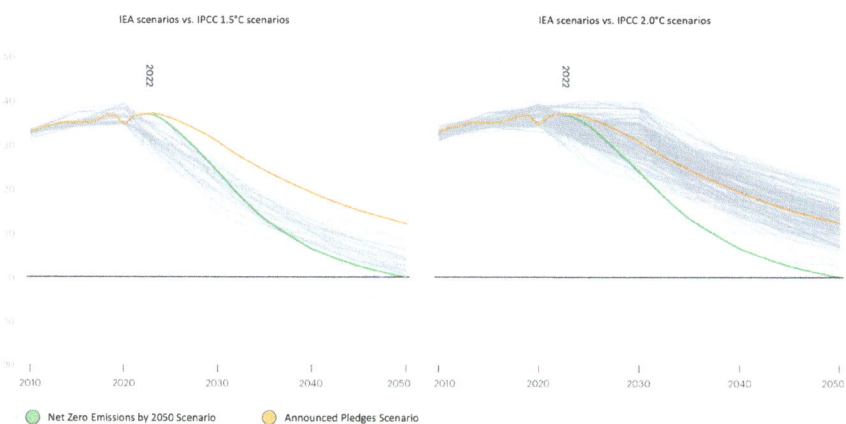

Fig. 8.3 Left Graph displays IEA scenarios vs. IPCC 1.5 °C scenarios: The Y-axis represents the amount of CO_2 emissions in gigatons. The green line represents the "Net-Zero Emissions by 2050 Scenario." The yellow line represents the "Announced Pledges Scenario." The gray lines represent various IPCC scenarios included in the comparison. Right Graph displays IEA scenarios vs. IPCC 2.0 °C scenarios. IEA. License: CC BY 4.0

8.3 Economics of Carbon Pricing

The concept of carbon pricing emerges from the understanding that CO2 and other greenhouse gases contribute to the greenhouse effect, trapping heat in the Earth's atmosphere and leading to global warming and climate change (Boyce, 2019). Carbon pricing aims to make the polluter pay for the external costs of carbon emissions, which are not accounted for in the market price of fossil fuels. Economists focus on externalities, which are the unintended impacts of decisions on others. Climate change represents a negative externality, where the production or consumption of a product can have harmful effects on others (Nordhaus, 2019). For example, burning coal for electricity releases CO2 into the atmosphere, contributing to global warming, yet neither the electricity producer nor the consumer bears the cost of this impact. This negative externality extends to future generations due to the delay between the emission of greenhouse gases and the resultant warming of the planet.

8.3.1 Economics of Carbon Pricing—Carbon Taxes and Cap-and-Trade Systems

There are two primary mechanisms for carbon pricing: cap-and-trade systems and carbon taxes (Stavins, 2019). Cap-and-trade systems establish a limit (cap) on the total allowable emissions for a specific sector or jurisdiction. The government issues tradable emission permits to emitters, allowing them to buy and sell permits within a designated market. This approach incentivizes entities that can reduce emissions below their allocated permits to sell their surplus permits to others who require additional allowances. This market-based approach aims to achieve emission-reduction goals at the lowest possible cost, as businesses with lower emission-reduction costs can sell permits to those with higher costs. However, cap-and-trade systems require careful design and management to avoid market manipulation and ensure that the cap is stringent enough to drive significant emission reductions.

A recent study (Narassimhan et al., 2018) evaluated eight emissions trading systems (ETSs) operating at the supranational, national, and sub-national levels in seven geographies—the EU, Switzerland, the Regional Greenhouse Gas Initiative (RGGI) and California in the US, Québec province in Canada, New Zealand, the Republic of Korea, and China's seven city and provincial pilots. The study used five criteria: environmental effectiveness, economic efficiency, market management, revenue management, and stakeholder engagement. The study emphasized that numerous ETSs appear to target a "dual dividend" approach to emission reduction. This strategy involves allocating a significant portion of the generated revenue back into activities that achieve additional emission cuts. The study also highlighted the importance of data availability since the economic efficiency and stakeholder engagement practices could not be gauged. On the other hand, a carbon tax directly sets a price on carbon by charging emitters a fixed amount for each

8.3 Economics of Carbon Pricing

ton of CO2 emitted. This method offers simplicity and predictability, allowing for straightforward implementation and administration.

However, a challenge with carbon taxes is setting the price high enough to effect change without causing economic disruption, especially in industries highly dependent on fossil fuels. The concept of carbon pricing in this context exemplifies a Pigouvian tax (Hawkins, 2020; Stern, 2007). These taxes are imposed on activities that generate negative externalities, affecting third parties not involved in the economic transaction. The primary goal of Pigouvian taxes is to rectify market outcomes by aligning private costs with social costs, effectively reducing or eliminating the negative externalities (Rezai et al., 2012). Real-world examples include congestion charges in cities like Singapore and London (Selmoune et al., 2020; Singichetti et al., 2021). New York City's congestion pricing tolls began on June 30, 2024; passenger vehicles pay $15 during peak hours.[1] The goals of the program are to reduce traffic and travel time, reduce air pollution and emissions, and improve quality of life.[2] Economists have long viewed climate change as a negative externality problem, advocating for carbon taxes to fully price greenhouse gas emissions.

Additionally, the endorsement of a carbon tax is rooted in its potential to enhance economic efficiency, decrease the production and consumption of fossil fuels, bolster government revenues, and establish restrictions on imports from countries such as China and India through a carbon border adjustment mechanism, as outlined by Costello (2024). The carbon tax has more visible and direct costs for consumers, which makes it a harder sell to the public.

Two concepts, spillover effects and social cost of carbon are relevant in this context. Nobel Prize winners in economics, Nordhaus (2019, 2021) and Romer, awarded the Nobel Prize in Economics in 2018 (along with William Nordhaus), explored how certain actions or innovations can have unintended impacts on others, called spillover effects or externalities (Romer, 1987; Jones, 2019). Carbon emissions from one place spread globally, contributing to climate change, and affecting everyone, now and in the future. Spatial externalities are significant as each region can potentially influence and be influenced by all other regions, not just its immediate neighbors (Fischer, 2011, 2018). Chapter 5 examines spatial dependencies in spatial econometrics. These externalities can have worldwide and lasting effects, and markets alone might not address the negative consequences efficiently. Therefore, Nordhaus and Romer argued that government intervention is necessary to manage these impacts.

The social cost of carbon attempts to quantify the economic damages associated with an additional ton of CO2 emissions. This estimation incorporates various impacts, such as health care costs, damage to property from extreme weather events, and agricultural losses. Nobel laureate William Nordhaus was recognized for his work in integrating the social cost of carbon into macroeconomic models, proposing methodologies for estimating this cost and its implications for policymaking (Nordhaus, 2017). The integrated assessment models (IAMs) enable simulations on how

---

[1] https://www.nytimes.com/interactive/2024/07/01/upshot/congestion-pricing.html.
[2] https://portal.311.nyc.gov/article/?kanumber=KA-03612.

the economy and climate would co-evolve in the future under alternative assumptions about the workings of nature and the market economy, including relevant policies. His models address questions about the desirability of different global scenarios and specific policy interventions. Different IAMs are constructed on diverse methodological approaches; some are scenario simulation models, some are computable general equilibrium (CGE) models, and others are dynamic optimization models (Nikas et al., 2019). However, if the tax revenue is returned to citizens, the net financial impact could be neutral, therefore incentivizing people to reduce their carbon footprint as they can save money by lowering their emissions.

Selecting the appropriate level for carbon pricing and deciding on the mechanism to use involves considering multiple factors including environmental effectiveness, economic efficiency, and equity concerns. The choice between a cap-and-trade system and a carbon tax can depend on the specific goals and circumstances of each jurisdiction, as both have their advantages and limitations. Both systems face challenges including political resistance, the complexity of implementation, and ensuring fairness across economic sectors and among populations, particularly those most vulnerable to climate change impacts.

The scope of carbon pricing policies—determining which sectors and sources of emissions are covered—is crucial for maximizing their environmental impact. Revenue generated from carbon pricing can be used in various ways, such as funding renewable energy projects, compensating affected communities, or returning it to citizens through dividends. This aspect of policy design is significant for ensuring that the transition to a low-carbon economy is just and equitable, particularly for communities disproportionately affected by climate change and pollution.

Both systems (ETS and taxes) face challenges, including political resistance, the complexity of implementation, and ensuring fairness across economic sectors and among populations, particularly those most vulnerable to climate change impacts (Stavins, 2020). Thus necessitating careful consideration of policy design to balance economic, environmental, and social goals. Ultimately, the challenge of carbon pricing lies in balancing the urgency of climate action with the need for economic and social fairness.

By putting a price on carbon emissions, society can make visible the hidden costs of fossil fuel consumption, incentivizing the shift toward a more sustainable and equitable future. As the global community grapples with the complexities of climate change mitigation, carbon pricing stands out as a critical tool in the arsenal of policy options, offering a path forward in the transition to a cleaner, healthier planet. In conclusion, while carbon pricing and cap-and-trade systems are not silver bullets, they are essential tools in the global effort to reduce emissions and mitigate climate change. By financially incentivizing the reduction of carbon emissions, these policies aim to steer economies toward a more sustainable and low-carbon future. The success of these mechanisms, however, depends on their design and implementation and the political will to enforce them.

8.3.2 Rationale Behind Carbon Pricing

Carbon pricing tackles climate change by making polluters pay for the environmental damage (CO_2 emissions) they cause. This economic pressure incentivizes a shift toward cleaner energy by making fossil fuels more expensive. Businesses reduce emissions to lower costs, driving innovation and a transition to a low-carbon economy. Environmentally, carbon pricing aims to curb CO_2 emissions, mitigating climate change's impacts like extreme weather and rising sea levels. The oldest operational carbon pricing scheme in the world was introduced via carbon taxes implemented in 1990 in Finland, Poland, Sweden, Norway, Denmark, and the Netherlands (Thisted & Thisted, 2020). This system focused on reducing emissions from industry and energy production sectors. However, setting the right price is crucial to balance economic disruption with effective emissions reduction (Ball, 2018; Klenert et al., 2018; Kolstad, 2020; Verbruggen, 2021).

Economically, as previously highlighted, carbon pricing addresses the issue of negative externalities, in which the environmental costs of carbon emissions are not borne by the emitter but by society at large. This misalignment results in a market failure where there is an overproduction and consumption of carbon-intensive goods. By putting a price on carbon, either through a carbon tax or a cap-and-trade system, carbon pricing seeks to internalize these external costs, reflecting the true cost of carbon emissions in the price of fossil fuels and goods that embody them. This incentivizes consumers and businesses to reduce consumption and invest in cleaner alternatives, fostering a shift toward a more sustainable economy (Stiglitz et al., 2017).

Carbon pricing also leverages the power of the market to find the most efficient ways to reduce emissions. It sets a clear, predictable price on carbon, providing a continuous economic signal for businesses and consumers to reduce their carbon footprint. By doing so, it can stimulate innovation and investment in renewable energy and energy efficiency, driving down the costs of these technologies over time. This can lead to significant environmental benefits, including reductions in air and water pollution, which have direct positive impacts on public health and biodiversity (World Bank & Ecofys, 2018). The revenue generated from carbon pricing mechanisms can further be used to fund renewable energy projects, improve infrastructure, or be returned to citizens through dividends or tax cuts, thereby potentially offsetting the regressive effects of carbon pricing on low-income households (Metcalf & Weisbach, 2009).

From an environmental standpoint, carbon pricing is a direct and potent tool for reducing GHG emissions. Making carbon-intensive activities more expensive naturally curtails the demand for fossil fuels, leading to a reduction in carbon emissions. This is critical for meeting the global emissions targets set under the Paris Agreement to limit global warming to well below 2 °C above pre-industrial levels. A well-designed carbon pricing system ensures that the environmental costs of emissions are factored into economic decisions, guiding economies toward a low-carbon transition in line with climate goals (Nordhaus, 2015).

In summary, the rationale behind carbon pricing as a strategy for mitigating climate change is deeply rooted in its ability to correct market failures by internalizing the external costs of carbon emissions. Its economic implications are profound, incentivizing the shift toward a more sustainable, low-carbon economy while fostering innovation and efficiency. Environmentally, it offers a straightforward, effective mechanism for reducing GHG emissions, essential for combating climate change and protecting the planet for future generations. As such, carbon pricing is not just an economic policy but a critical tool for ensuring environmental sustainability and social justice.

> **How to price carbon? Science fiction and reality can merge**
>
> Delton B. Chen (2019) proposed a financial incentive that would be offered for mitigated global carbon, facilitated through a novel financial instrument known as the "carbon currency" or "carbon coin," made famous in Stanley Robinson's (2020) Sci-Fi book "Ministry for the Future." Chen's Global Carbon Reward (GCR) presents an innovative approach that underpins policy by both a conceptual framework and a theoretical model and suggests establishment of a parallel economy dedicated to climate mitigation efforts. The global carbon reward initiative would incentivize actions that reduce emissions or remove atmospheric CO_2, complementing, rather than overhauling existing systems. Chen noted that this economy would function analogously to photosynthesis, absorbing carbon and rebalancing civilization's footprint.
>
> The carbon currency would not be money, but an asset awarded entities engaged in carbon reduction or sequestration. An international authority would set and enforce relevant standards. Entities demonstrating carbon reduction would make agreements, lasting up to 100 years, ensuring sustained commitment to mitigation. Upon verification of CO_2 removal, entities would receive carbon currency rewards from the enforcing authority. The currency could be traded on exchange markets for local currencies, thus transforming mitigation to capital.
>
> It would be critical to maintain the value of the carbon currency through strategies such as "carbon quantitative easing," by which central banks would purchase the currency, aiming to establish a floor price calibrated to meet international objectives such as those of the Paris Agreement. This approach would help stabilize the currency's value to ensure its effectiveness as an incentive for climate mitigation.
>
> Chen's proposal represents a shift towards a monetary policy framework for climate action, diverging from traditional fiscal measures like carbon taxes. This approach seeks to overcome the limitations of government-led initiatives, which are often stymied by disagreements and aversion to taxation. By leveraging monetary policy and financial markets, the global carbon reward policy would offer a comprehensive, long-term solution that aligns economic incentives with environmental sustainability.

8.3.3 Global Momentum and Challenges

Carbon pricing is gaining traction worldwide, with nearly 70 countries, states, and provinces implementing policies by 2022. The European Union, California, some northeastern US states, and China have cap-and-trade programs. British Columbia in Canada has a carbon tax with rebates to help residents adjust. These initiatives raise the cost of fossil fuels like coal, oil, and natural gas based on their carbon emissions, much like tobacco taxes discourage smoking. This approach incentivizes consumers and businesses to switch to cleaner alternatives such as renewable energy and electric vehicles. While carbon pricing can be initially contentious and costly, it promises a cost-effective path to reducing emissions and combating climate change by leveraging market mechanisms to find the most efficient solutions.

Figure 8.4 shows carbon taxes and ETSs implemented or under consideration. "Implemented" means that compliance obligations have been formally adopted by the government of the indicated country through legislation and are in force and enforced. "Under development" means the government is actively working toward implementation of a specific carbon pricing instrument and a mandate may have been established, but regulated entities do not yet face compliance obligations, and this has been formally confirmed by official government sources. "Under consideration" means the government has announced its intention to work toward the implementation of a carbon pricing instrument and this has been formally confirmed by official government sources. An "Abolished" instrument is one that has previously met the definition of "Implemented" but is no longer in place. The UK, as shown in Fig. 8.4, left (Brexit) the EU ETS but electricity generators in Northern Ireland are still subject to obligations.

Critics often argue that carbon pricing is politically unviable, but evidence suggests otherwise. In 2019, Canada, a major oil producer, enacted a national carbon fee and dividend program that increases annually. The European Union has also shown strong commitment, driving its carbon price above $100 per ton of CO_2. California covers around 80% of its carbon pollution with a rising price. In early 2023, Washington State joined these efforts, aiming to reduce emissions by 95% by 2050. Eleven

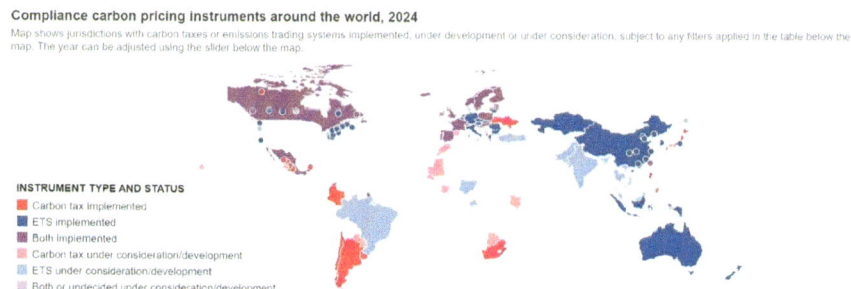

Fig. 8.4 Carbon tax and Emission Trading Scheme (ETS) pricing instruments are considered under the categories implemented or under consideration or under development *Source* World Bank

Fig. 8.5 Carbon pricing around the world in 2024; this heat map shows the level of the main price set by emission trading systems or carbon taxes in each jurisdiction (U$/tCO2e). The price ranges from $0.46 to $167 in Scandinavia in 2024. *Source* World Bank

northeastern states participate in the Regional Greenhouse Gas Initiative, which sets a carbon price on power sector emissions (Fig. 8.5).

Carbon pricing has gained traction and is now implemented in nearly 50 countries. Notably, the EU's trading system has seen carbon prices rise to 90 euros per ton, Canada is phasing in a carbon price of 170 Canadian dollars per ton, and China has introduced an emissions trading variant. Despite this progress, only a quarter of global greenhouse gases are currently subject to carbon pricing, with an average global price of $5 per ton. To meet temperature goals, a global price upward of $80 per ton by 2030 is needed.

Economists believe that a global carbon price of $75 per ton by 2030 could limit global warming to a manageable two degrees Celsius. Public opinion in the United States supports taxing carbon polluters to fund the necessary green transition. The feasibility and effectiveness of carbon pricing are well-documented, and with strong citizen advocacy, widespread implementation is achievable.

8.3.4 The Case of Canada

As of April 1, 2024, Canada's federal carbon tax is set at $80 per ton of CO2e, with an annual increase of $15 until it reaches $170 per ton by 2030.[3] This tax is

---

[3] https://www.energyhub.org/carbon-tax-rebate/.

8.3 Economics of Carbon Pricing

applied in Alberta, Manitoba, New Brunswick, Newfoundland and Labrador, Nova Scotia, Ontario, Prince Edward Island, and Saskatchewan, and partially in Nunavut and Yukon Territory. British Columbia, Quebec, and the Northwest Territories have their own carbon pricing programs. In 2024, the average Canadian qualifying individual received an annual carbon tax rebate of $516.92, while the average family of four received $1219 per year. In provinces fully subject to the federal carbon tax shown in Fig. 8.6, rebates are distributed quarterly according to the federal government schedule. In other regions (British Columbia, Northwest Territories, Nunavut, Quebec, and Yukon Territory), rebate payments are managed by their respective provincial and territorial governments.

Individuals in Alberta currently receive the highest carbon tax rebate ($900/yr) and individuals in Nunavut receive the lowest carbon tax rebate ($310/yr). There is no carbon tax in Quebec.

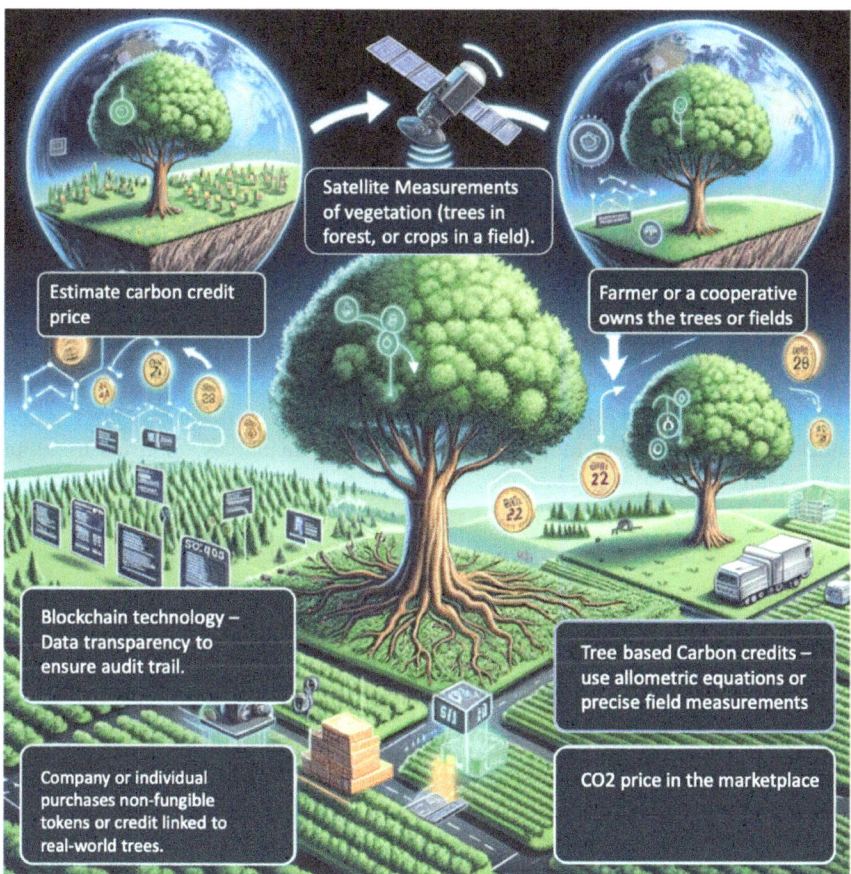

Fig. 8.6 The Fintech landscape showing the role of geospatial technology and blockchain technology

Every province and territory in Canada is subject to a carbon pricing mechanism. Some jurisdictions have developed their own programs, while others use one or both of the federal programs. In total, there are 12 different carbon pricing mechanisms in Canada. This includes two carbon tax programs, nine baseline and credit systems, and one cap-and-trade system. Below is the list of programs by province and territory.

- Federal Program: Applies to provinces without their own carbon pricing.
- Alberta: High carbon tax rebate and a baseline and credit system.
- British Columbia: Known for its comprehensive carbon tax program.
- Manitoba: Uses both federal carbon tax and a baseline and credit system.
- New Brunswick: Baseline and credit system in place.
- Newfoundland and Labrador: Baseline and credit system.
- Northwest Territories: Federal carbon tax program.
- Nova Scotia: Previously had a cap-and-trade system.
- Nunavut: Lowest carbon tax rebate and baseline and credit system.
- Ontario: Baseline and credit system.
- Prince Edward Island: Baseline and credit system.
- Québec: Cap-and-trade system, no carbon tax.
- Saskatchewan: Baseline and credit system.
- Yukon Territory: Baseline and credit system.

8.3.5 The US, the EU, and Japan

Private sector investment is crucial, with the majority of the necessary investment ideally coming from this sector. Policies like the US Inflation Reduction Act (IRA) can significantly reduce emissions but are less efficient than carbon pricing due to their narrower focus and higher fiscal costs. The EU's robust carbon pricing and border carbon adjustment mechanism create strong incentives for firms to adopt clean technologies.

Ira
An alternative approach to achieving emission reductions is through subsidies for renewable energy, which aim to enhance air quality, mitigate climate change, and generate new employment opportunities. However, their costs are often embedded within the larger government budget, making them less apparent. Additionally, the public tends to favor direct financial incentives from the government, such as rebates for heat pumps or tax credits for electric vehicles, over additional costs imposed on fossil fuel usage. The IRA introduces subsidies for electric vehicles with specific requirements. To qualify, vehicles must be assembled in North America, and certain components must be sourced from nations with which the United States has favorable trade agreements, with these requirements becoming more stringent over time.[4] Starting in 2024, any battery components originating from countries like China or

---

[4] https://siepr.stanford.edu/publications/policy-brief/clean-vehicle-tax-credit-new-industrial-policy-and-its-impact.

Russia will disqualify a vehicle from eligibility, with similar restrictions on critical minerals beginning in 2025.

European Union's Carbon Border Adjustment Mechanism (CBAM)
The European Union's CBAM is an instrument designed to assign an appropriate cost to the carbon emissions associated with the production of carbon-intensive goods imported into the EU. This mechanism aims to promote cleaner industrial production practices in non-EU countries by ensuring that imported goods bear a carbon cost equivalent to that of domestically produced goods. The CBAM is structured to comply with World Trade Organization regulations.

The CBAM functions by verifying that a carbon price has been applied to the emissions embedded in certain imported goods, thereby aligning the carbon cost of imports with that of domestic products. This alignment ensures that the EU's climate goals remain intact and are not compromised by imports from countries with less stringent carbon pricing mechanisms.

The CBAM is set to be fully implemented in its definitive regime starting in 2026, following a transitional phase from 2023 to 2025. This phased introduction coincides with the gradual elimination of free allowances under the EU Emissions Trading System (ETS), thereby supporting the decarbonization of EU industries.

Japan
Japan is introducing carbon pricing, a scheme that imposes a cost on carbon dioxide emitters, as part of its efforts to achieve carbon neutrality by 2050 (Mitsubishi, 2024; NRI, 2024). In February 2023, the Cabinet approved the Basic Policy on Green Transformation (GX), and on May 12, the Diet passed the GX Promotion Act (formally known as the Act for Promoting a Smooth Transition to a Decarbonized Growth-Oriented Industrial Structure). This initiative marks Japan's commitment to developing and deploying technologies for carbon neutrality, funded by GX Economic Transition Bonds, which aim to raise approximately ¥20 trillion over the next decade. Additionally, the Tokyo Stock Exchange (TSE) began trading carbon credits, which is a crucial component of Japan's strategy to combat climate change. As the world's fifth-largest carbon dioxide emitter, Japan is joining other Asian nations in establishing a carbon pricing mechanism and emissions trading system. The country aims to reduce emissions by 46% from 2013 levels by 2030 and achieve net-zero emissions by 2050.

8.4 The Role of Fintech in Carbon Pricing—Blockchain and Digital MRV

Financial technology, or Fintech, offers a suite of tools to mobilize capital and accelerate the transition to a low-carbon economy. Climate Fintech companies, for instance, develop solutions for data-driven carbon accounting, facilitating investments in renewable energy projects and streamlining carbon offset markets. These solutions can unlock new sources of funding, connect investors with sustainable projects, and ultimately accelerate the pace of decarbonization. However, existing carbon markets face challenges. One critical issue is ensuring the integrity and effectiveness of carbon offsets—tradable units representing a reduction in carbon emissions. This is where a specific technology, Blockchain, holds significant promise.

Blockchain is a decentralized, distributed ledger technology that records transactions across multiple computers in a way that is secure, transparent, and resistant to modification. It allows information to be stored in blocks that are linked together in a chain, hence the name "blockchain" (Wikipedia[5]). Blockchain technology was invented by an individual or group of individuals using the pseudonym Satoshi Nakamoto in 2008 to serve as the public transaction ledger of the cryptocurrency Bitcoin. While the true identity of Satoshi Nakamoto remains unknown, their invention of blockchain technology has had a significant impact beyond the realm of cryptocurrencies.

Blockchain technology offers several features that can help combat greenwashing in carbon trading. By providing a secure and transparent platform for trading carbon credits, blockchain can enhance the effectiveness of carbon markets. It ensures the integrity of transactions and the authenticity of carbon credits, encouraging companies to invest in carbon offsetting projects. Important areas of research are described below.

Increased Transparency: Immutable Record: Blockchain creates an unalterable record of carbon credits (Chen, 2018; Schulz & Feist, 2021). This allows anyone to track a credit's history, from its origin (project that generated it) to its current owner and retirement. This transparency makes it difficult for companies to misrepresent the source or impact of their carbon offsets.

Data Integrity: Blockchain uses cryptography to verify transactions, ensuring the data on carbon credits is tamper-proof (Khatoon et al., 2019). This reduces the risk of companies manipulating data to inflate the effectiveness of their carbon offset purchases.

---

[5] https://en.wikipedia.org/wiki/blockchain.

8.4 The Role of Fintech in Carbon Pricing—Blockchain and Digital MRV

Expert in Focus: Nick Zwaneveld

Nick Zwaneveld is the CEO of Coorest, based in Rotterdam, Netherlands. He is also a DeFi consultant, crypto investor, and trader. Coorest offers web3 solutions for traceable and verifiable CO2 compensation. By integrating satellite data on-chain, both businesses and individuals can trust the high-quality CO2 compensation provided by Coorest's decentralized platform. In addition to its environmental benefits, Coorest strives to make a positive social impact. The certified Coorest Carbon Standard enables smaller green projects and farmers to join the Coorest platform at no cost, allowing them to sell their CO2 and generate additional revenue to reinvest in their business and community. Coorest issues NFT in the form of CoorestTree tokens ("NFTrees") and Coorest's Carbon tokens ($CCO2) in proportion to the characteristics of their project and the CO2 absorbed by it.

The Tokens are part of the voluntary Market and can be operated, sold, and/or bought within the Coorest Dapp. Coorest is the first certified standard for blockchain-based CO2 compensation powered by smart contracts and satellite.

Expert Interview Nick Zwaneveld

At this moment, I primarily observe the convergence of multiple technologies. For instance, Floodlight Invest is leveraging satellite technologies for precise measurements, which I see as the starting point. These measurements are then translated into value through tokenization, where data around an asset, particularly a nature-based one, is converted into something valuable represented by a token. With the emergence of AI technology, we are entering a parabolic phase of development. AI simplifies platform development, concept building, and coding. It allows for AI-monitored measurements to be tokenized and transported globally. Blockchain technology, being borderless, eliminates barriers from traditional finance, particularly in developing countries. The convergence of monitoring, AI, and blockchain technology is propelling us into this accelerated development phase.

However, the carbon markets are currently in a difficult stage. They are highly political, with governments dictating the direction, unlike markets driven by natural supply and demand. This market, created to enforce environmental policies, is struggling. When it started over 20 years ago, few players and new technology led to monopolies, causing problems as many carbon credits are now inadequate. Efforts to correct this through blockchain technology and DRMRV face challenges due to the market's politicization and public skepticism. Current big lawsuits and potential scams exacerbate the difficulties, and I'm skeptical if blockchain alone can resolve these issues.

Blockchain must be combined with DRMRV because data verification is essential; without it, tokens are worthless. We are in a gray zone with uncertain outcomes. Efforts to combine data with tokens aim to enhance transparency and reliability, restoring trust in the market. However, the largest segment is the compliance market, involving trading emissions rights, which is unrelated to initiatives like tree planting. The compliance market is controlled by a few major players, creating a closed, cartel-like environment, with minimal retail participation.

Enhanced Traceability: Audit Trail: Every transaction involving a carbon credit is recorded on the blockchain, creating a complete audit trail (Al Sadawi et al., 2021; Ashley & Johnson, 2018). This allows stakeholders to track the use of credits and identify any potential inconsistencies between a company's reported carbon footprint and its offsetting activities.

Project Verification: Information about the project that generated the carbon credit can be linked to it on the blockchain (van der Gaast et al., 2018; Woo et al., 2021). This allows for independent verification of the project's legitimacy and its actual impact on emissions reduction.

Improved Accountability Through Smart Contracts: These self-executing contracts can be programmed to ensure specific criteria are met before a carbon credit is issued or traded (Duchenne, 2018). This can help enforce standards for project quality and ensure credits represent genuine emissions reductions.

Public Scrutiny: With a transparent and accessible record on the blockchain, companies' carbon offsetting activities are exposed to public scrutiny (RMI, 2022). This encourages companies to be more accountable and avoid misleading claims about their sustainability efforts.

Blockchain can't address all aspects of greenwashing.[6] Companies may still make misleading claims about their overall environmental impact, even if their carbon offsetting activities are legitimate (Kshetri, 2022). The effectiveness of blockchain in preventing greenwashing relies on the accuracy of data entered into the system. Robust verification processes are still needed to ensure the quality of project information linked to carbon credits.

Blockchain can play a crucial role in various aspects of the energy sector (World Bank, 2020) related to voluntary carbon markets. It can enable peer-to-peer energy trading, allowing consumers to produce, sell, and buy renewable energy directly among themselves without the need for traditional intermediaries. This democratizes energy distribution and can lead to increased adoption of renewable energy sources, thereby contributing to climate change mitigation. Some examples include:

Renewable Energy Trading: Blockchain enables the creation of decentralized energy markets, facilitating the trade of renewable energy between producers and consumers. This can significantly reduce the reliance on fossil fuels and contribute to reducing carbon emissions (Kang et al., 2018; Saxena et al., 2019; Thukral, 2021).

Smart Grids and Energy Management: Blockchain-based smart contracts can automate energy distribution and consumption processes in smart grids, optimizing energy use and reducing wastage. This contributes to more efficient and sustainable energy management (Kumari et al., 2020; Miglani et al., 2020; Xu et al., 2021).

Supply Chain Tracking: Blockchain can track the origin and lifecycle of energy resources, including renewable energy sources (Esmaeilian et al., 2020; Khanfar et al., 2021; Saberi et al., 2019). This enhances transparency and accountability in the energy supply chain, promoting sustainable practices.

Despite its potential, the integration of blockchain technology in the energy sector faces several challenges, including scalability (Schulz & Feist, 2021), energy consumption of blockchain operations (Chen, 2018), regulatory issues (Dorfleitner et al., 2021; World Bank, 2018), and the need for industry-wide standards (Espenan, 2023; Henly et al., 2018). Addressing these challenges requires ongoing research, development, and collaboration among stakeholders.

Future research should focus on developing more energy-efficient blockchain solutions, exploring hybrid models that combine public and private blockchains, and creating regulatory frameworks that support innovation while ensuring security and privacy. Moreover, interdisciplinary research combining blockchain with other emerging technologies, such as artificial intelligence (AI) and the Internet of Things (IoT), can unlock new possibilities for smart energy systems and climate change mitigation.

In conclusion, blockchain technology holds significant promise for transforming the energy sector by facilitating the transition to renewable energy, enhancing energy efficiency, and supporting climate change mitigation efforts. Continued innovation

---

[6] https://www.theguardian.com/environment/2023/jan/18/revealed-forest-carbon-offsets-biggest-provider-worthless-verra-aoe.

and collaboration across disciplines and industries are crucial for realizing this potential and addressing the challenges ahead.

8.5 Case Study—Floodlight

A Fintech startup, Floodlight Inc., brings carbon data "on-chain," a term used to describe bringing data onto the blockchain. These on-chain resources support smart contract solutions that revolutionize the way we approach climate change mitigation and adaptation. Through its decentralized oracle networks, Chainlink enables interoperable delivery of Floodlight's tracking and validation of greenhouse gas emissions data and environmental data, thereby strengthening robust digital Measurement, Reporting, and Verification (dMRV). Chainlink is a blockchain firm focused on working with various technical solutions to provide a comprehensive support for data "off chain" to be used "on-chain."

The data provided by floodlight serves as a powerful catalyst for automated carbon credit programs, reforestation through direct air capture, sustainable financing rates, parametric insurance, and more. Floodlight is serving Coorest for its carbon NFTree token—see interview with the CEO Nick Zwaneveld). Together, Chainlink and Floodlight are pushing climate markets into a new era of transparency and efficiency.

The overall approach to assessing the emissions is highlighted below.

1. Asset-level Measurement and Verification: Floodlight's satellite-based measurements of Greenhouse Gas emissions. By replacing traditional guesswork and manual surveys with direct, sensor measurements, it creates up-to-date emissions inventories swiftly, with unbiased accuracy. This will apply pre- and post-project when looking at development projects.
2. Blockchain Integration: Floodlight uses its BEACON solution to integrate blockchain technology, creating an immutable, transparent accounting of the carbon trail facilitating smart contracts. This enables Web 3.0 developers in accessing these data for usage in carbon accounting applications and auditing.
3. Collaborative Data Delivery: Floodlight is delivering greenhouse gas emissions data on-chain. In the near future, it supports a variety of programs, such as automated carbon credit programs, direct air capture reforestation, and sustainable financing rates.
4. Enhanced Transparency and Accountability: Floodlight is committed to driving transparency in climate markets by contradicting "greenwashing" and providing greater context to company disclosures. These will be through reports and dashboards delivered online and/or raw data.
5. Empowering Stakeholders: By providing precise, transparent, and unbiased data, Floodlight aims to enable businesses, analysts, and asset managers to accurately assess and benchmark its environmental footprint.

8.6 Conclusion

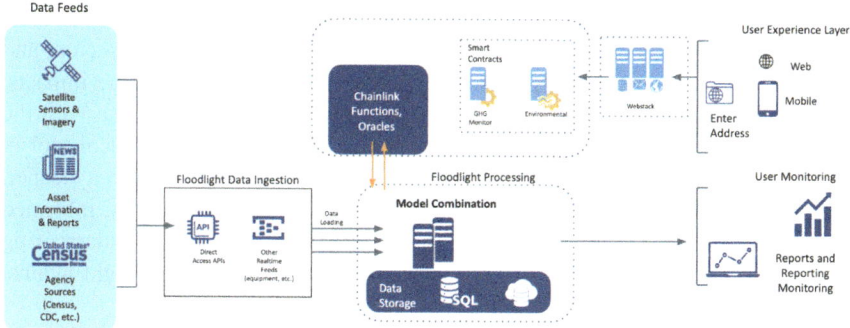

Fig. 8.7 Floodlight methodology for blockchain

As described in Fig. 8.7, the first step is data collection. Most of the sensor data arrives from satellite data collection and analysis. Advanced satellite technology is used to capture raw greenhouse gas emissions data (including CO_2, methane, and nitrous) from targeted assets. The satellite technology also collects data on flooding, natural hazards, and the biodiversity impact of the facilities under observation. These are combined with known asset information, such as ownership and parcel information.

Following the collection phase, the captured data is adjusted to specific asset locations, providing a comprehensive pre- and post-view of the emissions for a particular address or development project. Data is then accessed via smart contract methods to provide real-time data access. A Chainlink Oracle is a blockchain server that is set up to allow smart contracts to access data feeds from anywhere. The Oracle can effectively interact with our blockchain-stored data; this involves adjusting the Oracle's data call functions and ensuring that data retrieved from the blockchain is accurately represented when delivered to end-users.

Then the data is accessed by outside firms. One such firm is Coorest, a startup focused on matching CO_2 sequestration from trees to issue carbon tokens for each fraction of CO_2 sequestered. This allows farmers to put their field up to be monitored and tokens to be issued at regular intervals. These, in turn, can be accessed by investors globally to virtually "own" a fraction of one of the trees and the CO_2 tokens produced by the tree over time. These can be traded or re-invested, or used for offset planning.

8.6 Conclusion

In summary, carbon pricing is proving to be an effective tool in the fight against climate change. It is not only gaining global acceptance but also showing tangible results in reducing emissions and promoting cleaner energy alternatives. With continued support and political will, carbon pricing can play an important role in mitigating global warming.

Both carbon pricing mechanisms face challenges, including political resistance, complexity of implementation, and ensuring fairness across economic sectors and among populations, particularly those most vulnerable to climate change impacts. Ultimately, the challenge lies in balancing the urgency of climate action with the need for economic and social fairness. Carbon pricing stands as a critical tool in the arsenal of policy options, offering a path forward in the transition to a cleaner, healthier planet. However, its success depends on careful policy design, informed implementation, and strong political will to enforce these mechanisms, underscoring the importance of informed policymaking and public support in the fight against climate change.

Incorporating geospatial data into carbon pricing, particularly through innovations in Fintech, enhances the precision and transparency of these systems. For example, blockchain technology can integrate satellite data and vegetation indices to create more accurate and reliable carbon markets. This not only improves trust and accountability but also opens up new avenues for investment in sustainable projects.

As Fintech continues to evolve, its role in carbon pricing will expand, offering new tools for tracking, verifying, and trading carbon credits. The integration of geospatial data with Fintech solutions will be crucial for scaling these efforts, ensuring that carbon pricing mechanisms are both effective and equitable on a global scale. This synergy between technology and finance holds the potential to drive meaningful progress in the fight against climate change, making it a cornerstone of future policy and economic strategies.

References

Al Sadawi, A., Madani, B., Saboor, S., Ndiaye, M., & Abu-Lebdeh, G. (2021). A comprehensive hierarchical blockchain system for carbon emission trading utilizing blockchain of things and smart contract. *Technological Forecasting and Social Change, 173*, 121124.

Ashley, M. J., & Johnson, M. S. (2018). Establishing a secure, transparent, and autonomous blockchain of custody for renewable energy credits and carbon credits. *IEEE Engineering Management Review, 46*(4), 100–102.

Ball, J. (2018). Why carbon pricing isn't working: Good idea in theory, failing in practice. *Foreign Affairs, 97*, 134.

Boyce, J. K. (2019). *The case for carbon dividends*. Wiley.

Chen, D. (2018a). Utility of the blockchain for climate mitigation. *The Journal of the British Blockchain Association, 1*(1), 1–9.

Chen, D. B. (2018b). Central banks and blockchains: The case for managing climate risk with a positive carbon price. In *Transforming climate finance and green investment with blockchains* (pp. 201–216). Academic Press.

Chen, D. B., van der Beek, J., & Cloud, J. (2019). Hypothesis for a risk cost of carbon: Revising the externalities and ethics of climate change. *Understanding risks and uncertainties in energy and climate policy: Multidisciplinary methods and tools for a low carbon society* (pp. 183–222). Springer.

Costello, K. (2024). *The benefits of a carbon tax are probably exaggerated*. Available at SSRN 4747310.

References

Crippa, M., Guizzardi, D., Pagani, F., Banja, M., Muntean, M., Schaaf, E., Becker, W., Monforti-Ferrario, F., Quadrelli, R., Risquez Martin, A., Taghavi-Moharamli, P., Köykkä, J., Grassi, G., Rossi, S., Brandao De Melo, J., Oom, D., Branco, A., San-Miguel, J., & Vignati, E. (2023). *GHG emissions of all world countries*. Publications Office of the European Union, Luxembourg. https://doi.org/10.2760/953322,JRC134504

Dorfleitner, G., Muck, F., & Scheckenbach, I. (2021). Blockchain applications for climate protection: A global empirical investigation. *Renewable and Sustainable Energy Reviews, 149*, 111378.

Duchenne, J. (2018). Blockchain and smart contracts: Complementing climate finance, legislative frameworks, and renewable energy projects. In *Transforming climate finance and green investment with blockchains* (pp. 303–317). Academic Press.

Esmaeilian, B., Sarkis, J., Lewis, K., & Behdad, S. (2020). Blockchain for the future of sustainable supply chain management in Industry 4.0. *Resources, conservation and recycling, 163*, 105064.

Espenan, N. P. (2023). Improving voluntary carbon markets through standardization and blockchain technology. *Wyoming Law Review, 23*, 141.

Fischer, M. M. (2011). A spatial Mankiw–Romer–Weil model: Theory and evidence. *The Annals of Regional Science, 47*, 419–436.

Fischer, M. M. (2018). Spatial externalities and growth in a Mankiw-Romer-Weil world: Theory and evidence. *International Regional Science Review, 41*(1), 45–61.

Hawkins, J. (2020). One hundred years ago: The book that inspired the carbon price: Pigou's the economics of welfare. *History of Economics Review, 77*(1), 61–74. https://doi.org/10.1080/10370196.2020.1827759

Henly, C., Hartnett, S., Endemann, B., Tejblum, B., & Cohen, D. S. (2018). Energizing the future with blockchain. *Energy Law Journal, 39*, 197.

Howson, P. (2019). Tackling climate change with blockchain. *Nature Climate Change, 9*(9), 644–645.

Hubacek, K., Chen, X., Feng, K., Wiedmann, T., & Shan, Y. (2021). Evidence of decoupling consumption-based CO_2 emissions from economic growth. *Advances in Applied Energy, 4*, 100074.

IEA. (2023). *World Energy Outlook 2023*. IEA, Paris. https://www.iea.org/reports/world-energy-outlook-2023, License: CC BY 4.0 (report); CC BY NC SA 4.0 (Annex A)

IPCC. (2018). Global warming of 1.5°C. *An IPCC Special Report on the impacts of global warming of 1.5°C above pre-industrial levels and related global greenhouse gas emission pathways, in the context of strengthening the global response to the threat of climate change, sustainable development, and efforts to eradicate poverty* [V. Masson-Delmotte, P. Zhai, H.-O. Pörtner, D. Roberts, J. Skea, P. R. Shukla, A. Pirani, W. Moufouma-Okia, C. Péan, R. Pidcock, S. Connors, J. B. R. Matthews, Y. Chen, X. Zhou, M. I. Gomis, E. Lonnoy, T. Maycock, M. Tignor, & T. Waterfield (eds.)]. I

IPCC. (2023). Climate change 2023: Synthesis report. *Contribution of Working Groups I, II and III to the Sixth Assessment Report of the Intergovernmental Panel on Climate Change* [Core Writing Team, H. Lee & J. Romero (Eds.),] (pp. 35–115). IPCC, Geneva, Switzerland. https://doi.org/10.59327/IPCC/AR6-9789291691647

Jones, C. I. (2019). Paul Romer: Ideas, nonrivalry, and endogenous growth. *The Scandinavian Journal of Economics, 121*(3), 859–883.

Kang, E. S., Pee, S. J., Song, J. G., & Jang, J. W. (2018, April). A blockchain-based energy trading platform for smart homes in a microgrid. In *2018 3rd International Conference on Computer and Communication Systems (ICCCS)* (pp. 472–476). IEEE.

Khanfar, A. A., Iranmanesh, M., Ghobakhloo, M., Senali, M. G., & Fathi, M. (2021). Applications of blockchain technology in sustainable manufacturing and supply chain management: A systematic review. *Sustainability, 13*(14), 7870.

Khatoon, A., Verma, P., Southernwood, J., Massey, B., & Corcoran, P. (2019). Blockchain in energy efficiency: Potential applications and benefits. *Energies, 12*(17), 3317.

Kim, S. K., & Huh, J. H. (2020). Blockchain of carbon trading for UN sustainable development goals. *Sustainability, 12*(10), 4021.

Klenert, D., Mattauch, L., Combet, E., Edenhofer, O., Hepburn, C., Rafaty, R., & Stern, N. (2018). Making carbon pricing work for citizens. *Nature Climate Change, 8*(8), 669–677.

Kolstad, C. D. (2020). Subnational carbon pricing in the US. *Ifo DICE Report, 18*(1), 20–22.

Kshetri, N. (2022). Blockchain systems and ethical sourcing in the mineral and metal industry: A multiple case study. *The International Journal of Logistics Management, 33*(1), 1–27.

Kumari, A., Gupta, R., Tanwar, S., Tyagi, S., & Kumar, N. (2020). When blockchain meets smart grid: Secure energy trading in demand response management. *IEEE Network, 34*(5), 299–305.

Metcalf, G. E., & Weisbach, D. (2009). The design of a carbon tax. *Harvard Environmental Law Review, 33*, 499.

Miglani, A., Kumar, N., Chamola, V., & Zeadally, S. (2020). Blockchain for Internet of Energy management: Review, solutions, and challenges. *Computer Communications, 151*, 395–418.

Mitsubishi. (2024). *Carbon pricing in Japan: A policy perspective*. Mitsubishi Research Institute. https://www.mri.co.jp/en/knowledge/mreview/2023062.html

Narassimhan, E., Gallagher, K. S., Koester, S., & Alejo, J. R. (2018). Carbon pricing in practice: A review of existing emissions trading systems. *Climate Policy, 18*(8), 967–991.

Nikas, A., Doukas, H., & Papandreou, A. (2019). A detailed overview and consistent classification of climate-economy models. In H. Doukas, A. Flamos, & J. Lieu (Eds.), *Understanding risks and uncertainties in energy and climate policy*. Springer. https://doi.org/10.1007/978-3-030-03152-7_1

Nordhaus, W. (2015). Climate clubs: Overcoming free-riding in international climate policy. *American Economic Review, 105*(4), 1339–1370.

Nordhaus, W. (2019). Climate change: The ultimate challenge for economics. *American Economic Review, 109*(6), 1991–2014.

Nordhaus, W. D. (2017). Revisiting the social cost of carbon. *Proceedings of the National Academy of Sciences, 114*(7), 1518–1523.

Nordhaus, W. D. (2021). *The spirit of green: The economics of collisions and contagions in a crowded world*. Princeton University Press.

NRI. (2024). *Equilibrium carbon price for future carbon pricing in Japan*. https://www.nri.com/en/knowledge/publication/fis/lakyara/

Rezai, A., Foley, D. K., & Taylor, L. (2012). Global warming and economic externalities. *Economic Theory, 49*, 329–351.

RMI. (2022, November 11). *Beyond the buzz: What can blockchain do for carbon markets?* Rocky Mountain Institute. https://rmi.org/what-can-blockchain-do-for-carbon-markets/

Robinson, K. S. (2020). *The ministry for the future*. Hachette UK.

Romer, P. M. (1987). Growth based on increasing returns due to specialization. *The American Economic Review, 77*(2), 56–62.

Saberi, S., Kouhizadeh, M., Sarkis, J., & Shen, L. (2019). Blockchain technology and its relationships to sustainable supply chain management. *International Journal of Production Research, 57*(7), 2117–2135.

Saxena, S., Farag, H., Brookson, A., Turesson, H., & Kim, H. (2019, November). Design and field implementation of blockchain based renewable energy trading in residential communities. In *2019 2nd International Conference on Smart Grid and Renewable Energy (SGRE)* (pp. 1–6). IEEE.

Schandl, H., Hatfield-Dodds, S., Wiedmann, T., Geschke, A., Cai, Y., West, J., Newth, D., Baynes, T., Lenzen, M., & Owen, A. (2016). Decoupling global environmental pressure and economic growth: Scenarios for energy use, materials use and carbon emissions. *Journal of Cleaner Production, 132*, 45–56.

Schulz, K., & Feist, M. (2021). Leveraging blockchain technology for innovative climate finance under the Green Climate Fund. *Earth System Governance, 7*, 100084.

Selmoune, A., Cheng, Q., Wang, L., & Liu, Z. (2020). Influencing factors in congestion pricing acceptability: A literature review. *Journal of Advanced Transportation, 2020*(1), 4242964.

Singichetti, B., Conklin, J. L., Hassmiller Lich, K., Sabounchi, N. S., & Naumann, R. B. (2021). Congestion pricing policies and safety implications: A scoping review. *Journal of Urban Health, 98*(6), 754–771.

Stavins, R. N. (2019). *Carbon taxes vs. cap and trade: Theory and practice.* Harvard Project on Climate Agreements.

Stavins, R. N. (2020). The future of US carbon-pricing policy. *Environmental and Energy Policy and the Economy, 1*(1), 8–64.

Stern, N. (2007). *The economics of climate change: The stern review.* Cambridge University Press.

Stiglitz, J. E., Stern, N., Duan, M., Edenhofer, O., Giraud, G., Heal, G. M., La Rovere, E. L., Morris, A., Moyer, E., Pangestu, M., Shukla, P. R., Sokona, Y., & Winkler, H. (2017). Report of the high-level commission on carbon price. *International Bank for Reconstruction and Development and International Development Association/The World Bank.* https://doi.org/10.7916/d8-w2nc-4103

Thisted, E. V., & Thisted, R. V. (2020). The diffusion of carbon taxes and emission trading schemes: The emerging norm of carbon pricing. *Environmental Politics, 29*(5), 804–824.

Thukral, M. K. (2021). Emergence of blockchain-technology application in peer-to-peer electrical-energy trading: A review. *Clean Energy, 5*(1), 104–123.

van der Gaast, W., Sikkema, R., & Vohrer, M. (2018). The contribution of forest carbon credit projects to addressing the climate change challenge. *Climate Policy, 18*(1), 42–48.

Verbruggen, A. (2021). *Pricing carbon emissions: economic reality and utopia* (p. 262). Taylor & Francis.

Woo, J., Fatima, R., Kibert, C. J., Newman, R. E., Tian, Y., & Srinivasan, R. S. (2021). Applying blockchain technology for building energy performance measurement, reporting, and verification (MRV) and the carbon credit market: A review of the literature. *Building and Environment, 205*, 108199.

World Bank. (2020). *Using blockchain to support the energy transition and climate markets: Results and lessons from a pilot project in Chile.* World Bank.

World Bank and Ecofys. (2018). *State and trends of carbon pricing 2018 (May)", by World Bank.* https://doi.org/10.1596/978-1-4648-1292-7. "

World Bank Group. (2018). *Blockchain and emerging digital technologies for enhancing post-2020 climate markets.* World Bank.

Xu, W., Li, J., Dehghani, M., & GhasemiGarpachi, M. (2021). Blockchain-based secure energy policy and management of renewable-based smart microgrids. *Sustainable Cities and Society, 72*, 103010.

Chapter 9
GenAI: Unlocking Sustainability Insights and Driving Change in Fintech

> Generative AI is the key to solving some of the world's biggest problems, such as climate change, poverty, and disease. It has the potential to make the world a better place for everyone— Mark Zuckerberg

9.1 Introduction

Integrating sustainability and impact considerations into the Fintech sector has significantly increased the complexity and volume of data that investors and companies must process. Traditionally, agencies present these data through ESG ratings based on company sustainability reports. These company reports often combine quantitative metrics with qualitative disclosures, where subtle nuances in language and sentiment can reveal a company's genuine commitment (or lack thereof) to sustainable practices. Disentangling genuine sustainability efforts from greenwashing poses a significant challenge for asset managers, pension funds, and retail investors seeking to align investments with their values.

On the other hand, companies face their own set of challenges given the fragmented landscape of standards and frameworks governing sustainability reporting, including the Global Reporting Initiative (GRI), Greenhouse Gas (GHG) Protocol, Task Force on Climate-related Financial Disclosures (TCFD), International Sustainability Standards Board (ISSB), Partnership for Carbon Accounting Financials (PCAF), and UN Sustainable Development Goals (SDGs). These standards and regulations are discussed in detail in Chapter 5 of the book. While the GRI framework is divided into universal standards (applicable to all organizations) and sector-specific standards (tailored to particular industries), the PCAF requires financial institutions to calculate and report their financed emissions across different asset classes, including listed equity and corporate bonds, business loans and unlisted equity, project finance, commercial real estate, and mortgages. The UN SDGs are more global and have 17 goals to address global challenges such as poverty, inequality, climate change, environmental degradation, peace, and justice. The European Union (EU) has crafted an interconnected framework to promote sustainable economic activities and ensure transparent reporting across different sectors. While each framework has unique requirements tailored to specific aspects of sustainability, they all share a commitment to enhancing the transparency, accountability, and comparability of sustainability reporting. For companies, this means adopting a comprehensive approach that addresses the diverse criteria set forth by these standards and frameworks. Thus, navigating this reporting landscape requires a meticulous approach to ensure compliance and extensive reporting.

In this context of ESG and sustainable finance, GenAI (Generative Artificial Intelligence) and related LLMs (Large Language Models) can serve as powerful tools to translate sustainability reporting. Since LLMs are a subset of GenAI, the term GenAI is used throughout this chapter to mean this class of models known for processing and generating human-like text based on extensive data. GenAI can analyze existing disclosures, suggest areas for streamlining, and ensure compliance across multiple frameworks. Companies can focus their efforts beyond mere reporting, aiming for tangible progress in sustainability. While GenAI offers incredible insights, it does not offer us an ultimate solution for every problem. The GenAI results always need human validation. This includes expert review, comparing GenAI's analysis with traditional methods, and testing the models under different scenarios to ensure they remain accurate and unbiased. We discuss various ways in which GenAI helps in sustainable finance and reporting with relevant applications and case studies.

This chapter sets the stage for the application of GenAI, given the current regulatory, compliance, and reporting landscape for Fintech, sustainability, and impact investing. It also discusses the evolution and features of GenAI, prompt engineering, and technical modeling in sustainable finance. Figure 9.1 provides a broad overview of the GenAI/LLM in the sustainable Fintech space that is described in the following subsections.

9.1.1 Alignment to Financial Stakeholder Interests

In the evolving landscape of sustainable finance, various stakeholders have distinct roles and responsibilities to foster compliance, attract investment, and promote climate readiness. These roles are interconnected, driving the growth of sustainable practices and regulatory compliance across the financial ecosystem. Each of these stakeholders needs to save time and effort in complying with regulations and being responsible to their stakeholders. Increasingly, they must assess materiality and climate risks. GenAI has the potential to assist stakeholders in multiple ways, although further investigation is needed to fully realize these capabilities. A review of recent articles from a number of sources (EY Global, 2023; Google Cloud, 2024; SEB, 2024) provide these insights on validation. The potential applications for each stakeholder are discussed below:

9.1 Introduction

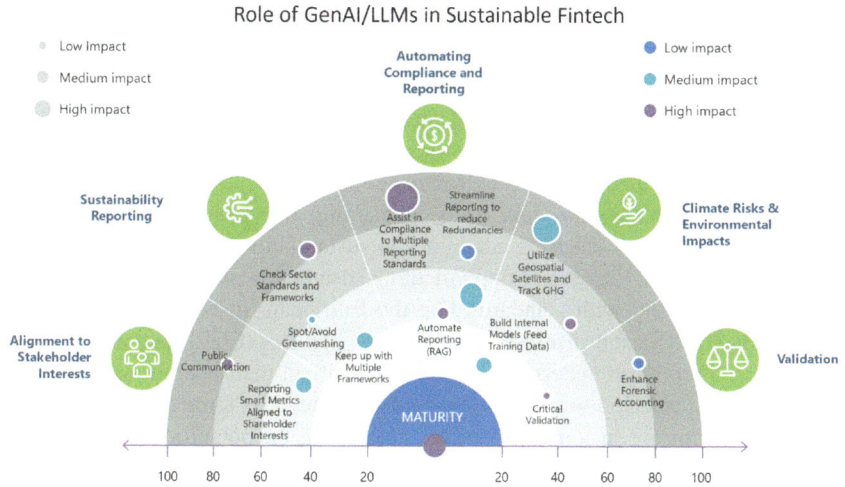

Fig. 9.1 GenAI/LLM assists stakeholder interests and reporting in the sustainable Fintech space

- Asset Managers play a pivotal role in integrating sustainability into investment decisions. They are responsible for ensuring their investment portfolios align with frameworks like the EU Taxonomy and Sustainable Finance Disclosure Regulation (SFDR). They may promote green bonds and other sustainable financial instruments to meet the increasing demand from investors. They assess and manage climate-related risks and opportunities within their portfolios to ensure long-term sustainability. Future trends indicate that GenAI can help with analysis of the vast amount of ESG data and provide insights on sustainability performance and compliance with regulatory frameworks.
- Asset owners, such as pension and sovereign wealth funds, are increasingly focused on sustainability to protect and grow their assets. Their responsibilities include defining investment mandates that prioritize environmental, social, and governance (ESG) factors, evaluating the ESG performance of their investments, and engaging with companies to improve sustainability practices. GenAI can analyze global ESG trends and regulations to help define forward-looking investment mandates. It can provide real-time assessments of ESG performance, benchmarking against industry standards. It can generate insights on best practices for engaging with companies to enhance their ESG practices.
- Wealth managers guide individual and institutional clients toward sustainable investment opportunities. They are responsible for informing clients about sustainable investing options and their potential benefits and aligning investment strategies with clients' ESG preferences and compliance requirements. GenAI-powered tools can provide personalized education materials on sustainable investing for clients. It can analyze client preferences and regulatory requirements to recommend tailored investment strategies. It can continuously monitor investment performance against ESG benchmarks and provide updates to clients.

- Banks facilitate the transition to a sustainable economy through financing and advisory services. Banks' green financing provides loans and underwrites bonds for sustainable projects, adhering to and promoting compliance with sustainability-related regulations and standards. GenAI can evaluate the sustainability impact of projects seeking financing, ensuring alignment with green financing criteria. It can assess environmental and financial risks associated with sustainable projects, improving decision-making. It can automate compliance checks and reporting, ensuring adherence to sustainability regulations.
- Corporations are at the core of implementing sustainable practices and reporting. They must comply with standards like the European Sustainability Reporting Standards (ESRS) and disclose sustainability impacts (EUR-Lex, 2022). They identify and report on material ESG issues that affect their operations and stakeholders (European Commission, 2024a, 2024b). They may attract green bonds and secure financing for sustainable projects. GenAI has the potential to automate the collection and reporting of ESG data, ensuring compliance with standards in EU or US or UK. GenAI can analyze and report on the sustainability impacts of corporate operations, highlighting areas for improvement. This requires a lot of effort and time in terms of training the algorithms so the results from GenAI are not greenwashed. Bias in reporting, which often relies on what is the available data, poses problems. For example, bricks are manufactured in Austria as well as in India. The emissions in each context are different and GenAI has to be explicitly trained with that data to provide a region specific emissions answer. GenAI can help identify and attract green bonds and other financing options for sustainable projects. Green bonds and other financial options are discussed in Chapter 3.
- Retail investors drive demand for sustainable products and can influence corporate behavior through their investment choices. They are responsible for understanding the impact of their investments on sustainability and using their shareholder rights to advocate for better ESG practices within companies. GenAI can create personalized educational resources to help investors understand ESG factors and their importance. For example, a Millennial investor interested in tackling gendered supply chains would be able to retrieve insights on where and how female labor force is employed in various companies and various sectors. GenAI can be trained to provide AI can provide detailed personalized analyses of sustainable investment options, helping investors make informed decisions. It can create climate scenarios for smarter analysis.
- Regulators and rating agencies ensure the integrity and transparency of sustainable finance. Their responsibilities include developing and enforcing sustainability reporting and compliance regulations and evaluating and rating the ESG performance of companies and financial products. For instance, the growing interest in biodiversity regulation has sparked considerable enthusiasm for green and blue bonds. Countries such as Belize are leading the way by utilizing these financial instruments to fund the protection of vital ecosystems, such as mangroves and coral reefs. By leveraging GenAI, Belize can enhance its regulatory framework, ensuring effective monitoring and enforcement of biodiversity conservation efforts. This approach not only supports sustainable development but also

preserves the natural heritage that is essential to Belize's environmental and economic health. GenAI can be trained to monitor and analyze ESG disclosures for compliance with regulations, identifying potential issues. In the long run, GenAI can enhance the accuracy and transparency of ESG ratings by integrating diverse data sources and advanced analytics. This will ensure that reporting and compliance are effective and aligned with global best practices. Nvidia CEO Huang proposes that countries must build sovereign AI infrastructure to protect their own culture and standards. Nvidia is at the forefront of the AI revolution making high-end AI chips.[1]

Each stakeholder contributes to a broader ecosystem that promotes sustainable growth, compliance with regulations, and readiness to address climate challenges. Their collaborative efforts are essential in driving the transition to a more sustainable and resilient financial system. Each stakeholder in the sustainable finance ecosystem can leverage GenAI to enhance their efficiency, accuracy, and impact. By automating data collection, analysis, and reporting, these technologies help stakeholders meet regulatory requirements, manage risks, and drive sustainable practices more effectively. This collaborative approach is essential for transitioning to a more sustainable and resilient financial system.

9.1.2 Sustainability Reporting

Unlike traditional annual reports, bound by strict reporting standards and balanced financial figures with narrative disclosures, corporate sustainability reporting utilizes a higher volume of narrative content and offers greater freedom for managerial discretion (Adams & Abhayawansa, 2022). These reports predominantly feature a narrative and qualitative format, with organizations often voluntarily sharing information, aligning with global voluntary initiatives such as the UN Sustainable Development Goals (SDGs) (Adams et al., 2020). The scope of sustainability reporting has broadened as corporations face increasing pressure to communicate the non-financial aspects of their operations to stakeholders. These disclosures, crucial for understanding the drivers and impacts of a company's performance, have become essential. The creation and examination of text in sustainability reports take on added significance amid rising concerns and accusations of greenwashing (Lyon & Montgomery, 2015). Studies have shown that corporate managers may prefer to report on social and environmental issues expected to positively influence their company's stock price (De Villiers & van Staden, 2011). This tactic challenges the integrity and credibility of sustainability reporting.

---

[1] https://www.reuters.com/technology/nvidia-ceo-huang-says-countries-must-build-sovereign-ai-infrastructure-2024-02-12/.

While the United Nations has provided initial general guidelines for incorporating ESG factors into the investment process, organizations such as the Sustainability Accounting Standards Board and the Global Reporting Initiative have developed and promoted sustainability accounting standards. Despite these efforts, each country still requires mandatory and voluntary ESG disclosure instruments to align with these general guidelines. One example of a voluntary disclosure instrument is the EU's Non-Financial Reporting Directive. However, this directive lacks a consistent standard for firms to follow in reporting their ESG information. Central to the EU reporting system is the EU Taxonomy, which provides a clear classification of what constitutes environmentally sustainable activities. It sets environmental goals and criteria for sustainable economic activities. It aligns financial and non-financial reporting with sustainability objectives. The EU taxonomy and regulatory framework is discussed in detail in Chapter 4. Other voluntary instruments include the Impact Reporting and Investment Standards and the Global Impact Investment Rating System, which assess the social and environmental impact of companies.

Mandatory disclosure instruments, such as the requirement for pension fund trustees to produce a statement of investment principles on ESG considerations or climate risks, aim to standardize ESG reporting. However, not all ESG disclosure instruments are mandatory, allowing firms to selectively disclose data or opt-out entirely. This leads to significant variability in the quality and content of ESG reports (Büyüközkan & Karabulut, 2018). As a result, stakeholders find it challenging to directly evaluate firms' transparency, performance, and corporate accountability in ESG aspects. They heavily rely on corporations' self-reported data, which may not accurately reflect their actual ESG performance, thus fostering potential greenwashing behavior (Van Halderen et al., 2016).

Case Study: Brick Manufacturing in India and Austria: This case study showcases the capabilities of a trained model in reporting on ESG (Environmental, Social, and Governance) metrics, specifically focusing on Scope 1 emissions (CO2e equivalent), gender pay gap ratios, and board diversity in the brick manufacturing industry in India and Austria.

In Fig. 9.2, the distributions in blue and red, drawn by GenAI using simulated data, make assumptions about the mean and standard deviations based on satellite data from known sites in the brick industry of both regions. These distributions represent estimates of emissions, pay gaps, and board structures derived from a trained model utilizing 30 examples from each setting. It is important to note that these results are estimates. More accurate and comprehensive training data will lead to better results in the future analyses. The authors are experimenting with various sectors and regions. Validation is critical in this context.

In this context, it is important to point out that if bricks, if imported from India, would be regulated also. The European Union regulates carbon emissions on imported products through the Carbon Border Adjustment Mechanism (CBAM). This regulation aims to prevent carbon leakage, where companies move production to countries with less stringent climate policies, and to ensure a level playing field for EU industries that are subject to the EU Emissions Trading System.

9.1 Introduction 351

ESG Metrics for Brick Manufacturing in Austria and India

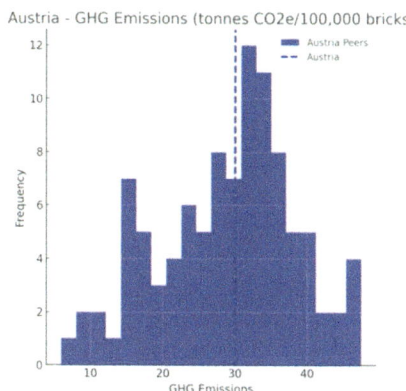
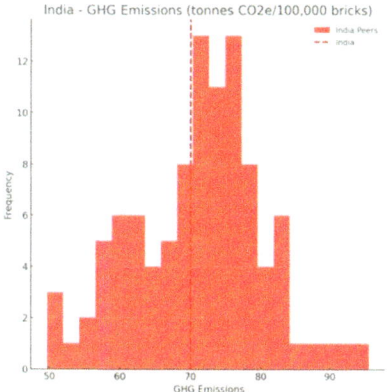

ESG Scores for Brick Manufacturing

Assume 100,000 bricks	GHG Scope 1 tonnes CO2e	Gender pay gap	Board gender diversity
Austria	30	€1.00:0.81	0.6
India	70	Rs1.00:0.30	0.3

Fig. 9.2 Trained GenAI model provides ESG metrics for entity level mandatory PAI indicators showing company's disclosures to EU SFDR, based on the case study of brick manufacturing in India and Austria

9.1.3 Issues in Automated Compliance Reporting

Companies are increasingly required to report a variety of sustainability metrics. Recent regulations, particularly from the European Union, aim to enhance data transparency, ensure consistency across reporting entities, and prevent greenwashing. The EU framework for sustainability reporting is detailed in the next subsection.

Table 9.1 presents the Principal Adverse Impact (PAI) indicators that are currently reported by Schneider Electric and Exxon Mobil for 2022–2023. Both companies have disclosed their greenhouse gas (GHG) emissions, either for Scope 1 or total emissions.

However, neither company has ever reported on other crucial PAIs such as biodiversity, gender pay gap, Scope 3 emissions, and violations of UN Global Compact principles, among others. This table underscores the significant reporting gaps that both companies need to address when the EU SFDR's PAIs rule is enforced. There is growing concern that the increasing regulatory burden on businesses is deterring investment and driving companies away.[2]

---

[2] https://oilprice.com/Latest-Energy-News/World-News/Exxon-Threatens-to-Take-Billions-of-Dollars-in-Climate-Investment-Out-of-the-EU.html.

Table 9.1 Exxon Mobil[3] and Schneider Electric currently report on a few PAIs. The boxes in dark gray are included in the SFDR PAI Mandatory Disclosures 2023[4]

Schneider Electric—What are relevant SFDR PAI Mandatory Disclosures		
Greenhouse Gas Emissions (2022)	Biodiversity	Social and Employee Issues
Total GHG emissions (CO2e) Schneider: 229,348 tons.	Activities negatively affecting biodiversity-sensitive areas (percent)	Violations of UN Global Compact principles and OECD guidelines
Carbon Footprint	Water	Lack of processes and compliance mechanisms to monitor compliance with UN Global Compact principles and OECD guidelines
GHG intensity of investee companies.	Emissions to water (ratio)	Unadjusted gender pay gap
Share of investments in companies active in the fossil fuel sector	Hazardous waste and radioactive waste ratio (ratio)	Board gender diversity
Share of non-renewable energy consumption and non-renewable energy production of investee companies from non-renewable energy sources compared to share of renewable energy sources, expressed as a percentage of total energy sources. 80-85% renewable energy.		Exposure to controversial weapons
Energy consumption in GWh per million EUR of revenue of investee companies, per high impact climate sector (gigajoules or similar)		

(continued)

---

[3] https://www.se.com/ww/en/assets/564/document/396656/2022-climate-report.pdf.

[4] https://corporate.exxonmobil.com/-/media/global/files/advancing-climate-solutions-progress-report/2023/2023-acs-ghg-data-supplement.pdf.

9.1 Introduction

Table 9.1 (continued)

Exxon Mobil—What are relevant SFDR PAI Mandatory Disclosures		
Greenhouse Gas Emissions (2022)	Biodiversity	Social and Employee Issues
Scope 1 GHG emissions (CO2e) Exxon Mobil: 97 million metric tons.	Activities negatively affecting biodiversity-sensitive areas (percent)	Violations of UN Global Compact principles and OECD guidelines
Scope 2 GHG emissions (CO2e) Exxon Mobil: 7 million metric tons	Water	Lack of processes and compliance mechanisms to monitor compliance with UN Global Compact principles and OECD guidelines
Scope 3 GHG emissions (tCO2e)	Emissions to water (ratio)	Unadjusted gender pay gap
Carbon Footprint	Hazardous waste and radioactive waste ratio (ratio)	Board gender diversity
GHG intensity of investee companies. Exxon Mobil: 23.2 (metric tons CO2e per 100 metric tons of throughput or production)		Exposure to controversial weapons
Share of investments in companies active in the fossil fuel sector		
Share of non-renewable energy consumption and non-renewable energy production of investee companies from non-renewable energy sources compared to share of renewable energy sources, expressed as a percentage of total energy sources.		
Energy consumption in GWh per million EUR of revenue of investee companies, per high impact climate sector (gigajoules or similar)		

9.1.4 Climate Risks and Environmental Impacts

GenAI can significantly enhance climate risk and environmental impact reporting. These technologies can process vast amounts of data, generate insights, and help in the accurate and comprehensive reporting of climate-related risks and impacts. They can integrate data from various sources, including IPCC climate models, SSP scenarios, and other climate risk indicators such as floods and hurricanes. GenAI can be set up to extract data on US SEC 10-K filings and company documents to mine for reported climate risk and environmental impact data (discussed in Chapter 4).

9.1.5 Validation and Increasing Compliance

Why is validation needed? The current landscape of Environmental, Social, and Governance (ESG) data disclosure faces numerous challenges. These include unaudited ESG data, the absence of a global governing body, various behavioral issues at the firm level, and a lack of specific regulatory guidelines to ensure the accuracy of reported ESG data (Friede, 2019; PRI, 2017). These impediments may allow companies to engage in ESG greenwashing. Stakeholders, discussed in subsection 9.1.1, find it challenging to directly evaluate firms' transparency, performance, and corporate accountability in ESG aspects. They heavily rely on corporations' self-reported data, which may not accurately reflect their actual ESG performance, thus fostering potential greenwashing behavior (Yu et al., 2020).

How can GenAI models help in validating and ensuring compliance? A review of recent articles from a number of sources (EY Global, 2023; Google Cloud, 2024; SEB, 2024) provide these insights on validation. Generative AI (GenAI) and Large Language Models (LLMs) like GPT-4 can significantly improve the transparency, consistency, and accuracy of ESG reporting, thereby reducing the risk of greenwashing. Cross-referencing with industry or sector data can be automated to compare a company's self-reported ESG data with industry benchmarks and statistics, identifying discrepancies and anomalies. GenAI can analyze ESG performance across sectors, providing comparative insights that highlight a company's standing relative to its peers, which can further assist in validation.

9.2 The GenAI Ecosystem and Its Transformative Impact

The last two decades have seen rapid advancements in artificial intelligence (AI), with natural language processing (NLP) being a focal area of development. The emergence of Large Language Models (LLMs) and Generative AI (GenAI) models, such as OpenAI's GPT series and Google's BERT, marks a pivotal moment in the progress of NLP. Unlike Generative Adversarial Networks (GANs), which primarily focus on image creation, models like ChatGPT, built on the Generative Pre-trained Transformer (GPT) architecture, prioritize NLP tasks. These models have undergone significant development, showcasing improvements in efficiency, scalability, accuracy, and broad applicability across different fields. One of the hallmark achievements in this space is GPT-3 by OpenAI, which, along with its successors, has redefined the benchmarks for AI in language understanding and generation (Brown et al., 2020). Trained on extensive datasets, these models can accurately comprehend, generate, and interpret human language, spanning across text, images, music, and more. This versatility is rooted in deep learning and neural networks, enabling GenAI models to dissect and produce outputs that closely mirror human capabilities.

9.2.1 GenAI Ecosystem

The evolution of GenAI is reshaping the landscape of AI, offering novel capabilities in language processing, content generation, and creative applications. Its impact on sustainable finance, among other fields, illustrates the potential for GenAI to contribute to more informed, efficient, and transparent financial practices. As we continue to witness the growth and integration of GenAI across various sectors, the collaboration between technology companies, researchers, and industry practitioners will be vital in harnessing this technology for positive societal impacts. The applications of GenAI are diverse, ranging from creating realistic images with models like DALL·E to generating human-like text with various GPT models. In the realm of sustainable finance, GenAI holds the potential to transform how data are analyzed, interpreted, and reported. By synthesizing complex datasets and generating insightful analyses, GenAI can assist in identifying sustainable investment opportunities, assessing environmental, social, and governance (ESG) factors, and enhancing the transparency and accuracy of sustainability reports. The discussion of AI advancements would be incomplete without acknowledging the role of semiconductor chip companies like Nvidia, AMD, and Taiwan Semiconductor. These companies are crucial in providing the hardware infrastructure that powers AI and GenAI developments. Thus, the GenAI ecosystem is complex and rapidly evolving, with new chips being designed, new LLMs being developed, and advancements in software engineering to enhance performance for various business use cases.

Figure 9.3 shows the branch called Large Language Models(LLM) containing ChatGPT (Generative Pre-trained Transformer) 3.5/4, Llama 3, Claude 3, Sonnet, Gemini Pro 1.5, and Mistral Medium. In addition, there are other models such as Perplexity GPT, a specific version or instance of a GPT, a specialized adaptation, emphasizing efficient and accurate search assistance, indicating it may involve some customization or fine-tuning specific to its intended use. These LLMs are supported across a wide array of cloud platforms including AWS, Databricks, Google Cloud, Hugging Face, Kaggle, IBM WatsonX, Microsoft Azure, NVIDIA's NIM, and

Snowflake, shown in Fig. 9.3. Additionally, these models are compatible with hardware platforms provided by leading technology companies such as AMD, AWS, Dell, Intel, NVIDIA, and Qualcomm.

We describe the applications of GenAI in the field of sustainable finance by examining the widely used models and some technical aspects described in the literature that impact the final results: Prompting, Tuning, Retrieval-Augmented Generation (RAG), and agentic reasoning. The history and evolution of models such as ChatGPT, LLaMA, Claude, Sonnet, Gemini Pro, Mistral, and Perplexity GPT illustrate significant advancements in NLP and AI. Here's a summary of their development and key characteristics:

- Google: Through initiatives like Google Brain and DeepMind, and tools like Bard, Google continues to expand the frontiers of AI, machine learning, and GenAI. Google Cloud is introducing a suite of new products that integrate Generative AI into its offerings, enabling developers to build with enterprise-grade safety, security, and privacy. This initiative kicks off with the launch of two key technologies: Generative AI Support in Vertex AI and Generative AI App Builder.[5]
- ChatGPT (Generative Pre-trained Transformer) 3.5/4: Developed by OpenAI, ChatGPT-3.5 and GPT-4 are known for their broad generative capabilities and fine-tuning potential across various tasks. The transition from GPT-3.5 to GPT-4 featured improvements in training techniques, data handling, and the ability to generate more contextually appropriate and nuanced text (OpenAI). A key investor in OpenAI, Microsoft has integrated GenAI tools like Copilot into its productivity suite, demonstrating the broad applicability and efficiency of scalable language models.
- LLaMA 3: Created by Meta, LLaMA (Language Model Meta AI) is designed to optimize performance across different computing environments including lower-resource settings. It focuses on efficient training and deployment to democratize access to state-of-the-art AI models (Meta AI). Meta is exploring applications in social media and virtual reality.
- Claude 3: Developed by Anthropic, Claude emphasizes safety and usability in human-AI interactions. The latest iteration, Claude 3, continues to improve understanding and generating human-like responses, aiming to be reliable and aligned with user intentions (Anthropic).
- Sonnet, Gemini Pro 1.5, and Mistral Medium: These models are examples of advancements by various organizations. Sonnet and Gemini Pro are tailored for specific applications like creative content generation and professional workflows, respectively, while Mistral Medium focuses on efficient language understanding and scalable deployments.[6]
- Perplexity GPT: This model is specialized for customizing LLMs to specific use cases, emphasizing tailored interactions based on particular user inputs or contexts (Perplexity AI).

---

[5] https://cloud.google.com/blog/products/ai-machine-learning/generative-ai-for-businesses-and-governments.

[6] https://en.wikipedia.org/wiki/large_language_model.

9.2 The GenAI Ecosystem and Its Transformative Impact

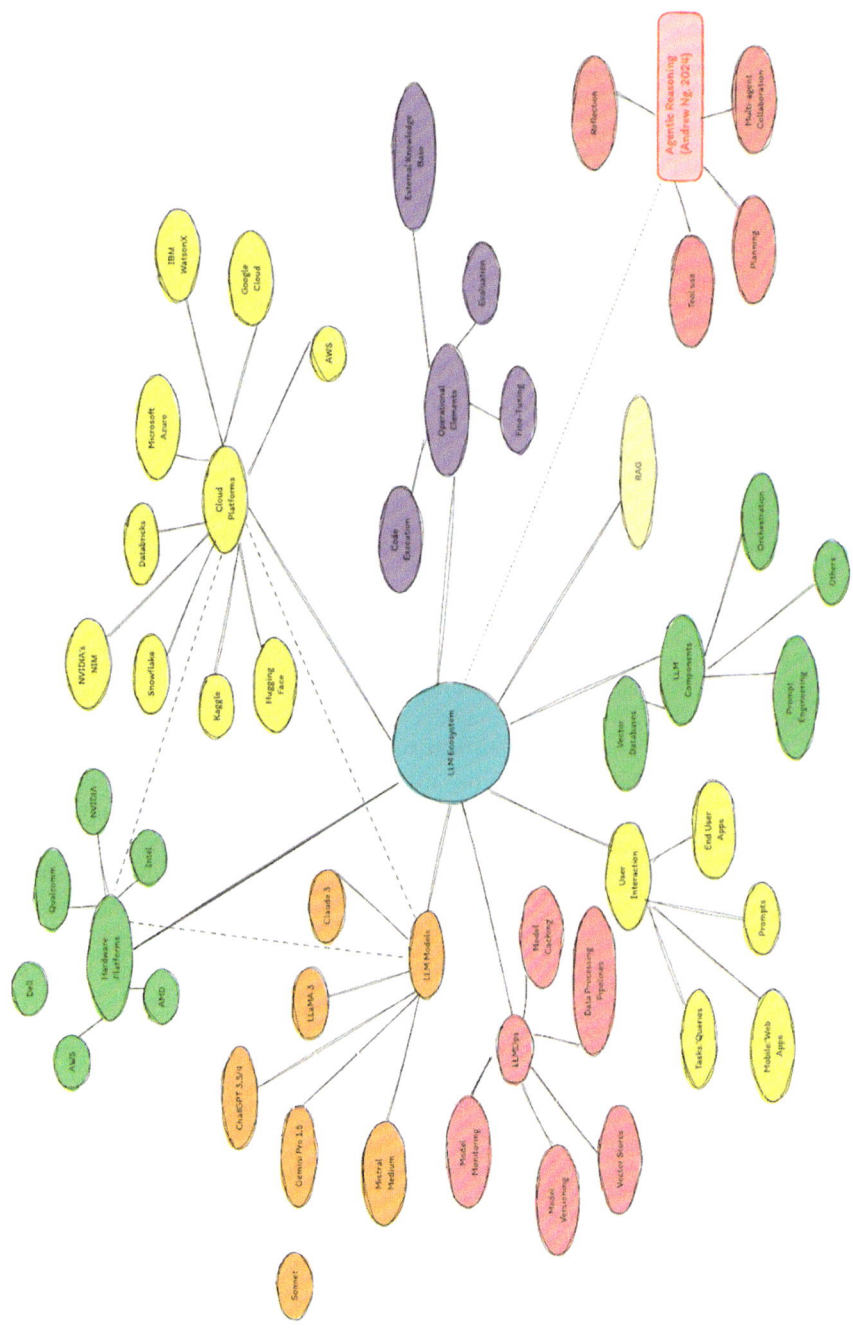

Fig. 9.3 Ecosystem of GenAI showing hardware, cloud, and other components

- Adobe: Adobe's exploration of GenAI in creative applications, such as design element suggestions and realistic texture generation, highlights the technology's creative potential.
- Amazon: By providing AWS with the necessary computing power for GenAI model training and experimentation, Amazon facilitates the broader development and application of GenAI.
- IBM: With its AI platform WatsonX, IBM focuses on the development and deployment of custom GenAI applications in healthcare, emphasizing responsible AI collaboration with healthcare providers and researchers.

These models have significantly impacted technology, the economy, and society, transforming how humans interact with information and enhancing tasks such as content creation, translation, and decision support. They continue to push the boundaries of what AI can achieve in understanding and generating human language (KPMG, 2023, 2024; McKinsey Digital, 2023). Prompt engineering is covered in subsection 9.2.2., fine-tuning in 9.2.3., and RAG in 9.2.4.

9.2.2 Prompt Engineering: Unleashing GenAI's Potential

ChatGPT distinguishes itself in the field of NLP with features that enhance its utility across various applications. Its sophisticated contextual comprehension facilitates engaging dialogue by generating pertinent responses. The model's language generation proficiency allows for the creation of coherent and grammatically sound text, suitable for tasks like content creation and summarization. ChatGPT's versatility is further underscored by its adaptability to specific tasks, encompassing a spectrum from customer service to educational assistance. Its proficiency in numerous languages broadens its global applicability, while its scalable architecture meets diverse computational needs. Notably, ChatGPT exhibits capabilities for zero-shot and few-shot learning, which minimizes the necessity for extensive training datasets. Finally, its fine-tuning feature allows for task-specific optimization, and the utilization of prompt engineering significantly improves interaction efficacy with AI models (Giray, 2023).

- Contextual Understanding: One of the most significant advancements in ChatGPT is its ability to understand context in text-based conversations. By comprehending the meaning of sentences and phrases, ChatGPT can generate relevant and coherent responses, making its interactions with users more natural and engaging (Bansal et al., 2024; Ray, 2023).
- Language Generation Capabilities: ChatGPT has exceptional language generation capabilities, producing text that is coherent, contextually accurate, and grammatically correct. Its fluency in text generation allows it to be used for various applications such as content writing, summarization, and rewriting (Chang et al., 2023)

- Task Adaptability: ChatGPT can be adapted to a wide range of tasks, making it versatile across industries and domains. With fine-tuning, it can be customized for specific use cases such as customer support, content creation, tutoring, translation, and more. This adaptability allows developers to harness ChatGPT's capabilities to create tailored solutions for their needs (Haleem et al., 2022; Kocoń et al., 2023).
- Multilingual Proficiency: ChatGPT is proficient in multiple languages, enabling it to be used in global applications and cater to diverse user bases. Its multilingual capabilities are essential for applications such as translation, sentiment analysis, and multilingual content generation (Team, 2023)
- Scalability: The architecture of ChatGPT allows it to be scaled according to the available computational resources and desired response times. This scalability ensures that it can be used in applications with varying requirements, from small-scale projects to large-scale enterprise solutions (T. Wu et al., 2023b).
- Zero-Shot and Few-Shot Learning: ChatGPT can perform zero-shot and few-shot learning, enabling it to understand new tasks without extensive training. In zero-shot learning, the model can generate responses for tasks it has never seen before, while in few-shot learning, it can learn new tasks with just a few examples. This ability reduces the need for large, labeled datasets and extensive fine-tuning, saving time and resources in the development process (Mishra et al., 2018; Wei et al., 2023).
- Fine-Tuning: Fine-tuning is a crucial feature of ChatGPT, allowing developers to adapt the model to specific tasks or domains. By training the model on a smaller dataset tailored to the target application, ChatGPT can generate more accurate and relevant responses. Fine-tuning enables developers to create highly customized solutions using ChatGPT as the foundation (Zhong et al., 2023)
- Prompt Engineering for ChatGPT: Prompt engineering plays a significant role in enhancing the user experience and ensuring effective communication when interacting with AI models like ChatGPT. By employing prompt engineering techniques, users can guide the AI model to generate more accurate, relevant, and useful responses (Short & Short, 2023). Section 9.5 will outline how prompt engineering can be used in ChatGPT conversations to optimize the interaction.

9.2.3 Fundamentals of Fine-Tuning

Large Language Models (LLMs), such as Generative Pre-trained Transformers (GPT), have significantly advanced the capabilities of machines in understanding and generating human-like text. The fine-tuning of these models is critical for enhancing their application in specialized domains such as finance, healthcare, law, and customer service. This process involves adapting a general, pre-trained model to better meet the specific needs of these fields. A brief description of the methodology and importance of LLM fine-tuning is given below:

The Mechanics of LLM Fine-Tuning: Fine-tuning begins with a base LLM that has been trained on a broad corpus of text. This is called a pre-trained model; this foundational training equips the model with a general understanding of natural language, covering aspects like syntax, grammar, and basic semantics. However, the model lacks depth in specialized knowledge areas (Brown et al., 2020). The essence of fine-tuning lies in utilizing smaller, highly relevant training data (corpus) tailored to a specific domain. For instance, enhancing a model for sustainable finance might involve incorporating data from environmental, finance, and regulatory journals and company/industry reports (Howard & Ruder, 2018). During fine-tuning, the model's parameters are finely adjusted to reduce prediction errors relevant to the new domain. These adjustments are designed to be minimal to preserve the model's broad linguistic capabilities while improving its domain-specific performance (Devlin et al., 2018). A reduced learning rate is used in fine-tuning to prevent significant deviations from the model's foundational training. This cautious approach helps maintain the model's general linguistic abilities while allowing it to adapt to new contexts. In the sustainable finance industry, fine-tuning a model involves training it to deeply understand ESG terminology and practices. For example, the abbreviation "ESG" is specifically recognized as "Environment, Social and Governance" in a sustainability company report. This specificity enables the model to participate more effectively in ESG discussions, enhancing its utility for sustainability reporting.

Fine-tuning improves the model's accuracy and relevance, making it particularly valuable in fields that require specialized knowledge such as providing legal or medical advice (Liu et al., 2019). Fine-tuning allows for the customization of a general model to meet the particular needs of various sectors, making it a versatile tool across different industries (Kishore, 2024). Organizations can optimize their existing investments by refining a pre-trained model for multiple uses, rather than developing a new model from scratch for each application (Zhuang et al., 2023). A fine-tuned model provides a more intuitive and contextually appropriate interaction for users, making technology not only powerful but also user-friendly. To summarize, the fine-tuning of LLMs is a crucial process that greatly enhances the utility of general AI models across diverse specialized domains. It allows for the precise and context-aware application of AI, transforming general models into indispensable, tailored tools for specific industries.

9.2.4 ABC's of Retrieval-Augmented Generation (RAG)

While the process of LLM fine-tuning traditionally involves training a pre-trained model on a smaller, domain-specific dataset, the integration of Retrieval-Augmented Generation (RAG) enhances LLMs' performance further. RAG merges retrieval-based systems with generative models, addressing the inevitable gaps that arise in a general LLM's training data. This becomes especially critical when new information surfaces after a model's training or when responses require access to proprietary data not included in initial model training (Lewis et al., 2020). RAG operates by fetching

9.2 The GenAI Ecosystem and Its Transformative Impact

relevant documents from an extensive dataset in real time, allowing the model to incorporate these data into its responses. This method provides a richer, context-specific understanding, transforming a general LLM into a specialized one capable of delivering precise answers to complex queries (Guu et al., 2020).

In sustainable finance, understanding the impact of specific environmental or social factors on investments is crucial. To illustrate, let's consider a scenario involving carbon emissions and water usage impacts on a company's sustainability performance. Presented with a question such as, "What's the effect of Company X's carbon emissions and water usage on its overall sustainability score?" a fine-tuned Language Model (LM) understands the basic environmental context—that "carbon emissions" and "water usage" are significant environmental metrics, and "Company X" is the variable under analysis. It might explain that "Company X has reported emissions levels that are above industry standards and high water usage, which negatively impacts its sustainability score." This demonstrates the fine-tuned LM's capability to provide contextually relevant information based on predefined data (Devlin et al., 2018).

However, this query also implicitly asks about the interactions between these metrics and their cumulative impact on the company's overall sustainability profile and market performance. This complex requirement might surpass the capabilities of a fine-tuned LM alone. Here, Retrieval-Augmented Generation (RAG) comes into play, accessing a vast database to retrieve detailed reports and data on "Company X's" carbon footprint and water management practices, and their direct and indirect effects on the company's sustainability score and long-term financial stability (Choi et al., 2020). In the carbon emissions example, the basic context with a fine-tuned LM can provide insights into how high carbon emissions from Company X contribute to climate change and regulatory risks, potentially leading to increased operational costs or penalties.

But complex interactions involving RAG can delve deeper into how these emissions specifically affect investor perceptions and stakeholder relationships and compare these metrics against industry benchmarks. For instance, accessing reports from sources like the Carbon Disclosure Project (CDP) or sustainability assessments from S&P Global can provide a more nuanced view. While fine-tuned LMs provide a solid understanding of basic sustainability metrics and their immediate impacts, advanced tools like RAG offer deeper insights into complex interactions and long-term risks associated with these factors. Combining these approaches allows for a comprehensive analysis that is crucial for informed decision-making in sustainable finance.

The adoption of and demand for Retrieval-Augmented Generation (RAG) systems vary significantly across different industries, shaped by each sector's unique requirements, the volume of data managed, and their reliance on AI-driven processes. Notably, the technology and IT sectors show a heightened demand due to their direct engagement with AI, machine learning, and data analytics innovations. In these fields, RAG is primarily utilized to enhance functionalities in search engines, elevate code generation processes, and augment the development of AI-driven tools and solutions.

Industry-Specific Applications of RAG:

1. RAG in Marketing and Advertising of ESG or Social Impact Investment Products: In marketing and advertising, RAG systems revolutionize how companies craft their communications. By retrieving and integrating data-driven insights, businesses can create highly personalized advertisements tailored to individual consumer preferences. This targeted approach significantly boosts engagement rates, improves conversions, and enhances the return on investment (ROI) by ensuring that marketing messages resonate more effectively with their intended audiences for social finance or sustainable investments. Social finance refers to financial investments that seek to generate social benefits alongside financial returns while sustainable investments refer to investments that consider ESG factors to generate long-term competitive financial returns and positive societal impact.
2. Customer Service and Support: RAG technology greatly benefits the customer service sector by providing instantaneous responses to customer queries. The system leverages a vast repository of historical interaction data, allowing for responses that are not only timely but also contextually informed. This capability substantially decreases response times and enhances the quality of customer support, fostering greater customer satisfaction and loyalty.
3. RAG Integration into Existing Systems: The integration of RAG models into current business infrastructures involves several critical steps:

    - Infrastructure Evaluation: Assess the existing technological setup to ensure it can support the computational demands of RAG, including adequate processing power, memory, and data storage.
    - Data Alignment: Standardize data formats and structures to meet the requirements of the RAG model, ensuring efficient data retrieval and processing.
    - Application Programming Interface (API) Development: Create APIs or interfaces that facilitate seamless communication between existing systems and the RAG model, enabling smooth data exchange and integration.
    - Continuous Learning: Implement mechanisms that allow the RAG model to continuously learn and update itself with new information, maintaining its relevance and accuracy.
    - Performance Monitoring: Establish a framework to monitor the system's performance, ensuring the RAG model consistently delivers accurate and reliable outputs.

By integrating RAG models, businesses enhance their capabilities in generating high-quality content and performing complex data analyses, thereby increasing operational efficiency and driving innovation. These diverse applications highlight how RAG systems can be tailored to meet the specific needs of sustainable finance and related industries, enhancing their capacity to leverage AI for improved automation, decision-making, and customer engagement.

9.2.5 The Emerging Agentic Workflow

At the Sequoia Capital AI Ascent 2024 conference, artificial intelligence luminary Andrew Ng unveiled a novel concept he termed "Agentic Workflow."[7] Ng (2024) explained how agentic reasoning enhances the efficiency of generative pre-trained transformers (GPTs), such as GPT-3.5, producing superior outputs compared to traditional zero-shot prompting methods like those used in GPT-4.[8] It is necessary to differentiate between agentic vs. non-agentic workflows to see the benefits and elements of this paradigm. In a typical non-agentic or zero-shot workflow, a prompt is provided to a model-like ChatGPT, which then generates a response in a single session without iteration—akin to writing a first draft without revision. In contrast, an agentic workflow embodies a more natural iterative process involving research, consultation, and revision, much like how humans typically refine their work.

Ng highlighted the effectiveness of agentic workflows with a practical example from coding. His team used the HumanEval coding benchmark dataset to compare the traditional zero-shot prompting with the agentic workflow approach. While GPT-3.5 achieved only a 48% accuracy and GPT-4 a 67% accuracy with zero-shot prompting, the agentic workflow allowed GPT-3.5 to surpass even GPT-4's zero-shot performance by breaking down tasks into multiple steps such as problem analysis, iterative coding, testing, and debugging.

Ng suggested four design patterns elaborated below:

a. Reflection: This involves the AI reviewing its answers, identifying errors, and refining its response. This iterative self-feedback mechanism improves the output's quality and accuracy, applicable not just to programming but across various domains including writing and design. The Self-Refine (Madaan et al., 2024) uses feedback and repeated iterations to improve the accuracy and quality of outputs from large language models. The key feature is that it improves itself without needing human input. On the other hand, the Reflexion (Shinn et al., 2024) method strengthens language models by using verbal feedback to help them make better decisions. It stores feedback in a memory system and can adapt to different kinds of feedback, which enhances its performance across many tasks.

b. Tool Use: Ng discussed the integration of specialized tools like Microsoft Co-Pilot, MidJourney, and Wolfram Alpha for tasks ranging from research to image generation. This pattern leverages external APIs to enhance the model's capabilities, reflecting early computer vision techniques in which visual tasks were outsourced to specialized functions. For example, Gorilla (Patil et al., 2023) is a large language model enhanced to make effective API calls. It specifically excels beyond GPT-4 by improving how it generates input parameters and reducing errors in content generation, known as hallucinations. MM-REACT (Z. Yang

---

[7] https://www.deeplearning.ai/the-batch/issue-242/.
[8] A. Ng, Agentic Design Pattern, April 2024, [online] Available: https://www.deeplearning.ai/the-batch/how-agents-can-improve-llm-performance/?ref=dl-staging-website.ghost.io.

et al., 2023b) is a method that equips ChatGPT to handle tasks that require understanding and integrating different types of data, like text, images, and web content. The development of these models emphasizes enhanced planning, reasoning, and action capabilities, suggesting that the future of LLMs will involve much broader applications beyond traditional text processing. This evolution will potentially make AI tools even more integral to solving complex problems and performing sophisticated tasks across different domains.

c. Planning: This pattern trains AI to autonomously plan, decompose, and execute complex tasks. A provided example involved an AI that identifies an image's posture, synthesizes a new image accordingly, and complements it with generated text. Recent studies (Shen et al., 2024; Wei et al., 2022) have collectively advanced the functionality of LLMs by equipping them with more structured reasoning abilities and the capability to interact with and utilize other specialized AI models. The Chain-of-Thought Prompting technique provides a framework for LLMs to break down and reason through problems methodically, significantly enhancing their problem-solving accuracy. Meanwhile, HuggingGPT exemplifies how integration with diverse expert models can expand the utility of LLMs beyond simple text-based tasks to include sophisticated multimodal interactions. Together, these methodologies not only improve the immediate effectiveness of LLMs in specialized tasks but also pave the way for broader applications in real-world scenarios, suggesting a future when AI can potentially handle increasingly complex and varied challenges across multiple domains.

d. Multi-Agent Collaboration: This involves multiple AI agents collaborating, simulating roles like a CEO or an expert programmer to enhance problem-solving capabilities. This approach encourages a division of labor among AIs to optimize output quality. ChatDev (Qian et al., 2023) is a framework where large language models operate as team members in software development. Each model plays a distinct role, such as a designer or developer, engaging in continuous dialogue to refine product requirements and generate code. Another development is AutoGen (Q. Wu et al., 2023a) is another framework that exemplifies the power of multi-agent collaboration. It integrates multiple language models, each responsible for different aspects of a task, such as analyzing requirements or designing software architecture. This setup demonstrates significant improvements in handling various programming tasks, showcasing the feasibility and effectiveness of collaborative AI in software engineering.

Ng's presentation emphasized that agentic workflows could significantly advance AI capabilities, making them more dynamic and contextually aware. This method promises to improve how AI systems analyze, plan, and iterate, potentially revolutionizing fields from software development to content creation. These advancements suggest a paradigm shift in AI application, moving away from static response generation to dynamic, context-aware processes that mimic human cognitive workflows. The agentic workflow not only maximizes the efficiency of existing models but also sets a foundation for the development of more sophisticated AI systems, marking a significant step toward achieving Artificial General Intelligence (AGI).

9.3 GenAI: A New Dawn for Sustainability Reporting

How can GenAI/LLM help in finance and accounting in general? Generative AI facilitates the automation of routine tasks such as data entry, categorization, and the generation of reports, thereby minimizing human error and reducing operational costs. Furthermore, these models support compliance efforts by ensuring conformity with changing regulations and advancing forensic accounting methods. A prior study demonstrated the use of ChatGPT (see Sect. 9.2.1) to analyze ESG reporting, evaluate corporate culture, and perform sentiment analysis on various aspects of company reporting (Cao & Zhai, 2023).

GenAI models excel in processing large datasets, improving the efficiency of algorithmic trading, bolstering risk management practices, and elevating fraud detection mechanisms. GenAI as used by Kim et al., (2023) provides reliable summaries of lengthy text documents, significantly reducing their length while maintaining or enhancing their informational content, proving its economic usefulness. This development is beneficial not only for academics but also for regulators and investors, who often grapple with the prohibitive costs of processing extensive disclosure information. GenAI could represent a significant technological leap in financial reporting, paralleling past innovations such as the SEC's introduction of EDGAR (Kim et al., 2023). The impact of "bloated" disclosures using GenAI highlights its potential to detect greenwashing and improve the clarity and effectiveness of financial disclosures. The role of GenAI in finance and accounting, as evidenced by its application in automating routine tasks and supporting compliance efforts, signifies a profound potential for revolutionizing the financial sector. The multiple uses of GenAI in the field of sustainable finance are shown in Fig. 9.4.

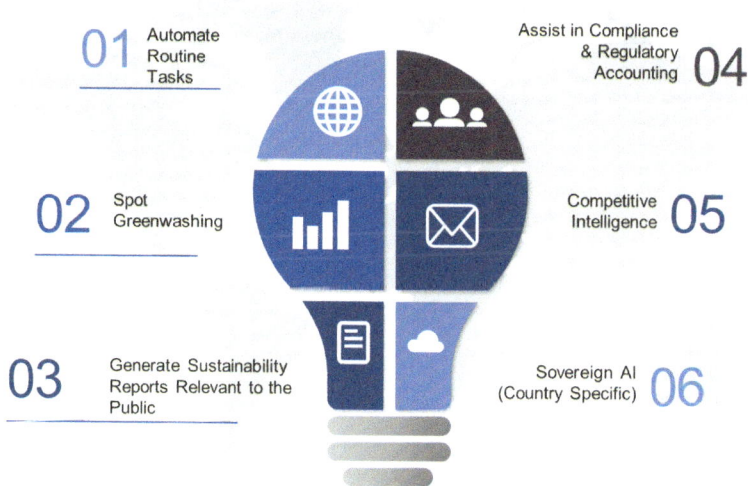

Fig. 9.4 Multiple uses of GenAI for sustainable finance

How can GenAI help in sustainability reporting aligned to a framework such as UN SDGs, GRI, or TCFD? For companies, GenAI can analyze existing reporting frameworks and suggest ways to streamline and harmonize disclosures across GRI, GHG, TCFD, and more. This reduces redundancies and improves transparency. GenAI has the potential to aid financial market participants map their activities to relevant Principal Adverse Impact (PAI) indicators. It can even suggest ways to mitigate negative impacts and report on progress, ensuring smoother compliance.

ChatGPT/Gemini has the potential to help companies map their activities to the UN SDGs' PAI indicators. This clarifies which environmental and social issues a company's operations potentially influence. ChatGPT/Gemini has the potential to help companies identify potential negative impacts and suggest mitigation strategies. It can even assist in reporting progress on these efforts, ensuring smoother compliance with regulations and stakeholder expectations. The true magic lies in the synergy between these functionalities. Streamlined reporting frees up resources to focus on the strategic aspects of sustainability. By mapping impacts and mitigating risks, companies can proactively address sustainability challenges and demonstrate leadership in a responsible future. In the next few years, these LLM models will be improved with better training data, eliminating obvious bias and limitations.

Our interview with **Per Edin**, Board Committee Chair and Artificial Intelligence Leader at KPMG shows the promise and the potential of AI in industry.

> **Expert in Focus: Per Edin**
>
> Per Edin serves as the Board Committee Chair and AI Go-to-Market leader at KPMG in the US. In his role, Per oversees the development of strategy services for the Technology, Media & Telecommunications (TMT) sector as a partner within the US firm's Advisory Services team. He provides guidance to both corporate and private equity clients on strategies aimed at driving growth, enhancing profitability, and transforming business models.

9.3 GenAI: A New Dawn for Sustainability Reporting

Per's career began at the European Space Agency, working on using space technology to mitigate natural disasters and developing civil applications of drones for Broadband satellite communications. He holds master's degrees in electrical engineering, Telecommunications, Computer Sciences, and Space Applications from the Royal Institute of Technology in Stockholm. With over 30 years of experience in Artificial Intelligence, Per is passionate about leveraging technology to boost human productivity and creativity in business, catering to both corporate and private equity clients. He collaborates with C-suite executives to shape strategies and implement strategic initiatives that accelerate growth, improve operations, and build essential capabilities. Since the launch of Chat-GPT 4, he has led the KPMG GenAI Rapid Response team, supporting over 1000 client engagements across various sectors and functions. He frequently collaborates with boards, C-suite leaders, and investors, sharing insights on GenAI, AI, and advanced analytics.

The 2023 KPMG Global Tech Survey (KPMG, 2024) reveals that three out of five respondents believe AI, including machine learning and Generative AI, will be crucial for achieving their business goals over the next three years. In the financial services sector, KPMG aims to connect technology, business, and specific problem-solving needs. They approach technology costs and investments in three categories: maintaining outdated systems, upgrading technology and related cultural changes, and ensuring future adaptability without increasing technical debt.

Prioritizing the timing, location, and scale of investment in AI transformation for 2024 is a complex task. One significant challenge highlighted by Per Edin (KPMG, 2024) is the 'last mile challenge of AI.' This issue is often overlooked.

Per explains, "Even if AI can help knowledge workers free up a third of their time in studies and pilots, this only translates into real productivity gains if all knowledge workers adopt the tools and re-invest hours saved into something more productive — for example, taking on more volume or higher value-add tasks."

Per further emphasizes, "These are major behavioral changes that cannot be ignored if PE firms are to deliver the productivity gains that AI promises. Success will require a carefully crafted transformation program with a portfolio of actions that hit all behavioral change barriers simultaneously. Solving this, at scale, may be the biggest value creation challenge GenAI will face, and not a muscle well trained in prior technology-driven disruptions."

Finally, the rapid adoption of AI heightens risks such as data privacy breaches, more sophisticated cyberattacks, and legal issues stemming from inherent biases in AI models. To mitigate these risks, it's crucial to implement a human-in-the-loop approach for many applications, establish 'Trusted AI' governance frameworks, and use third-party software solutions. A recent initiative by KPMG, Cranium, exemplifies this approach. Cranium is a software platform developed in the US to provide technology solutions that help organizations safely adopt and deploy AI models.

In the second article, the KPMG report (KPMG, 2024) on board oversight of Generative AI (GenAI) highlights several critical issues and offers guidance for boards to navigate this emerging technology (KPMG, 2024). As GenAI moves from experimentation to broad company-wide adoption, it presents both significant opportunities and challenges. The discussion centers around strategic importance of GenAI, behavioral and organizational challenges, evolving risks and governance needs and the role of the board and leadership. The report suggests the importance of careful oversight and strategic planning by boards and management teams.

9.3.1 Automating Routine Tasks

LLMs are transforming the finance industry by automating routine tasks, thus enabling financial institutions to operate more efficiently and effectively (Yan et al., 2023). This automation not only reduces operational costs but also enhances accuracy and customer satisfaction. FinGPT, a financial GPT, streamlines the analysis of

9.3 GenAI: A New Dawn for Sustainability Reporting

large datasets by automatically curating and interpreting financial data. This capability is crucial for generating comprehensive reports and insights without manual intervention (H. Yang et al., 2023a). LLMs can efficiently summarize lengthy financial documents, such as earnings reports and regulatory filings, providing quick and actionable insights (Phogat et al., 2023). LLMs enable chatbots to handle a wide range of customer queries, from account inquiries to transaction details. Advanced LLMs power virtual assistants that can conduct personalized interactions such as helping customers with financial planning and advising on products suited to their needs. LLMs analyze transaction data in real time to detect and flag unusual patterns indicative of fraudulent activity. This proactive monitoring helps in minimizing financial losses due to fraud (Chu et al., 2023). Thus, LLM automation not only reduces operational costs but also enhances accuracy and customer satisfaction.

9.3.2 Can GenAI Be Trained to Spot Greenwashing?

By analyzing language patterns and nuances, GenAI can be trained to flag potential greenwashing, helping investors see beyond misleading claims. GenAI can be a transformative tool in sustainable accounting and reporting, capable of enhancing the accessibility and quality of sustainability disclosures for a wide range of stakeholders.

Given the likelihood that training datasets for AI assistants like ChatGPT include both greenwashed information and more accurate portrayals of corporate sustainability performance, there is a risk that AI-generated content could perpetuate greenwashing. If GenAI is used to draft sections of sustainability reports, the issue of greenwashing would be of more significant concern, given misinformation and bias. Nonetheless, AI offers promising applications for cross-verifying narrative information against other sources, potentially safeguarding against greenwashing practices. As sustainability reporting aims to foster greater trust and transparency between companies and their stakeholders, it becomes imperative to critically assess the role and future implications of AI in the sustainability reporting landscape. There is a lot of work to be done in this area.

9.3.3 GenAI for Complying to Different Standards and Frameworks

GenAI can serve as a powerful tool, acting as a translator for sustainability reporting. It can analyze existing disclosures, suggest areas for streamlining, and ensure compliance across multiple frameworks. Companies investing in GenAI can then focus beyond mere reporting, aiming for tangible progress in sustainability. Asset managers and ESG rating companies can use GenAI to dissect the mountains of sustainability reports issued by companies. GenAI can turn qualitative reports into quantifiable metrics. Quantitative reporting empowers investors to compare companies based on tangible sustainability data, enabling more informed investment choices that align with their values. In the future, companies could leverage ChatGPT/Gemini to navigate the complexities of sustainability reporting. ChatGPT/Gemini has the potential to promote transparency by harmonizing disclosures across different frameworks including GRI, GHG, and TCFD, identifying redundancies, and suggesting ways to streamline data collection and reporting. This use case will be developed ensuring different guardrails are in place for training these models. This creates a clear and consistent picture of a company's sustainability efforts.

9.3.4 Bridging Compliance and Reporting Gaps

GenAI is a powerful tool that can transform how we approach sustainability and compliance. As we continue to explore the capabilities and limitations of GenAI, it is imperative to foster a balanced understanding of its role in sustainability reporting. The ultimate goal is to enhance trust and transparency between companies and their stakeholders, paving the way for a more sustainable future. Understanding its potential from both company and investor perspectives can unlock a more transparent and sustainable future. However, remaining cognizant of the ethical considerations and potential biases inherent in AI technologies is crucial. Ensuring transparency in how AI models are trained and applied is essential to maintaining trust and integrity in sustainability disclosures.

9.3.5 Competitive Intelligence

Incorporating LLMs into sustainability initiatives helps companies improve their competitive position in the rapidly evolving green economy. Businesses are striving to achieve their sustainability goals more effectively and stay ahead in the market using GenAI/LLM and other tools. There is work to be done in this area to position companies as well as cities to gain the right positioning in a competitive marketplace.

9.3.6 Sovereign AI

Generative AI holds the potential to significantly boost global GDP growth and transform white-collar work over the next decade. However, its rapid adoption may adversely affect labor and economic prosperity in developing countries that previously thrived on trends like outsourcing and digitization. Nations worldwide, from the Philippines to India, are facing the economic disruptions of AI, leading to actions aimed at protecting their sovereign interests. The UN Commission on Science and

Technology for Development[9] as well as tech leaders such as Jensen Huan[10] (CEO of NIVIDIA) and Michael Dell[11] (CEO of Dell Technologies) see the opportunities and the necessities of developing sovereign AI.

The fast-paced growth of AI, termed "flash growth," is dominated by a few Big Tech firms that shape how technologies like LLMs (e.g., ChatGPT) operate. This concentration of control raises concerns about economic dependence on a limited number of companies and the potential reversal of capacity building in less developed nations. Additionally, these Generative AI systems must be "taught" societal values, placing ethical decisions in the hands of a few.

To counter these risks, many governments are implementing AI regulations and exploring the development of sovereign AI systems, independent of Big Tech. For example, the EU AI Act and the US AI Executive Order are steps toward managing AI's societal impact. However, creating sovereign AI is costly and complex, potentially widening the digital divide. Collaborative efforts, such as shared computing resources among nations, and leveraging academic expertise, are essential strategies for overcoming these challenges. The future of AI offers immense promise if guided by responsible, inclusive policies that democratize its benefits.

9.4 Overcoming Challenges with GenAI

Within the scientific domain, ChatGPT's integration presents multifaceted challenges and ethical considerations that demand attention. Concerns range from ensuring the reliability and factual accuracy of AI-generated content to mitigating inherent biases within the model, stemming from its training data. The need to avoid overreliance on such tools is imperative to preserve critical thinking and problem-solving skills in the research community. Continuous monitoring and refinement of these models are essential for quality control and to address issues of dataset bias, which can adversely affect decision-making in critical sectors. Further, the model's complex nature poses difficulties in explainability, crucial for transparency and trust. Environmental considerations also emerge from the substantial energy requirements for operating these AI systems. Moreover, privacy concerns and the potential for generating harmful content necessitate the development of robust safety and privacy protocols. Lastly, improving real-time responsiveness and addressing cultural and linguistic biases are key to enhancing the model's inclusivity and utility.

ChatGPT's capabilities, while impressive, are marred by various biases and limitations stemming from its training data, such as inaccuracy, bias, and outdated knowledge. The model's challenges include struggles with contextual awareness, ethical dilemmas, and maintaining conversational context. Its text-based nature restricts it

---

[9] https://unctad.org/news/sovereign-gpts-aligning-values-ai-development.

[10] https://blogs.nvidia.com/blog/world-governments-summit/.

[11] https://indianexpress.com/article/technology/artificial-intelligence/michael-dell-india-ai-attractive-market-9341741/.

from generating visual content and hinders its ability to manage ambiguous or inappropriate queries effectively. These shortcomings underscore the need for continuous model improvements and responsible AI use (Agarwal & Mishra, 2021; Astobiza et al., 2021).

9.4.1 How Do Cognitive Biases and Fallacies in Human Decision-Making Impact GenAI Training?

When making decisions under risk and uncertainty, people often rely on heuristics—simple decision rules that allow them to make judgments without processing all available information. In complex situations or under time pressure, heuristics help individuals manage their limited capacity to process information by simplifying decision-making. How can GenAI System be trained in understanding these heuristics to provide better decision-making for sustainable finance? Behavioral finance examines (Baker & Nofsinger, 2010) the availability heuristic (Tversky & Kahneman, 1973) leads people to assess the likelihood or importance of an event based on how easily examples come to mind. In sustainable finance, this can cause investors to overemphasize recent or highly publicized environmental, social, and governance (ESG) issues while overlooking less visible but equally important factors. For example, a pension fund manager might prioritize investments in renewable energy projects following a major climate conference (such as UN or World Economic Forum) or disaster, while underweighting other critical areas like sustainable agriculture or water conservation, simply because they are less prominent in the media (Kahneman & Tversky, 1972).

Representativeness heuristic (Tversky & Kahneman, 1973) causes people to judge the probability of an event based on how closely it resembles their existing mental models or stereotypes. In the context of sustainable finance, this can lead to misjudgments about the true impact or sustainability of investments. Investors might assume that a company with a green logo or marketing campaign is more sustainable than it actually is, leading to potential greenwashing, where funds are directed toward companies that do not truly meet ESG criteria. Anchoring bias occurs when people rely too heavily on the first piece of information they receive when making decisions. In finance, initial evaluations or ratings can unduly influence the assessment of an investment's sustainability.

Anchoring bias (Tversky & Kahneman, 1974) occurs when people rely too heavily on the first piece of information they receive when making decisions. In finance, initial evaluations or ratings can unduly influence the assessment of an investment's sustainability. If a sustainable investment fund is initially rated as high-performing based on certain metrics, such as GHG emissions, fund managers may continue to favor it even if later data suggests declining performance or emerging risks, potentially leading to poor long-term outcomes.

Thus, when training a GenAI model for sustainable finance related decision-making, understanding and incorporating these heuristics can both enhance the model's effectiveness and help mitigate potential biases.

9.4.2 The Need for Human Validation

This Sect. 9.4.2.expands on the critical need for expert review and continuous testing of GenAI models to ensure their reliability and trustworthiness in sustainable finance. The necessity for human validation in the utilization of Generative Artificial Intelligence (GenAI) models within sustainable finance is underscored by the potential risks associated with misinformation, lies, whitewashing, and greenwashing. When financial institutions increasingly rely on GenAI to process, analyze, and report sustainability data, the accuracy and integrity of these outputs become paramount.

Expert review plays a crucial role in validating the outputs of GenAI models. Professionals with domain expertise in sustainability and finance are essential for scrutinizing AI-generated reports and analyses to detect any inaccuracies, biases, or misrepresentations. Experts can assess the context, relevance, and credibility of GenAI insights, ensuring they align with established sustainability principles and reporting standards (Adams & McNicholas, 2007; Eccles & Krzus, 2010). For instance, sustainability reports reviewed by experts can help identify instances when GenAI might have inadvertently amplified greenwashing claims by misinterpreting data or language nuances (Lyon & Montgomery, 2015). Improving the real-time responsiveness of GenAI models and addressing cultural and linguistic biases are key to enhancing their inclusivity and utility. The chapter discusses advanced prompt engineering techniques in Sect. 9.5 to maximize GenAI's potential and ensure it serves a diverse user base effectively.

Continual testing of GenAI models under various scenarios is vital to assess their robustness and adaptability over time. This involves subjecting GenAI systems to a wide range of data inputs, including edge cases, to evaluate their performance and accuracy in different contexts (Raj & Seamans, 2019). Such rigorous testing can uncover potential weaknesses in AI algorithms that might lead to misleading or erroneous sustainability assessments. Moreover, it ensures that GenAI models remain up-to-date with evolving sustainability reporting standards and regulations, such as the Global Reporting Initiative (GRI) or the Task Force on Climate-related Financial Disclosures (TCFD, 2017).

The integration of human validation and continual testing is crucial for mitigating the risks of misinformation and greenwashing in sustainable finance. By involving experts in the review process, financial institutions can enhance the credibility of their sustainability disclosures and investment products (Sullivan & Gouldson, 2017). Additionally, systematic testing of GenAI models helps in refining their analytical capabilities, reducing the likelihood of errors that could mislead investors or stakeholders about a company's environmental or social impact (Christensen et al., 2019).

9.4.3 Ethical Considerations and Bias

The integration of Generative Artificial Intelligence (GenAI) in sustainable finance brings to the forefront a myriad of ethical considerations and challenges related to bias and transparency. These issues are particularly pronounced when considering the varied contexts of developing countries (the Global South with less information-rich environments) and advanced economies.

The foundation of trust in GenAI-driven sustainable finance solutions lies in their transparency and integrity. Ethical challenges emerge when these technologies are opaque, making it difficult for stakeholders to understand how decisions are made or how data are processed (Mittelstadt et al., 2016). This lack of transparency can obscure the presence of biases in AI models, undermining their integrity and the trust stakeholders place in them. AI systems, including GenAI, inherit biases from their training data. In the context of sustainable finance, such biases could skew investment recommendations, risk assessments, and sustainability ratings, potentially disadvantaging certain regions, industries, or companies based on incomplete or biased data (Barocas et al., 2019). The challenge is more acute in developing countries (the Global South), where data may be less available, less reliable, or not representative, leading to models that are less accurate or fair when applied in these contexts. This leads to bias.

Developing countries often suffer from a lack of representation in global datasets, a situation is termed as "data colonialism" (Couldry & Mejias, 2019). This lack of representation can lead GenAI models to produce outcomes that are less relevant or accurate for these regions, reinforcing existing inequalities and potentially directing sustainable investments away from where they might be most needed. This leads to inequities caused by data representation. For example, indigenous/tribal populations across the world depend on ecosystem services provided by nature. Their valuation of such services is difficult to gauge using a Western or developed mindset. One needs to put on an "indigenous tribal lens."

Addressing the challenges is a necessity in the increasing use of AI related to enhancing transparency, bias mitigation, inclusive data practices, and sustainable AI development. Adopting explainable AI (XAI) principles can help mitigate these ethical concerns by making GenAI systems more transparent and understandable to all stakeholders, including those in the Global South (Arrieta et al., 2020). Developers must employ strategies to identify and mitigate biases in AI models. This involves diversifying training datasets, employing fairness-aware algorithms, and continually monitoring and updating models to ensure they remain fair and equitable across different regions and demographics (Mehrabi et al., 2021).

Actively including diverse and representative data from the Global South in training datasets can improve the relevance and fairness of GenAI applications in sustainable finance. Collaboration with local stakeholders to collect and validate data can enhance the accuracy and applicability of AI models in these contexts. Prioritizing energy-efficient AI training methods and using renewable energy sources for data centers can help reduce the environmental footprint of GenAI technologies.

Additionally, developing lightweight models that require less computational power without compromising performance can contribute to more sustainable AI practices.

In conclusion, while GenAI holds significant promise for advancing sustainable finance, addressing its ethical challenges, particularly around transparency, bias, and environmental sustainability, is crucial. By adopting ethical AI practices, the financial sector can leverage GenAI to not only enhance financial returns but also contribute to a more equitable and sustainable world.

9.5 Unlocking Potential: Prompt Engineering for Sustainable Fintech—Use Cases

Large Language Models (LLMs) are revolutionizing natural language processing (NLP) due to their ability to learn with minimal data. This section first explores the basics of prompt engineering and then describes three key techniques that unlock potential applying few-shot, zero-shot, and multimodal chain-of-thought prompting. These models are celebrated for their ability to effectively learn from minimal examples or even in the absence of task-specific training. Illustrative examples are drawn from sustainable Fintech. This section will delve into practical examples of GenAI-driven sustainability data analysis. Methods for ensuring the accuracy and trustworthiness of GenAI-generated insights will be presented.

9.5.1 Mastering Effective Prompts: Extracting Insights from the Web with ChatGPT/Gemini

This subsection 9.5.1 provides some specific examples using ChatGPT/Gemini for applications in sustainable finance.

The basic case involves clear and specific prompts: To obtain the desired response, ensuring prompts are explicit and unambiguous is important. Ambiguous prompts may lead to unsatisfactory or irrelevant responses.

For example:

Less effective prompt: *"**Which S&P 500 company has the best and most comprehensive sustainability report?**"*

Evaluation Criteria

The companies above are recognized for their comprehensive reporting based on several criteria:

- **Detail and Transparency**: Providing in-depth data and clear narratives on their sustainability performance.
- **Scope of Coverage**: Addressing a wide range of ESG factors, including environmental impact, social responsibility, and governance.
- **Commitment to Goals**: Setting and tracking ambitious sustainability goals.
- **Third-Party Verification**: Many of these reports are independently audited or verified, adding credibility to their claims (S&P Global) (S&P Global) (The Center for Audit Quality).

Conclusion

While many S&P 500 companies produce high-quality sustainability reports, Microsoft, Apple, Tesla, Alphabet, and Johnson & Johnson are frequently recognized for their outstanding efforts. Each of these companies not only reports comprehensively but also leads in setting ambitious sustainability targets and demonstrating transparent progress.

For more details on their reports, you can visit their respective sustainability pages:

- Microsoft Sustainability
- Apple Environment
- Tesla Impact Report
- Google Sustainability
- Johnson & Johnson Health for Humanity

More effective prompt: *"What are the GHG emissions of a cement, oil and gas and steel company in the US?"*

Summary of Emissions

Industry	Company	Total GHG Emissions (2022)	Scope 1 and Scope 2 Emissions
Cement	Cemex USA	10.2 million metric tons CO2e	Direct and indirect emissions from production
Oil and Gas	ExxonMobil	108 million metric tons CO2e	Emissions from operations and energy use
Steel	Nucor Corp	24 million metric tons CO2e	Emissions from steel production processes

References:

1. **Cemex USA:** Cemex Annual Report 2022
2. **ExxonMobil:** ExxonMobil Sustainability Report 2022
3. **Nucor Corporation:** Nucor Sustainability Report 2022

These reports provide detailed information on the GHG emissions and sustainability efforts of each company.

A more advanced case provides context and background information: Offering context or background information when necessary to help ChatGPT understand the subject matter generates informed responses. For example:

Less effective prompt: *"What was the contribution of steel companies to emission in the US?"*

More effective prompt: *"What are Scope 1 and Scope 2 emission contributions of Nucor Steel or Cleveland Cliff?"*

Specify desired format and structure: Guiding ChatGPT toward a specific response format or structure ensures the output meets the user's expectations. For example:

Less effective prompt: *"Give me some emission reduction tips."*

More effective prompt: *"Give me some ways in which steel companies can reduce their emission footprint."*

A third case applies constraints and limitations: Setting boundaries on the response, such as character limits, timeframes, or scope, maintains focus and conciseness. For example:

Less effective prompt: *"Tell me about the use of GenAI."*

More effective: *"List the use of GenAI in sustainability finance products highlighting 5 key contributions."*

The next case is iterative prompting: If the initial response did not meet the user's expectations, refining the prompt or breaking it down into smaller sub-questions guides ChatGPT toward the desired information. For example, ChatGPT 4o produces a complete answer.

Initial prompt: *"**What are the business impact of China's naval exercises and missile strikes in the South China Sea on Taiwan?**"*

Revised prompts: "How to quantify this risk to the US market? What are the business impact of China's naval exercises and strikes in the South China sea on Taiwan? How do you quantify this risk to the US markets?"

Which response do you prefer?

China's naval exercises and strikes in the South China Sea, particularly targeting areas around Taiwan, have significant business and economic impacts. These impacts extend to Taiwan's economy and can indirectly affect US markets. Here are some key points to consider:

Business Impact on Taiwan

1. Trade Disruption:
   - Taiwan is a major global hub for semiconductor manufacturing, with companies like TSMC (Taiwan Semiconductor Manufacturing Company) playing a critical role in the global supply chain. Any disruption in Taiwan's

China's naval exercises and strikes in the South China Sea, particularly targeting areas around Taiwan, have significant geopolitical and economic implications. These actions contribute to heightened regional tensions and can disrupt global markets, including those in the US. Let's break down the business impacts and how to quantify the risks to the US markets.

Business Impact on Taiwan

1. Supply Chain Disruptions:
   - Semiconductor Industry: Taiwan is home to TSMC (Taiwan Semiconductor Manufacturing Company), a critical supplier of semiconductors globally. Military activities can disrupt

9.5.2 What's in a Name? Few-Shot, Zero-Shot, and Multimodal Chain-Of-Thought Prompting

This subsection 9.5.2 explores three key techniques of prompting with relevant examples from sustainable Fintech. Prompting is an art form that produces more effective and complete responses matching the user's expectations. For example,

9.5 Unlocking Potential: Prompt Engineering for Sustainable Fintech—Use ...

 What is the GHG emissions of a cement, oil and gas and steel company in the US? provide actual examples

Show drafts

Unfortunately, I cannot directly access and share private data on specific companies' emissions. However, I can guide you on how to find the GHG emissions of cement, oil & gas, and steel companies in the US using actual examples:

1. Company Websites:

Most large companies publish sustainability reports which often include data on greenhouse gas emissions (GHG). Here's how to find them for specific examples:

- **Cement: Eagle Materials Inc.** (https://eaglematerials.com/) is a major US cement producer. Look for their "Sustainability Report" under the "Investors" section.
- **Oil & Gas: Exxon Mobil** (https://corporate.exxonmobil.com/) is a leading US oil & gas company. Search their website for "Sustainability Report" or "Environmental Performance" within the "Sustainability and Reports" section.
- **Steel: Nucor Corporation** (https://nucor.com/) is a prominent US steel producer. Search their website for "Sustainability Report" or "ESG Report" under the "Investors" section.

2. Financial Databases:

If you have access to financial databases like S&P Global Market Intelligence or Bloomberg, you can search for these companies and find their ESG data, which might include greenhouse gas emissions.

Zero-shot prompting is a technique used in large language models (LLMs) to generate text or perform tasks without being explicitly trained on specific examples for those tasks. Here, the LLM leverages its pre-trained knowledge and understanding of language to complete tasks without any specific training examples. The user simply provides a clear and concise prompt that instructs the LLM on the desired task or outcome. The prompt does not include any specific examples or training data related to the task. Zero-prompt may include classification questions, question answering, translation, and creative text generation. However, these models might struggle with complex tasks or require very specific prompts to achieve desired results. A question and answer prompt, such as "What are the reported greenhouse gas emissions of Exxon in 2023 and 2023 in terms of CO2e," provides quite a lengthy response.

Which are the ten ESG mutual funds in the US that have shown the highest returns in the past 5 years?

Unfortunately, I can't provide a definitive list of the top 10 mutual ESG funds in the US with the highest returns over the past 5 years for a few reasons:

- **Market Volatility:** Fund performance fluctuates constantly, especially within the ESG sector where market trends and investment styles can rapidly shift. What was top-performing yesterday may not be today.
- **Reliable Data:** Identifying the absolute top 10 requires up-to-the-minute, accurate data across a vast number of funds. This often requires subscription-based financial data services.
- **Defining "ESG":** ESG funds have diverse strategies and focuses (environmental focus, social, governance). A fund excelling in one area might underperform another considered "top-ranked" overall.

However, I can guide you to find this information reliably and make informed choices:

Resources:

- **Financial News Websites:**
    - Morningstar (https://www.morningstar.com/): Offers fund screening tools, ESG ratings, and performance data.
    - MarketWatch (https://www.marketwatch.com/): Provides financial news and analysis, sometimes ranking top ESG performers.
    - Bloomberg (https://www.bloomberg.com/): Robust financial data, often with an ESG angle in their reporting.
- **ESG-Specific Resources:**
    - USSIF (https://www.ussif.org/): The Forum for Sustainable and Responsible Investment offers fund screening tools and resources.
    - Your Future Planet ([invalid URL removed]): News and rankings focused on ESG investing.

Things to Consider:

- **Your Investment Goals:** What matters most to you? High returns, specific environmental focus, social impact, etc. This narrows your search.

Few-shot prompting is a technique used in Large Language Models (LLMs), which bridges the gap between zero-shot prompting and traditional training with large datasets. It provides a little more guidance than zero-shot prompting, aiming to improve the accuracy and control of the model's output. The user provides the

9.5 Unlocking Potential: Prompt Engineering for Sustainable Fintech—Use ...

LLM with a prompt that describes the desired outcome or task. But unlike zero-shot prompting, the user includes a few examples (usually 1–10) that demonstrate the desired format or output. These "shots" act as a mini-training session.

The LLM utilizes its pre-trained knowledge, the prompt instructions, and the provided examples to generate text or perform tasks more accurately aligned with the user's expectations.

To summarize, few-shot prompting involves training the model on a limited set of labeled examples tailored to a particular task, which, despite the availability of larger datasets, remains a preferred approach due to the high resource demands of data labeling and extensive training processes. Conversely, zero-shot prompting bypasses the need for task-specific training altogether, leveraging pre-trained models to make predictions on both familiar and novel categories without any labeled examples or fine-tuning, offering significant savings in computational resources and time. Thus zero-shot represents a forward-thinking approach to learning, enabling models to tackle tasks without any direct training examples by using model instructions or "prompting" techniques. These prompts can be crafted either manually or through automated processes. Studies have shown that while models like GPT-3 exhibit promising capabilities across various tasks using zero-shot, one-shot, and multi-shot prompts, their performance in zero-shot settings often falls short compared to when they are provided with a few examples. This discrepancy is believed to stem from the challenge models face in adapting to prompts that differ from their pre-training data formats.

Innovations such **as Multimodal Chain of Thought prompting (CoT)** have emerged to improve LLMs' performance in zero-shot scenarios by guiding them through a step-by-step reasoning process, significantly enhancing their reasoning capabilities without task-specific examples. These models incorporate data from various modalities, such as images and videos, alongside text-based prompts. Furthermore, advancements combining images and text, such as Img2LLM, a plug-and-play module (Guo et al., 2023), have introduced modules for generating effective prompts from image content, enabling LLMs to address zero-shot visual question-answering tasks without comprehensive training. Additionally, new frameworks like ChatIE (Wei et al., 2023) have been developed to exploit LLMs like ChatGPT for zero-shot information extraction through a multi-turn question-answering approach, showcasing the expanding versatility and application potential of LLMs in various domains. While promising, multimodal CoT prompting presents challenges. Developing LLMs capable of handling diverse data formats and reasoning processes is complex. Additionally, interpreting the reasoning steps, especially for intricate scenarios, can be difficult.

Prompt given *"**What is the relevance of this image to Scope 1,2,3 GHG of the fossil fuel industry?**"*

Source https://www.ucsusa.org/resources/hidden-costs-fossil-fuels

◆ The image you sent is of a smoke stack emitting smoke from a coal-fired power plant. This image is partially relevant to the Scope 1, 2, and 3 GHG emissions of the fossil fuel industry, here's why:

Relevance to Scope 1 Emissions:

- **Partially Relevant:** Coal-fired power plants are not directly part of the oil and gas extraction or refining processes that generate Scope 1 emissions for the oil industry.
- **Indirect Contribution:** However, coal-fired power plants are a major source of greenhouse gas emissions from the fossil fuel industry in general. Many utilities that generate electricity with coal might also sell fossil fuels like natural gas. In that sense, the image indirectly depicts a source of Scope 1 emissions within the broader fossil fuel industry.

9.5 Unlocking Potential: Prompt Engineering for Sustainable Fintech—Use …

Relevance to Scope 2 Emissions:

- **More Relevant:** If the oil and gas company operates the coal-fired power plant in the image, the emissions would be directly relevant to their Scope 2 emissions. Scope 2 covers purchased electricity and heat.
- **Uncertain Applicability:** Without knowing the owner or operator of the power plant, it's impossible to say for sure if the emissions contribute to an oil and gas company's Scope 2 emissions.

Relevance to Scope 3 Emissions:

- **Least Relevant:** Scope 3 emissions are from a company's value chain but outside their direct control. The emissions from this power plant would not be part of the oil and gas company's Scope 3 emissions unless the oil and gas company is somehow responsible for the downstream use of the electricity generated by this plant (e.g., a very specific contractual agreement).

Overall, the image has limited direct relevance to the oil and gas industry's Scope 1 emissions, but it is more relevant to Scope 2 emissions if the oil and gas company operates the plant. It has minimal relevance to Scope 3 emissions.

In conclusion, few-shot prompting involves training models with a small set of labeled examples tailored to specific tasks, offering an effective but resource-intensive approach. In contrast, zero-shot prompting bypasses the need for task-specific training by leveraging pre-trained models to make predictions on novel categories without labeled examples or fine-tuning, saving significant computational resources and time. Zero-shot prompting represents a forward-thinking approach that allows models to tackle tasks using model instructions or "prompting" techniques, either crafted manually or through automated processes. While models like GPT-3 show promising capabilities, their performance in zero-shot settings often lags behind scenarios where a few examples are provided, due to challenges in adapting to new prompt formats. Innovations like Multimodal Chain of Thought (CoT) prompting have emerged to enhance reasoning capabilities in zero-shot scenarios by guiding models through step-by-step processes. These models integrate various data types, such as images and text, improving performance in tasks like visual question answering without extensive training. Despite these advancements, challenges remain in developing models capable of handling diverse data formats and reasoning processes, indicating the need for continued innovation in the field.

9.5.3 Extracting Specific Information from US SEC 10-K Filings

This subsection 9.5.3 presents extensive analysis on the types of risks mentioned in 10-K filings of 90 companies. US companies file form 10-K annually or semiannually to the US Securities and Exchange Commission (SEC), which describes a company's business and the risks it faces including natural disasters, climate change, and impacts on supply chains and operations. A list of 50 key words (Appendix) was utilized to filter the Edgar database[12] for specific weather related mentions in the reports. This analysis resulted in 90 companies that had mentioned words such as droughts, hurricanes, floods, wildfires, and other disasters impacting their business in their 10-K filings. Each LLM is given the following prompt: *On a scale of − 1 to 1, where − 1 is the most negative and 1 is the most positive, what is the sentiment value of the following text in the context of each of the fifty words.* The programming was done in Python.

Companies usually report natural disaster risk and exposure information in their 10-K filings. Our analysis from this database reveals that companies provide sentiment about the risks in a qualitative manner to assure their shareholders of their awareness. Sometimes these statements are negative or positive and sometimes neutral. We gauge these sentiments around various natural disasters. ChatGPT provides the following list of companies that show the highest negative sentiment overall concerning their hazards. However, ChatGPT does not provide insights on why they are facing negative sentiments around hazards:

- Exponent, Inc. is an engineering and scientific consulting firm that provides technical solutions and litigation support to industries like energy, manufacturing, and transportation.
- Avista Corporation is an energy holding company that operates electric and natural gas utilities in the western United States.
- JBG Smith Properties is a real estate investment trust (REIT) that invests, develops, manages, and leases office and residential properties in the Washington, D.C. metro area and other key markets in the United States.
- Clean Energy Fuels Corp. is a provider of natural gas and renewable natural gas (RNG) for vehicles and a developer of renewable natural gas infrastructure.
- Imperial Oil Limited is an integrated oil and gas company that explores for, produces, refines, transports, and markets petroleum products in Canada.
- Murphy Oil Corporation is an exploration and production company engaged in the exploration, development, and production of crude oil and natural gas in the United States and internationally.

ChatGPT provides the following list of companies with the worst negative sentiment:

---

[12] https://www.sec.gov/edgar/search/#/q=climate&dateRange=1y&filter_forms=10-K. Sample search using climate in 10-K filing for one tax year 2023 results in 4345.

- ADT Inc. ADT provides electronic security services for homes and businesses in the United States and Canada. https://www.adt.com/
- Federal Home Loan Bank of Topeka. This is a regional wholesale bank that provides financing to member institutions, primarily community banks, credit unions, insurance companies, and community development financial institutions. https://www.fhlbtopeka.com/
- Chubb Limited. Chubb is a publicly traded insurance company that provides commercial and personal property and casualty insurance, accident and health insurance, reinsurance, and life insurance. https://www.chubb.com/us-en/
- Assured Guaranty Ltd. Assured Guaranty is a financial services company specializing in credit enhancement products, such as financial guaranty insurance, for the public finance and structured finance markets. https://assuredguaranty.com/investor-information
- Murphy Oil Corporation. Murphy Oil Corporation is an exploration and production company engaged in the exploration, development, and production of oil and natural gas in the United States and internationally. https://www.murphyoilsoap.com/
- Hallador Energy Company. Hallador is a coal producer with active mining operations in Pennsylvania, West Virginia, and Maryland. https://halladorenergy.com/overview/default.aspx
- Alliance Resource Partners, L.P. Alliance is a coal producer that mines and sells coal to electric utilities and industrial customers in the United States. https://www.arlp.com/
- MasTec, Inc. MasTec is a leading infrastructure construction company specializing in the engineering, procurement, construction, and maintenance of energy, communication, and utility infrastructure. https://www.mastec.com/

The user can delve into negative climate risks. Google Gemini provided the following answer to the prompt: **Why would these companies face drought risk?**

While the companies you mentioned operate in diverse sectors, they can still face indirect risks from droughts due to the interconnected nature of the economy and infrastructure. Here's how:

1. *Disruptions to their supply chains: Droughts can impact the availability and cost of resources required by these companies in various ways:*

   - *Energy companies: Droughts can affect water levels in rivers used for transportation, hindering the delivery of coal or other resources to power plants. Additionally, droughts can disrupt agricultural production, impacting the availability of biofuels used in some energy generation.*
   - *Financial institutions: Droughts can negatively impact the financial health of borrowers in drought-stricken regions, potentially increasing loan defaults and impacting the financial performance of banks and insurance companies.*

- Infrastructure companies: Droughts can strain water resources used in construction projects, potentially impacting project timelines and costs. Additionally, droughts can increase the risk of wildfires, which can damage infrastructure and disrupt construction activities.

2. Increased costs: Droughts can lead to higher energy prices due to reduced hydropower generation and potential reliance on alternative, more expensive sources. This can impact the operational costs of all the companies listed, regardless of their specific industry.
3. Regulatory changes: Droughts can lead to stricter water use regulations, impacting the operations of various companies:

    - Energy companies: May face restrictions on water usage for cooling power plants, potentially forcing them to reduce output or invest in alternative cooling methods.
    - Construction companies: May face limitations on water usage for construction activities, impacting project timelines and costs.

4. Reputational risks: Companies operating in water-stressed regions may face public scrutiny and reputational risks if perceived as not being water-conscious or contributing to the problem.

    It's important to remember that the severity of these risks will vary depending on the specific company, its location, and its water usage. However, it's crucial for companies to be aware of the potential indirect impacts of droughts and take steps to mitigate them, such as:

    - Diversifying their supply chains to reduce reliance on resources from drought-prone regions.
    - Implementing water conservation measures to reduce their water footprint.
    - Developing contingency plans to address potential disruptions caused by droughts.
    - Engaging with stakeholders to address concerns about water usage and demonstrate responsible water management practices.

Drought impacts the shareholder perception of risk and valuation. By taking proactive measures, these companies can minimize the potential impact of droughts on their operations and reputation. GenAI and LLM models have a large role in sifting through the filings of companies for specific instances of risks and valuation.

9.6 The Elephant in the Room: Are GenAI and Other AI Models Increasing GHG Emissions?

The environmental impact of training and running large AI models presents an ethical paradox in the application of GenAI for sustainable finance. The significant energy consumption associated with these processes (Strubell et al., 2019) can contribute

9.6 The Elephant in the Room: Are GenAI and Other AI Models Increasing ...

to the very environmental degradation that sustainable finance seeks to mitigate, highlighting the need for sustainable practices in AI development and deployment. A whole field called **Sustainable AI** is emerging (Dauvergne, 2020). Sustainable AI is a movement and field of practice that aims to minimize the environmental impact of artificial intelligence (AI) technologies while maximizing their positive social and economic contributions. This field encompasses two key aspects. First, using AI for sustainability addresses environmental and social challenges such as climate change mitigation, biodiversity protection, and resource efficiency (Vinuesa et al., 2020). The second aspect focuses on sustainability of AI, which is reducing the carbon footprint and resource consumption associated with the development, training, and deployment of AI models (Van Wynsberghe et al., 2023). This field holds the perspective that the environmental impact of AI is not just a technical issue; it's an ethical one. Environmental sustainability must be considered alongside other ethical concerns as AI becomes more widespread. There is research now on energy usage of data centers.

Data centers are essential for the digital world, storing and processing vast amounts of information that power everything from online shopping to video streaming. However, their operations come with a significant environmental cost,[13] primarily due to their high energy consumption. Datacenters are filled with power-hungry servers, storage units, and network equipment that constantly generate heat. Powerful cooling systems are needed to prevent overheating, further adding to the energy demand. The growing reliance on digital services is expected to lead to an increase in the number and size of data centers, potentially worsening the problem.

In 2022, International Energy Agency[14] noted that datacenters globally consumed around 240–340 TWh1, or around 1–1.3% of global final electricity demand. This amount (TWh) of electricity annually is equivalent to the annual consumption of several European countries. It translates to 3.5% of global greenhouse gas (GHG) emissions, equivalent with the entire aviation industry. A recent report from Morgan Stanley[15] warns that there is a 70% increase in energy demand every year, from under 15 terawatt hours in 2023 to an estimated 224 TWh in 2029. Another report from Price Waterhouse Cooper[16] shows how GenAI models training and deployment impact sustainability, detailing consumption patterns. The substantial increase in energy consumption not only raises sustainability concerns but also amplifies potential contributions to climate change. Despite efforts to use cleaner energy sources, the spike in power usage could mean more reliance on fossil fuels, challenging global efforts to reduce carbon emissions (Masanet et al., 2020; Siddik et al., 2021).

---

[13] https://www.technologyreview.com/2019/06/06/239031/training-A-single-ai-model-can-emit-as-much-carbon-as-five-cars-in-their-lifetimes/.

[14] https://www.iea.org/energy-system/buildings/data-centres-and-data-transmission-networks.

[15] https://www.morningstar.com/news/marketwatch/2024013144/ai-sector-is-on-course-to-use-as-much-electricity-as-spain-by-2027-new-report-warns.

[16] https://www.pwc.com/us/en/tech-effect/emerging-tech/impacts-of-generative-ai-on-sustainability.html#:~:text=GenAI's%20biggest%20contribution%20to%20increasing,will%20have%20a%20greater%20impact.

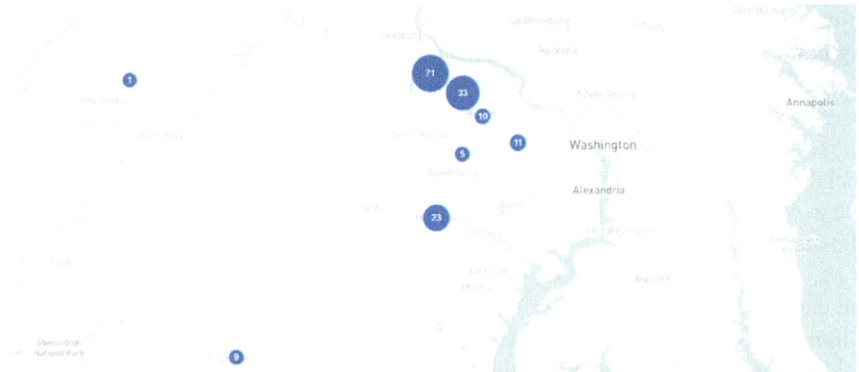

Fig. 9.5 Map of an area in Virginia, showing data centers being built in proximity to the Washington DC metropolitan area

There are ten data centers[17] in Lagos, Nigeria, where scarce water resources are being used for cooling instead of supplying drinking water to people in the area, who are now demanding accountability for water usage (Oson, 2024). Northern Virginia, home to the world's largest data center market, has experienced a significant increase in energy use due to data centers. Figure 9.5 shows a map of northern Virgina, where Ashburn has 71 data centers and Sterling has 33, in proximity to Washington DC. This is called the "Data Center Alley" (see Fig. 9.5).

Mitigating the Environmental Impact of datacenters is on the radar as advancements in technology lead to more efficient hardware and cooling systems, reducing energy consumption per unit of processing power. Data centers are increasingly shifting toward renewable energy sources like solar and wind power. New data center designs prioritize energy efficiency through air-free cooling and optimized server placement for better airflow. Google Cloud is the first major company to use 100% renewable energy. Governments can play a role by incentivizing or mandating the adoption of energy-efficient technologies and renewable energy sources by data center operators. Clearer reporting standards for energy consumption and GHG emissions can encourage responsible practices and inform consumer choices. Collaboration between technology companies, policymakers, and energy providers is crucial to develop and implement innovative solutions for sustainable data centers. In conclusion, data centers are vital for the digital age, but their environmental impact cannot be overlooked. By embracing technological advancements, renewable energy, and collaborative efforts, we can ensure that these facilities power the digital world in a more sustainable way.

While energy-intensive, GenAI models show great potential in addressing environmental challenges. Strategies to reduce their carbon footprint include optimizing computing locations and using fine-tuned models. Importantly, GenAI solutions often produce significantly fewer emissions than traditional human-driven methods.

---

[17] https://www.datacentermap.com/nigeria/lagos/.

However, evaluating the full environmental impact of GenAI—positive and negative—requires further research. This has to be scoped out in every project to justify the use of GenAI.

9.7 Conclusion: Charting the Path Forward

Generative AI (GenAI) stands at the forefront of revolutionizing the Fintech sector by addressing sustainability challenges through advanced data analysis and reporting mechanisms. The deployment of GenAI technologies offers significant opportunities for enhancing the accuracy, efficiency, and comprehensiveness of sustainability disclosures, which are essential for investors, companies, and regulatory bodies aiming to align financial practices with environmental, social, and governance (ESG) criteria.

One of the primary opportunities presented by GenAI is its ability to process and analyze vast amounts of unstructured sustainability data, transforming qualitative reports into quantifiable metrics. This capability enables a more nuanced understanding of a company's sustainability efforts, facilitating informed decision-making and investment strategies that prioritize long-term environmental and social value. Additionally, GenAI aids in harmonizing reporting standards across different frameworks, such as the Global Reporting Initiative (GRI) and the Task Force on Climate-related Financial Disclosures (TCFD), thereby simplifying compliance and enhancing transparency.

However, the integration of GenAI into sustainability practices in Fintech also necessitates careful consideration of ethical and environmental concerns. The development and operation of AI technologies consume considerable computational resources, leading to significant energy use and potential increases in greenhouse gas (GHG) emissions. Therefore, it is crucial to pursue sustainable AI practices, such as optimizing data center energy efficiency and leveraging renewable energy sources, to mitigate the environmental footprint of AI infrastructure.

Moreover, ethical considerations are paramount in ensuring that GenAI applications do not perpetuate biases or misinformation, particularly in the context of sustainability reporting. Ensuring the integrity of GenAI-generated insights requires robust validation mechanisms including human oversight and continual model testing under diverse scenarios. Transparency in AI development and application processes is essential to maintain trust and reliability in GenAI-enhanced sustainability disclosures.

In conclusion, GenAI holds transformative potential for addressing sustainability challenges in the Fintech sector by offering advanced tools for data analysis and reporting. However, realizing this potential requires a balanced approach that not only harnesses the opportunities of GenAI but also addresses the ethical and environmental implications of AI development. By prioritizing sustainable AI practices and ethical considerations, the Fintech industry can leverage GenAI to advance toward a more transparent, efficient, and sustainable financial ecosystem.

References

Adams, C. A., & Abhayawansa, S. (2022). Connecting the COVID-19 pandemic, environmental, social and governance (ESG) investing and calls for 'harmonisation' of sustainability reporting. *Critical Perspectives on Accounting, 82*, 102309.

Adams, C. A., & McNicholas, P. (2007). Making a difference: Sustainability reporting, accountability and organisational change. *Accounting, Auditing & Accountability Journal, 20*(3), 382–402.

Adams, T., Kishore Kumar, S., Goggins, J., & Manton, R. (2020). *Embedment of UN Sustainable Development Goals (SDG) within Engineering Degree Programmes.*

Agarwal, S., & Mishra, S. (2021). *Responsible AI: Implementing Ethical and Unbiased Algorithms.* Springer International Publishing.

Arrieta, A. B., Díaz-Rodríguez, N., Del Ser, J., Bennetot, A., Tabik, S., Barbado, A., García, S., Gil-López, S., Molina, D., Benjamins, R., Chatila, R., & Herrera, F. (2020). *Explainable Artificial Intelligence (XAI): Concepts, taxonomies, opportunities and challenges toward responsible AI.* Information Fusion.

Astobiza, A. M., Toboso, M., Aparicio, M., & López, D. (2021). AI ethics for sustainable development goals. *IEEE Technology and Society Magazine, 40*(2), 66–71.

Baker, H. K., & Nofsinger, J. R. (Eds.). (2010). *Behavioral finance: Investors, corporations, and markets* (Vol. 6). Wiley.

Bansal, G., Chamola, V., Hussain, A., Guizani, M., & Niyato, D. (2024). Transforming Conversations with AI—A Comprehensive Study of ChatGPT. *Cognitive Computation, 16*(5), 1–24.

Barocas, S., Selbst, A. D., & Raghavan, M. (2019). Fairness and abstraction in sociotechnical systems. *ACM Conference on Fairness, Accountability, and Transparency* (FAT*).

Brown, T., Mann, B., Ryder, N., Subbiah, M., Kaplan, J. D., Dhariwal, P., Neelakantan, A., Shyam, P., Sastry, G., Askell, A., Agarwal, S., Herbert-Voss, A., Krueger, G., Henighan, T., Child, R., Ramesh, A., Ziegler, D. M., Wu, J., Winter, C., & Amodei, D. (2020). Language models are few-shot learners. *Advances in Neural Information Processing Systems, 33*, 1877–1901.

Cao, Y., & Zhai, J. (2023). Bridging the gap–the impact of ChatGPT on financial research. *Journal of Chinese Economic and Business Studies, 21*(2), 177–191.

Chang, Y., Wang, X., Wang, J., Wu, Y., Yang, L., Zhu, K., Chen, H., Yi, H., Wang, H., Wang, Y., Ye, W., Zhang, Y., Chang, Y., Yu, S. P., Yang, Q., & Xie, X. (2023). A survey on evaluation of large language models. *ACM Transactions on Intelligent Systems and Technology, 15*(3), 1–45.

Choi, D., Choi, P. M. S., Choi, J. H., & Chung, C. Y. (2020). Corporate governance and corporate social responsibility: Evidence from the role of the largest institutional blockholders in the Korean market. *Sustainability, 12*(4), 1680.

Christensen, H. B., Hail, L., & Leuz, C. (2019). Adoption of CSR and sustainability reporting standards: Economic analysis and review. *Journal of Accounting and Economics, 67*(2–3), 1–19.

Chu, S., Oldford, E., & Wang, J. (2023). Corporate social responsibility and corporate fraud in China: The perspective of moderating effect of board gender diversity. *International Review of Economics & Finance, 88*, 1582–1601.

Couldry, N., & Mejias, U. A. (2019). *The costs of connection: How data is colonizing human life and appropriating it for capitalism.* Stanford University Press.

Dauvergne, P. (2020). *AI in the wild: Sustainability in the age of artificial intelligence.* MIT Press.

De Villiers, C., & Van Staden, C. J. (2011). Where firms choose to disclose voluntary environmental information. *Journal of Accounting and Public Policy, 30*(6), 504–525.

Devlin, J., Chang, M. W., Lee, K., & Toutanova, K. (2018). *Bert: Pre-training of deep bidirectional transformers for language understanding.* arXiv preprint arXiv:1810.04805

Eccles, R. G., & Krzus, M. P. (2010). *One report: Integrated reporting for a sustainable strategy.* Wiley.

References

EUR-Lex. (2022). Directive (EU) 2022/2464 of the European Parliament and of the Council of 14 December 2022 amending Regulation (EU) No 537/2014, Directive 2004/109/EC, Directive 2006/43/EC and Directive 2013/34/EU, as regards corporate sustainability reporting (Text with EEA relevance; Document 32022L2464; PE/35/2022/REV/1). https://eur-lex.europa.eu/legal-content/EN/TXT/?uri=CELEX:32022L2464

European Commission. (2024a). *Corporate sustainability reporting.* https://finance.ec.europa.eu/capital-markets-union-and-financial-markets/company-reporting-and-auditing/company-reporting/corporate-sustainability-reporting_en

European Commission. (2024b). *The European Green Deal. Striving to be the first climate-neutral continent.* https://commission.europa.eu/strategy-and-policy/priorities-2019-2024/european-green-deal_en

EY Global. (2023). *How can AI help us accelerate the pace of change the world needs?* Ernst & Young. https://www.ey.com/en_gl/insights/sustainability/how-can-ai-help-us-accelerate-the-pace-of-change-the-world-needs

Friede, G. (2019). Why don't we see more action? A metasynthesis of the investor impediments to integrate environmental, social, and governance factors. *Business Strategy and the Environment, 28*(6), 1260–1282.

Giray, L. (2023). Prompt engineering with ChatGPT: A guide for academic writers. *Annals of Biomedical Engineering, 51*(12), 2629–2633.

Google Cloud. (2024). *Green shoots, AI roots: Responding to crises and building sustainable futures with gen AI.* Google. https://cloud.google.com/transform/gen-ai-crisis-response-sustainability-google-org-nonprofit-ai-incubator

Guo, J., Li, J., Li, D., Tiong, A. M. H., Li, B., Tao, D., & Hoi, S. (2023). From images to textual prompts: Zero-shot visual question answering with frozen large language models. In *Proceedings of the IEEE/CVF Conference on Computer Vision and Pattern Recognition* (pp. 10867–10877).

Guu, K., Lee, K., Tung, Z., Pasupat, P., & Chang, M. (2020, November). Retrieval augmented language model pre-training. In *International Conference on Machine Learning* (pp. 3929–3938). PMLR.

Haleem, A., Javaid, M., & Singh, R. P. (2022). An era of ChatGPT as a significant futuristic support tool: A study on features, abilities, and challenges. *BenchCouncil Transactions on Benchmarks, Standards and Evaluations, 2*(4), 100089.

Howard, J., & Ruder, S. (2018). *Universal language model fine-tuning for text classification.* arXiv preprint arXiv:1801.06146. https://eur-lex.europa.eu/legal-content/EN/TXT/?uri=CELEX:32016L2341

Kahneman, D., & Tversky, A. (1972). Subjective probability: A judgment of representativeness. *Cognitive Psychology, 3*(3), 430–454.

Kim, A. G., Muhn, M., & Nikolaev, V. V. (2023). *Bloated disclosures: Can ChatGPT help investors process information?* Chicago Booth Research Paper (23–07).

Kishore, Y. (2024). Optimizing enterprise conversational AI: Accelerating response accuracy with custom dataset fine-tuning. *Intelligent Information Management, 16*(2), 65–76.

Kocoń, J., Cichecki, I., Kaszyca, O., Kochanek, M., Szydło, D., Baran, J., Bielaniewicz, J., Gruza, M., Janz, A., Kanclerz, K., Kocoń, A., Koptyra, B., Mieleszczenko-Kowszewicz, W., Miłkowski, P., Oleksy, M., Piasecki, M., Radliński, Ł., Wojtasik, K., Woźniak, S., & Kazienko, P. (2023). ChatGPT: Jack of all trades, master of none. *Information Fusion, 99*, 101861.

KPMG. (2023). *KPMG global tech report 2023.* https://kpmg.com/xx/en/home/insights/2023/09/kpmg-global-tech-report-2023.html

KPMG. (2024). *Quarterly webcast: A boardroom lens on generative AI.* https://kpmg.com/us/en/board-leadership/webcasts/2024/boards-lens-on-generative-ai.html

Lewis, P., Perez, E., Piktus, A., Petroni, F., Karpukhin, V., Goyal, N., Küttler, H., Lewis, M., Yih, W., Rocktäschel, T., Riedel, S., & Kiela, D. (2020). Retrieval-augmented generation for knowledge-intensive NLP tasks. *Advances in Neural Information Processing Systems, 33*, 9459–9474.

Liu, Y., Ott, M., Goyal, N., Du, J., Joshi, M., Chen, D., Levy, O., Lewis, M., Zettlemoyer, L., & Stoyanov, V. (2019). *Roberta: A robustly optimized bert pretraining approach.* arXiv preprint arXiv:1907.11692

Lyon, T. P., & Montgomery, A. W. (2015). The means and end of greenwash. *Organization & Environment, 28*(2), 223–249.

Madaan, A., Tandon, N., Gupta, P., Hallinan, S., Gao, L., Wiegreffe, S., Alon, U., Dziri, N., Yang, Y., Gupta, S., Majumder, B. P., Hermann, K., Wellbeck, S., Yazdanbakhsh, Y., & Clark, P. (2024). Self-refine: Iterative refinement with self-feedback. *Advances in Neural Information Processing Systems, 36.*

Masanet, E., Shehabi, A., Lei, N., Smith, S., & Koomey, J. (2020). Recalibrating global data center energy-use estimates. *Science, 367*(6481), 984–986.

Mckinsey Digital. (2023, June 14). *The economic potential of generative AI: The next productivity frontier.* https://www.mckinsey.com/capabilities/mckinsey-digital/our-insights/the-economic-potential-of-generative-ai-the-next-productivity-frontier

Mehrabi, N., Morstatter, F., Saxena, N., Lerman, K., & Galstyan, A. (2021). *A survey on bias and fairness in machine learning.* ACM Computing Surveys.

Mishra, A., Verma, V. K., Reddy, M. S. K., Arulkumar, S., Rai, P., & Mittal, A. (2018, March). A generative approach to zero-shot and few-shot action recognition. In *2018 IEEE Winter Conference on Applications of Computer Vision (WACV)* (pp. 372–380). IEEE.

Mittelstadt, B., Allo, P., Taddeo, M., Watcher, S., & Floridi, L. (2016). The ethics of algorithms: Mapping the debate. *Big Data & Society, 3*(2), 21.

Ng, A. (2024). *Andrew Ng's vision for AI's future: Unlocking agentic workflows.* https://nextbrain.ai/blog/andrew-ngs-vision-for-ais-future-unlocking-agentic-workflows

Oson, N. (2024). Effect of green computing initiatives on energy consumption in data centers in Nigeria. *American Journal of Computing and Engineering, 7*(2), 1–13.

Patil, S. G., Zhang, T., Wang, X., & Gonzalez, J. E. (2023). *Gorilla: Large language model connected with massive apis.* arXiv preprint arXiv:2305.15334.

Phogat, K., Harsha, C., Dasaratha, S., Ramakrishna, S., & Puranam, S. (2023). *Zero-Shot Question answering over financial documents using large language models.* ArXiv, abs/2311.14722. https://doi.org/10.48550/arXiv.2311.14722

PRI. (2017). *PRI reporting framework 2017. Principles for Responsible Investment.* https://www.unpri.org/Uploads/k/w/q/2017_pri_indicator_methodology_574171.pdf

Qian, C., Cong, X., Yang, C., Chen, W., Su, Y., Xu, J., Li, D., Liu, Z., & Sun, M. (2023). *Communicative agents for software development.* arXiv preprint arXiv:2307.07924.

Raj, M., & Seamans, R. (2019). Primer on artificial intelligence and robotics. *Journal of Organization Design, 8*(1), 11.

Ray, P. P. (2023). ChatGPT: A comprehensive review on background, applications, key challenges, bias, ethics, limitations and future scope. *Internet of Things and Cyber-Physical Systems, 3*, 121–154.

SEB. (2024). *The Green Bond your insight into sustain able finance.* https://sebgroup.com/siteassets/cision/documents/2024/20240618-sebs-the-green-bond-report-can-ai-support-the-sustainability-transition-en-gb-0-3464645-4851806.pdf

Shen, Y., Song, K., Tan, X., Li, D., Lu, W., & Zhuang, Y. (2024). Hugginggpt: Solving AI tasks with Chatgpt and its friends in hugging face. *Advances in Neural Information Processing Systems, 36.*

Shinn, N., Cassano, F., Gopinath, A., Narasimhan, K., & Yao, S. (2024). Reflexion: Language agents with verbal reinforcement learning. Advances in Neural Information Processing Systems, 36.

Short, C. E., & Short, J. C. (2023). The artificially intelligent entrepreneur: ChatGPT, prompt engineering, and entrepreneurial rhetoric creation. *Journal of Business Venturing Insights, 19,* e00388.

Siddik, M. A. B., Shehabi, A., & Marston, L. (2021). The environmental footprint of data centers in the United States. *Environmental Research Letters, 16*(6), 064017.

References

Strubell, E., Ganesh, A., & McCallum, A. (2019). Energy and Policy Considerations for Deep Learning in NLP. *Proceedings of the 57th Annual Meeting of the Association for Computational Linguistics* (pp. 3645–3650).

Sullivan, R., & Gouldson, A. (2017). The governance of corporate responses to climate change: An international comparison. *Business Strategy and the Environment, 26*(4), 413–425.

Task Force on Climate-related Financial Disclosures (TCFD). (2017). *Final report: Recommendations of the Task Force on Climate-related Financial Disclosures.* TCFD.

Team, I. (2023). *Internlm: A multilingual language model with progressively enhanced capabilities.* https://github.com/InternLM/InternLM

Tversky, A., & Kahneman, D. (1973). Availability: A heuristic for judging frequency and probability. *Cognitive Psychology, 5*(2), 207–232.

Tversky, A., & Kahneman, D. (1974). Judgement under uncertainty: Heuristics and biases. *Science, 185*, 1124–1131.

Van Halderen, D., Bhatt, M., Berens, G. A., Brown, T., & Van Riel, C. (2016). Managing impressions in the face of rising stakeholder pressures: Examining oil companies' shifting stances in the climate change debate. *Journal of Business Ethics, 133*, 567–582.

Van Wynsberghe, A., Vandemeulebroucke, T., Bolte, L., & Nachid, J. (2023). *Towards the sustainability of AI multi-disciplinary approaches to investigate the hidden costs of AI.* MDPI.

Vinuesa, R., Azizpour, H., Leite, I., Balaam, M., Dignum, V., Domisch, S., Felländer, A., Langhans, S. D., Tegmark, M., & Fuso Nerini, F. (2020). The role of artificial intelligence in achieving the Sustainable Development Goals. *Nature Communications, 11*(1), 1–10.

Wei, J., Wang, X., Schuurmans, D., Bosma, M., Xia, F., Chi, E., & LE, Q. V., & Zhou, D. (2022). Chain-of-thought prompting elicits reasoning in large language models. *Advances in Neural Information Processing Systems, 35*, 24824–24837.

Wei, X., Cui, X., Cheng, N., Wang, X., Zhang, X., Huang, S., Xie, P., Xu, J., Chen, Y., Zhang, M., Jiang, Y., & Han, W. (2023). *Zero-shot information extraction via chatting with ChatGpt.* arXiv preprint arXiv:2302.10205.

Wu, Q., Bansal, G., Zhang, J., Wu, Y., Zhang, S., Zhu, E., Jiang, L., Zhang, X., Zhang, S., Liu, J., Awadallah, A. H., White, R. W., Burger, D., & Wang, C. (2023a). *Autogen: Enabling next-gen LLM applications via multi-agent conversation framework.* arXiv preprint arXiv:2308.08155.

Wu, T., He, S., Liu, J., Sun, S., Liu, K., Han, Q. L., & Tang, Y. (2023b). A brief overview of ChatGPT: The history, status quo and potential future development. *IEEE/CAA Journal of Automatica Sinica, 10*(5), 1122–1136.

Yan, B., Chen, S., He, Y., & Li, Z. (2023). *Model-agnostic meta-learning for natural language understanding tasks in finance.* ArXiv, abs/2303.02841. https://doi.org/10.48550/arXiv.2303.02841

Yang, H., Liu, X., & Wang, C. (2023a). *FinGPT: Open-source financial large language models.* ArXiv, abs/2306.06031. https://doi.org/10.48550/arXiv.2306.06031.

Yang, Z., Li, L., Wang, J., Lin, K., Azarnasab, E., Ahmed, F., Liu, J., Liu, C., Zeng, M., & Wang, L. (2023b). *Mm-react: Prompting chatgpt for multimodal reasoning and action.* arXiv preprint arXiv:2303.11381.

Yu, E. P. Y., Van Luu, B., & Chen, C. H. (2020). Greenwashing in environmental, social and governance disclosures. *Research in International Business and Finance, 52*, 101192.

Zhong, Q., Ding, L., Liu, J., Du, B., & Tao, D. (2023). *Can chatgpt understand too? A comparative study on chatgpt and fine-tuned bert.* arXiv preprint arXiv:2302.10198

Zhuang, W., Chen, C., & Lyu, L. (2023). *When foundation model meets federated learning: Motivations, challenges, and future directions.* arXiv preprint arXiv:2306.15546

Chapter 10
Buds, Thorns, and Roses: Navigating the Landscape of Sustainable Finance and Climate Resilience

> There is enough in the world for everyone's need; there is not enough for everyone's greed—
> Anonymous, The Upanishads

10.1 Introduction

As we look to the future of sustainable and resilient solutions, it's clear that the landscape is a complex mix of opportunities, challenges, and cautionary tales. In this chapter, we will explore the promising developments ("buds"), the obstacles and pitfalls ("thorns"), and the successful initiatives ("roses") that are shaping the global response to climate change and sustainability. This short chapter sketches the buds, thorns, and roses related to sustainable finance.

This chapter explores the transformative role of sustainable finance in addressing the global challenges of climate change and environmental degradation. This book's previous nine chapters delved into how financial institutions are pioneering new strategies to integrate sustainability into their core operations, driving both global and local impact. It highlights the critical role of development finance and multilateral banks in supporting these efforts, particularly in developing countries and regions most vulnerable to climate change. By leveraging advanced technologies, such as AI, geospatial data, and renewable energy solutions, these entities are not only mitigating environmental risks but also unlocking new economic opportunities. It's clear that the landscape is a complex mix of opportunities, challenges, and cautionary tales.

10.2 Buds: Emerging Opportunities and Innovations

The "buds" represent the promising developments and innovations that hold the potential to transform our approach to sustainability and resilience. One of the most significant areas of growth is in renewable energy technologies. The United Nations Sustainable Development Goals (UN SDGs) have sparked global interest in renewable energy, particularly in the Global South. Countries and companies alike are increasingly investing in offshore wind, solar, and geothermal energy projects. This focus is not only helping to reduce greenhouse gas emissions but also fostering economic development in regions that are often underserved by traditional energy infrastructure. The emergence of green hydrogen, next-generation batteries, and modular nuclear plants further exemplifies the technological advancements that are paving the way for a more sustainable future. The emerging innovations were covered in Chapter 2 as well as in Chapters 6–9 of the book.

In the United States, the Inflation Reduction Act has committed substantial funding to building the climate infrastructure needed to support these innovations. This legislative action is catalyzing investment in new technologies and accelerating the transition to a low-carbon economy. Similarly, the European Union's stringent sustainability standards and regulations are driving countries within the EU to critically examine and improve their environmental impact, leading to a surge in data providers and other Fintech companies focused on sustainability. These topics were covered in Chapter 5 of the book.

10.3 Thorns: The Challenges and Pitfalls

Despite these promising developments, the journey toward a sustainable future is fraught with challenges—the "thorns" that can hinder progress. One of the most significant issues is the inadequacy of global development finance. At recent G20 summits and United Nations Climate Change Conferences (COPS), there has been much discussion about the responsibility of wealthy nations to support developing countries, particularly those that are most vulnerable to the impacts of climate change. Unfortunately, the financial commitments made by these wealthy nations have often fallen short of what is needed. The amount of money pledged to funds intended to support developing countries and island nations is insufficient to address the scale of the climate crisis they face. This disparity highlights a fundamental challenge in achieving global climate justice and underscores the need for more robust and equitable financial mechanisms.

Another challenge lies in the rush to capitalize on the burgeoning sustainability sector. As the demand for climate solutions grows, a slew of new companies has emerged, many of which are focused on providing data or developing new technologies. However, there is a need for caution—the science behind these innovations must be sound. In the haste to enter the "golden pond" of sustainability, there is a risk that some solutions may be more hype than substance, leading to inefficiencies, wasted investments, and potentially, negative environmental impacts. Greenwashing should not take more hues and saturations as companies rush to satisfy regulations in EU, Asia, Australia, UK, and California. It is critical that the scientific rigor behind these innovations is maintained, and that data-driven approaches are validated and trustworthy. Chapters 6, 7, and 9 talked about such issues. Chapter 9 raised red flags on ethics and bias in GenAI.

10.4 Roses: Success Stories and Positive Impacts

Amid the challenges and emerging opportunities, there are "roses"—success stories that demonstrate the positive impact of sustainable and resilient solutions. The adoption of the UN SDGs by nations and companies is one such example. These goals have provided a clear framework for measuring and achieving sustainability, and many organizations are now examining their impacts against these metrics. This has led to a more structured approach to sustainability, where businesses and governments alike are held accountable for their environmental and social impacts.

The focus on renewable energy in the Global South is also yielding positive results. By investing in sustainable energy sources, developing nations are not only reducing their carbon footprints but also gaining access to reliable and affordable energy. This is helping to improve the quality of life for millions of people, while also fostering economic growth and resilience.

In the financial sector, the rise of Fintech companies that specialize in sustainability is another success story. These companies are developing innovative solutions that help businesses and investors manage their environmental impacts more effectively. For example, data providers are offering sophisticated tools that enable organizations to measure and report on their sustainability performance, thereby improving transparency and accountability.

10.5 Conclusion: Navigating the Future of Sustainability

As we move forward, the future of sustainable and resilient solutions will depend on our ability to navigate the complex landscape of opportunities and challenges. While the buds of innovation and the roses of success are encouraging, we must remain vigilant against the thorns that can derail progress. By maintaining a critical eye on the science behind new technologies, ensuring that financial mechanisms are equitable and sufficient, and continuing to build on the successes of the past, we can create a future that is not only sustainable but also resilient and just.

In the spirit of John Lennon's "Imagine," we envision a world where the barriers of today are dissolved by the unity of purpose and the collective will to overcome adversity. A world where nations, communities, and individuals come together to protect our planet and ensure a thriving, equitable future for generations to come. As authors of this work, we remain steadfast in our hope that humanity will rise to the challenges before us, creating a world where the dream of a better, more sustainable planet becomes our shared reality. Imagine all the people, living life in peace, where sustainability is not just an aspiration, but a way of life—this is the future we strive to build.

The manufacturer's authorised representative in the EU is Springer Nature Customer Service Centre GmbH, Europaplatz 3, 69115 Heidelberg, Germany. If you have any concerns regarding our products, please contact ProductSafety@springernature.com

Printed and bound by CPI Group (UK) Ltd, Croydon, CR0 4YY

25/03/2026

02078171-0014